D1213071

PERSONALITY CHANGE

PERSONALITY CHANGE

edited by Philip Worchel

PROFESSOR OF PSYCHOLOGY, UNIVERSITY OF TEXAS

and Donn Byrne

ASSOCIATE PROFESSOR OF PSYCHOLOGY, UNIVERSITY OF TEXAS

John Wiley & Sons, Inc., New York · London · Sydney

Contributors

Robert R. Blake
    Ph.D., University of Texas
    Professor of Psychology, University of Texas

Donn Byrne
    Ph.D., Stanford University
    Associate Professor of Psychology, University of Texas

I. E. Farber
    Ph.D., State University of Iowa
    Professor of Psychology, State University of Iowa

Leon Festinger
    Ph.D., State University of Iowa
    Professor of Psychology, Stanford University

Jonathan L. Freedman
    Ph.D., Yale University
    Assistant Professor of Psychology, Stanford University

Eugene Gendlin
    Ph.D., University of Chicago
    Research Coordinator, Psychotherapy Research Group,
    Wisconsin Psychiatric Institute, University of Wisconsin

Ernest A. Haggard
    Ph.D., Harvard University
    Professor, University of Illinois College of Medicine

Robert R. Holt
    Ph.D., Harvard University
    Professor of Psychology, New York University
    Research Center for Mental Health

Martin M. Katz
  Ph.D., University of Texas
  Research Psychologist, Psychopharmacology Service Center,
  National Institute of Mental Health

Raymond G. Kuhlen
  Ph.D., Ohio State University
  Professor of Psychology, Syracuse University

Lester Luborsky
  Ph.D., Duke University
  Associate Professor of Psychology in Psychiatry,
  University of Pennsylvania Medical School

William Madsen
  Ph.D., University of California
  Research Associate, Institute for the Study of Human Problems,
  Stanford University

Neal E. Miller
  Ph.D., Yale University
  Professor of Psychology, Yale University

Jane S. Mouton
  Ph.D., University of Texas
  Assistant Professor of Psychology, University of Texas

E. J. Murray
  Ph.D., Yale University
  Associate Professor of Psychology, Syracuse University

Theodore R. Sarbin
  Ph.D., Ohio State University
  Professor of Psychology, University of California

Jean Schimek
  Ph.D., University of California
  Chief Clinical Psychologist, Albert Einstein Medical Center,
  Philadelphia, Pennsylvania

Ross Stagner
  Ph.D., University of Wisconsin
  Professor of Psychology, Wayne State University

Philip Worchel
  Ph.D., Cornell University
  Professor of Psychology, University of Texas

Leon J. Yarrow
Ph.D., State University of Iowa
Research Psychologist and Director, Infant Research Project,
Family and Child Services, Washington, D.C.

Marian Radke Yarrow
Ph.D., University of Minnesota
Social Psychologist, National Institute of Mental Health

Joseph Zubin
Ph.D., Columbia University
Professor of Psychology, Columbia University,
Chief of Psychiatric Research (Biometrics),
State of New York, Department of Mental Hygiene

Preface

Over the past years, in a series of seminars and informal discussions concerning research in the area of personality, a recurring topic of interest was that of personality change. It seemed clear that investigations in a number of diverse areas could be seen as sharing a common characteristic: the study of induced changes in personality structure and functioning. Within the field of personality, a considerable amount of theory development, experimental effort, and applied activity deals with "personality variables"—changes in the relatively stable and enduring characteristics of individuals.

The broad outlines of our thinking about the problem of personality change ran along the following lines. Many theories of personality and all theories of learning are directed toward specifying the conditions under which a change in characteristic behavior is effected. Any consideration of personality change would necessarily require a close look at important similarities and differences in existing theoretical formulations. Similarly, a growing body of research deals with the problem of altering personality, often with respect to psychotherapy as a technique of change. Psychotherapy does not stand alone as a change agent, however, and there is increasing applied and theoretical interest in quite different approaches to behavior alteration. Examples include forcible indoctrination or "brainwashing," the laboratory approach to human relations training in industry, the use of psychopharmacological agents, and the long-standing interest in various techniques for changing attitudes and beliefs about topics ranging from racial intolerance to international tensions. In addition, there are still other areas of research which deal not with deliberate attempts to alter personality but with changes which occur as an incidental consequence of natural events: isolated living conditions, confrontation of divergent cultures, disruption of family life, and the many events associated with growing old.

Despite the apparent differences in the various approaches to change, it seemed that sufficient commonality was involved to suggest possible advantages in considering these topics as a conceptual unit. Much of the material on behavior change is widely dispersed in different texts, different courses, and even in different disciplines. As a way of bringing together a number of investigators working in diverse areas on the common problem of change, a Symposium on Personality Change was organized.

Our first task was to outline a tentative list of topics and contributors. Each contributor prepared a paper for oral presentation at a colloquium at the University of Texas, provided a written version of the paper for inclusion in the present book, and spent two or three days in Austin meeting with small groups of students and staff members in formal and informal groups. A United States Public Health Service training grant made it possible to bring this series of visitors to our campus.

The symposium was initiated in June of 1961 when Ross Stagner spoke on the reduction of international tensions and was completed in April of 1962 when Jean Schimek delivered the paper on psychoanalytic theory which he coauthored with Lester Luborsky. Perhaps it should be mentioned that our original notion was to collect these presentations in book form for use by research workers in areas in which the problem of personality and personality change is relevant. As it developed, however, this collection of papers would seem to be of value in graduate courses in personality theory, in developmental psychology, and in social psychology, and in courses which cover personality change more broadly than do technique courses in psychotherapy. In addition, there seems to be much that may be of interest to the literate layman.

The success of projects of this sort is, of necessity, the result of the contributions of many people. Our special thanks go to the contributors who accepted our invitation and were most patient with all our pressures to complete the task. The support of the entire staff of the Department of Psychology and, in particular, Fillmore Sanford, helped to make the project a more pleasant experience. Finally, we would like to express our appreciation to Mrs. Shirley Perryman, Mrs. Evelyn Stewart, and Mrs. Eddy Lou Ayers for their invaluable secretarial assistance.

PHILIP WORCHEL
DONN BYRNE

Austin, Texas
January, 1964

Contents

PART ONE

INTRODUCTION

In dealing with the phenomenon of personality change, a number of topics recur throughout this book: the definition of personality, the way in which change is investigated by behavioral scientists, the place of theoretical formulations in this endeavor, and the problems associated with obtaining adequate assessment of the relevant variables. In the first two chapters, these topics are explored in some detail.

Farber outlines a framework for the study of personality in the initial chapter. The term "personality" refers to reaction systems and their susceptibility to change. Therefore, there is no meaningful distinction between the study of personality and the study of behavior. Any relatively comprehensive theory of behavior is a theory of personality and personality change. Basically, the behavioral scientist assumes that behavior is a function of its antecedents and that laws relating these elements can be discovered empirically. Hypotheses and theories are evaluated in terms of their ability to yield accurate predictions of consequents rather than their ability to yield "understanding." This thorough-going determinism is, Farber suggests, unpalatable to many personality theorists. He discusses a number of issues which have created disagreements among personality theorists; included are the assumption of lawfulness, the meaning of causation, and the implications of behavior control. Still another issue is the wide discrepancy between the complex behavioral problems facing mankind and the simple behavior studied by the psychologist in the laboratory. Farber attempts to clarify the rationale of the latter approach by indicating that generalization to more complex situations and the application of a knowledge of behavioral laws must await the slow accretion of scientific knowledge. With this discussion as a background, he takes up the function of theory in science, utilizing Hull-Spence learning theory as an example.

In Chapter 2, the focus is on the problem of measurement. Byrne defines personality as that area of psychology concerned with dimensions of individual differences. Research on personality change involves the determination of those conditions which bring about alterations in an individual's characteristic position on these dimensions. Obviously, the accurate measurement of personality variables and their alteration is a prime methodological requirement. Psychometric concepts of test evaluation are discussed in terms of their applicability to personality research. Reliable measurement is a function of the extent to which the experimenter is able to maintain stimulus consistency and is able to select consistent responses to form his units of measurement. Validity of measurement resolves itself to the basic question, "To what are scores on the instrument related?" Because of the scarcity of reliable and valid measures, the researcher in personality usually must face the problems involved in constructing instruments to measure that which he wishes to study. It is proposed that as researchers pay more attention to problems of measurement, theory building will proceed more rapidly. As an illustration of the measurement issues under discussion, the development of the Manifest Anxiety Scale is outlined along with a summary of studies of its reliability, validity, and of changes in manifest anxiety.

chapter one

A Framework for
the Study of Personality
as a Behavioral Science

I. E. Farber

Almost half a century ago, Watson (1919) had, among other things, this to say about personality:

> Let us mean by the term personality an individual's total assets (actual and potential) and liabilities (actual and potential) on the reaction side. By assets we mean first the total mass of organized habits; the socialized and regulated instincts; the socialized and tempered emotions; and the combinations and interrelations among these; and secondly, high coefficients both of plasticity (capability of new habit formation or altering of old) and of retention (readiness of implanted habits to function after disuse). Looked at in another way, assets are that part of the individual's equipment which make for his adjustment and balance in his present environment and for readjustment if the environment changes.
>
> By liabilities we mean similarly that part of the individual's equipment which does not work in the present environment and the potential or possible factors which would prevent his rising to meet a changed environment (p. 397).

And, again:

> During the whole process of human development from infancy to old age, . . . there goes on not only the process of acquisition of habit and the modification of hereditary reaction but also and equally important that of the elimination of reaction systems which work only up to a certain age. Old situations give way to new and as the situation changes old ways of reacting should be cast off and new ones formed (p. 415).

In my opinion the point of view expressed in these passages is neither tendentious nor antiquated. Among other things, it emphasizes the importance of two aspects of the study of personality: personality as product or structure,

Work on this paper was supported by a PHS research grant, M-2296, from the National Institute of Mental Health, Public Health Service.

the state at any given moment of the ceaseless stream of processes and activities that constitute behavior; and personality as process, change, development. Personality can be fully understood in its cross-sectional aspects only if we know the nature of the events and circumstances of which it is the result, and in its developmental aspects, only if we know the particular behaviors or processes that are modified.

But this view does more than assert the importance of specifying the nature both of reaction systems and their modulators. It treats the probability or degree of susceptibility of the various systems to change in particular ways and degrees under given conditions as fundamental descriptive characteristics of personality. Insofar as personality is described in these terms, it may be unnecessary and even misleading to distinguish between the concept of personality and that of personality change.

The foregoing portrayal of personality differs from others, of course, as other current approaches differ among themselves, in respect to the conceptualizations of the systems or processes that are subject to change, and of the dimensions whereby change may be described. At the same time, divested of metaphysical implications and of commitment to any particular hypotheses concerning the determinants of behavior, this formulation appears quite consonant with a good many others frequently characterized as "dynamic," in at least one sense of this much-abused term. With this salute to good company, one may classify it a little more definitely, because of its evident concern with behavior and the learning process, as a behavior- or learning-theoretical view. Though I should be comfortable with these designations, the label "behavioral science" or "behavioral approach" may be preferred by those who consider the adjective "theoretical" gratuitous. None of these terms is altogether unobjectionable, but insofar as they refer to attempts at systematic formulations of the determinants of the acquisition, maintenance, and elimination of particular kinds of behavior or behavior tendencies, they will serve to identify the perspective of the present paper.

THEORIES OF BEHAVIOR VERSUS THEORIES OF PERSONALITY

Whether any behavior system or theory can be at once comprehensive enough and detailed enough to encompass the mysteries of personality and personality change is still an open question. One reason why some psychologists are skeptical is that such formulations do not seem to refer at all to a special class of concepts or phenomena called "personality," but rather to behavior in general, or to predispositions inferred from behavior in general. I believe this observation to be quite accurate. Behavior theorists ordinarily do not distinguish between the task of explaining or predicting personality and that of explaining or predicting behavior. To be sure, in discussing personality they are likely to stress certain processes or concepts such as learning and motivation, but this is characteristic of their general approach to psychology. In their typical view, the study of personality is essentially coterminous with the study of behavior.

I must confess to a certain puzzlement concerning some other views of personality, especially in regard to the distinctions between those behaviors or processes that are supposed to comprise or reflect personality and those that are not. Statements such as "Personality is what a man really is" are simply not helpful, since any kind of behavior or hypothetical variable that might reasonably be used to account for behavior, e.g., habit, libido, press, or positive self-regard, seems equally realistic. Nor does the following amplification seem more satisfying: "Personality is the dynamic organization within the individual of those psychophysical systems that determine his unique adjustments to his environment" (Allport, 1937, p. 48). Except for the term "unique," which is better calculated to reassure people than enlighten them (cf. Eysenck, 1952; Meehl, 1954), this statement does not appear to exclude from consideration any aspect of behavior or a single variable of which behavior in general may be considered a function. Indeed, at the risk of offending both sides, one might point out that the two definitions, the one by Watson and the other by Allport, seem more remarkable for their similarities than their differences.

Still, discussions of personality do not, as a rule, cover every aspect of behavior, though some, even of a non-behavioral sort (e.g., Murphy, 1947), come close. Most frequently, as Hall and Lindzey (1957) observe in their excellent text, they concentrate on motivational variables, i.e., those used to account for the apparently purposive, striving, goal-directed aspects of behavior. Thus, performance on an intelligence test may not be regarded as an index of personality unless there is reason to suppose it is affected by such variables as boredom, achievement needs, anxiety, or hostility toward the tester. Since any kind of behavior, including that involved in taking an intelligence test, running the hundred-yard dash, or whatever, might conceivably be affected by such variables, there seems no clear basis for excluding any kind of behavior from consideration.

I would maintain, therefore, that any relatively comprehensive theory of behavior, especially if it includes variables of a motivational sort, qualifies as a theory of personality. The relative adequacy of the various behavioral approaches in accounting for the complexities of human behavior is, of course, another question.

PRESUPPOSITIONS AND ASSUMPTIONS

If behavior theories are, at least in principle, like theories of personality in their emphasis on the variety and interdependence of variables influencing behavior, particularly those of a motivational sort, how do they differ from personality theories? Or, to put the question differently, since behavior theories show great diversity, and especially, perhaps, in regard to their treatment of motivation (Brown, 1961), what do they have in common that distinguishes them from other kinds of theories?

The answers to these questions are not easily formulated and, to the extent that they seem easy, are likely to be banal and superficial. They lie, I believe, not in any considerable agreement concerning substantive or systematic issues, such as what variables determine what behaviors under what conditions, but rather in certain characteristic views concerning the nature of science and scientific method and their place in psychology. The agreements among behavioral scientists and their disagreements with other formulations lie mainly in the area of metatheory, i.e., their methodological assumptions, or orienting attitudes, if you will.

I must confess to some uneasiness about my competence to treat these issues. They are enormously complicated, and seem to engender disagreement even among highly trained philosophers of science. Fortunately, many of them have been ably discussed elsewhere in the context of general psychological theorizing (e.g., Bergmann, 1943, 1951, 1953, 1956; Bergmann and Spence, 1941; Spence, 1944, 1948, 1956, 1957), so what follows presumes to do little more than to point, without technical elaboration, to some of the presuppositions of behavioral scientists that, in my opinion, underlie their approach to the study of personality. To some, particularly to experimental psychologists, the explicit statement of some of these assumptions and beliefs may appear gratuitous. But they are not by any means taken for granted by all personality theorists, perhaps, as Hall and Lindzey (1957) suggest, because "the stiffening brush of positivism has spread much more lightly over the personality psychologist than over the experimental psychologist" (p. 7).

Lawfulness, Freedom, and the Analysis of Mental Contents

The basic assumption of behavioral scientists is that behavior is a function of its antecedents. These antecedents are natural events in the natural world, and the laws relating behavior to its antecedents can be discovered in the manner of other natural sciences, by the observation and analysis of empirical events. These laws of behavior are, at least in principle, susceptible of discovery. Not all will, as a matter of fact, be known at any given time, since they are exceedingly complex, and new information tends to uncover new complexities. But this is merely a recognition of pragmatic difficulties. It does not make a virtue of obscurantism nor elevate ignorance of ultimate causes to the status of a scientific principle. Once the laws of behavior, or enough of them, are known, the behavior can be predicted. And if the determinants, or enough of them, are manipulable, the behavior can be controlled.

One might suppose that these assumptions, which involve little more than the denial of transcendental or supernatural causation, would be accepted as a matter of course, but, in fact, they seem to arouse intense dissatisfaction. One reason is that, for some, lawfulness implies fatalism, and a second is that, for some (usually the same people), lawfulness implies coercion.

These objections are not usually among those voiced by psychologists, and can be quickly disposed of. In the fatalistic view, certain consequences are inevitable regardless of the antecedent conditions. The antecedents may change, but the consequence does not. This, of course, is exactly the opposite of a deterministic view, which considers consequences to be a function of their antecedents, i.e., if the antecedents change, the consequences change. In the one view, behavior is lawful; in the other, it is unlawful.

The notion of scientific laws as mandatory or coercive results from confusing scientific laws with judicial or legislative laws. If one does not obey a judicial law, one is punished; but if one does not obey a scientific law, the law is inaccurate and must be modified. Scientific laws do not make anything happen. They are merely statements of what does happen under certain conditions. Natural phenomena do not depend on scientific laws. Rather, the converse is true—the statement of the law depends on the nature of the observed phenomena.

Although psychologists do not usually object to determinism on the foregoing grounds, many join the humanists in the protest, on related grounds, that it relegates man to the level of a robot, a senseless and purposeless machine reacting to every fortuitous change in the external and internal environment. Instead, they insist, men actively select the environmental changes to which they respond, and actively decide what responses they shall make.

This position certainly has a strong emotional appeal, as evidenced by the storm of protest raised against both Watson and Freud, in part because of their insistence on a thorough-going determinism. Most people not only do not want to believe they are mere robots; they do not actually feel that they are. Whether there is any autism in this self-perception may be a moot question. Practically, anyone who regards himself as a machine is likely to be subjected to therapeutic treatments aimed at modifying this view. Certainly, normal phenomenological experience runs counter to the notion that people are helpless victims of inexorable circumstances. Rogers (see Murray et al., 1961) has recently affirmed both his acceptance of this position and his conviction of its untenability: "I prefer to live with what seems to me to be a genuine paradox, . . . that in our pursuit of science, we are fools if we do not assume that everything that occurs is a portion of a cause-and-effect sequence, and that nothing occurs outside of that. But I also feel that if we adopt that point of view in our living as human beings, in our confrontation with life, then that is death" (p. 575).

It seems to me this statement epitomizes a rather widespread attitude, that the rules of the scientific game are all very well on the home grounds—in the laboratory, in dealing with insentient objects—but ought not be applied to the study of real persons in the real world. By contrast, behavioral scientists insist on attempting to apply these rules under all conditions, even in the face of the complexities of human personality.

It is important, at this point, to distinguish between the contention on phenomenological grounds that behavior is unlawful, and the possible role of an analysis of mental events in constructing psychological concepts. To the best of my knowledge, no one these days denies the existence of mental events. Watson did on occasion, but in Bergmann's perspicuous phrase, "Watson's particular mistake was that in order to establish that there are no interacting minds, which is true, he thought it necessary to assert that *there are no minds,* which is not only false but silly" (1956, p. 266). To follow Bergmann's analysis, no one doubts that there are such things as mental contents, awarenesses, cognitive states, percepts, etc. However, to any statement containing such terms it is possible, at least in principle, to coordinate another ". . . which mentions only behavioral, physiological, and environmental items, such that they are either both true or both false. Otherwise one would have to maintain that we can, literally and not metaphorically speaking, directly observe other people's states of mind" (p. 270). Thus, mental events exist, and in a commonsense way we know what we mean when we refer to them, but it is unnecessary to appeal to them in a thorough-going account of behavior.

So far as I understand this view, it does not preclude the possibility that some kinds of systematic analyses of mental contents, i.e., the contents of observable indexes or reports of mental states, may serve a useful purpose in the discovery of behavioral laws. It is undoubtedly true that psychologists' preoccupation with such analyses has declined since the heydey of Structural Psychology. But I doubt whether this occurred, as Koch (1959) has recently implied, because of the pernicious influence of behavioristic epistemology. It occurred, I believe, because the particular contents emerging from the structuralists' analyses were simply inadequate to the ordering of the kinds of psychological phenomena in which most psychologists had become interested. It may be time, as McClelland (1955) and Koch (1959) maintain, for psychologists generally to recognize that other kinds of experiential analyses *can* be useful to psychological science. One might offer a slight demurral to Koch's (1959) conclusion that current theoretical formulations show a *trend* in this direction, on the grounds that many of the authors cited were never persuaded that significant psychological laws could be discovered by any method other than the analysis of mental contents. But this would be somewhat irrelevant. So long as such analyses are concerned with the formulation of psychological laws, including those relating experiential data to behavior, they do not oppose, but rather support a deterministic view of behavior.

It is a curious fact that the claims of phenomenological experience apparently still lead some psychologists, who are otherwise at a polar extreme from Watson, to his own mistaken conclusion that admission of the existence of private experience is prejudicial to the notion of lawfulness. An examination of both the methodological positions (cf. Skinner, 1953, p. 257 ff.) and the research strategies of those within the behavioral camp reveals no reluctance to use introspective reports or any other observable indexes that might be coordinated to mental events. Indeed, insofar as the concept of mediating processes relates to such events, they have been used for a long while (vid. Goss, 1961). And their current utilization within the framework of behavior theory in investigations of such problems as stimulus equivalence and distinctiveness (e.g., Spiker, 1962), concept formation (e.g., Kendler and Kendler, 1962), and human operant conditioning (e.g., Farber, 1963), speaks for itself. It is true that these formulations frequently refer to language, but as the Kendlers (1962) carefully point out, it is neither necessary nor desirable to identify mediational events with any particular process. It is only necessary to demonstrate that such concepts are useful elements in the understanding and prediction of behavior.

Causation, Finalism, and Explanatory Fictions

The preoccupation of personality theorists with motivation, the apparently purposive, striving, goal-directed aspects of behavior referred to earlier, has sometimes led to the adoption of a finalistic or teleological view of behavior. The biological counterpart of this view has been aptly summarized by Simpson (1950):

The distinctive finalist belief is that of progression toward a goal or end. The end is not reached, the finalist believes, because of what goes before, but what goes before is but a means for reaching the end. The end, although later in time, is, then, the cause and the preceding course of history is the effect. The history of life is thus to be viewed as purposeful, and (it almost goes without saying) finalists usually consider man as the essential feature of that purpose (pp. 126–127).

The degree of conviction with which this belief has been held by some theorists is indicated in the following quotation from Adler's (1930) chapter in the *Psychologies of 1930:*

Individual Psychology insists absolutely on the indispensability of finalism for the understanding of all psychological phenomena. Causes, powers, instincts, impulses, and the like cannot serve as explanatory principles. The final goal alone can explain man's behavior (p. 400).

To the typical non-scientist man-in-the-street this view seems not only reasonable but self-evident. Asked why an acorn planted in the ground grows as it does, he is likely to reply, "So that it can become an oak tree." Or, if he has had the benefit of a liberal education, asked why people sleep, he may answer, "To restore homeostasis." Even psychologists who know better fall into the habit of explaining one kind of behavior or another by referring to the goals to be attained.

Quite apart from the reversal of the order of materialistic cause and effect, such explanations tend to account for either too little or too much. They account for too little when the expected goal is not reached. Not all acorns become oak trees. Some rot and others are eaten by hogs. People and animals who have suffered injury to the anterior portion of the hypothalamus may be unable to sleep. And people all too frequently fail to achieve goals or achieve them by the most diverse means. Such explanations are too comprehensive when they are used to account for every conceivable kind of eventuality. To explain all behavior in terms of "adjustment" or "satisfaction of the pleasure drive," for instance, explains nothing, since one must still account for the different kinds of behavior.

I must confess to the belief that some constructions of the concept of self-actualization, which in one form or another appears to have wide currency in personality theories, suffer from this defect. Rogers, for instance, assigns to human beings only a single motive, the actualizing tendency. "This is the inherent tendency of the organism to develop all its capacities in ways which serve to maintain or enhance the organism" (1959, p. 196). It includes the concepts of tension reduction, growth motivation, differentiation of organs and functions, enhancement through reproduction, autonomy, and indeed, so far as I can tell, almost any predisposition one can think of that results in the expanded effectiveness of the organism. This seems equivalent to saying that organisms tend under all conditions to do those things that are "good" for them, in a vague sense of the word "good." Unfortunately, even if one adopts this optimistic view of man, one still does not know what a given individual will do, or why one individual differs from another. To know this, one would have to identify the particular factors, whether hereditary or environmental, that occasion different behaviors. This is not to say that the postulated correlates of the actualizing tendency, e.g., originality, creativity, and spontaneity, are fictitious or unimportant. On the contrary, precisely because they are important, a behavior science ought to be adequate to their prediction and explanation. And this can be done, not by defining them as the culminating aspects of a universal *élan vital,* but by discovering their particular determinants. In the present view, if we knew the independently defined variables of which such behaviors or behavior characteristics are a function, we would dispense with such overarching concepts as self-actualization.

It is interesting to contemplate the number of concepts that might be dispensed with in psychology, if we only knew more about the determinants of given kinds of behavior. For instance, behavior theorists, like everyone else, occasionally talk about the phenomenon of "choosing." It is notable, however, that the term "choice" usually refers to nothing more than the descriptive fact that an organism behaves in one way rather than another. Suppose we know that a person has repeatedly heard a tone just before receiving an air puff on the cornea of his eye. If we then note that he blinks when the tone is presented, we add nothing to our explanation by saying he chose to blink. Similarly, when after prolonged food deprivation, a person identifies an ambiguous picture as a steak rather than something else, it is trivial to say this is because he decided to say "steak." Since the evidence of the decision is the behavior itself, attributing the behavior under these circumstances to choice is exactly as useful as attributing it to demons. Note should be made of the qualification, "under these circumstances." If the definition of choice is made independently of the behavior it is supposed to explain, this concept may, of course, be useful.

In general, the frequency of appeals to such explanatory fictions is an index of our ignorance of the antecedents of the phenomenon under consideration. All too often, the sole evidence for the supposed cause is the very behavior it is supposed to explain. Thus, as Skinner (1961, p. 535) has observed, it is useless to say that forms of life that have survived did so because they had survival value, if all we know is that they survived. And it is useless to argue that people adjust to their environment because of some special capacities such as intelligence, if these are defined in terms of their adjustive value. Similarly:

When we say that a man eats *because* he is hungry, smokes a great deal *because* he has the tobacco habit, fights *because* of the instinct of pugnacity, behaves brilliantly *because* of his intelligence, or plays the piano well *because* of his musical ability, we seem to be referring to causes. But on analysis these phrases prove to be merely redundant descriptions (Skinner, 1953, p. 31).

The Control of Behavior

It was stated earlier that, if the determinants of behavior were known, and if enough of them were susceptible to manipulation, then it would be possible to control behavior. It was also noted that this proposition arouses the most intense annoyance and anxiety in many people, including psychologists, who for good reasons, abhor the idea of a totalitarian technocracy (Bergmann, 1956). In its superficial aspects, one can rather readily understand why the concepts of "control" and "despotism" are sometimes equated. If behavior can indeed be controlled by manipulating its determinants, then individuals with the requisite knowledge could and very possibly would exercise this control. In this light, any deterministic view of behavior may be suspect. For instance, psychoanalytic theory, which on other grounds does not perhaps qualify as a behavioral approach, has, because of its thoroughgoing determinism, also been accused of sinister and exploitative advocations.

The reaction against the proposition that behavior is susceptible of manipulation tends to take two different and rather contradictory forms. At one extreme, it emerges as a flat denial—the use of the Freudian term is not unintentional—that behavior, particularly implicit behavior, is controllable or even predictable. According to this view, the deterministic thesis, as applied to human behavior, is simply false. At the other extreme, it consists of the condemnation and proscription of attempts to discover the laws of behavior. According to the latter view, behavior is not only lawful and predictable, but the laws are already well-known and the techniques for their effective application all-too-readily available. Couched in less extreme terms, the two arguments, oddly enough, frequently appear in a single context, without recognition of their inconsistency.

Some aspects of the first objection concerning the essential unpredictability of behavior have already been referred to. Beliefs to the contrary rest on philosophical assumptions not subject to empirical proof or disproof. It might be commented, not altogether frivolously, that anyone who sincerely believes *as a matter of principle* that behavior is unlawful and unpredictable ought to complain about the expenditure of his tax dollar for such things as schools and mental hospitals, since they are established on the supposition that at least some behaviors are somewhat amenable to control.

The second reaction, that the laws of behavior are well-known, and are even now being applied in one or another program of exploitation, is, despite allegations from the best-seller list, unwarranted by the facts. The facts are that, at present, much human behavior is unpredictable because its laws, though discoverable, are as yet largely unknown. This is not exactly news to informed individuals, and affords psychologists scant basis for self-congratulation. It may conceivably comfort those who regard the acquisition and application of psychological knowledge as a threat to human welfare, including, paradoxically, some psychologists who appear to see in the advancement of behavioral science only the grim prospect of 1984. As Skinner (1955) observes:

> Such predictions of the havoc to be wreaked by the application of science to human affairs are usually made with surprising confidence. They not only show a faith in the orderliness of human behavior: they presuppose an established body of knowledge with the help of which it can positively be asserted that the changes which scientists propose to make will have quite specific results—albeit not the results they foresee (p. 61).

The essential ingredient in such views is a distrust of science. Those who bemoan our lack of knowledge concerning the factors governing intersocietal and interpersonal relations are frequently the same people who condemn the use of those procedures best calculated to achieve that knowledge—the methods of science. If these forebodings were taken seriously, we should have to conclude that even if we knew how to make our educational system more effective, even if we knew what kinds of conditions in our homes would increase the probabilities of our children's becoming responsible and useful citizens, we nevertheless ought to refuse to establish such conditions on the grounds that this would constitute undesirable control; even if we knew how to allay those suspicions and change those motives or cognitive structures of individuals, the consequences of which threaten our country with racial upheaval or the world with nuclear disaster, we ought not act because this would violate men's freedom.

Surely, few persons would care to push the argument for the inviolability of human freedom so far. Nevertheless, the issue is not a simple one, and will certainly not be resolved here. I merely wish to point to the illogicality of an automatic rejection of any plan calculated on the basis of scientific knowledge to modify the behavior of individuals or societies.

On the one hand, we must recognize that different societies and different individuals have different goals. What is desirable or reinforcing for one may be frustrating and punishing for another. We are only too liable to the delusion that our own goals are the only reasonable ones. Thus, when I try to change a person's behavior or attitudes, I am appealing to his better judgment; when you try to do so, you are using propaganda; and when "they" do so, they are brainwashing. To complicate matters further, this multiplicity of motives and goals extends to the intrapersonal sphere. The behavior that is instrumental to the satisfaction of one motive may frustrate the satisfaction of another.

On the other hand, our respect for the rights of others to their particular goals and the instrumental acts whereby they are achieved should not lead us to the romantic delusion that these are spontaneous products of unfettered choice. No one escapes control by the physical environment short of death; and no one escapes control by his social environment short of complete isolation. Almost the entire period of childhood is given over to the acquisition of new behaviors, goals, and motives, under the guidance of parents, family, and teachers. Be it wise or unwise, deliberate, impulsive, or unconscious, such guidance inevitably has its effects. It is difficult, in fact, to think of any kind of social interaction that has absolutely no effect on behavior. That the effects are unintentional or unwanted does not negate them. There is some feeling among those who read popular discussions of persuasive techniques that frank and open appeals to frank and open motives such as hunger and thirst may be tolerable; but disguised and subtle appeals to disguised and possibly disreputable motives such as sex or dominance are illegitimate. This reaction probably results from the belief that behavior related to the first class of motives is more liable to self-control and less liable to control by others. This is extremely doubtful. But, in any event, those who would proscribe the use of such techniques on the grounds that they constitute unwarranted control are usually not nearly so concerned with the ethical implications of their own proposal to control the attitudes and behavior of others. The plain fact is, the obdurate refusal to arrange circumstances for influencing others, on ethical or moral grounds, may simply serve as a mask for indecision and irresponsibility. Furthermore, such refusal ignores the evident fact that we influence others in unintended and unplanned ways.

Even non-directive psychotherapists adopt their procedures on the assumption that they have certain behavioral consequences. If refusing to say or do something produces given effects, this constitutes control no less than does active intervention. Which of these kinds of antecedents is more closely related to the desired behaviors is an empirical matter, not to be decided on a priori philosophical grounds. Advocates of a non-interventionist approach to psychology know this, of course, since they frequently refer to empirical evidence indicating that their procedures are more effective than some others.

It seems to me there is much more agreement concerning the kind of world most of us want and the kinds of people we should like to have in it than one would suppose from the interminable arguments about such matters. The disagreements among social scientists or, for that matter, between social scientists and humanists, relate not so much to goals as to the means by which they can best be achieved. For example, in a recent symposium (Murray et al., 1961), Rogers suggests that an alternative to control is the release of potentialities and capacities, leading to ". . . behavior that is more variable, more spontaneous, more creative, and hence in its specifics, more unpredictable" (p. 575). Surely no one would question the desirability of such behavior. We might question whether the optimal conditions for creativity and spontaneity are those of laissez-faire or accident. And we might question whether such conditions do, as a matter of fact, constitute an alternative to control, since some sorts of controls by parents, teachers, and many other individuals and institutions are inevitable. Whether such fortuitous controls are likely to encourage or stifle creativity needs to be investigated, not taken for granted.

There may be some who would deny the desirability of such empirical investigations, presumably on the principle that ignorance is bliss. But if, as a result of investigations such as those Rogers himself has inspired, there were good reason to suppose that certain conditions have a greater likelihood than others of eliciting behavior upon whose worth almost all can agree, then I doubt that one could reasonably argue against the deliberate institution of such conditions on the grounds of ethical propriety. We are mainly ignorant about the controls that now exist, so we can only be sure they are man-made and far from perfect. It seems inconceivable and, indeed, a contradiction in terms to suppose that controls based on scientific knowledge would be worse. Unfortunately, influential writers, including some psychologists in the field of personality, seem otherwise persuaded.

Prediction versus Understanding

It is possible that we have been setting up a straw man, since relatively few individuals in our time would condemn the pursuit and application of empirical knowledge, though not many years ago a congressional committee investigating the social sciences heard such complaints. However this may be, there are certainly differences of opinion concerning the criteria whereby knowledge may be verified. In one aspect, they relate to the foregoing discussion of prediction and control. Thus, Maslow, in the aforementioned symposium (Murray et al., 1961), suggests that the testing of scientific hypotheses in terms of prediction and control implies an "overactive and interfering conception of science" (p. 572). He prefers a conception whose "key characteristics are receptivity to knowledge . . . , understanding as the main goal of science, rather than prediction and control . . . , the freer use of intuition, empathy, and identification with the object of study, a greater stress on experiential knowledge, a less pragmatic attitude" (p. 572).

This statement addresses two somewhat independent problems which may be easily confused. The one has to do with techniques or modes of acquiring knowledge; the other with procedures for verifying knowledge.

In respect to the first, one may note that we frequently do not know the circumstances that yield useful hunches concerning the determinants of behavior in specific instances. The context of discovery, to use Reichenbach's (1938) excellent term, is uncertain. This is so, not because the determinants of useful hunches are in principle unknowable, but because we are as yet relatively ignorant about them. We do know that many hunches, including those asseverated by psychologists, turn out to be mistaken. Citing the conclusion of one investigator, that non-psychologists appear to be able to judge others more accurately than do clinical psychologists, Allport suggests that the present training of psychologists merely ". . . leads them to a *knowledge about,* rather than an *acquaintance with,* human nature in its concrete manifestations" (1961, p. 543). This may be so, and we may be training our students badly. This should not be surprising, since psychologists, like other educators, know less than they should about the conditions of effective training for various purposes. Though I very much doubt that psychological training generally impairs one's ability to judge others, it is unquestionably true that others can do a better job than psychologists of predicting behavior under some circumstances.

Sometimes the reasons for this are perfectly evident. On occasion, my neighbor, who is a dentist, can predict the behavior of my dog—understands its personality, if by that one means its behavioral tendencies—much better than I, because, for good reasons, it spends its time around his garden bed and garbage cans. On the other hand, I can occasionally predict the condition of my children's teeth better than he, because I am in a better position to control their predilection for sweets. In these instances, as in all others, successful prediction depends on the amount and kind of information available. Psychologists, including personality theorists, simply do not predict behavior in general. They can only say, given such and such conditions, a given behavior should ensue. As Dollard and Miller (1950) nicely point out in respect to the cultural determinants of behavior, they may not always be in a position to know just what these conditions may be in specific instances.

In this regard, we may frequently be impressed with the perceptiveness of politicians, salesmen, and animal trainers. Many of the more highly educated in our society are even more likely to be impressed with the insights of novelists, poets, biographers, and the great religious and social essayists who have written so well and wisely about the nature and condition of man. We should certainly not disparage such insights as these persons may have. Psychologists have no monopoly of access to the cues that may serve as the basis for successful prediction and evaluation of behavior.

But this recognition of the variety of sources of possible knowledge, that is, the diverse contexts of discovery, should not blind us to the second problem, the necessity for verifying knowledge. The context of justification (Reichenbach, 1938) has its own ineluctable requirements. The accuracy of statements by those whose writings appear to embody the wisdom of the ages must, like those by dentists and psychologists, be evaluated in the light of their predictive value.

The deficiencies of speculative wisdom, as of intuition and empathic understanding generally, lie not in their inaccuracy. They may be quite accurate. Their fault is that they give no adequate basis for knowing whether or not they are accurate. As Campbell (1959) has observed, the speculative wisdom of the ages has often proposed contradictory resolutions of the same problem. The insights of classical wisdom, in contrast to scientific knowledge, are notoriously equivocal and non-cumulative. The reason is that science insists that insights and hypotheses be tested and sets up a machinery for this purpose, whereas classical wisdom is content with the mere experience of certitude. Even the putative wisdom of Allport's commonsensical homespun philosopher must be tested, else we should never know when he is truly being wise and when, like the rest of us, he is merely a victim of undisciplined conviction.

On the Significance of Psychological Concepts

One may accept the view that personality and its changes are lawful, that their antecedents are discoverable by the methods of natural science, that statements concerning the relations between personality variables and their antecedents must be verified by predictive test, and that once known, information concerning such laws ought to be used for the benefit of individuals and society. Granting all this, one may still regard the whole enterprise, in its present stages, at least, as a fantastic network of trivialities. We need, desperately, to solve the social and political problems of our times; meanwhile, the behavioral scientist busies himself with the variables determining a rat's speed of running down a straight alley, the rate of bar-pressing in a Skinner box, and eyeblinks. And perhaps, judging from the disagreements concerning even such simple matters, busying themselves none too successfully, at that.

The justification for such interests may not be readily apparent to those concerned with the threat of thermonuclear warfare, or, as in the case of many personality theorists, to those concerned with the problems of mental illness, education, or group productivity. If behavioral science can do no more, many people believe, the whole sorry business really ought to be abandoned.

It would be foolish to suppose that behavioral science promises solution of our social and personal problems in the foreseeable future. Many behavioral scientists would regard any proposal that their activities be justified on this ground as impertinent and insulting. But they are even more likely to point out that preoccupation with such problems, even by those most vitally concerned with them, is not necessarily the best guarantee nor even a very good guarantee of their solution. Science differs from speculative wisdom in its cumulative nature. Each advance rests on the broad structure of what is already known, and without that substructure further advance is often impossible. As Campbell (1959) has noted, "Science has solved important problems, but this final achievement should not obscure the modesty and caution of the initial steps." Nor are the initial steps usually oriented toward those problems to whose solution they may lead. We may be quite sure that in 1912, when Rutherford was measuring the deflection of alpha particles by gold foil, he was not thinking of a hydrogen bomb. Yet, according to historians of physics (Condon, 1955), this work led directly to the nuclear atom model which was the basis for all subsequent work in physics.

Spence (1956) has pointed to two major deterrents to the establishment of a scientific body of psychological knowledge:

The first of these . . . is reflected in . . . the tendency to criticize theoretical concepts in this field as being too elementaristic, too mechanistic, and as failing to portray the real essence or true nature of man's behavior. In particular, these critics have complained about the artificiality of the objective types of concepts such as offered by the behavioristic psychologist (p. 20).

The second factor is the tendency to evaluate the significance of psychological concepts and research in terms of the degree to which they are applicable to some immediate practical or technological problem rather than the extent to which they enter into or contribute toward the development of a body of lawful relations . . . (p. 21).

The notion that behavioral scientists pursue what is precise at the expense of what is important appears to be one of those insights so highly regarded by admirers of speculative wisdom. I, for one, doubt whether the principles thus far derived by behavior theoretical approaches are demonstrably less useful for the understanding of complex social problems than those deriving from other approaches. But more importantly, the view that precision implies triviality mistakes the nature of scientific laws and theories.

A concept is trivial only if it is isolated, i.e., does not enter into a system of interlocking laws. Stated otherwise, a concept may be considered significant only insofar as it enters into such a nomological network (Cronbach and Meehl, 1955). In physics, for instance, the test of the accuracy of theories of very great power may depend on the precise measurement of phenomena that would in themselves be quite inconsequential. Certainly, precision does not guarantee significance. On the other hand, concepts having any great degree of imprecision are unlikely to have a useful function in the development of a systematic body of lawful relations. Such concepts, no matter how profound or compelling they may appear, are truly trivial. An important part of the history of physical and even behavioral science deals with the abandonment of just such meretricious concepts.

The work of behavioral science, or any science, may seem rather pedestrian, not suited to men of grand vision and extravagant expression. But it does not seem beside the mark to note that some three thousand years of the application of the speculative wisdom of the best minds of the ages have failed to illuminate very much the problems of behavior (cf. Campbell, 1959). As Spence (1956) puts it:

> The science-oriented psychologist merely asks that he be given the same opportunity to develop a scientific account of his phenomena that his colleagues in the physical and biological fields have had. If there are aspects of human behavior for which such an account cannot ever be developed, there are not, so far as I know, any means of finding this out without a try (pp. 20–21).

SOURCES OF INFORMATION CONCERNING THE DETERMINANTS OF BEHAVIOR

We know, of course, that the variables influencing behavior are many, and their interactions extremely complex. For this reason, if one wants to know whether a given kind of behavior is some function of one, or, at most, a restricted set of these variables, one must either construct or find situations such that the effects of the one variable or the particular set of variables may be isolated. This can be done by eliminating the other relevant variables, holding them constant, or in some way measuring their effects.

This does not imply the expectation that in other combinations the variable(s) under consideration will invariably affect behavior in ways clearly evident from their relatively isolated effect on behavior. It merely presupposes that the study of the effects of restricted sets of variables on the behavior of relatively simple organisms may lead to useful hypotheses concerning their effects in more complex combinations and in more complex organisms. This method of science is usually necessary because "it is seldom possible to proceed directly to complex cases. We begin with the simple and build up to the complex, step by step" (Skinner, 1953, p. 204).

Now, nothing is more certain than the fact that relations found in such simple instances will sometimes, perhaps usually, fail to hold in more complex instances. No one would deny that changes in the combinations of variables may affect behavior. But unless one has fairly precise notions about the conditions under which a given kind of behavior occurs, it seems exceedingly unlikely that one can decide with any certainty what particular aspects of different or more complex conditions are responsible for a change in that behavior.

Generalizing from the Laboratory to Real Life

Those who argue that the observation of behavior under the artificial and highly controlled conditions of the laboratory has no predictive value for behavior under "real life" conditions sometimes appear to fail to understand the necessity for doing more than simply pointing to the change. What we wish to know is the nature of the variables of which that change is a function. In any event, there is universal agreement on one point: before one generalizes from observations of behavior in the laboratory to real-life situations, one had better consider very carefully the differences between the laboratory conditions and those in real life.

In the light of this recognition of the necessity for considering the variables involved, it is puzzling why anyone who objects to generalizations from laboratory findings should consider it safe to generalize from behavior in one complex, uncontrolled situation to behavior in another. Obviously, circumstances change from one uncontrolled situation to another. When one does not know what variables have changed, generalizations from one real-life situation to another are at least as uncertain as those from controlled situations to real-life situations. An added disadvantage lies in the relatively greater difficulty of disentangling the particular variables that have changed. This is not easy, whether one deals with either controlled or uncontrolled conditions, but under any circumstances the lack of control or information concerning the effects of specific variables can hardly be regarded as a positive aid to understanding and prediction.

Generalizing from Animals to People

In view of the well-known differences between rats, which are non-social and non-verbal, and human beings, who are exceedingly social and verbal, it is not surprising to find a good deal of skepticism concerning the applicability of rat laws to human behavior. Occasionally, there is an autistic element in such criticisms. Some people consider it degrading to be compared with rats, just as some consider it insulting to be compared with infants, as in psycho-analytic theory. But most criticisms of this sort are based on the objective fact that rats and people differ in many and possibly crucial respects. Koch (1956) has expressed in eloquent detail his disbelief in the probability of generating the essential laws of human behavior from rat data. He points out that one may not even be able to generate decent laws concerning rats by observing rats, especially if they inhabit different laboratories.

In regard to the latter observation, that one cannot generalize from rats to rats without risk, one can only agree that animal experimenters ought perhaps to describe their experimental conditions more adequately, or to try harder to discover those conditions whose variation is responsible for the reported inconsistencies. I do not believe animal psychologists are generally regarded as unusually deficient in their specification of the variables they know about or in their zeal to discover the ones they do not know about. But perhaps they ought to be doing a more careful job. It is important to note that this calls for more analytic precision, not less.

In regard to the former observation, that one cannot generalize from rats to human beings, it seems fair to repeat that frequently one also cannot generalize from human beings to human beings. Koch (1956) for instance, in describing his own "B states," i.e., his experiences while deeply engrossed in work, maintains that despite the importance of such states, despite their exemplification of behavior in its most organized, energized, and motivated form, current psychological theories are inadequate to the recognition of such states, let alone their explanation. "Subtle and organized descriptive phenomenologies of B states are badly needed by science—but not from individuals whose B-state products are 'creative' only by extravagant metaphor" (p. 68). Whatever one thinks of this pronouncement, it is certain that B-states cannot be observed in rats, and unlikely that they could be even partially accounted for in terms of principles based on rat behavior. But, as Koch himself suggests in the foregoing quotation, it would be rash to suppose that all human beings share these experiences. And in view of the restriction imposed, even among those who might have such experiences, very few could claim the privilege of attempting to communicate them. This is not to say that B-states do not exist, nor that they are unimportant. It does suggest the uncertainties of attempting to generalize from what may be discovered about Koch's B-states to the experiential states of people whose phenomenological descriptions may be limited to a phrase such as "Man, it's the most!" There is grave risk in generalizing from both rats and human beings when important variables differ.

Despite these cautionary notes, I think it possible to point to some instances of successful generalizations from animal as well as other human behavior, i.e., to hypotheses that have turned out to be fruitful. Instead, I should like to tell of an "Aha!" experience I recently had while listening to Frank A. Logan describe some of his animal experiments at Yale, in which delay of reward was balanced against amount of reward in simple choice situations. The experimental results showed that, within limits, rats will choose a longer delay, if the reward is large enough, in preference to shorter delays with lesser rewards. Probably because of obtuseness, it had never before occurred to me in quite the same way that the morality of human beings in giving up the pleasures of this world for the sake of eternal salvation may have something in common with the morality of rats in giving up an immediate reinforcement for the sake of a bigger piece of Purina dog chow. Now, this is undoubtedly a specious analogy at best. It ignores the many disanalogies in the two instances, and may be utterly foolish. But until this has been demonstrated, it suggests some, not by any means all, of the variables of which even such sublime sentiments may be a function. Of course, it goes without saying that no matter how intriguing this notion may appear in the context of discovery, it must make its scientific way in the context of justification.

The distaste of some psychologists for animal studies frequently extends to conditioning studies as well, in part because the conditioned reflex appears characteristic of subhuman or subnormal behavior. Again, we might attempt to show how the laws of conditioning have been used as a basis for predicting some relatively complex human activities, such as verbal learning. Instead, we can point to a curious inconsistency in our treatments of such concepts. According to the earlier Gestalt psychologists, insight, or perception of relations, is also a primitive process, altogether characteristic of animals. Yet we seldom hear the argument that this concept is, therefore, useless for the understanding of human behavior. Unfortunately, judgments of what is scientifically useful are all-too-frequently confounded with judgments of what is good or bad. Thus, the successful efforts of Communists to modify beliefs and actions are likely to be attributed to the use of Pavlovian conditioning techniques, which work only if men are reduced to the level of witless automatons (cf. Farber, Harlow, and West, 1957); our own successful efforts, on the other hand, are likely to be attributed to methods engaging the higher mental processes. It seems just possible, does it not, that many of the same determinants may be operative in both instances?

Proponents of a behavioral approach are likely to answer this question affirmatively because, for the most part, they distrust the doctrines of emergentism. While the variables influencing animal behavior are certainly different and less complex than those influencing human behavior, most behavioral scientists, nevertheless, prefer to look for continuity in the explanatory principles involved. Similarly, they look for continuity between the laws of child and adult behavior, between social and non-social behavior, and between normal and abnormal behavior. Whether this sort of search is useful may be open to question. At this stage of the game there appears to be no way of deciding this to everyone's satisfaction.

General Laws and the Individual Case

The foregoing discussion has dwelt on two apparently contradictory principles. The one stresses the necessity for caution in generalizing from one circumstance to another, in the face of inevitable changes in the variables represented. The second holds to the optimistic belief that generalization is frequently possible, even in the face of changes in some of the variables affecting behavior. Behavioral scientists, like others, differ in their relative emphases on these two principles, depending in part on the relative strengths of their empiricist or theoretical predilections; but they are likely to agree that the question whether one can successfully predict from one context to another can be answered only by empirical test.

Some personality theorists, however, appear to consider this a methodological rather than an empirical issue. They may deny, for instance, even the possibility of applying general laws to the prediction of individual behavior. Since, they argue, the variables influencing a given individual's behavior are not exactly duplicated for any other person, and since these variables interact in complicated ways, it is simply not possible to predict anything about one person from laws based on the observation of others. Since each individual is unique, the only legitimate predictions concerning any given person must be based on what is known about that person. Curiously enough, this reasoning is ordinarily not extended to the intraindividual case. If it were, we would have to deny the possibility of predicting an individual's behavior even on the basis of what is known about that person, since the variables influencing his behavior at one time can never be exactly duplicated at any other time. At the very least, the ordinal positions of the two occasions differ.

Most behavioral scientists believe that general laws can be reasonably and usefully applied to individuals (Eysenck, 1952; Meehl, 1954). At the same time, they can readily agree that predictions about a given individual will frequently be more precise if they are based on the observation of his own past behavior. Perhaps the main reason for this is that many of the important determinants of his past behavior are likely to persist as determinants of his future behavior. Individuals carry such determinants around with them, so to speak, in the form of their inherited and learned predispositions.

Nevertheless, if there is reason to suppose that present conditions are quite different from those in the individual's past, predictions are likely to be more successful if they are based on the behavior of others for whom we know these conditions have obtained. It is gratuitous to say so, but this merely means it may be more useful, in predicting the effects of aging on a given person, to look at old people than at that person at age two; or it may be more useful, in predicting the effects of a certain drug on a person's behavior, to observe other people drunk than that person sober. Of course, the more nearly alike the reference group and the individual in question, the more accurate the prediction. This simply means that the probability of successful prediction from one instance to another is some positive function of the communality of their behavioral determinants (cf. Meehl, 1954).

We should note that this formulation of the issue does not dispose of the empirical question whether general laws can at present be usefully applied to a particular individual in any given instance. The hard job of ascertaining just what the important variables are in any given context, and when a change in one variable changes the significance of another, must still be done. We may hypothesize to our hearts' content about such matters. But we should not mistake the hypothesis, no matter how firmly held, for empirical proof.

PERSONALITY VARIABLES AND BEHAVIORAL LAWS

The preceding section has barely touched on the exceedingly complicated problem of general versus individual prediction. One aspect of this problem relates to the interaction between situational or environmental variables and individual differences variables. Early in this discussion it was stated that behavioral scientists ordinarily find no clear-cut basis for distinguishing between the study of personality and the study of behavior in general. What view does this imply concerning the role of individual differences, especially those customarily classified under the heading of personality? According to many personality theorists, the existence of individual differences constitutes the most significant datum of psychology, yet the general psychologist persists in regarding them as mere annoyances, sources of error variance, to be eliminated or disregarded.

It is a matter of historical fact that, traditionally, experimental psychologists have been primarily interested in variables whose main effects or interactions are more or less independent of the kinds of subconditions known as individual differences. They have never denied the existence or even the importance of individual differences. After all, the classical Structuralists did not restrict their investigations to normal, adult, human observers because they supposed the observations would be unaffected by such variables as psychopathology, age, or species membership. They simply were not interested in the interactive effects of such variables. Many experimental psychologists still are not very interested in these kinds of variables, though this picture has been changing somewhat.

Many personality theorists, on the other hand, are frequently interested only in the kinds of variables that do interact with individual differences. They, in turn, do not usually deny that there may be important situational variables whose main effects override individual differences of one sort or another, but they are simply not so interested in them. We may find intransigents in both camps who absolutely deny the importance of any kinds of variables except the ones they happen to be interested in, but such persons are fortunately not numerous.

Environmental Events, Intervening Variables, and the Individual

Psychologists who deplore the traditional emphasis by experimental psychologists on manipulable environmental variables, to the denigration, as they suppose, of the role of the behaving organism, frequently state their position in a characteristic way, by pointing to the necessity for considering not only the external event, but also its meaning to the individual, or how the individual perceives it.

In a commonsensical way, there is no doubt they are correct. If a physicalistically defined stimulus is presented to an organism, our estimate of the probability of a given response is always contingent on certain assumptions, usually implicit, concerning some characteristics of that organism, e.g., adequate sensory and motor equipment, a relatively intact nervous system, and so on. Woodworth's well-known suggestion that the S-R formula ought to be modified to read "S-O-R" was designed to take account of such contributions by the organism to its own behavior, though he undoubtedly intended the "O" to include more than physiological structures and processes.

Behavioral scientists differ, as we have noted, in their estimates of the usefulness of attributing to organisms such hypothetical, non-observable characteristics as habits, intentions, cognitions, etc. Though all would agree with Skinner that one must beware of the dangers of hypostatization and reification, many are convinced that empiricism is quite compatible with the use of abstract concepts and theories. The construction of intervening variables, for instance, represents one sort of attempt by behavior theorists to delineate the kinds of organismic characteristics that might be useful in accounting for behavior (cf. Spence, 1952). Thus, intervening variables are inferred characteristics of organisms, calculated, among other things, to explain why different individuals, or the same individual at different times, may sometimes behave differently under the same environmental conditions, and sometimes similarly under different environmental conditions. This portrayal may remind some of Allport's definition of a trait as a "neuropsychic system . . . with the capacity to render many stimuli functionally equivalent, and to initiate and guide consistent (equivalent) forms of . . . behavior" (1937, p. 295). According to a behavioral view, of course, the usefulness of the concept of a trait, as of that of any other intervening variable, is not assured by the simple expedient of tacking on a reference to unspecified neuropsychic events.

In light of the foregoing analysis, it might be startling, but not altogether beside the mark, to maintain that a theory such as Hull's is the exemplar of personality theories, on the assumption that some of his intervening variables, or some of the constants defining their growth or decline, differ from person to person in a relatively consistent way. One may not like the particular intervening variables Hull has proposed, because they may not appear to bridge the gap between stimulus and response in a satisfactory manner, or because there is reason to suppose that different characteristics or classifications of characteristics would do a better job. It is apparent to everyone, including those who have been influenced by Hull, that more precise and comprehensive conceptualizations are needed to account for behavior. It is simply suggested that the construction of such systems will, as a matter of course, increase our understanding of the individual.

In brief, whatever their particular nature and interrelations, the states and processes conceptualized as intervening variables are indisputably the properties of the individuals from whose behavior they are inferred. Of course, abstract properties do not literally occupy a place in space, but this does not imply that such concepts as drive level, self-regard, or cathexes are not attributes of "real" flesh-and-blood people (cf. Bergmann, 1953).

Despite this happy unanimity of concern for the nature of the behaving organism, it does not necessarily follow that stimuli ought to be *defined* in terms of their meaning to the organism. Rather, the meaning itself must be accounted for in terms of objective factors in the past and present states of the organism and its environment (cf. Bergmann, 1943). From a behavioral standpoint, meanings are certainly important, and conceptualized as mediating processes, play a prominent role in current theoretical formulations. Thus, it is useful, in a variety of situations, to suppose that external events elicit some sort of implicit response whose stimulus components in one way or another modify the overt response to the external event. Familiar examples of such mediating processes are the fractional anticipatory goal response $(r_g\text{-}s_g)$, emotional states $(r_e\text{-}s_e)$, and anticipatory frustration $(r_F\text{-}s_F)$ discussed by such theorists as Spence (e.g., 1956) and Amsel (e.g., 1962).

Another sort of mediating mechanism is the one discussed by Kendler and Kendler (1962), among others, representing a symbolic response to external cues. This implicit response and its accompanying stimulus components can be used to explain a wide variety of phenomena, including, as we have noted, stimulus equivalence and distinctiveness. Since the hypothetical implicit stimulus may serve to explain why ostensibly different environmental events may elicit the same response, and apparently similar environmental events may lead to different responses, one may be tempted to regard the "real" stimulus as consisting of both the external event *and* its accompanying mediator, or even to consider the external event inconsequential, the only relevant factor being the nature of the mediational process, i.e., the "meaning" of the external event. I must leave the question of what can reasonably be meant by "reality" to those more competent to discuss the philosophical issues, but it seems to me that if one insists that stimuli be defined in terms of one sort of inferred process, i.e., symbolic mediation, one could with equal justification insist that they be defined in terms of any or all the others, e.g., motives, expectancies, inhibitory states, and so on. This sort of equating of observable events with inferred events, i.e., intervening variables, seems a dubious basis for clarifying theoretical problems.

Although I believe it necessary to distinguish between stimuli as observables and inferred characteristics of the organism as non-observables, it seems reasonable to consider behavior as the invariable function of both. If we think the stimulus is unimportant, we might try substituting a very different stimulus, to see whether the response does not change; and if we think the organism is unimportant, let us substitute a bag of potatoes in place of the usual psychological subject (Bergmann, 1951).

To say that every response is a function of both stimulus conditions and the organism is to say it is not possible to attribute any behavior exclusively to either the one or the other. There is something puzzling, for instance, about the supposition that the effects of length of a word list or the degree of similarity of the items in the list are attributable to extraorganismic factors, whereas the arousal of disgust by the same items is due to an intraorganismic factor. Why should variations in motivation or inhibitory tendency due to massing of practice be considered the result of extraorganismic variables exclusively, but variations in the same states due to anticipation of failure because of the same antecedents be considered the result of intraorganismic variables exclusively?

A case in point is Gill's (1959) recent classification of ego-functions, including perception, thought, memory, and concept formation as intrapsychic, but interpersonal and social factors as extraorganismic. We wonder how interpersonal and social factors are to have any effect on the organism independently of the processes of perception, thought, and memory. Perhaps all that is meant in this instance is that environmental events and hypothetical organismic processes or states can, and ought to be, independently defined. If so, this and similar formulations are in good accord with the behavior theoretical view that stimuli ought not be defined in terms of "what they mean" to the individual.

A consideration of the historical roots of the widespread tendency to classify behaviors according to inner or outer determinants would take us far afield. It may be of interest, however, to observe that one historical basis for this dichotomy appears to be the conventional distinction between associative and non-associative determinants of behavior. In the old days of classical associationism, ideas were endowed with their own adhesive qualities. They came together, stuck, or were separated in accordance with certain principles; but though their locus was presumably somewhere inside the organism, the power of association resided, not in the organism, but rather, in some sense, in the ideas themselves. Some psychologists may suppose that behavior theorists, particularly since they typically use an S-R terminology, still conceive of the association between environmental events and behavior according to this old associationistic formula. It must be admitted that they often speak as though associative strength is a characteristic of stimuli. But this is merely a verbal shorthand, perhaps an unfortunate one, if it is so liable to misunderstanding. Let it be noted that it is the organism, not the stimulus impinging on his receptors that does the associating. The term $_sH_R$ refers to an intraorganismic process, just as much as do the terms relating to motivation or emotion.

After all this, it may be salutary to recall the reservations held by behavioral scientists, in common with Skinner, respecting explanations of behavior in terms of inferred characteristics of the organism. Such inferences must be made on the basis of observations that are independent of the particular instance of behavior the characteristic is supposed to explain. There is no use saying a person runs away because he is afraid, if the fear is inferred wholly from his running away. If we observe that a given person habitually behaves in an inconsiderate, selfish, and malicious way, whereas in the same situations another habitually behaves in a kind and considerate way, it may be useful to characterize these behaviors, or for that matter, the persons, as respectively "mean" and "generous." But saying that these people behave in their respective ways *because* the one is mean and the other generous is to appeal to the kind of empty explanatory fiction Skinner and many others warn against. When we know the objective conditions under which a given behavior or behavioral characteristic occurs, we can explain any relevant behavior in terms of those conditions. We need not appeal to some hypothetical characteristic to which they supposedly give rise. This caveat applies as well to intervening variables. If they do no more than account for the particular behavior from which they are adduced, they are fatuitous.

Traditionally, the kinds of objective conditions to which behavior theorists have given most attention have been temporally antecedent events, i.e., they have relied more on historical than on ahistorical laws. This does not imply that anyone supposes that the variables affecting behavior can be anything but contemporaneous. Events in the past history of organisms can influence current behavior only insofar as they are represented in their current traces. Anyone who thinks otherwise believes in ghosts. Historical laws are used, *faute de mieux,* in the absence either of satisfactory measures of these traces that are independent of the observable behaviors they occasion, or of techniques for manipulating them directly.

This strategy involves no basic theoretical issue. Thus, behavioral scientists fully appreciate the current advances in our understanding of the physiological processes and anatomical structures mediating behavior, recognizing that this knowledge is indispensible to the bridging of the gap between past events and current behavior. From their view, the import of the breakthrough in physiological psychology lies precisely in its departure from the dismal tradition of inferring physiological processes solely on the basis of the behaviors they are intended to explain. It is the definitional independence of the variables in a law that is important, not their reference to historical rather than ahistorical events.

Response-Defined Concepts

Behavioral scientists differ, as we have indicated, in their evaluation of the usefulness of attempts to explain behavior in terms of hypothetical states or processes of the organism. And they are particularly skeptical when the inferred characteristics are defined in terms of behavior rather than environmental conditions. Even apart from the dangers referred to, the difficulties in attempting to decide on the basis of behavior alone whether variations in a given performance are more probably due to variations in one class of hypothetical determinants than another are formidable (vid., Brown and Farber, 1951). Everyone, so far as I know, takes it for granted that every kind of behavior is multiply determined, and that the determinants may interact. To use an obvious example, at any given moment two people may perform in the same way because one has high drive and low habit strength and the other high habit strength and weak drive. It is not easy to devise techniques that permit the disentangling of these different strands.

A related difficulty to which experimentalists are likely to point is the fact that many behavioral measures may be intrinsically interrelated. For instance, to use only one of innumerable possible examples, it is known that the correlation between Manifest Anxiety Scale scores and those on the psychasthenia (Pt) scale of the MMPI is about +.70 to +.80 for college sophomores, even after the common items are removed. Pt scores are sometimes considered a measure of emotional expressiveness, as contrasted with repressiveness. The correlation of the MAS scores with the K-Scale of the MMPI is frequently found to be about −.70. K is supposedly a measure of defensiveness. And Edwards (1957) reports a correlation of −.84 between the MAS and his Social Desirability Scale, which is supposed to measure strength of desire to make a good impression. In the face of these impressive relations, how can one say whether the MAS measures drive level, emotional expressiveness, lack of defensiveness, or disinterest in making a good impression, or any, or all of these? And what about all the other tests, present and future, whose relations with the MAS, though not yet computed, will undoubtedly reach comparable orders of magnitude? What, then, does the test measure?

In one sense, this is a trivial question, and requires but a trivial answer, though, unfortunately, one that constructors and users of tests sometimes fail to see, namely, that giving tests different names does not guarantee that they reflect different characteristics, and giving them the same names does not necessarily mean they reflect the same determinants. If all these highly interrelated measures are related to all other kinds of behaviors in the same way, they measure the same thing, regardless of their labels.

Occasionally, however, this confusion among the characteristics inferred from behavior is not merely nominal. For instance, height and weight are highly correlated in the general population, yet no one supposes they are merely different names for the same thing. What if defensiveness and desire to make a favorable impression are independent, but nevertheless empirically related in a given population? How, then, could we decide whether they reflect different organismic states or processes? Or better, if the one measure is related to some other mode of behavior, which hypothetical variable is responsible for the relation?

These are not trivial questions, and their answers are not easily come by. One kind of answer is simply the observation that there is never any guarantee in science against the inaccurate identification of determinants. And this holds as well for experimental variables, i.e., those that are directly manipulable, as for differential variables, whose values must be selected wherever and whenever they occur. Suppose, for instance, the number of food responses in a free association test or, for that matter, speed of running in a straight alley, is shown to be a function of length of food deprivation. How do we know these results are not due to variations in blood-sugar level, or changes in bodily weight, or any number of other variables associated with food deprivation? As Miller (1959) points out, in attempting to specify behavioral antecedents "It is possible to proceed down the scale to an almost infinite number of possible empirical independent variables; even the most detailed operational description of procedure involves assumptions about the general applicability of the terms used. It is impossible for a theorist to be completely certain in advance whether or not these assumptions are justifiable. It is equally impossible for a person who believes himself to be a pure empiricist to avoid such assumptions" (p. 215).

It is usually possible, given skill and patience, to tease out ever-finer specifications of the variables entering into behavioral laws. So too with response-defined variables; by careful selection of cases, statistical correction, or the elimination of errors of measurement, we can frequently decide which of several variables, even though they be highly correlated, determine the form of the relation under consideration. If it turns out, as it frequently does, that a given behavior is a joint function of several response variables, the circumstance is one quite familiar to experimentalists. For instance, no one is unduly disturbed by the finding that the probability of drinking is a function of both dryness of the mucous membranes and general water deficit. The additional fact that these two variables are themselves frequently related under many conditions is a complication, to be sure, but not an insuperable one.

All we can reasonably ask in regard to either experimental or differential variables is that they be specified as precisely as possible. We should then be prepared to discover, soon enough, that more precise and detailed specifications are necessary.

THE NATURE AND FUNCTION OF THEORIES

Thus far, relatively little of our discussion has been directly concerned with the nature or role of theory in psychology, at least as this term is typically used by personality theorists. It has been mainly concerned, instead, with some fundamental propositions: that behavior is lawful; its antecedents are discoverable by naturalistic methods; guesses as to the antecedents of behavior are best verified by the method of prediction; the laws relating behavior to its antecedents are initially most easily discovered by observing simple behavior in simple situations; at least some of the variables and laws identified in simple situations are likely to be useful, in interaction with new factors, in explaining more complex behavior in more complex situations; it may sometimes be useful to infer or guess at certain characteristics or properties of organisms that might account for variations in behavior under ostensibly similar environmental conditions; and, finally, these hypothetical properties, whether defined in terms of behavioral antecedents or some aspects of behavior itself, might reasonably be considered as personality variables. Clearly, only the last two points bear very closely on the question of theory.

Behavior Theories and S-R Language

It will be recalled that this entire discussion started with the question: "What do behavioral approaches to personality have in common, and how do they differ from other views?" A partial answer, with some elaborations and digressions, has been given in terms of the foregoing propositions. What they come to, in a word, is an emphasis on the formulation of empirical laws and the analysis of the variables comprising them. As we have noted, the assumption that it is the business of behavioral science to explicate the relations between objectively defined environmental and behavioral events is in itself no theory, but rather a metatheoretical or pretheoretical preference. Those who adopt this approach, especially if they have an interest in the phenomena of learning, are likely to use the terms "S" and "R" to refer, respectively, to the environmental and behavioral events, and the familiar formula "S-R" to indicate a relation between these two classes of variables. In addition, those who use this terminology are perhaps more than others committed to the view that complex behavior can be understood, at least in part, in terms of concepts and relations adumbrated in the observation of simpler sorts of behavior. Not all theorists, not even all behavior theorists, entirely share the belief that S-R concepts are adequate to this task (cf. Koch, 1959). Kendler and Kendler (1962) have commented on one reason for such misgivings:

> Much of the objection to S-R language stems from the apparent discrepancy between active, flowing behavior and the inert, static, single S-R association. Using S-R language does not mean complex behavior *actually* consists of S-R connections. After analyzing the concept of light, Toulmin (1953) concludes: "We do not *find* light atomized into individual rays: we *represent* it as consisting of such rays" (p. 29). Applying the same idea to the concept of the S-R association: "We do not *find* behavior atomized into individual S-R associations: we *represent* it as consisting of such S-R associations." The concept of S-R association, therefore, must be judged not in terms of its ability to provide a clear image of behavior, but rather in its capacity to represent the facts of behavior (p. 3).

Although S-R formulations share a certain strategy, as the foregoing quotation indicates, the notion of S-R is not a theory either, but rather a pretheoretical model. Thus, its adoption does not imply a single level or kind of conceptualization of either "stimulus" or "response" (Brown, 1961; Miller, 1959). It does not imply that S-R laws are the only ones of importance in psychology (Spence, 1948). It does not imply any particular stand with respect to the necessity or desirability of introducing hypothetical constructs in accounting for behavior. And it certainly does not imply any substantial agreement concerning either the specific observable variables or hypothetical variables of which particular responses or response classes are a function. In brief, "S-R" is simply a type of terminology employed by some empirically-minded psychologists, including some who are also theoretically inclined.

What, then, is meant by a "behavioral theory"? In physics, the term "theory" refers to a system of interrelations among highly abstract concepts which serves to organize a very large number of laws that were previously unrelated (Spence, 1956, 1957). Comprehensive theories, i.e., those serving to organize a considerable number of laws, depend on the state of knowledge in a given area. If many empirical relations are known, then the theories may unify a large area. In psychology, at least according to the view of behavior theorists such as Spence, the development of a body of empirical laws is still in its early stages, so the possible unifying power of theory is relatively small.

This rather modest conception of theory is a far cry from the grandiose conceptualizations of some personality theorists. One reason for this is the insistence that every term in the system, no matter how abstract, be referable in some way to observable events. This requirement, sometimes referred to, not altogether correctly, as that of "operational definition," simply states the necessity for indicating more or less unambiguously the nature of the circumstances under which the term is to be used. Furthermore, these circumstances ought to be of a sort concerning which there is a high degree of intersubjective agreement. Theories that achieve apparent comprehensiveness by the use of concepts that have no clear-cut referents of this sort may have a certain suggestive value in the context of discovery, but in the context of justification their ambiguity precludes any rigorous test of their purported relations. It is apparently possible, however, for behavior theorists to take somewhat different stands in respect to the methodological implications of this requirement, as the recent discussions of the notion of construct validity amply demonstrate (e.g., Bechtoldt, 1959; Campbell, 1960; Cronbach and Meehl, 1955).

The Economic Function of Theories

Theories, even of such limited scope as those now existing in psychology, seem to serve two functions, the one economic and the other integrative. The economic function appears to have been the one emphasized by Tolman (1936) when he introduced the concept of the "intervening variable." He noted that the function relating any kind of behavior to its many determinants is likely to be exceedingly complex, and also, that these functions differ for different sets of antecedent conditions and for different kinds of behaviors. Therefore, he proposed that certain hypothetical notions be introduced to decrease the number of statements necessary to indicate all these relations. Feigl (1945), observing that the concept "electric current" has precisely this status of an intervening variable between numerous causal conditions and numerous effects has clearly indicated the nature of this stratagem:

> If there are m causal conditions and n possible effects we would need mn statements in order to formulate all possible observable relations. If, however, we introduce our auxiliary concepts the number of statements required shrinks to $m + n$. For large numbers m and n the conceptual economy is accordingly quite considerable (p. 257).

Miller (1959) has recently suggested how one might design experiments to test the hypothesis that various kinds of behavioral indexes in various experimental contexts might actually be accounted for in terms of a single construct of this sort.

There is some reason to believe that the economic function of such theorizing is served in part by Skinner's procedure of classifying antecedents of various kinds under the same rubric, e.g., "motivation," because they bear the same kinds of functional relations to a given aspect of behavior. As he says of the concept of "drive":

> The term is simply a convenient way of referring to the effects of deprivation and satiation and of other operations which alter the probability of behavior in more or less the same way. It is convenient because it enables us to deal with many cases at once. There are many ways of changing the probability that an organism will eat; at the same time, a single kind of deprivation strengthens many kinds of behavior. The concept of hunger as a drive brings these various relations together in a single term (1953, p. 144).

Thus, despite his renunciation of theory, Skinner's procedure, and even its rationale, appears to bear a certain resemblance to those followed by self-acknowledged behavior theorists. Perhaps, as Miller (1959) has suggested, Skinner has not been too impressed with the theoretical significance of this procedure, because he tends to deal with only one index of behavior, rate of bar-pressing. Obviously, even if the number of m causal variables is very large, if the number n of response variables is only one, mn will always be less than $m + n$. Consequently, no simplification can ensue from the use of intervening variables.

The Integrative Function of Theories

The second function of a theoretical structure is to integrate various empirical laws within a given domain, by linking the constructs used to account for one set of laws with those used to account for other sets. In this way, one may establish a "network of connected concepts" (Feigl, 1945). In a theoretical structure detailed enough to include statements of relations among several hypothetical variables, the deductive consequences of the supposition that an empirical variable is related to one or another of these intervening variables may be quite far-reaching, and in some cases may lead to unexpected conclusions.

Since such abstract statements about the merits of theory are rather unconvincing, we might consider an example of such guessed-at interrelations and their empirical implications, even at the risk of getting finally to some substantive issues. This example is from the theoretical structure formulated by Hull and Spence—only because it is the one I am most familiar with. There is no implication that different formulations would not yield equally pertinent instances.

Consider the consequences of the supposition that a given variable Y is related to general drive level (D). If it is further assumed that the strength of responses is some function of habit strength (H) multiplied by drive level ($R = H \times D$), one can make a rather large number of predictions concerning the effects on behavior of variations in Y. For instance, increases in the value of Y should lead to the following consequences: improved performance in situations in which the strongest habit is correct, but poorer performance when the strongest habit is incorrect; greater responsiveness to generalized stimuli, but better discrimination between the training and generalized stimuli when presented simultaneously; steepened slopes of psychophysical functions relating to sensory thresholds, but no change in the absolute threshold. All these, and a substantial number of other consequences may be deduced from the Hull-Spence theory, on the hypothesis that Y is a drive factor (e.g., Brown, 1961; Spence, 1956). These consequences depend, of course, on the assumed relations between empirical variables and intervening variables as well as those among the intervening variables.

In the case of any particular variable Y, of course, the predicted consequences may not appear. In this eventuality, one must conclude either that Y is not a drive variable, or some of the assumptions relating drive to other constructs and to behavior are incorrect, or both. The point is, unless one has a theory in which these relations are made explicit, there would be no reason even to look for these possible effects on behavior.

In an earlier section, note was taken of the wide variety of tests that have yielded scores highly correlated with those on the Manifest Anxiety Scale. A few years ago, Davids (1955) asked a question that has probably occurred to many psychologists: in view of these high relations between MAS scores and those on other, well-established instruments, some of which may be even more valid measures of anxiety, why has there been so much emphasis on the MAS? In my opinion, the answer is obvious: because of the supposition that these scores might be related to one of the intervening variables in the Hull-Spence theory and, consequently, to variations in all the kinds of behaviors theoretically affected by this variable. In other words, the popularity of the MAS resulted, not necessarily from any intrinsic value of the test itself, and certainly not from its title, which is in some respects misleading, but from its presumptive relation to constructs within a comparatively highly integrated theory.

Since, as Spence (1958) has stated, the primary function of the sort of theoretical scheme he employs ". . . is to provide for the unification of what, without the theory, would be a multiplicity of isolated or unconnected facts and laws" (p. 140), assigning any variable to a place in the theory permits the deduction of a variety of behaviors which would otherwise not be suspected. For example, it is quite probable that MAS scores represent, in part, the strength of the desire to make a good impression (Edwards, 1957). But I wonder whether anyone seriously believes that this conceptualization would have led to studies of eyelid conditioning, or psychophysical functions, or the steepness of stimulus generalization gradients, or paired-associates learning, or for that matter Davids' own investigation of productivity in a word association test (Davids and Eriksen, 1955).

It may be of some interest to note that many of the predictions based on the assumption that the MAS measures drive level have been borne out; in other instances, the predictions have met with but indifferent success. Indeed, if the Hull-Spence theory is correct, then some of these findings demonstrate that the MAS also measures characteristics other than D. Since no one, to the best of my knowledge, ever doubted this (Farber, 1954, 1955), these demonstrations are not too surprising. Whether the evidence indicates that it measures D at all is perhaps still a moot question. Indeed, in a larger context, it may be questioned whether it is necessary or useful for theoretical purposes to posit a non-associative concept of D at all (e.g., Brown, 1961; Estes, 1958; Postman, 1953).

These questions are of the utmost importance. Nevertheless, in considering the metatheoretical nature and functions of theory, they are in a sense quite irrelevant. If the MAS does not measure D, perhaps some other indexes, such as certain kinds of autonomic or cortical activity will do so. Perhaps no kind of behavior indexes will prove useful for this purpose. Perhaps the kinds of behavioral phenomena accounted for in terms of the Hull-Spence theoretical formulation will be better integrated within new theoretical systems, which may not contain the construct of drive level at all. Theories are not sacrosanct. They are formulated for only one purpose—to account for the behavioral data. If they fail to do so, they must be modified or discarded.

I believe a number of behavior theories have proved useful in providing a basis for predicting behavioral phenomena of interest even to those who consider such approaches too simplistic to account for the complexities of personality. Miller's studies of fear and conflict, Skinner's studies of operant conditioning, and the extension of both to the area of psychotherapy are cases in point. New theories are being constructed and older ones revised, the better to incorporate and account for new findings. It is in the very nature of behavior theoretical formulations that they be modified on the basis of empirical facts. Since the empirical facts of psychology include those relating to individual differences, one may anticipate that as behavior theories become more precise and more comprehensive they will encompass more and more phenomena now referred to under the rubric of "personality." I, for one, look forward to the day, which I do not expect to see myself, when personality theories are regarded as historical curiosities.

chapter two

Assessing Personality Variables and Their Alteration

Donn Byrne

Among the hallmarks of a mature scientific discipline are (1) a network of interrelated theoretical constructs which provide a high degree of predictive accuracy over a wide range of phenomena and (2) reliable and valid instruments with which to measure all relevant variables. The former is the goal of science, and the latter is a necessary concomitant of that goal. It seems clear that, with reference to these criteria of maturity, the field of personality is at best in its preadolescence.

The greater portion of this book is devoted to theoretical considerations. However, in the present chapter attention will be focused on the second of the above characteristics. In discussing the role of assessment in personality research, some of the general problems of measurement will be examined. The intention is to explore the difficulties involved in attempting simultaneously to build a theory of behavior and to develop appropriate measuring instruments.

The author would like to express his appreciation to the following individuals who were kind enough to offer helpful comments and criticisms of the original draft of this chapter: John Altrocchi, Barbara Blaylock, I. E. Farber, June Goldberg, Austin Grigg, Fred Hine, Lester Luborsky, Louis J. Moran, Jean Schimek, Al Simmons, Ross Stagner, and Joseph Zubin.

Appreciation of a different order, but equally important, should be expressed to those individuals who were helpful in furthering the social aspects of the symposium by offering their hospitality to our visitors. These include the Oliver Bowns, the Alfred Castanedas, the Harry Helsons, the Carson McGuires, the Glenn Ramseys, the William Sloans, and the William Wolfes. A very special word of thanks is due to Ann and Fillmore Sanford and to my wife, Lois, for their continuous support throughout the project.

PERSONALITY AS A FIELD OF PSYCHOLOGICAL RESEARCH

It would seem that few areas of psychology are defined in as many diverse ways by as many different individuals as is personality. Before the problems of personality measurement are discussed, an initial digression to define the field is in order. Courses and texts dealing with "personality" range in subject matter from problems of personality adjustment to summaries of psychoanalytic theory to the identification and description of factorially pure traits to an outline of methods for obtaining global descriptions of individual clients. Without arguing that a particular definition is the only acceptable one, the meaning of "personality" as used in this chapter is indicated in the following discussion.

The Two Disciplines of Scientific Psychology

As psychology has developed through the past century, two major emphases in the study of behavior may be distinguished. On the one hand, there are efforts to determine general behavioral regularities. Antecedents are found to be lawfully related to consequents, and the resultant theoretical formulations are assumed to hold across individuals. In the terminology employed by Bergmann and Spence (1944), these relationships are of the form $R = f(S)$. Most of the work in areas such as perception, cognition, and learning falls within this framework.

With all organisms, but especially with human beings, a major problem arises in employing this approach. That is, a large proportion of the antecedent conditions which contribute to a given behavior are likely to be unobserved by the investigator. It is not that man is exempt from lawful antecedent-consequent relationships; rather, the investigator is often unable to control, measure, or even observe the crucial antecedents. If we do not know about a given individual's early interactions with his mother or his genetic structure or his diet over the preceding year and if the lasting effects of such variables determine the responses under investigation, how might we go about building laws of behavior? With many dependent variables, such unobserved antecedent conditions may prove of negligible importance compared to antecedents in the stimulus situation itself. For example, if amount of reward is being varied by the experimenter in order to determine its effects on a motor learning task, it may be that no variable based on childhood experiences is related to this dependent variable. Or, if some variable such as "maternal warmth" does affect the learning of this task, one's sampling procedures are usually such that the effects of the uncontrolled variable are distributed across experimental conditions. The proportion of unexplained variance is increased, but one can still establish lawful relationships between S and R. Recognition of the possible importance of such variables is indicated by an extension of the S-R formula, e.g., R = f(S, T, D, I).[1]

What happens, however, when the influence of an unobserved antecedent condition is of such magnitude that it affects the response to a greater extent than does the manipulated stimulus? It is here that an experimenter must (1) take on the difficult and sometimes impossible task of seeking out the crucial antecedent variable, (2) abandon the investigation of this particular dependent variable, or (3) utilize an approach in which the antecedents are studied indirectly in the form of personality variables. An emphasis on the third of these alternatives constitutes the field of personality as defined in this chapter.

Integrating the Experimental and Differential Approaches

There is nothing inherently incompatible about an interest in individual differences and adherence to an S-R or antecedent-consequent conceptualization. Perhaps the diagram shown in Figure 1 will help make this clear.

In the experiment suggested by the drawing, the investigator manipulates S_1 and measures variations in response R_1. However, the effect of variations in a particular class of past events (S_x) has an influence on R_1 which is great enough to obscure the S_1-R_1 relationship. If we can assume that the effects of S_x on the organism brought about lasting changes which influence other responses besides R_1 and that these effects represent relatively stable characteristics of the organism, an indirect approach to S_x becomes possible. That is, in a second and perhaps separate research session, another stimulus (S_2) is presented to the subject and his responses (R_2) obtained. This approach makes it possible to predict the dependent variable (R_1) by a combination of S_1 and R_2. Presumably R_2 is relevant only because both it and R_1 are partially dependent on the effects of S_x. Thus, the necessity of including S_x and the difficulties involved in doing so make it imperative in much of the research at the human level to include variables obtained in the S_2-R_2 manner.

It is here that individual differences or personality variables can be of vital importance. In the example given, the unobserved variable was suggested as a particular class of childhood experiences. The example could just as well have been one involving variations in heredity. In an analogous way, unobserved events (in this instance, genetic variations) result in relatively per-

[1] Response is a function of stimulus, training or previous experience, drive, and innate individual differences.

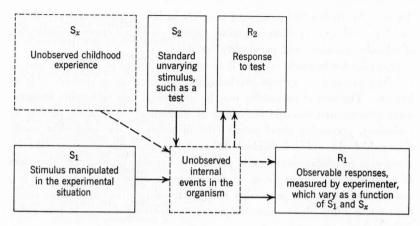

Figure 1. A stimulus-response analysis of an experiment in which a stimulus variable and a personality variable jointly influence a response variable.

manent and stable organismic characteristics. In either example, the changes brought about by S_x would be such that R_2 would be likely to remain approximately the same over a period of time, barring specific types of interventions. Among other implications, this would mean that the determination of R_2 could be at a point separated in time from the determination of R_1. These response characteristics, designated as personality variables, can thus be utilized in long-range prediction.[2]

Returning to the diagram, an investigation of the relationship between S_1 and R_1 would be designated as a study falling in the realm of general experimental psychology, and the findings would deal with relationships between stimuli in the present situation and responses that hold for all individuals. Any investigation in which R_2 was utilized would be designated as a study falling in the realm of personality. Furthermore, it seems probable that work with human subjects will involve an integrated approach to an increasing

[2] There are other unobserved and uncontrolled antecedent conditions which differ from personality variables in that they fluctuate over short periods of time. Such variables include unidentified external stimulus changes (e.g., barometric pressure) and unobserved internal events (e.g., hormone production). If neither barometric pressure nor hormone production were under experimental control and if their variation resulted in measurable response differences, the most direct solution would be to seek to operationalize the responsible stimuli. An alternative approach would be to consider their effects as personality variables. In this instance, however, the determination of R_2 and R_1 must be at approximately the same time. It might be useful to classify personality variables as either relatively stable (analogous to weight measured by a scale) or relatively subject to fluctuation (analogous to temperature measured by a thermometer).

degree.   As Meili (1961) suggests, progress in both experimental and differential psychology will almost certainly depend on simultaneous consideration of stimulus variables and personality variables.

Primarily for heuristic reasons, it is sometimes useful to divide the sort of activities pursued by various psychologists into even more specific fields of interest. The area of personality may be subdivided into personality measurement (the construction and evaluation of instruments to measure personality variables), personality development (the discovery of the antecedent conditions which determine individual differences), personality structure (the investigation of relationships among personality variables), personality dynamics (the simultaneous investigation of the effects of stimulus variables and personality variables), and personality change (the determination of those conditions which bring about either temporary or enduring changes in personality variables).

MEASUREMENT IN PERSONALITY RESEARCH

Science and the Measurement of Variables

PHYSICAL SCIENCES AND BEHAVIORAL SCIENCES.   In many respects, the basic assumptions of science run contrary to beliefs widely held in our culture. The benefits of the technology which grows out of science are obvious and are highly valued. The scientific enterprise itself is neither obvious in its functioning nor highly valued as an activity. Individuals engaged in basic research seldom find themselves honored by ticker-tape parades. And, until it has achieved a given success, there seem to be widespread doubts about science's reaching its goals. As one of the original *F*-scale items phrases it, "Science has its place, but there are many important things that can never possibly be understood by the human mind" (Adorno, Frenkel-Brunswik, Levinson, and Sanford, 1950, p. 256).

Even more resistance is met when we go beyond the physical sciences. There seems to be a greater degree of scepticism about the possibility of building a science of behavior, for example, than about the possibility of building a science of inorganic matter. Perhaps one underlying source of doubt lies in McClelland's (1951) suggestion that Western Civilization has been influenced to some extent by the Hebrew tradition that man's wish to know about man is presumptuous and sinful.

The behavioral sciences have to face a variety of lay criticism ranging from the notion that human behavior is unpredictable (as a function of the operation of free will or divine planning or some other non-operational construct) to the notion that having one's own behavior predicted is undesirable.   The latter reaction is exemplified by William Whyte's (1956) suggestion that prospective employees should cheat on personnel tests in order to subvert the selection process. Martin Gross (1962) goes so far as to assert that even the attempt to predict the behavior of individual men is immoral because it is a violation of personal destiny. Both the notion that human behavior is unpredictable and that "the human mind can be weighed" have yet to be generally assimilated in our culture. Obviously behavior could, in fact, turn out to be largely unpredictable and unmeasurable, but that possibility is becoming an increasingly unlikely one.

Another somewhat curious sort of distinction has been made, often at a relatively sophisticated level, by individuals both inside and outside of our field. That is, social and physical sciences are sometimes differentiated along an abstract-concrete dimension. For example, Robert S. Morison (1960) of the Rockefeller Foundation made the following points in an address at the 1959 APA convention:

> The elementary facts in the physical sciences are concrete entities which present themselves immediately to the senses. . . . Psychology, insofar as it is different from biology and ascends from sensory physiology to that obscure realm in which bits of data are put together into perceptions, memories, and complex motor acts, does not present itself immediately to the senses of the observer. The mind is after all an inference, and it is hard to study the morphology of an inference. By the very nature of its material, psychology has been deprived of the morphological phase which has provided such a solid groundwork for the other sciences . . . (pp. 195–196).

Morison offers a way out of this handicapped position. Psychologists can become more biological in outlook and method by moving toward such fields as ethology and neurophysiology. Work in these areas helps give "material substance to what have hitherto been rather misty and abstract concepts" (p. 196).

Perhaps the fairest statement to make in reply to such characterizations is to suggest that the writer must entertain certain misconceptions about the subject matter of psychology. Actually, he is distinguishing science and non-science. Anyone would be hard pressed to defend the proposition that the content of various scientific disciplines differs along such dimensions as "concreteness," "availability to the senses," or "abstractness." On the contrary, planetary motion and authoritarian behavior are equally concrete, equally available to the senses, equally lawful, and equally measurable. Psychology is at an early stage of development compared to relatively mature fields such as astronomy, physics, and chemistry, but the initial problems and procedures in any developing field of knowledge are quite similar. As an example, we can consider an early physics problem (speed of falling objects) as compared with a current psychological one (conformity). Without necessarily claiming that our conceptual systems are as developed or as generalized in their implications as those of physics at the end of the sixteenth century, essential similarities may still be noted.

MEASURING SPEED AND MEASURING CONFORMITY. Most of the gross methodological problems dealing with the measurement of such variables as time or distance or weight or temperature have been solved relatively well by our colleagues in the physical sciences. There is, of course, no end point at which one can say that the measurement of a variable is infinitely precise and hence no longer a problem. However, when improvement is perceptible, it is possible to appreciate the lack of precision of previous eras. For example, there is a considerable difference in the precision of atomic clocks which vary one second in 1500 years compared to the ponderous clocks in the village square a few centuries back which varied as much as two hours a day. It is difficult to conceive the future impact of comparable improvements in psychological measurement.

It was probably very early in the history of our species when someone verbalized the notion that "all that goes up must come down." A considerable period of time was to pass, however, before much progress was made in answering or even in asking such questions as "How fast do they come down?" or "Why do they come down?" As an essential step in achieving this progress, an approach had been made over the centuries toward conceptualizing and measuring weight, distance, time, and speed. Sufficiently adequate solutions had been devised by the year 1589 to make it possible for Galileo to conduct experimental work on these problems. By using an inclined plane, he found that the distance covered by falling bodies per unit of time increases as the square of the time involved in their fall, and he concluded that in a vacuum all objects would fall with exactly equal velocities. It is obvious that this work would have been impossible prior to the development of the necessary techniques to quantify the relevant variables. Time, for example, was measured by weighing the amount of water poured from a special spout while the object was descending. To underline this point, it might be noted that Galileo hypothesized that light had a finite velocity, but he was unable to verify this possibility experimentally because of inadequate measuring instruments. Thus, he had tools which were of sufficient reliability and validity to answer some questions but not others. The reciprocal relationship between developments in theory-building and developments in the construction of measuring devices is a familiar one in many fields.

It was very likely at a relatively more recent date when someone first verbalized the idea that some individuals are more likely than others to alter their opinions in order to conform with the majority view. And, it was not until half-way through this century that an experimental procedure was employed to deal with questions such as "Under what conditions do people conform?" or "Why do some people conform more than others?" Our experimental equipment must equal or exceed Galileo's in crudity, but it is sufficiently advanced to make possible the undertaking of a varied array of investigations. A respectable body of literature gives us information about stimulus variables and individual differences variables which determine conforming responses as indicated by frequency of yielding to an incorrect majority. There is little reason to doubt that our conceptualizations about conformity and our ability to measure it and the variables relevant to it will improve as much in the next three and a half centuries as have the conceptualizations and methodology of physics in dealing with gravitational phenomena over the past 350 years. If so, the hypotheses tested, the instruments utilized in experimentation, and the theories constructed by psychologists of the future would almost certainly be unrecognizable to the primitive behavioral scientists of the twentieth century.

THE EVOLUTION OF MEASUREMENT IN SCIENCE. Still another example of the parallel between the development of physical measures and of behavioral measures was given by Zubin (1961) at a recent symposium at Columbia.

The question is often raised about the lag between measurement in personality and in the physical sciences. We regard personality evaluation as still highly intuitive, subjective, and hence, unreliable and invalid. But all measurement began in this fashion. The first measures of length, weight, time, temperature, touch, etc. were originally subjective, self-referred and intuitively based. Let us look at the measurement of subjective warmth. Since there is no documentary evidence for man's initial attempts at gauging the cause and degree of subjective warmth, we shall resort to fantasy. Come with me to a cave in some prehistoric Ice Age, before fire was invented, and listen to a symposium on the origin of subjective warmth feelings. One savant declares that warmth depends on the number of skins covering the body. Another claims that it depends on duration of exposure to the sun. A third postulates swift running as the source of warmth and the distance covered as a measure. The medicine man in their midst raises a controversy because of his claim that his patients often report and feel warm without the benefit of any of the other factors mentioned. The symposium ends without a resolution. But someone later invents fire and demonstrates that by adding faggots to the fire, subjective warmth is raised in all the inhabitants of the cave and by the same token removal of faggots reduces it. The first break-through has occurred. Man can manipulate an external agent to raise and lower the temperature at will. But this is still far from measurement. The first known historical break-through occurs in Egypt, where rating scales are developed for measuring warmth in four steps—with warmth likened at one extreme to the hottest day of summer, and at the other extreme to the coldest day of winter. Eventually, the expansion of mercury with increase of subjective warmth is noted, and the thermometer is born, and finally, humidity and air pressure are recognized as important factors, and the present day discomfort index emerges. What were the essential steps in the process? First, the discovery of a means of inducing a subjective experience by external control. Second, the development of an external criterion for measurement independent of the self-referred subjective experience. The same process, no doubt, held true of the other measures which have attained great objectivity. Pain is still a subjective phenomenon without an external criterion, and without measurable ways of inducing it, though recent efforts along these lines show considerable promise. Intelligence tests became objective when mental age scales were substituted for subjective impressions. Anxiety, depression, elation, are still in the rating stage. In my fantasy, I sometimes imagine that we may find a life-bearing planet, somewhere in space, where anxiety has already been measured, but where warmth or length are still on the intuitive level.

As general truisms, it seems that quantification is an essential step in science, and that the history of most fields reveals a gradual development of increasingly more precise measuring instruments. It is also clear that theoretical advances and advances in measurement proceed hand in hand. As theories expand, the need for precise measurement increases. As precise measuring instruments become available, the possibility of testing and extending theories increases correspondingly. In the next section, attention is turned to some of the specific measurement concerns in personality research.

Reliability of Measurement

Baughman and Welsh (1962) describe a clever classroom demonstration of the effects of differentially reliable measuring instruments on measurement consistency. The width of a classroom lectern was measured successively by a visual estimate, a 3×5 card, and a finely divided yardstick. Consistency of measurement by the classroom group increased across these three techniques as shown by the progressively smaller ranges and standard deviations.

The task of measurement is that of ordering events along a dimension of discriminable differences. Reliability refers to the consistency with which this ordering is done. Measurement error refers to inconsistency in measurement. At the risk of laboring the obvious, to the extent that the measuring instruments are inconsistent, they provide data which combine the variance we are attempting to predict with unpredicted "error" variance. The possibility of building a cumulative body of interlocking findings is not notably enhanced by the use of rubber rulers, variable interval clocks, leaking thermometers, or equally unreliable behavioral measures. As elementary as these statements appear, it is hardly uncommon to find that one experimenter in psychology measures a response variable with instrument A of low (or unknown) reliability and discovers that his results are inexplicably incompatible with the results of another experimenter who measures that response variable with instrument B which is also of low (or unknown) reliability. It appears that variations in methodology and unconcern with reliability of measurement are by no means atypical in some areas of psychological investigation (Byrne and Holcomb, 1962).

Four types of reliability were defined by the committees who produced the APA publication which dealt with technical recommendations for tests (APA, 1954). These types will be included in the following discussion, but they will be approached in a slightly different fashion.

STIMULUS CONSISTENCY. The term "reliability" is not generally applied to stimulus variables. However, the major source of inconsistency or unreliability of measurement probably lies in unintentional stimulus variability.

A very simple situation is depicted in Figure 2. A stimulus is presented to an organism, and a response is elicited. Variations in that response across individuals or within one individual over time may be the result of (accidental) variations in the external stimulus, inaccuracies in recording the response, or internal stimulus variables. The first two possibilities are sources of error variance and should be eliminated. If they are eliminated to a satisfactory degree, the remaining variations in the response constitute a legitimate problem for a personality approach.

Unintentional stimulus variations occur in two ways. Figure 2 shows what is generally identified as the stimulus in a given experiment: the operationally defined independent variable manipulated by the experimenter. It is obviously extremely difficult to control or even to specify all of the external stimuli which are impinging on the receptors of the organism. It is obvious, nevertheless, that many stimulus variables other than the operationally defined ones are acting in the situation. These peripheral stimuli are at

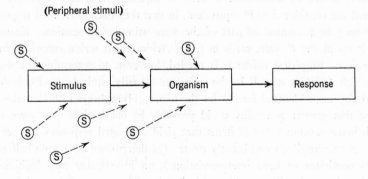

Figure 2

times partially operationalized by the experimenter. For example, an experimenter might measure or even regulate room brightness but fail to consider room temperature.

As a minimal operational statement, an attempt is made to identify that stimulus or stimulus complex which is believed to be primary in eliciting the responses which constitute the dependent variable. The defined stimulus may be a simple cue in a psychological investigation or the 566 printed items in a questionnaire. Ideally, this stimulus is defined with sufficient clarity that any investigator is able to reproduce it with exactness. Though in many instances even the specification of the central stimulus is faulty, probably the greatest source of stimulus inconsistency in otherwise well-designed studies lies in the peripheral stimuli.

The suggestion that uncontrolled peripheral stimuli contribute to error variance is not entirely an academic spinning of wheels. Examples of such variables which have been found to affect certain kinds of responses are age of experimenter (Mussen and Scodel, 1955), room decor (Maslow and Mintz, 1956), race of experimenter (Ranking and Campbell, 1955), anxiety and hostility of the experimenter (Sanders and Cleveland, 1953), sex of experimenter (Doris and Fierman, 1956), information about the purpose of the investigation (Henry and Rotter, 1956), and the presence of other subjects (Kimble, 1945). In addition, we could suggest a host of possibilities such as subject procurement procedure, time of day, day of week, season of the year, room temperature, and atmospheric pressure. No experimenter has attempted to determine and report all such peripheral stimuli; the necessity of doing so depends on empirical demonstrations of their influence on a given response.

When a stimulus is a complex one in that it consists of a combination of discrete stimuli, it is assumed that the stimuli being combined are actually equivalent. The combining of non-equivalent stimuli is probably the second greatest source of measurement error in psychology. First, whenever two stimuli are considered to be equivalent, in that they elicit correlated responses, they may be presented as part of the same stimulus dimension. Examples are items in the *F* scale, cards in the *n* Achievement series, questions in an interview. Empirical evidence is needed, however, to determine the degree to which different stimuli in the series are actually equivalent. Equivalence need not mean identical format for the items. Humphreys (1962) makes the point that greater generality could probably be obtained if tests were built with heterogeneous *types* of items that yield correlated responses. When responses to stimuli do consistently covary (as determined by a split-half reliability coefficient or item intercorrelations), an investigator may legitimately employ those stimuli as a dimensional unit. Thus, a coefficient of internal consistency provides evidence that a given stimulus complex is not simply a haphazard collection of unrelated units.[3]

Similarly, when two stimuli or sets of stimuli are utilized on separate occasions as equivalent means of eliciting responses, evidence is required that one is actually using interchangeable stimuli. The correlation between responses elicited by the two instruments is the coefficient of equivalence.

Thus, with respect to stimulus consistency, reliable measurement implies a striving for (1) sufficient identification of the central and peripheral stimuli to be identical across experiments, (2) the utilization of stimuli which elicit correlated responses to form a dimension, and (3) the interchangeable use of different sets of stimuli only if they have been found to be equivalent.

RESPONSE CONSISTENCY. Two of the familiar types of reliability determination deal with inconsistencies in quantifying responses. First, a necessary, but not sufficient, condition for the measurement of any variable is interscorer agreement. Two or more experimenters must be able to arrive independently at essentially the same score. With some scoring systems (such as a scoring template for a true-false answer sheet), it is usually assumed that any two normally functioning experimenters would report the same score. With other variables (such as affiliation imagery in thematic apperception protocols), it is quite possible for two different judges to assign scores which differ considerably. Whenever any subjectivity enters into the scoring process, interscorer agreement must be determined by correlating the scores recorded by at least two judges working independently, using the same definitional material. If such a correlation is not in the neighborhood of .90 or better, further work is needed in defining the variable and/or in training the scorers.[4]

The second aspect of response consistency is that of stability over a period of time. The coefficient of stability (test-retest reliability) indicates the extent to which a subject's responses are consistent over time. Instead of assuming that lack of consistency reveals measurement errors, the position could be taken that variations in scores on reliable measuring instruments

[3] It should be noted that a high split-half reliability is not a guarantee of homogeneity. If a test were made up of a random arrangement of two or more sets of homogeneous but unrelated series, the correlation of odd with even items would be high. Only a study of item intercorrelations or a factor analysis would reveal that more than one dimension was contained in the test.

[4] Even with high interscorer correlations, there may be unreliable scoring. For example, two scorers could disagree on many specific items and still arrive at equal total scores. Or, the correlation could be high even though one judge assigned consistently higher scores than another. A percentage agreement index is a useful supplement to interscorer correlations.

reflect meaningful personality variations. Such coefficients offer a way to evaluate the extent to which a given personality variable is stable over time. Obviously, if a variable is assumed to be a stable one and if long-range predictions are made on the basis of such scores, a high coefficient of stability is essential. Perhaps this coefficient might be conceptualized as an indication of the feasibility of labeling a given personality variable as relatively stable or as relatively subject to fluctuation.

Validity of Measurement

In many respects, the question of the validity of a particular measurement has been clouded by concepts borrowed in their entirety from a psychometric tradition in which they were used more appropriately than in personality research. Most descriptions and definitions of validity are appropriate in the evaluation of ability tests which are used only to predict a specific performance. Especially in applied fields, it is essential to know the relationship between one's predictor instrument and the criterion variable. Thus, using the standard terminology, it is reasonable to ask the validity of a scholastic aptitude test, a personnel selection device, or a psychological instrument designed to detect organicity. The higher the validity coefficient, the better is the predictive value of the measuring instrument.

However, such concepts tend to be inappropriate and often troublesome in personality research. Except for specific tests designed to predict specific behaviors, there is no one validity coefficient which could sensibly be interpreted as indicating the value of a test. Thus, terms such as "construct validity" have come into widespread use; "construct validity is evaluated by investigating what psychological qualities a test measures . . ." (APA, 1954, p. 14). And, as Meehl (1959) suggests, the great majority of validation problems which are posed by personality tests are problems of construct validity.

It seems to the author that the term "validity" as it is traditionally used is outmoded and is often a source of confusion. Ebel (1961), among others, has recently made a strong case against the usual conception of test "validity." Following his lead, it is proposed that the following sort of approach be used in evaluating measuring devices used in personality research. The only meaningful validational question is simply "To what are scores on the instrument related?" Response measures should not be conceptualized as an imperfect index of an underlying "real" trait nor as an inadequate substitute for some "real life" behavior in which the tester is primarily interested. Rather, test scores are operationally defined samples of behavior which should be investigated in their own right. The status of these behaviors in psychological theory is determined by the relationship of a given personality dimension to stimulus variables, response variables, and other personality variables.

Another way of asking the validational question is, "What is the best name to apply to the responses measured by this instrument?" As simple (or simple-minded) as this question appears, much of the controversy centering around many tests resolves itself to the naming problem. Hopefully, the name designated for any measured behavior may be thought of as tentative. Perhaps the following qualifying statement should be assumed wherever the name of a test appears: "In view of the item content of this test and its relationships with other variables, at this time the instrument appears best to be conceptualized as a measure of _____."

Finally, and least important at the present time, whenever scores on a given test are used to make specific predictions about some other behavior (as in applied settings), it is essential to determine the validity of the test *for this particular predictive use*. The question here is the familiar one of "How well does the instrument predict variable *X*?" Clearly, this question is only a limited part of the more general question of relationship.

Constructing Reliable Measuring Instruments

The simplest sort of response measure is a unitary one which either involves a two-point scale (present-absent, true-false, etc.) or longer scales along a single dimension (seven degrees of agreement, five-point self-ratings of intensity, etc.). Test construction in such instances generally consists of carefully defining the item and, if appropriate, determining interjudge consistency. If alternate forms are proposed, their intercorrelations should be high. If the measured behavior is conceptualized as a personality variable, its stability over time is of interest. If the response is believed to vary primarily as a function of external or internal stimulus conditions, it should be shown to vary appropriately with stimulus magnitude.

When such items or scales are combined to form longer measuring instruments, complications arise in building instruments which are internally consistent. Essentially, the experimenter is combining imperfectly correlated responses, and the frequency with which a subject gives a particular class of response is taken to indicate the magnitude of that response class. Thus, on an intelligence test the correct repetition of five digits may be scored as one point and the correct definition of "nail" may be scored as another point. If the two responses are correlated and if they make theoretical sense as falling together in a behavior dimension, they may be added as units of intelligence. In this simple, two-item example, the possible total scores are 2, 1, and 0, and the intelligence of anyone measured by this scale would be indicated by his position along this ordinal scale. As more items are added, this measuring device can become an increasingly discriminating one. As suggested in the discussion of reliability, however, when items which elicit unrelated responses are added to the test, inconsistency of measurement is the result. It is here that most test construction inadequacies arise. Perhaps it would be helpful to review the three basic ways in which stimulus items are combined to form a psychological test.

INTUITIVE APPROACH. In any test-construction procedure, the first step is that of assembling items, at least some portion of which may prove useful in measuring the desired behavior. In the other two approaches to be discussed, procedures are described by which an investigator may verify the value of the initial selection process. In the intuitive approach, the initial selection is assumed to be sufficient for measuring purposes.

The experimenter (or a group of judges) selects items which may reasonably be combined. The basis may be theory, logic, guesses about a behavior dimension, common sense, or whatever. On the face of it, it does not seem probable that such a procedure will produce a highly reliable behavior measure which is suitable for the experimenter's purpose, though there are numerous examples in the literature which demonstrate its utility. For example, the author (Byrne, 1956) used a thirty-two-item humor test which was constructed on the basis of unanimous agreement among five judges as to cartoon content. When subjects were asked to sort the cartoons into hostile and non-hostile categories, the resulting Hostility Judging Score yielded a corrected split-half reliability of .86.

The intuitive procedure can obviously be useful as a first step in test construction. With care, it is often possible to select a series of items which yield sufficiently reliable scores for exploratory research. It is assumed that, should the measure prove useful, more effort will be expended on subsequent improvements in the measuring instrument.

When intuitively constructed tests are used, the experimenter is obliged to determine and report the appropriate types of reliability. Such information is helpful in determining the value of the instruments and in interpreting the meaning of the research findings. For example, a test with a split-half reliability of .50 which is consistently related to other variables suggests that (1) the obtained relationships would be considerably greater if a better measuring device were available, and (2) it is probably worthwhile to spend time in improving the measure.

Besides the obvious problems involved when a science is based on data involving poorly measured variables, there is one other danger in relying on intuitively constructed tests. If actual relationships are obscured by inconsistency of measurement, the incidence of Type II errors increases. It seems likely that a mountain of unpublished "negative" findings is stored in our files and that many potentially rewarding avenues of research have been abandoned because our measuring instruments are inadequate for a given problem.

BOOTSTRAP OR INTERNAL CONSISTENCY APPROACH. It is possible to improve item selection beyond simple intuitive judgments about their properties by determining the extent to which presumably similar responses are actually related.

One such procedure is to administer the proposed testing instrument to a relatively large number of individuals, score their responses on the basis of the intuitive scoring system, and determine the relationship between the score on each item and the total score obtained on all the items. A good item is one which is consistent with the intuitive scoring system in that it measures some portion of the same dimension. This procedure is frequently utilized in one form or another. In the successive revisions of the Authoritarian Scale, Adorno et al. (1950) employed internal consistency item analyses, determining the Discriminatory Power of each item for each sample. The average split-half reliability coefficient for their final scale was .90.

A similar, but more elaborate, method is to assemble items, administer them to a sample of subjects, and then employ factor analytic procedures to determine those items which covary. In this way, factorially pure and internally consistent scales may be obtained.

EXTERNAL CRITERION APPROACH. Whenever an adequate external criterion is available, it is possible and usually desirable to use it for the selection of items. Thus, items are retained in the test if they share the property of relationship with an external variable. This method can be further subdivided into experimental and correlational approaches.

When an experimental technique is used, the test constructor manipulates relevant peripheral stimuli such that one group experiences a given experimental procedure while a second group does not. Any differences in responding to the central stimulus which is common to both groups are attributed to differences in the peripheral stimuli. Application of the test in subsequent groups under neutral conditions is assumed to indicate characteristic differences in the presence of stimuli analagous to the peripheral ones. For example, if certain items were answered in specifically different ways by subjects exposed to hostility arousal conditions than by subjects exposed to neutral conditions, responses by subsequent subjects like those of the hostility group would suggest the presence of internal cues similar to those present in the experimental group. This approach has been utilized primarily in developing scoring systems for projective measures of motivation, including need for achievement (McClelland, Atkinson, Clark, and Lowell, 1953) and need for affiliation (Shipley and Veroff, 1952).

A more common technique is a correlational one. Group differences or differences along a dimension are determined by other procedures, and then the proposed test items are correlated with this criterion. Those items which are significantly related to this external variable are retained. This method has been widely used; examples include each of the clinical scales of the MMPI (Hathaway and McKinley, 1940) and the occupational scales of the Strong Vocational Interest Blank (1943).

With all of these techniques, of course, cross validation of the item analysis procedure should be carried out, and the appropriate types of reliability should be determined.

GENERALIZATION OF TEST CONSTRUCTION METHODOLOGY. In much of this discussion and most others about reliability, validity, and test construction, it may sound as if the only type of behavior measure under consideration is some sort of paper and pencil test. Procedures such as item analysis are described most clearly in the context of a true-false questionnaire, for example. Nevertheless, the same rules and procedures apply for any type of behavior measure and for any attempt to combine responses to measure a personality variable or a response variable.

Any scoring scheme for projective tests, for example, should be evaluated in this way. And measurement of overt physical acts fits into this same conceptual system. If we were interested in measuring overt hostile behavior on the part of mothers toward their children, the same problems and procedures would apply as in measuring manifest anxiety by means of a series of true-false questions. An investigator should have the same concerns about consistency in the stimulus (e.g., child placed in experimenter's waiting room) and consistency in response measurement (e.g., observation of hostile maternal responses through one-way screen). And if different responses were to be combined to obtain a dimensional score (e.g., hitting, scolding, restricting), the same test-construction considerations would apply. However, test construction methodology has not been frequently applied beyond the bounds of paper and pencil tests.

To what extent *should* measurement considerations influence psychological research? Should test-construction be regarded as a necessary prerequisite to research or as a tidying-up procedure for technicians once the theories are in relatively final form? A number of issues are involved and the solutions have been quite different for different investigators as will be discussed in the following section.

TEST CONSTRUCTION VERSUS THEORY BUILDING

Even though it is possible to obtain general agreement about the goal toward which psychology aims and about our present inadequacies, a point of disagreement arises in the choice of research strategies by which best to advance knowledge in our field. One of the continuing unresolved controversies in the area of personality is determining the relative precedence which should be given to theory building and hypothesis testing in contrast to test construction and the refinement of methodology. This is a special kind of chicken and egg problem; which should come first?

A Problem in Research

SELECTING A BEHAVIOR MEASURE. Perhaps a way of getting this strategy problem into concrete terms is to consider the sort of problem faced by any experimenter, as for example the contributors to this symposium.

It is easy to reach agreement when ideal conditions are being discussed. Ideally, any researcher who is interested in any aspect of personality change would prefer to utilize the most precise of measuring instruments. No one selects inadequate assessment techniques as a matter of choice. If someone were interested in changes in personality variable Y as a function of experimental manipulation X, it might be decided to measure Y before, immediately after, and several months after the occurrence of X. He would turn to the International Index of Standard Tests and select three parallel measures of Y. The three instruments would be of nearly perfect reliability and the validity of the instrument as a measure of Y would be clear from a series of correlational and experimental investigations. The three forms of the test would have equal means, variances, and covariances. Their intercorrelations would be above .90.

Back here in the real world, however, an investigator's actual procedure is likely to be considerably different from that described. Let us say that an experimenter has some hypotheses about the effect of a laboratory manipulation or a naturalistic occurrence on achievement need. On the basis of theory or observation, he has reason to propose that the specified stimulus events would result in an increase in the motive to achieve. In attempting to select appropriate operations for the measurement of this personality variable, several difficulties arise. There is no International Index of Standard Tests, and no one has developed a parallel series of achievement tests of the sort desired.[5] In fact, scores on three widely used measures of achievement

[5] With few exceptions (e.g., Moran, Kimble, and Mefferd, 1960), parallel series of measures do not exist for any behavioral variables.

need are unrelated to one another. Correlations which do not differ significantly from zero are found when the thematic apperception measure (McClelland et al., 1953), the French Insight Test (French, 1958), and *n* Ach on the Personal Preference Schedule (Edwards, 1954) are investigated simultaneously (Atkinson and Litwin, 1960; Himelstein, Eschenbach, and Carp, 1958; Marlowe, 1959). These are not interchangeable measuring instruments. The task of choosing the one which most closely approximates the investigator's definition of achievement and of solving the pre-experimental and post-experimental comparison problem is a formidable one. Problems are involved for which no universally accepted solution has been found.

With many other personality dimensions and response variables, there are even more difficult stumbling blocks to adequate assessment. It is not an uncommon experience to talk to a student who has an intriguing research idea which involves a personality variable such as dependency or anal retentiveness or organization-mindedness. When he is asked how he plans to measure the dimension in question, he says, "I thought there must already be some test to measure that." Very quickly he finds that "Quite unlike the biological sciences, personality research has not developed standard methods or instruments of investigation" (Brenglemann, 1960, p. 294).

It is at this point that any investigator must make decisions about the best strategy for research. In one sense, there is a continuum of values which ranges from an emphasis on measurement and methodology to an emphasis on theory and hypotheses. Perhaps it would be helpful to look at the issues involved in more detail.

Inductive and Deductive Biases

DIFFERENCES IN STRATEGY. Though not many psychologists seem explicitly to label themselves in the following way, it is possible to observe decided differences in their preferences for one of two types of experimental strategy. Those with a deductive bent tend to begin with a theoretical problem (either their own or someone else's) and then design an experimental test of hypotheses deduced from the theory. The particular operations used in a given experiment are somewhat arbitrary and somewhat irrelevant. That is, the variables are defined by the theory and any one of a variety of different operations could have been employed in a given investigation. On the other hand, psychologists with an inductive bent tend to begin with a methodological technique (either their own or someone else's) and then generate data which must be explained by a theory induced from the findings. The particular theoretical statement which is formulated is somewhat arbitrary in that any set of findings can be explained in some way or other by an inventive investigator. The problem is defined by the existence of a consistent body of data which result from a specific set of operations; different operations can be substituted only if they are known to yield equivalent data.

Obviously, it is impossible to have a purely deductive or inductive approach. All theorizing is based on some sort of data and all data gathering involves some direction if only by implicit theories. Nevertheless, the differences in emphasis do exist, and these differences have many implications for research.

With respect to measurement, these value differences are reflected in rather specific ways. Is it best to build theories and test hypotheses with admittedly inadequate data measurement or is it preferable to concentrate on problems of measurement as a step preliminary to experimentation? An investigator's orientation on the deductive-inductive continuum should determine the answer which is made. Both ways of proceeding have their strengths and weaknesses. The primary advantage of giving measurement a secondary position is that the initial theories and subsequent experimental findings provide guidelines which indicate what it is that is worth measuring. The primary advantage of giving precedence to measurement is that one's experimental results are not based on the shifting sands of error variance.

In the field of personality, it should be possible to place each investigator at some point along the continuum. On one side of the median are investigators such as Cattell who has explicitly and cogently argued for the precedence of measurement and the delineation of basic variables (Cattell, 1959). In his view, of course, these initial steps can best be accomplished using multivariate methodology.

Psychologists lying on the other side of the median have not been as vocal in relegating measurement problems to a secondary position. Rather, they have simply tended to stress the hypothetico-deductive approach; their relative de-emphasis of measurement as a preliminary problem is best seen in their actual work. Much of the work in experimental psychology exemplifies one sort of solution to the measurement problem. It is possible for investigators to concentrate all of their research work on a limited number of dependent variables which can be easily quantified, often along physical dimensions (speed of running in a straight-alley runway, frequency of pressing a lever, number of trials to reach criterion, etc.). Thus, it is possible to concentrate on theory and experiment, utilize physical measures, and remain apart from the controversy. In personality investigations, more complex variables are measured, because such measurement is sometimes necessary in testing hypotheses. Levy (1961) suggests that research activity may be determined primarily by the existence of problems or by the existence of techniques. He feels that researchers whose activity indicates that they fall in the former category are likely to be labeled theorists, while those in the latter category are likely to be known as methodologists. Furthermore, he indicates that the theorist label is more socially desirable and that when techniques are the stimulus for research, opportunism is implied.

STRATEGY DIFFERENCES AND PERSONALITY RESEARCH. The basis for these differences in approach and in bias is a part of the historical division which Cronbach (1957) characterizes as experimental and correlational psychology. Though the field of personality is primarily identified with correlational psychology, both camps have contributed to its present form.

All areas of scientific inquiry have their roots in philosophical speculation, and personality is no exception. However, twentieth century physics seems a long qualitative and quantitative distance from the speculations of Lucretius, while twentieth century personality is still to a great extent influenced by the theorizing analogous to that of the poet-physicist of the first century B.C. A familiar approach to the study of personality has been the theorist who is interested in constructing a broad, descriptive framework to account for his myriad observations of human behavior in everyday life or in psychotherapeutic interactions. Primarily as a function of the training of most such theorists, the original empirical referents of their constructs are often not made explicit. And the possibility of utilizing these theories for making specific and accurate predictions about behavior is often non-existent. From the point of view of the theorists, the primary aim was to make sense out of behavior by constructing after-the-fact explanations limited only by man's imagination. Within such a context, the test of a theory's value consists of making a subjective judgment as to whether one's new observations are consistent with the structure of the theory.

Obviously, such an approach to personality has not given rise to a notable concern with the measurement of behavior and has not made any direct contribution to measurement methodology. However, many personality variables were described, and a good many later tests have had their origins in these global accounts of human behavior. Personality theorists of this sort have generally been content to leave the measurement of such variables as orality, inferiority feelings, and parataxic functioning to others. Moreover, attempts to measure such variables have usually met with something short of enthusiasm on the part of the theorists and their adherents. A common criticism has been that the underlying meaning of a given construct was lost in the sterility of operationism. Such criticism leaves the research-oriented psychologist in a conflict not faced by the clinical theoretician. He must either decide that the construct has no operational referent and is hence relegated to the realm of non-science, or he must decide to sacrifice "conceptual richness" and the blessings of the initiated in order to bring the construct into the empirical world of science.

Most psychologists are quite willing to make the indicated sacrifices. However, much of the initial research in personality placed considerably greater emphasis on theory and experimentation than on assessment techniques. Thus, the experimentally oriented personality researchers shared many theoretical biases with the global theorists but differed from them in being scientists rather than clinicians. Among psychologists, those who carried out most of the early experimental work in personality shared many scientific biases with their correlational colleagues but differed from them with respect to orientation toward measurement. For example, in a widely quoted report published in 1940, Sears, Hovland, and Miller were interested in exploring further some of the implications of the frustration-aggression hypothesis. In order to do so, they recognized the desirability of developing appropriate methods for the measurement of aggressive behavior. These experimenters attempted to devise and evaluate a number of measures of aggression. The instruments ranged from a Joke Test with aggressive and non-aggressive items to an Annoyance Test on which subjects rated the degree to which various things annoyed them. In putting together these tests, there were no item-analysis procedures, and independent evidence of validity was presented for only two of the eight instruments. With respect to consistency of measurement, split-half reliability was reported for one instrument and interjudge consistency for another. In the experiment itself, the evidence for the validity of the instruments was largely negative, but there was no indication of the way in which a better procedure might be employed to construct a test or tests to measure aggressive behavior. The experimenters concluded that "The utter failure of the several paper and pencil tests to reflect this aggression in any consistent and objectively measurable way leaves little hope that the problem of momentary aggression can be studied with their aid" (p. 293).

It would appear that in the late 1930's and early 1940's even some of our most distinguished colleagues had not gone far in solving problems of measurement. In fact, examples of experimentalists who fail to indicate the reliability of their instruments or to report independent evidence of validity may be found in the present decade as well (Byrne and Holcomb, 1962). In experimental work in personality, test construction tends to involve an intuitively based selection of items, and an interest in reliability seldom goes beyond interjudge consistency.

While clinical theorists were weaving theories to explain all of man's behavior and experimenters were beginning to bring interest in such variables into science, still a third group of individuals was working in the field of personality. Primarily within the context of attitude scaling and achievement and aptitude testing, the theories and techniques of psychological measurement were developing rapidly. The overall emphasis was strongly statistical and often involved applied interests. Measurement of such variables as intelligence, job aptitude, scholastic ability, or ethnic prejudice is obviously a part of the field of personality as it is defined here. The tendency for the experimental work and the psychometric work to evolve relatively independently left the former short on measurement and the latter short on theory.

RAPPROCHEMENT IN THE FIELD OF PERSONALITY. It was inevitable that the experimental and psychometric approaches would be combined by some investigators and that the special advantages of each would contribute to the general advancement of behavioral science. As has been indicated by others (Bindra and Scheier, 1954; Cronbach, 1957), such a fusion is characterized by a simultaneous interest in the manipulation of stimulus variables and the determination of individual differences variables as additional factors influencing dependent variables. Of greater importance is the potential payoff in which personality theories are built on an experimental data base consisting of reliably measured variables.

While the deductive-inductive differences do affect various aspects of research activity, it is possible to make certain methodological compromises in which the strengths of each approach to personality research should be combined to benefit the field.

The primary task of science is to obtain knowledge. It seems clear that the building of theories and the testing of hypotheses have proven their usefulness as ways to increase man's knowledge. Measurement is a tool, and an essential tool, in this more general endeavor. However, effective experimental work should include the best possible measurement of personality variables and response variables. Such measurement should be an aid rather than a stumbling block to research.

Let us say that an investigator is interested in the effect of hostility as a personality characteristic on response to different degrees of frustration. Let us say that he knows how he wishes to create degrees of frustration and that he also has an adequate response measure for aggressive responses. However, he is unable to find an appropriate measure of hostility. Two major alternatives present themselves based on the sorts of differences that have been discussed in reference to strategy. On an intuitive basis, the investigator might simply devise some sort of personality test which would have face validity as a hostility measure (a TAT scoring system, a true-false questionnaire, a behavior rating scale, etc.). The only investigation of the test would be as a personality variable in the experiment itself. A second alternative would be to undertake a full-scale test construction project with a large number of subjects, cross-validation samples, determination of the relevant reliability coefficients, independent determinations of validity, establishment of normative data, and possibly an attempt to construct at least two forms of the test simultaneously. In the former alternative, either positive or negative results leave many unanswered questions because the measuring instrument is of unknown precision and doubtful meaning. In the second alternative, a great deal of research time and effort may be spent on building a precise measure of a variable which leads to unfruitful research.

A third possibility seems more reasonable than either extreme. A hostility test could be constructed with greater care than simply assembling test materials and making up an ad hoc scoring system and with less care than would go into a test construction project. Whenever an intuitive scoring procedure is devised, its reliability should be determined and reported. If it is found to be inadequate, a more elaborate item selection technique should be undertaken, either by an internal consistency analysis or through utilization of an external criterion. Even if the sample is small by test construction standards, an important step has been taken toward creating a useful measuring instrument. Reliability can be established on another sample of subjects, and again a relatively small group can be used. If, at this point, reliability is respectably high, one has greater confidence that *something* is being measured in a consistent way. If reliability is still low, further attention might be turned to improving the measure rather than wasting time with an experiment in which data are dependent on an unreliable tool.

With this much attention given to the construction of a personality measure, experimental work can proceed with the knowledge that hypothesis testing is not hampered by the use of rubber yardsticks. Then, given a series of successful investigations using the instrument, it may well turn out that the personality construct is of such validity that it warrants additional work in terms of improved measurement. In the field of personality, the day must eventually arrive when we are concerned not only that there is a difference between groups but how much; not only that there is a relationship but its magnitude; not only that X influences Y but the shape of the curve representing its function.

To work toward such precision, we need to construct the best possible measures for our variables at a given stage of theoretical development. It is difficult to generate much enthusiasm for test construction in the absence of knowledge of the importance of the variable to be measured. And it is equally uninspiring to stumble along with experiments in which poor measurement is the rule.

Obviously, the procedures outlined in the "compromise" are familiar in the actual practice of many investigators. With the exception of the final step of making a serious psychometric effort, many workers in experimental personality have been paying more than lip service to problems of adequate measurement. Familiar examples are the measures of achievement need, anxiety, authoritarianism. Though we have not progressed very far down the alphabet as yet in measuring personality dimensions, it seems clear that whenever more than passing attention is paid to the measurement of an important personality variable, a productive flood of research is almost certain to follow. Levy (1961) may be right that we are more technique oriented than problem oriented, but it would seem that we now have a considerably greater number of well-stated problems than we do of adequate techniques.

And this brings us to another major point concerning the construction of measuring instruments. In spite of our desire to emulate the older sciences, our attempts at theory construction and theory testing are obviously in beginning stages, especially in personality. Theories are essential devices for making sense out of a mass of data, for tying together empirical relationships, for generating new predictions, and for pointing to hitherto unthought of implications. Our present data in the field of personality are not such that our theories rest on firm foundations. Therefore, a measuring device is more than simply a tool for hypothesis testing. It can, and usually does, become a primary means by which further data can be obtained. For example, we may notice—in the course of psychotherapy, or riding a bus, or observing our relatives—that there are consistent individual differences in behaviors which may be given the label "compulsive." Such an observation may lead to notions about how these differences came to be, with what other concurrent behaviors they are related, and what future behaviors they will predict. However, such speculations and hunches are several steps removed from actually testing them. And, once a measuring device for compulsivity is actually constructed, experimental results are unlikely to correspond to a high degree with the original "theory." These unpredicted data plus any other incidental data gathered through the use of the instrument now become a primary set of facts to be explained by a theory. And it is the author's opinion that facts derived from research activity are more likely to lead to fruitful theories than the original uncontrolled observations. There is a constant interaction between inductive and deductive processes; thus, good measuring devices have value beyond simply allowing us to test existing theories. The use of the microscope and telescope has not been that of simply verifying hypotheses originated before the development of these instruments.

As an illustration of the problems of measurement and of the utility of possessing adequate measuring devices, one approach to measuring anxiety will be discussed.

MEASURING ANXIETY AND CHANGES IN ANXIETY

Both as a response variable and as a personality variable, the concept of anxiety holds a pervasive and extremely important position in many theoretical formulations about human behavior. This is especially true in the field of personality as is cogently discussed by Murray in Chapter 8, and by Luborsky and Schimek in Chapter 3.

Definitions of anxiety have varied both in terms of specific content and in terms of operational referents. The measurement of anxiety has included such diverse approaches as simple self-rating scales and elaborate physiological indices. The single anxiety measure which has perhaps had the greatest use in psychological research has been Janet Taylor Spence's Manifest Anxiety Scale.

The Manifest Anxiety Scale

CONSTRUCTING AN ANXIETY MEASURE. In attempting to measure anxiety, experimenters have usually concentrated either on a response measure which fluctuates in response to internal and external cues or on an enduring personality variable which is relatively constant across situations. Taylor (1953) focused on the latter sort of definition of anxiety. Her purpose in building such a scale was to utilize a measure of manifest anxiety as an index of drive level.

Essentially, her initial step was the utilization of the intuitive approach to test construction. A definition of manifest anxiety was given to five clinicians along with 200 MMPI items. Their instructions were to judge which of the items appeared to measure anxiety as defined. She obtained 80 per cent or better agreement on 65 of the items.

Successful research efforts with this intuitively constructed anxiety test led Bechtoldt (1953) to attempt to improve the measuring instrument by means of an internal consistency analysis of the items. The result was a 50-item scale made up of those items which had the highest correlations with the total score. The internal consistency of the test appears to be high even with the original 65-item test for which a split-half reliability coefficient of .92 has been reported (Hilgard, Jones, and Kaplan, 1951). As given in the "Biographical Inventory" form, the MAS was found to have a test-retest reliability of .89 over a three-week period, .82 over a five-month period, and

.81 over nine to seventeen months. Since the means also remained relatively constant over time, this test would appear potentially useful for measuring changes in a relatively stable personality characteristic. Even better, of coruse, would be the development of one or more scales which are equivalent to the present MAS, so that repeated measurement could be on different instruments. The IPAT 8-Parallel-Form Anxiety Battery developed by Scheier and Cattell (1960) is an example of the sort of parallel instruments which are needed.

VALIDITY: TO WHAT IS IT RELATED? In attempting to gain an empirical understanding of the meaning of scores on this test, perhaps it is well to omit studies in which test scores were utilized as an index of drive level. The orientation of the learning and performance experiments was not toward "anxiety" per se, and a summary of that use of the test requires a more extensive analysis than is appropriate here. Even though Taylor was not directly interested in the study of anxiety, her test was obviously destined to be widely used for that purpose. It is in this context that the following summary is offered.

When MAS scores are compared with behavior ratings of anxiety, a positive relationship of relatively low magnitude is generally reported. For example, MAS scores have been found to be significantly related to anxiety ratings made by psychologists, psychiatrists, and counselors by Buss, Wiener, Durkee, and Baer (1955), Gleser and Ulett (1952), Hoyt and Magoon (1954), Lauterbach (1958), and Siegman (1956).

Other tests which are used as anxiety measures are sometimes found to be related to the MAS, sometimes not. In general, the closer the other instrument approaches the MAS with respect to a true-false questionnaire form, the higher is the relationship. The MAS is positively correlated with the Welsh Anxiety Index on the MMPI (Windle, 1955), measures of test anxiety (Raphelson, 1957; Sarason, 1961), the Saslow Screening Test of anxiety-proneness (Gleser and Ulett, 1952), and the Elizur Rorschach Content measure of anxiety (Goodstein, 1954). However, it has been found unrelated to anxiety as measured by the Iowa Multiple-Choice Picture Interpretation Test (Goodstein, 1954) or the Discomfort-Relief Quotient (Lebo and Applegate, 1959).

Individual variations in physiological indices of anxiety are generally found to be unrelated to MAS scores. Jackson and Bloomberg (1958) report no relationship between MAS and either palmar sweating or blink rate, while Raphelson (1957) reports that the MAS and skin conductance are independent. Sarason (1960) suggests that such negative findings may be a function of failure to study *patterns* of physiological responding and failure to measure subjects' physiological responses under stress conditions. For example, Berry and Martin (1957) found no relationship between scores on the test anxiety questionnaire and GSR; however, Kissel and Littig (1962) did find a relationship between these two measures when GSR's were obtained in a failure situation. Still another possibility is Hunt's (Strupp and Luborsky, 1962) report that *changes* in palmar sweat in a threatening condition are predicted by the MAS; studies with negative results may have used inappropriate physiological indices. It is also possible that the personality variable measured by the MAS and the response variable measured by various physiological indicators are simply unrelated and hence should not be given the undifferentiating label of "anxiety." Such increases in the specificity of the meaning of concepts are to be expected.

A final sort of validity data has to do with pathology and the MAS. Since a characteristic of many pathological states is a relatively elevated level of anxiety, it is reasonable to expect a purported measure of anxiety to differentiate normal and abnormal individuals. The evidence here supporting the MAS is overwhelmingly positive. For example, compared to normals, significantly higher MAS scores are obtained by psychiatric patients (Taylor, 1953) and by dysthymics and hysterics (Eysenck and Claridge, 1962). Patients with a diagnosis of anxiety reaction score higher than those in any other diagnostic category (Siegman, 1956), and MAS scores are positively related to the Total Pathology Score of the Clinical Psychiatric Rating Scale (Shatin, 1961). In addition, on the MMPI the MAS is positively related to scores on the Winne Neuroticism Scale (Holtzman, Calvin, and Bitterman, 1952; Kerrick, 1955; Windle, 1955) and to the neurotic triad (Windle, 1955), is virtually interchangeable with the psychasthenia scale (Brackbill and Little, 1954; Eriksen and Davids, 1955), and is correlated with a variety of other MMPI scales and combinations of scales.

It would seem, then, that scores on the Manifest Anxiety Scale are related to a number of other test and non-test behaviors, the totality of which contributes to the definition of this measuring device. Further, enough of these other measures are relevant to the term "anxiety" that this seems to be a reasonable name for that which the MAS measures. This is not to say that all behaviors which have been given this label are measured by the MAS. As noted, palmar sweating and the verbal behavior indicated by the Discomfort-Relief Quotient are not. Nevertheless, until more accurate and noncontradictory labels are agreed upon, it appears to be justifiable to use the MAS as one measure of what is meant by "anxiety."

Measuring Personality Change

CHANGES IN MANIFEST ANXIETY. Even without the series of parallel forms suggested as ideal a little earlier, it has become possible to utilize Taylor's scale to measure changes in anxiety. The same test is administered on two different occasions; if effective change-inducing events intervene between the two measurement periods, test scores should change. Fruitful research of this type should lead to developments in several directions. The existence of a measuring device makes it possible to test the efficacy of various change agents. At the same time, positive results in this and other work with the MAS should act as an inducement for the development of more refined anxiety measurement. And, as the focus shifts from validating the MAS to validating the agents of change, it should prove possible to include such studies in an overall experimental program designed to build a theory of personality change. To date, what is the evidence with respect to various types of stimulus manipulations as effectors of changes in anxiety?

Psychotherapy is a complex process designed to alter behavior, and one expectancy would be that successful psychotherapy should bring about anxiety reduction. Changes in MAS scores would be expected to indicate this reduction if (1) psychotherapy is effective in altering this personality variable and if (2) the MAS does, in fact, measure the sort of behavior that therapists believe that they are changing. Thus, a double validation is involved.

An investigation of the effect of psychotherapy was reported by Lorr, McNair, Michaux, and Raskin (1962). Patients at a number of VA Mental Hygiene Clinics took the MAS along with a series of other measures at the beginning of treatment and after 4, 8, and 12 months. Only for the latter comparison was there a significant pretherapy to post-therapy change in MAS scores. Another investigation involved the effects of client-centered therapy with 42 college students at the clinic at Pennsylvania State College. Gallagher (1953) tested the proposition that therapy influences anxiety, using the MAS as a measure of what he called "anxiety stress." As Gallagher suggested, a necessary but not sufficient criterion of successful therapy is the reduction of anxiety. Along with other measures of anxiety, MAS scores were significantly lower after the termination of therapy than at the beginning of therapy. Also, the magnitude of the change in anxiety scores was significantly related to several indices of therapeutic success.

Another investigation in which the effect of a therapeutic activity on anxiety was studied was that of Lebo, Toal, and Brick (1958). Carbon dioxide therapy has been used in clinical settings as a means of reducing anxiety symptoms. In this investigation, prisoners were selected who had been diagnosed as having symptoms of manifest anxiety; half were given carbon dioxide therapy and half were not. The MAS was given before therapy began and after it was completed. Compared to the control group, the experimental group revealed a significant reduction in anxiety scores.

Situational stress which continues over a sufficiently long period of time would be expected to bring about an elevation in anxiety level. And anxiety reduction should occur when the situation is resolved. For example, impending surgery, loss of employment, or notification of induction into the armed services should raise MAS scores. When the operation is completed, a new job is obtained, or adjustment to the service has taken place, MAS scores should diminish. Davids, DeVault, and Talmadge (1961) measured anxiety among women during pregnancy and following child birth. Though their primary interest was in comparing anxiety scores of women whose offspring did and did not have abnormalities at birth, their data do suggest that the MAS scores of both groups of mothers decreased after the birth of a child.

Finally, anxiety can apparently be raised by hypnotic suggestions involving fear and tension. Grosz and Levitt (1959) induced anxiety in a group of twelve students by means of hypnotic suggestion. Significantly higher MAS scores were obtained following such suggestions than in either a waking state or a simple trance state.

COMBINING DATA FROM EXPERIMENTS. Among other advantages, the existence of a reliable measuring instrument which is used by a series of investigators makes it possible to compare data across experiments. For example, a question such as "Is psychotherapy effective in reducing anxiety?" can be changed to "Is client-centered psychotherapy more effective than carbon dioxide therapy or than a given environmental change in reducing anxiety?" As such questions receive answers, further questions beginning with "Why" must inevitably be raised and answers must be sought. As a sample of how such comparisons would look, data from the five studies just cited are given in Table 1.

Two points become evident when one attempts to construct such a table. First, it would be of great value to be able to obtain comparable measurement from different experimenters investigating independent problems. Second, existing data are not satisfactory for this purpose. For example, carbon dioxide therapy appears to exert a relatively important reduction effect on anxiety. Then, one notes that the anxiety level of the prisoners *after* therapy is higher than that of college students *before* client-centered therapy. One of the problems is that of population differences. A more frustrating one is that with an instrument such as the MAS, investigators are not prone to be particularly concerned about stimulus consistency even though such consistency could be easily obtained. In general, the MAS is *not* administered in the same form by different experimenters. For example, in the studies reported in Table 1, Taylor (1953) administered the 225-item Biographical

Table 1.   *Measuring Changes in Anxiety: MAS Mean Scores*

High Anxiety		Normal Anxiety	Change	p	Source
		Introductory psychology students in neutral conditions	14.56		Taylor, 1953
Veterans beginning outpatient psychotherapy	29.9	Veterans after one year of outpatient psychotherapy	26.4	3.50	<.01	Lorr, McNair, Michaux, and Raskin, 1962
Students requesting psychotherapy	17.28	Students after completion of client-centered psychotherapy	13.76	3.52	<.01	Gallagher, 1953
Prisoners with diagnosis of anxiety symptoms	28.50 *	Prisoners after completion of carbon dioxide therapy	19.00 *	9.50	<.05	Lebo, Toal, and Brick, 1958
Pregnant women	18.95	Women after birth of baby	16.16	2.79	not reported	Davids, DeVault, and Talmadge, 1961
Hypnotic trance with anxiety suggestions	25.00	Hypnotic trance without anxiety suggestions	12.67	12.33	<.001	Grosz and Levitt, 1959

* Median scores.

Inventory (the 50 MAS items plus buffers), Lorr et al. (1962) used a 50-item modified version of the MAS, Gallagher (1953) administered the entire MMPI but scored only 34 of the 50 MAS items, Lebo et al. (1958) administered 49 MAS items, Davids et al. (1961) apparently administered the 50 items as a separate test, and Grosz and Levitt (1959) do not indicate the manner in which they administered the MAS. In view of these differences, comparisons across experiments would seem to be on shaky ground.

Nevertheless, it is obvious that measuring techniques will gradually improve, and attention to precision in measurement will increase hand in hand with theoretical progress. Hopefully, theoretical concepts about personality and its alterations will grow in sophistication and in power. In a decade or two, it is to be hoped that a Symposium on Personality Change will contain tight theoretical formulations built on precisely quantified data. And perhaps it is not unfair to speculate that as our measuring devices go, so goes our science.

PART TWO

THEORETICAL CONSIDERATIONS

Antecedent conditions responsible for change are a matter of empirical determination. How these antecedents operate to produce consequents is a problem for the theoretician. Theorists have postulated widely diverse constructs to link antecedent and consequent events. The following chapters present five approaches to a theory of personality change.

Psychoanalytic theory holds an important place in theories of change both historically and in terms of contemporary influence. Luborsky and Schimek compare change produced by psychoanalytic treatment with change as a consequence of development. They review the basic aspects of Freudian theory and contrast psychoanalytic treatment with supportive psychotherapy. To Freud, changes in the personality were primarily ego changes which may be brought about by the interpretive activity of the analyst. As the conscious control of the ego is extended, libidinal energy is transferred from symptoms to behavior involving enjoyment and achievement. Change is facilitated if the patient maintains a high level of drive and if he identifies with the therapist. Developmental change is an equally important aspect of psychoanalytic theory. Particular emphasis is placed on the first five years of life. Maturational changes involve a gradual strengthening of ego functions as evidenced by the dominance of the reality principle and secondary process. The authors also discuss in some detail many of the difficulties involved in assessing and predicting change.

As a representative of another major psychotherapeutic approach, Gendlin presents a theory of personality change from the viewpoint of a self theorist. He criticizes existing personality theories with respect to their adequacy in dealing with the phenomenon of change. He suggests that we must deal with the paradigms of repression and content to account for changes in personality. How can we become aware of repressed material and how can the entities of personality undergo alteration? Within most personality theories, it is proposed that change involves an intense internal feeling process and usually occurs in an ongoing interpersonal context. Rogers, he feels, went a step further than his predecessors and discovered in practice the way in which the individual can be helped to overcome repression. It is Gendlin's position, however, that Rogerian theory fails to account for personality change. The therapist may respond to the felt, implicit meanings of experiencing without encountering resistance, and a succession of such responses leads to a self-propelled reorganizing change process in the individual. Gendlin presents his own theory of personality change as a series of twenty-six theoretical assertions in the framework of a general theory of experiencing. His theory of change is based on a phenomenological approach and the observed process of personality change during psychotherapy.

In Chapter 5 Neal Miller indicates the implications of S-R theory to some of the specific problems of personality change and psychotherapy. Working with behavior theory and the conflict models he developed in collaboration with John Dollard, he discusses various types of therapeutic techniques and patient behavior in therapy. He stresses that clinicians should use new change-inducing techniques, based on direct application of behavior theory, rather than accept the restrictions of the techniques of the typical approaches to psychotherapy. In somewhat of a departure from his earlier theoretical emphases, Miller also discusses the interaction of organic factors with learning capacity and the course of learning. In addition, the problems of change and resistance to change are outlined in terms of the conditions which produce stable or unstable equilibrium.

Still another sort of psychological theory which deals with personality change is that of role theory as described by Sarbin. The most general proposition is that change is brought about when an individual engages in role-playing behavior. Sarbin presents evidence which indicates that role enactment brings about changes in somatic processes, performance, attention, and dispositional characteristics. Role theory is concerned with the importance of the status, positions, or roles assigned by a society to each individual in it. There are variations in the quality of the role enactment, and these variations are a function of expectations about the role held by the individual and by others in the group, perception of the role to be enacted, the implicit demands of the role, differences in role-taking aptitude, the extent to which the role is congruent with the self, and the reinforcement properties of the audience. Taking these formulations as a base, Sarbin goes on to demonstrate the utility of role theory in various types of psychological research: hypnosis, attitude change, and behavior pathology.

Leon Festinger's formulation of dissonance theory is a circumscribed framework which deals with a particular type of motivation. Over the past several years, it has proven extremely fruitful in stimulating a variety of research efforts. Basically, it proposes that dissonance is produced when an individual holds two psychologically inconsistent cognitions, and the individual is motivated to bring about dissonance reduction. The factors responsible for bringing about dissonance and its reduction are relevant for explaining and predicting a variety of behaviors. In Chapter 7, Festinger and Freedman present a brief outline of dissonance theory and then apply it to one type of change: the acquisition of moral values. Among the desired components of acculturation is the internalization of society's moral values with respect to those behaviors which are considered undesirable. A series of investigations is described in which the effects on moral values of such variables as strength of admonition to avoid proscribed actions, magnitude of temptations to violate moral codes, and participation in censuring moral violations by others are derived from dissonance theory. Finally, the authors postulate the relatively complex relationship which should hold between the combined actions of strength of deterrents and effectiveness of deterrents on the internalization of moral values.

chapter three

Psychoanalytic Theories of Therapeutic and Developmental Change: Implications for Assessment

Lester Luborsky and Jean Schimek

Parts of the psychoanalytic theory of personality and neurosis formation are widely known. However, we will review its main tools and tenets for two reasons. First, the whole of psychoanalytic theory is not well known. It is only the clinical theory which is generally understood, as Rapaport says (1960, p. 140): "The general theory, far from being well-ingrained dogma, is a waif unknown to many, noticed by some, and closely familiar to few." Secondly, the very volume of psychoanalytic writings necessitates a review of the theory itself as a background for a survey of the theory of change.

Therefore, we will start with the basic conceptual tools of the theory. Our focus in most of the paper will be on comparing and contrasting the theories of change through psychoanalytic treatment with theories of change through development. Beyond this, we will show how the theories of change imply certain principles for assessment and prediction of change.

THE PSYCHOANALYTIC THEORY OF PERSONALITY AND NEUROSIS

Conceptual Tools of the Psychoanalytic System

Any theory of change has to answer at least two basic questions: What entity or process is changing? What makes it change? The answer to these questions will determine the kind of selected observations and explanations that each theory has to offer. The conception of change in all theories is logically and empirically inseparable from their conception of *lack* of change, that is, permanence or stability; what is changing can only be described and conceptualized by comparison with what is not.[1] A psychoanalytic theory of change deals with the *psychological causes* of change occurring within a *mental apparatus* or personality structure. Let us examine what is implied by these two terms.

Psychoanalytic theory remains at a psychological level of analysis; that is, it does not seek to reduce behavior to selected units suitable to the laws of physics, physiology, or biology. It does not ignore physical, somatic, or social determinants of behavior, but rather it deals only with their *psychological representations,* their experience as feelings, perceptions, thoughts, memories, etc. Experience does not mean *conscious* experience. In order to explain behavior by psychological causes, Freud assumed that "the mental is in itself unconscious," consciousness being only a restricted and fugitive condition.

Even the fundamental psychoanalytic concept of instinctual drive is primarily a psychological and not a biological one. It does not concern itself directly with somatic processes or physiological stimuli, but with their mental representation (for instance, the experience of hunger and not with stomach contractions). According to Freud's definition (Freud, 1915, p. 121 ff.), "an instinctual drive appears to us as a concept on the frontier between the mental and the somatic, as the psychical representative of stimuli originating from within the organism and reaching the mind, as a measure of the demand made upon the mind for work in consequence of its connection with the body." (For a detailed discussion of this crucial point, see Rapaport (1960*b*)).

Psychoanalytic theory views change and stability in behavior as multiply determined by the interaction of physical, biological, and cultural factors which are all selectively mediated and integrated within the framework of an individual personality structure. In other words, the concept of a personality structure, or, to use Freud's term, "the mental apparatus" is the main intervening variable (closely tied to the more specific construct of unconscious determinants) between multiple external causes and resulting behavioral change.

This principle of multidimensional psychological causality is described in its broadest sense by what Erikson (1950) calls "the relativity in human existence." At each stage of personality development, change has to be considered in terms of three interrelated series of determinants: physical (somatic), cultural, and individual (ego). "A human being is at all times an

---

[1] Because most psychological theories have been committed to a search for what is recurrent, general, and predictable, they have been more successful in dealing with the problem of stability and regularity in behavior, rather than discontinuity and change, and psychoanalytic theory is no exception on this point.

organism, an ego, and a member of society and is involved in all three processes of organization. An item in one process gains relevance by giving significance to and receiving significance from items in the others."

The most extensive and systematic presentation of the conceptual structure of psychoanalytic theory has been given by Rapaport (1960a). Here we can only quote his listings of the basic propositions which define the general orientation of psychoanalytic theory:

(a) the subject matter of psychoanalysis is behavior (the empirical point of view); (b) behavior is integrated and indivisible (the Gestalt point of view); (c) no behavior stands in isolation (the organismic point of view); (d) all behavior is a part of a genetic series (the genetic point of view); (e) the crucial determinants of behavior are unconscious (the topographic point of view); (f) all behavior is ultimately drive determined (the dynamic point of view); (g) all behavior disposes of and is regulated by psychological energy (the economic point of view); (h) all behavior has structural determiners (the structural point of view); (i) all behavior is determined by reality (the adaptive point of view); and (j) all behavior is socially determined (the psychosocial point of view).

The Mental Apparatus

Personality is conceptualized as consisting of the interactions of three parts or agencies. The most primitive and impersonal of these is the id which represents essentially the psychological manifestations of biological drives (inborn and unfolded through maturation). The drives seek the pleasure of immediate tension release, regardless of reality consequences or the long-range survival of the individual. Survival and adaptation to the demands of external reality are functions of the ego, which is the more organized and individualized part of the personality, molded by the specific and accidental influences in the individual's life history and environment. In its adaptive function, the ego has to be able to control and delay the discharge of instinctual drives and to channel these drives towards specific objects and goals while avoiding others and bringing about modification in the external world so that the object of drive satisfaction will be available. For this task, the ego explores and stores knowledge of external reality through the functions of perception, memory, and learning; it is also in control of voluntary movement and actions. The ego is the psychological—that is internalized, intrapsychic—manifestation of the demands and pressures of the external environment, just as the id is the psychological expression of the somatic demands of the organism. Finally, the third agency, the superego, is the internalized expression of the earliest and most basic parental and social goals and prohibitions which the child has acquired through the parents' influence and by identification with them. The superego is mostly responsible for the sense of guilt and the need for punishment.

The ego has to make workable compromises between the demands of instinctual drives, the limitations and opportunities provided by the physical and social environment, and the prohibitions and goals of the superego. Its function is not only one of control, but also of synthesis; it is a cohesive organization, providing the personality with a sense of sameness, continuity, and individual identity. The mental processes of the id, superego, and to a large extent the ego, are unconscious.

Defenses, Fixations, and Neurotic Conflicts

The ego is often too weak to accomplish its task of control, adaptation, and synthesis successfully, particularly in the early years of childhood when it is still very incompletely developed. It cannot run away from internal drives, and its capacity for actively changing the external environment is very limited. In trying to avoid the threat of being overwhelmed by external pressures or by internal drives, the ego has to resort to various "defense mechanisms." For instance, the ego will attempt to ignore or repudiate the existence of internal or external threats, or at least keep them out of conscious awareness (denial and repression). Or it can use such primitive controls as deflecting the drive against itself (for instance, aggression turned against the self which can also serve the need for self-punishment), or of avoiding altogether certain areas of behavior (for instance, phobias and inhibitions). These and many other defenses are essentially emergency measures which the ego uses when it is still developmentally weak, at times when the demands of instinctual drives are unusually strong (for instance, at puberty), or when the stress of environmental demands and deprivations is unusually great (traumatic situations). These defense mechanisms are universal and not necessarily maladaptive.

A neurosis or disturbance of the ego is created when these primitive defenses become permanent and *fixated* and, therefore, cannot be superseded by the more adaptive, flexible, and voluntary controls which later development provides. The conflict between a specific early pattern of drive expression and drive inhibition remains basically unchanged in the unconscious; the drive, prevented by the rigid defense from finding an adequate outlet, produces more and more substitute derivatives (in the form of neurotic symptoms and character traits) which get increasingly dissociated from the rest of the changing personality and out of touch with changes in the external environment. The ego has not been able to solve conflicts between early expressions of sexual and aggressive drives and the demands of external reality, except by becoming fixated to ineffective primitive defense measures. Thus, neuroses are essentially disorders of the ego or a breakdown of ego unity and synthesis. They represent obstacles to change and partial arrests of normal development. The usual results of such neurotic conflicts are inhibition in various areas of behavior, waste of energy, and suffering through symptoms. The multiple-level causation of these neurotic fixations can be stated in a most general way as follows: a fixation is likely to occur through either severe frustration or overindulgence at a certain level of development in an individual whose constitutional endowment and previous developmental history make him particularly sensitive to external trauma at this particular level.

THE PSYCHOANALYTIC THEORY OF PSYCHOTHERAPEUTIC CHANGE

Most of what has been written on the psychoanalytic theory of change deals with *psychoanalytic* treatment—much less theoretical concern has been devoted to the rationale of other forms of treatment. What follows remains in the mainstream; it applies mainly to change via psychoanalysis. For contrast, however, we will review briefly the theory of change in a common form of treatment known as "supportive psychotherapy."

We will distinguish between (*a*) concepts concerning *what* is the nature of change and (*b*) concepts concerning *how* the change is supposed to come about. The latter involves the theory of the process and technique of psychoanalytic treatment as well as the *obstacles* to change.

Freud's Theory of Change via Psychoanalysis

The theory of psychotherapeutic change is almost explicit in the theory of personality and neurosis which we have just reviewed. No more authoritative or better expressed statement of the theory exists than Freud's. What follows is summarized from his work. In one of his earlier statements on theory of treatment (1920, pp. 394–398), consisting of three courses of lectures delivered in 1915–1917, Freud discusses the mechanism of recovery, with strong emphasis upon the libido concept. The specific incapacities of the neurotic are (*a*) incapacity for enjoyment and (*b*) incapacity for achievement. The incapacity for enjoyment Freud attributes to the fact that the "libido was attached to no real object"; i.e., it is associated with fantasied objects. The incapacity for achievement is the result of energy that would otherwise be available, being "expended in maintaining the libido under repression." It is the conflict between the ego and the libido that consumes the energy.

The emphasis here (and in Freud's other writings) is upon changes in the ego. For example, "the ego becomes wider by the work of interpretation, which brings unconscious material into consciousness." Or, the ego acquires "new capacity to expend a certain amount of the libido in sublimation." He did not believe that the instinctual energies changed much. The change was mainly in ways of handling these energies; the changes were, therefore, ego changes.

Treatment works by loosening the libido from its attachment to the symptoms which offer it substitute satisfaction. To dissolve the symptoms, one must go back to the point at which they started and find new solutions. Revising the repression can only partly be effected by reviving the memory traces of the conflict via free association. The main work is accomplished by dissolving the new editions of the conflict that appear in the relationship to the therapist (that is, through the transference phenomena).

Freud wrote the final statement of his theories in *An Outline of Psychoanalysis* (1949) in London in the few weeks following July 22, 1938. His formulations in the chapter on "The Technique of Psychoanalysis" are basically the same as the earlier work summarized. He again emphasizes that in neurosis, the ego is not able to meet the demands from reality, the id, and the superego. Much energy is expended in keeping down the claims of the id and the crippling action of the superego, both of which may alter the person's relationship to reality.

Change is induced through the role and activity of the psychoanalyst which provide the patient's ego with an ally in his struggles. The patient and the psychoanalyst enter into a pact in which the patient is to say everything that comes to mind. The psychoanalyst's job is to provide interpretations. These facilitate insights which help the ego regain mastery over the id, superego, and reality functions.

Freud (1919) assigned a role in facilitating change to the condition of abstinence and the elevated frustration level of the patient. For the treatment of phobias especially, Freud believed in the value of putting up with the anxiety of engaging in the feared activities. For the patient this procedure gains access to the relevant associated memories with which the conflicts can then be resolved.

Restatements and Reformulations by Others

Latter-day psychoanalysts have attempted to restate systematically the essence of the technique of change in psychoanalytic treatment. These presentations typically involve special emphases, even though they are presented as restatements. Karl Menninger, for example (1958), provides a set of useful diagrammatic representations of the main components of Freud's theory revolving around the nature of the initial compact between the patient and the analyst and the transactions between them. His analysis, however, gives more emphasis than most theorists do to the role of the frustrating aspects of the analytic situation (e.g., not giving in to patient's pleas and demands, etc.) as a motivator of change. Through this "controlled frustration" the patient comes to know his "style of, and conditions for, loving and hating."

A successful and succinct integration of the aspects of technique is accomplished by Ekstein (1956). While the conceptual ingredients listed by Ekstein are Freud's, the role of the capacity to endure regression is especially stressed for its value in the strengthening and expanding of ego functions. Ekstein presents a diagram of the main concepts that are relevant in the "ideal" psychoanalytic treatment. In this diagram, the patient at the beginning of treatment is pictured as having two deficiencies in his ego. One is the result of those aspects which are repressed, and another is due to those aspects of ego functioning which are undeveloped functions of the mature ego. During the progress of analysis there is an expansion of the self-organization in both directions. There emerges an appropriate availability of primitive (originally repressed) functions as well as mature (originally undeveloped) functions of the ego. The transference neurosis gradually develops to a high point and then gradually dissolves as a more mature, objectively perceived relationship to the analyst is formed. The strengthening of the ego occurs through the interpretive process and the consequent insight along with an increasing capacity for appropriate regression.

Obstacles to Change

Later in his life, Freud (1937) concluded that the question of how analysis effects change had been amply described; it was the obstacles to change which needed more exploration. He discerned three main factors which limit change: (a) the degree to which the illness is the result of a trauma (the more focally traumatic, the greater the possible change); (b) the constitutional strength of the instincts (the stronger the instincts—relative to the strength of the ego—the less change is possible); (c) the degree of "modification of the ego" (the greater the distortion, the less the possible change).

Earlier, Freud (1926) had listed types of interferences or "resistances" which impede the progress of psychoanalysis: ego resistances, i.e., repression resistance, transference resistance, and the gain of the illness; superego resistances, i.e., especially from the sense of guilt or need for punishment; and id resistance which may show up in the form of the "repetition compulsion."

Theory of Change via "Supportive Psychotherapy" in Contrast to Psychoanalysis

We have chosen "supportive psychotherapy" to contrast with psychoanalysis, since the two are quite different in the way change is supposed to be accomplished, and supportive psychotherapy is even more commonly used than psychoanalysis itself. Psychotherapies can be compared along many dimensions. The following seem especially relevant: (*a*) goals, (*b*) techniques, (*c*) subject matter, and (*d*) most suitable patients (Luborsky et al., 1958).

In terms of goals, the aim is "the strengthening of defenses" rather than the analysis of them as in psychoanalysis, according to Gill (1951), who has identified the basic ingredients of supportive psychotherapy. In psychoanalysis the goals are most ambitious: changing the character structure and impulse-defense configurations to make the ego able to meet its tasks with minimal energies devoted to defensive needs and maximal neutralized energies available for subliminatory and creative activities (Wallerstein et al., 1956). The goals of other treatment modalities are less than this in varying degrees.

In terms of technique, Bibring (1954) classifies all techniques into five groups: (*a*) suggestive, (*b*) abreactive, (*c*) manipulative, (*d*) clarifying, and (*e*) interpretive. In psychoanalysis, interpretive techniques are most heavily emphasized. At the other end of the spectrum, in supportive psychotherapy, techniques for strengthening defenses are stressed; for example, the encouragement of adaptive combinations of instinct and defense, and the avoidance of uncovering or interpreting defenses which are essential to the patient's equilibrium.

In terms of subject matter, psychoanalysis is more likely to make use of dream and fantasy material and explicit interpretation of transference manifestations than is supportive psychotherapy.

The most suitable patients for psychoanalysis are those in the neurotic range. Supportive psychotherapy may be used occasionally for basically healthy people who are temporarily overwhelmed by catastrophe and are not functioning with their usual ego resources. Most often it is used for ego-disturbed people (as opposed to primarily intact neurotic individuals). For such patients, uncovering or expressive types of treatment might lead to regression because of the unbearable anxiety that would be engendered. Typically, such patients seek treatment at the point of imminent collapse. The primary aim is to restabilize the individual.

Principles of Change via Psychoanalytic Treatment

From the above sections, a number of principles emerge concerning *what* changes occur in psychoanalytic treatment:

1. Greater ability to make satisfactory compromises among the demands of reality, id, and superego. This partly involves a shift away from the dominance of the pleasure principle to more consideration of the reality principle.

2. Increased capacity for enjoyment (as the attachment to real objects supplants attachments to fantasied objects).

3. Increased capacity for achievement (some of these achievements may represent sublimations). The increased capacity derives from the freeing of energy bound in holding the libido under repression.

4. Increased availability of unconscious material to consciousness. This has been expressed in the terse formula "where id was, there shall ego be." It can also be described more prosaically as "increased insight."

5. Increased capacity for appropriate regression (this is closely related to (4)). It has been described as "regression in the service of the ego" by Kris (1952) and Schafer (1958).

The main principles of *how* change comes about in psychoanalysis include:

1. The retracing of steps back to the point at which the symptoms started via reviving memory traces of the conflict in the course of free association sessions.

2. The dissolving of the new editions of the conflicts as they are re-experienced in the relationship to the analyst (i.e., the development and working through of the transference).

3. The toleration during this process of elevated frustration levels and anxiety.

4. The alliance of the analyst and patient in the task of coming to know the patient and his defensive struggles. The analyst provides interpretations; the patient gradually develops (through imitation and identification) the therapist's principal tool, his observing ego.[2]

[2] According to Rapaport (1960*a*), the theory of therapeutic technique is part of the still largely unfulfilled program of psychoanalysis.

It was so treated by Freud in the prehistory of psychoanalysis (Breuer & Freud, 1895, Chap. III), in some of the "Papers on Technique" (Freud, 1910–1919) and in "Analysis Terminable and Interminable" (1937). Nevertheless, this program is still far from fulfillment. Even the most systematic (Fenichel, 1941) of the few extensive (Glover, 1928;

THE PSYCHOANALYTIC THEORY
OF DEVELOPMENTAL CHANGE

Historical Development

From the beginning, Freud strove to develop a general psychological theory of the mind and of personality functioning, and not just a clinical rationale for the understanding and treatment of neuroses. But it is obviously the more specific clinical theory which remained in the focus of psychoanalytic studies. Therefore, the psychoanalytic theory of personality development is essentially an extension of the more specific theory of neurosis formation. Psychoanalytic theory, due to its origin in the clinical theory of neurosis, tends to emphasize the development of libidinal sexual drives and of defenses against them rather than the development of perception, memory, learning, and other functions more commonly studied by general psychology. Also, it has more to say about development from birth to puberty than it does about changes in later life. The psychoanalytic theory of development is so much tied in with the development of psychoanalytic theory itself that it is the latter which we will first summarize.

(*a*) Psychoanalysis started with an attempt at a psychological explanation of neurotic symptoms, considered as the result of unconscious conflicts around the expression of infantile sexual drives. Therefore, early psychoanalytic theory concentrated mostly on the developmental stages of libido; the vicissitudes of instinctual drives were seen as a main factor in development just as unresolved conflicts at various stages of this libidinal development were seen as the main cause of later neurotic symptoms. The well-known theory of the development of infantile sexuality and its three main stages need not be restated here. These stages are seen as a biologically determined sequence whereby one body zone after another (mouth, anus, genitals) becomes a focus of the child's sexual and aggressive impulses and fantasies, determining

Lorand, 1946) treatments of technique contributes little toward the theoretical program. E. Bibring (1954) has penetrated into these problems further than most have. Recently Eissler (1953) and Gill (1954) have also made relevant contributions. The importance of this program and the difficulties in its way are equally great. Progress may require not only the study of the techniques of psychoanalysis and those of other schools of therapy, but also the development of a psychoanalytic theory of communication (p. 132). Data for building such a theory are needed. The data and concepts of the existing attempts at a communication theory do not seem to be relevant. The focus of such a theory must be the laws which govern the tendency of communication to engender or to prevent reciprocal communication. Moreover, it should be a theory in which the communicants' becoming conscious of something is equivalent to (latent) verbal or nonverbal communication (see Rapaport, 1949, 1953). The methods by which data relevant to such a theory can be obtained have yet to be worked out (p. 136).

his interaction with external objects, that is, mostly with his parents and other significant persons.

(*b*) In a second stage, starting roughly about 1920, increasing emphasis was put on defenses. The growth of the drive-controlling functions of the ego (which had never been altogether ignored) became another crucial impetus in personality development (A. Freud, 1936).

(*c*) Finally, in the last fifteen or twenty years, the emphasis on the crucial role of ego development has been continued and amplified. The ego is seen as not only the result of a battle between drives and the frustrating impact of external reality. It is assumed to have a constitutional basis in the motor, perceptual, and intellectual endowment of the individual and a relatively autonomous development (i.e., not directly tied to conflicts surrounding libidinal development).

Similarly, cultural patterns are seen not only as obstacles to full-fledged drive development, but as patterns that give content, meaning, and consistency to both drive expressions and drive controls. Drive development itself becomes a predetermined sequence of potential behavior patterns rooted in the structure of the organism and preadapted to an average expectable environment. These potentialities can only become actualized by being met by specific cultural patterns and corresponding levels of ego functioning. These conceptions have been more specifically spelled out by Erikson (1950), who described an epigenetic sequence of personality development throughout "eight stages of man"; each stage is characterized by its specific crisis which is universal, while its solution varies from society to society and is individually unique. The stages are named by their most universal successful or unsuccessful outcome (e.g., guilt versus initiative for the Oedipal period, or identity versus role diffusion for the adolescence crisis).

Development in the Middle Years (*Approximately Ages 25 to 45*)

There are few concepts and studies within the framework of psychoanalytic theory which deal with normal change after adolescence. For the classical psychoanalytic conception of development, centered around libidinal stages, the optimum end point is the achievement of "genitality." The concept of genitality, either in the narrow sense as mutuality of orgasm with a heterosexual partner or, in the broader sense, as a culturally determined ideal of love and family relationship, can tell us little about the normal process and stages of change after adolescence. The clinical psychoanalytic theory usually describes postadolescent development in terms of the reasons and ways in which this genital ideal has *not* been achieved.

As we have seen in the preceding sections, psychoanalytic ego psychology can give us some formulations as to the general direction of development after adolescence. We can assume that the general development of stable structures, defenses and controls, and a sense of identity will produce more sameness and consistency in behavior. As the character structure becomes more fixed, the frequency and amplitude of changes to immediate external events or to bodily changes is reduced and modulated. The more crystallized personality structure becomes more and more an *active* and autonomous agent of change. After the experimental branching out in many directions which is often found through adolescence, we usually find in later years a funneling effect, a selective concentration on certain patterns and areas of behavior while others are discarded, or remain as mere potentialities. There is more depth and less spreading out.

But beyond assuming a general trend towards stability and consolidation, one cannot ignore the continuous and often drastic changes that do occur after the years of adolescence and often even in the absence of gross changes in the environment. This process of intrapsychically determined personality growth or maturation is still very poorly understood. The most comprehensive psychoanalytic formulation of these problems is that of Erikson (1950), who has extended his conception of an epigenetic sequence to the whole life cycle. After the period of adolescence where the basic ego conflict is that of identity versus role diffusion, the following stages are also described as successive crises tied to each level of ego development and the corresponding social and somatic environment: intimacy versus isolation, generativity versus stagnation, integrity versus despair. Each crisis has a potential for new development or for regression to earlier stages. The "generativity crisis," for example, reflects the more or less gradually formed conclusion by the person about the productivity and worthwhileness he has achieved in his life.

There have been few studies (even in the general psychological literature) of personality changes in adult life as people develop without the benefit of psychotherapy. These less known years are the ones just after college which are so full of career making that the individuals are hard to recruit for psychological research. This is especially true for the exceptional but significant instances of people who, even in their middle years, make drastic changes in their life orientations and goals (for instance, religious, political, or artistic "conversions") which involve—at least on the surface—a giving up of almost everything they have been doing or striving for previously.

Recent work which illustrates and extends these observations to the middle years has been done by White (1952) on the later lives of college students, Holt and Luborsky (1958, Chapter 5), and Holt (1959) on psychiatric residents. The observations in these reports suggest that development continues actively in these years and that many large changes occur. Many of the young adults in the psychiatric resident group (ages 25 to 35) were still working out the resolution of Oedipal conflicts and particularly efforts to free themselves from dependence upon their parents. Prominent changes were in the areas of: (*a*) the deepening of interests, (*b*) the development of self-insight, (*c*) the development of mature relationships with people, and (*d*) the stabilizing of ego identity.

Principles of Change via Development

Without going into a description of specific stages of development, we can summarize certain general principles that characterize the psychoanalytic theory of personality development:

1. Experiences during the earliest years (particularly the first five years) when organic and psychological maturation occurs at a much faster rate, have a crucial role in determining later development. It is in these early years that the most basic and lasting personality patterns are established, setting the general framework of all further change.

2. Early levels of development never completely disappear, and continue to coexist with later superimposed levels. This is implied by the concept of fixation and regression and accounts for the obvious observations that anyone's behavior will fluctuate between more advanced and more regressed levels at different times and under different circumstances. But more basically it states that personality functioning *at any one time* is multiple layered and overdetermined. Any item of behavior has both conscious and unconscious motivations and meanings which have their roots in different levels of development. It is likely that personality development, especially after puberty, consists not so much in completely new stages of development being added, but rather in changes in relationship between the already existing levels of personality structure—for instance, in the relative dominance of one level over the other and in the degree of synthesis, conflict, or autonomy between them. It is essentially this kind of change that analytic therapy aims to bring about; that is, an increase in synthesis between conflicting levels and some removal of barrier between them, thus permitting better integration.

3. The main trend of development is conceptualized as a progressive shift from the dominance of the pleasure principle and primary process to the dominance of the reality principle and secondary process; that is, a strengthening and widening of the adaptive ego functions. With the establishment of more stable defenses and control, there is more sameness and consistency in behavior and the personality acquires its specific identity and individuality. The

personality structure becomes both more solidified and more differentiated. There is an increased differentiation between external reality and the ego, between objective and subjective. The formation of a well-delineated and stable ego is paralleled with the development of the experience of an external objective reality in terms of stable objects; indeed, just as "the concept of reality creates the concept of the ego" (Fenichel, 1945, p. 35), the concept of ego creates the concept of an external reality. As the ego becomes more organized and differentiated, behavior is less and less determined by the immediate and changing balance of external stimuli and drive stimuli, and more and more through autonomous ego factors. There is an increasing capacity for consistent action and long-range planning with more active mastery of the external environment and ability to modify it. This means that there is less overall change, but also a different kind of change. The ego is more of an active agent of change, has more conscious and deliberate goals. Or, to put it colloquially, the person will be more able to change because he wants to, rather than just because he has to.

COMPARISON OF THE THEORIES OF PSYCHOTHERAPEUTIC AND DEVELOPMENTAL CHANGE

The two theories are fundamentally similar, since the developmental theory is historically and conceptually an extension of the theory of psychotherapeutic change. In the most general way, one could state that psychoanalysis aims to bring about in neurotic individuals changes which are normally expected to occur through favorable development. It aims to undo obstacles to normal development which have occurred in the form of fixations and partial regressions to earlier levels of development.

The general developmental theory, especially in its classical formulation, puts a heavy emphasis on constitutional factors and a universal biologically determined sequence in the maturation of drives and drive controls. By contrast, for the psychotherapeutic understanding of the individual patient, we are most concerned with the sequence of specific events in his life and his patterns of interaction with the environment. In short, while the theory stresses nature, in our practice we deal more with nurture, finding it more accessible to our knowledge and, we hope, to our influence.

Even within this general formulation, there are many aspects that we know little about. Most of these are still untouched by human research. (*a*) When we do see significant changes in patients, it is hard to tell whether the process of treatment is responsible, or other factors in the patient's "natural" personality development. We cannot arbitrarily assume that any personality change in analysis is a function of analysis only. We must also enquire to what degree intrapsychic conflicts can be resolved by changes in the environment—for instance, love, death, war, illness, or certain "lucky breaks." (We shall return to this in the section on prediction of change, see p. 97.) (*b*) The technique of psychoanalytic treatment probably involves a unique relationship which is not the same as the parents' personality-molding influence on the child. Nor is it exactly like any other social interaction in other usual life situations. The outcomes of treatment versus development should show some differences, just as outcomes of different types of treatments should. One hopeful tradition of opinion maintains that analyzed people have certain special superiorities, for example, in capacity for self-insight.[3] It would be interesting to investigate differences between people with comparable levels of mental health or personality integration who have achieved it as a result of successful psychoanalysis or by "natural outcome of development." For example, one could compare an analyzed with a non-analyzed group of people who had been matched on a scale such as the Health-Sickness Rating Scale (Luborsky, 1962).[4]

IMPLICATIONS FOR ASSESSMENT OF CHANGE AND PREDICTION OF CHANGE

The original data, from which the psychoanalytic theory of development was derived, were clinical ones obtained through the reconstruction during psychoanalytic treatment of the developmental history of adult neurotics. They were supplemented later by the direct observation of young children, either in treatment, or in a nursery, or family setting. An increasing number of studies have dealt with direct cross-sectional or longitudinal observation of infants (Escalona and Heider, 1959). Most of these studies give a description of certain aspects of change, but they do not contain significant modifi-

---

[3] For example, Freud (1937, p. 328) ". . . analysis produces a state which never does occur spontaneously. . . . Analysis enables the mature ego to review these old repressions, with the result that some are lifted, while others are accepted but reconstructed from more solid material."

[4] An experience with psychiatric residents (Holt and Luborsky, 1958. Vol. I, p. 68, Vol. II, Appendix 5.3, p. 20–23) *may* bear on the issue of developmental versus treatment-induced change. In this study we compared the amount of improvement in performance of psychiatric residents over the three-year period for two groups: a group who received treatment during residency, and a group who did not. No significant difference emerged in improvement *in performance as a resident*. Possibly the treatment accomplished little that influenced the residents' work. But more likely, the people who went into treatment were different from those who did not. Those who did not may have been more able to develop properly in their performance as residents, while those who went into treatment required the treatment to make a comparable change.

cation or specification of the general principles of the theory. Considering the mass of accumulated observations, the harvest of crucial findings is relatively meager. The same conclusion applies to the yield from the mass of psychotherapy research reports (Luborsky and Strupp, 1962).

One obvious requisite for doing research in this area is too often neglected. In order to make observations that will be relevant to the psychoanalytic theory of change, the researcher must be familiar with the concepts and principles of such a theory, for as Rapaport (1960) has observed, "Observations demonstrate theoretical relationships only to those who already conceive of the observed in terms of the theory's concepts." The obvious danger is that the observer is likely to see in the data only what his theory expects him to find there. This difficulty could only be solved by the establishment of certain criteria of evidence and verification, and there seem to be no such accepted standards for the interpretation of clinical observations.

General Principles for Assessment of Change

THE INTRAPERSONALITY INTERACTION PRINCIPLE. Difficulties in assessing change come from the fact that *change through development or treatment is multiple leveled and multiple determined,* and changes on any level influence changes on other levels. Many "objective" and non-clinical developmental studies—most longitudinal ones, for instance—are limited to dealing with gross observable changes in behavior without knowledge of the inner dynamics; whereas clinical data derived from psychoanalysis or psychotherapy usually lack the more "objective" knowledge of the patient's life environment and of his behavior during the twenty-three hours when he is not in the therapist's office (Strupp and Luborsky, 1962). Some efforts have been made to remedy this by a multiple-level approach, using both clinical and observational data (Kris, 1957). The inherent difficulties of such an approach are more practical than theoretical (e.g., questions of privacy, therapeutic advisability, motivation on the part of the subject, and, in general, the question of how far people can be manipulated for purposes of study and experimentation).

The personality configuration may be altered by a change on any level and in turn influence changes on other levels. Therefore, *favorable changes in patients do not always imply that all symptoms are gone.* Symptoms may sometimes be present after treatment, even though the patients may have accomplished much change. An illustrative story is told of a man who had suffered from enuresis since early childhood. He was advised to undergo analysis and he did. Several years later he ran into a friend, Dr. R, who, in the course of getting reacquainted, asked him about the treatment. The reply was that the analysis had been successful. Dr. R then asked, "And how is the enuresis?" The man replied, "Oh, I still pee in my pants, but it doesn't bother me now." The humor conveys the serious point that through treatment the symptom can become part of a new context in which it no longer stirs up as much conflict and discomfort as previously. In assessing development, the interaction principle is equally true: growth does not imply that conflicts will no longer be discernible.

It is a corollary of the principle that *small changes can make a huge difference in the total functioning,* as Brenman (1952) suggests, since *any change alters the entire configuration.* Schafer (1958) makes a similar point in the analysis of retest results: "Significant ego changes are often indicated only in relatively small score changes or thematic changes. If test protocols are subjected only to interindividual comparisons, the scope of these changes may be underestimated."

The interaction principle directly implies that *no aspect of change can be evaluated in isolation.* No single criterion of adjustment is sufficient. For psychological tests, no single score is sufficient. Change involves altered interaction with other areas of the personality and with the external environment. (This view is expressed in the principle of change via psychoanalysis, "a greater ability to satisfy the demands of reality, id, and the superego.") Changes in one area may sometimes be achieved at the expense of changes in other areas, and at times even have unpleasant consequences to the person or society. A probably apocryphal instance is on record of a man who paid fifty dollars to a psychiatrist to cure his inferiority complex. On the way home he was fined another fifty dollars for talking back to a policeman!

THE DEGREE TO WHICH CHANGE IS BASED UPON RESOLUTION OF CONFLICT AND ACHIEVEMENT OF "AUTONOMOUS FUNCTIONING." The interaction principle does not mean that emergent qualities in patients will always remain *tied* to conflict; the changes in the patient may become relatively autonomous. This fits with the concept of "autonomous functioning of the ego" introduced by Hartmann (1939). Orderliness, for example, can have an autonomous functioning of its own; it can be "conflict free," and not necessarily tied to the anal struggles of childhood. The principle applies equally well to qualities such as orderliness that come about either developmentally or through treatment.

Rapaport (1958) provides an excellent example of the autonomy of the ego from the id in the personality change that was attributed to Moses:

. . . Moses' portrait was brought to an Oriental king whose astrologers and phrenologists concluded from it that Moses was a cruel, greedy, craven, self-seeking man. The king, who had heard that Moses was a leader, kindly, generous, and bold, was puzzled, and went to visit Moses. On meeting him, he saw that the portrait was good, and said: "My phrenologists and astrologers were wrong." But Moses disagreed: "Your phrenologists and astrologers were right, they saw what I was made of; what they couldn't tell you was that I struggled against all that and so became what I am." In other words, the ego, which arises in the course of life's struggles, can become unlike the original impulses—can be relatively autonomous from them—and can control them.

Consistent with the principle of autonomous ego functioning, Schafer (1958) stresses the importance of assessing "changes in the patient's attempts at relatively pure secondary process functioning, as brought out by intelligence tests particularly. Significant leads will be found regarding the steady availability of relatively free ego energy and the autonomy of ego function from conflict."

The concept of *"structural versus non-structural change"* was mainly constructed for its bearing on the issue of whether a change is based upon resolution of conflict versus other determinants. It is a structural change in the ego "when the newer more adaptive patterns are not just altered techniques of adjustment through transference effects or shifts in tension-relieving devices; they are more permanently different ways of dealing with stress based on resolution of the older inhibiting conflict-bound ways . . ." (Wallerstein et al., 1956, p. 258). It is "more than an adaptation to a particular interpersonal relationship . . . it has more general applicability." Probably the key statement is, "based on *resolution* of the conflict-bound ways." It is not only a question of permanence, although that is important—the shift in personality of Alexander the Great (which is described below) might have been relatively permanent, but there had been no resolution of conflict, merely an avoidance of it.

The Menninger Foundation Psychotherapy Research Project has attempted to estimate the degree of structural change of each patient (Luborsky et al., 1958). They reported that the judges had difficulty in applying the concept to some patients and concluded that it probably needs even more specific definition than has been provided for it so far.

THE DEGREE TO WHICH CHANGE IS ADAPTIVE IN RELATION TO THE LIFE SITUATION. The psychoanalytic theory postulates that all behavior can be seen from an adaptive point of view (Rapaport, 1960). Specifically, one of the principles of change, whether through treatment or development, is increasing ability to reconcile the demands of reality, id, and superego.

Any change must, therefore, be judged from the point of view of the extent of its adaptiveness to the individual's life situation. The "average expectable environment" is much too general a concept to apply to each person—the life situation is often not average or expected. We need to know the extent to which changes will be blocked or supported, or even facilitated by the life situation. A small change might make a huge difference because of its special congruence for a person. The ability of an adolescent away at college to be awakened by a clock instead of by parents may make a huge difference in his being able to adapt away from home without parents. A child who becomes more independent may meet parental disapproval or approval with very different consequences for the change. A woman who is ready for a normal sexual relationship but whose husband is impotent may have a very difficult time of it. Examples are easy to find.

We do not mean to imply that the life situation is thought of as immutable. In fact, we are impressed with the extent to which it can be altered to meet the person's needs when interpsychic conflicts are resolved. The woman who considers herself unattractive and, therefore, unable to find a husband, may find, after changes in herself through treatment, that she is sought after.

In sum, it is important to assess the life situation in evaluating a change to determine (*a*) the extent to which the change is likely to be inhibited or facilitated by the life situation, and (*b*) the extent to which the change can be seen as a product of an altered life situation, rather than a product of a developmental or treatment-induced change. The life situation, therefore, can be seen as a two-way street: it can be seen as having been constructed by the person and altering when the person alters, and, conversely, changes in the life situation can be seen as having an influence upon the person and changing him. (For assessing treatment results some detailed lists of life situation variables are available: Sargent et al. (1958) and Voth et al. (1962)).

THE DEPENDENCE OF TYPE OF CHANGE UPON THE INITIAL MENTAL HEALTH LEVEL (OR, INITIAL DEVELOPMENTAL LEVEL). There is accumulating evidence from diverse psychotherapy research projects that patients starting at all levels of initial mental health show improvement. Studies reporting this finding include one on client-centered therapy patients (Rogers and Dymond, 1954), one on psychoanalytic patients (Klein, 1960), and one on long-term psychotherapy and psychoanalytic patients (Luborsky, 1962). The last two suggest that patients improve in relation to their initial position. In fact, Luborsky found a high correlation between initial position and termination position (on the Health-Sickness Rating Scale). Klein (1960) reported that patients improve approximately the same number of degrees regardless of where they start, suggesting to her some sort of limit to the modifiability of patients.

A common misconception has been to consider amount of improvement as an increment, without considering the position from which each patient started. This error is especially egregious in comparing the results of different therapies for different groups of patients. A patient who at the start of treatment is "hallucinating" and then recovers, has made a change which is difficult to compare on the same scale and in the same units with a patient who overcomes a phobic response to a teaching situation. This is an extreme example of a common problem in comparing changes in different patients (Luborsky, 1961).[5]

THE DEPENDENCE OF TYPE OF CHANGE UPON TYPE OF TREATMENT. What we try to change and how we structure the treatment differs for different patients, as we illustrated in the comparison of supportive psychotherapy and psychoanalysis. Therefore, the outcomes of treatment may not be the same for patients in different forms of treatment, even though the change might be labeled "improvement." Eissler (1950) drives home this point by his story of Alexander the Great who once was beginning to feel quite guilty about an egregious wrong he had done one of his subjects. The guilt was easily removed by a flattering advisor saying how great Alexander was; *he* needn't worry about such things. The outcome was "improvement" (via a role-playing sup-

---

[5] Schafer (1958*a*) lists a number of other technical principles for psychoanalytic study of test-retest evaluations of patients in psychotherapy. These actually apply to any clinical evaluation of change whether it is the result of treatment or development. (1) ". . . the patient [should] be compared with himself, and not only compared or averaged with other individuals before therapy and then after therapy. . . . The appearance of oral content or an increase of it may signify a noteworthy liberation within the individual or a noteworthy regression, again depending in part on the original and subsequent matrices." Schafer believes, therefore, that the judge should always know which set of test records was first, and which second, since otherwise significant trends would be obscured. (2) Any attempt to establish the part played by therapy in observed changes must include control groups of either comparable patients who have not been treated, or comparable patients treated by other techniques. Schafer suggests this since we may find, for example, changes that reflect developmental advances occurring relatively independent of therapy (of course, control groups are still going to be short of a full answer to this question). (3) ". . . practice effects on retests may be significant indicators of personality change." (4) "The research unit should be interpretations and not scores or theme counts. Only then may we continue to work in context, which is to say, work with clinical data clinically. Scores, content, sequence, attitudes, behavior, and style of verbalization must all feed into the interpretation. Any one of these by itself is not a reliable, specific, and hierarchically localized indicator." (5) Since interpretations are the research unit, ". . . the quality of the data and judges can hardly be over-emphasized. Good formal design will be of little help when inexperienced psychiatric residents and graduate students are relatively independently gathering the therapeutic and test data and processing them." (6) "Independent judges must be used to establish reliability of interpretation." (7) "Blind analysis of the test protocols is required to avoid contaminated interpretations." "Blind" in the context of test re-evaluation, however, should only mean that the judge is ignorant of the clinical history and the nature and course of therapy, not of certain actuarial characteristics of the patient, such as age and sex.

portive type of treatment). Another type of advisor might have allowed Alexander the Great to try to live with his guilt and talked with him about it. If, eventually, the outcome was better ego controls to avoid similar behavior in the future, Alexander the Great at that point would also be "improved" (via an analytic type of treatment). Both treatments might result in a reduction of guilt by the posttreatment point, yet the patient emerges differently from both. (Similarly, in terms of development, we know that differing environments and parental techniques will produce children of different personality structure.)

Application of Principles to the Study of Some Major Dimensions of Change

We will try now to be concrete about how the principles of assessment apply to some specific dimensions of change. Our accent here will be upon assessing change through treatment, although the principles apply as well to change through development. Rather than trying to be exhaustive, five crucial areas—crucial according to the principles of change in psychoanalytic theory—will be discussed: anxiety level (and anxiety tolerance), insight, regression in the service of the ego, neutralization, and transference resolution. (Wallerstein et al., 1956, provide a more complete survey of dimensions along which change is expected, according to psychoanalytic theory.)

ANXIETY LEVEL AND ANXIETY TOLERANCE. Anxiety is one of the main movers of change in behavior. Yet it plays a dual role: both in the context of treatment or in ordinary life, anxiety can be an overwhelming obstacle to change or a compelling motive for it.[6] The need to avoid and master anxiety will lead people to make changes in themselves and in their environment; or, on the other hand, anxiety will bring about a fear of anything new, unknown, or unstructured, and a rigid clinging to the past. Within the context of psychotherapy, anxiety is the most common symptom of inner conflict, and the suffering it causes is the main factor which leads people to seek treatment. Once treatment is started, a certain amount of anxiety is necessary to keep treatment going and therefore acts as a motivation for improvement. Yet the desire to stay away from anxiety-arousing memories and feelings is the basic cause of all resistances in the course of treatment.

To understand this apparent paradox, one has to look at the changing role and function of anxiety within the development of the ego. Anxiety is essentially a painful affect, an experience of dread or anticipation of unknown

[6] E. J. Murray in his chapter in this volume devotes a large section to the central role of anxiety in change in psychotherapy.

danger (accompanied by certain physiological reactions in heart rate, breathing, muscular tonicity, etc.). In its most primitive and acute form, anxiety is an experience of helplessness of the ego in reaction to overstimulation which the ego cannot master except through an emergency discharge reaction along pre-established, inborn physiological channels. The main danger situations that provoke anxiety are developmentally, culturally, and individually determined; Freud has listed their genetic sequence as: helplessness, absence of the parent, loss of love, castration, loss of approval of conscience (guilt), loss of social approval. Through development, the ego acquires an increasing capacity for controlling anxiety and using it as an anticipatory signal for danger situations. Anxiety thus becomes a signal for change in behavior. At first the changes are merely passive ones such as flight from external or internal (drive) stimuli through various primitive defenses; later on, however, these changes bring about an active adaptive modification of the environment and the signal of anxiety becomes a tool of learning and personality development.

Therefore, the way of handling anxiety depends on the developmental level of the ego function—specifically, the ability of the ego to tolerate anxiety without regressing, and its capacity to make an active use of it. (Cf. the assessment principles on pp. 89 and 90.) Clinically, the presence of overt anxiety can be a favorable or unfavorable prognostic sign, depending on the ego state of the patient.

Clinical experience and research findings indicate that a high degree of initial anxiety is favorable to change, but only in the absence of severe character pathology or ego disturbance. In a report on twenty-four patients (Luborsky, 1962), the correlation of rated initial anxiety level with change (in Health-Sickness Rating) was .44. (The scattergram shows a clear-cut trend line, with the exception of only one atypical patient.) Those patients who were low in the Health-Sickness Rating did not show the relationship as strongly. An independent study (Siegal and Rosen, 1962) on the same patients points in the same direction: the capacity to utilize signal anxiety (i.e., anxiety tolerance) is crucial for change.

INSIGHT. Increase in a patient's self-insight is assumed to be one of the main changes during psychoanalytic therapy. Insight was originally equated with a lessening of repressions, bringing the unconscious into the conscious. When the conscious verbalization of an inner experience does not bring about the desired change, it is usually assumed that this is not "true" insight, that defenses other than repression are operative (e.g., isolation of affect and intellectualization) and thus limit the curative value of insight. The problem is broader, however, than a question of defense mechanisms. The difference is between insight as the capacity to verbalize an experience and insight as an understanding of experience, its causes, consequences, and its relation to the overall context of our behavior and self-image; this understanding requires the ability to accept responsibility for a part of our self which was denied and alienated. In short, it is the difference between a temporary awareness and a lasting structural change in the ego.[7]

Here again we see the parallel between the development of insight through therapeutic change and as the normal developmental process of ego functions, involving reality testing, capacity for objective judgment, identity formation, etc. Some of these points could be illustrated clinically by the relative ineffectiveness of insight—in the sense of conscious verbalization of inner experiences—with ego-disturbed or borderline patients. For these patients, the lack of effective insight does not seem to be due to repressions or other defenses in specific areas, but to a more general impairment of ego functions which cannot make an active synthesis and translate increased awareness into increased conscious controls and a change in behavior. Insight as such can even have a disruptive role on weak ego structures which rely essentially on primitive defenses.

From a psychotherapy research point of view, this approach would require comparing change during therapy with the amount of verbalized insight, and take into account the character diagnosis of a patient and the general context in which this material was presented. One would probably have several categories: great change accompanied by much verbalized insight, great change with relatively little verbalized insight, and no change or even regression in spite of a lot of verbalized insight.

REGRESSION IN THE SERVICE OF THE EGO. To evaluate behavior changes which may seem regressive, we need to take into account the personality context (cf. the intrapersonality interaction principle, p. 88). Ego functioning after the person matures or after the person emerges from successful psychotherapy is not necessarily devoted to secondary process rational thinking under all circumstances. In fact, according to the psychoanalytic theory of change through psychoanalytic treatment, the person should become more capable of regressive thinking. This concept has been elevated by a special designation

---

[7] This difference parallels the dual aspects of the psychoanalytic theory of consciousness. On the one hand, consciousness is a mere descriptive term, a quality of subjective experience, a degree of awareness. On the other hand, consciousness is meant as an awareness of awareness, which means descriptively not only having the experience of something but being aware of ourselves as having this experience. This ability is closely tied to the development of reality testing and differentiation of objective and subjective; it implies the functioning of a superordinate ego structure which can take distance and look at the rest of the self as an external observer would look at an external object.

of its own: regression in the service of the ego. Kris (1952) stresses the great importance of this capacity, particularly for artistic and other types of creative thinking. Schafer (1958, 1961) lays great stress upon the importance of assessing regression in the service of the ego in psychological tests as well as in therapy.

"NEUTRALIZATION" OF THINKING. The concept of neutralization may have value in judging the degree of autonomy of the ego functions (which bears on our principle concerning autonomous functioning on p. 89). The concept, according to Kris (1951) and Hartman (1950) refers to the degree to which thinking is organized along primary versus secondary process lines, because of the extent of neutralization (desexualization, deaggressivization) of the energy of the thinking. Holt (1960) has gone about providing an operational definition of the concept via a scoring key which is especially applicable to the Rorschach. Responses are rated on a scale depending on the degree to which the response contains explicit aggressive or sexual qualities. This measure has been applied fruitfully in a number of investigations, including, for example, a Ph.D. dissertation from New York University (T. Saretsky) studying change induced by chlorpromazine in schizophrenics. He found evidence of significant movement in the direction of more neutralization; also better *control* of primary process generally. A project is under way to study psychotherapeutic change with before-after Rorschachs, using this scoring system.

TRANSFERENCE RESOLUTION. The term "transference" refers specifically to treatment. It is typically defined as the appearance in the treatment of new editions of archaic relationships with important figures in the patient's past. Everyone who writes on the topic of what is supposed to change in psychoanalysis assigns the central position to transference resolution. In the course of development there is an obvious counterpart to transference resolution, although it is not called that in development. It is the growing out of, or the giving up of, the predominance of archaic revivals in present relationships. This kind of loosening of the bonds of one's biography has obvious adaptive value.

The principle of the dependence of type of change upon type of treatment (p. 92) is especially relevant here, since transference resolution is especially crucial for psychoanalytic treatment, and not necessarily for other treatments. It is not that transference does not emerge in other forms of treatment, but that often it is either not recognized, or assigned no important theoretical place. Psychoanalytic treatment is defined by its consistent emphasis upon the resolution of these transferred archaic relationships.

No one has yet gone far into the measurement and the assessment of this concept. The most that has been done is in the Menninger Foundation's Psychotherapy Research Project in which a team of clinicians initially attempted to assess the transference potentials and to record their conclusions in the form of a discursive description. At termination, another team of clinicians attempted to make a similar description of the transference patterns that emerged and were or were not resolved.

PREDICTION OF CHANGE

Predictions are based on the assumption of continuity, on projecting in the future consistent and regular patterns found in the past. One of the basic psychoanalytic concepts is that of a multiple-layered personality structure. One dimension along which these levels differ is the extent to which they are stable or subject to change, and consequently the extent and manner in which they are predictable. Let us contrast briefly the "deeper" levels (more primary process, more unconscious and genetically earlier) with the more surface ones (more conscious, secondary process and developmentally advanced). The deeper levels are assumed to be relatively fixed and unchanging after the first years of life; they are little influenced by changes in the external environment and not subject to conscious or voluntary control. The surface levels are constantly changing and directly influenced by external events and conscious goals and controls. The deeper levels usually do not manifest themselves directly but only in a derivative way, by influencing the *general* trend and sequences of overt behavior and specific actions; therefore, on this basis alone we cannot predict *specific* outcomes and choices in a concrete situation but only potentialities and long range trends, usually with several linked alternatives.

To give a simplified illustration, a young male patient in his pattern of relation to women tends to repeat his relationship to a domineering mother and will go through a cycle of submissive, dependent, "good boy" behavior alternating with rebellious "naughty boy" behavior with attempts to assert himself and prove his masculinity. To make predictions of change in *the pattern,* we have to know (*a*) how much pain and disruption of his life the pattern causes, (*b*) how much insight the patient has into this pattern, (*c*) how much conscious desire to alter it, and (*d*) how much ability he has to modify his behavior by conscious and deliberate actions (the old fashioned "will" or the modern "ego strength"). Finally, to make predictions as to how he will act in a specific situation (e.g., whether he will stay married to a certain woman or get divorced), we have to know a great deal about the external reality he is faced with (his wife's character, his socioeconomic circumstances, etc.).

For specific predictions, we need a knowledge of the surface layers, including the individual's conscious intentions, values, abilities, and how these fit with the details of his external reality situation. Obviously the deeper levels can only be inferred from a long-range knowledge of the individual and his past history, whereas the surface levels and their momentary manifestations can be easily observed and checked. Our best predictor would be a full knowledge of the individual's present personality structure, including both overt behavior traits and underlying unconscious motives, conflicts, and defense patterns.[8] Even in the absence of such an ideal synthesis, we have to keep our predictions multileveled, separating the more stable and predictable areas from those that are more fluid and changing. We may be more successful in delineating *areas* of potential change than in predicting the exact nature and specific outcome of these changes.

Just as any one individual is stable and predictable in certain areas and less so in others, different individuals differ greatly in the extent to which their behavior is consistent and predictable. As a start, one can try to differentiate three basic types of personality in terms of the amount and kind of change they are likely to show.

(*a*) The first type would be the person who behaviorally is constantly changing in accordance with momentary external pressures and expectations. This is the chameleon type of reaction which is likely to be superficially adaptive, but often leads to disturbances clinically described as psychopath and impulse disorders. Even a small environmental change would bring about a great change in overt behavior. Such a person's specific behavior is highly changing and unpredictable, but what is predictable and likely to be fairly stable is his very pattern of change, his consistency in his apparent inconsistency.

(*b*) At the other extreme, we have the rigidly stable and unchanging type who depends on fixed routines in his environment and on very tight controls of his impulses (clinically associated with various types of inhibitions, projections, and obsessive-compulsive defenses, and socially has been described— for better or worse—under the label of "authoritarian personality"). This type of person is likely to show no reaction to small changes in the environment, to react to a great environmental change by an increase in his rigidity and tightness, and if the external pressures become very great, to regress severely and become completely passive and helpless.

(*c*) The third type has stable and flexible inner controls with both capacity for consistency and continuity and also for development and change. Change

---

[8] This conclusion is consistent with one of the recommendations from the experience in predicting the performance of psychiatric residents (Holt and Luborsky, 1958).

is likely to be more selective, deliberate, and inner determined. His personality is more an autonomous active agent of change, rather than just passively following or passively resisting all external influences as in the two previous types. For this type of person we could predict that he will not be greatly influenced by small external factors, but will react to greater external changes by a moderate and consistent internal change and will be able to regress under great external pressures in a temporary and limited way without total and lasting disintegration. This last condition is, of course, developmentally more mature and overlaps with what is usually described as ego strength.

Our emphasis here is, however, on patterns of reaction to external change and degree of predictability. It is also clear that these three patterns are never encountered in pure form, and that one of the ways in which people differ from each other and change in their life development is in the extent to which they make use of *all* of these three patterns.

In summary, we have seen that psychoanalysis has a dual relationship to the theory of change: as a method of treatment, it is a technique for inducing personality change; as a general psychological theory, it stresses sameness and consistency underlying apparent change and the determining influence of the past upon present behavior. This duality is built into the psychoanalytic view of personality as a multilayered structure whose overt and covert levels are differentiated by their degree of stability, rate of change, and susceptibility to external influences. Psychoanalytic concepts are especially suited to the understanding of consistency and stability in personality development, and for helping us differentiate what is changing from what is more permanent.

We have extracted some principles from the theory that are especially applicable to research projects in which one must assess or predict change: (1) the intrapersonality interaction principle, (2) the degree to which change is based upon resolution of conflict and achievement of "autonomous functioning," (3) the degree to which change is adaptive in relation to the life situation, (4) the dependence of type of change upon the initial mental health level, and (5) the dependence of type of change upon type of treatment. The way these principles can be applied in assessing change was illustrated in terms of five crucial variables: (1) anxiety level and anxiety tolerance, (2) insight, (3) regression in the service of the ego, (4) "neutralization" of thinking, and (5) transference resolution.

chapter four

A Theory of Personality Change

Eugene T. Gendlin

After a few pages which state two main problems and two observations, a theory of personality change will be presented. The theory is another step in the continuing work on "experiencing" (Gendlin, 1957, 1962b; Gendlin and Zimring, 1955). The theory of experiencing provides a frame of reference in which theoretical considerations are viewed in a new way.

A theory requires terms, defined words with which to specify observations, and a formulation of a chain of theoretical hypotheses. The theory presented here is developed within this basic structure, and special notice should be given to the new terms which are introduced and defined. These terms are pointed out and numbered. (We can have a genuine theory only with carefully defined terms, and only by using defined terms can we later modify, improve, and extend theory.)

PROBLEMS AND OBSERVATIONS

In most theories, the static content-and-structure aspects of personality are primary, and therefore personality change is an especially difficult problem. The present theoretical frame of reference is especially suited to account for change, since it employs concepts that apply to the experiencing process, and to the relationships between that process and content aspects of personality.

I am grateful to Malcolm A. Brown for many helpful and clarifying discussions, which greatly aided the process of writing this chapter, and to Dr. Sidney M. Jourard, Marilyn Geist, Dr. William Wharton, Joe T. Hart, David Le Roy, and Ruth Nielsen for their valuable comments and editorial help.

Personality Theory and Personality Change

Personality theories have chiefly been concerned with the factors that determine and explain different individuals' personalities as they are, and the factors which have brought about the given personality. What is called personality maintains its character despite circumstances. Aspects of an individual fail to puzzle us if his current situation explains them. We do not even attribute it to his personality when an individual shows all sorts of undesirable behavior under overwhelmingly bad circumstances, or when he becomes likable and secure under the influence of events which (as we say) would make almost anybody likable and secure. What we do attribute to personality is the reverse: when an individual remains likable and secure under overwhelmingly bad circumstances, and when an individual remains afraid and in pain despite apparent opportunities and good luck. Thus, it could be said that, far from explaining personality change, our theories have been endeavoring to explain and define personality as that which tends not to change when one would expect change.

To some extent this view of personality as factors which resist change is justified. We usually think of a person as involving identity and continuity through time. However, the contents and patterns in the theories are a *type of explanatory concept* which renders change impossible by definition. The structure of personality (in theories) is formulated in such a way that it is said to maintain itself against all new experience which might alter it. The individual is viewed as a structured entity with defined contents. These explanatory concepts can explain only why an individual cannot change.

Personality theory, then, has concentrated upon the factors which explain why an individual is as he is, how he has become so, and how these factors maintain him so, despite circumstances, fortunes, and opportunities. Such explanatory concepts of content and structure tell us what prevents an individual from being changed by experience, what factors will force him forever (by definition) to miss or distort everything that might change him unless (as we commonly say) his personality (somehow) changes first.

Since structure and content do tend to maintain themselves and distort present experience, we can account for personality change only if we can show exactly how this change resistance yields to change.

Theories in the past have not wanted to portray personality change as impossible. On the contrary, the theories assert that change does actually occur. The chief personality theories have sprung from psychotherapy—that is to say (when psychotherapy is successful), from ongoing personality change.

Quite paradoxically, as personality change occurs before their eyes and with their participation, therapists find their minds formulating what has been wrong. Even the individual, himself, as he searches into his feelings and expresses these, speaks as if the whole endeavor were to investigate what has been wrong—what has constituted the aspects of his personality which have prevented ordinary adaption and change. And, usually, such an individual becomes aware of much which, he then says, has been true all along but of which he has not been aware.

Thus, psychotherapy regularly gives us this observation of an individual "uncovering" or "becoming aware" of these stubborn contents and his previous inability to be aware of them. So well have the various personality theories formulated these contents and this self-maintaining and censoring structure that, while we have concepts to explain what makes an individual as he is, we cannot formulate how he can change. Yet all the time the individual has been changing just these "uncovered" factors which we formulate in terms of static explanatory contents.[1]

I will now present in more detail the two main ways in which much current formulation of personality makes change appear theoretically impossible. I call these two impossibilities "the repression paradigm," and "the content paradigm." [2]

Since these theories, nevertheless, also assert that change does occur, I will then take up the two main ways in which theories attempt to account for change. I will try to show that theories usually cite two observations: a *feeling process;* and a certain *personal relationship.*

Two Problems

THE "REPRESSION PARADIGM." Most personality theories (in different words and with somewhat different meanings) share what I call the "repression paradigm." They agree that in an individual's early family relations he introjected certain values, according to which he was loved only if he felt and behaved in certain ways. Experiences which contradicted these demands on him came to be "repressed" (Freud), or "denied to awareness" (Rogers), or "not me" (Sullivan). Later, when the individual encounters experiences of

---

[1] This tendency to view ongoing change in terms of the static contents it reveals can be seen also in the very many research projects which have employed psychotherapy and hospital situations to study diagnostic and classificatory aspects of people as compared with the very few researches which have employed these treatment settings to study change. Our psychometric instruments do not as yet have standardized or even defined indices of personality change, having been used so rarely before and after psychotherapy. This is another example of the way we tend to think most about the change-resistant contents of personality, even in treatment situations.

[2] "Paradigm," or model, refers to the *theoretical* models used in these theories, regardless of whether they use the words "repression" and "content" or not.

this contradicting sort, he must either distort them or remain totally unaware of them. For, were he to notice the contradictory experiences, he would become intolerably anxious. The ego (Freud), or self-concept (Rogers), or self-dynamism (Sullivan), thus basically influences awareness and perception. This influence is termed "resistance" (Freud), or "defensiveness" (Rogers), or "security operation" (Sullivan), and a great deal of behavior is thereby explainable. A personality is as it is, and remains as it is, because it cannot take account of these experiences. Or if, somehow, repression is forcefully lifted and the individual is made to become aware of these experiences, the ego will "lose control," the self will "disintegrate," and intolerable "uncanny emotions" will occur. In psychosis, it is said, the individual is aware of such experiences and the ego or self-organization has indeed broken down.

If the individual needed merely to be reminded, or to have the "repressed" factors called to his notice, he would soon be straightened out. There are always helpful or angry people who attempt this, and many situations grossly demand attention to these factors. The individual, however, represses not only the given factors within him but also anything outside him which would relate to these factors and remind him of them.[3] He misunderstands or reinterprets so as to prevent himself from noticing the aspects of events and persons which would bring these factors to his awareness.

Thus, the specific personality structure maintains itself and change is theoretically impossible. Whatever would change the individual in the necessary respects is distorted or goes unnoticed just to that extent and in those respects in which it could lift the repression and change him.

Now, this explanation (shared in some way, as I have tried to indicate, by the major personality theories of the day[4]) is based on the striking way in which the individual during psychotherapy becomes aware of what (so he now says) he has long felt but has not known that he felt. Moreover, the individual realizes how powerfully these previously unaware experiences have affected his feelings and behavior. So many individuals have now reported this that there is no longer much doubt that it is a valid observation. The open question is how we are to formulate it theoretically.

Once we formulate theory along the lines of the repression paradigm, we cannot then blithely turn around and "explain" personality change as a "becoming aware" of the previously repressed. Once we have shown how

[3] The repression paradigm in its most oversimplified form can be noticed in use when person A insists that person B has some content he cannot be aware of, because it is "unconscious." B's own experiences and feelings are, by definition, undercut and "thrown out of court." No way to the supposed content exists which B can use.

[4] S. Freud, 1914 (p. 375), 1920 (pp. 16–19), 1930 (p. 105). H. S. Sullivan, 1940 (pp. 20–21, 205–207), 1953 (pp. 42, 160–163). C. R. Rogers, 1957, 1958, 1959a and b, 1960, 1961a and b, 1962.

anything will be distorted which tends to bring these experiences to awareness, we cannot then consider it an explanation to simply assert that personality change is (by definition supposedly impossible) a becoming aware. Change happens. But, to say that is not to offer an explanation—it is only to state the problem. We may take the "repression paradigm" to be one basic aspect of personality change—one of the two basic factors with which this chapter will be concerned. To account for personality change, we will have to account for how this crucial becoming aware really does occur, and then we will have to go back and reformulate our theory of repression and the unconscious.

THE "CONTENT PARADIGM." The second basic aspect of personality change (and the second way in which current modes of formulating make change theoretically impossible) concerns the view of personality as made up of various "contents." By "contents" I mean any *defined* entities, whether they are called "experiences," "factors," "S-R bonds," "needs," "drives," "motives," "appraisals," "traits," "self-concepts," "anxieties," "motivational systems," "infantile fixations," "developmental failures," or whatever.

If we are to understand personality change, we must understand how these personality constituents can change in nature.

To account for this change in the nature of contents, we need a type of definition (explanatory constructs) which also can change. We cannot explain *change* in the nature of the *content* when our theory specifically defines personality only as content. Such theory can formulate what needs to be changed, and later it can also formulate what has changed, and into what it has changed; but it will remain theoretically unexplained how such change is possible, so long as all our explanations are in terms of concepts of this or that defined content.

We require some kind of more basic personality variable to formulate an account of how, under what conditions, and through what process, change in the nature of contents can occur.

Thus, for example, chemistry defines the elements in terms of more basic activities of electrons and protons, and thereby we can account for the subatomic processes by which elements engage in chemical change reactions, and through which an element can be bombarded with subatomic particles and turned into a different element. Without these concepts, which view elements as motions of something more basic, we could not explain the chemical and atomic *change* we observe, nor operationally study and define the conditions under which it occurs. We could state only that at t_1 the test tube had certain contents A, B, while at t_2 the contents were C, D. Only if A, B, C, D, are not themselves the *ultimate* explanatory concepts can we expect to explain changes from one to another. And so it is with personality change. If our ultimate explanatory constructs are "contents," we cannot explain the change in the nature of just these contents.

Our conclusion here is not simply that defined contents of personality do not exist. Rather, it is that if we define personality as contents and in no further, more basic way, then we cannot expect to use the same concepts to explain just how these contents change. And, inasmuch as it will have been just these contents which define the personality (and the respects in which change must occur if it is to be important personality change), exactly this theoretically impossible task is posed when personality theories come to explain change.

For example, during psychotherapy the patient finally comes to realize these essential contents (they will be conceptualized in whatever the vocabulary of the particular theory the psychotherapist uses). He realizes now that he has been full of "hostility," or that he has felt and acted from "partial, fixated sexual desires," or that he "hates his father," or that he is "passive-dependent," or was "never loved as a child." "Now what?," he asks. How do you change such contents? No way is given. The fact that these contents actually do change is our good fortune. The theories explain the personality in terms of these defined contents, these "experiences," or "needs," or "lacks." The theories cannot explain how these contents melt and lose their character to become something of a different character. Yet they do.

Our second basic problem of personality change, then, is this "content paradigm." The question is, "In what way should the nature of personality definitions change so that we can arrive at a means of defining that will fit the process of change in personality contents?" In answering this, we will describe something more basic or ultimate than defined contents. Then we will consider how defined contents arise in this more ultimate personality process.

Two Universal Observations of Personality Change

Now that two basic *problems* of personality change have been stated (becoming aware and change in the nature of contents), we will turn next to two basic *observations* of personality change. In contrast to the aforementioned *theoretical* impossibilities, most theories of personality cite two *observations,* which they assert are nearly always involved in personality change.

1. Major personality change involves some sort of intense affective or feeling process occurring in the individual.

2. Major personality change occurs nearly always in the context of an ongoing personal relationship.

THE FEELING PROCESS. When major personality change occurs, intense, emotional, inwardly felt events are usually observed. I would like to give the name "feeling process" to this affective dimension of personality change. The word "feeling" is preferable to "affective," because "feeling" usually refers to something concretely sensed by an individual. In personality change the individual directly feels an inward reworking. His own concepts and constructs become partly unstructured and his felt experiencing at times exceeds his intellectual grasp.

In various contexts it has been noted that major personality change requires not only intellectual or actional operations, but also this felt process. For instance, psychotherapists (of whatever orientation) often discuss the presence or absence of this feeling process in a particular case. They discuss whether the individual, in a given psychotherapy hour, is engaged in "merely" intellectualizing, or whether (as they phrase it) he is "really" engaged in psychotherapy. The former they consider a waste of time or a defense, and they predict [5] that no major personality change will result from it. The latter they consider promising of personality change.

Now, although this difference is universally discussed, it is most often phrased so unclearly, and the words following "merely" ("merely" intellectualizing, defending, avoiding, externalizing, etc.), and the words following "really" ("really" engaged, facing, dealing with) are so undefined that we may as well simply refer to this difference as the difference between "merely" and "really." Although it may not be phrased well, what is always meant or referred to by "really" is a *feeling process* which is absent when something is termed "merely."

A similar distinction between "merely" and "really" is talked about in education: There has always been much concern with the contrast between "mere" rote learnings of facts and "really" learning something (making it one's own, becoming able to "integrate," "apply," and "creatively elaborate" it).

"Really" learning is predicted to result in observable behavior changes, while "mere" rote learning is predicted to result in little (or different) be-

---

[5] Throughout, the new concepts and words defined here are intended to lead to new and more effective operational variables. Where research is cited, the theory has already led to some operational variables. One must distinguish *theoretical concepts* from *operational variables*. For example, above, "feeling process" is a theoretical concept. The operational variables (and there will be many specific ones) which a theoretical concept aids us to isolate and define are indices of behavior and exactly repeatable procedures whereby these can be reliably measured.

When it is held that the difference above between "really" and "merely" is a "subjective" difference, this only means that we have *not yet* defined the observable variables which enable a common-sense observer to predict differential behavioral results.

havior change. The learning process is said to differ in the two instances, depending upon the degree of the individual's "internal motivation," his way of "taking the new material in," his "application of himself to what he learns," his genuine grasp of meanings. These metaphoric phrases indicate that, here again during learning, the difference between "really" and "merely" refers to a certain participation of the individual's feelings in the learning process.

Let me give some further aspects of this observation from psychotherapy.

An Adlerian therapist some years ago told me: "Of course interpretation is not enough. Of course the person doesn't change only because of the wisdoms which the therapist tells him. But no technique really expresses what makes the change itself. The change comes through some kind of emotional digesting; but then you must admit that none of us understand what *that* is."

Therapists often miss this fact. They labor at helping the individual to a better explanation of what is wrong with him, yet, when asked how the individual is to *change* this now clearly explained maladaption, nothing very clear is said. Somehow, knowing his problem, the individual should change, yet *knowing* is not the process of changing.

A good diagnostician, perhaps with the aid of a few psychometric tests, can often give a very accurate and detailed description and explanation of an individual's personality. Therapist and client often both *know*, after such testing and a few interviews, a good deal of what is wrong and what needs to be changed. Quite often, after two years of therapeutic interviews, the description and explanation which was (or could have been) given at the outset appears in retrospect to have been quite accurate. Yet it is clear that there is a major difference between knowing the *conceptual* explanation of personality (which one can devise in a few hours) and the actual *feeling process* of changing (which often requires years). Relatively little has been said about this process,[6] how one may observe and measure it, and just in

[6] Rogers discovered how, in practice, the individual can be helped to overcome the repression paradigm.

His discovery is that defensiveness and resistance are obviated when one responds to an individual "within his own internal frame of reference." This phrase means that the psychotherapist's response always refers to something which is directly present in the individual's own momentary awareness.

Rogers at first found that even if the therapist did nothing more than to rephrase the client's communication—that is to say, if the therapist clearly showed that he was receiving and exactly understanding the client's moment-by-moment communications—a very deep and self-propelled change process began and continued in the client. Something happens in an individual when he is understood in this way. Some change takes place in what he momentarily confronts. Something releases. He then has something else,

what theoretical way this feeling process functions to permit personality change.

THE PERSONAL RELATIONSHIP. Just as the feeling process is observed as essential in personality change—while little is said to delineate, observably define, or theoretically account for it—so also the personal relationship is always cited. Can theory define this enormous and critical difference which it makes to the individual to live in relation to another person?

We observe that when the individual thinks about his experiences and emotions by himself, there is often little change. We observe that when he speaks about these things to *some* other people, equally little change occurs.

further, to say; and if this, again, is received and understood, something still further emerges which the individual would not even have thought of (nor was capable of thinking), had not such a sequence of expressions and responses taken place.

Rogers next found that if he aimed to conceptualize exactly what the client now wished to communicate, and if he kept this aim visible and known to the client, he could formulate the client's present message much more deeply and accurately than the client had done. Perhaps the client gave a long series of externalized reports of incidents and his generally angry reactions. The therapist, after listening, could sense the specific felt meaning which the client was inarticulately struggling to communicate to himself and to the therapist. Thus, in response to some long situational reports the therapist might say, "It frightens you to think that you are helpless when that sort of thing happens."

Rogers found that, while interpretations, deductions, and conceptual explanations were useless and usually resisted, the *exact* referring to the client's own momentarily felt meaning was almost always *welcome* to the client and seemed to release him into deeper and further self-expression and awareness.

I like to think of this diagrammatically, as two dimensions of a communication. Along one (say the horizontal) direction one may deduce or adduce from what an individual says quite a lot of other things about him—his background, his usual behavior, his probable emotional patterns, traits, etc. One does this by moving from what he now feels, through concepts and generalizations, *to other* things, which he does *not now feel.*

The other (vertical) dimension depends on the fact that any communication refers inwardly to a mass of feelings, perceptions, intentions, judgments, wishes, etc., which *are now felt.* While a communication *says* only a little in verbal form, it *rests on* a great deal that is felt now in the speaker's awareness. Thus, one can respond very superficially or very deeply and yet remain within what is now awarely felt by the speaker.

Rogers discovered how a response can get to, and affect, the individual's felt events *before* the defensive limits are widened. Once we can explain exactly how the individual can take such a response in at all, we will find it possible to explain also how his defensive limits are thereby widened. But, the problem had been that, given the individual's repressions and their limits and force upon anything current, how was anything ever to enter which did not already conform to his defenses?

I term it the "discovery" of Rogers' because it is not a theory, not a hypothesis, but an observation. Anyone may confirm it. It has two parts:

1. Along the "vertical" dimension of response to presently felt meaning in awareness, deep responses are welcome and taken in.

However, when we come to the "therapeutic" or "effective" personal relationship, we say that "suggestion," or "libidinal support," or "approval and reinforcement," or the other person's "therapeutic attitudes," or the "conversation between the two unconsciousnesses," somehow obviates the factors which otherwise shape all his experiences and personal relations to keep the individual as he is. Somehow, now, he is said to "become aware" of what he previously could not be aware of, he is "influenced" by suggestions, he "overcomes" the transference, his "libidinal balance" is altered, he somehow now "perceives the attitudes" of the therapist, where he has always distorted and anticipated the attitudes of others. This is really the problem, not the explanation, of personality change.

2. Successive responses of this sort give rise to a deeply felt and profoundly reorganizing change process in the individual which is self-propelled and moves from one fresh self-expression to another and another, along a chain of feeling quite unpredictable and quite different than either client or therapist may have planned or expected.

One import of this discovery must first be pointed out. The response can enter *before* the defensive limits are widened, *because* the response has for its referent not the individual's concepts, not his self-structure or construct, but something which he can now *experience* (or "feel"). If only concepts and constructs were given in the individual, the therapist would either have to conform exactly to these, or he would exceed the defensive limits. But since there is present in the individual at any moment a realm of felt, but largely unsymbolized, "meaning" or "feeling" or "experience," it is possible for the therapist to respond to that as it was implied in the individual's words, rather than just to his words. Words and concepts have only just the specific meaning they have. On the other hand, *an individual's personal communication always involves not only the meanings of his words, but also the whole realm of momentarily felt, but not fully stated, experiential meanings. These constitute his "internal frame of reference."*

Thus, Rogers' discovery of how to enter responsively within the defensive limits adds the consideration of direct experience to the theory of personality.

Rogers' theory retains the "self" as an organization of appraisals consisting in part of appraisals of the self by others:

Self, Concept of self, Self-structure. These terms refer to the organized, consistent conceptual gestalt composed of perceptions of the characteristics of the "I" or "me" and the perceptions of the relationships of the "I" or "me" to others and to various aspects of life, together with the values attached to these perceptions (Rogers, 1959b, p. 200).

We note that the self here is a "conceptual" gestalt, as indeed the words self-*concept* and appraisal indicate. But, this view of the self (agreeing as it does with past views of what makes personality) really gives us only the negative, artificial, non-adaptive or maladjusted side:

At the fixed [maladjusted] end of the continuum we find that personal constructs are extremely rigid, unrecognized as constructs, but thought of as external facts. Experience seems to *have* this meaning; the individual is quite unaware that he has construed experience as having this meaning (Rogers, 1959a, p. 103).

Here Rogers defines as maladjusted both the rigidity of personal constructs and the fact that the individual views himself and his experience *as* personal constructs. The mal-

But we do *observe* that almost always these changes occur in the context of a personal relationship. Some definitions of the kind of relationship which does (and the kind which does not) effect personality change have been offered (Rogers, 1957, 1959*b*). Very little has been said about how relationship events affect the conditions making for repression and the nature of contents, so that these alter.

So far we have formulated two problems of personality change and we have then cited *two observations;* the feeling process in the individual; and the personal relationship.

Our two observations and our two problems are related: simply, we may say that, while it is *theoretically* impossible for the individual to become aware of what he must *repress* and to change his personality *contents* into other *contents,* we *observe* that both occur *when* the individual is engaged in a deep and intense *feeling process* and in the context of a *personal relationship.* We need a theoretical account of this observed possibility, and we need to reformulate the theory of repression and the definitions of personality constituents, so that observed changes can be theoretically formulated.

adjusted individual does not recognize that he is construing *experience.* He takes his construct as a fact, and as what he is.

Rogers then describes more adjusted stages of personality:

The self becomes increasingly simply the subjective and reflexive awareness of experiencing (Rogers, 1961*a*, p. 153).

[At the most adjusted end of the continuum] the self exists in the experiencing of feelings. . . . At any given moment the self *is* the experiencing (Rogers, 1959*a*).

. . . the self is primarily a reflexive awareness of the process of experiencing. It is not a perceived object, but something confidently felt in process. It is not a structure to be defended, but a rich and changing awareness of the internal experiencing (Rogers, 1959*a*, p. 103).

In the last ten years during which I worked with Rogers, I have contributed some aspects of the above formulation, although the basic *intent* of that formulation was as it is today before the theory of experiencing came upon the scene. Fred M. Zimring collaborated with me in helping to formulate this aspect of Rogerian theory.

Also, it should be noted that while the older definitions, now the maladjusted aspects, invariably consist of constructs, judgments, and structures, Rogers always views the more basic and adaptive aspect of personality as consisting directly of *experience.* What we "introject" from others are constructs, judgments (conclusions without the process of arriving at them), appraisals, which we employ *instead of* experience. In optimal adjustment we do not replace these judgments with other judgments. We base evaluations and behavior directly on experience instead.

In my opinion, these basic additions of Rogers stem directly from his practical discovery that, aside from the individual's defenses, constructs, and concepts, one can respond directly to the *experienced* or felt data which he momentarily confronts. This directly experienced dimension more basically and concretely *is* the human being, and through this directly experienced dimension a positive and corrective change process can occur, and a much more adaptive and constructive personality can result.

THE THEORY

Basic Concepts—What Are Psychological Events?

1. EXPERIENCING.

(*a*) The "ing" in the term "experiencing" indicates that experience is considered as a *process*. (We will have to define the theoretical conceptions which go to make up a process framework.)

Now, of course, the above is not really a definition, since the usage of the word "experience" is currently confused and various. The field of psychology lacks a theory of experience. However, the theory of experiencing (Gendlin, 1962*b*) attempts to provide a process for determining a theory of experience.

Since the term "experiencing" is extremely broad, more specific terms will be defined for specific aspects of experiencing. Anything in particular which we may consider will be a particular *manner* or *mode* of experiencing, or a particular *function* of it, or a particular logical pattern we choose to impose. The term "experiencing," then, denotes all "experience" viewed in terms of the process framework.

(*b*) The word "experience" in psychology, wherever employed, means concrete psychological events. The same is the case here. Experiencing is a process of concrete, ongoing events.

(*c*) Finally, by experiencing we mean a *felt* process. We mean inwardly sensed, bodily felt events, and we hold that the concrete "stuff" of personality or of psychological events is this flow of bodily sensing or feeling.

Experiencing is the process of concrete, bodily feeling, which constitutes the basic matter of psychological and personality phenomena.

2. THE DIRECT REFERENT. Both in social talk and in theory we so largely emphasize external events and logical meaning that it almost seems as if it were difficult to notice that, in addition to external objects and logic, we also have an inward bodily feeling or sensing. This is, of course, a commonplace that can be readily checked by anyone.

At any moment he wishes, one can refer directly to an inwardly felt datum. Experiencing, in the mode of being directly referred to in this way, I term the "direct referent."

Of course, there are other modes of experiencing. Situations and external events, symbols, and actions may interact with our feeling process quite without any reflexive attention paid to the direct referent. We are aware and feel without this direct attention as well as with it.

One can always refer directly to experiencing.

3. IMPLICIT. It is less apparent, but still easily checked by anyone, that this direct referent contains meaning. At first it may seem that experiencing is simply the inward sense of our body, its tension, or its well-being. Yet, upon further reflection, we can notice that only in this direct sensing do we have the meanings of what we say and think. For, without our "feel" of the meaning, verbal symbols are only noises (or sound images of noises).

For example, someone listens to you speak, and then says: "Pardon me, but I don't grasp what you mean." If you would like to restate what you meant in different words, you will notice that you must inwardly attend to your direct referent, your *felt* meaning. Only in this way can you arrive at different words with which to restate it.

In fact, we employ explicit symbols only for very small portions of what we think. We have most of it in the form of *felt* meanings.

For example, when we think about a problem, we must think about quite a number of considerations together. We cannot do so *verbally*. In fact, we could not think about the meaning of these considerations at all if we had to keep reviewing the verbal symbols over and over. We may review them verbally. However, to think upon the problem we must use the *felt* meanings—we must think of how "this" (which we previously verbalized) relates to "that" (which we also previously verbalized). To think "this" and "that," we employ their *felt* meanings.

When felt meanings occur in interaction with verbal symbols and we feel what the symbols mean, we term such meanings "explicit" or "explicitly known." On the other hand, quite often we have just such felt meanings without a verbal symbolization. Instead we have an event, a perception, or some word such as the word "this" (which represents nothing, but only points). When this is the case, we can term the meaning "implicit" or "implicitly felt, but not explicitly known."

Please note that "explicit" and "implicit" meanings are both *in awareness.* What we concretely feel and can inwardly refer to is certainly "in awareness" (though the term "awareness" will later require some reformulations). "Implicit" meaning is often confusingly discussed as if it were "unconscious" or "not in awareness." It should be quite clear that, since the direct referent is felt and is a direct datum of attention, it is "in awareness." *Anything termed "implicit" is felt in awareness.*

Furthermore, we may now add that even when a meaning is explicit (when we say "exactly what we mean") the felt meaning we have always contains a great deal more implicit meaning than we have made explicit. When we define the words we have just used, or when we "elaborate" what we "meant," we notice that the felt meanings we have been employing always contain implicitly many, many meanings—always many more than those to which we gave explicit formulation. We find that we employed these meanings. We find they were central to what we did make explicit, that they made up what we actually meant, yet they were only felt. They were implicit.

4. IMPLICIT FUNCTION (IN PERCEPTION AND BEHAVIOR). So far we have thought of implicit meanings as existing only in the direct referent; that is to say, only if and when we directly refer to our experiencing as a felt datum. However, quite without such direct reference to experiencing, most of life and behavior proceed on implicit meanings. (Explicit meanings serve only a few special purposes.) We say, for example, that our interpretation of and reactions to present situations are determined by our "past" experiences. But in which way are our past experiences here *now*? For instance, if I am to observe an immediate situation and then describe it, in what way are there present my knowledge and experiences of past events, my knowledge of language, and my memories of this situation which I have just observed so that they function now? To describe the situation I just observed, my words will arise for me from a felt sense of what I have observed, reacted to, and now mean to say. Rarely, if at all, do I think *in words* what I now observe. Nor do I think each of the past experiences which function in this observing. Rarely do I think in explicit words what I will say. All these meanings *function implicitly as my present, concretely felt* experiencing.

5. COMPLETION; CARRYING FORWARD

6. INTERACTION. Implicit meanings are *incomplete*. Symbolic *completion*— or *carrying forward*—is a bodily felt process. There is an *interacting*, not an equation, between implicit meaning and symbols.

I must now make it quite clear that "implicit" and "explicit" meanings are different in nature. We may feel that some verbal statement says exactly what we mean; nevertheless, to feel the meaning is not the same kind of thing as verbal symbols. As we have shown, a felt meaning can contain very many meanings and can be further and further elaborated. Thus, the felt meaning is not the same in kind as the precise symbolized explicit meaning. The reason the difference in kind is so important is because if we ignore it we assume that explicit meanings are (or were) already in the implicit felt meaning. We are led to make the felt, implicit meaning a kind of dark place in which countless explicit meanings are hidden. We then wrongly assume that these meanings are "implicit" and felt only in that they are "hidden." I must emphasize that the "implicit" or "felt" datum of experiencing is a sensing of body life. As such it may have countless organized aspects, but this does not mean that they are conceptually formed, explicit, and hidden. Rather, we *complete* and form them when we explicate. Before symbolization, the "felt" meanings are *incomplete*. They are analogous, let us say, to the muscle movement in my stomach which I can call "hunger." This sensation certainly "means" something about eating, but it does not "contain" eating. To be even more graphic, the feeling of hunger is not a repressed eating. It does not contain within itself the search for an animal, the killing and roasting of this animal, the eating, digesting, and absorbing of food particles, and the excretion and burying of wastes. Now just as all these steps (some of them patterned in the newborn organism, some of them learned) do not exist within the hunger sensation of muscle movement, so also the symbolic meaning "hunger" does not exist within it. Symbols must interact with the feeling before we have a meaning. The verbal symbol "hunger," just as "food," must interact with it before we carry forward the digestive process. The symbol "hunger," like other aspects of the search for food or my sitting down at a table, is a learned step of the digestive process and carries that process forward. Before that occurs, the feeling of the muscle movement implicitly contains the body's patterned readiness for organized interaction but not the formed conceptual units. Implicit bodily feeling is *preconceptual*. Only when *interaction* with verbal symbols (or events) actually occurs, is the process actually carried forward and the explicit meaning formed.[7] So long as it is implicit, it is *incomplete,* awaiting symbols (or events) with which it can interact in preorganized ways.

Thus, to explicate is to *carry forward* a bodily felt process. Implicit meanings are *incomplete*. They are not hidden conceptual units. They are not the same in nature as explicitly known meanings. There is no equation possible between implicit meanings and "their" explicit symbolization. Rather than an equation, there is an *interaction* between felt experiencing and symbols (or events).[8]

[7] Experiencing is essentially an *interaction* between feeling and "symbols" (attention, words, events), just as body life is an *interaction* between body and environment. In its basic nature, the physical life process is interaction. (This is an application of Sullivan's basic concepts.) For example, the body consists of cells which are interaction processes involving the environment (oxygen and food particles). If we apply this concept of interaction to experiencing, we can view it as an interaction of feeling and events ("events" here includes verbal noises, others' behaviors, external occurrences—anything that can interact with feeling).

[8] For the full theory of affect and meaning see Gendlin (1962*b*). As will be seen later (definitions 15–18 and 26), the discussion here lays the ground for a view of personality which avoids the "content paradigm"; i.e., the erroneous assumption that psychological events involve conceptually formed static units.

The Feeling Process—How Change Takes Place in the Individual

7. FOCUSING. "Focusing" (or, more exactly, "continuous focusing") will be defined in terms of four more specific definitions (8–11) below. "Focusing" is the whole process which ensues when the individual attends to the direct referent of experiencing.

We noted earlier that direct reference is one mode of experiencing. The feeling process we term "experiencing" also occurs in an individual's awareness without direct reference to it as a felt datum. In these other modes, also, experiencing has important functions in personality change. We will discuss them later.

"Focusing" refers to how one mode of experiencing, the direct referent, functions in ongoing personality change.

The foregoing definitions (1–6) will be employed in the following discussion, and four more definitions concerning focusing will be formulated.

Focusing will be analyzed in four phases. The division into these phases is more a result of my way of formulation than of any inherent four-step divisibility in the process. Although it may occur in these clearly separable phases, more often it does not.

8. DIRECT REFERENCE IN PSYCHOTHERAPY (PHASE ONE OF FOCUSING). A definitely felt, but conceptually vague referent is directly referred to by the individual. Let us say he has been discussing some troublesome situation or personal trait. He has described various events, emotions, opinions, and interpretations. Perhaps he has called himself "foolish," "unrealistic," and assured his listener that he really "knows better" than to react in the way he does. He is puzzled by his own reactions, and he disapproves of them. Or, what amounts to the same thing, he strongly defends his reactions against some real or imaginary critic who would say that the reactions make no sense, are self-defeating, unrealistic, and foolish. If he is understandingly listened to and responded to, he may be able to refer directly to the felt meaning which the matter has for him. He may then lay aside, for a moment, all his better judgment or bad feeling about the fact that he is as he is, and he may refer directly to the felt meaning of what he is talking about. He may then say something like: "Well, I know it makes no sense, but in some way it does." Or: "It's awfully vague to me what this is with me, but I feel it pretty definitely." It may seem as if language and logic are insufficient, but the trouble is merely that we are not used to talking about something which is conceptually vague, but definitely and distinctly *felt*.

If the individual continues to focus his attention on this direct referent (if he does not break off attending to it because it seems too foolish, or too bad, or too doubtful whether he isn't just coddling himself, etc.), he may become able to conceptualize some rough aspects of it. For example, he may find: "I feel that way whenever anyone does such-and-such to me." Or: "I think there is something about that kind of thing which could make something completely terrible and frightening happen to me, but that's silly. You have to accept things like that. That's life. But that's the way it feels, kind of a terror."

Having conceptualized some such rough aspect of "it," the individual usually feels the felt meaning more strongly and vividly, becomes more excited and hopeful about the process of focusing within himself, and is less likely now to settle for the conceptual explanations, accusations, and apologies. It is a profound discovery for most people when they find it possible to continue direct reference. It comes to be deeply valued as "I am in touch with myself."

As the individual continues to focus on such a direct referent, he may puzzle over what a funny kind of a "this" he is talking about. He may call it "this feeling," or "this whole thing," or "this is the way I am when such-and-such occurs." Very clearly it is an inwardly sensed referent in his present experiencing. Nothing is vague about the definite way he *feels* it. He can turn to it with his inward attention. Only *conceptually* is it vague.

A very important and surprising fact about direct reference to felt meanings is that if the matter under consideration is anxiety producing or highly uncomfortable, this felt discomfort *decreases* as the individual directly refers to the felt meaning. One would have expected the opposite. Certainly the opposite is true, for example, when the individual chooses between various topics for discussion. The prospect of talking about this difficult, anxiety-provoking matter certainly makes the person more anxious than the prospect of talking about some neutral or pleasant subject. Thus, he may be in quite a lot of inward pain as he decides to bring the matter up at all. However, once into the topic, the more directly he attends to the direct referent, the felt meaning, the less his discomfort and anxiety. If he momentarily loses track of it, the anxiety flares up again, and the diffuse discomfort of the topic returns.

As the individual symbolizes some aspect of the felt meaning, he senses its rightness partly by the degree of *easing* of the anxiety which he feels.

In contrast to the anxiety or discomfort, the felt meaning itself becomes sharper, more distinctly felt, as he refers to and correctly symbolizes what it is. In fact, his sense of whether or not he has "correctly" symbolized is partly just this sense of increased intensity of the felt meaning.[9]

---

[9] The word "correctly" here really refers just to this interaction between the felt referent and the symbols which we are describing. The fact that, a few minutes later, the *same* type

This decreased anxiety is a very surprising fact, much against the general assumptions about anxiety-provoking material. We generally assume that to focus directly on the experiencing makes us more anxious. My observations indicate that increased anxiety comes from topic choice, and it is this which we generally expect. On the other hand, given the topic, the more we focus directly upon the felt meaning, and the more of it we symbolize correctly, the more relief we feel. Even a little error in symbolizing ("no, what I just said isn't quite it") again increases the anxiety.

We may theoretically interpret this observation in terms of definitions 5 and 6 and our use of the work of Mead and Sullivan. To symbolize a directly felt implicit meaning carries the organismic process a step forward. It is felt so. It also appears from this that we should consider the direct reference (or the giving of attention), as itself, already a kind of symbolizing. Direct reference, as well as the resulting symbolizations, involves bodily felt tension relief.[10]

There are other ways of describing the individual's focusing on a direct referent of experiencing. We may say that, at such moments, his experiencing is "ahead of his concepts." It "guides" his concepts. He forms concepts and "checks them against" his directly felt meaning and, on this basis, decides their correctness.

As he continues to refer directly to the felt meaning (he is probably calling it "this"), he may find that his previous formulation which felt correct must be replaced by another which now feels more correct. The listener can help by pointing his words also at "this" and by helping to find words and concepts that might fit it.[11] The listener, of course, cannot judge the

of interaction with further symbols can again produce a very different, yet now "correct" further conceptualization shows that "correctness" does not imply that a given set of symbols means what the felt referent alone means. Rather, "correctness" refers to the experienced effect which certain symbols produce and which is described above, and in definitions 5 and 6.

[10] Research (Gendlin and Berlin, 1961) employing autonomic correlates has borne out this observation operationally. Individuals were given tape-recorded instructions to engage in various processes. After each instruction there was a period of silence in which to carry it out. It was found that galvanic skin resistance (also skin temperature and heart rate) indicated tension reduction during the period when individuals were instructed to (and reported later that they did) focus inwardly on the felt meanings of a troublesome personal problem. It has continued to be difficult to define and check individuals' performances after this and other instructions. Therefore, this research remains tentative. Nevertheless, several replications have supported the observation that, while threatening topics in general raise tension, direct inward focusing involves tension reduction.

[11] It is extremely important that the listener refers his words to "this" felt datum in the individual and that he shares the sense that the datum itself decides what is correct and what is not. It is much less important whether or not the listener's words turn out to be accurate.

correctness. Not even the individual himself judges it but, we might say somewhat poetically, his direct referent does the judging. Both persons may thus be surprised by the direction which the symbolizing takes.

The above has been a description of how an individual may directly refer to or "focus on" a direct referent of experiencing which, for him, constitutes the felt meaning of some topic, situation, behavior, or personality aspect.

9. UNFOLDING (PHASE TWO OF FOCUSING). Sometimes, in focusing on a directly felt referent, there is a gradual step-by-step process of coming to know explicitly what it is. Yet, it may "open up" in one dramatic instant. Most often there is both a gradual coming to know it better and some instants during which there is a very noticeable "opening up." With a great physical relief and sudden dawning, the individual suddenly knows. He may sit there, nodding to himself, thinking only words such as "yes, I've got it" quite without as yet finding concepts to tell himself what it is he "has got." However, he knows that now he *can* say. It is possible that, if he is now suddenly interrupted, he may "lose it," so that later he can only say, "I really felt I knew what it was at that moment, but I've lost it now." Usually, however, he will as swiftly as possible find concepts and words to say what has opened up. It is almost always a number of things. For example:

Yes, *of course* he is afraid, he realizes. He has not permitted himself even to think about dealing with *this* and *this* aspect of the situation, and this has been because he has not believed that these aspects really existed. Well, yes, he did realize they existed, but he also felt compelled to blame himself for them as if he merely imagined them. And if they do exist (and they do), he does not know how he could possibly live with them. He has not allowed himself to try to deal with them (he now realizes) or even to consider them anything other than merely his imagination, because, my God, if they are really there, then he is helpless. Then there is *nothing* he can do! But they are there. Well, it is a relief to know at least that.

This example illustrates the multiplicity one generally finds in an implicit meaning which was felt as one "this." It may, as in the example, be a multiplicity which can still be thought of as "one thing." Experiencing has no given definite unit experiences.

The example also illustrates that, often, the meanings one finds with such great relief are not at all pleasant or good. The problem is not at all resolved. Quite the contrary, now it *really* looks impossible. Now it seems clear why one has been so anxious. It *does* seem hopeless. Yet it is a great and physically experienced tension reduction when the directly felt referent "unfolds" in this way.

The unfolding of a direct referent always involves a surprising and deeply emotional recognition of the good sense of our own (previously so seemingly irksome) feelings. *"Of course,"* we say over and over, "Of course!" Or, we say, "Well, what do you know, that's what that was!"

Because what was previously felt now actually "makes sense," problem resolutions can occur at this stage. For, we may see that *given this or that judgment,* or perception, or event, or situation, "of course" we felt as we did, but we do not now judge it in the same way. However, my example illustrated that even when the solution seems further away than ever, still the physiological tension reduction occurs, and a genuine change takes place. I believe that this change is really more basic than the resolution of specific problems.

A whole vast multiplicity of implicit aspects in the person's functioning and dysfunctioning is always involved. For, when a direct referent of experiencing "opens up," much more change has occurred than the cognitive realization of this or that. This is most dramatically evident when, after the "unfolding," the individual still sees no way out. He says, "At least I know what it is now, but how will I ever change it or deal with it?" Yet, during the following days and in the next therapy hour, it turns out that he is already different, that the quality of the problem has changed and his behavior has been different. And, as for a good explanation of all this resolution . . . "well, it just seems all right now." There is a global change in the whole manner of experiencing in this regard. From this *felt change,* with its lack of logical description, come some of our simple-minded notions: "Just accept it," we tell ourselves and others. We can recall that we have observed individuals, such as I just described, *report* a basic change in such a simplistic way:

"How is everything different?"

"Well, it just seems OK now!"

"Do you still feel that such-and-such might happen and you couldn't deal with it?"

"Yes, but now I kind of feel, well, that's life. That's the way it is, you have to accept things like that."

And that is just what he had said to himself over and over again, *without any effect,* before the process in which he focused on the felt meaning and it unfolded!

Thus, as I have said, only sometimes does *what* is unfolded lead to a solution in an explicable way. More often, deep global feeling change occurs as one unfolds the direct referent, even when it seems to open into something which sounds worse and more hopeless than one had expected. Whether or not some specific resolution is noticeable, the change appears to be broad and global. It is not just this problem resolved, or that trait changed, but a change in many areas and respects. We can say that the broad multiplicity of aspects which are implicit in any felt meaning are all of them changed—thus the global change. Or we can say that meanings are aspects of the experiencing process and that the very *manner of* experiencing changes, hence also the quality of all of its meanings.

As one client put it: "Until now I always saw this problem in black and white terms, and I struggled for a solution that would be gray. But now, this new way isn't black or white, *or* gray. It's in color!" Thus the unfolding of a felt referent does not just inform one about what was involved but, rather, it changes the whole manner in which one experiences.

10. GLOBAL APPLICATION (PHASE THREE OF FOCUSING). This global way in which the process of direct reference and unfolding affects many aspects of the person is noticeable not only in his later reports of the resulting difference, but also in the moments which immediately follow the unfolding of a felt referent. The individual is flooded by many different associations, memories, situations, and circumstances, all in relation to the felt referent. Although conceptually they can be very different, they share the same felt meaning with which he has been dealing. Except for this they may concern quite different and unrelated matters.[12] "Oh, and that's also why I can't get up any enthusiasm for this-and-this." "Yes, and another thing about it is, this comes in every time somebody tells me what to do or think. I can't say, well, what *I* think is more important, because, see, this way of making myself wrong comes in there." "Oh, and also, back when this and this happened, I did the *same* thing."

During this "wide application" period which often follows the unfolding of a felt referent, the individual may sit in silence, only occasionally voicing some of the pieces from this flood.

I realize that some of the foregoing observations have been termed by others as "insight." I believe that is a misnomer. First, the global application is in no way a figuring out, nor is it chiefly a better understanding. Rather, insight and better understanding are the results, the by-products, of this process, as a few of its very many changed aspects call attention to themselves. One can be sure that for every relation or application the individual here explicitly thinks, there are thousands which he does not think of, but which have, nevertheless, just changed. Not his thinking about the difference which the unfolding has made, but the unfolding itself, changes him

---

[12] We can always apply logic after the process and formulate the relationships implied, but we can almost never choose correctly ahead of time which of the thousands of possible relations between various problems and topics will function in a concretely felt process as described above.

in all these thousands of respects. The change occurs whether or not he thinks of any such applications, and whether or not he considers the unfolding to be a resolving. For, as I emphasized, he may well walk out saying, "I have no idea what I can do with this, or how I change it." But, it has already changed, and the great multiplicity of respects in which "it" *implicitly functions* have all changed.

11. REFERENT MOVEMENT (PHASE FOUR OF FOCUSING). A definite alteration or movement in the direct referent is felt. This "referent movement" often occurs after the three phases just described. When there has been *direct reference,* dramatic *unfolding* occurs, and when the flood of *global application* subsides, the individual finds that he now refers to a direct referent which feels different. The *implicit* meanings which he can symbolize from this direct reference are now quite different ones. It is a new direct reference; and so the four-phase process begins again.

But focusing is not always such a neatly divisible four-phase process. As noted before, *unfolding* can occur with or without a noticeable flood of *global application.* Unfolding can also occur quite undramatically, in very small steps of successive symbolization. And, even without unfolding, even without any symbolization which feels "correct," the individual's direct reference can *carry forward* the feeling process and is experienced with bodily tension relief. What we are here calling the fourth phase of focusing, the *referent movement,* can occur at any of these times. Usually, direct reference alone does not change or move the direct referent, but does make it stronger, sharper, and more distinctly felt. It increases its intensity as a feeling and diminishes the diffuse tension, discomfort, and anxiety. However, sometimes the mere process of continuous direct reference will change or "move" the direct referent. More often, such a movement occurs after at least some unfolding and symbolizing, and especially after the felt flooding of global application.

The individual distinctly feels a change in the quality of the felt referent. It is not only a change but a directly experienced "give" or "movement" which feels right and welcome. Its tremendous importance lies in the fact that after such a referent movement (even very small), the implicit meanings are now different. The "scenery," as it were, which one confronts, changes.

It is just this referent movement which is usually missing when one *talks at* oneself, when one has recited all the good reasons, considerations, and ways one should feel and would be more sensible to feel, etc. Most often, thereafter, the *same unchanged* felt referent is still there, and the same diffuse anxiety as well. From this lack of referent movement, one knows that nothing has really changed.

Conversely, after referent movement, the meanings and symbolizations one formulates are different. The relevant considerations are different. The whole scene is different. Of course, most often in one such step one does not find "solutions." The individual may say: "Well, that doesn't help me either, because now this helpless feeling, it just seems like the worst crime in the world to be helpless, weak, just let everything happen to you. I can't stand that either. I don't know what is so bad about it, I mean, if actually, in reality, I can't do anything about it anyhow." Here we see that there is no hint of anything like a solution, but the relevant surrounding considerations have now changed. What he looks at and symbolizes is different as the felt referent to which he directly refers is different.

Reference movement gives direction to the focusing process. The individual's attention and symbolizing tends to follow that direction which produces referent movement.

Without reference movement, what is said is "merely" talk, "merely" intellectualization, "merely" hair splitting, or "merely" reporting.

Reference movement is the direct experience that something more than logic and verbalization has occurred. The movement can often be logically analyzed (that is to say, logical relationships can be formulated between what he said earlier and what he says now). However, such logical analysis can be made between any verbalizations, whether or not there has been reference movement. And, often, for a small bit of reference movement the logical or conceptual shift is extremely large. Even a *slight* reference movement can make for what conceptually looks like a totally different vantage point.

Reference movement is a change in the felt meaning which functions in symbolizing.

I hope I have conveyed something of the overlapping character of what I call the four phases of focusing. To summarize them: phase one, *direct reference* to a felt meaning which is conceptually vague but definite as felt; phase two, *unfolding* and the symbolizing of some aspects; phase three, a flooding of *global application;* phase four, *referent movement,* and the process can begin again with phase one.

These four definitions (8–11) define "focusing." [13]

[13] I must now describe some common sorts of so-called "internal" attention which do not involve direct reference and thus are not *focusing.*

Since the term "experiencing" includes any kind of experience at all, so long as we consider it as inwardly *felt* and apply to it the theoretical formulation of *process,* misunderstandings have arisen concerning the mode of experiencing called the *direct referent.* By this latter, more specific term we do not at all mean just anything at all which can be called inward attention.

Especially since the direct referent is "felt," it has been confused with emotions. (Emotions are also said to be "felt.") But the direct referent is internally complex and an in-

12. THE SELF-PROPELLED FEELING PROCESS. As the individual engages in focusing, and as *referent movement* occurs, he finds himself pulled along in a direction he neither chose nor predicted. There is a very strong impelling force exerted by the direct referent just then felt. The individual may "get off the track," "talk about something else," or put up with considerable distracting comments and useless deductions by his listener; and still the given felt, direct referent remains strikingly as the "next thing" with which he must deal. If the listener's responsiveness makes it possible, the individual finds himself moving from one referent movement and unfolding to another and another.

dividual feels "in touch with himself" when he refers to it, while emotions are internally all one quality . . . they are "sheer." They often keep him from sensing that in himself which is the complex ground of the emotion.

This and other distinctions will become clearer in the following list of kinds of occurrences in an individual which are not direct reference and thus are not focusing.

Direct reference is not:

1. *Sheer emotions.* The emotions of guilt, shame, embarrassment, or feeling that I am "bad" are *about* me or this aspect of my experience and its meaning to me. These emotions are not themselves the experience and its meaning to me. The emotions as such are not a direct reference to the felt experiencing. I must, at least momentarily, *get by* these emotions *about it* (or about myself) in order to refer directly to what all this means to me, why and what makes me feel ashamed. For example, I must say to myself: "All right, yes, I *am* very ashamed; but for a minute now, although it makes me feel very ashamed, I want to sense *what* this is in me."

For example: One client spent many sleepless hours each night with anxiety, shame, and resentment. He blamed himself for his reactions to a certain situation. He felt foolish and ashamed of the whole thing. As he tried to resolve it, he alternately felt resentful (he would decide to confront them, fight it out, not back down, etc.), and alternately he felt ashamed (he was a fool, and humiliatingly so, etc.). Only in the psychotherapy hour did it become possible for him to focus directly on "this," what it was, how it felt, and where it "lived" in him. In "this" he found a good many valid perceptions concerning the other people and the situation which he had not been able to specify before, and a good many personal aspects of himself. During a number of hours he directly referred to successive direct referents and felt meanings. Yet between hours he was unable to do this alone, but felt only shame or resentment. Only by moving temporarily "on by" these emotions could he refer directly to "this," "what I feel," about which, granted, I also have these emotions.

It seems quite striking and universal that we feel guilt, shame, and badness, *instead* of feeling that concerning which we feel shame, guilt, and badness. It is almost as if these emotions themselves preclude our feeling what it all is to us—not so much because they are so unpleasant, as because they skip the point at which we might complete, symbolize, respond or attend to that which centrally we feel. I am inclined to hypothesize that guilt, shame, and badness are emotions which occur as responses instead of the response which, by action or symbolizing, we would otherwise give our felt referent. These emotions seem to complete but actually "skip" the incomplete implicit meanings. It is like an animal whose response to hunger is to bite itself in the leg. Instead of responding with a behavior which in some way "symbolizes" the hunger and carries forward the organ-

Each time the inward scene changes, new felt meanings are there for him. The cycles of the four phases set into motion an overall feeling process. This feeling process has a very striking, concretely felt, self-propelled quality. As a psychotherapist I have learned that I must depend on this self-propelled feeling process in the client. This is an important principle, because I have the power to distract him. When I do so (by too many explanations or insights of my own into what he says), then this feeling process does not oc-

ismic digestion process, such an animal would be most aware of the pain in its leg and would behave accordingly. At any rate, the preoccupation with these emotions is not to be confused with the felt meaning which, though connected to these emotions, needs the focusing.

One client describes it in terms of a hurricane: "If you only go so far into something, it's like going into a hurricane and getting terribly blown around. You have to go into it and then keep going further and further *in* till you get to the eye of the hurricane. There it's quiet and you can see where you are." This beautifully expresses the fact that the direction of focusing is definitely into the emotions, not away from them, yet also that focusing involves something qualitatively very different than merely "being blown around" by the emotions. The illustration also captures something of the centrality, depth, and quiet which one finds—the quality which others have called "being in touch with myself." The felt referent, for the moment, *is* "me." It *unfolds* and is a thousand things. In comparison, the emotional tone which attaches to it and precedes it is not itself a thousand things. To remain with it merely feeds it. There is always a "breath-held," tense, tight quality about most of these emotional tones. Yet to turn away from the emotion is to turn away also from the direction in which one "finds oneself." Thus, one must "move into" and "through," or "on by," these emotional tones to the direct referent which is the *felt meaning* of it all.

The difference between focusing and "wallowing" or "being trapped in" certain emotions is most dramatically evident when one compares the usual experiences of an individual when he works on a personality difficulty alone and when he does so in the presence of an understanding other person. The difference is dramatic, because during many hours he has gone round and round, feeling the same series of emotions and lacking any *referent movement*. In contrast, often even just saying to the other person a little of what one has been feeling and thinking produces direct reference and referent movement. Later I will discuss this role of the other person in making focusing and other therapeutic processes possible. Another person's responses to the emotions, for instance, can make it possible to "grant them," "let them," and "get by" them, so as to refer directly to the felt meanings. It is often possible, though always unsteady and difficult, for the individual to focus by himself.

2. Circumstantial orbit. Just as one may get lost in the sheer emotions of guilt, shame, or badness, so one may also get lost in an inward recitation of circumstances, such as: what one ought to have done or did do; what others did, or might have done, or can be imagined to have done, etc. Such circumstantial play and replay, the inward repetitions of conversations, and dramatic re-enactings are clearly different from the felt meaning all this has and on which the individual could (perhaps, with help) focus. Often the client arrives for the therapy hour after sleepless nights and tired days of this kind of circumstantial "runaround" and finds, with a few responses to the felt meaning of "all this," that with great relief he now directly refers to and unfolds the felt meaning. No matter what cur. On the other hand, I have also learned that my questions and self-expressions can be useful, provided I always intend what I say to refer to the individual's felt referent and I show that I would like him to continue to focus on it.

In order to permit the feeling process to arise, we must sometimes remain silent, at least for some brief periods. If either he or I talk all the time, little

a bad look it turns out to have, the physically felt and verbalized steps of focusing are clearly and relievingly different from the circumstantial orbit.

3. *Explanatory orbit.* Attempts at explanations are different from direct reference: "Is it just that I'm so hostile?" "It must mean that I'm projecting some latent homosexuality." "This means I have a need to fail." "It's just that I'm trying to be right." "I'm just trying to get the love I didn't get as a child." "This is paranoid." "Other people don't get upset at this, so it must be that I'm not grateful for what I have."

Whether the explanatory concepts are simple and foolish, or sophisticated and quite correct, they are useless unless one employs them as pointers to momentarily name and hold onto a directly felt meaning. Without that, one cogitates in a vacuum and gets "no further." The explanatory "runaround" races the mental engine, disengaged from the wheels. It makes one tired and confused, and it is quite different from focusing on the felt meaning. Even one small step of the focusing process can change the inner scene so that one's whole set of explanatory concepts suddenly becomes irrelevant. In comparison with the felt meaning, explanatory concepts are so gross, so general, so empty, that even when they are accurate they are helpless abstractions.

4. *Self-engineering.* A fourth runaround consists in something that might be called "self-engineering." In this also one does not attend to one's felt meaning. Instead, one "talks at" oneself, inwardly. One is very active and constructive, arranging and rearranging one's feelings without stopping to sense quite what they are. This self-engineering is clearly different from focusing on a felt referent and the sensing and symbolizing of its implicit meaning.

Self-engineering is not always futile. In fact, it can succeed exactly to the extent to which one's experiencing in the given regard functions implicitly. The trouble with will-power and engineering is not, as Sullivan held and Rogers sometimes seems to assume, that there is no such thing. There is. One is not always automatically "wafted" into action or self-control. Willpower, decision, and self-engineering are often necessary. However, they cannot be effectively exerted at points where experiencing does not implicitly function. In such regards self-responses or the responses of others are required first, so that the process can be carried forward and experiencing then does implicitly function.

This focusing may be what has always been meant in religious terms by "listening to the still small voice." This has more recently been confused with conscience (and, only in very well-adjusted people can one identify conscience with direct reference). All but a few people have been puzzled as to where inside to "listen" and "hear" this "voice." The above indicates that to "listen" really means to keep quiet, to stop "talking at" yourself, and to sense just what is there, bodily felt, meaningful, and about to become clearer and then verbalizable.

The rule for focusing—a rule to be applied inwardly to oneself—is "Keep quiet and listen!" Then, by referring to the concretely felt referent, it will unfold; the sense of its meaning, and then the words, will come into focus.

direct reference can take place. Therefore, when he has stopped talking and I have stopped responding, I am glad if there is a little silence in which he can feel the meaning of what we have been saying. I am especially glad if the next thing he then says follows not simply and logically from what we have said, but shows that he has been immersed in something felt. In this way I can notice that a felt referent has provided the transition from what he did say to what he now says. This "descent" into himself, this focusing, and the overall feeling process which arises, give verbalization to the underlying flow of events of personality change. This self-propelled feeling process is the essential motor of personality change.

Once this feeling process has arisen, it continues even between the times the individual engages in the four-phase focusing process I have outlined. Thus, during the several days between two psychotherapy hours, the client may find important thoughts, feelings, memories, and insights "coming" to him. He may find a generalized "stirring," an inward "eventfulness," even without a specific symbolized content. Thus the overall *feeling process* comes to be self-propelled and broader than just the four phases of focusing I have described.

The Role of the Personal Relationship—How Another Person's Responses Affect the Individual's Experiencing, and How Personality "Contents" Are Inherently Changeable Thereby

We tend to be so concerned with content (symbolized meanings) that we sometimes discuss psychological questions as if personality were nothing but contents. We forget the obvious differences which exist not only in *what* an individual's experience is at a given moment, but also in *how* he experiences. Thus we ask a question such as this: What difference does the personal relationship make, since the individual can think and feel the same contents when he is alone as he can when he talks to another person?

Often a psychotherapist (or any listener who wants to be helpful) will feel that he must "do something," "add something," bring in some new content or insight, so that he will be helpful and make a difference.

Yet, there is already all the difference between *how* one thinks and feels *alone* and *how* one thinks and feels *with another person*. The conceptual content may (for a time) be the same as the individual can think and feel by himself; but, the *manner* of experiencing will be totally different. Consider, for example, the type of listener who interrupts with his own concerns and is inclined to be annoyed and critical long before he understands what is said. With him, my manner of experiencing will be quite constricted. I will think of less and feel less than I do when I am alone. I will tend to say what I must in round, general, swiftly finished terms. I will *not* tend to feel deeply, or intensely, or richly. Certain things will never occur to me when I am with him or, if they do occur to me, I will save them for the time when I am alone, and can feel them through without the constricting effects of his responses. We all know this difference between the manner of our experiencing with certain persons as compared with when we are alone.

Similarly, there are others (we are fortunate to know one) with whom we feel more intensely and freely whatever we feel. We think of more things, we have the patience and the ability to go more deeply into the details, we bear better our own inward strain when we are speaking to this person. If we are sad and dry-eyed alone, then with this person we cry. If we are stopped by our guilt, shame, and anxiety, then with this person we come to life again, inwardly, as being more than these emotions. If we have showered disgust and annoyance on ourselves to the point of becoming silent and deadened inside, then with this person we "come alive" again. As we tell this person some old, familiar, many times repeated story, we find it richer and freshly meaningful, and we may not get all the way through it for the many facets of personal meaning which now unfold.

How shall we theoretically explain these differences in the *manner* in which we experience in different relationships and alone?

13. MANNER OF EXPERIENCING. Whatever the content which we are said to experience, there is also the manner in which we experience. Few terms in our formal psychological language denote differences in *manner of experiencing*. Let us, therefore, define some more terms. (These terms overlap, so that fully explicating one of them would give us the others.)

Immediacy of Experiencing. Immediacy can be contrasted with disassociation or postponement of affect. Descriptive and poetic terms are usually invented by individuals to describe immediacy and its opposites: "I do everything right, but I'm not in it"; or "I am a spectator of my own behavior"; or "What it means to me so occupies me that I don't feel what is going on at all"; "Life is going on all right, but I'm in some back room. I merely hear about it, I'm not living it."

Presentness. Am I reacting to the present situation? Am I feeling a *now,* or is the present situation merely an occasion, a cue for a familiar, repetitious, structured pattern of feeling?

Richness of Fresh Detail. Any moment's experience has a host of fresh details that I experience implicitly, some of which I could symbolize and differentiate. In contrast, the structured feeling pattern consists of only a few emotions and meanings. Sometimes, however, I have none of the richness of the present, only the same old, stale feeling pattern. In such instances psychologists are inclined to notice chiefly the content of the stale pattern. We say: "This is a protesting reaction against authority," or "this is a need to dominate," or a "partial" infantile sex drive such as "voyeurism," or "exhibitionism," or a "passive-aggressive need." We tend to neglect the fact that such feeling patterns are also different in *manner* from an immediate, present, and richly detailed experiencing. It is not only that I react poorly to authority. Rather, I react this way to *every* person whom I perceive as an authority. And, more important, I react *only* to his being an authority, not to him as a person, and to the very many present facets of him and our situation which are different from any other situation. The "authority pattern," or any similar pattern, is really only a bare outline. My experiencing is *structure-bound* in manner, when I experience only this bare outline and feel only this bare set of emotions, lacking the myriad of fresh detail of the present. I might resent my boss's behaviors even if my manner of experiencing were optimal. Too much time and attention is wasted in deciding whether my reaction to him is to be blamed on me or on him. It does not matter. What does matter is the *manner* of my experiencing. No matter how obnoxious he may really be, if my experiencing is structure bound, I do not even experience *his* obnoxiousness except as mere cues for the experience of my old bare structure.

Frozen Wholes. We often speak of contents or "experiences" as if they were set, shaped units with their own set structure. But this is the case only to the extent that my experiencing is structure bound in its manner. For example, when I listen as you tell me something of your feelings I may occasionally think of my own experiences. I need the feelings and meanings of my own experiences in order to understand yours. However, if I must keep thinking of my experiences explicitly as such, then I cannot grasp the meanings yours have to you. I will then insist that your experiences are the same as mine (or, if I am wise, I will know that I am not understanding you). Unless *my* experiences *implicitly function* so that I can newly understand *you*, I cannot really understand you at all. Insofar as my experiencing is structure bound, it does not implicitly function. It is not "seamlessly" felt by me with its thousands of implicit aspects functioning so that I arrive at some fresh meaning, something you are trying to convey to me. Rather, in this regard, my experience is a "frozen whole" and will not give up its structure. Whatever requires the implicit function of experiencing in these regards makes me feel my whole frozen structure and nothing new.

Repetitive versus Modifiable. Since within the bare structured *frozen whole* experiencing does not function in interaction with present detail, the structure is not *modified* by the present. Hence, it remains the same, it repeats itself in many situations without ever changing. So long as the manner of experiencing remains structure bound, the structures themselves are not *modifiable* by present occurrences.

Optimal Implicit Functioning. It is clear from the above that, to the extent the manner of experiencing is structure bound, the implicit functioning of experiencing cannot occur. Instead of the many, many implicit meanings of experiencing which must interact with present detail to interpret and react, the individual has a structured feeling pattern.

These terms define *manner of experiencing.*

14. IN PROCESS VERSUS STRUCTURE BOUND. Experiencing is always in process and always functions implicitly. The respects in which it is *structure bound* are not experiencing. The conceptual content *in an abstract way* can *appear* to be the same with different manners of experiencing. However, in the structure-bound manner the experiencing process is, in given respects, missing. By "missing" we mean that from an external viewpoint we may notice that the implicit functioning of experiencing ought to be there, but there is only the process-skipping structure, *and the experiencing surrounding it and leading up to it.* Thus we say that *structure-bound* aspects are not *in process.*

15. RECONSTITUTING. Earlier we said that symbols, or events can *carry forward* the process of experiencing. Experiencing is essentially an *interaction* between feeling and "symbols" (attention, words, events), just as body life is an *interaction* between body and environment. In its basic nature, the physical life process is interaction. It requires not only the body's respiratory machinery but also oxygen. And the body's respiratory machinery itself consists of cells which again are chemical processes involving oxygen and food particles. If we apply this conceptual model of interaction process to experiencing, we can consider it an *interaction* of *feeling* and events ("events" here includes verbal noises, others' behaviors, external occurrences—anything that can interact with feeling).

If we formulate the theory of experiencing in this way, we can formulate why the other person's responses so basically affect the individual's manner of experiencing.[14] For, *if there is a response, there will be an ongoing interaction process.* Certain aspects of the personality will be *in process.* However, without the response, there will not (in these respects) be a process at all.

Subjectively, phenomenologically, people describe this as "coming alive

---

[14] Our formulation here may be seen as an extension of Sullivan's basic concepts referred to earlier at the beginning of our discussion of Sullivan.

inside," or as "feeling many more facets" of oneself. *Responses* can *reconstitute* the experiencing process in respects in which, before the response, there was no process (no interaction between feeling and something else and hence no *ongoing* interaction process).

The peculiar condition of "experience" which is not *in process* has puzzled psychology for many years. It has been called "unconscious," [15] "repressed," "covert," "inhibited," "denied," etc. The fact is that we observe individuals awarely and actively feeling (in ways which were missing before) when they are responded to in certain ways. The individual feels that the feelings "have always been there in some sense, but were not felt." Psychology cannot deny this common observation. One way of formulating it is as the *reconstituting* of the experiencing process.

16. CONTENTS ARE PROCESS ASPECTS. What is a "content" of experience (or *"an* experience," when that is meant to refer to a given content)? We noted (definitions 3 and 5) that the felt implicit meanings of experiencing can be put into interaction with verbal symbols. We then say that the symbols "mean" or "represent" what the experience is "of" or, more simply, that the symbols symbolize the experience. Such a *symbolized unit is a content*.[16]

Thus, in order for there to be a content, some aspect of *implicit function* (see definition 4) must be ongoing in interaction with symbols.

But what if there are not, as yet, any *verbal* symbols? Is there then no ongoing experiencing either? The answer is that verbal symbols are not the only events with which feelings can be in an interaction process. External occurrences, other people's responses, even our own attention, can interact with feeling so as to constitute a process.

Therefore, it is often the case that there is an ongoing experiencing process without verbal symbols. In fact, most situations and behaviors involve feeling in interaction with nonverbal events. Experiencing *functions implicitly* with countless meanings which, as felt (without verbal symbolization), are aspects of the ongoing interaction.

The respects in which experiencing is ongoing are also those in which we *can* verbally symbolize contents. The respects in which it is not ongoing (no matter how it may appear externally) cannot be verbally symbolized. Only pale, useless, general meaning can be given to concepts of the supposed contents which are not at this instant process aspects. Contents are aspects of ongoing felt process. That is to say, contents are *process aspects*.

---

[15] Recall our earlier discussion of the repression paradigm. Also see later discussion of the unconscious, definition 24.

[16] Compare our earlier discussion of the "content paradigm."

17. THE LAW OF RECONSTITUTION OF THE EXPERIENCING PROCESS. An individual can symbolize only those aspects which are *already* implicitly functioning in ongoing experiencing.

In any experiencing (that is to say, in any ongoing interaction of feeling and events) a great many implicit meanings are process aspects (so-called "contents"). Thus, for any moment's ongoing experiencing one can symbolize a great many contents. These are *incomplete* (definition 5) until some symbols (or events) *carry forward* the process in these respects.

Thus there are two different definitions: to *carry forward,* and to *reconstitute.* To "carry forward" means that symbols (or events) occur to interact with *already* implicitly functioning aspects of ongoing experiencing. To "reconstitute" means that the process has become ongoing and implicitly functions in respects in which it previously was not ongoing.

We can now state a *law of the reconstitution of experiencing process:* When certain *implicitly functioning* aspects of experiencing are *carried forward* by symbols or events, the resulting experiencing always involves *other* sometimes newly *reconstituted* aspects which thereby come to be *in process* and *function implicitly* in that experiencing.

18. HIERARCHY OF PROCESS ASPECTS. If contents are viewed as process aspects —that is to say, as implicitly functioning aspects of ongoing experiencing— then *the law of reconstitution* implies that *certain* contents (process aspects) must be symbolized before certain *other contents* (process aspects) can thereby become process aspects that are capable of being symbolized.

This fact gives the individual's self-exploration an ordered or hierarchical character. It is as if he can "get to" certain things only via certain other things. We must let him travel his "own road," not because we believe in democracy, and not because we like self-reliance, but because *only* when the experiencing process has been reconstituted, so that certain aspects become implicit in it, can he symbolize these.

19. SELF-PROCESS. To the extent that experiencing does *implicitly function,* the individual may respond to himself and may *carry forward* his own experiencing. This interaction of the individual's feelings with his own (symbolic or actual) behavior,[17] we term "self." A more exact term: *self-process.*

To the extent that experiencing does not implicitly function, the individual cannot respond to himself and carry forward his experiencing. In what-

---

[17] Compare George Herbert Mead (1938, p. 445): "The self . . . grows out of the more primitive attitude of indicating to others, and later arousing in the organism the response of the other, because this response is native to the organism, so that the stimulation which calls it out in another tends to call it out in the individual himself."

ever respects it does not function (is structure bound), responses are needed first to *reconstitute* the interaction process of experiencing in these respects.

Why is it that the individual himself does not *carry forward* his already *implicitly functioning* experiencing in ways which would newly reconstitute *structure-bound* aspects of it? Of course, he cannot respond to the structure-bound aspects, as such (they are not implicitly functioning), but neither can the psychotherapist. The psychotherapeutic response can be defined as one which responds to aspects of experiencing which *are* implicitly functioning, but to which the individual himself tends not to respond. More precisely, his own response is a whole frozen structure which does not carry forward the felt experiencing process in these respects.

20. THE RECONSTITUTING RESPONSE IS IMPLICITLY INDICATED. The response which will *reconstitute* the experiencing process (in some now *structure-bound* respect) is already implied [18] in the individual's experiencing. One must respond *to the functioning experiencing, not to the structure*. In practice this means that one must take at face value and give a personal response to the *functioning* aspect of the person. No one is greatly changed by responses and analyses of how he does not function (though we are often tempted in this direction). We see that the individual's work behavior actually defeats his desire to work, that his sexual behavior turns away opportunities for genuine sexuality, that his desire to please makes him annoy people, that his way of reaching out to people actually turns people away, that his self-expression is dramatized and hollow. Yet these structures are his responses *to* his *actually functioning* desire to work, his actually functioning sexuality, his actually functioning desire to relate to people and be close to them, and his actual self-expressive urge. Only if we respond to these actually functioning aspects of his experiencing (despite the obviously opposite character of his behavior and symbolic self-responding) can we carry forward what is now actual and reconstitute the process where he himself had (symbolically and actually) responded only with structure.

21. PRIMACY OF PROCESS. We tend to neglect the fact that contents are process aspects. We pay the most attention to contents as symbolized meanings with specific logical implications (which they also are). Hence we often discuss self-exploration as if it were purely a logical inquiry in search of conceptual

---

[18] This point has been made by others. Freud said that the energy of the defense comes from the repressed—i.e., that the *concrete force* which motivates the behavior is the *real* one, despite the opposite and *unreal* nature of the *structure that determines the behavior*. Rogers said that the most therapeutic response is to take the basic, intended felt meaning of the individual's self-expression at face value, no matter how obvious the defensiveness and rationalization. But we may add specificity to these more general statements.

answers. However, in psychotherapy (and in one's private self-exploration as well) the logical contents and insights are secondary. Process has primacy. We must attend and symbolize in order to carry forward the process and thereby reconstitute it in certain new aspects. *Only then,* as new contents come to function implicitly in feeling, can we symbolize them.

In definition 9 we noted that "unfolding" can occur as a felt "now I've got it," quite without symbolization. This is a direct experience of *reconstituting.* The process is felt as ongoing in newly reconstituted respects. Reconstituting occurs when one symbolizes meanings which, in the previous moments, have already been implicit. The carrying forward of these implicit meanings turns out to involve the wider process which reconstitutes the new aspects.

In psychotherapy, therefore, the situation is not that first we figure out what is wrong with an individual and how he must change—and then, somehow, he does it. Rather, his experiencing with us is *already* vitally different with us than it previously could be. From this different experiencing arise the solutions of his problems. The changes are already occurring as he speaks. *Our* responses (as verbal symbols *and as events*) interact and carry forward *his* experiencing. Our gestures and attitude, the very fact that he is talking *to* us, the differences which each moment he makes to us—all of this interacts concretely with what implicitly functions in him, his felt experiencing. Conceptually it may look like a futile statement and restatement of problems. Or, conceptually, we may arrive at *the* most basic causes and factors—the ways in which an individual ought to change, the reasons and lacks which prevent him from so changing—but no genuine *solution* is *conceptually* arrived at. The conceptual search ends by shrugging and attaching some blameful label to the individual who, through bad will or constitution, is said to lack these or those basic essentials. Yet, *given certain interpersonal responses, he is already different.*

By *primacy of process* over conceptual content, we mean this fact: [19] The presently ongoing experiencing process must be *carried forward* concretely. Thereby it is in many respects reconstituted, made more immediate in its manner of experiencing, more full of differentiable detail. Thereby new

[19] I call it a fact, because in psychotherapy we observe it. In the above context it is a matter of theoretical formulation, not of fact.

Some observable research variables have been defined: Assents to one set of descriptions of "immediacy" were found to increase significantly in successful psychotherapy (Gendlin and Shlien, 1961). One group of therapists observed significantly more of the above described new experiencing during the hour in success cases (Gendlin, Jenny, and Shlien, 1960). Successful clients were judged significantly higher on scale-defined variables called immediate manner of experiencing and expression (concerning self, personal meanings, the therapist, problems . . . any content), as compared with failure clients.

process aspects (contents), "solutions," and personality changes arise. Most often these solutions seem terribly simple,[20] conceptually (see definition 9), and cannot possibly be the reason for the change. Rather, they are rough conceptualizations of a few aspects of a broadly different process.

22. PROCESS UNITY. There is a *single* process which involves all of the following: environmental interaction, body life, feeling, cognitive meanings, interpersonal relations, and self. The concretely occurring process is one, although we can isolate and emphasize these various aspects of it. Our "thing language" tends to present whatever we discuss as if it were a separable object in space. In this way we artificially separate environment, body, feeling, meanings, other people, and self.[21] When they are discussed as separable things, their obvious interrelations become puzzling: How can *feelings* be involved in (psychosomatic) body illnesses? How can *cognitive* thought be influenced by *felt* needs? How is it that expressing ourselves *interpersonally* results in changes in the *self?* At every juncture the "separate thing" view of these phenomena builds these puzzles into our discussions. Instead we can employ a frame of reference which considers the *one* process which concretely occurs. I want to give the name *process unity* to the way in which the one concrete process is basic to these various aspects.

We have tried to show that *feeling* is a bodily affair, an aspect of physiological process. We have shown that *cognitive meanings* consist not only of verbal or pictorial symbols, but also of a *felt* sense which is implicitly meaningful and must function in interaction with symbols. *Interpersonal responses* (like other types of events) can interact with *feeling* and carry forward the concrete process. Now we will try to show that the *self* (the individual's own responses to his implicitly functioning experiencing) is also an aspect of the one concretely felt process, continuous with body, feeling, meanings, and interpersonal relations.

23. THE SELF PROCESS AND ITS INTERPERSONAL CONTINUITY. Throughout this discussion we have been dealing with one concretely occurring interaction process between *feeling* and *events.* Interpersonal events occur before there

[20] This is a trouble with most concepts about personality change and psychotherapy, as well as with most concepts of ideals, moral values, and life wisdom: The concepts tell a little something of how it seems when one has arrived at the aim, but they tell nothing of the process of getting there. Such concepts make all sorts of mischief because we tend to try to fit them without allowing ourselves the very different process of getting there. Better concepts about the process of getting there can remedy this age-old problem.

[21] Many contemporary writers point to the essential interpersonal relatedness of the human individual. Daseinsanalyse, Sullivan, Mead, and Buber point out that individual personality is not a self-contained piece of machinery with its own primary characteristics which is *then* placed into interaction. Rather, *personality is an interacting.*

is a self. Others respond to us before we come to respond to ourselves. If these responses were not in interaction with feeling—if there were nothing but other people's responses as such—the self could become nothing but the learned responses of others. But interpersonal responses are not merely external events. They are events *in interaction with the individual's feeling.* The individual then develops a capacity *to respond to* his feeling. The self is not merely a learned repertoire of responses, but a response process *to* feeling.

If feeling did not have implicit meaning, then all meaning would depend totally on the events or responses which occur. Again then, the self could never become anything but the repetition of the responses of others. The individual would always have to interpret himself and shape his personal meanings just as others had interpreted him.

But feeling has implicit meanings. Therefore, to the extent that a feeling process is ongoing, we can *further* respond to it differently than others have. However, to the extent to which we respond to our own feeling so as to skip or stop the process rather than carry it forward, to that extent we need others to help us be ourselves. Not only the genesis, but the adult development of the self also may require interpersonal responses. Such responses are required not because of their appraisal or content, but because we need them concretely to reconstitute the feeling process. If in certain respects the process is not ongoing when we are alone, it does not help to recite to ourselves some content or happy appraisal which we may remember from a person with whom we felt "more ourselves"; that person's effect on us was brought about not by his appraisal or evaluation, which we can recite to ourselves. Rather, the effect occurred through his responses to our concrete feeling process and, in some respects, reconstituted it and carried it forward. If we can do *that* alone, we are independent selves in that respect.

Thus, personality change in us is not a result of our perceiving another's positive appraisals of us or attitudes toward us. It is true that rejecting attitudes toward us are unlikely to carry forward our implicit meanings. However, that is not because of the negative appraisal as such, but because rejection usually ignores the implicit meanings of my feeling. To reject is to turn away or push away. In contrast, someone's "unconditional positive regard" toward us is not only an appraisal or attitude. They respond and carry forward the concretely ongoing process with their responses.

We must, therefore, reformulate Rogers' (1959*b*) view that personality change depends on the client's *perception* of the therapist's attitudes. The present theory implies that the client may perceive the therapist's attitudes correctly, or he may not. He may be convinced that the therapist must dislike him and cannot possibly understand him. Not these *perceptions,* but the *manner of process which is actually occurring,* will determine whether personality change results. In many cases, the client can perceive positive therapist attitudes only after the concrete personality change process has already occurred.

The change-effective factor is not the perception of a content, an appraisal, an evaluation, or an attitude, considered apart from the concrete process.

Personality change is the difference made by *your* responses in *carrying forward my* concrete experiencing. To be myself I need your responses, to the extent to which my own responses fail to *carry* my feelings *forward.* At first, in these respects, I am "really myself" *only when I am with you.*

For a time, the individual can have this fuller *self-process* only in just this *relationship.*[22]   That is not "dependence." It should not lead one to back away, but to fuller and deeper responses carrying forward the experiencing, which, for the time being, the individual says he can feel "only here." The continued *carrying forward* into *ongoing interaction process* is necessary to *reconstitute* the experiencing long enough for the individual himself to obtain the ability to carry it forward as *self-process.*

[22] Only in verbal and conceptual content is "self-exploration" in psychotherapy distinguishable from the personal "relationship." As an ongoing experience process they are the same. The individual may say "only here am I myself" (showing the process to include both self and relationship), or he may speak mostly about the *relationship,* or mostly about *himself.* It is the same process whether the content seems to be mostly about self or mostly about the relationship.

One research finding (Gendlin, Jenny, and Shlien, 1960) employed some operational variables related to this point. Psychotherapists were asked to make ratings of the extent to which "therapy, for this client, focuses chiefly on his problems, or . . . on his relationship with you." These ratings were *not* associated with outcome.

On the other hand, outcome did correlate with the following two scales: "How important to the client is the relationship as a source of new experience? Examples: 'I've never been able to let go and just feel dependent and helpless as I do now'; or, 'This is the first time I've ever really gotten angry at someone.' " Another scale which also correlated with outcome was: "To what extent does the client *express* his feelings, and to what extent does he rather talk *about* them?" These findings indicate that outcome is not affected by whether the *content (topic)* is the self or the relationship. Rather, it matters whether the individual is engaged in a *manner* of ongoing interaction process which involves newly reconstituted aspects of experiencing.

This research illustrates the usefulness of process concepts as compared to content concepts to generate operational research variables. Earlier research (Seeman, 1954) had posed the problem by finding no significant association between success in psychotherapy and discussion of the relationship with the therapist. The finding seemed to contradict the importance of the relationship. New research replicated that finding and added scales concerning the ongoing interaction *process.*

We need theory to create operational definitions. The most effective kind of theory for that purpose is one which employs process concepts in reference to experiencing. We must carefully distinguish from theory the operational terms (to which it leads) that are then defined by procedure and observation, not by theory.

Repression and Content Definitions Reformulated

24. THE UNCONSCIOUS AS INCOMPLETE PROCESS. When "ego" or "self-system" are said to "exclude" some experiences from awareness, usually it is assumed that these experiences nevertheless exist "in the unconscious" or "in the organism." Our discussion, however, leads us to the conclusion that they do not. *Something* exists, to be sure, but it is not the experiences as they would be if they were optimally ongoing. Rather, what exists is a felt and physiological condition which results when, in some regards, the body interaction process is stopped—i.e., is not occurring. What kind of condition is that?

We have shown how the resulting dysfunction will be such that something is "missing," but we should not place what is missing into the unconscious (any more than we should place *eating* into the unconscious when someone is *hungry*). Rather, the unconscious consists of the body's stopped processes, the muscular and visceral blockage—just as a stopped electric current does not consist of a current that is going on under cover, but rather of certain electric potentials which build up in various parts (not only at the interruption) of the circuit. When a conductor re-establishes the electric current, different events occur than were occurring in its interrupted condition—yet, of course, the two are related. We say that this is the electrical energy which existed (in static form) before the current was reconstituted. This is "the unconscious."

When we say that certain experiences, perceptions, motives, feelings, etc. are "missing" from our awareness, it is not that *they* exist "below" awareness (somewhere under there in the body or in an unconscious). Rather there is a narrowed, or in some respects blocked, interaction and experiencing. The manner of experiencing which we have described is one in which, in a good many regards, the experiencing and body life process is *not* "completed" or fully ongoing.

Does this mean that there is no "unconscious"? Only what we are aware of exists? To put the matter in that too simple way ignores important observations. The present theory must be able to account for these observations.[23] Therefore, we are basically reformulating the theory of the uncon-

---

[23] I will choose two observations and show how the reformulation accounts for them:

1. A sequence of words is flashed, each for fractions of a second, on a screen by means of a tachistoscope. When the individual is unable to read the word it is flashed again and again. Now, for example, an individual may be able to read the words "grass," "democracy," "table," "independence," with an average number of repetitions, but for the word "sex" he requires twice as many repetitions. The theories of the unconscious explain this as follows:

The organism can discriminate a stimulus and its meaning for the organism without utilizing the higher nerve centers involved in awareness.

The current theories have this assumption in common: Words such as "unconscious,"

scious rather than in any simple way throwing it out. The unconscious is redefined as *incomplete process*.

Since there is no sharp distinction between *carrying forward* what is implicitly felt, and *reconstituting* experiencing in previously stopped respects

"repression," "covert," "not me," "denial to awareness," "subception," all involve the uncomfortable but seemingly necessary assumption that there is a discrimination before an aware discrimination takes place, and that the experience or *content* which the individual misses in awareness actually exists somewhere in him. How else can one account for the above example and the many other observations just like it?

But we need not assume that something in the individual first reads the word sex, then becomes anxious about it, and then forces it to remain outside of awareness. Rather let us try to interpret this observation as a case where the individual does not ever read it until he does so in awareness. Why then does he take so long to read just that word when he could read the others in half the time? We have tried to show earlier (definitions 4 and 16) that, in order to read a word and to say what it is, the function of *felt* experiencing is necessary. We read without *explicitly* thinking the meanings of what we read. We have the sound images and *we have the felt meaning*. Now if for some reason our felt process cannot interact with the words, our eyes may continue, but we cannot say what we have read.

To explain the matter, process theory must take the place of content theory. The process of interacting with the symbols, of "reading them," requires the function of experiencing (the inwardly felt body process). If this felt process is not functioning in some regards, then the expected discriminating will not occur in these regards. Aspects which ought to be "implicit" will not function and, therefore, cannot interact and interpret the present situation. Hence, in these regards, the individual may misconstrue or simply miss (be unable to complete) the process, without this implying that he first interpreted these fully and then keeps them out of awareness.

The difference can be put simply: content theories assume that one completes the process of knowing, experiencing, interpreting, reacting, but that some of this process does not reach awareness. The present theory holds that the process does not completely occur.

2. A second observation:

An individual leaves a certain situation feeling quite happy. Four days later he becomes aware that really he has been quite angry about what happened. He feels that he "has been" angry all along but "wasn't aware of it."

Now, our theory denies that what he now calls anger was in his body all along, without awareness. Rather, *there was something, but not the process of being angry*. He calls it being angry *now*, because *now* he is engaged in that process, and he clearly feels the releasing (see definition 8) quality which physiologically lets him know that his present anger "satisfies," "discharges," "releases," "symbolizes," "completes"—in short, *has some deeply felt relation to*—the condition he physically felt during the four preceding days. The process *was not* occurring, and that made for a physiological condition which is *only now* altered. When "structure bound" experience "goes to completion," we feel that we *now* know what it was *then*; we did not know it then, because the ongoing process of now is different from the stopped condition of then.

Only by *completing* the process by response to the feeling or felt meaning that is there (and is *not* anger) does the individual then "become aware" of anger. If we view this in terms of content, it is all very puzzling. First the content is not there, and then, later (the former will involve the latter),[24] the felt datum which *is* there, in a sense, contains everything. In what sense does it? In the sense that, *given fully carrying forward responses* to it, everything will be here as aspects of ongoing process.

Therefore, in practice the rule is: "Never mind what is not being felt. Respond to what is being felt."

25. EXTREME STRUCTURE-BOUND MANNER OF EXPERIENCING (PSYCHOSES, DREAMS, HYPNOSIS, CO_2, LSD, STIMULUS DEPRIVATION). Throughout, we have been discussing the *felt, implicit functioning* of the interaction process we term "experiencing." We have been pointing out that all appropriate behavior and interpretations of present situations depend on this *felt* functioning. It constitutes the thousands of meanings and past experiences which determine appropriate present behavior. In addition, it is this felt functioning to which we can respond ourselves, and this is the *self-process*. The functioning I am discussing is *felt,* meaning that we can refer to it ourselves. For example, as we read this page the words are sound images for us. These sound images are all we explicitly have in mind. However, we also have the *meanings* of the sound images. How? We do not *say* to ourselves what it all means. We *feel* the meanings of what we read as we go along. They function implicitly. This feeling process is an interaction between the symbols on the page and our feeling. This felt *interaction* process is now *ongoing* and gives us appropriate feelings and meanings.

When the *interaction process* is greatly curtailed (as in sleep, hypnosis, psychosis, and isolation experiments), the inwardly felt experiencing is thereby curtailed. The individual then lacks the implicit function of felt experiencing and loses both his sense of "self" and his capacity to respond to and interpret present events appropriately. Both require the felt process just illustrated.

The peculiar phenomena which occur under these circumstances are somewhat more understandable when they are considered in terms of curtailment or stoppage of the *interaction* process and *implicit function* of *felt* experiencing.

on, it is said to have been there all along (hidden in there, somewhere). But in terms of process it is precisely this deeply felt relationship of the later anger to the previously felt condition that tells us that a previously stopped process has only now been completed.

We, therefore, need not assume that there are two minds in the individual—one being an unconscious mind that first perceives a content and then permits or prohibits the aware mind to perceive it. Rather, the aware feeling (whatever it is—let us say it is a tension or a dissatisfaction, not at all anger) must be responded to and carried forward. Only thereby does the process go to completion and anger (or whatever supposed content) come to be an aspect of the reconstituted process.

[24] See definition 17, the law of reconstitution.

I would like now to state some of the characteristics of this (hallucinatory or dreamlike) *extreme structure-bound manner of experiencing.*

Structures Are Perceived as Such. Ordinarily, past experiences and learnings function implicitly in felt experiencing, so that we interpret and perceive the present, not the past experiences themselves. Yet under hypnosis, in dreams, and in hallucinations, we may perceive rigid structures and past events as such. Characteristically, we do not then have the relevant aspects of felt process which usually function. Thus hallucinations and dreams are not understandable to the present individual. He is puzzled or aghast at them. They often seem to him "not his." The felt experiencing that would give him a sense of their being "his," and would let him know their meaning, is not ongoing. Dreams and hallucinations are, so to speak, decomposed pieces of what would otherwise be a functioning, felt process. This interaction process with the present is not ongoing, and hence the felt meanings are not functioning.

Let me now trace through these several different kinds of circumstances how in each the interaction process is first curtailed, and how in each the function of felt experiencing is then missing.

Extreme Structure-Bound Manner Occurs Whenever the Interaction Process is Greatly Curtailed. Dreams, hypnosis, psychosis, CO_2 and LSD, and stimulus deprivation share at least one factor, the curtailment of ongoing interaction.

In sleep there is a great reduction of external stimuli. Dreams occur with this curtailment of the usually ongoing interaction process with the environment.

In hypnosis, too, the subject must shut off his interaction with present stimuli, and must cease his own self-responsiveness. He must concentrate on a point.

Psychosis, as has often been remarked (for example, Shlien, 1960), involves both in its genesis and later, an "isolation," a curtailment of interaction between feeling and events. Also, physical isolation from people can, in some individuals, bring on hallucinations.

Certain poisons (CO_2, LSD) are inimical to the physiological interaction process of body life. CO_2 narrows (and eventually stops) the process of respiration.

Experiments in which individuals are placed in soundproof and lightproof suits that also prevent touch stimuli result (after a few hours) in psychotic-like hallucinations.

The peculiarly similar experiences which arise under these widely different conditions hint at something similar. At least one factor they all share is the curtailment of the ongoing interaction process which, as felt, is experiencing.

We would thus expect a lack of the implicit functioning which ongoing experiencing usually provides.

And indeed this is shared by the phenomena which occur in all these circumstances. The peculiar character of these phenomena is understandable as a rigidity or lack of this *felt functioning* which usually interprets every present situation for us, and to which we respond in *self-process*. Thus appropriate interpreting of situations and sense of self are lost.

Lack of Implicit Function. The implicit function (see definition 4) of felt experiencing becomes rigid (not *in process*) or "literal" in all these conditions. In hypnosis, for example, when the individual is told to "raise your hand," he will lift the palm of his hand up by his wrist. He will not, as when awake, interpret the idiomatic phrase appropriately (it means, of course, to raise one's whole arm up into the air). The same "literal" quality occurs in dreams and in psychosis. Much of what has been called "primary process," "schizophrenic thinking," or the schizophrenic's inability to "abstract" his "concrete" thinking, his "taking the part for the whole" (Goldstein, 1954), really consists of this *literal* and rigid manner in which experiencing functions. As in dreams and hypnosis, the *felt* process of experiencing is curtailed and does not provide its implicit functioning.

The many implicit *felt* meanings that are needed for appropriate interpretations and reactions do not function, since the *felt* process (of which they are process aspects) is not ongoing. That is exactly what "literal" means: the lack of functioning of *other* meanings which should inform our interpretation of a given set of words or events.

"Loss of Self." Another characteristic shared by dreams, hypnosis, psychosis, and the phenomena obtained in stimulus-deprivation and LSD, is the loss of a sense of self. In dreams what we perceive is beyond the control, interpretation, ownership, of the self (or ego). In hypnosis the individual specifically accepts another's suggestions for his own and totally permits them to replace his own self-responding. And in psychosis so often the patient complains: "I didn't do that. Something made me do it"; or "I'm not myself"; or "These voices are not mine"; or, "Inside me I'm nothing at all." The hallucinations, voices, and things in his head are not *felt* to be his own. He lacks the sense of self. If he does have a sense of self (an "intact ego"), this felt sense does not inform the hallucinatory phenomena. In regard to these, he has no sense of self that implicitly contains their meaning.

This loss of self is due to the missing felt functioning of experiencing. Just as outward events (to the extent of psychosis) are not interpreted and interacted with on the basis of felt experiencing, so also this felt experiencing is missing for self-responses.

We have defined the self as *self-process*. The self exists to the extent that the individual can carry his felt process forward by means of his own symbols, behaviors, or attention. Experiments with stimulus deprivation have found that individuals who develop psychosis more slowly have a greater capacity to respond to themselves (the most "imagination" and "creativity," it was called). The finding would corroborate our views since, to the extent the individual can carry forward his own experiencing, he will be maintaining (by symbols and attention) his interaction process. When the interaction process is greatly narrowed, not only do psychotic-like experiences occur, but the sense of "self" is lost. The felt process to which there can be self-response becomes static and the individual has *unowned* perceptions.

Static, Repetitious, Unmodifiable Manner. Insofar as the implicit function of felt experiencing is rigid, there is no way for present situations to interact with it, and to modify it so that it becomes an interpretation of the present situation. Instead we perceive a repetitious pattern that is not modified by the present situation. The sequence may "go off" as a result of being "cued" by present events, but it is not an interpretation of, or response to, present events.

The Universality of Psychotic "Contents." Experiences in the extreme structure-bound manner are not *process aspects*. They occur precisely to the extent that the felt process is not ongoing. It is striking how certain themes universally recur—usually the familiar "oral, anal, and genital" themes. It seems that this is the stuff of which we are all composed . . . and into which the usually ongoing process decomposes, insofar as it is not ongoing.

Psychotic Experiences Are Not "the Repressed." It is fallacious to consider these structure-bound manifestations as repressed experiences which have now "emerged" or "erupted." To so consider them raises the puzzling question: On the one hand many theories hold that adjustment requires awareness, and that repression makes maladjustment, but on the other hand they hold that the psychotic is "too aware" and needs to "rerepress" all these experiences.

A better formulation, I think, would be to interpret this observation as follows: Optimally these universal past experiences function implicitly in felt experiencing. When that ongoing process ceases, decomposed static patterns occupy the center of the sensorium.

The implications of this reformulation can be seen, for example, in the following. "The psychosis," in this view, is *not* these supposedly underlying contents (in that sense everyone is "psychotic"). Rather, *"the psychosis" is the curtailment or cessation of the interaction process of feeling and events.* When, therefore, we label an individual "borderline psychotic," this does *not* mean that certain dangerous *contents* lie down there in him. Rather, he is "isolated," "uninvolved," "not quite there," "withdrawn," or "out of touch with himself"; i.e., his *manner* of experiencing is highly structure bound. To prevent "the psychosis" from occurring, one must respond as much as possible to such feelings as do implicitly function, so as to carry forward and reconstitute ongoing interaction and experiencing.

The view of *"latent psychotic contents"* leads to two dangerous errors: either one decides that the individual's feelings of difficulty and trouble had better be ignored (lest they "blossom into" full psychosis), or one "interprets" them and "digs" them "out." Either decision denies and pushes away the personal interaction and the individual's *implicitly functioning* feelings. Either decision will result in psychosis—they involve the same self-verifying misconception that "contents" are psychotic.

There is nothing "psychotic" about any "underlying contents." What is psychotic is the structure-bound manner of experiencing, the absence or literal rigidity of felt experiencing and interaction.

Whether "borderline" or seemingly "gone," the person will "come alive" if interaction and experiencing [25] is reconstituted by personal responses which carry forward what does still function.[26]

[25] In the large research (Rogers, 1960, p. 93) into psychotherapy with schizophrenics in which I am now engaged, we are applying process variables to the behavior changes of psychotics. The findings so far (Rogers et al., 1961) indicate that improvement on diagnostic tests is associated with operational behavior variables of a less rigid, less repetitive, less structure-bound manner of experiencing, and a greater use of felt experiencing as a direct referent and as a basis for behavior, expression, and relating. These tentative findings are defined in terms of rating scale variables and rating procedures.

[26] Therapist's self-expression used to reconstitute process:
When the client's verbalization or behavior gives us a sense of the implicit, felt meanings from which he speaks, then responding to that (even if it is not at all clear) carries the process forward and reconstitutes it as well. However, when the client is silent or speaks only of external matters, then *the therapist's* voicing his own feelings is an important mode of response which can reconstitute *the client's* experiencing process.

There are several other kinds of difficulties. Sometimes the client's talk is bizarre and hard to understand. If there are bits which do make sense, one must repeat these carefully, checking one's understanding. This gives the isolated individual a moment-by-moment sense of contact—something like the pier is for a drowning man. I do not want to be merely poetic in saying that. I want to point up the need for a concretely felt sense of the interacting listener which, where welcome to the client, should be given every few moments during talk that is hard to follow.

Sometimes there is no understandable *logical* content, but the symbolic images do add up to a feeling. (Client: "The Austrian army took all my possessions. They're going to pay me a million dollars." Therapist: "Somebody did you dirt? Took everything away from you? You want to make them pay back?").

Sometimes even less is understandable, but one can be sure the individual is suffering,

26. CONTENT MUTATION. As *implicitly functioning* felt meanings are *carried forward* and the process is *reconstituted* and made more immediate in *manner,* there is a constant change in "content." As *referent movement* occurs, both symbolization and direct referent change. There is a sequence of successive "contents." Sometimes these successive contents are said to "emerge" as if they had always been there, or as if the final basic content is now finally revealed. But I prefer to call this *content mutation.* It is not a change only in how one interprets but, rather a change both in feeling and in symbols. The contents change because the process is being newly completed and reconstituted by responses. What the contents will be depends greatly on the responses.

An example of *content mutation* has already been given (definitions 8–9). Here are more examples of content mutation:

The client is in terror. She says there will be "doom." The world will fly to pieces. Something awful will happen. There is a monster.

Here is "the psychosis" someone might say. At any rate, a common enough psychotic *content.*

lonely, hurt, having a rough time. The therapist can talk about any of these without needing any confirming response from the client.

Sometimes the therapist must simply *imagine* what *might* be going on in the client. If the therapist says he does not know, would like to know but need not be told, and imagines so-and-so, the therapist can speak about what he imagines and thereby an interaction process is restored.

The client may not say a word, but what is occurring is a felt interaction process in which articulation and symbolization is given his feelings. One person's behavior can *reconstitute* the interaction and experiencing process of the other person (see definition 23).

During silent hours the therapist can express what might go on in a troubled person uncomfortably sitting there; or, what goes on in the therapist as he wishes to help, wishes to hear, wishes not to pressure, hates to be useless, would be glad if he knew the silent time was useful, or imagines many feelings and perhaps painful ones going through the client's mind which he is not ready to talk about yet.

These therapist self-expressions require four specifications:

1. They are expressed explicitly *as the therapist's own.* If they imply anything about the client, then the therapist says he is not sure it is so, he imagines it, has this impression, etc. It needs no affirmation or denial from the client. It is the therapist, speaking for himself.

2. The therapist spends a few moments *focusing* on the feeling he might express. He seeks some aspect from all he feels, some bit which he can safely and simply say. No one can say all of the thousand *implicit* meanings he feels at one moment. One or two—especially those which, at the moment, seem too personal or bad or embarrassing—become, after a moment's *focusing,* an intimate and personal expression of present interaction.

Perhaps it is hard for me that we are silent and I am perhaps useless to him. There! That is something I can tell him. Or, I wonder if in this silence he is doing anything at

She is awfully afraid, she says. I respond that she is afraid and that I want to keep company and be with her, since she is afraid. She repeats that she *is* afraid. No matter how much or little meaningful symbology there is to the "doom," she is *afraid now.*

Minutes or months later she can say:

"I'm afraid of being lost. I'm lost. I'm *so* lost!"

"For years I have had to know exactly what to do every moment. I'd plan to know exactly what to do so I'd be distracted. It's like blinders. I'd be afraid to look up, sort of. I need someone or something to hold on to, or I'll disappear."

This is more understandable than world doom. The *content* seems now to be "object-loss" or "passive-dependent needs." Whatever it is, the response needed must provide contact: I grasp her hand; or I talk gently, saying something, pertinent or not—something from me to maintain contact and not to talk away the fear of being lost. In terms of *process unity* such talking and such touching are really the same, in that they both *re-establish interaction.*

all. I find that I am glad to be silent if that gives him time and peace to think and feel. I can express that. Such expressions are a warmly personal interaction. But they require a few moments of self-attention during which I *focus* on and *unfold* my present experiencing in this interaction.

3. The phrasings and meanings which arise in us are very strongly influenced by our overall feeling toward the person to whom we speak. The therapeutic attitude toward the client as a person is an attitude of being totally for him—Rogers' (1957) "unconditional regard." Whitehorn (1959) terms it being like the patient's "lawyer." It is an attitude that whatever we both dislike about this trouble, *the individual as a person is "up against" that in himself.* I can always truly assume that. (This attitude has nothing to do with an overall approval or agreement or liking for this or that behavior, trait, attitude, or peculiarity.) Often I must imagine the person inside, who is "up against" all this. Only months later do I come to love and know that person.

It is amazing what a definable and concrete attitude this is. One can depend on it. There is always a person *"up against"* anything dislikable in him.

4. When the client expresses himself, a response to *that* is needed. At such times therapist self-expression can get in the way.

When one has an opportunity to respond to the client's feeling, to *his* specific felt meaning, and the exact way of perceiving and interpreting something, responding exactly to that is the best and most powerful response. The self-expressive modes of responding fit those clients who give little to which one can respond.

Therapist self-expression as a mode of responding is important with those among the people labeled psychotic, who express little feeling, only externalized situational descriptions, or who sit in pure silence. However, there are many well-functioning persons with whom it is difficult to form a deep interaction because they do not express themselves. Kirtner (1958) found that individuals can be predicted to fail in therapy if their *first* interview shows little inward attention. Recently we are learning that therapist self-expression can help reconstitute the interaction and experiencing process of such individuals.

To do so it must be personal and it must convert the *need* to "hold on" into a successfully *ongoing* contact, real or symbolic.

"I need to hold on, but I'm a monster. No one can love me. You must be sick of me. I need so much, all I do is need. I'm just selfish and evil. I'll suck you dry if I can. I'm just a horrible mouth."

Oral needs, oral incorporation, are now the contents that might be proposed.

But her need *does feel* endless, infinite, hungry. "Sure," I say, "It feels endless, bottomless, and awful to you. It's like you want to be fed and held forever."

Then, or some other time, she may say: "I'm just a baby. I hate that child. An ugly child. I *was* an ugly child. Nobody could like me the way I am."

But we have come a long way when the monster is now a child! A child is quite a nice thing. What became of the monster? A child is quite a human, every day, daylight thing. What became of the terror? *The psychosis?*

Such *content mutation* can occur within a few minutes or over months. It may occur in such words and symbols as above or in purely socially acceptable language, or with bizarre incoherent words, or in silence. The point I am trying to make is that *the content changes as one responds* and thereby carries forward and reconstitutes an interaction process. Such interaction constitutes felt experiencing, and contents are always aspects thereof. As the process changes, the contents change. I term it *content mutation.*

Content mutation occurs strikingly with so-called "psychotic contents." The monsters, weird fears, infinite hungers, and doom-expectant terrors are so often aspects of isolation, loss of self and interaction. They are not psychotic "things" in a person, but a narrowed or stopped interaction process. As the interaction process is restored the contents change and, also, they become more understandable and commonly human.

But *content mutation* occurs not only with quite dramatic expressions, such as in the above example. It occurs equally with the often silent, unexpressive, and "unmotivated" individuals with whom we have so largely been working in the current research on psychotherapy with schizophrenics (Rogers et al., 1961; Gendlin, 1961*b*, 1962*a*, 1962*c*), although these individuals often conceptualize so little of what they are feeling. The following is a further example of *content mutation:*

An individual talks about a chain of circumstances which disturb him. Numerous patterns, characteristics, and personality "contents," seem noticeable in his report of these circumstances.

Perhaps with the aid of responses, he goes on to find that this chain of circumstances really makes him very *angry*. That's it! He is furious. He wishes he could harm and destroy the people involved. He is afraid he will attack them when he next sees them. He hopes he will be able to control this destructive desire. He is amazed at his own *hostility* and his own fear of it. He hardly needs further to report the circumstances, so deeply true is his experience of this anger and destructive need. Again, now, we are tempted to consider personality "contents." Our first deductions now seem too broad. Here, really, we have some contents of this man's personality. We are familiar with this fear of one's own hostility and what some of the bases of the hostility probably are.

But let us say the man continues (and I continue to respond to his *felt meanings*). He imagines himself attempting to vent his anger at these people. He finds now that he is not afraid he will uncontrollably attack and harm them. It is more likely (of all things!) that he will not be able even to yell at them, because perhaps he will cry. His voice would choke up, he is sure. In fact, it is somewhat choked up right now. This thing is not really hostility, it now appears. It is rather that he feels so *hurt!* They should not have done this to him! They hurt him, and . . . what can he do? And now he feels, with some relief, that he finally is in touch with what all this really means to him. (We may now propose a third group of personality contents, again different.)

But, as he continues, it turns out that the circumstances as such do not really matter. No wonder! It seemed all along quite a petty thing to be so upset about. The content is really something else and that is what hurts. And he finds now it is not a hurt after all. Rather, it brought home to him that he feels weak and helpless. "I'm not really hurt" (he now finds), "it's more that it points up to me how I can't make it in the world" (passivity, castration, we may now say).

The term "content mutation" can be applied to this sequential shifting of what seems to be the "content." Contents are process aspects of ongoing feeling process. They can be symbolized because they function implicitly in that feeling process. As it is carried forward, there is referent movement and change in what can be symbolized. It is not merely a shifting of interpretation. There is *referent movement*—that is to say, *that which is being symbolized* is changing.

Content mutation does not imply that all our concepts are simply inapplicable. Often they are correct in terms of predicting the individual's other behaviors, and often they enable us to guess or be sensitively ready for a next content mutation.   However, the concepts of personality contents are static and much too general [27] and empty.   They are never a substitute for *direct reference, referent movement,* and *content mutation.*

[27] A note on the many new terms:
In the realm of personality *change* we largely lack sufficiently specific concepts to discuss and define observations.   The present theory attempts to offer such concepts.   It is hoped that with these concepts (and others) our thinking and discussing will be advanced and our ability to isolate and define observations sharpened.

There may be some difficulty in holding fast to new definitions such as *direct referent, referent movement, carrying forward, reconstituting, manner of experiencing, implicit function.*   It cannot be hoped that all twenty-six definitions will succeed in entering the language.   Nevertheless, we need these (or better) terms to discuss personality change.

chapter five

Some Implications of Modern Behavior Theory for Personality Change and Psychotherapy

Neal E. Miller

In this chapter a variety of topics relevant to personality change and resistance to such change will be covered. Since psychotherapy is an attempt to change personality, it will be shown how the conflict model and the type of analysis put forward in collaboration with John Dollard can be applied to a variety of quite different types of therapy—Freudian and non-Freudian; the use of behavior theory will be urged as a basis for radical innovations which are badly needed in the treatment of mental disease. We will discuss the interactions of organic factors with learning and the importance of changes produced by early experience. We will analyze some of the factors responsible for resistance to change, or, in other words, for the remarkable psychological homeostasis which many individuals show. We will contrast factors producing functional effects analogous to negative feedback, and hence leading to stable equilibrium resisting change, with those producing effects analogous to positive feedback, and hence producing unstable equilibrium susceptible to change. We will try to point out the relevance of some of the more recent results of laboratory studies of learning—especially those on schedules of correlated reinforcement. We will deal with an extension of the type of cybernetic analysis originally evolved to deal with copying behavior, and a few words will be said about the problem of unity or disunity of personality.

Work on this paper and some of the studies in it was supported by Grant MY2949 and Grant M647 from the National Institutes of Health, Department of Health, Education and Welfare, Public Health Service, Bethesda, Maryland.

APPLICATIONS OF BEHAVIOR THEORY TO RADICALLY DIVERGENT TYPES OF PSYCHOTHERAPY

Although certain successful cases can be enormously convincing—especially to the therapist who is exposed at first hand to the detailed observations—the fact remains that some are baffling and tragically unsuccessful. Furthermore, there is distressingly little rigorous proof that the average improvement of treated patients is better than the spontaneous improvement of untreated ones. Although part of this lack of proof may be due to difficulties inherent in the complex social situations involved, techniques that regularly produce better outcomes would surmount such difficulties. Finally, the social needs for psychotherapy far exceed our ability to provide it with the present laborious and costly techniques. For all these reasons there is an urgent need to improve our techniques. We need to try a number of quite different innovations in our methods of helping these people to change for the better. I believe that modern learning theory can be a useful guide to such innovations in remedial personality education, or, in other words, psychotherapy.

A Variety of Implications of the Conflict Model

Conflict seems to play a central role in many forms of mental disturbance. Let us examine some of the implications of a simple theoretical model which is supported by a considerable body of experimental data and which seems to fit many clinical facts.[1] The chief relationships are summarized in the first three figures. These involve the following assumptions which have been studied one at a time in separate simple experiments and verified; a number of the deductions from the joint action of these assumptions in more complex situations have also been verified (Miller, 1944; 1959). The main assumptions are: (a) the tendency to approach a goal is stronger the nearer the subject is to it (gradient of approach); (b) the tendency to avoid a feared stimulus is stronger the nearer the subject is to it (gradient of avoidance); (c) the strength of avoidance increases more rapidly with nearness than that of approach (greater steepness of avoidance gradient); (d) the strength of the tendencies to approach or avoid varies directly as the strength of drive upon which they are based (increased drive raises height of entire gradient).

[1] For more details see Miller (1944; 1951; 1961), and Dollard and Miller (1950). The reader who is already familiar with these materials can skip directly to *New Implications for Various Tactics* on page 154 of this chapter.

Let us look first at the weak approach and avoidance in Figure 1. When the subject is to the left of the point at which the gradients intersect, approach will be stronger, so that he will move nearer. But if he moves beyond the point of intersection, avoidance will be stronger so that he will retreat. Therefore, the free-moving subject will tend to remain in the region of the point of intersection. You can see that, when the avoidance is relatively weak, the subject will approach near to the goal even under weak motivation to approach. Then a slight increase of the strength of approach (from weak to moderate) will cause the subject to reach the goal.

The amount of avoidance, and presumably also of fear, actually elicited will depend upon where the subject is, which will be the point at which the two gradients intersect. The fear elicited is represented by the vertical, double-headed arrows. It can be seen that the increase from weak to moderate approach that causes the subject to go the short additional distance for-

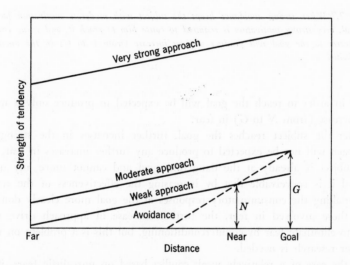

Figure 1. When the subject is farther from the goal than the point at which the gradients intersect, approach is stronger than avoidance so that he should continue to approach until he passes the intersection, at which point the greater strength of avoidance should stop him.

When the avoidance is weak, so that the subject is able to approach near to the goal, a small increase in the strength of approach (from weak to moderate) causes him to reach the goal and produces only a small increase (from N to G) in the amount of fear elicited.

Throughout, linear gradients are used for clarity, but similar deductions could be made for any curves with a continuous slope steeper for avoidance than approach at each point above the abscissa.

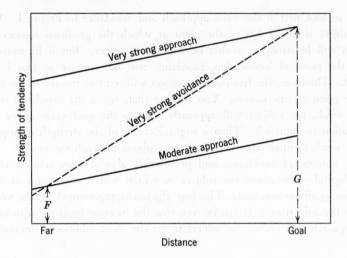

Figure 2. When strong avoidance keeps the subject with moderate motivation far from the goal, very strong motivation is required to cause him to reach it, and going considerably nearer to the goal will produce a great increase (from F to G) in the amount of fear elicited.

ward in order to reach the goal will be expected to produce only a moderate increase (from N to G) in fear.

After the subject reaches the goal, further increases in the strength of approach will not be expected to produce any further increases in fear, since the subject is already at the dangerous goal and cannot move any nearer. Indeed it is conceivable that by increasing the effectiveness of the reward, and making the consummatory responses at the goal more clearly dominant over those involved in fear, the further increase in approach drive might help to eliminate fear by counterconditioning, but this is a problem on which further research is needed.

In the case of a relatively weak conflict based on unrealistic fears, it presumably is relatively easy to produce therapeutic changes by moderate increases in the strength of the drive to approach, so that the subject reaches the goal, extinguishing and counterconditioning his fears. Even in the case of realistic fears based on mild punishment, the subject may tolerate the punishment in order to achieve the goal. Such therapy can come about readily by natural increases in the drive to approach, or be facilitated by associates who use various means to enhance the attractiveness of the goal, encourage the subject, or even add motivation to escape mild ridicule to the other factors motivating approach. Presumably most subjects whose avoidance is weak enough so that they can be induced to change in this way do not reach a psychotherapist.

The situation that we have been describing may be contrasted with the one represented in Figure 2 in which strong avoidance is motivated by strong fear, so that the subject with moderate motivation to approach remains far from the goal. In this case it can be seen that it will take very strong approach motivation to bring him to the goal and that inducing such motivation will prduce a great increase (from *F* to *G*) in fear. If strong enough motivation to approach is not available, the subject may never reach the goal where he would have the most effective opportunity for extinguishing fear, but may be near enough to it so that he suffers intolerable fear and conflict. Thus, psychotherapists have found that trying to force severe neurotics nearer to the goal that is the source of their fear is not an effective way of producing a favorable change. But as we have just seen, this finding should not be generalized to subjects who are in a weaker conflict so that they are nearer to achieving the goal.

In the same case of a strong conflict, Figure 3 shows what happens when the same amount of advance to the goal is produced by lowering the gradient of avoidance. One can see that, as the subject considers the goal to be

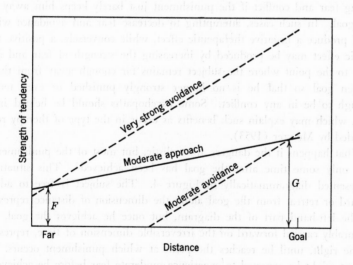

Figure 3. While very strong avoidance keeps the subject far from the goal, decreasing the strength of avoidance so that he comes very near to the dangerous goal will increase the strength of fear. The increase produced in this way, however, is not as great as that produced when, as in Figure 2, the same distance of approach is elicited by increasing the strength of motivation to approach.

less dangerous and moves nearer to it, we would expect a paradoxical increase (from F to G) in the strength of fear actually elicited. Such increases have been observed by clinicians and are called a negative therapeutic effect. You can also see, however, that the increase produced in this way is much less than the one to be expected when exactly the same advance toward the goal is produced by increasing the strength of motivation to approach. This difference apparently supplies the rationale for concentrating therapeutic efforts on lowering unrealistic fears, or in other words, analyzing the resistance first. After such fears have been reduced enough so that the subject is quite near to achieving the goal, he is in a situation represented by Figure 1 so that it may be all right to move him the additional distance by trying to increase the strength of approach.

New Implications for Various Tactics

This much of the analysis has been presented in detail before. Now let me draw some further implications which are readily apparent, but apparently have been relatively overlooked. Suppose the fears are realistic, so that the subjects will get severely punished for achieving the goal. In that case the subject will either suffer punishment if he achieves the goal, or strong fear and conflict if the punishment just barely keeps him away from the goal. In such cases, attempting to decrease fear and avoidance will indeed produce a negative therapeutic effect, while conversely, a positive therapeutic effect may be produced by increasing the strength of fear and avoidance to the point where the subject remains far enough away from the forbidden goal so that he is no longer strongly punished or even tempted enough to be in any conflict. Some psychopaths should be helped in this way, which may explain such benefits as occur in the type of therapy recommended by Mowrer (1953).

What happens if the dangers are realistic, but most of the punishment occurs only some time after the goal has been achieved? This situation is represented diagrammatically in Figure 4. The subject is free to advance toward or retreat from the goal along the dimension of distance represented by the left-hand part of the diagram, but once he achieves the goal, he is inexorably carried forward on the irreversible dimension of time, represented to the right, until he reaches the point at which punishment occurs. The subject might be expected to experience moderate fear before he achieves the goal, but strong fear (commonly called guilt) afterwards. In such a case it can be seen that increasing the height of avoidance might produce great therapeutic changes.

In order to bring out most clearly the essential dynamics, we have greatly

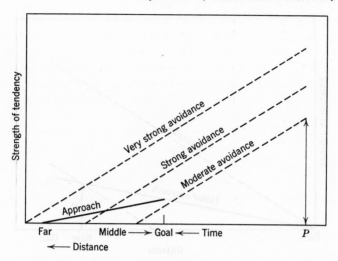

Figure 4. When delayed punishment is given (at time P) after achieving the goal, fear should mount rapidly during this delay. The strongest fear actually encountered should be greatly reduced (from P to Far, respectively) when the strength of avoidance is increased, so that the subject is prevented from reaching the goal or kept far from it.

oversimplified the foregoing examples. The experienced clinician or student of personality can readily supply his own details and can work out further extensions. We have time here to mention only a few such adaptations.

For example, the intense fear (guilt) elicited after achieving the forbidden goal may motivate various symptoms. In some cases one of the symptoms may be an approach to the same forbidden goal which will initiate a vicious spiral, as in the case of the alcoholic who drinks to relieve his fears and thereby produces a realistic basis for additional fears and guilt.

To take another approach, one may assume that the gradient of approach can vary in steepness, being steeper the more the drive motivating the approach is subject to arousal by external cues, as for example, seems to occur with sex (Miller, 1959). From Figure 5 it can be seen that the paradoxical decrease in fear with increase in height of the gradient of avoidance is greater when the gradient of approach is steeper. This leads to a prediction concerning the circumstances under which a greater negative therapeutic effect should occur from attempting to reduce unrealistic dangers, or similarly a greater paradoxical positive therapeutic effect from increasing the fear of real dangers.

To follow yet other implications, it is apparent that therapeutic changes from increasing the height of avoidance are more feasible in situations in

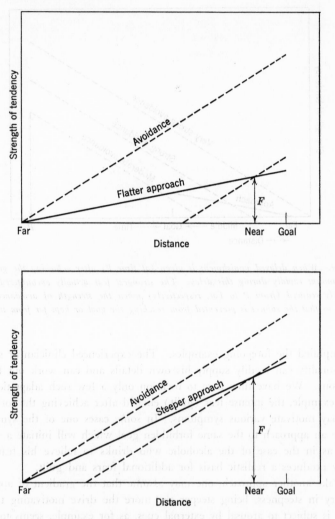

Figure 5. If the gradient of approach is steeper, the positive and negative therapeutic effects become greater; there is more difference in the amount of fear (F) elicited at the near and far points, and less of a change in the strength of avoidance is required to cause the subject to move from one of these points to the other.

which either the drive responsible for approach does not continue to mount to great heights in the absence of the goal response, or alternative means of satiating the drive are available. Often alternative means are available. In some cases these are blocked by neurotic or unrealistic fears so that the subjects are motivated to approach realistically dangerous, tabooed goals. For example, certain individuals are driven by fears of sexual enjoyment with the spouse to seek extramarital affairs. In such cases the theory suggests increasing the avoidance of the realistically dangerous goal while at the same time decreasing that of the unrealistically feared one. But one might have to work also on the generalization of fear from one situation to the other by using labeling and other techniques to increase the ability to discriminate between the two types of goals.

Discrimination versus Counterconditioning of Fear

In *Personality and Psychotherapy* (Dollard and Miller, 1950) we worked out the details of a learning-theory analysis of repression. We showed how the inhibition of cue-producing responses, or what Pavlov (1957) called "the second signal system," would be expected to interfere with social control and the individual's ability to use the higher forms of problem solving to adapt to changes in his environmental conditions. On the one hand, restoring the cue-producing response, largely verbal, indicates that a certain amount of extinction of fear already has occurred; on the other hand, it provides a basis for better discrimination between realistic and unrealistic fears. Thus restoring the ability to think is an important part of therapy.[2]

Conversely, if the neurotic subject is responding to safe situations with sentences or images which elicit strong fear, teaching the subject not to respond with these inappropriate mediating responses should eliminate the unrealistic fears. This latter process appears to be the goal of the therapy described by Ellis (1962).

Another part of the process, which we certainly included, but perhaps did not emphasize enough, is the experimental extinction and counterconditioning of unrealistic fears. As we pointed out, the extinction of fear can be helped by drugs, provided the extinction of fear will transfer from the drugged to the normal state. Considerable work is now being done along this line; a great deal more is needed. We need laboratory work to develop and screen more effective fear-reducing drugs and determine the principles involved in the best ways of using them (Miller and Barry, 1960; Miller, 1961). We also need clinical work to translate these principles into the most effective techniques of using drugs in both traditional and radically new types of psychotherapy.

[2] But the removal of repression should not be confused with license to be immoral. We cannot be well adjusted if our behavior deviates too widely from the standards of our society. Thus in describing psychotherapy, Dollard and Miller (1950, p. 221) say: "The result is not an escape from the mores of his group. To attempt this escape would almost certainly be maladaptive. In fact the foresight that comes with the removal of repression may help the patient to be on his guard and to exercise socially useful restraint."

Similarly, we need additional research on the principles involved in the extinction and counterconditioning of fear. We need to try radically new means of applying these principles to the therapeutic situation. Wolpe (1958) seems to have made an interesting beginning, but a great deal remains to be done, especially in using the behavior of a social group, instead of that of only a single therapist, in extinguishing and counterconditioning fear. Finally we need more work on the problem of learning to resist pain and fear (Miller, 1960). We also need more ingenious attempts to reward positive tendencies and to train subjects in missing social skills—a task for which the resources of a therapeutic group or community should be more adequate than those of a single therapist working alone.

We also need additional research on the basic mechanism of reinforcement and on whether or not glandular and visceral responses and general levels of activation or depression can be modified, like instrumental somatic responses can, by rewards as well as by classical conditioning. Such problems, and a new hypothesis concerning reinforcement, are discussed elsewhere (Miller, 1963).

Freedom to Innovate

In order to free clinical workers to try the radical innovations that may lead to the improvements that are needed, we first must get rid of some of the unrealistic fears that are inhibiting innovations in psychotherapy. Psychotherapy, as it presently is conducted, often is an extremely difficult and delicate process. Thus one can understand the therapist's unwillingness to deviate from any procedures that he has found to be successful. But the very conditions of current psychotherapy, namely, a rather high incidence of unpredictable successes and failures, with strong rewards for success and strong punishments for failure, are those which are most likely to produce stereotyped superstitious behavior that is strongly resistant to extinction.

One of the superstitions of the past has been that the recording of therapeutic interviews, which is essential for superior research and training, would be extremely difficult and dangerous to the therapeutic relationship, and perhaps even highly unethical. When the therapist overcomes his own fears and merely says something like, "Instead of taking notes I use the modern method of tape recording," many of the anticipated difficulties fail to appear.

Another of the superstitions is that the therapist must learn about the social conditions of the patient's life and his social behavior only through what he can decode from the patient's behavior toward the therapist and his free associations during the therapeutic hours. This rule of the game sometimes can lead to absurd situations in which a patient gives even an experienced therapist an entirely misleading impression of his social behavior and real problems. I believe we need to experiment more extensively with other ways of learning about the patient's social conditions, his behavior, and the actual changes that are, or are not, occurring.

If the therapist is in better touch with the conditions of the patient's life and his actual social behavior in these conditions, he may be in a better position to guide him in securing the rewards which will hasten and consolidate the process of change. But from the point of view of learning theory, one of the things that often makes therapy so difficult is the fact that the therapist does not have direct control over the important rewards and punishments in the patient's environment. Ingenious and courageous attempts to deal with this problem should be fruitful. Perhaps responsibility for a therapeutic regime could be divided between two people: one who is responsible for manipulating the reality conditions of the patient's life, and another who is in the more conventional therapeutic role of trying to help the patient to adjust to these conditions. We have not yet explored all of the possible combinations of individual and group therapy, therapeutic communities and clubs or associations, drug therapy, and re-education that can be suggested by a thorough analysis in terms of the principles and the conditions of social learning. Research along such lines will be expensive but much less so than manned exploration of the moon or than the enormous personal and social burdens of mental disease.

INTERACTION OF ORGANIC FACTORS WITH LEARNING

The capacity to learn, which plays such an important role in personality change, is of course itself an innate capacity dependent upon the organic nature of the human species. Thus the principles of learning must have an organic basis which in most cases is not yet understood. Organic factors also influence the course of learning. To take a very simple example, physiological experiments show that the suitable stimulation of the isolated spinal cord of the cat can elicit well-coordinated locomotor reflexes of different types—stepping, hopping, trotting. Such reflexes in the spinal cord presumably are a part of the innate wiring diagram and enormously facilitate the learning of various forms of locomotor behavior by making adaptive responses infinitely more likely to occur than they would be if the cat had to learn by sheer trial and error to time correctly the proper combinations of muscular contraction. By facilitating the learning of certain characteristic types of locomotor behavior, such innate patterns also shape the course of learning so that certain gaits are characteristic of certain species. But the learning that occurs in acquiring habits of approaching or avoiding specific objects and learning how to cope with unusual obstacles or terrains tends to disguise the original innate patterns which have so greatly facilitated and shaped that learning.

Similarly, electrical stimulation by a chronically implanted electrode of specific points in the unanesthetized cat's lower brain centers can elicit complex patterns. Stimulation in one location regularly elicits coordinated rage responses including dilation of the pupils, hissing, flattening back of the ears, and striking viciously with the unsheathed claws. Such attack is flexibly directed at specific objects such as a stick or a gloved hand inserted into the cage. Stimulation at another point regularly elicits a quite different pattern of cowering and slinking. The uniform localization and patterns of these complex reactions must be innately organized. The normal rage or fear behavior of the cat shows many of the same components, but under specific circumstances, the pattern is considerably modified, and hence disguised, by learning.[3]

These are but a few of the examples that emerge from a careful study of mammalian behavior. It seems highly probable that far more complicated innate patterns exist, that they play an important role in the development of human social behavior, and that these instinctual patterns are modifiable enough so that they tend to be disguised by learning although they may play crucial roles in motivating, facilitating, and shaping socially learned behavior.

Specifically, it is possible that some of the social learnable drives, which I used to think were based on more primary drives, actually have an organic basis of their own, but are subject to channeling, and possibly also to potentiation, by learning which tends to disguise this innate basis. But I have discussed elsewhere (Miller, 1959, pp. 262–272) this possibility and other new trails for research on motivation.

For producing change, the practical importance of a particular class of factors is determined by the range through which it is varied. This range may change with various circumstances, such as the development of new techniques. For example, the organic defect of congenital deafness used to be a catastrophic handicap because it removed the victim from social communication. It was widely thought to include a general deficit in both intellect and personality. With the development of psychological and educational techniques for teaching deaf people sign language, lip reading, and speech, deafness became much less important. The invention of these new

---

[3] A somewhat similar role is played on the sensory side by innate mechanisms at various levels in the nervous system that process sensory information in ways which help to provide various stable cues related to selected attributes of stimulus objects (Miller, 1959, p. 251; Ratliff, 1961; Hubel and Wiesel, 1962).

psychological techniques dramatically altered the prognosis for this organic defect. Conversely, new operations on the ear can cure certain types of deafness. The importance of manipulating the organic factor in these cases is increased by these operative techniques.

Critical Sensitive Periods

A dramatic example of the care that must be used in unraveling the roles of organic and experiential factors is presented by some of the recent work of Fuller (1962) and his associates in the Jackson Memorial Laboratory at Bar Harbor. Rearing puppies in isolation from the ages of three to twelve weeks is known to produce relatively long-lasting deficits in their social and manipulative responses. Using a series of carefully standardized tests, Fuller and his colleagues studied these effects. A natural conclusion from these results would be that there is a sensitive period for the learning of the types of behavior in which the deprived dogs were deficient, and that the dog loses his capacity for the type of learning required after the sensitive period is over. However, Fuller found that, if puppies reared in isolation were given a tranquilizer, chlorpromazine, during their first test session, their behavior was much more normal. After three days the drug was withdrawn with no regression of behavior.

These observations indicate that the rich normal environment was not necessary for the gradual learning of the items of behavior in question, which probably were developing primarily by maturation, and/or were learned very quickly during the test sessions under drug. Thus, it was not the deprivation per se which did the lasting damage, but the sudden emergence from the deprived to the complex "normal environment." Apparently this sudden emergence elicited traumatic fears which were learned and which interfered with the performance (and/or very rapid learning) of behavior of which the animal was perfectly capable. The trauma was avoided by the temporary use of the tranquilizer at this crucial juncture.

The factors supposedly involved are summarized in Figure 6. In this case, the capacity for the desired behavior develops in spite of isolation, but as the animal matures his capacity to perceive the complexity and strangeness of the normal situation, so that traumatic fear is elicited by a sudden introduction to it, also begins to develop. These interfering tendencies develop at an increasing rate so that, after the critical period, they are dominant and prevent the normal behavior. When animals are reared in the normal situation, the gradual development of their ability to perceive its complexities prevents them from being overwhelmed by any sudden change.

Hinde (1955) and Moltz (1960) already have applied a similar type of

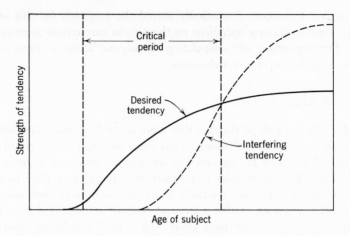

Figure 6. During the critical period the desired tendency is stronger than the interfering one, so that desired responses can be elicited and reinforced. Before the critical period, the desired tendencies have not matured; afterwards, they are inhibited by the interfering ones.

analysis to another example of a "critical period," that for imprinting with certain birds. Hess (1957) found that chlorpromazine would prolong the critical period during which Mallard ducklings could be imprinted to follow a moving object. In this case the interfering tendency might be thought of as something like "fear of strangers" which becomes strong enough after a certain age to prevent the occurrence of following. It can be seen that a critical period may be explained by the acquisition of a habit, or maturation of an instinctual tendency, interfering with the learning or performance of the desired behavior, rather than by a loss of the capacity to learn or perform it, although the latter cannot be ruled out in all cases.

What I have just said should not be taken as a definitive answer to the problem of critical periods, but rather as an example of the type of experimental and theoretical analysis that is needed before we can understand the roles which such periods seem to play in certain types of personality change.

Various Other Bases for Importance of Early Experience

We have been discussing how maturational processes might contribute to critical periods, but there are other factors which also may contribute to the importance of early experience. As Dollard and I (1950) have emphasized, the human infant is unusually dependent and hence highly motivated for certain types of learning, and susceptible to severe traumas that are less likely to occur in later life. Thus it seems easier to acquire neuroses during certain periods of childhood, but when soldiers are subjected to similar extreme situations during combat, they acquire neuroses even though they are adult. Similarly, those trying to produce the drastic changes described as "brainwashing" take care to subject the victims to extreme conditions of dependency, helplessness, isolation, and other conditions that create strong motivations in many respects paralleling those occurring in infancy.

The same conditions that determine the earliest learning are likely to persist into later life. The kind of parents who allow an unusually traumatic experience to occur in early childhood may continue, for a considerable span of years, to reinforce maladaptive learning or to fail to reward certain adaptive habits. Thus the importance of the single dramatic incident may be overestimated. Indeed, in some cases the importance of earlier experiences may be overestimated because the infant does not yet possess the capacity to learn from them, and hence is not affected as much as an older child would be.

Society sets up an age-graded program for shaping many important kinds of social behavior. Once an individual gets far enough out of step, he may not be likely to encounter the types of shaping situations that will elicit and reward the missing habits. There is a need for special therapeutic training sequences to restore such individuals to their appropriate level.

Another quite different reason for the importance of early experience is that responses being learned then do not have to compete with habits already established by previous experience. This aspect of early experience leads us on to the discussion of conditions of unstable equilibrium.

PSYCHOLOGICAL HOMEOSTASIS—
STABLE VERSUS UNSTABLE EQUILIBRIUM

Let us now consider some additional factors determining susceptibility to, or resistance to, change. One of the most striking features of the human personality is its ability to maintain what might be described as psychological homeostasis in the face of many vicissitudes. This capacity is especially impressive when one tries to perform experiments on fatigue, stress, or distraction. The experimental subjects often show great ability to compensate for rather extreme conditions, so that their performance is affected relatively little. And such effects as do occur are often in the form of sudden rather major breaks, which, however may be only momentary. Similar abilities to compensate, sometimes followed by sudden breaks, are observed in the natural social environment. On the other hand, people sometimes change gradually, or even fairly rapidly.

What are the factors responsible for either psychological homeostasis or progressive change? I believe it is useful to rephrase the problem in terms of the conditions producing stable versus unstable equilibrium.

Figure 7 represents graphically several different dynamic possibilities. Let us first examine these simple physical analogies, and then turn to the psychological principles and environmental conditions that would be expected to produce similar effects.

Figure 7(*a*) is a weight on a horizontal surface with friction. A change in position is produced when a force acts; there are no marked discontinuities.

Figure 7(*b*) represents a ball on top of a dome in a situation of unstable equilibrium. A relatively small force in either direction will produce a relatively big effect which is difficult to reverse. The dynamics are analogous to those of positive feedback. We have this situation when two or more quite different weak responses are initially of approximately equal strength and each likely to be rewarded. Whichever one occurs will be strengthened, thus be more likely to occur again and be still further strengthened, so that a progressive change toward that response pattern continues to gain momentum and becomes increasingly difficult to reverse. In such cases, the conditions determining which response occurs first may be crucial. This may be the

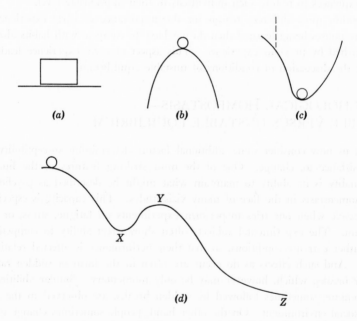

Figure 7. Graphic illustrations of different types of equilibrium discussed in the text.

basis for the old adage, "as the twig is bent, so the tree will grow." It is one of the reasons for the importance of early experience.

Figure 7(c) is representative of the situation of stable equilibrium—the further the ball is moved off center, the stronger the forces to return it toward center. We shall examine situations of this kind which tend to produce psychological homeostasis, or the equivalent of negative feedback. To the right we have illustrated the situation in which, once a certain amount of change is produced (i.e., getting the ball over the top), there is a sudden break. On the left side we have represented a situation with the dotted line in which there is a limit on lateral movement; the solid line illustrates a situation that has a point beyond which resistance decreases but does not stop.

In 7(d) we have represented the interesting situation in which a change started in a given direction is likely to be maintained for a distance, but then encounters a region of stable equilibrium—the valley at X—where the ball is likely to remain trapped. As we shall see, there are a number of conditions of this kind which tend to limit personality and social development.

Effects of Correlated Reinforcement

In the past, most experiments on learning have studied extremely simple relationships between response and reward. For example, a correct response is rewarded 100 per cent of the time with a fixed amount of reward and an incorrect response is never rewarded. Skinner (1938; Skinner and Ferster, 1957) and his students have made the valuable innovation of studying more complicated schedules of reinforcement and the effects of rewarding specific rates of response. Logan (1960) has extended this work with his program of investigating correlated reinforcement, a topic which is particularly relevant to problems of human personality development.

Under conditions of correlated reinforcement the amount, or the promptness, of reward depends on the speed, amplitude, or some other dimension of performance. It can readily be seen that the situation in which a particular type of behavior is maximally rewarded, and deviations from this optimum receive progressively less reward, will produce effects like those diagrammed in 7(c), if one thinks of the maximum rewards occurring at the lowest point in the U-shaped valley. The sharper the correlation (producing a V instead of a U), the more the variability should be reduced after thorough learning. This greatly reduced variability should also produce resistance to change, because different responses are unlikely to occur and thus cannot be learned, even when conditions have changed so that they might now be more strongly rewarded.

Logan's (1960) experimental results confirm the predictions of greatly reduced variability and also show that correlations of this kind can produce extreme resistance to extinction. The response is likely to remain almost exactly the same for many non-rewarded trials; when change does finally occur, it comes as a sudden rather complete breakdown of performance. In short, we have seen how appropriate conditions of correlated reinforcement can produce the characteristics of stable equilibrium, or, in other words, psychological homeostasis.

To date only some of the simplest conditions of correlated reinforcement have been studied experimentally, but it is a relatively short step to deduce the effect of certain other patterns of reinforcement, and to test these deductions by experiment. I believe that the effects of certain discontinuities in correlated reinforcement have especially interesting implications for problems of personality change.

Let us consider a situation analogous to that represented in Figure 7(d). The greater amounts of reward should be thought of as occurring at lower levels on the ordinate of the diagram, so that the valley in which a ball would tend to be trapped represents a region of greater reward. It can be seen that, although the subject would receive greater rewards for changing his behavior further towards Z, he is likely to remain "trapped" at X because he has to pass through the zone of diminishing reward at Y in order to get to Z.

To take a simple example, a tennis player who has learned to hit the ball only with a good chop may have to go through a period of losing more points if he wants to practice and develop a good drive. Or a child, who has learned to get his way by highly developed skills of aggression on the playground, may be less rewarded if he changes and tries to be pleasant, because half-way aggression may not work, and he may not be very skillful at getting his way by being pleasant even though this might be more rewarding in the long run.

Often a worker promoted to foreman may lose the reward of equal association with his old friends before gaining the potentially greater rewards from his new position and thus have to go through a difficult period of readjustment analogous to the region Y in Figure 7(d). Some workers recently promoted to foremen actually ask to be demoted and others do not work for, or even turn down, the opportunity to be promoted. During a transition period of social mobility a person's old friends may punish him for deserting them, while his new associates may resent his intrusion.

In dealing with the general problem of social mobility, yet other factors may contribute to the type of equilibrium we have been discussing. The parents who realize the American dream of giving their children better opportunities than they had, who send their children to a better school for more education and expect them to do better than they did, may suddenly discover that, as their children are moving up and ahead, they are also moving farther away. They want their children to change for the better, but are unhappy when they find them becoming different. Personality changes may frustrate others, conflict with their habits, including perceptual expectancies, and force them to learn new habits. Therefore one's associates may punish change and reward constancy. Even in psychotherapy, the spouse or family may not like the neurotic person's progress toward becoming more self-assertive, and may try to force him back into his former role. Similar factors opposing change sometimes appear when a talent-mobile man is married to a very young, pretty, but intellectually and socially limited, girl. As the man moves into new and more stimulating environments, his personality changes while the girl does not change, so that a formerly happy marriage becomes unhappy.

This brief discussion has been able to illustrate only a few of the factors which can oppose changes in the habits that constitute personality. A far more detailed theoretical and empirical analysis of the conditions producing stable equilibrium, and hence resistance to change, is needed and should be highly profitable.

Factors Favoring Unstable Equilibrium, and Hence Change

We have just been discussing factors favoring stable equilibrium, or resistance to change. But there are other factors which tend to produce positive feedback, unstable equilibrium and hence to facilitate change. For example, there is what might be called "the lucky spiral up." In the academic field which I know best, there is the bright, energetic student who has the good fortune to hit on a topic for a Ph.D. dissertation which comes out strikingly well and is timely. He is likely to get a position at a leading university which gives him a reasonable teaching load and good research space. It is easy for him to get a sizeable research grant which gives him the chance to do enough additional studies so that, with reasonable luck, he is on his way to becoming a productive well-known scholar, moving in a stimulating and supportive environment which will favor continued success. As the saying goes: "Nothing succeeds like success."

The foregoing case may be contrasted with the student who has the bad luck to run into a string of unexpected difficulties on his dissertation. He may get a position at a poorer university with a heavier teaching load, fewer research opportunities, less chance to get a good research grant, and less stimulation to continue with research. Especially if his next problem should happen to turn out badly, it will be extremely difficult for him to get established. Now, I realize that a talented man is more likely to select a good problem, or to drop a bad one soon, but I also am impressed with the fact that the process of groping forward into the unknown inevitably involves a considerable element of chance.

I would theoretically expect the chance success or failure that has been described to have a general effect on the personality—with success generating optimism, confidence, pride, ambition, and other favorable social traits which will help to contribute to further success. Similarly, failure can lead to frustration, bitterness, insecurity, resignation, or a shift toward different goals in life. While other factors than professional success or failure certainly can play important roles in personality development, I believe that the role of success deserves considerable study and will be found to be a significant factor in cases in which the direction of causality can be determined clearly—for example, brothers settling on arid farms, but with one happening to contain oil.

EFFECTS OF CHANGING SOCIAL GROUPS

As the source of a great many of the rewards and punishments in life, the social group has a great effect on shaping personality. One could devote an entire lecture to the effects of culture, nationality, region, social class, and occupation. Thus, when an individual makes a radical change in his membership in any of these social groups, it is likely to produce eventually a considerable change in his personality. Considerable research has been done on the roles of such social factors, but much much more remains to be done. For example, there is considerable evidence that psychiatric disturbances are related to group factors, and that they are especially likely to occur in disorganized communities.[4] But the factors of cause and effect are difficult to disentangle in such cases; we need studies that are much more extensive, penetrating and analytical.

A HUMAN RESEARCH DECADE

Since it is impossible deliberately to set up conditions that will produce severe mental disorder in human subjects, and difficult to set up those that will produce other forms of drastic personality change, much of the research has to take advantage of natural experiments. The differences among the various cultures of the world are, therefore, an invaluable source of information about the effects of social conditions on human development. The

[4] Some of the studies on this topic are: Hollingshead and Redlich (1958); Leighton (1959); Myers and Roberts (1959); Sarason and Gladwin (1959); Srole et al. (1962).

study of the effects of large differences in the social conditions of these cultures affords a unique opportunity, not only to learn more about the basic principles involved in personality development and in mental disease but also to study medical and biological problems, such as the effects of diet on the cardiovascular system and of various environmental conditions on cancer.

Furthermore, the rapid changes that are occurring in such cultures with the explosive spread of western technology afford unusual opportunities to study the effects of changes in social conditions on personality. However, these opportunities are fleeting. The introduction of technology is homogenizing old cultures at an ever-increasing rate, and enormously reducing the range of differences in relevant variables. If the effects of these cultural differences, and the rapid changes in them, are not studied soon, it will be too late. A human research decade should be organized to take advantage of this unique opportunity before it is lost forever (Miller et al., 1962).

COPYING AND CYBERNETIC BEHAVIOR

Let us now turn to a theoretical formulation that is relevant to a number of topics—flexible cybernetic behavior, reactions to dissonance, self-images, and psychological homeostasis. We shall start with the original example of a subject learning to match a model by singing the same note (Miller and Dollard, 1941). The subject learns to make a relative response, tensing the vocal cords, to the cue of the direction of a difference, namely, too low a pitch. He stops correcting when the cue of the difference disappears. Had the term been coined then, this type of responding would have been called "cybernetic" (Weiner, 1948). As in a servo system, the behavior is controlled by feedback with stable equilibrium at the closest match.

Another simple example is reaching for a pencil. The subject learns to respond to the discrepancy of being too far to the left by the correction of moving to the right, and to make similar corrections for being too far to the right, and too high or too low. Thus he "homes in" on the pencil.

Making the plausible assumptions which, however, need additional experimental study, that there is a great deal of similarity between the cue of a given difference (such as being too far to the right) in many absolute contexts, and much similarity among the responses of moving more to the left from a variety of postures, it can be seen that it will be easy to generalize such a skill so that it produces a very flexible type of behavior. Thus this type of formulation is a solution to one of the fundamental dilemmas—namely, explaining the flexibility and goal orientation of behavior—that has plagued S-R theories since their inception.

Further steps in refining the skillful performance of cybernetic behavior are learning to respond to larger differences with larger corrections, and also learning to respond to a discrepancy with the arousal of a learned drive and to the reduction in a discrepancy with a learned reward. With this step, the subject automatically motivates himself to match, and rewards himself for closer matches. The relevance of this mechanism to goal-directed, learned drives has been discussed elsewhere (Miller, 1959; 1963).[5]

It is obvious that this type of analysis is in many respects similar to one later elaborated upon by Mowrer (1960a). But there are some important differences. First, it is not assumed that all responses are necessarily of this kind; allowances are made for rapid, ballistic responses that are not guided all the way to the goal by proprioceptive feedback (Miller, 1959).[6] Secondly, it is assumed that learning can connect a response (either peripheral movement or central image) to the cue of a specific discrepancy (or to other cues), while Mowrer assumes that learning modifies only the motivational values of cues. On the basis of his assumption, it is difficult to see how a response could be selected rapidly from among a large number of alternatives without many of them having to occur incipiently, so that they may be automatically rejected or selected according to the motivation that has been conditioned to cues of feedback from them. It is obvious that this difficulty becomes

[5] A somewhat similar mechanism was proposed by Miller and Dollard (1941, p. 68) for some of the unconscious copying involved in shaping the infant's first learning of speech, as follows:

At the same time that the child is practicing his own crying responses, he is learning to respond to the voices of others. Adults who are feeding, fondling, and otherwise caring for infants usually talk to them; thus certain tones of the human voice acquire a reward value and may later be used to soothe the fretful child. It seems possible that this acquired reward value of the sounds in the language generalizes to sounds which the child makes while he is babbling and helps to reinforce the babbling behavior. . . .

It would be interesting to compare the babbling behavior of different children after an attempt had been made to give different phonemes a special acquired reward value. One child would be talked to with a certain phoneme while being fed and with a different but equally pronounceable phoneme while being dressed or having some other routine performed which seems to annoy him. A second child would be talked to with the first phoneme while being dressed and the second while being fed. The babbling behavior of the two children would then be compared. The prediction would be that the child would learn to babble with the phoneme which had been given an acquired reward value more than with the other.

Subsequently this hypothesis has been discussed by Mowrer (1950) at greater length, but he is wrong in concluding that our consideration of a second and additional mechanism means that we must have discarded the first one.

[6] This conclusion would seem to be supported by the fact that workers in Konorski's laboratory (e. g., Gorska and Jankowska, 1960) have found that learned responses can be established in completely deafferented limbs, although it is possible that the motor neurons in the cortex that are responsible for these responses have connections, the firing of which can serve as cues so that a certain amount of central feedback may be involved.

progressively worse, when there are a larger number of alternatives—as in choosing the appropriate word out of the many thousands in the subject's vocabulary—or when the behavior must be extremely rapid as in making the correct finger movement in a fast cadenza on the piano. Mowrer (1960*b*, pp. 286–288) is aware of this difficulty, but does not solve it.

Discrepancy and Dissonance

The idea that a difference can serve as a cue to arouse motivation obviously is relevant also to some of the phenomena which have been described recently as dissonance (Festinger, 1957). But again, there are important differences. While it is conceivable that some motivation may be produced innately by conflict, such as that between anticipatory goal responses and the responses elicited by the absence of the goal object (Miller and Stevenson, 1936; Miller, 1959), it is clear that the motivational reactions to many differences are learned. In the example of learning to match the pitch of a note sung by a model there does not seem to be any innate motivational value to the difference. The same is true of an individual's reactions to a discrepancy in balancing a checkbook.

To take somewhat more complex examples, whether we react with reward, aversion, or indifference to the dissonances of ultramodern music depends on our previous learning. As I have pointed out before (Dollard and Miller, 1950, p. 120; Miller, 1944, p. 457), children do not necessarily react with distress to logical inconsistencies, but after considerable social training, they may come to do so. Many forms of incompatibility are learned; I have speculated elsewhere about some of the mechanisms that could be involved (Miller, 1944; Dollard and Miller, 1950, p. 209).

I believe that it would be profitable to carry the brilliant analyses by some of the proponents of dissonance theory one step further by analyzing some of the different reactions to dissonance in terms of previous learning. In certain cases, this might help to get this type of theory out of the dilemma of being able to give a highly satisfying explanation of what has occurred, but often being able to explain equally easily also the exact opposite.

Reaction to Discrepancies and Psychological Homeostasis

Responding to the cue of a difference with motivation which is proportional to the size of that difference can be a very economical mechanism for supplying motivation only when it is needed (Miller, 1959). For example, a professor may have an approximate schedule of times to be at different places in driving to meet an eight o'clock class or to catch a plane. As long as he is on schedule, little motivation is apparent; we might think that the responses are being performed solely because they have been associated by contiguity. But if a series of unusual conditions in traffic puts him far behind schedule, he starts to respond to the increasing discrepancy between the time on his watch and the time of the schedule with increasingly obvious motivation, and he will attempt to drive faster or take alternate routes to get there on time. Responding to the cue of the difference provides an automatic mechanism for bringing in additional motivation, exactly when it is needed to keep the behavior on schedule. This might be described as a simple example of psychological homeostasis.

A similar mechanism may be involved in compensating for the effects of fatigue or distraction, and in overcoming other difficulties. With sufficient practice, of course, some of the motivation to pull ourselves together and compensate for difficulties can become attached to the cues of the difficulties encountered, so that we react before any signs of poorer performance are apparent.

The same mechanism, analogous to that outlined for copying, can apply to the matching of a variety of internal standards involving either images or verbal cue-producing responses. Thus, the student who has a "gentleman's C" as a standard for academic accomplishment may be expected to relax when his grades are above this, and to try harder when they fall too low. Other examples of what might be called ideals, self-images, or standards will readily occur to you—being able to take it like a man, being a gentleman, being honest, fair, or scientific. The definition of these standards and the attachment of motivational value to them, involves a great deal of social learning. Often the first step is to copy other individuals, and then to copy one's own concept of the standards. We have already pointed out how some of this copying can be unconscious (Miller and Dollard, 1941). What I want to emphasize here is that this cybernetic mechanism can play an important role in the phenomena of psychological homeostasis. With strong motivation to maintain well-defined standards, the person resists changes that would otherwise be elicited by fluctuations in the environment, but if the standards change, the personality changes.

Some Problems of Equilibrium in Responding to Discrepancies

The foregoing type of analysis is obviously sketchy; many problems need more detailed investigation, such as the nature of the central images or verbalized principles involved, and the details of how the mechanism develops during socialization. An experimental program is needed to determine exactly the types of differences that can serve as cues, how widely the responses to such differences will generalize, and the detailed laws of perceptual learning that may be involved. I believe that the study of such problems will be very fruitful.

Yet, other problems will suggest themselves. I have time to sketch only a few. Let us consider how the response might be expected to vary with the size of the discrepancy. At one limit, when the discrepancy is too small to be discriminated, there will be no response, as we have already pointed out. In many situations, a subject will have learned to make a larger response to larger discrepancies. But will this tendency continue indefinitely? Are some discrepancies so large that they are not likely to be perceived as on the same continuum?

We would expect that the responses to increasingly larger discrepancies would depend on the way that such responses have been correlated with reinforcement under particular conditions of learning. As long as the subject has been more strongly rewarded (e. g., by escaping stronger punishments) for correcting larger discrepancies, we may expect him to try harder the further he is off, and hence show increasingly stronger resistance to more drastic changes. If he has never experienced discrepancies of the test magnitude, his reaction should depend upon principles of stimulus generalization, which have not yet been, but easily could be, experimentally studied with the direction of a difference as a cue. Will the relationship "the greater, the more" be extrapolated, at least for a distance, or will a gradient of stimulus-generalization decrement begin to be encountered with the first novel size of difference?

In some situations, the subject will have routinely experienced failures for trying to copy models that are too different, and may even have been specifically punished for being presumptuous. In yet other cases, there may be a sharp discontinuity in the conditions of reinforcement at a specific point, such as going bankrupt, being sent to prison, or committed to an institution. We might expect such conditions to favor increased struggle up to a certain point, and then a relatively sudden break as illustrated on the right-hand side of Figure 7(c). We need a great deal more theoretical and empirical analysis of such problems.

UNITY AND DISUNITY IN PERSONALITY

Some aspects of social behavior and motivation are relatively easy to change; others are extremely resistant to change. In the latter case serious alterations often occur throughout the whole personality before the specific item in question will change. We need to know much more about what is responsible for such differences (Miller, 1951).

An attempt should be made to apply to this problem the principles that have already been studied as describing the persistence of simple habits under various schedules of reinforcement and strengths of motivation. The roles of stimulus (and response) generalization in producing unity should be investigated. The relationship of the particular item of behavior to various standards or models of the types we have just been discussing and the conditions of reinforcement for these standards should also be relevant. It can be seen that these standards, or certain general rules such as "honesty is the best policy" provide a basis for learned generalization (Dollard and Miller, 1950, p. 106).

The social conditions of learning are also important. The principle of stimulus generalization operating in other people tends to lead them to generalize with respect to the subject, so that they expect him to respond more consistently, or are frustrated by departures from their simplified stereotype of him, and exert a variety of pressures for conformity to this stereotype. Operating over generations, these forces toward consistency in individuals and cultures can snowball, especially under conditions where certain constellations function better than others, as so convincingly documented by Murdoch (1949). These constellations of interrelated cultural conditions tend to turn out individuals with certain types of personalities. In fact, people in certain social-class cliques all show remarkable similarities. To the extent that the social conditions are unified, the personality will be unified.

On the other hand, from a distance, it is easy to overestimate the similarities in a given culture or social class, and also to overestimate the unity of the different aspects of an individual personality. It is easy to make the error of the Chinese visitor, who says: "All you Americans look alike!" We should not overestimate the unity of personality.

Where patterns of reinforcement are different in different contexts, we will expect discriminations to be learned, so that behavior will be different in these contexts. For example, Asratyan (1961) has trained a dog in one room to salivate to a bell signaling food, and withdraw his paw to a light signaling shock; and in another room to do exactly the opposite, show the approach and salivary responses to the light and the defense responses to the bell. Many analogous social conditions are encountered and produce analogous inconsistencies. The parents who teach the child always to tell the truth may be embarrassed when he does so in certain social situations and teach him to tell "white lies." Thus, it is not surprising that Hartshorne and May's (1928) classical studies showed that honesty is not a unitary personality trait.

Similarly, the student who shows the most courage on the football field may not be the most courageous when asked to make a short speech before a large group. Children may behave differently at home or when visiting a friend's home. The person who displays such a gracious and cooperative personality to the big boss may display quite a different personality to his subordinates. Generally kind people can be cruel in certain situations, and vicious criminals can be kind to a child, so that as Gilbert and Sullivan have said: "A policeman's lot is not a happy one."

Membership in groups which reward different patterns of behavior should be especially likely to produce disunity of personality, and in fact, it appears to do so. In some cases this disunity produces conflicts, but in other cases the individual does not seem to sense any incompatibility. Has the latter person merely learned to discriminate different contexts? We need a great deal more research on the social conditions and psychological principles of learning that produce unity or disunity in the personality and that cause people either to compartmentalize effectively or to display conflict over "incompatible" personality traits.

chapter six

Role Theoretical Interpretation
of Psychological Change

Theodore R. Sarbin

By way of an introduction, the constructs of role theory cited here are drawn from the drama and from everyday life. In this chapter, some data and some interpretations to support the general thesis that role enactment influences psychological change are presented first. Then the concepts derived from role theory that are useful in accounting for role enactment are outlined, and finally some recently completed and ongoing research which stems from this orientation is discussed.

It would be instructive to dwell for a moment on the meaning of the term psychological change. In the literature on psychological change, four referents are employed. These referents provide the background for criterion measures used in field or laboratory studies of change. These referents may be identified as

(*a*) somatic changes, which may be monitored by various kinds of sensing apparatus such as sphygmomanometer, EKG, or by observation;

(*b*) changes in performance (skilled acts, verbal or motoric), which may be monitored by observational procedures or by the inspection of the outcomes of performances;

(*c*) changes in preferences for attention deployment, which must be inferred from observation or from self-reports; and

(*d*) changes in cognitive dispositions, attitudes, values, opinions, and be-

I am deeply indebted to Messrs. Vernon Allen, Eldred Rutherford, Milton E. Andersen, Karl E. Scheibe, Robert Sullivan, and Rolf Kroger, members of the Tuesday Morning Group, who read earlier drafts and made many valuable suggestions, most of which have been incorporated into the text. I am also grateful to Professor Seymour Feshbach for reading this chapter and offering some pertinent comments.

liefs which must be inferred from observation of performances or from self-reports.

It is important to note that these criteria of change are not independent one from another. The employment of one type of criterion may be dictated by personal preferences, convenience, or by the nature of one's theory of personality. The non-independence of these criteria is illustrated by the psychological changes following a man's participation in a physical conditioning program for six months. In terms of somatic changes, one could observe improved posture and better tonus. In terms of performance changes, he could now perform such acts as woodchopping and mountain climbing, which he had been unable to do before. In terms of attention deployment, he now scans the ecology for opportunities to use instrumental acts instead of focussing on bodily symptoms as a retreat from problems, and finally, in terms of cognitive dispositions, inferences may be constructed about changes in his self-concept from biographical statements taken before and after the physical conditioning program. The self had been characterized by such adjectives as weak and passive and now is characterized by the adjectives virile, strong, and active. The further inference should not be drawn that these four types of criteria are necessarily related in any systematic way.

THE EFFECTS OF ROLE ENACTMENT

We will first demonstrate that role enactment can in fact produce changes in somatic processes, in performances, in attention deployment, and in cognitive dispositions. Before proceeding, however, a tentative definition of role enactment is offered; a more detailed treatment of it will be given later.

Role enactment is the performance of patterned behaviors where the antecedent conditions include assignment to a position in the social structure. The size and complexity of the social structure may range from a two-person group to a national collectivity. The assignment may be in a contrived setting, as in a play or in an experiment, or in a naturalistic setting, as in a factory or a family. In all cases, the role enactment is to a real or imagined audience.

Evidence that Role Enactment Influences Somatic Processes

Somatic changes have usually been the province of medical science. In studying the responsiveness of organs and organ systems physiologists have usually formulated the antecedent conditions as "stimuli." For example, in studying muscular function an electric current may be used as a stimulus. Or, in studying gastric function the ingestion of certain nutrients may be regarded as stimuli. However, those of us interested in social psychological processes see the "stimulus" of the physiologist only as intermediary effects of a complex set of events centered around the social act. If we were to use the model of the physiological laboratory then we could share the idea of assessing "stimuli" as the antecedents of somatic processes. However, we are not constrained to adopt the physiological laboratory model, but rather may adopt a model with the social act as the antecedent for somatic changes. The studies of Wolf and Wolff (1942) illustrate these two orientations. For example, in Chapter 4 of "Human Gastric Function," the authors report on their investigations of the effects of various chemical agents on gastric functions. In Chapter 8, they move from studying chemical agents to "life situations" as antecedent events. For example, in Tom, their famous laboratory subject with the gastric fistula, "apprehension over social disgrace" was shown to produce marked gastric changes.

Most psychological experimentation that employs somatic changes as dependent variables does not as a rule specify antecedent conditions in terms of role enactment or other social psychological formulations. For example, studies of GSR changes characteristically describe stimulus events which elicit anxiety, anger, and so on. The focus is on the emotional state as the antecedent. I would argue that the more proper antecedents are the social psychological conditions that elicit emotional responses which in turn lead to the somatic effects.

Perhaps the area in which this formulation may be applied directly is in the study of the effects of certain kinds of influence communications, such as hypnosis, on various bodily functions.

Recent research has demonstrated unequivocally that the antecedent conditions in hypnosis experiments may be described as role enactment. (At this point I can point not only to my own studies but to those of Orne (1959), Barber (1960, 1961), and Fisher (1954).) Despite the resistance of some authors to role terminology, their explanations in effect deal with the relationship between an experimenter and a subject each holding expectations reciprocal to each other.

One study that was reported by Lewis and Sarbin (1941) some years ago demonstrated the influence of role enactment on gastric hunger contractions. In this experiment the subjects appeared in a laboratory without having had food for fifteen hours. They were hypnotized and attached to the Carlson balloon manometer apparatus. This apparatus consists of a balloon to which is attached a very fine tube. After the subject swallows the balloon it is inflated. To the other end of the tube is attached a manometer which activates a recording instrument. As the stomach contracts, air is displaced so that the amount of pressure in the stomach is given a meter reading.

We first obtained typical records of each subject so that we knew approximately the length of the hunger cycle. During the middle of a period of acute hunger the subject was given instructions to imagine eating a normal breakfast. In several ways, he was told to take the role of a person about to satisfy his hunger. Those subjects who had been rated as "good role takers," which was operationally defined as a high score on the Friedlander-Sarbin scale of hypnotic depth, were able to inhibit the gastric contractions. Refined analysis of their responses to the role-taking instructions indicated that the good role takers exhibited such role-relevant behaviors as chewing, swallowing, salivating, smacking the lips, and other eating behavior. The purpose of reviewing this experiment is to illustrate that role enactment under hypnosis may influence vital somatic processes. The physiologist in performing this study would concern himself, for example, with the effect of increased salivation on the reduction of hunger contractions, or the physiochemical properties of saliva on gastric mucosa. On the other hand, our purpose is to focus on the social psychological events which are antecedent to and presumably determinative of such salivary changes.

Another illustration of the effect of role enactment on somatic processes is the inhibition or suppression of pain. Barber (1959) reviewed a number of studies in which pain thresholds are raised as a result of instructions and placebos. When the physician administers the placebo, at the same time performing appropriate role behaviors, he activates certain role expectations in the patient—that is, the patient's expectations are that of a person about to receive a pain reliever (morphine)—whose response is indistinguishable from that of a person to whom the drug is actually administered.

The placebo response may be viewed as a direct function of the "stimulus"; however, the "stimulus" is not the ineffective inert compound, but the entire situation which includes the "drug," the word [and other role behaviors] of the physician and the patient's previous experience with physicians and drugs (Barber, 1959, p. 463).

These observations are cited merely to demonstrate that for one kind of consequent variable, somatic changes, the antecedent variable can be considered one of role enactment.

Evidence that Role Enactment Influences Changes in Performance

In the context of social psychological work, it would seem that the observations of performances—overt actions—would be the preferred criterion. This is not to gainsay the importance of somatic or cognitive consequents, but rather to emphasize the central importance of overt behaviors in dyadic and other social psychological relationships. A demonstration that role enactment can influence performance has been the subject of many literary efforts, among them Shaw's *Pygmalion* and Barrie's *Admirable Crichton*. In both these plays we have a central character who is assigned a role and whose behavior is consistent with the role assignment. In the case of Eliza Doolittle, the assignment follows preparation in the vocal and gestural behaviors appropriate to the role; in the case of Crichton, he already possesses in a latent form the requirements of the leadership role which is demanded by the emergency shipwreck situation.

The same elements are contained in the pioneer work of Moreno (1934). He developed the psychodrama as a procedure for modifying conduct, the changes in performance serving as the criterion of the effectiveness of the psychodramatic method. In the psychodrama the patient is assigned various roles, some of which lead to a better understanding of the total role situation in which he finds himself, and some of which lead to changes in performance in much the same way as for Eliza and Crichton. Moreno's innovation has led to the use of role playing as a technique for modifying performances of many kinds. One might mention, for example, the pioneering work of J. R. P. French who utilized role-playing procedure for the training of foremen in an industrial organization (1945).[1]

The behavior changes which occur in the case of Eliza are too obvious to mention. She is being asked to play the role of a lady and must acquire the necessary, specific behaviors of speech and manner which the role demands. In the case of Crichton, he already possesses those survival skills which the shipwreck situation demands, hence, his change in performance. Or, to put it another way, Eliza acquires a set of acts to validate her illegitimate occupancy of the role of lady, Crichton performs heroic actions as a result of an emergent social structure and achieves the role of leader.

The importance of studying performances as a criterion is apparent when one considers the effects of the role enactment in these two situations. We find that as a consequence of performing the role of a lady, Eliza can no longer return to the slum, and to the role of a street urchin. Instrumental in this effect are the feedback properties of her behavior: in acting like a lady other persons now have expectations that she will continue to perform

---

[1] At this point, a distinction ought to be made between performances that are role-specific, such as the way to intone "to be or not to be," and performances that go beyond the role, so as to affect performances of other roles. To continue the illustration from *Hamlet,* sustained and involved enactment of the role might lead an actor to perform non-stage roles in a vacillating and indecisive manner. In studying the effects of role enactment, we are obliged to specify whether the dependent variable is measured in terms of role-specific performances or performances of a non-specific kind.

in this new role and they may, indeed, provide reinforcement for her continuing in this role. As she had experienced difficulty in acquiring the new role, she experienced even greater difficulty in relinquishing the role. The effect of her role performance was to set up persisting expectations in members of the new reference group, such expectations functioning as role demands which she perceives and which she cannot ignore.

In the case of Crichton, the performance as leader has modified the expectations of the other members of the social group, so that the role demands made on Crichton have changed, and, as a result, his performance changes to meet these role demands. The dramatist makes capital of the incompatibilities when the original positions are restored, and Crichton is again assigned the role of butler. The occupants of the complementary roles experience great difficulty in re-establishing the previous social structure. The explanation, of course, lies in the conflict of role demands which have now come into play—on the one hand are the traditional role expectations for servant, and on the other the role expectations acquired through Crichton's performance in the emergency.

We can apply a similar analytic framework to a study reported by Milton (1957) dealing with differences in problem solving between sexes. Subjects who were categorized in terms of sex-role identification showed variable performance on problem-solving tasks. Females who were classified as adopting the male role were better solvers than those who did not. This is probably due to the differential role expectations we have in our society for males and females. The achievement orientation of males is probably not as intensely demanded of females. The implication of this finding for social learning is that a modification in sex-role identification will produce changes in problem-solving skills. Some preliminary support for this hypothesis has been offered by Carey (1958).

Evidence for the Effect of Role Enactment on Deployment of Attention

By attention deployment I mean the direction and manner of a person's search of the ecology for inputs. It is my hypothesis that the kinds of inputs that influence the way in which a person defines the situation—locates the other and himself on role dimensions—is a function of the position he occupies. That is to say, the performance of appropriate role behaviors is dependent upon the accurate perception of the role of the other or others in an interaction situation. Examples from everyday life can be readily cited. The umpire in an athletic contest is oriented towards perception of behaviors which are infractions of rules. When he is not performing his professional role, and becomes a spectator or a player, he is oriented towards stimulus events more in keeping with the demands of these other roles.

In a study reported by Bugenthal and Lehner (1958) the authors were interested in studying two leadership roles in terms of the accuracy of social perception. They identified two types of leaders, popular leaders (the center of affect within the group), and "true" leaders, who guide the group toward group goals. They found that popular leaders were more sensitive to interpersonal traits and group dimensions than the "true" leaders. The inference may be drawn that enacting the role of "true" leader leads to the search for inputs that may be related to decisions affecting group goals; enacting the role of popular leader, on the other hand, leads to the search for inputs that are related to decisions promoting group harmony.

When a person is placed in a social situation where the role of other interactants are unknown or ambiguous, he must place the others on role dimensions in order to perform (define) his own role. In order to reduce the ambiguity he will direct his attention to behaviors emitted by the undefined persons. Attending to such inputs may reduce the amount of effort he can expend in the solution of group tasks. Ewart Smith (1957) reported a study that demonstrates nicely the effects of clear and unclear role expectations on productivity. In this study the roles of all participants were defined in one group, but in the other no information about their roles was given to any of the participants. Smith found significantly less productivity in those groups whose members' roles were undefined than in groups whose roles were unambiguously defined. The implication of the study is this: when a person must devote an inordinate amount of time in searching for inputs to establish the roles of others and, complementarily, of himself, he has less time to attend to inputs relevant to the task at hand.

Evidence that Role Enactment Produces Changes in
Dispositional Characteristics

Of the four types of psychological change, perhaps the most thoroughly investigated is the study of change in inferred cognitive structure as a result of antecedent variables, many of which can be conceptualized as role enactments. The usual paradigm for the experiment is to pretest subjects on some belief, value, or attitude, and then to place them under various experimental treatments, after which the subjects are retested. The independent variables may be in the form of persuasive communications, the presentation of selected stimuli under controlled conditions, the observation of the behaviors of other persons, or role enactments. (I shall be concerned with the latter.)

The hypothesis that role enactment may influence changes in dispositional characteristics originated in folk psychology. It is a belief among many primitives that certain personality characteristics accrue to persons who have performed certain specified social roles. For example, once a person has been adjudged to be a criminal his social group expects that he will have criminal tendencies as a part of his personality makeup. Similarly, if a person has been assigned the sick role and committed to a mental hospital, other members of the community will believe that there are permanent effects on the personality stemming from such role enactment. Merton (1940) has written a clear and concise description of the bureaucratic personality. He shows that the rigid and impersonal attention to rules and regulations results in a depersonalization of relationships. In a similar vein, Waller (1932) has reported the effects of enacting the role of teacher on dispositional characteristics. He found that prolonged enactment of the teacher role may produce recognizable changes in attitude, in style of solving problems, and even in speech and mannerisms.

A study which is destined to become a classic was reported by Lieberman (1956). Lieberman's hypothesis was that individuals who are assigned a role will take on attitudes that are congruent with the role. He tested this hypothesis by examining the attitudes of factory personnel in regard to labor-management questions. This was a field study—the experimenter manipulated no variables. Twenty-three of the employees became foremen, and thirty-five became union stewards during the period of study. Results indicated that those who were promoted to the job of foreman saw the factory as a better place to work, developed more favorable perceptions of management, and expressed more favorable attitudes towards the incentive system. The new stewards showed more favorable attitudes toward labor unions, they were more positive in their perceptions of union officers, and tended to prefer seniority as a criterion for promotion.

Lieberman had the opportunity of studying the relative permanence of these attitude changes. As a result of an economic slowdown a number of men were laid off, and some foremen and stewards returned to non-supervisory worker roles. Demoted foremen showed consistent changes in the direction of their earlier (preforeman) attitudes. The demoted union stewards showed less difference, but this was probably because the original change was not so great as that of the foremen.

The author interprets his study as demonstrating that the performance of the role influences attitudes. He goes on to elaborate an interpretation, suggesting that a change in role results in a change in reference group which, in turn, brings about a new frame of reference. By shifting one's attitudes so that they are consistent with one's actions, it helps the role occupant be "at one" with himself, and facilitates effective performance on the job. An alternate interpretation is that new role demands arise as a result of change in status. In order effectively to meet these demands, both attitudes and overt actions must be consistent with the role. If one is a foreman, he is also a representative of management, he has contacts and associations with other management personnel. There are demands, subtle and obvious, created both by superiors and subordinates that he represent management. In order to do so convincingly, he must acquire appropriate supporting beliefs and attitudes.

A large number of studies have been reported which were aimed directly at throwing light on the influence of role enactments on opinion and attitude change. Two studies are reported as examples. Scott (1957) obtained opinions from a number of student subjects, then arranged for them to participate in a debate on the side opposite his expressed opinion. The audience was presumably polled to determine which side had "won" the debate. The experimenter faked the count and announced "winner" or "loser" by preplan. There was a post-test on the same attitudes. It was found that the attitudes of the debaters who were "winners" changed significantly more in the direction of the assigned position than did the "losers," or the non-debater controls. The interpretation offered by Scott is one derived from reinforcement theory. It is suggested that the subjects tentatively modified their attitudes as a result of active participation in the debate. The announcement of "win" is a positive reinforcement and in effect told the debater that his arguments influenced the audience. The announcement of "lose" told the debater that his arguments had no effect on the audience. In my view, the reinforcement properties of the audience were crucial in fixing the tentative shift in attitude brought about through active participation. (A little later in discussion I will report a related experiment from my own laboratory.)

A similar method was used by Janis and King in two studies. No direct reinforcements were given at the conclusion of the debate; however, in their studies attitude change seemed to be a function of the amount of improvisation introduced by the debaters to support the assigned position. In my framework improvisation is another way of describing the *degree of self-involvement* in a role. A high degree of self-involvement exhibited in a public setting constitutes a commitment to the role. This commitment comes about because of expected negative sanctions in the form of social disapproval for demonstrating inconsistent behavior. It is the commitment to the role, then, which initiates the modification of attitude so that it is more consistent with the subject's publicly expressed opinion.

Illustrative of the influence of role enactment on role-taking aptitude is an experiment reported by Mann and Mann (1958). In this experiment all subjects at the beginning and at the end of the experimental period participated in a situational test in which they were observed and rated on various role-playing dimensions. When compared with two control groups, the role-playing experience was shown to increase general role-taking aptitude or skill. Among the measures which led to this conclusion were the following: ratings made by members of the audience; by other role-players; by judges listening to tape recordings of the situational tests; and by observers of the situational test.

I am not yet prepared to claim that *all* personality change is mediated by role enactment. From the observation of persons who enact occupational and familial roles over time, the inference may confidently be drawn that effective role enactment does leave behavior changes that may be monitored in various ways. Empirical research of the kind reported by Newcomb (1943) in the Bennington College studies emphasizes how social attitudes are generated and modified through group membership, and, by extension, through the enactment of role behaviors demanded by such group membership.

The analysis of religious conversion fits neatly into the role-enactment scheme. What better way to describe the convert than to say that he now enacts a role in keeping with the expectations and demands of significant others. That the level of involvement of the self in a role is high can be inferred from self-reports of persons who have passed through a religious crisis.

Catastrophic events, such as floods, wars, plagues, and revolution are attended by far-reaching changes in personality organization. In terms of our theory, such occurrences upset the social organization in various ways. The disequilibrium is followed by confusion and misperception of the positions of others, partly because such positions are no longer functional. The roles enacted by persons in non-functional positions fail to elicit reinforcement from significant others. Under such conditions, persons are thrust into, or seek out, novel positions where the validating role enactments are accepted and given sanction through real or ritualized rewards.

Changes following psychotherapeutic intervention may be seen as the effects of role enactments over time reinforced by appropriate reinforcements on the part of therapists and other significant audiences.

Space limitations do not allow me fully to document my belief that behavior changes, such as those just mentioned, can best be conceptualized with the aid of role concepts. However, we may claim that effective role enactment is the antecedent variable in many recorded instances of psychological change. However, this antecedent-consequent relationship is not an invariant one. Our next task is to suggest some of the sources of variance in valid role enactment, using as guideposts a set of concepts that are grouped under the label role theory.

ROLE THEORY

At this juncture, I should like to offer a digest of the principal constructs of role theory. Role theory is a special kind of orientation in that it attempts to bridge the constructs of both psychology and sociology. Therefore, a short sociological overture is demanded in order to give the concepts appropriate clarity.

The maintenance of a human group depends upon the smooth functioning of its participants in working toward shared culturally defined goals. In order for the group to operate with a modicum of efficiency, functions are segregated so that only members of certain categories perform assigned tasks. Learning to recognize which classes of persons engage in which performances is one of the main features of the enculturation process. The organization of functions may be formally codified as in a table or organization where the units are jobs. More often, the table of organization is in the form of a set of implicit expectations held by members of a collectivity. Patterns of such implicit expectations are the units of societal organization and are variously called status, position, or office. (We use these terms interchangeably.) A status is defined by the expectations held by members of a group. Members of the social group hold expectations that the occupant of a given status will perform motoric and/or verbal actions paying attention to sequence, timing, involvement, etc. The content of these expectations are *acts*. Further, expectations are held that the occupant will perform in ways that will allow inferences to be drawn about qualities or traits. The content of these expectations are imputed dispositions. To illustrate the two types of expectations: the status denoted by the label "village chief" is defined by expectations held by members of his village that he will perform certain acts in civic and religious ceremonials (performance can be specified in considerable detail), and that he will perform in such a manner that he will be regarded as dignified, honest, efficient, and proper.

Role Enactment

We have said little so far about the specification of effective role enactment. Since role enactment is a matter of complex response processes, how do we go about assessing performances in social situations? Suggestions have been made from time to time that performances be dimensionalized according to such characteristics as tempo, flexibility, and motility. Such suggestions have not been taken up primarily because of the equivalence of different acts in meeting the demands of a given situation. The assessment of the validity, effectiveness or convincingness of a performance must be carried on chiefly through the medium of the human observer as recorder and evaluator. To be sure, some aspects of formal role enactments may be assessed through mechanical devices, such as structured examinations, but the assessment of *ongoing* behavior must be channeled through human observers.

In principle, there are two ways of assessing the validity of a performance. The first is through observing the presence or absence (or degrees of presence) of certain characteristics which may be relevant to a particular role enactment. Example: a short, stocky man walks up and down before a group of observers in the personnel office of a department store. At frequent intervals, he utters "Ho, Ho, Ho," and asks several stereotyped questions. On an adjective check list, the observers check such words as kindly, jolly, warm, humane, generous, understanding, and so on. These characteristics are central traits in the role of department store Santa Claus. His performance, then, is judged effective because of the high degree of overlap between the codified behavior and the role expectations. The second method calls for a "global" assessment. The observer is asked: "How well does this person's performance meet your criteria of what a Santa Claus should be like?"

Both methods were used in the study reported by Sarbin and Jones (1956). In this study, attention was directed toward the performance of the daughter role in a contrived situation. Members of our audience, after observing a five-minute verbal interaction of a subject with a man assigned the role of father, checked qualitative aspects of her role enactment on a two-hundred-word adjective check list. These check lists had been filled out earlier for the role expectations of the typical daughter in contemporary society. The measurement of effectiveness of role enactment was determined through a comparison of the number of adjectives checked by the observers with the list of adjectives that made up the qualitative role expectations. This method allowed us to identify those subjects whose enactment was conformant with the prescribed role expectations. The second method was simply a ranking of the six role players in terms of their *adequacy* of portrayal of the role of daughter. In this second type of assessment, the audience presumably compared the performances with their own implicit role expectations.

In the first method, the observer in the audience is not asked to take an evaluative attitude—that is, he is not asked to play a critic's role in which his conduct is guided by the question "How well is the subject enacting the role?" Rather he is asked to take a neutral stance, and search for inputs that will allow certain non-evaluative ratings to be made. The actual evaluation of role enactment is made by a third person who compares the ratings with some set of expectations. In the second method, members of the audience cannot take a neutral stance, but must assess the conduct in terms of their own expectations or of those provided for the particular situation.

The assessment of the effectiveness of role enactment, then, must be achieved through the intervention of an audience. Which of the two methods is used will depend upon the needs and theoretical predilections of the experimenter. Complications arising from the reinforcement properties of the audience will be discussed later.

The remainder of this section of my paper is devoted to a discussion of the variables that influence the effectiveness of role enactment. In order, I shall discuss briefly the following: role expectations, role perception, role demands, role-taking aptitude or skill, self-role congruence, and reinforcement properties of an audience.

Role Expectations

The term *role* is assigned to the patterns of behavior emitted by the occupant of a status that are relevant to validating his occupancy of that status. Thus, expectations held by an individual or by a collection of individuals about the performance of any person assigned a status may legitimately be called role expectations. We infer the existence of role expectations in two ways: on the stimulus side, from the person's previous commerce with regularities in others' behavior; and on the response side, from his practice of grouping together a number of acts and qualities and assigning the label of a social status to the grouping. Role, on the other hand, is the set of *performances enacted* by the occupant of a status. The extent to which the role enactment corresponds to the expectations held by relevant others is the efficiency, convincingness, or validity of the enactment.

Lest you regard this formulation as overly simplified, let me add that persons usually occupy multiple statuses—some of which may be compatible, such as male, professor, scientist, and some of which may be incompatible, such as clergyman and military officer. Furthermore, the occupant of a specific position not only enacts relevant behaviors to validate his status in the macrocosmic social role system, he also performs acts which validate his statuses in microcosmic personal role systems. Goffman (1961) has conceptualized the latter type of system as providing the opportunity for *encounters*. While the macrosystem dictates the kinds of role behaviors appropriate to regularly occurring situations, miniature systems grow up where the units must be expressed in terms of idiosyncratic preferences and/or non-consensual expectations, such as a group of roommates in an apartment, members of a combat platoon, or a surgical team.

The problems of assessing role expectations are the same as in the assessment of any cognitive structure. Expectations must be inferred from some overt behavior, or from self-reports. The investigator may make his inferences from answers provided by respondents to the direct question: "What behavior should one expect typically from a person who is a father, Santa Claus, priest, sweetheart, neighbor, etc.?"

In order to assess role expectations in a systematic way, various instruments have been developed. I have been interested in the qualitative aspects of role enactment and have employed a two-hundred-word adjective check list to assess role expectations in terms of qualities. For example, in the study already mentioned (Sarbin and Jones, 1956), we determined the consensus of role expectations for the "daughter in contemporary American society" by asking all the respondents to check those adjectives that characterize this role. Among the adjectives checked by at least 40 per cent of the group were the following: informal, imaginative, pleasure seeking, well mannered, warm, gentle, feminine, modest, cheerful.

In another study, we used the same instrument to assess the qualities of middle-level supervisors in a government agency. By collecting the qualitative role expectations of top management and of line workers, we were able to construct a scale of adjectives that was a composite for both groups. (Sarbin and Jones, 1955*b*). Among the adjectives that make up this scale are the following: industrious, serious, stable, intelligent, fair-minded, tactful, reasonable, etc.

Out of the consensus of role expectations arise group norms. Bates and Cloyd (1956) have shown how group norms in small group studies are made up of a set of agreed upon expectations which include acts and qualities, such as members of the group should stick to the subject, be interested in the discussion, be dependable, and be even tempered.

Although my discussion has centered on the consensual aspect role expectations, one must not lose sight of the fact that a person may hold idiosyncratic expectations. Observations of overt behaviors allow certain inferences about idiosyncratic expectations such as in the following fragment of a juvenile hall counselor's report: "Whenever John was approached by a woman, he drew back as if he expected to be scolded, punished or beaten." The behavior of the person holding non-consensual expectations, however, is likely to be marked by surprise, disappointment and/or frustration until non-fulfillments provide the basis for correcting the role expectation so that it more nearly coincides with the consensus.

The sentence completion method may also be used to study role expectations. Thomas, Polansky, and Kounin (1955) employed sentence completions to assess the role expectations of a potentially helpful person (such as social worker, psychologist, minister, etc.). Examples of the incomplete sentences are: "After I told this person what my problem was, he/she. . . ." "While talking to this person, I had the feeling that he/she expected me to. . . ." This study demonstrated that such a procedure could produce a consensus of role expectations, and further, that the expectations could be modified under conditions of anticipated interest and attention on the part of the potential helper.

Role Perception

The proposition has been asserted that in order for a person validly to enact a role, he must know what role to enact, or, in other words he must locate himself in the role system. Such locating or positioning occurs as the result of an assessment of the other(s) in the situation in relation to one's self. The accuracy of locating the other (and reciprocally one's self) in the role system determines to a large extent the validity of enactment. (Parenthetically, we use the term perception in its broadest sense, and it is roughly equivalent to cognizing, recognizing, knowing. Our preference is for the term role instantiation because we regard a set of cues as being an instance of a general class. However, the term instantiation does not yet have wide currency.)

To perceive the role of the other, one must attend to the other's behavior. Cues that locate others on age and sex dimensions are readily available. In some groups, signs or badges of office enable participants to recognize the other's position in the social structure. In interactions that have some continuity, the actor must be able to take into account the behavior of the other. One of the cues readily available for instantiating a person on various dimensions is posture. Because our language is impoverished with regard to the infinitude of postures, we (Sarbin and Hardyck, 1955) constructed a set of stick figures where all cues—including age and sex cues—were eliminated except postural cues. This has been used as a role-perception test in a number of studies. The procedure is to present the stick figures, one at a time, and ask the subject to check one of five words or phrases which are descriptive of the figure. The frequencies of response for the five choices follow a J curve. On standardizing groups, the modal response contains at least 70 per cent of the choices. When a person's protocol for the forty-three figures shows many choices from the modal response category we call his role perceptions conformant.

In the first published report (Sarbin and Hardyck, 1955) we demonstrated that schizophrenics in a state hospital chose the modal response category no more frequently than the low response categories. When we studied juvenile delinquents, we found a significant relationship between scores on the stick-figures test and severity of maladjustment. The more disturbed delinquents selected fewer modal responses (Sarbin and Jones, 1958). In some further work on this procedure, we identified 25 of the stimuli as calling for *inferences* about a covert state, e.g., happy, sad, angry, and thinking. The other 18 cards we identified as non-inference figures; they were essentially descriptions of the stimuli, e.g., standing at attention, running, and sleeping. Krasner, Ullmann, and Weiss (1961), used these categories in a further study of schizophrenia. Comparisons between schizophrenics and non-hospitalized control groups showed no significant differences in perceiving the modal response for "non-inference" figures, but a very large difference for the "inference" figures ($p = .001$). This finding lends support to the proposition that psychiatric patients are characterized by an inability to place persons in the role-system when they must depend on interpreting cues that reflect feelings and other covert states.

The failure of schizophrenics to infer qualities on the basis of limited acquaintance is the subject of a report by Helfand (1956). After reading an autobiography, patients took a specially prepared Q sort. These sorts were correlated with the Q sort of the author of the autobiography. Chronic patients were inferior to privileged (less severe) patients, both patient groups were inferior to normals. The chronic patients showed the greatest variance. The author concludes that members of the patient group are idiosyncratic in their perceptions of the person as revealed through his autobiography. Another formulation could be borrowed from G. H. Mead (1934)—the schizophrenic patients lack a "generalized other"—that is, the schizophrenic does not use conventional dimensions or roles to group available cue properties of the ecology.

Role Demands

Let us say that a person correctly locates the status of the other on the basis of age and sex-role cues, social class and occupational cues, etc. Furthermore, let us suppose that this same person has a set of role expectations which will facilitate his interaction with the other. At this point, of course, the possible acts have been reduced from near infinity to a small number. Certain additional features of the situation must be taken into account, however, which may further limit the choices of the interactant. These are *role demands*—usually implicit. These demands differ from the expectations generated by the set of instructions delivered to a subject in a psychological experiment. Take one of the early experiments on perceptual defense (McGinnies, 1949). The explicit role expectations, not necessarily verbalized at the moment, were: "I am the experimenter, you are the subject. When you see a flash

on the screen, I shall expect you to tell me what you see." In addition to
the explicit instructions directed toward the experimental procedures, the experimenter implicitly invoked the norm of cooperation, a norm that has all
the properties of a cultural role—a set of behaviors expected by all, or
nearly all, members of a group simply in virtue of membership. But there are
other implicit role demands in the form of propriety norms for age, sex,
and class statuses. The performance of the propriety role sets the background for the specific enactment of experimental subject. So when a student subject dimly recognizes a dirty word flashed on the screen, the implicit norm of propriety creates the demand not to respond, i.e., to withhold
the response. In so doing, of course, he or she is validating the implicit
propriety role. However, when the exposure time or illumination is increased so that the word is clearly recognized, then the more obvious role
demands of the instruction take over. Some of the mystery vanishes when
perceptual defense is seen as response suppression in order to validate one's
adherence to a normative role.[2]

The experiment by Postman et al. (1953) may be interpreted along similar
lines. They tried to bring the implicit role demands under experimental
control by incorporating them in the explicit role demands; that is, in the
experimenter's instructions. The facilitation of response to taboo words was
encouraged by instructions which implied that difficulty in seeing and reporting dirty words was a sign of maladjustment and mental illness. To
inhibit recognition of taboo words, instructions were given which implied
that having difficulty with seeing and reporting taboo words was equivalent
to positive mental health and social adjustment. It is interesting to note
that a third instruction, which merely told the subjects to expect some taboo
words but where no attempt was explicitly made to create role demands,
produced the same order of recognition thresholds as the *inhibition* instruction. One interpretation of this finding is that the norm of favorable self
presentation was operative as an implicit role demand. We recently repeated
this study in our laboratory, employing three types of stimulus materials and
three types of response measures. Only the variable of role demands, as
manipulated through pre-experimental communications, accounted for differences in response measures (Chun and Sarbin, 1961).

A series of experiments by Martin Orne (1959, 1961) contain the most
forceful arguments for considering the role-demand variable in any social
psychological setting—including laboratory experiments. In his first series of
studies, he demonstrated that the role enactment of subjects motivated to

[2] Role demands, as used here, are equivalent to the mores as described by Sumner
(1900).

simulate the role of the hypnotic subject could not be differentiated from the role enactment of subjects where role demands were created through the traditional hypnotic induction in appropriately predisposed subjects. The implications of this and other studies in hypnosis relevant to role demand will be discussed presently. Orne's second series of studies is concerned with the social psychology of the psychological experiment. One of these studies demonstrates the differential role demands created when subjects recognize or infer that they are in experimental or control groups. In a setup that simulated sensory deprivation experiments, including an examination by a physician and the presence of a panic button in the experimental room, *but in the absence of actual sensory deprivation,* experimental subjects reported many, if not all, of the phenomena attributed to actual sensory deprivation. Subjects who were told that they were *control* subjects received the same experimental treatment (the panic button was removed) but they reported none of the sensory-deprivation phenomena. In short, different role demands produced different experimental results. In this experiment, the assignment to experimental or control group was made explicit. In the usual experiment, the subject is left free to speculate whether he is in the experimental or in the control group. He will use whatever cues are available to help define his role.

The implications of Orne's work strengthen my argument that implicit role demands are important determinants of role enactment. For the experimental subject the norm of contribution to science operates to create a demand to perform nearly any kind of conduct when identified as a scientific experiment. When the sophisticated experimenter tries to control for this demand by a postexperimental inquiry, he may receive responses which lead him to say that the subjects were ignorant of the purposes of the experiment. However, the denial requires examination. As I shall discuss presently in connection with hypnosis studies, another norm that is operative is the face-saving norm. The subject may try to save the experimenter the embarrassment which would follow his announcement that he saw through the experimenter's subterfuge.

Role demands are created by implied differences in power of the interactants in a social situation. Sheehan has provided me with some data to illustrate the effect of differently identified listeners on stuttering. The subjects read standard passages five times before listeners identified as faculty members or as fellow students. The number of speech "blocks" was greater in the condition where the listeners were faculty members. For this group of subjects, the hierarchal position of the listener implicitly created a demand which served as a stressor (Sheehan, 1961).

Among other norms which operate as silent role demands are commitment as a result of a public declaration and the norm of reciprocity. We shall discuss their operation in the context of social influence studies in a later section of this chapter.

Role-Taking Aptitude

Cameron (1947), Gough (1948), Newcomb (1950), Sarbin (1954), and others, following the speculations and observations of G. H. Mead (1934), have presented arguments for the existence of an aptitude that facilitates role enactment and subsequent social interaction. This aptitude is parallel to other aptitudes, presumably acquired early in life. It is a property of the person and must be inferred from samples of behavior. It is not difficult to rationalize such an aptitude from observation of the ease with which some persons shift their role behaviors as they respond to minimal information in the ecology, while others seem to require a great deal of information before they can assign the correct status to the other, and complementarily to self. The absence of this aptitude or skill, according to Cameron (1947) accounts for the invalid and desocialized enactment of schizophrenic patients. Similarly, interpreted as the inability to take the role of the other (Gough, 1948; Sarbin, 1954), this lack of skill accounts for certain kinds of delinquent and criminal conduct.

The role-taking aptitude seems to contain several components. These may be inferred from studies carried out in attempts to find a general factor of role-taking skill. The criteria for such studies have included ratings on improvisations of various kinds, filling out paper and pencil tests as if the subject were the target person, replying to standard questions in the same way as some specified class of persons, such as the majority of Americans, college graduates, fellow-prisoners, etc.

I cannot go into detail here, but my analysis of the criteria used in such studies leads me to suggest four components: a general cognitive component (role expectations); a general motoric component; an empathetic component (role perception); and a specificity component.

The cognitive component arises from acquaintance with the role system of the person about whom an inference is being made. If the subject knows his role system, he will know the expectations that make up this system and, from this knowledge, can extrapolate to any individual occupying a status in the system. The frequently cited work of Gage (1952) illustrates this point. Predictions of conduct were more accurate when based upon general role expectations or stereotypes rather than upon perceived idiosyncracies of the target person. I should make clear that knowledge of the role system includes knowledge of microsystems in which role expectations may be codified along different dimensions from the wider social structure. To tap this component, Sarbin and Jones (1956) developed an as-if test—a simple face valid procedure where subjects write an answer to the question: "In what way could your life have been different if you had been born a member of the opposite sex?" Scores based on content analysis correlated with effectiveness of role enactment in a contrived situation.

The general motoric component is one that has not been systematically studied except in the context of dramatic acting. Where the criterion of the presence of role-taking skill includes overt gestural, verbal, and motoric actions, the careful investigator will raise the question of the generality of these actions in situations other than the test situation. Like the general cognitive component, this aspect of role-taking skill presupposes a broad acquaintance with, and practice of, the overt role behaviors associated with many statuses. While each person's repertory of verbal and gestural acts and bodily movements will differ from every other, there is a minimum which is required for carrying on social transactions. Recognition of such an aptitude is important in experiments where the consequent variable includes verbal, gestural, or other motoric performances. Unless the experimenter controls for this general aptitude, he may err in his interpretation of the relationship to the antecedent conditions specified in his experiment. As we shall point out in a later section, this aptitude is an important one in hypnosis experiments where the criterion is made up of various gestural and motoric actions.

The empathetic component is the one so frequently sought in person-perception experiments. On the basis of minimal acquaintance with a target person, the subject must make predictions or postdictions of the target person's behavior. These predictions must have an accuracy greater than predictions based on knowledge of the role system alone. In short, idiosyncratic behavior (i.e., events with low base rates) of the target person are inferred from cues supplied in the interaction situation. Some writers make the assumption that the inference follows from kinesthetic feedback as a result of taking the posture of the target person. This assumption has not been satisfactorily tested. Most experiments that claim to have discovered this empathetic skill, when properly analyzed, show the confounding of some general role expectations, as in assumed similarity. However, Cline and Richards (1960) have consistently found a general empathetic trait in a series of carefully controlled experiments in which subjects make inferences about the social behavior of target persons after watching sound motion pictures.

The specificity component is analogous to specific abilities in the context of personnel testing. Certain roles demand highly specialized skills. The role of the dentist requires fine manual dexterity and eye-hand coordination.

The role of the quarterback requires speed and ability to pass, run, and kick. These specific role-taking skills may be perceptual, verbal, or motoric. It it important to recognize the possibility of the skill factor operating when one is using a criterion of enactment that has low base rates. Barber (1960) has shown that the role enactment that includes a gross modification of the Babinski—usually attributed to hypnotic induction procedures—is just an application of the specific skill in using certain muscles. As we shall spell out presently, hallucinations—when part of the criteria of role enactment—occur only in persons who are specially skillful in imagining the presence of certain absent physical stimulus objects.

Self-role Congruence

From folk psychology we have acquired the principle that a role is performed better if its requirements are congruent with the self. For our purposes we shall define the self as a cognitive structure, the residue of the human organism's commerce with objects and events, including other humans. These residues are the referents for the symbol "I." Although referents for the term "I" may be found in a number of ways, we have found two procedures particularly useful: adjectives and I-statements. In our language system the most frequently employed device for talking about the self-structure of persons is the adjective. A person can describe his self as a catalog of adjectives or traits, such as, friendly, helpful, hostile, clean, rugged, etc. The assessment device that uses this assumption is the familiar adjective check list. I-statements, of course, are the backbone of most personality and preference inventories. The respondent indicates various predicates when I is the subject, in this way expressing his fears, hates, preferences, attitudes, feelings, etc. The particular dimensions used for organizing such sentences into scales are invented for particular purposes by the experimenter, or distilled through various analytic procedures (Washburn, 1961).

If we have the requirements of a role and these can be codified in terms of adjectives or statements, then it is possible to compare the qualitative or action requirements of the role with the self-characteristics of the person. When these are congruent, we may say that the person has a potential or actual attachment to, or liking for, the role. When the self and role characteristics are antagonistic, however, then we expect an unconvincing performance, and very little, if any, behavior change, other things being equal. This feature of role theory is called the motivational variable.

An example of the way in which role and self-characteristics may be systematically varied is contained in a recent study by Smelser (1961). He selected persons who were high and low on the trait of dominance (derived from the California Psychological Inventory, Gough, 1957) and placed them in a cooperative work situation, systematically assigning dominant and submissive roles. The most productive groups were composed of pairs in which the dominant subject was assigned the dominant role and the submissive subject the submissive role. The least productive groups were composed of pairs with these roles reversed.

We have become so attached to this self variable that we are prescribing its use in most studies that are processed through our laboratory. For example, in an operant verbal conditioning study, self characteristics were assessed by various scales from Schutz' FIRO-B (1958). For subjects who performed according to the expectations built into the experiment (the subjects who were conditioned), a highly significant negative correlation (rho $= -.71$) was found between conditioning scores and a characteristic of the self inferred from a series of I-statements and labeled by the experimenter "resistance to influence communications" (Kroger, 1961).

Another way of looking at this variable is in terms of involvement of the self in the role. Forced compliance to the requirements of a role whose attributes are not congruent with an individual's self-conceptions will not lead to permanent changes. Attempts to indoctrinate prisoners of war in alien ideology generally fail because of the lack of self-involvement in the role, even though the person may appear to give adequate motoric and verbal performances.

Reinforcement Properties of the Ecology

The orientation central to this paper is that we must look at the continuities in conduct, rather than at small samples of outcome behaviors. The essence of the notion of role is that the person engages in conduct that is complementary to the behavior of another, or of a group of others. The effectiveness of his role enactment, of course, will be related to his perception of occurrences in the ecology, some of which may appear as a result of his own actions. We shall not concern ourselves here with non-social aspects of the ecology—although these will have effects, such as the changes in role enactment observed when it suddenly rains.

We can push our analysis along by regarding the significant aspect of the social ecology as an audience. The audience is frequently one person (as in studies of the psychotherapeutic process or studies in operant verbal conditioning), a small group (as in some of the work done on the dynamics of the discussion or work group), or a large assemblage (as in mass meetings, the theater, and athletic contests). The audience may serve two functions: it may provide cues enabling the actor flexibly to continue the enactment of his role; and it may provide cues that are reinforcing. For example, in the mental status examination, the clinical psychologist may ask the patient: "Do you ever feel lonely?" The question is a cue that gives the patient some information regarding the expectations of the one-person audience, the examining psychologist. At the termination of the interview in which the patient reported his dreams, the psychologist might say: "You did well today." This statement has the potential for acting as a reinforcing cue and increasing the probability of dream reporting on subsequent occasions.

The situation frequently exists where the person rehearses without an audience but with the expectation that he may be asked to enact a role before an audience. The imagined presence of an audience may have effects on performance. For example, Burri (1931) found that when subjects learned pairs of words under the anticipation of recall before an audience, the time required to learn the list was longer, and eventual recall was poorer. Grace (1951) showed that the anticipation of a female audience affected the order of recall of objects, which were masculine, feminine, and neuter. Zimmerman and Bauer (1956) showed that an imagined audience characterized as holding certain attitudes that were incongruent with material to be learned and remembered influenced the retention of material. Such material was not retained as well as material that was congruent with the attitudes of the imaginary audience.

Recent work in operant verbal conditioning is pertinent to our analysis. Verplanck (1955), Lindsley (1956), and Krasner (1958), to mention a few, have shown how certain features of the social ecology can increase the frequency of words of a given response class. The features are generally located in the verbal or gestural behavior of a person acting as an experimenter. Ullman, Krasner, and Collins (1961) have demonstrated that the reinforcing effects of a one-person audience to emotionally toned words apparently generalized to the effectiveness of a role enactment calling for verbal behavior. The subjects were patients who were members of therapy groups in a VA hospital. The criterion of change was the ratings of group therapists before and after the conditioning experiment.

UTILITY OF ROLE THEORY IN PSYCHOLOGICAL RESEARCH

Having sketched some of the principal constructs of role theory, let us now return to a demonstration of their utility in psychological research. The problem of psychological change is implicit in our work. We approach persisting problems in social and clinical psychology with the basic question: "What characteristics of persons and/or situations lead to change (or lack of change) on specified dimensions? In my own work, the questions have been addressed to three types of problems. The first is in the field of social influence, in that special area traditionally identified as hypnosis and suggestibility. The second is also in the field of social influence, in the area called attitude change. The third is in the field of behavior pathology, focussed around the area of juvenile delinquency and also around problems in constructing a useful taxonomy of social psychological stressors.

In the remainder of this chapter, we shall present some selected recent and ongoing research in an effort to demonstrate the utility of the role-theoretical concepts outlined before. Although we shall talk of hypnosis, behavior pathology, and attitude manipulation, the concepts are intended to be applied generally to social psychological phenomena.

To recapitulate, before embarking on a discussion of this research: we have asserted that psychological change, no matter how specified, may be brought about through effective role enactment. This antecedent-consequent relationship is not an invariant one, however, so our efforts must be directed toward discovering the sources of variation. This discovery is aided by guideposts derived from role theory. So we turn to the question: "What are the conditions of effective role enactment?" Consider the general formula: effective role enactment $= f$ (accuracy of perception of roles of the other(s) and of role demands, a set of valid role expectations, role-relevant skills or aptitudes, and self-role congruence and reinforcement properties in the social ecology.)

Hypnosis and Suggestibility

The role enactment formula may be employed in the typical hypnosis situation. Effective role enactment is defined by the subject's performing in such a way as to lead a qualified observer to say "the subject is hypnotized." The reference behaviors are those considered a part of the role by the observer and may include such diverse elements as catalepsy, reported sensory changes, posthypnotic behavior, amnesia, and hallucinations. Since individual differences in role enactment are the rule in hypnotic experiments, we have tried to nail down the sources of variation in a number of experiments (some of which go back twenty-five years).

THE ROLE-EXPECTATION VARIABLE. It is a matter of common sense that a person cannot enact a role unless he knows what behaviors are appropriate and relevant to that role. The assessment of role expectations may be achieved through the administration of an inventory, the items of which are the behaviors and conditions of the traditional hypnotic experiment. Among college students who make up most of our experimental samples, the range of variation in role expectations is restricted. This is no doubt a function of relatively uniform exposure to mass media, to accounts in novels and textbooks, and to movies and television. In spite of this restriction, we find a significant correlation between expectations and performance on a group suggestibility task (Sarbin and Andersen, 1961). We have collected a large number of interesting clinical anecdotes which illustrate ineffective or inept role enactment where the subject has little or no conception of the role expected of him by the hypnotist.

THE ROLE-PERCEPTION VARIABLE. To perform in any interaction situation the actor must be able to specify the role of the other in order to know what reciprocal role to play. As in the perception of any object or event, the person attends to the behavior of the other and assigns him a location in his personal and social space. On the achievement of this classificatory act, the person's choice of behavior alternatives is reduced to manageable proportions. If the subject does not instantiate (classify) the other as influencer, hypnotist, healer, or something similar, then one cannot expect the subject to choose the complementary hypnotic role. It should be emphasized that the subject may penetrate subterfuges used in psychological experimentation, including hypnosis. Even though the experimenter may assiduously avoid the use of the term hypnosis, trance states, challenges, etc., and may talk about "everyday suggestion," some subjects will interpret the instructions as equivalent to the hypnotic induction and will perform a convincing "hypnotic" role enactment. The postexperimental inquiry is an important procedure in our experiments and is becoming a necessary part of any experimental design. How the subject perceives the experimenter, the accomplices, and even the physical surroundings, may have more to do with the type of role-enactment variables monitored than the independent variables presumably under control. This will be discussed more fully under role demands. Suffice it to say that the choice of one's own role in the hypnotic situation is related to the nature of one's perception of the complementary role.

ROLE DEMANDS. As was stated before, the nature of the situation may allow for a limited number of alternative role enactments. In some situations, the expectations of the other(s) may have such saliency that the person is obliged to enact a prescribed set of behaviors even though such behaviors may be alien to his self conception. In the typical two-person situation, there is a built-in set of mutual expectations based upon the norm of reciprocity. This is not unlike the "exchange of favors" system observed in some bureaucratic organizations: if you expend energy and take time in your role vis-à-vis me, then I am obliged to behave in a reciprocal way. In the typical two-person hypnosis experiment, the hypnotist spends time and presumably effort in order to bring about a particular role enactment. In keeping with the norm of reciprocity, the subject is under an obligation to reciprocate—to give the hypnotist a yield for his time and effort. Other things being equal, the subject, within the limits of his role-taking skill, will enact the prescribed role. The role demands in this instance are covert and dictated by the norm of reciprocity. When the same hypnotic instructions are used in a mass induction experiment, the proportionate number of subjects who perform the hypnotic role is less. The time and effort of the experimenter is spread among many subjects, making reciprocal behavior unnecessary. Considerations other than the norm of reciprocity are operative for those subjects who perform the enactment.

We have some data that bear on this point. From an undergraduate class who had participated in a mass experiment in suggestibility, we obtained twenty-one volunteers for the two-person experiment. They represented the entire range of suggestibility. The instructions were slightly modified in keeping with the nature of the two-person situations. In addition, each subject was told that he would be paid three dollars for his time. All the subjects who responded to the social influence in the mass experiment also responded in the two-person situation; half the subjects who failed to respond in the mass situation, however, moved up on the scale of suggestibility. That is, they were low scorers in the mass experiment, where they were relatively anonymous and where the role demands were minimal; but when they were put into the two-person situation, they performed the role of the hypnotic subject; their anonymity was removed, role demands were increased presumably in virtue of the operation of the norm of reciprocity reinforced by the financial reward.

To illustrate further the subtle nature of role demands within the context of hypnosis studies, we may direct our attention to an observation made by a number of investigators, although not clarified by systematic research. Experienced hypnotists report that if volunteers are hypnotized before a large audience, the number of subjects who enact the role satisfactorily is larger than when subjects appear one at a time in the laboratory without an audience. Operating as a role demand to perform according to the instructions of the hypnotist is another subtle norm—the prevention of embarrassment or face-saving—which may function conjointly with the norm of reciprocity. The refusal of the subject to respond favorably before a large audience has the potential of embarrassing or shaming the experimenter. If we recognize that social conduct may be conceptualized as a set of acts performed in such a manner and at such a time as to facilitate the achievement of group goals, then any embarrassment is potentially threatening to the entire group. In the two-person group, where the audience is made up of only *one* person, the degree of embarrassment is less. The data for this statement is derived from postexperimental inquiries conducted by persons not associated with the hypnotist.

Related to the norm of reciprocity and the norm of face-saving is another subtle condition that creates a demand for the subject to perform the role. This is the norm of commitment. Social life, as we all know, becomes more predictable and less risky when persons enter into contractual arrangements one with the other and these contractual arrangements are honored. In subtle and informal ways, people enter into social arrangements they cannot repudiate without the threat of negative sanctions being imposed upon them. Commitment to a role is seen in everyday life where, let us say, I accept in 1960 an invitation to appear at a University of Texas symposium. Even though other responsibilities and obligations interfere, one cannot repudiate the implied contract. I am committed to the role of symposiast.

The degree of participation in the role of the hypnotic subject in public settings can be readily understood with the aid of the notion of role commitment. A volunteer may stand before the audience "for kicks," to impress his friends, to demonstrate his willpower, and so on. The skillful hypnotist will lead the subject into commitment, through asking for the performance of simple, non-threatening motoric acts. As the interaction proceeds, the tasks become more and more demanding, such as tests of analgesia and age regression. After performing the simple non-threatening tasks, the subject becomes committed to performing all the rest even though he may be asked to act like a fool. Incidentally, the more he acts like a fool, the more certain one can be of amnesia for the event—amnesia in this case being equivalent to response suppression.

So much for role demands in the hypnotic setting. From our analysis of role demands in this special influence situation, we have learned some important lessons for the analysis of other types of experiments (to be discussed below).

ROLE-TAKING APTITUDE OR SKILL. Certain role enactments require more than the bare minimum demanded for ordinary social intercourse. For example, the dramatic actor must have a high degree of this aptitude in order to shift rapidly from role to role as demanded by his assignments. Because hypnosis is a matter of role taking in which motoric and gestural behavior plays a large part, we would expect persons who perform well in the hypnotic role also to perform well in other contrived roles. An experiment conducted in our laboratory gives considerable support to the statement that good hypnotic role takers would perform improvisations effectively. Student volunteers were given a standard hypnotic induction in the two-person situation. They were scored on effectiveness of role enactment by using the Friedlander-Sarbin (1938) scale of hypnotic performance. Later, these same students individually were sent to the Dramatic Arts department where they performed pantomime improvisations before several dramatics instructors who rated their performances. The rank-order correlation between ratings on the two performances was .52 (Sarbin and Lim, 1963).

Many of the dramatic features of hypnotic performances can be readily understood, if we invoke the concept of role-specific skills. Such phenomena as hypnotic analgesia, hallucinatory behavior, and control of certain physiological processes are usually attributed to the effects of a postulated trance state—a state that is in some mysterious way discontinuous from the normal waking state.

The position of role theory in regard to hypnotic behavior provides a skeptical view about the necessity of a special state or trance to bring about certain effects. The viewpoint of a required special state contains the silent assumption that these special phenomena, for example, analgesia, have base rates approximating zero. Save for statements by the present author (1943, 1950), and more recently by Orne (1959), Sutcliffe (1960, 1961) and Barber (1961), the assumption has hardly been questioned. We can see the operation of this silent assumption (zero base rate) in a study recently reported by Harold Underwood (1960). In this study, certain atypical behaviors were attributed to the effects of the so-called trance state. Through an extensive selection procedure, Underwood sought subjects who could meet certain rigorous criteria for producing consistent "deep" hypnotic behavior. Only six persons out of 196 tested met these criteria. Included in the criteria was the requirement of being able reliably to produce vivid hallucinations. The experimental task set for his selected subjects was to hallucinate the presence of a non-existent field in a figure-ground illusion. Underwood proposed that if the non-existent field were effectively hallucinated, a superimposed figure would be distorted as in the actual figure-ground illusion. As is usually the case in two-person hypnosis studies, Underwood's subjects were faced with strong role demands to hallucinate the missing background in the figure-ground illusion. The control subjects, on the other hand, were merely told to *guess* how the figure would look if the field were actually present. Five of the six subjects identified as "deeply hypnotized," under instructions to hallucinate the ground, were actually able to report a distorted figure.

We raised the question: "Could the hallucinatory effects be attributed to events other than the so-called hypnotic state?" Our reasoning was as follows. Since the hypnotized 3 per cent of Underwood's subjects could hallucinate the ground in the figure-ground illusion, could this be one of those phenomena where base rates are low but reliably greater than zero? Or, to put it another way, were these five subjects particularly skillful in the role-specific performance requested by the experimenter?

We proceeded to test the base rate of this phenomenon without the use of any induction procedures. A total of 120 subjects in three different groups was used. All were given detailed and careful instruction to arouse, enhance, and support the free use of imagination. That is to say, the subjects were encouraged to imagine the presence of the non-existent field. Eleven of our subjects (or 9 per cent) were able to demonstrate this skill. Thus, we concluded that the hallucinatory behavior found by Underwood was not necessarily due to hypnosis per se but to the careful preselection of subjects on the ability to utilize visual imagery. (The answer to the query: "Why did we get nine per cent and Underwood only 3 per cent?" is probably in the fact that Underwood had multiple criteria for inclusion in the "deeply hypnotized" group. With several independent criteria, of course, the probability of any one subject being included in the criterion group is diminished.) (Sarbin and Andersen, 1963.)

The implications of this study for research on psychological change is that the experimenter must be certain that the criterion measure reflects the operation of his experimental treatments and not merely the activating of unmeasured pre-experimental skills or traits.

CONGRUENCE OF SELF AND ROLE. This brings us to the report of a large scale study which we have had under way at Berkeley for the past two years. Earlier we pointed out that the concept of the self is required in order to account for many individual differences in role enactments. The utility of this construct for hypnosis studies has been asserted in previous papers (Sarbin, 1943; 1950; 1952; 1954). However, attempts to find a consistent picture of self-characteristics that are congruent with the role of the hypnotic subject have not been too fruitful. In 1941, R. W. White found small but significant correlations between valid hypnotic role enactment and need autonomy (negative) and need deference.

Earlier work attempted to use assessment procedures that had not been devised for the prediction of the specific role enactments of hypnosis. The use of such instruments as the Bernreuter Personality Inventory, MMPI, California Psychological Inventory, and the Rorschach test have sometimes yielded correlations with such scales as Hy (MMPI), Dominance (CPI), W/D ratio (Rorschach). Replications generally have not confirmed these findings.

In a study soon to be reported, we approached the problem of assessing self-characteristics through a preliminary logical analysis of the behavioral requirements of the person enacting the typical role of the hypnotic subject. In this analysis we came up with the following set of categories:

(*a*) ability to become engaged or involved in the role as shown through absorption, concentration, and so on;

(*b*) attachment to the role as shown in readiness to accept altered attentional and mood experiences which are concomitants of intense role involvement.

We constructed for the special purpose a questionnaire which contained one hundred and seventeen items especially written to tap these dispositions and administered it to two large classes. In addition, we employed a questionnaire that dealt specifically with attitudes toward hypnosis, and several other measures designed to tap intrapersonal characteristics which appeared congruent with the hypnotic role.

Before giving the details of the experiment, let me digress for a moment to point out that the role behaviors that made up our dependent variable were derived from settings that might be called mass suggestion or mass persuasion. In this series of studies the subjects were treated en masse, and the assessment of performance was accomplished through self-ratings on specially prepared answer sheets. We have data that demonstrate in what ways this situation and the two-person situation are not the same and what ways they have some elements in common.

In one study, we used eight of the twelve tests for assessing depth of hypnosis that make up the Stanford Hypnotic Susceptibility Scale (developed by Weitzenhoffer and Hilgard, 1959). We compared frequency distributions of the Stanford sample with our own. The Stanford sample showed the effect of standard two-person hypnotic situations (with the experimenter assessing the quality of the role enactment), the Berkeley sample, the effect of suggestibility tasks given in the classroom to scores of students (with the subject making his own assessment of the quality of his role enactment). The graph shows the relationship between the two frequency distributions. Both samples show the relative ease with which hand lowering can be elicited, and the greater difficulty in eliciting arm immobilization (Figure 1).

To return to the experiment. Early in the Spring semester 1960, the various questionnaires were administered to ninety-three subjects as part of an ongoing study on student attitudes. Late in the semester, the instructor announced an exercise in suggestion and then distributed especially prepared rating scales for the self-report of responsiveness to the suggestions. There were ten criterion tasks, including such items as taste hallucination, hand lowering, eye closure, arm rigidity, and a rating of overall responsiveness. With some minor modifications, the study was repeated in the Spring semes-

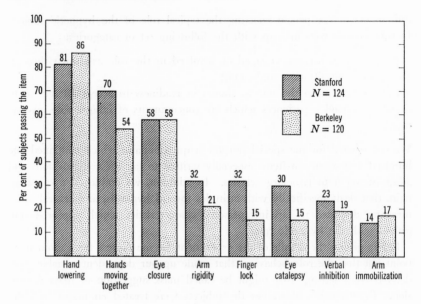

Figure 1

ter 1961 with a somewhat larger sample. The distributions of the criterion items were similar for the two samples.

Remember we were interested in discovering dispositional characteristics (aspects of the self) with which the role of the hypnotic subject would be congruent. From our initial pool of one hundred and seventeen items, twenty-three discriminated between persons high and low on role enactment. A logical clustering of these items allowed us to compose five clusters. The first two are related to degree of role involvement or role engagement and its concomitants, the third to the degree of attachment to or liking for the role. The highly responsive subject describes himself as (1) able to concentrate and become absorbed in appropriate tasks and activities, (2) ready to accept mood changes and altered states of consciousness, (3) enjoying new experiences, fantasy, and as-if behavior, (4) interested in hypnosis and cognate phenomena, and (5) unconcerned about responsibilities and social reinforcements and non-reinforcements.

Illustrative of the items in the first cluster are the following:

"I sometimes become absorbed in a task so that I am forgetful of other less important aspects of the daily routine." (True)

"I can study a subject rather well even when I'm tired." (True)

Illustrative of the items on the second cluster are the following:

"I would hesitate to take drugs that produce mood changes out of the ordinary." (False)

"I would be afraid of anything that would temporarily change my awareness of my surroundings." (False)

It is noteworthy that our two most significant clusters, (1) and (2), which may be described as *role absorption* and *acceptance of altered processes deriving from intense role involvement* are very similar to two dispositions isolated by Åas (1962) of the Stanford group. In the latter work, the criteria were assessed by experimenters in the two-person hypnotic situation. Space limitations here prevent reporting more of the findings of this study. Suffice it to say only that we found high correlations between certain items on the attitude inventory dealing exclusively with hypnosis as an object of evaluative judgment. Furthermore, on several different measures, we found a lack of concern for extrinsic social rewards as a correlate of effective role enactment of the hypnotic subject; rather, the responsive subject seemed more concerned with the intrinsic reward of the experience for its own sake.

We have just completed a study that taps dispositional characteristics in a way which probably has not been tried before. Consider the typical induction instructions for the two-person hypnotic situation. It is made up of a number of sentences that tell the subject what is expected of him, and it is usually recited slowly, monotonously, with emphasis on relaxation, concentration, etc. When the same induction is given to a number of subjects, some respond with relevant role enactments, others with no enactment. Other conditions being equal, then, we would expect that the uniform induction would be interpreted differently by responsive and unresponsive subjects. The differential interpretation would follow from different dispositional characteristics, self conceptions, and the like.

Early in the Spring semester, 1960, the Friedlander-Sarbin standard hypnotic induction was taped. This induction was comprised of 37 sentences. The tape was presented to an undergraduate class in psychology along with 37 answer sheets on each of which were the ten semantic differential scales listed herewith:

voluntary—compulsory
conflicting—harmonious
soothing—interesting
elevated—depressed
skeptical—believing
uninfluential—influential
feeble—vigorous
spacious—constricted
relaxed—tense
improbable—probable

The subjects rated each sentence on the ten scales during a twenty-second pause between sentences. Correlations between these scale values and self-rated performances on group suggestibility tasks administered two months later were computed. The first 10 sentences of the induction recital are in the nature of general instructions and reassurances and are not contained in this analysis. An analysis of the correlation between the criterion of role enactment and the ratings of the remaining 27 sentences (which comprise the induction proper) shows the following. (The end of the scale checked by the "good subjects" is given first.)

Probable-Improbable	21 sentences correlated significantly with criterion
Depressed-Elevated	20 sentences *
Influential-Uninfluential	18 sentences
Harmonious-Conflicting	15 sentences
Constricted-Spacious	11 sentences
Believing-Skeptical	10 sentences
Voluntary-Compulsory	8 sentences

* The opposite of depressed on this scale is elevated, not elated. The many references in the patter to heavy eyelids, eyelids pushing down, down, down, probably influenced this correlation.

In brief, the meanings attributed to the hypnosis induction recital by persons who effectively enact the prescribed role are different from the meanings attributed by persons unable or unwilling to enact the same role. Inasmuch as the objective stimulus situation is the same for all subjects, we may entertain the inference that the source of variation in the attribution of meanings to the influence communication is in the set of cognitive dispositions called the self. The congruence of such dispositions with the demands of the role is apparent. The readiness to interpret the sentences as probable, influential, harmonious, and so on, contributes to taking a role—the component acts of which depend upon assigning a high probability to sentences uttered by the experimenter, to interpreting communications emanating from the experimenter as influential, to seeing harmony rather than conflict in the ambiguous communication, etc.

Reinforcement Properties of the Social Ecology

So far we have tried to show that variation in role enactment in the context of a particular social influence situation can be accounted for by variations in the accuracy of role perception, in role expectations held by the subject, in the nature of implicit and explicit role demands, in role-specific skills, and in the congruence of dispositions with role demands. Now we turn briefly to the influence of variations in reinforcement properties of the social ecology.

Too often we are content with demonstrating the relationship between antecedent variables and a consequent variable monitored over a short period of time. The employment of an attitude scale is a case in point. We manipulate various influence variables, then assess the attitude during a brief interval. Such a procedure gives us little information on the lability of the subject's cognitive or motoric behavior. Where we wittingly let role enactment serve as the independent variable in the study of psychological change, we have the opportunity of observing changes in role enactment as the ecology changes. The usual hypnotic performance occurs over a thirty- to sixty-minute time interval. During this period, the experimenter may introduce changes in the interaction situation, through redefining the situation. Fisher (1954) demonstrated, for example, that the acceptance and enactment of the hypnotic role shifted with the presence or absence of a contrived set of cues designed to alter the subject's role perceptions. In an unpublished study, I have shown how changing the label of the experimenter from professor to student resulted in a change in role enactment in the direction of less involvement. Dorcus et al. (1941) demonstrated the changes in role enactment when the ecological setting was changed through the sudden departure of the experimenter. The subjects discontinued their enactment of the so-called trance.

We have already indicated the importance of the audience in creating role demands through providing discriminable cues. The audience has another function—a reinforcement function. As the person enacts a role to validate his status, the occupants of complementary statuses are also performing. To the extent that the audience provides feedback through indications of acceptance, approval, attention, reward, etc., for relevant and appropriate enactments, the role-enactment will continue. To the extent that the audience indicates disapproval, disappointment, inattention, etc., the actor will modify his performances (within the limits set by other parameters). In the two-person hypnotic situation, the hypnotist generally indicates through word or gesture his satisfaction or dissatisfaction with the way things are going. This variable—the reinforcement function of the audience—is usually neglected where hypnosis is used as an avenue for the study of cognitive processes (Blum, 1961; Rosenberg, 1960). When the hypnotic role enactment is rewarded through positive reinforcements, the possibility exists for the subject to generalize to special roles within the hypnotist-subject interaction. (The much publicized Bridey Murphy was a case in point.)

So much for the application of role concepts to the study of hypnosis, one kind of social influence phenomenon. Admittedly, the conceptualization is not complete. We recognize that the variables we have described are not necessarily independent one from the other. The task facing us now in social influence research is the more detailed specification of the variables and their interactions.

Attitude Change

We will next investigate a second type of influence process—how the enactment of a role which is incongruent with one's dispositional structure influences attitudes. We have already alluded to the work of Janis and King (1954), Scott (1951) and others, where a situation is created in which the subject must publicly take a stand on an issue contrary to his privately expressed beliefs. Under some conditions, such enactment produces a change in attitude in the direction of the publicly endorsed position. A number of investigators are concerned with the mechanism through which such change is effected. Janis and King, for example, relate such changes to the amount of improvisation; Festinger, to the reduction of dissonance; Scott, to reinforcement.

We have approached this as a problem in social influence through role enactment and are attempting to study it with the aid of role concepts. Sarbin and Allen (1961) set up an experiment similar to that of Scott where subjects are asked to debate a position contrary to their privately held views. Although the role enactments are typically completed in five or ten minutes, there is still ample opportunity for the debater to respond to cues in the ecology, specifically, reinforcement cues emitted by the audience. In our study, we manipulated the ecology by arranging for the audience to provide positive reinforcements or negative reinforcements during the presentation of the arguments. The audience was made up of 10 students who were trained to provide positive reinforcements during the debating period by showing attention, by nodding approval, by making notes, and so on, and to provide negative reinforcements by appearing uninterested, by yawning, by looking out of the window, and so on.

From our point of view, type of audience feedback by itself is not sufficient to account for attitude change. The self characteristics of the subjects must be taken into account. We posit need reinforcement as a dimension of the self. That is, the need or preference for positive social reinforcement may be construed as a variable. Those subjects who lie at the high end of this dimension will be influenced differently by audience feedback from subjects who lie at the low end of the dimension. Although we could not find a ready made assessment device labeled need reinforcement, we were able to approximate the construct by combining two of Schutz's FIRO-B scales "wanted inclusion" and "wanted affection." These scales measure preferences for being with people and for being close and personal with people, respectively. We also obtained a rough estimate of one of the role demands generated in the experiment, degree of commitment. It is assumed that commitment in a public context creates some demand which leads to various kinds of motoric or cognitive shifts, including attitude change. The degree of commitment was inferred from a postexperimental inquiry which dealt with amount of involvement, improvisation, enthusiasm, vigor, etc.

We used two types of controls: (1) subjects who filled out the test instrument twice, and (2) subjects who received the same instructions as the debaters but who were excused from actually debating.

The differences between control groups and experimental groups were significant. That is, the mean change in the direction of the position assigned in the debate was a significant one. What of the effects of differential need reinforcement? The attitudes of those scoring high on the FIRO-B scales change more, on the average, than those scoring low. What of the effects of different reinforcing properties of the audience—of differential reinforcement? Subjects receiving negative reinforcement changed *more* than those receiving positive reinforcement. This may appear contrary to common sense but we have some additional information that makes this finding more plausible. The postexperimental inquiry revealed that the role demands for those exposed to negative reinforcements produced greater involvement, improvisation, vigor, and enthusiasm. It was as if the subjects, in order to fulfill their roles as debaters, put more effort into convincing an audience that was "sitting on its hands." The role demands remained relatively constant during the debating period for subjects in the positive reinforcement group. (Parenthetically, we have just designed a study to assess directly the degree of involvement during successive phases of role enactment under different reinforcement conditions.)

As is usually the case, the experiment raises more questions than it answers. However, it does show the utility of studying the interaction of reinforcement properties of the audience and self-role congruencies in the social influence situation.

In the same context, I would like briefly to offer an interpretation of a widely cited study on attitude change. Festinger and Carlsmith (1959) reported a study within the context of dissonance theory. Subjects were given a series of repetitive manual tasks, and it was assumed that this would lead all subjects to hold the belief that the task was dull and monotonous. At the conclusion of this experiment each subject was led to believe that a research assistant who was to conduct another phase of the experiment was unable to appear, and the subject for the next experiment (an accomplice) was waiting. The first subjects were asked to serve as assistants and help out the experimenter. Half of the first subjects were offered $1 for this service, the other half were offered $20. The task for the subject was to tell the next subject that the experiment she was about to do was interesting, exciting, inspiring, etc. This latter statement, of course, was incompatible with the assumed belief about the dull and monotonous nature of the tasks. Festinger predicted that subjects in the $20 group would show no shift in attitude about explaining the dull and uninteresting task as exciting, but that subjects in the $1 group would reveal a shift in attitude in the direction of remembering and describing the tasks as not so dull and uninteresting. The postexperimental inquiry was done in another context and provided data for inferences about attitude change. The predictions were confirmed. The explanation, somewhat oversimplified here, is that the subject in the high-reward group does not experience dissonance because the $20 is the reward for selling out. The high reward is not incompatible with the ongoing events. Since there is no dissonance, then there will be no attitude change. The subject in the low-reward group experiences tension because of the public expression of a statement which he did not believe; therefore, he changes his beliefs so he would not be saying something contrary to his beliefs.

If we interpolate between the $1 and $20, dissonance theory would predict something like a straight line representing the relationship between attitude change and amount of payment. In fact, we might say the $10 would produce an effect somewhere between the effects of $1 and $20, and, extrapolating, fifty cents would produce more change than $1.

Role theory would not make the same predictions as dissonance theory. Role theory would say that in the $1 condition, subjects were being asked to perform a role for which $1 was an appropriate payment, this would be at the rate of about $2 an hour—the going rate for student assistants. To the degree that the subjects become attached and committed to the role of research assistant, to that degree would we expect postexperimental statements about psychological experiments to be consistent with the second cognition—that *the tasks were interesting.* The offer of $20 for a half-hour's work places different role demands on the student subject. The payment of so much money can lead the subject to engage in a set of private cogitations about the money, wondering, for example, whether he would be allowed to keep it, etc. Because so much attention is deployed to these cogitations, less attention could be given to the task at hand so that the subject could not become committed to the role of research assistant. My prediction for the two payment conditions would be the same as Festinger's, but I would not predict a continuous relationship between amount of reward and attitude change. My prediction would show a discontinuity. If the amount of payment offered is perceived as being appropriate to the role of student assistant—say a range of $1 to $2.50 for a half hour's work—then, other conditions being equal, I would expect change in the direction of the second communication. When the amount of payment exceeds that which is appropriate for the position of student assistant, then the subject's role perception is characterized by uncertainty, lack of clarity, and doubt, and his performance would lack conviction and involvement.

We have planned a study along these lines in which a range of rewards are offered. As a preliminary we tested, in an informal fashion, the notion that subjects' attention would be deployed in attempts at justifying the payment of $20. We wrote out a one page description of the Festinger-Carlsmith experiment prefaced by the following statement: "Suppose you are a volunteer in a psychology experiment and. . . ." Then the steps in the experiment were described in detail, for example, "You spent a half hour turning blocks, etc., and then you were asked by the experimenter to serve as student assistant, etc., and were offered $1.00 ($20.00) for your services, what thoughts would occur to you?" We used two sections of our elementary psychology course, in one section the instruction sheets had the $1 offer, in the other, the $20 offer.

Of course, we did not expect to replicate Festinger's findings in this exercise. The report of as-if behavior allows the student freedom to cogitate about all kinds of events, which he cannot do under the demands of making a decision to accept the offer and to follow through. However, one fact stands out. The subjects in the $20 group had doubts about the genuineness of the experiment but were *more concerned about the money and why it was offered*. The subjects in the $1 group had plenty of doubts about the experiment, too, but the doubts were *not focused* on money. Until we complete the experiment, our speculation that differential role demands are central to the outcome can be considered as a possible alternate to Festinger's interpretation.

Behavior Pathology

I would like to turn now from the application of role theory to problems of social psychology to problems in behavior pathology. Very briefly, let me outline two projects where we have found the role theoretical formulations exceedingly useful. The first is the development of a new model of behavior pathology which is fully described elsewhere by the author (Sarbin, 1964), and the second is an attempt to account for the etiology of certain forms of juvenile delinquency (Baker and Sarbin, 1955; Jones, Livson, and Sarbin, 1955; Sarbin, 1955; Sarbin and Jones, 1955).

The behavior pathology model has three major components: (*a*) stressors, the antecedents of pathological behavior patterns, in part formulated in terms of role demands which exceed the capacities of the person; (*b*) arousal, the intervening process, seen as cognitive strain and physiological perturbations; and (*c*) adaptation, interpreted in terms of role enactments designed to validate the occupancy of irregular, autistic, unconventional statuses, or statuses with minimal obligations.[3]

We shall focus here on the adaptational phase. Consider a person subject to severe and prolonged stressors which produce discomfort and strain. His search for relief may be a blind (but not random) trial and error process (Campbell, 1960), in which he explores various role enactments until he finds a role for which he has or can develop role-specific skills. As an illustration, let us take the typical state-hospital patient diagnosed as schizophrenic. From the reading of numerous case histories and talking to patients and members of their families it is possible to reconstruct a picture which, broadly conceived, looks something like this. The stressors are probably in the area of incompatible role demands which produce strain and discomfort. Furthermore, since the source is in the immediate family setting, the stressors are omnipresent (Bateson et al., 1956). The typical patient has tried a number of role enactments in order to meet the demands imposed upon him but without achieving relief. In the course of his trials, he has hit upon withdrawal as a technique for reducing the amount of social participation, and concomitantly, for reducing the demands for the enactment of ascribed roles. For these roles he has not acquired relevant expectations, or the general and specific skills, or the appropriate self characteristics. Withdrawal, usually described as one of a catalog of defense or escape mechanisms, is a redeployment of attention. The patient focuses on socially irrelevant objects or events or on his fantasies instead of on the relevant behavior of others. The result of this shift in attention deployment is, of course, defective role perception leading to role enactments regarded as invalid by members of the society.

The next step in the development of the invalid social role is in the demands made upon members of the family. Because the patient engages in conduct which is embarrassing to the family group, he must be removed.

---

[3] The full treatment of the behavior pathology model makes use of seven components: (*a*) the social ecology, (*b*) inputs, (*c*) belief-value systems, (*d*) instantiation on threat dimension, (*e*) arousal, (*f*) adaptive techniques designed to reduce arousal, and (*g*) distal effects on persons in the social ecology who can give or withhold reinforcements.

For certain historical reasons which are not difficult to document, persons regarded as disturbed, deranged, crazy, or mentally ill infect the family with a burden of shame. The family's search for a solution which will reduce the component of shame is rewarded in western societies by the discovery and utilization of a ready made status: *the sick person.* Through the assimilation of the concept of illness to disordered behavior, the sick role includes not only persons suffering from tuberculosis, hardening of the arteries, and sprained wrists, but also persons unable successfully to enact ascribed social roles.[4] The sick role has minimal social obligations, so the non-enactment of standard social roles is excused.

However, the sick role of the mental patient is not identical with the sick role of the surgical patient. The surgical patient and the physician may enact complementary roles focused on the physiological antecedents for a temporary stay in the hospital. To validate his occupancy of the role of a sick person, the mental patient is supposed to exhibit symptoms that fulfill the expectations of the person engaged in enacting the complementary role, the physician or his surrogate. In the enactment of his role, the physician communicates to the patient that he is expected to perform in certain ways, to show deference, to be cooperative, to accept without a show of affect the invasion of his privacy and the withdrawal of his civil rights, to describe his mental life, to report delusions and hallucinations, and so on. Because of the absence of physical symptoms that have a degree of reality, the mental patient's role is less clear than the surgical patient's. To validate his status as a sick person, then, he must acquire performances to meet the role expectations of the others in the social organization. In the typical state mental hospital, where medically oriented practitioners regard patients as occupying the status of sick people, demands are created for the patients to enact the sick role. When a patient does not accept the sick role, all the forces of the hospital are directed toward shaping his behavior so that he does. If he objects vigorously, say, to having his matches taken away, the patient may be sent to a punitive ward in order to "cool off." Through selective rewards and punishments, the patient acquires the components of the "sick role" in the mental hospital. For example, one patient told me,

[4] Elsewhere I have argued that persons labeled deviants in any culture are those who do not perform, within the limits of tolerance, *ascribed* social roles. These are sex roles, age roles, kinship roles, and a set of cultural roles which are incorporated into all conventional social roles: the latter may be described as propriety roles and include (*a*) patterned behaviors to control in-group aggression, (*b*) complementariness in behavior (communication norms), and (*c*) modesty norms. The failure to perform *achieved* or *assigned* roles may be regarded as "failure" and is met with disappointment but not with the intense affect with which members of a collectivity regard the violation or non-enactment of ascribed roles.

The doctors never paid much attention to me until I began talking to myself in the corner of the room. They asked me if I heard voices and I said yes I heard voices, I heard *their* voices. Then Dr. X asked me if I heard voices when there were no people around. I said sure, I could hear voices when people weren't around. I was thinking of voices on the radio but I didn't tell him that. After that, Dr. X would come in and talk to me every day and write down what the voices told me. He seemed disappointed on days when I didn't have anything to tell him.

I do not want to extend the argument and assert that schizophrenia is an iatrogenic disorder, rather my purpose is to emphasize that the social structure of the mental hospital contributes to the final shaping of the product after the initial shaping in the family and community structures. The same paradigm may be applied to any of the standard nosological categories, hypochondriasis, hysteria, neurasthenia, and so on. The choice and style of symptom complex are functions of the reinforcements provided by an audience or by reinforcements which are anxiety-neutralizing, or both.

In this connection, the concepts of primary and secondary gain require some re-examination. The usual formulation holds that the performances that are successful in reducing anxiety are *primary* and tend to fix the successful act; sympathy and attention from other persons are *secondary* gains, that is, these responses are provided by others *after* the pathological response pattern has become fixed and are in keeping with standard role performances vis-à-vis sick people. It can be demonstrated that the sympathy and attention provided by others can be reinforcing and, as a consequence, serve as the agency of anxiety neutralization.

This sample of my views on behavior pathology must suffice. Much more needs to be said to convince those who endorse the view that behavior disorders are parallel to physiological disorders. As we move away from the conception of behavior pathology as disease and approach it from the point of view of learning in a social setting, we shall find more and more use for role theoretical concepts and their derivatives.

About ten years ago, prompted by some hypotheses suggested by role theory, we began a series of studies in an attempt to learn something about a group of persons who consistently perform invalid role enactments—juvenile delinquents. We were not interested in the casual offender, nor in the offender who was frankly feebleminded or psychotic, but in the run-of-the-mill delinquent who begins an antisocial career early in his teens, and despite (or because of) attempts by social and penal agencies to rehabilitate him, perseveres in unlawful conduct.

The role enactment of the delinquent may be regarded as invalid in that he fails to pay heed to certain implicit role demands—those cultural norms that have been codified as laws. We have carried out a number of experiments to try to tie down the sources of these persistently invalid role enactments. A sample of the results is herewith presented.

ROLE PERCEPTION. The delinquent's role perception is faulty. Although perception of the non-social ecology is not deficient, his classifications of persons suffer from a failure to notice or respond to cues that have to do with intentions, attitudes, feelings, and other covert or semicovert behaviors. As pointed out before, the severity of delinquency is related to the inability to use the conformant response on the stick figures (Sarbin and Jones, 1958). Delinquents are inferior to normals on the Street-Gestalt test (made up of incomplete or fractured figures), the differences being due to stimuli that are classified as human (Jones, Livson, and Sarbin, 1954).

The readiness to perceive human, rather than non-human, characteristics in ambiguous situations may play a part in the development of sympathy, empathy, taking the role of another, and similar interactional processes. Barron (1955) has argued that the human movement concept of the Rorschach test may tap this fundamental dimension. He developed the "M" threshold test, a set of twenty-six achromatic inkblots, arranged in order of difficulty of eliciting human movement responses. The blots are shown one at a time to the subject who gives one response to each. The test gives two scores, a latency score and total number of human movement responses. Using this procedure on delinquents and non-delinquents, we found that delinquents have longer latencies, i.e., do not see human movements as quickly as the controls, and offer fewer responses of this type.

CONGRUENCE OF SELF AND ROLE. Most of our work has been addressed to the problem of assessing the self of the typical delinquent. In short, we ask, what are the dispositional characteristics that predispose him to enact behaviors that are judged as ineffective, improper, and invalid?

The self characteristics of the delinquent may be inferred from his responses to I-statements. Gough has shown how his CPI scale, socialization, differentiates delinquents and other persons characterized as antisocial from normals. We have used a modification of this scale in our own research and have found that it is the best single instrument for discriminating delinquents from controls. The inference to be drawn from the use of the scale is that the delinquents are undersocialized—that is, they see themselves enacting roles more fitting to the normative demands for younger children. At present, we can only speculate about the origin of this failure of socialization. We see it as a failure to assimilate generalized social reinforcers.

Congruence of self and role may be perceived in terms of accuracy of perception of the external world in the light of one's own skills, traits, etc. To assess the accuracy of self-perception in a test situation we used a level of aspiration procedure. This involved a pretraining period to a criterion for each subject to throw darts at one of a set of different-sized targets. Following the pretraining period, which was designed to equate subjects on the number of successes obtained, ten test trials were run, with the subject free to choose any target from the test at each trial. The targets ranged from very small ones (about the size of a quarter) with high point values, to large targets with small point values; the subject's task was to make as high a score as possible on the series of ten trials. The disparity between aspiration and achievement over all ten trials is taken as a measure of reality orientation. The delinquent group showed a substantially greater disparity ($p = .01$) between aspiration and achievement. One way of interpreting the results is that the delinquents were less accurate in assessing "reality."

ROLE DEMANDS. The Bender Gestalt test was administered to our delinquent and control groups. This is a copying test which calls for the continual assessment and checking of one's behavior. The delinquents were deficient in this task. Their protocols are characterized by carelessness and the absence of checking. Another procedure that differentiates between delinquents and non-delinquents is one which, at first, was difficult to rationalize. This is the tapping subtest of the McQuarrie Mechanical Ability test. All that is required of the subject is to tap three times in each of a series of circles. He is encouraged to go fast and not to be concerned about accuracy. In three different experiments, the delinquents were inferior to normals, that is, they were slower. This test has no correlation with general intelligence. It is so simple that it cannot be considered a test of skill. To solve the puzzle created by this finding, we suggest the following. What are the role-demands that serve to bring about fast performance? In the non-delinquent, it is the norm of cooperativeness with its implied reward in the form of social reinforcement. That is, the examiner asks the subject to do something, and when he has completed the task, there is an implicit or explicit "thank you." We argue that the poorer performance in the delinquent groups follows from the fact that they have not assimilated the norm—they have not acquired the characteristic readiness to respond merely for *social* reinforcements. The same speculation holds for the poorer performance on the Bender Gestalt copying test.

A test of this formulation is now being carried out. The hypothesis is this: that delinquents will be less responsive to reinforcement cues from the personal or social ecology. We have some preliminary data to show that undersocialized delinquents do, in fact, show less verbal learning than normals in an operant verbal conditioning situation.

The preceding pages record some ideas that stem from the application of a model of psychology that is borrowed from the drama and from everyday life. I am not under any illusion that this theory is the only road to the truth. The demands that I make on theory are modest ones—that the theory tell me where to look for facts. The test of a theory is its utility; if role theory is useful in pointing to the possible sources of variation in behavior and in organizing facts, then it serves its purpose.

I prefaced this chapter with a four-way classification of the criteria used in studying psychological change. Effective role enactment, I submitted, can induce psychological change—no matter how monitored. Since role enactment is not always effective, the way to study psychological change is to study the sources of variation in role enactment. I presented six constructs and offered some specifications for their assessment—they all contribute to the validity of role enactment. These constructs are listed as if they are independent. They are probably not. Further work will show which of these variables, if any, are the master ones, and which are subsidiary.

The test of the utility of a theory, as I just suggested, is its power for generating testable hypotheses. The third part of this paper illustrated some of the research that is being done within the framework of role theory. The knotty problems of influence communication, some of which have been identified with hypnosis and suggestion, are becoming disentangled through research stemming from role theory. Similarly, some of the problems of social influence as they affect attitudes are illuminated by role concepts. Perhaps most important, through role theory, we can reconstruct the psychology of behavior pathology without depending on outworn demonological concepts.

chapter seven

Dissonance Reduction
and Moral Values

Leon Festinger and Jonathan L. Freedman

One of the more important areas with which psychologists concern themselves is that dealing with the process of acculturation. A human being is born and grows up in a specific social and cultural milieu, and somehow in the course of the person's life he acquires certain behavior patterns, and he accepts and internalizes certain cultural and moral values. Our understanding of, and knowledge about, this process is relatively limited. The theories concerning it come mainly from simple extensions of reward theories of learning or from complicated extensions of psychoanalytic theory. The extent to which these theories, singly or in combination, are adequate to explain the processes of acculturation has never been adequately tested empirically. Our own opinion is that there are obvious germs of truth in these theories, but that they certainly do not represent the whole truth.

It will be the purpose of this chapter to propose a rather specific theoretical mechanism by means of which values become internalized. We will support the theory with some experimental evidence. Before beginning, however, it should be made completely clear that we are not proposing *the* theoretical explanation for internalization of values. We are going to explicate one process which we believe does occur. There are undoubtedly others which also occur.

COGNITIVE DISSONANCE

Since this discussion will be based primarily on the theory of cognitive dissonance (Festinger, 1957), let us present a brief outline of this theory before dealing with its application to the problem at hand. The central proposition of the theory is that when a person holds two cognitions that are psychologically inconsistent with each other, dissonance is produced; that the existence of this dissonance is uncomfortable, and that the person experiencing it will try to reduce the dissonance and achieve consonance. In other words, the presence of dissonance serves as a motivating force in much the same way as do other drive states.

To begin with, it is important to be quite clear about the definition of dissonance. The theory states that "two elements are in a dissonant relation if, considering these two alone, the obverse of one element would follow from the other." Cognitive elements are considered any knowledge, opinion or belief about the environment, about an individual or about his behavior. Thus, for example, if a person believes that all lions are yellow and sees a black lion, these two cognitions are dissonant. Or if a person knows that he is honest and also that he just stole a loaf of bread, the two elements are in a dissonant relation.

With this quite general definition, it is apparent that dissonance between two cognitions may stem from a number of different sources:

1. Dissonance could arise from logical inconsistency between two cognitions. If a person believed that man would reach the stars in three years and also believed that nothing can travel faster than the speed of light, these two cognitions are dissonant with each other. The obverse of one follows from the other on logical grounds, since even traveling at the speed of light it would take over four years to reach the nearest star. Note, however, that these cognitions would not be dissonant with each other if the person holding the two cognitions did not know how far away the stars were or did not make the logical connection among the cognitions.

2. Dissonance could arise because of cultural mores. A person at a formal dinner who uses his fingers to pick up some elusive peas on his plate should feel dissonance because the knowledge of what he is doing is dissonant with his knowledge of formal dinner etiquette. In this case the dissonance exists because the culture defines what is consonant and what is not. In some other culture these two cognitions might not be dissonant at all.

3. Dissonance may arise because a particular opinion or course of action is included, by definition, in a more general opinion. If in a given election someone who considers himself a Democrat votes for the Republican candidate, the cognitions corresponding to the knowledge of his belief and his action are dissonant with each other because "being a Democrat" includes, as part of the concept, favoring Democratic candidates.

4. Dissonance may arise because of past experience. A person who stood in the rain and somehow did not get wet would experience dissonance because he knows from experience that getting wet follows from standing in

the rain. If he had never had any experience with rain, these two cognitions would probably not be dissonant.

These various examples are probably sufficient to illustrate how the conceptual definition of dissonance, together with some specific meaning of the phrase "follow from," would be used empirically to decide whether two cognitive elements are dissonant or consonant. It is clear, of course, that in any of these situations there might exist many other elements or cognitions that are consonant with either of the two elements under consideration. Nevertheless, the relation between the two elements is dissonant if, disregarding the others, the one does not, or would not be expected to, follow from the other.

The magnitude of dissonance produced in a given situation would seem to depend upon a number of factors. If two elements are dissonant with one another, the more important the elements are to the person, the greater will be the magnitude of the dissonance produced. If a person gives ten cents to a beggar knowing full well that the beggar is not really in need, the dissonance that exists between these two cognitions is rather weak. If he gives a hundred dollars, the dissonance is much greater. If a person knows he is honest and that he just stole a grape from a fruit stand, very little dissonance will be produced. If he stole the whole fruit stand, the magnitude of dissonance will be considerably greater.

When we think about the total amount of dissonance between a given cognition and all other relevant cognitions, the *number* of consonant and dissonant elements becomes crucial. Assuming for the moment that all the elements in question are equally important, the total amount of dissonance between the given element and the rest of the person's cognitions will depend on the proportion of all relevant elements that are dissonant with the one in question. If most of the relevant cognitions are consonant with a particular element, little dissonance will be produced; while if most of them are dissonant, a great deal of dissonance will occur. Thus, taking both factors together, the magnitude of dissonance will be determined by the importance of the elements and the proportion of dissonant elements in the given context.

To return to the original proposition, it should be remembered that the existence of dissonance is thought to operate in a manner similar to other drives such as hunger or thirst. The existence of dissonance is uncomfortable. The more dissonance there is, the more uncomfortable it is. Thus, people try to reduce dissonance, and the greater the magnitude of dissonance, the greater the pressure to reduce it.

There are several quite distinct ways in which dissonance reduction may be accomplished. The person may change one of the cognitive elements. In the example given earlier, the man who saw a black lion and thought that all lions were yellow could decide that what he had seen was a leopard or that not all lions are yellow. Either of these changes would effectively reduce the dissonance.

Another mode of dissonance reduction is the addition of consonant elements. The honest man who stole the loaf of bread might find it very difficult to change either of these two cognitions, but he may be able to add the cognition that his family was starving, and therefore the theft was justified. He would presumably not feel any dissonance because even an honest man may steal something to save the lives of his family. There are, of course, numerous variations on these two major modes of dissonance reduction. The major point is that in a given situation that mode of dissonance reduction will be chosen which reduces the dissonance most effectively and is the easiest to employ. Those cognitive elements which are the least resistant to change will be the ones that are altered to reduce the dissonance.

A considerable amount of research has been done to support these central propositions and to extend them to a variety of situations. Much of the research has centered around the effects of a decision on subsequent attitudes and behavior. If a person is asked to make a choice between two alternatives, after the choice, the positive aspects of the unchosen alternative and the negative aspects of the chosen alternative are dissonant with the choice. That is, the cognition "I chose X" is dissonant with the cognition "X is bad" or "Y is good." This dissonance may be reduced by increasing the relative attractiveness of the chosen alternative by rating it more favorably and the unchosen less favorably. Thus, the theory would predict that after a decision the difference in attractiveness of two alternatives will be greater than before the decision.

Brehm (1956) conducted a study in which housewives were asked to choose between two small kitchen appliances to receive as a gift. The women first rated the attractiveness of eight appliances and were then asked to choose between two of these. After they had chosen and received the gift, they rerated all of the appliances. As predicted, in the second rating the difference between the chosen alternative and unchosen was significantly greater than before the decision had been made. An additional factor in the study was that some women were asked to choose between two items they had given quite close ratings, while others were given items they had rated far apart. Presumably, when the items are close there will be more dissonance after the decision than when they are initially already far apart. It was, therefore, predicted that the greater the dissonance (i.e., the closer the alternatives), the more relative change there would be in the ratings of the items after the choice. The results supported this prediction. Thus, the study shows that after a choice, dissonance is reduced by increasing the attractiveness of the chosen alternative and decreasing the attractiveness of the unchosen; and that the greater the dissonance, the greater is this effect.

A closely related area of research concerns the effects of so-called forced compliance. In these situations a person is induced to engage in behavior which is discrepant from an opinion he holds or which is in some way unpleasant (e.g., stating an opinion which disagrees with his actual opinion). The inducement may be in the form of a reward, social pressure, or various other reasons for performing the act. Under these conditions dissonance should be produced by the discrepancy between the knowledge that the act was performed and the knowledge that it disagrees with a personal opinion or inclination of the subject. This dissonance may be reduced by changing the private opinion to make it more consistent with the act; and several studies have demonstrated that this does, in fact, occur (Festinger and Carlsmith, 1959; Freedman, 1963).

An additional prediction from the theory is that the greater the reward or justification of any kind that the person is given for performing the act, the less opinion change will occur. The idea here is that the more reason given for committing the discrepant act, the less dissonance is produced. If a person is forced (e.g., by enormous social pressure) to say something he does not believe, there should be less dissonance than if he makes the same statement under little or no pressure. The pressure or justification serves as a consonant element in the situation. The cognitions "I said X" and "I believe not-X" are dissonant. But, the cognition "I was forced" is consonant with saying not-X when you actually believe X. Similarly a large reward serves as a consonant element. In other words, the justification gives the person a reason for acting the way he did, and thus reduces the amount of dissonance. Since the amount of opinion change is a function of the amount of dissonance, there should be less change with higher justification.

To test this prediction, Festinger and Carlsmith had subjects make a statement which was contrary to a private opinion. (As has already been described in Chapter 6, in one condition they were given twenty dollars for making the statement; in another they received only one dollar.) It was found that there was more opinion change after making the statement in the low reward condition than in the high reward condition. A related experiment by Freedman extended this finding to the situation in which two degrees of justification were produced by telling subjects that an unpleasant task was either very useful or not very useful. Subjects rated the task more enjoyable when it was described as not very useful than when it was described as very useful. These studies, together with several others, support the analysis in terms of cognitive dissonance of forced compliance situations. The basic point is that if a person is induced to perform an act he would rather not perform, maximum opinion change (in the direction of consistency with the act) will occur if the pressure to comply is just great enough to cause the person to perform the act. Any less pressure will produce less change because the person will not commit the discrepant act; any more pressure will provide additional justification and reduce the amount of dissonance produced by the performance of the discrepant act.

Let us describe just one more deduction from the theory before getting into our discussion of how all of this relates to moral values. In the study by Freedman, the person was induced to do something unpleasant under conditions of high or low justification, and he rated the task more enjoyable when there was low justification. A similar situation is one in which a person does something unpleasant for a specific reason, and the unpleasantness of the behavior is varied. Under these circumstances it would be expected that, given the opportunity to rate the quality of the justification, the more unpleasant the behavior, the higher the person would rate the reason he was given for doing it. The more unpleasant the behavior, the more dissonance is produced by the person's knowledge that he voluntarily underwent it, and the greater the justification that would be necessary to reduce that dissonance.

Aronson and Mills (1959) conducted an experiment in which college women volunteered to join a discussion group. The women were divided into three groups: severe initiation, mild initiation, and no initiation. In order to get into the group the severe initiation subjects were required to take an embarrassment test consisting of reading aloud obscene words and lurid passages from novels; the mild initiation group merely read some relatively genteel sexually oriented words; and the other group had no test to take. All subjects then listened to a tape recording of a discussion which they believed was a live discussion among the members of the group they were going to join. This discussion was purposely made extremely dull and disorganized. The subjects then rated the quality of the discussion and the group members. The severe initiation subjects rated the group more attractive than either the mild initiation or no-initiation subjects. Whereas both of the latter groups rated the discussion relatively low, the severe initiation group, which underwent the most unpleasant experience in order to join the discussion group, felt that the discussion was interesting and the group members were quite intelligent.

Thus, the theory of cognitive dissonance has been investigated in a variety of different situations, and a number of deductions from the theory have been supported. Now that the general theory has been outlined, how may it be related to the specific problem of the formation of moral values?

DISSONANCE AND MORAL VALUES

Let us narrow the scope of our inquiry somewhat and also give some specific definition to some of the concepts and terms with which we will deal. We will concern ourselves, specifically, with some of the conditions under which some kinds of moral values develop and change. We will not concern ourselves with all kinds of moral values. We will concern ourselves only with the particular moral values about those kinds of behavior that human beings frequently are inclined to engage in, and which our culture defines as bad and undesirable. For example, it would be a rare person who has never had a strong impulse to be overtly aggressive and destructive; it is highly doubtful that there has ever been a school child who, at one time or another, was not tempted to cheat; almost everyone in the course of their life has at least felt the inclination to steal something that he wanted. All of these behaviors—stealing, cheating, destructive aggression—are frowned upon and considered morally wrong in our culture.

Most of us, by the time we are adults, have internalized the cultural values about these behaviors. The only thing meant here by the word "internalized" is that we accept these values as our own. An adult who does not believe these behaviors to be morally wrong is usually a bit of a problem to our society. Someone who is able to steal, cheat, and destroy for personal gain without feeling that he is doing wrong represents a distinct failure of the acculturation process.

What, then, are some of the conditions which determine whether or not such values become internalized? We would like to answer this question in a somewhat roundabout manner. Let us first present the results of an experiment recently completed by Aronson and Carlsmith (1963) which is quite clearly relevant to the preceding discussion.

The Aronson and Carlsmith experiment was conducted with children who ranged in age from 3.8 to 4.6 years. Each child was individually brought into a large play room that contained a one-way observation mirror. On a table in the room were five rather attractive toys. After the child had an opportunity to play briefly with each of the toys, the experimenter obtained a preference order of the toys using the method of paired comparison. The experimenter then spread four of the toys around the room on the floor. That toy which had come out to be second most preferred in the preference order was left on the table. The child was then told that the experimenter had to leave for a few minutes to do an errand but would be back soon. In one condition, which we will call the No Threat condition, the experimenter told the child that it could play with any of the toys in the room until the experimenter returned. He then left taking the second-ranked toy from the table with him out of the room. In a second condition, the Severe Threat condition, the experimenter told the child it could play with any of the toys except the one on the table, namely, the one ranked second in preference. Furthermore, the threatened punishment if the child did play with the forbidden toy was rather strong. A third condition, the Mild Threat condition, was identical to the preceding one except that the threatened punishment for playing with the forbidden toy was rather weak.

The experimenter then left the room and observed the subject for ten minutes through the observation mirror. In the No Threat condition the child could not possibly play with the second ranked toy, of course, since the experimenter had taken it with him when he left the room. In the two threat conditions, none of the children violated the prohibition against playing with the second-ranked toy which was on the table. Several gave evidence of being attracted to it but none even picked it up.

After ten minutes of observation, the experimenter returned to the play room and each child was again permitted to play briefly with each of the five toys. The paired comparison procedure was then repeated to obtain another preference ranking of the toys. Thus, we may examine the effects of the three experimental procedures on the preferences among the toys.

Table 1 presents these data in a rather simple fashion, namely, the number of subjects who increase, decrease, or do not change their ranking of the forbidden toy. Only 11 children were used in the No Threat condition of the experiment. Of these 11 children, 7 increase their evaluation of the toy that the experimenter took out of the room with him. The other four children do not change. This condition was, of course, used as a control group by

Table 1.   Change in Preference for Forbidden Toy
(from Aronson and Carlsmith)

	Preference		
	In-creased	Un-changed	De-creased
No Threat (N = 11)	7	4	0
Severe Threat (N = 22)	14	8	0
Mild Threat (N = 22)	4	10	8

the experimenters. It was simply intended to show what would happen to preference if it was impossible to play with one of the toys under conditions where no threats of any kind were employed. Thus, the results in the other two conditions can be compared to this condition to determine the effect of prohibition using threat. Before we move ahead, however, we might point out that the results of this No Threat condition are quite suggestive all by themselves. The suggestion is, of course, that people are correct in what they have long suspected—something which is forbidden is likely to become more attractive.

Let us now examine the results of the other two experimental conditions. In the Severe Threat condition (that is, under circumstances where the children refrained from playing with the forbidden toy because of strong threatened punishment) the results are almost identical to those of the No Threat condition. Out of 22 children in this condition, 8 do not change their evaluation of the forbidden toy, while 14 increase their rating of it. Just as in the No Threat condition, there are no instances of a child decreasing his evaluation of the toy he could not play with.

The Mild Threat condition, however, shows a rather different picture. It will be recalled that in this condition the children refrained from playing with the forbidden toy because of only a mild threat. And in this condition 8 out of the 22 children *decrease* their evaluation of that toy. Only 4 children increase their evaluation and 10 of them do not change. In other words, where a prohibition was enforced by means of only mild threats, there was a tendency to regard the forbidden thing as less attractive. The differences between the Mild Threat condition and the other two conditions are both highly significant statistically.

We now come to the important questions. How are we to explain these findings, and what is the relevance of these results to the process of acquisition and change of moral values? The authors of the experiment, Aronson and Carlsmith, interpret their results in terms of the theory of dissonance. They say:

> The results clearly support the theory of cognitive dissonance. In the severe threat condition, an individual's cognition that he did not play with an attractive toy was consonant with his cognition that he would have been severely punished if he had played with the toy. There was no need for him to provide further justification for his abstinence. However, when he refrained from playing with the toy in the absence of a severe threat, he experienced dissonance. His cognition that he did not play with the toy was dissonant with his cognition that it was attractive. In order to reduce dissonance, he derogated the toy.

Clearly, this suggests a mechanism whereby beliefs and values may be developed and changed. Here is a situation where the child has tendencies to play with the toy. It is an attractive toy for him and he would like to play with it. If one manages to restrain the child from playing with the toy by means of very weak threats, then the child develops "internalized" opinions which justify his restraint. Too much threat does not produce the same effect.

If we make the analogue to behavior involving the kind of moral values we wish to talk about, such as cheating or stealing, we can imagine the following kind of situation. A parent may discover that his four-year-old son stole something. The parent regards such behavior as wrong and, consequently, punishes the child in an endeavor to teach the child that stealing is bad and in order to prevent a recurrence of the act. If the child has been punished very severely, and the same treatment is threatened explicitly or implicitly if there is a recurrence, it will undoubtedly affect the child's behavior. The next time the child has an impulse to steal something he will probably refrain. There will, however, be little or no attitudinal consequences for the child. The knowledge of the severe punishment that is being avoided is sufficient justification for not stealing.

If, however, the parent had punished the child only mildly, a quite different situation is created. If the child refrains from stealing the next time he is tempted, the knowledge of the punishment which is avoided is not, by itself, sufficient justification for having not taken a desired object. The child will provide itself with additional justification and, thus, there will be attitudinal consequences.

But what are these attitudinal consequences and how do we get our discussion around to moral values? In the experiment we described the "attitudinal consequences" measured were how much the child liked the toy. And we could imagine a similar effect in the case of not stealing after very mild threat. The child could persuade himself that the object he did not steal was really not very desirable.

This kind of change in the evaluation of external objects is, of course, one means of reducing dissonance in the situation, but it is only one of several possible means. There are at least two other ways in which the dissonance may be reduced. The child could exaggerate the severity of the punishment which was experienced and was threatened. This would also provide him with more justification for resisting temptation. Or the child could persuade himself that stealing itself is a bad thing to do. This also provides justification for not stealing. It is obvious that this last means of dissonance reduction would lead to the development of moral values. In the experiment by Aronson and Carlsmith one would expect that, in addition to the changes in evaluation of the toy, there would have been some changes in the child's values concerning obedience and disobedience. For the point we wish to make in this chapter, it is unfortunate that the authors did not measure this latter attitude.

To make our point more forceful, that is, to apply convincingly the theory of dissonance to the development of moral values, it would be important to show experimentally two additional things. One, it would be valuable to show that in such situations changes do indeed occur in the moral value itself and, two, to show that the punishment variable is not crucial. Variation in rewards ought to produce the same effects. That is, restraining undesirable behavior by means of very large promised rewards should be similar to severe threats in terms of attitudinal consequences. A large reward for not engaging in a given behavior can also provide sufficient justification for restraint. Small rewards which effectively restrain behavior would be similar in their effects to mild threats. The size of a reward or punishment must, of course, be considered in relation to the magnitude of the temptation. A threat of punishment, or a promise of reward, which may be quite sufficient justification for refraining from some mildly attractive action may not be at all sufficient justification when the temptation is very strong.

An experiment reported by Mills in 1959 presents data relevant to some of these considerations. This experiment also dealt with the attitudinal consequences of succumbing to, or resisting, temptation. The experiment was specifically concerned with the effect of cheating, or of refraining from cheating, on moral attitudes toward cheating. The design of the experiment was quite straightforward. Sixth grade students were given a questionnaire to determine their opinions concerning cheating. They then participated in a contest either in which they could win a large prize or in which no prize was offered. The contest was so arranged that it was impossible to win without cheating and easy to win if they cheated. Furthermore, it was made easy to cheat. Two days after the contest the questionnaire concerning attitudes toward cheating was readministered. Different experimenters ran the contest and administered the attitude questionnaires so that the two would not be connected in the minds of the subjects. Two different contests were used in the experiment. Since the results are virtually identical for both of them, we will describe and give the results of just one of them.

The experimenter told the class that he was conducting a contest on dot counting because he was interested in measuring the ability to count things quickly and accurately. The experimenter stressed how important this ability was. He then passed out answer sheets, asked the students to write their names on them, and told them that their task would be to count the number of dots in each of twenty squares.

Your score will be the number of squares you have counted correctly. If the number you write down on your answer page next to the letter of a square is not the exact number of dots in that square, your answer will be wrong.

The first task sheets were passed out face down and the students cautioned not to begin until told to do so. Four forms of the task sheets with different numbers of dots in the squares were used to minimize cheating by copying answers from nearby students. It was made clear that students sitting near each other did not have the same form, and that the forms were all equally difficult but had different correct answers.

The substance of the instructions was repeated and the experimenter urged them to work rapidly and to stop counting as soon as they were told to.

After the subjects had worked for two minutes on the task, they were told to stop and the task sheets were immediately collected. The experimenter then announced that there would be a second trial similar to the first but more difficult. He continued:

> They are very tricky so be particularly careful to be accurate. I'd like to see if you can improve your scores on this second sheet. In order to make it more interesting and get you to really try, I am going to make this into a contest. I am going to come back in a couple of days and announce the names of those people who do better on the second sheet than they did on the first. . . .

Here the motivation to cheat was manipulated. Nothing further was mentioned about prizes in the low motivation groups. In the high motivation groups the experimenter added that everyone who improved would get a five-dollar gift certificate.

The second task sheets were then passed out, again face down. The second trial was conducted just as the first one and the task sheets were collected immediately afterwards. The opportunity to cheat was then introduced. The experimenter told the students that, before collecting their answer sheets, he would write the correct answers on the blackboard so that they could see for themselves how well they had done. They were told to "mark those you got right so that you can keep track of your score." The experimenter then wrote down the correct answers for the first trial. After this he proceeded to write down the answers for the second trial. These latter, however, with a few exceptions, were not really the correct answers. They differed by three or four from the actually correct answers. It was obviously rather easy for the students to cheat if they wanted to by changing their answers on the second answer sheet or by adding more answers so as to improve their score from the first trial. Most of the time the experimenter's back was turned as he was writing the supposedly correct answers on the blackboard. For purposes of analysis of the data, however, cheating could readily be detected, since it was highly improbable that anyone would honestly have obtained the precise answers that they were told were correct for the second trial. A day or two following the second administration of the attitude toward cheating questionnaire, the experimenter returned, told them that he had made a mistake in the answers he had written down for the second trial and that, while no one had actually improved, they had all done so well that he would award ten dollars to the class treasury. This satisfied the students very nicely.

To summarize the experimental design, all students were put in a situation where there was some temptation to cheat. In one condition the temptation was low, while in another condition the temptation was rather high. Within each of these conditions we may examine the data separately for those who succumbed to, and for those who resisted, the temptation. Clearly, the psychological situation for those who resisted temptation in this experiment is very similar to the situation for the children in the Aronson and Carlsmith experiment which we discussed earlier. In both cases a desire to engage in some activity which is frowned upon is resisted. Aside from the age of the subjects, the only difference is that Aronson and Carlsmith varied the severity of threatened punishment for succumbing to temptation while Mills varied the magnitude of reward to be obtained for yielding to temptation. If our interpretation in terms of dissonance theory is correct, the high threat of punishment should be psychologically equivalent to low magnitude of temptation. In both of these conditions, less dissonance is created when temptation is resisted than in the low threat or high temptation conditions. In short, among those who did not cheat, we would expect attitude change in the direction of feeling that cheating was a bad thing, and the amount of change should be greater in the high temptation condition than in the low temptation condition, since in the latter less dissonance is introduced.

Those who do succumb to temptation and do cheat should show an inverse pattern. Here dissonance is greatest if they violate their moral values for very little reward, and so for cheaters the dissonance is greatest in the low temptation condition. Consequently, we would expect cheaters in that condition to change their attitudes in the direction of feeling that cheating was not a very bad thing. Let us look at the data which are presented in Table 2.

First of all, we may examine the evidence concerning the effectiveness of the experimental manipulation. Of 84 subjects in the high temptation condition, 37 per cent succumb to temptation and cheat. Of the 90 subjects in the low temptation condition, only 16 per cent cheat. Clearly, the high temptation condition was more tempting than the low—thus the evidence is that the manipulaion was successful. Next we must satisfy ourselves as to whether or not the behavior of cheating in this situation was, indeed, in violation of their moral values as measured in the questionnaire. If not, we can hardly

Table 2. Temptation to Cheat (from Mills)

		High	Low
Number of subjects		84	90
Per cent cheating		37	16
Initial score	Cheaters	36.0	34.8
	Honest	38.4	38.0
Final score	Cheaters	36.6	33.3
	Honest	39.7	38.6
Change	Cheaters	+.6	−1.5
	Honest	+1.3	+.6

speak of dissonance having been created. It can be seen in the table, however, that their moral values about cheating, as measured on the questionnaire, were relevant to their cheating behavior. In both conditions those who cheat have initially lower scores on the questionnaire—in other words, those who initially feel that cheating is not so bad are more likely to be the ones who cheat. This is, of course, very obvious but very comforting from a methodological point of view.

The last two rows of the table give the data on attitude change. It is clear that the theoretical expectations are supported. The cheaters in the low temptation condition change appreciably in the direction of becoming more lenient toward cheating. The non-cheaters in the high temptation condition change appreciably in the direction of becoming more severe toward cheating. The other two conditions change very little, both in a positive direction.

The interpretation of these data are, of course, somewhat less clear than those from Aronson and Carlsmith's experiment because of the problems created by self-selection of who cheats and who does not cheat. Thus, for example, the slight positive change of the cheaters in the high temptation condition may be due to statistical regression effects. After all, these cheaters are initially low and regression effects could produce this slight positive change. It is clear, however, that such regression effects cannot possibly account for the cheaters in the low temptation condition changing appreciably in a negative direction or for the honest subjects changing in a positive direction.

Thus, it seems plausible to accept these data as consistent with the results of the Aronson and Carlsmith experiment and as supporting the idea that variation in magnitude of temptation together with variation in magnitude of threatened punishment affect the development of, and changes in, moral values concerning the tempted behavior. Maximal internalization of the culturally desired moral value should occur if the person resists temptation under conditions of high motivation to succumb and low threat for yielding. If the person yields to temptation, however, value changes occur in a direction opposite to that which, presumably, the culture is attempting to inculcate.

We would not want to leave the impression that engaging in, or not engaging in, prohibited behavior is the only mechanism mediating or controlling the development of moral values or that the magnitudes of temptation and threatened punishment are the only variables affecting the amount of change in moral values that occurs. Certainly, the extent to which social support is available for the moral value will be an important determinant of the effectiveness with which dissonance can be reduced by changing one's moral values. Thus, for example, if parents continually tell a child that cheating is bad, it will certainly be easier for this child to persuade himself that cheating is, indeed, bad after some instance when he has refrained from cheating. Similarly, it might be harder for the child to persuade himself that cheating is a good thing to do after he has succumbed to temptation.

It might be noted, however, that the nature of the arguments the parents use may be a crucial factor in the development of moral values. It appears that modern day parents tend to avoid simply telling a child that something is bad. Instead they try to explain why it is bad by giving reasons in terms of social consequences, etc. So, they might tell the child that cheating is bad because he will not learn anything if he cheats, that he is only cheating himself, and that he would not like it if someone cheated from him. These arguments may be quite convincing and will prevent the child from cheating under most circumstances. However, note that they provide the child with justification for not cheating in much the same way that punishments or rewards do.

It will be remembered that in the study by Freedman (1963) mentioned earlier, justification in the form of reasons for performing a task operated in much the same way as did rewards. Subjects who were given good reasons for performing a dull task apparently experienced less dissonance as a result of performing the task and changed their ratings of the task less than did subjects who were given poor reasons. This would seem to suggest that the child who has sufficient reasons for not cheating—whether it is in terms of desire to receive a reward, avoid a punishment, or avoid social consequences— would feel less dissonance as a result of not cheating than a child who has less good reasons. Since the child has sufficient reasons and feels little dissonance, he may not develop a moral value or restriction against cheating. He may not cheat because he is convinced it is a bad idea, but, on the other hand, he may not think that cheating is bad per se. In some sense he will be freer in that he does not blindly follow a moral code, but he is also freer in that under appropriate circumstances he may feel free to cheat in much the same way that a child who refrains only from fear is free when the fear is removed. In other words, the child who is given good reasons for not cheating may not develop as strong a moral code as a child who is given less good reasons and told merely that it is wrong. Although the study mentioned above gives some indirect support for this idea, there are, unfortunately, no data directly concerning this problem.

The social interactive process does, undoubtedly, provide many complications for any simple model concerning the development and change of moral values. Once we begin to consider these complications, we immediately think of other behaviors, apart from simply succumbing to or resisting temptation, which would also affect the moral values involved. Let us imagine, for example, a situation in which a person sees someone else engage in a prohibited act such as cheating. According to considerations from dissonance theory, the person's responses and reactions to this kind of situation should also have attitudinal consequences, that is, should affect his own moral evaluation of the prohibited behavior.

Let us imagine, for example, that we observe another person in the act of cheating and we do nothing about it. Dissonance then exists between our knowledge concerning our own behavior in the situation and the knowledge that we have, perhaps, suffered some loss through the other person's cheating and have also, at a minimum, condoned an antisocial act. We can well imagine how this dissonance might be reduced by persuading oneself that cheating is, after all, not a terrible thing. On the other hand, if after seeing the other person cheat, we reported this behavior to the appropriate authorities, our knowledge concerning this action is then dissonant with a variety of other values we hold. We should not harm others, we should not inform on others, and the like. This dissonance could well be reduced by persuading oneself that, really, cheating is a terrible offense and quite inexcusable. In other words, in addition to our own behavior with respect to something like cheating, our moral attitudes are also fashioned as a reaction to our behavior with respect to these actions in others.

A recent experiment by Festinger and Gumpert (1962) was designed to test whether this hypothesized process does occur and whether the magnitude of change in attitudes is responsive to the same variables that determine the magnitude of dissonance reduction in other kinds of situations. The basic purpose of the design of the experiment was to create a situation in which subjects observed someone cheating. One condition was to be experimentally controlled so that the subject reported the cheating. In another condition the subject would not report the cheating. We would then be able to assess whether this difference in induced behavior made a difference in the subsequent attitude of the subject.

Subjects were recruited for the experiment by an advertisement in the student newspaper stating that some interesting and rather well-paid jobs were available for qualified undergraduate women as interviewers in a survey being conducted. Those interested in applying for such a job were asked to phone and make an appointment. Thus, the subjects had no idea that this was an experiment. They found themselves in a real situation in which they were applying for, and hoped to get, a good part-time job.

When the applicant for the job arrived at the time scheduled for her appointment, she found that there were two other applicants also being considered simultaneously. These two other applicants were actually confederates. The same two confederates appeared with every subject and played the roles which will be shortly described.

The experimenter told the three girls that he knew it was somewhat unusual to see three applicants simultaneously, but since a large number of applicants would have to be interviewed, this procedure was being followed in the interests of economy. The experimenter then told them something about the nature of the interviewing job for which they were applying, making it sound rather attractive, and emphasizing that particularly sensitive persons were needed to do the interviewing. Because of this latter need, the applicants were asked to take an "interviewer aptitude test" in order to compete for the job. The girls were told that the aptitude test was rather valid for our purposes. They were also told that there were about three times as many applicants as there were jobs available and so it had been decided to give a job to that girl in each set of three who scored highest on the aptitude test.

They were then each handed a booklet of questions, an answer sheet, and told to start. The experimenter explained that as soon as they had finished he would score the tests with the scoring key he had brought along so that they would know immediately which one had obtained the job. He then left the room telling them that if they finished before he got back, they could have some coffee which was ready in a nearby room.

About five minutes after the experimenter had left the room, one of the confederates, the cheater, got up, walked over to where the experimenter had left his materials, picked up the scoring key and, also carrying her own answer sheet, started to leave the room. In order to guarantee that the subject noticed at least part of what was going on, at this point the second confederate, the informer, asked the cheater where she was going with that material. The cheater simply replied, "Oh, I'll be right back" and left.

After about five minutes, the cheater returned to the room, replaced the scoring key with the materials the experimenter had left, put her test booklet and answer sheet on the desk where the experimenter had asked for them to be left and, obviously finished with the aptitude test, again began to leave the room. At this point, in order to be sure that nothing was lost on the subject, the informer queried the cheater, "Was that the scoring key you had?" After the cheater replied in the affirmative, the informer asked, with an incredulous note in her voice, "You didn't use it, did you?" The cheater simply said, "Sure," in a pleasant, matter of fact tone and left the room.

The subject and the informer then continued working on the aptitude test which took about another fifteen or twenty minutes to complete. The informer then suggested that the two of them go and have some coffee since the experimenter had not yet returned. The cheater was not around, of course. This was done to prevent any further direct interaction between the cheater and the subject. In the coffee room, after some small talk, the informer went into one or another routine to manipulate whether the subject joined the informer in reporting the cheating to the experimenter or whether the informer reported it all by herself and on her own. In order to be sure that the condition the subject was to be in did not affect the behavior of either of the confederates in the preceding episodes, neither of the confederates knew which condition the subject was to be in until this moment. At this point, by the position on the table of a cup and spoon, the informer discovered which of the two experimental conditions was to be created.

If the subject was to be in the participation condition the informer said, "What do you think we ought to do about that girl? It seems to me we really are going to have to do something." Then, after some comments about the cheater's behavior, the informer suggested that they both write a note to the experimenter simply describing what had happened. The informer then wrote the note, which was, of course, standardized, and used whatever gentle social pressure was necessary to induce the subject to join her in signing it. In almost all cases, the subject signed the note after simply being asked to. Thus, in this condition, the subject participated in reporting the cheating behavior.

If the subject was to be in the no participation condition, the informer began in the identical manner up to the point where she suggested that they both write and sign the note. In this condition, instead, the informer simply stated that she was going to write a note to the experimenter describing what had happened. She then proceeded to write the note, of course the same standardized note, signed it and simply read to the subject what she had written. Thus, in this condition, the cheating was also reported to the experimenter but the subject herself had had no part in it.

Afterwards, both girls returned to the room where they had taken the test. The informer put the note to the experimenter with her own answer sheet on the experimenter's desk, and the two waited for the experimenter to return. About a minute later the cheater returned and, very soon thereafter, the experimenter came in. He asked them if, while he was scoring the tests, they would mind filling out an interpersonal sensitivity scale which had nothing to do with the job but which he would be interested in having for other purposes. They, of course, agreed and the experimenter distributed copies of it to them. The interpersonal sensitivity scale simply contained a lot of filler material until the very end where the data concerning our dependent variable were collected.

While the applicants were answering the filler questions, the experimenter scored the answers to the aptitude test. He, of course, quickly found the note which had been left for him, looked up and told the cheater in a very severe voice that she was disqualified and could leave now, and that furthermore, he and Professor _____ would both like to see her the next afternoon at two o'clock. The cheater simply nodded and left. The experimenter finished scoring the aptitude tests and told them that both of them had done very well but that _____ had done better and so had the job. For half of the subjects in each condition the informer obtained the job while for the other half, the subject herself got the job. Thus, we could see whether reward, or goal attainment, would affect the results.

The girls continued filling out the sensitivity questionnaire, coming to the important questions only after all of the above had taken place. It would have been nice, of course, to have obtained measures directly concerning their attitudes about cheating but it was feared that after all the drama that had gone on, this would provoke suspicion. We consequently contented ourselves with asking how much they liked each of the other girls. It seems not too unreasonable to suppose that how much they liked the cheater would depend, in part at least, on how serious a breach of ethics they thought cheating was and whether or not they could find excuses for her. This, then, was the major dependent variable.

Before we examine the results, let us review the design and our theoretical expectations. It is clear that the difference between the participation and nonparticipation conditions in the experiment is a very small one. In both conditions the behavior of the cheater was identical; in both conditions the condemnation of the cheater's behavior by the informer was identical; in both conditions the cheater was reported to the experimenter and the experimenter's behavior toward the cheater was identical. The only difference between the two conditions lies in whether or not the subject signed the note reporting the cheater's behavior. Thus, any difference between the two conditions in their attitude toward the cheater must be due solely to whether or not they participated in reporting the behavior. If the interpretation from dissonance theory is correct, helping to report the cheating should result in greater dislike of the cheater by the subject. Table 3 presents the data.

Let us first look at the top row of figures. On a scale which went from 0, representing "like very much," to 5, representing "dislike very much," the subjects in the participation condition who did not get the job show an average of 3.84—rather severe dislike. This is, of course, the condition in which dissonance should have been maximal since no reward occurred partially to justify the behavior of reporting the cheater. Subjects in the non-participation condition who did not get the job show an average rating of 2.84, only slightly on the negative side of neutral. The difference between these two conditions is significant at the 1 per cent level.

The second row of figures shows the comparable data for those subjects who were told that they themselves got the job. We would, of course, expect that getting the job would, by itself, reduce dissonance somewhat in the same way that in the Mills experiment, less dissonance was created by cheating for a large prize than by cheating for a small prize. Thus, in this condition we would expect the cheater to be disliked less than in the participation–no-job condition. The difference between these two conditions, that is, between the average ratings of 3.84 and 3.46, is in the expected direction and is significant at about the 10 per cent level.

The one surprising figure in the table is that for the no-participation–got-the-job condition. The average rating of 3.26 is unexpectedly high and is significantly higher than the other no participation condition at the 5 per cent

Table 3. Liking for Cheater (from Gumpert and Festinger)

	Participation	No Participation
Did not get job	3.84	2.84
	(11)	(12)
Got job	3.46	3.26
	(11)	(12)

0 = Like to 5 = Dislike

level. Why the dislike is so high in this condition is a problem about which one can speculate but we do not have any good, demonstrable answers. It may be, for example, that when the subject got the job they realized more fully that the cheater was attempting to do them personal harm and so disliked her more. There are any number of other possible hunches also. At any rate, the data on the whole support our point concerning the attitudinal consequences of behavior with respect to others who yield to temptation.

ACQUISITION OF MORAL VALUES IN VARIABLE, REAL LIFE SITUATIONS

A theory concerning the internalization of moral values should, however, be able to say more than we have so far stated. It should be possible to say something about the effects of repeated experiences on these moral values. After all, values are acquired over periods of many years. It would be easy to say simply that the same experience repeated again and again would have a cumulative effect. For example, if every time a person had any impulse to be aggressive this impulse were restrained by an appropriately weak external pressure, the cumulative effects of dissonance reduction would be the development of a simple and uncomplicated moral attitude that aggression is a very bad thing. Such consistency of experience and behavior from time to time is not, however, to be found in the actual life of people. If we are, then, to attempt some explanation for the development of moral values, we must apply the things we have said earlier to more complex types of situations.

Let us examine the nature of the complications with which we must deal theoretically. Imagine a child who, from time to time, has impulses to be aggressive toward his younger brother. The strength of this impulse will undoubtedly vary considerably at different times. There might also be considerable variation from time to time in the strength of the punishment which he anticipates for being aggressive toward this younger sibling. The consequence of this would be that sometimes when he has an impulse to, say, hit his little brother, he refrains; while at other times he goes ahead and does it. According to our theory, in the former instance, when he refrains from aggression he would persuade himself that aggression was a bad thing in order to reduce dissonance while in the latter instance, where he *is* aggressive, he would persuade himself that aggression is a good thing. Thus, it is unclear that the cumulative course of dissonance reduction in a variable environment would lead to the development of clear and unambiguous moral values.

At first glance, this conclusion might seem to make our theory unacceptable. On further consideration, however, it is not unacceptable at all. Indeed, the moral values that most people develop about such things as aggression, cheating, and stealing are not clear and unequivocal. They are usually surrounded with qualifications and conditions. Very few persons would maintain, for example, that overt aggression is always a bad thing. Most people will want to say that it depends on many factors in the situation. Thus, a theory concerning a process of development of moral values which leads us to expect some equivocation and contradictoriness within such values may indeed appropriately mirror reality.

Let us then examine what, and how much, we can say concerning the nature of the moral value that develops under variable conditions. We will take aggression as an example and illustrate our speculations by means of Figure 1. At one extreme, the situation is rather clear. We could imagine parents who convincingly threaten such extreme punishment for overt aggression that, no matter how strong the aggressive impulse in the child is, he restrains himself because the anticipated punishment is so overwhelming. Perhaps one or two such punishments would have to materialize to make it

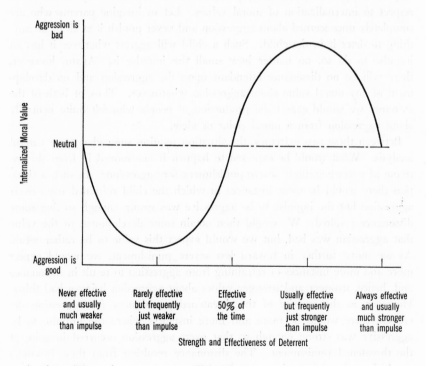

Figure 1

convincing but a few such instances would probably be relatively insignificant for the development of the moral value over a long period of time. A child in this kind of situation would not show overt aggression near his parents but would not suffer much dissonance either. The situation would be similar to the strong threat condition in the Aronson and Carlsmith experiment described earlier. The knowledge the child has concerning the punishment he has avoided is sufficient justification for having restrained himself. Without dissonance to be reduced, there would be no internalization of moral values concerning aggression. We would expect such a child to grow up feeling that aggression was neither a good nor a bad thing. Morally he should feel quite neutral about it.

Parenthetically, let us make it quite clear that this analysis is still highly oversimplified. We are ignoring other possible bases for internalization of moral values and ignoring all the situations which the child would encounter and react to outside of the home. But some oversimplification is necessary to talk about the situation in terms which are conceivably testable empirically.

The other extreme of the distribution of possible environments is also quite easy to analyze and, strangely, produces results that are very similar with respect to internalization of moral values. Let us imagine parents who are completely unconcerned about aggression and never punish it at all or do anything to deter it in the child. Such a child will aggress whenever it has an impulse to do so, no matter how small the impulse is. Again, however, there will be no dissonance attendant upon the aggression and no development of any moral value about aggression whatsoever. Thus, at both of the extremes we would expect the production of people who felt quite neutrally about aggression from a moral point of view.

Between these two extremes, the situation requires somewhat more careful analysis. What would be expected to happen if one moved in from the extreme of overwhelmingly severe punishment for aggression? In such a situation there would be some instances in which the child refrained from overt aggression but the impulse to be aggressive was strong enough so that some dissonance resulted. We would then obtain some development of the value that aggression was bad, but we would expect this value to be rather weak. As we move further in toward less severe punishment, we would expect more and more instances of refraining from aggression to result in dissonance and, hence, stronger and stronger values about aggression being a bad thing. However, as the severity of the threatened punishment for aggression decreases, there would be more and more instances where the impulse to be aggressive was strong enough so that overt aggression occurred in spite of the threatened punishment. The dissonance resulting from these instances would be reduced by seeing some good aspects to aggression. There is, thus, some maximum point on the curve and weakening of threatened punishment beyond this results in a more ambiguous negative moral evaluation of aggression.

The point in the middle of the curve is of particular interest theoretically. We might imagine this point on the abscissa to be one where the deterrent to aggression is equal to the average impulse the child has toward aggression. Then, assuming a symmetrical distribution of impulses toward aggression, the child would refrain half the time and would show overt aggression half the time. Furthermore, the dissonance to be reduced by persuading himself that aggression was a bad thing would be equal to the dissonance to be reduced by persuading himself that aggression was a good thing. Overall, we would then expect an internalized moral value that averaged out to "neither good nor bad." It is important, however, to distinguish carefully between this point and the neutrality of the extremes. This middle point would undoubtedly represent highly conditional internalized values. That is, there would be specific elaboration of when aggression is morally bad and when it is morally good.

As we move past this middle point, one gets to the area where impulses to aggress are expressed overtly more often than they are controlled. Little more need be said here. The preponderance of dissonance is reduced by persuading oneself that aggression is a good thing and the curve on this side is theoretically similar in all ways to the other half of the curve, but reversed in direction of the value which is acquired.

It would be very dramatic if we could now present some data which tested this rather complicated theoretical speculation. Unfortunately, there are no such data and, what is more, it seems that it would be difficult to obtain good relevant data. One of the major problems, of course, is the specification of, and the measurement of, the variable of severity of punishment. This cannot be regarded as simply the absolute magnitude of deterrent but must be the deterrent in relation to the strength of the impulses which the child has to be aggressive. The difficulties of getting any reasonably accurate measure of such a variable are obvious and need no comment. Nevertheless, we may be able to find some indirect ways of validating this speculation. At least we can say that it has some basis in laboratory investigation.

PART THREE

THE INDUCTION
OF CHANGE

A shift from theoretical considerations of the variables responsible for change to a more specific consideration of actual procedures used involves more than simply a change of emphasis. To some extent, there is also a shift from the scientific goal of prediction to that of control. As we learn about the conditions that are effective in eliciting changes in behavior, it is obvious that this knowledge will be applied in non-laboratory settings. It is also obvious that such application raises new issues centering around questions of values. Academic discussions of psychoanalytic theory and laboratory investigations of cognitive dissonance have much in common. They represent a search for knowledge, and hence predictability, in the universe. On the other hand, when psychotherapy is utilized to reduce anxiety, or "brainwashing" techniques are applied to alter political ideology, or human relations training procedures are used to alter the climate of an industrial concern, something qualitatively different is involved. Whenever there is application of scientific knowledge in an attempt to exercise control, value judgments enter, and the decisions which must then be made are not those that are traditionally a part of the scientific endeavor. Physicists were thrown into the middle of this dilemma by the atomic age. Psychologists will increasingly share in this problem in the years to come. In the following five chapters, there are thoughtful discussions of the application of theory to applied problems, the benefits to theory from work on such problems, and the value-laden issues which are raised by applied behavioral science.

Though psychotherapy has been the focus of the two earlier chapters on psychoanalytic theory and self theory, Murray deals more specifically with psychotherapy as a way to bring about a particular kind of change: the reduction of anxiety. And, he takes the position that psychotherapy can best be studied in the context of a learning-theoretical framework. Thus, his paper serves as a bridge between the S-R approach to behavioral science outlined by Farber and the work of a practicing therapist. Since anxiety appears to be a central causative factor in symptom-formation and in most forms of psychopathology, the ability of therapeutic procedures to reduce anxiety is a crucial question. By utilizing the concepts and terminology of S-R learning theory, Murray discusses many of the typical phenomena observed in therapy such as initial reduction in anxiety, vacillation in discussing dynamically significant material, the extinction of anxiety by the permissiveness of the therapist, and reinforcement of behavior by therapists. His presentation of content analysis as a way to study the behavior which occurs in therapy is an important methodological innovation. In addition, there is a discussion of other types of therapy and therapeutic approaches in terms of personality change as social learning.

While most of us would agree that attempts to change behavior via psychotherapy represent an admirable endeavor, the connotation of personality change via "brainwashing" is a negative one. However, Holt's discussion makes it clear that the principles involved in attempting to bring about changes by forcible indoctrination are similar to those considered in conjunction with other techniques aimed at changing behavior. He discusses the specific techniques utilized by communist interrogators, and indicates the crucial elements of these techniques which seem to bring about behavior changes. The major elements seem to be designed to bring about a childish or regressed state, to evoke shame and guilt rather than anger, and to require active participation by the prisoner. Holt indicates that the indoctrination procedures have been extremely effective in extorting false confessions from prisoners, but not at all effective in bringing about lasting ideological changes. He also discusses findings with respect to individual differences in responsiveness to these indoctrination procedures. Holt concludes that personality can be changed if there is a modification of the environment, if existing psychic structures are broken down and replaced by new ones, and if there is continuing environmental support for the new behavior. However, it is difficult and almost impossible to "break down existing psychic structures." To the extent that the personal identity is strong, an individual is not likely to yield to indoctrinational pressures.

In a setting quite different from that of the therapist's office or the prison interrogation room, attempts are made to effect changes in industrial organizations. Blake and Mouton describe the application of the techniques of human training laboratories to the solution of interpersonal problems in large organizations. A program of planned change involves diagnosing the existing problem, identifying the unit of behavior to be changed, establishing goals, and developing techniques to bring about the change. With a detailed presentation of Managerial Grid theory, they indicate the various ways in which concern for production and concern for human relationships may interact. They make the point that the behavioral sciences have not developed appropriate theories and techniques which are capable of solving organizational problems. Outlining their experiences in a series of factories, they draw tentative conclusions about the variables which are important in bringing about changes in this setting. The role of the behavioral scientist throughout this program is made explicit.

In Chapter 11, Zubin and Katz explore the effects of drugs on changes in personality. They indicate that it is still an open question as to whether drugs are capable of producing enduring changes in personality. The effects of drugs on personality have primarily been studied with respect to temporary factors such as mood. They concur with the points emphasized in Chapter 2 that the lack of an adequate methodology for the study of change is retarding development in the field of personality. The authors present a model for the study of drug effects on personality and review much of the relevant literature as an illustration of this model. They conclude that the field of personality is in the doldrums and might be improved by replacing psychophysical and clinical methods with classification on the basis of response to chemical substances. This, they suggest, might get at much deeper levels of functioning than do our present techniques.

Efforts to change attitudes, beliefs, opinions, values, and related dimensions of individual differences have long formed an important area of research. In considering the effects of religious intolerance, racial bigotry, political controversy, and nationalistic hostility, it may be seen that such attitudinal differences have important and far-reaching effects on man's behavior. In the era of thermonuclear weapons, such attitudes along with traditional beliefs about how to resolve differences constitute a threat to mankind itself. Stagner addresses himself to the problem of attitude change as a prerequisite to the reduction of international tensions. Rather than viewing international questions as problems of reality, he deals with the psychological processes related to them: attitudes, values, and decisions. He conceptualizes attitude changes as the process of inducing expectancies different from those already established. In world affairs, nationalism and ethnocentrism are seen as the nucleus of tension-arousing attitudes. He reviews the findings on attitude change and then applies the principles to the problem of altering nationalistic beliefs through modifying national images. As an example of such change in action, he describes Osgood's graduated reciprocation proposal as a method for changing national images. Stagner is not, however, very optimistic about the prospects of the success of such efforts at behavior modification.

chapter eight

Sociotropic-Learning Approach to Psychotherapy

Edward J. Murray

In a very real sense, the phenomena of psychotherapy form the foundation for a discussion of personality change. It is inconceivable that the very topic would have become prominent in psychology without the achievements, claims, and hopes of several generations of psychotherapists. Even now, when the cold, hard statistics of success and failure seem to be running against psychotherapy, it is the image of the haggard, perplexed neurotic emerging from therapy with self-confidence and maturity which leads us to think that man can change his destiny through education, rehabilitation, and international cooperation. Yet we know so little about psychotherapy!

The future of psychotherapy rests on research efforts, but such efforts can be ultimately unproductive without some sort of conceptual framework in which to order the data. Self theory, psychoanalytic theory, role theory, and many other systems offer such conceptual frameworks. The purpose of this chapter is to relate psychotherapy to the conceptual framework provided by learning, or behavior, theory. Why learning theory? The principles of learning, to the extent that they are known, constitute an attempt to account for the acquisition, performance, and elimination of all forms of behavior. Since psychotherapy may be viewed as a method of changing behavior, it follows that the principles of learning should apply.

Naturally, it is not all that simple: psychotherapy is a complex phenomenon with many forms and variations. It is necessary to specify which psychotherapy is under discussion and what particular aspect of that therapy. It is well known, furthermore, that there is less than perfect agreement among learning theorists as to the basic laws and their application. While there is a common pool of information about learning which will be drawn upon, the ideas of Skinner, Hull, Tolman, Lewin, and, especially, Miller and Dollard have strongly influenced the author.

One significant feature of the interpretation of psychotherapy by Dollard and Miller (1950) is their interdisciplinary approach. This is extremely significant for understanding the role of learning theory in explaining, predicting, and modifying psychotherapy. The principles of learning are quasi-mathematical relationships between abstract entities such as stimuli, responses, reinforcements, drives, and so on. Coordinating definitions between these abstract entities and the experimental operations in the laboratory in which they were studied are known, but they may be quite unspecified and totally different in the clinical setting to which they are applied. For example, a food pellet may be well established as a reinforcement in a laboratory experiment, but it was a long time before we realized that certain sounds, such as the ubiquitous therapeutic "Mm," were reinforcing events.

This is where the findings of psychoanalysis and the social sciences are useful. They provide the content of the conflicts; the conditions of social learning; the meaning of stimulus, response, drive, and reinforcement in a given situation with a given individual. Thus, psychoanalysis points to intrafamilial competition for affection while sociology suggests middle-class mobility striving as sources of psychopathology. Not that this is without controversy! In fact, much of the disagreement between various schools of psychotherapy boils down to the question of critical content: sex, independence, security, identity, self-actualization, or what have you. The fields of personality and social behavior will have to answer these questions; learning theory is concerned with relationships and, like the computing machine, cannot operate until the proper information is fed into it.

The informed reader will know by now that the position being taken is not shared by all of those who advocate a learning approach to psychotherapy. The English group (Eysenck, 1960), for example, would disagree with much that has been said so far and we with even more of what they say. The fact of the matter is, that there are many ways of using a theoretical system, as the history of psychology has shown, so that theorists starting with essentially similar principles may, by making different ancillary assumptions, arrive at quite different conceptions of the same phenomenon.

The various applications of learning theory to psychotherapy can be placed along a continuum ranging from "biotropic" to "sociotropic" approaches (Murray, 1963). At the extreme biotropic end are Eysenck (1960), Wolpe (1958), Salter (1961), and their followers. At the other end are Dollard and Miller (1950), Shoben (1949, 1953), Mowrer (1953), and others. Some of the characteristics of these two positions are shown in Table 1. It can be seen that they differ radically in explanatory principles, conceptions of psycho-

Table 1. *Two Approaches in the Application of Learning Principles to Psychotherapy (after Murray 1963)*

Biotropic	Sociotropic
1. Relatively greater reliance on classical Pavlovian conditioning.	1. More emphasis is placed on operant, or instrumental, learning.
2. Direct transposition of laboratory hardware into clinic, e.g., PGR conditioning, bar-pressing apparatus.	2. Translation of laboratory findings into verbal and expressive techniques.
3. More use of reinforcement based on physiological drives, e.g., electric shock, candy bars, erotic pictures.	3. Social reinforcement and acquired drives are more important, e.g., approval, empathy, interest, understanding, respect, and life goals of individual.
4. Primary stimulus generalization and discrimination central to psychopathology and therapy, e.g., trains, buses, and cars in phobias.	4. Secondary, or mediated, generalization and discrimination of most importance, e.g., verbal symbols and feelings.
5. Restriction of interest to overt muscular responses and peripheral autonomic reactions in naïve behaviorist tradition.	5. Recognition of important, although difficult to measure, cognitive processes such as thinking, fantasy, and dreams (which on the physiological level would be central brain mechanisms).
6. Transference is not part of treatment—"personal relations are not essential."	6. The therapeutic relationship is seen as the key learning experience in all forms of therapy.
7. Causal factors in neurosis are seen as primarily genetic, physiological, and medical.	7. Cultural variables play a great role in determining disturbance, e.g., social class, family relations, and social learning.
8. Affinity for the directive-organic school of psychiatry.	8. Affinity for the analytic-psychological school of psychiatry.
9. Techniques deemed of most importance include hypnosis, suggestion, progressive relaxation, drugs, and overt manipulation.	9. Point to techniques such as insight, labeling, permissiveness, and other subtle means of influencing behavior.
10. Learning theory presented as an alternative to traditional psychotherapy.	10. Adopt a strategy of first reinterpreting and then extending and modifying traditional therapy.

pathology, therapeutic techniques, and basic views of human nature. The approach in this paper will be sociotropic.

The present learning interpretation of psychotherapy will be built around the concept of anxiety. Anxiety, stemming from childhood experiences, motivates symptoms and appears central to the forms of psychopathology most often encountered in psychotherapy. Whatever else psychotherapy does, and by whatever means, it must have some effect on this key phenomenon, if therapeutic progress is to take place. Nearly all theorists—learning or otherwise—have recourse to this notion, but just what is anxiety? Before making a theoretical analysis of psychotherapy, it is incumbent upon any writer to discuss the nature of anxiety. The following hypothesis about anxiety is designed to relate it to social and personal processes, so that the concept will be more meaningful in a sociotropic-learning explanation of personality change in psychotherapy.

THE NATURE OF ANXIETY

It is widely agreed that anxiety is a psychophysiological emergency reaction to conditions which threaten the survival of the organism. Under some conditions the aroused state is adaptive, and under others, not. Anxiety has drive properties and may motivate the learning of new responses (Miller, 1951). These responses, when maladaptive in various situations, constitute symptoms such as phobias, obsessions, hallucinations, delusions, alcoholism, sexual abnormalities, or, sometimes, criminal acts. While these symptoms may result in greater problems over the long run, they serve as immediate anxiety reducers and thus are reinforced (Dollard and Miller, 1950).

From a learning point of view, the reason the neurotic or psychotic develops anxiety, and/or its symptoms, is that the individual is in conflict (Miller, 1944). For example, a person may be in a sex-anxiety conflict; the closer he approaches a sexual goal, the greater the anxiety. The drives which may be in conflict with anxiety range from sex and aggression to social mobility and achievement (Dollard and Miller, 1950). As long as these drives are strong and the conflict exists, the individual will be driven toward the goal which arouses anxiety and, thus, toward the development of symptoms.

An issue of great significance here is what is the original source of the anxiety in normal and pathological personalities. That is, what arouses the anxiety in the first place? The answer given by most learning theorists is that pain is the unconditioned stimulus for anxiety. This position has been very ably criticized by Kessen and Mandler (1961), who cite evidence suggesting that pain is neither a sufficient nor necessary antecedent of anxiety.

Stimulus patterns which are strange or startling also evoke anxiety (Tin-bergen, 1951; Hebb, 1949). In Harlow's movies, the fear reactions of mon-keys to startling stimuli, open spaces, and strange places are quite striking. It is possible that internal drives, such as hunger, also produce anxiety. Thus, the sources of anxiety are varied and widespread.

Still, these physical sources do not account for all the anxiety seen in chil-dren—much of it stems from threats to the child's relationship to the parents and other significant persons. Child (1954) has reviewed empirical evidence showing that love-oriented punishment, not physical, is the antecedent of a good deal of social anxiety, or guilt. Furthermore, the effectiveness of even physical punishment is dependent on maternal warmth (Sears, Maccoby, and Levin, 1957).

The importance of parental approval and affection in socialization is usu-ally explained by learning theorists in terms of secondary reinforcement. Through association with primary reinforcement, such as food or the re-moval of a source of anxiety, the parent's presence, or activity, functions as an acquired reward (Dollard and Miller, 1950) or a generalized reinforcer (Skinner, 1953). This explanation accounts for some, but not all, of the attachment of a child for its parents, however.

The studies of affectional responses in monkeys demonstrate that the in-fant prefers stimulus objects offering some degree of maternal contact com-fort to those associated with feeding (Harlow, 1958; Harlow and Zimmer-man, 1959). Lactation does have some effect, but only in combination with contact (Igel and Calvin, 1960). Also of importance, here, are the observa-tions in the Israeli Kibbutzim, where the children's caretaker is responsible for the socialization of the "instincts," yet the primary attachment is to the mother, who provides only affection (Yarrow, 1961). It would seem that there is some innate adience for contact comfort, succorance, love, or call it what you will.

There appears to be a reciprocal relationship between anxiety and the so-cial contact just mentioned. The presence of another member of the same species has a damping effect on the physiological reaction to stress (Bovard, 1959). Specific innate anxiety inhibitors, such as sucking, maternal con-tact, rocking, etc., are proposed by Kessen and Mandler (1961). In his analysis of imprinting, Moltz (1960) points out that the critical period just after birth is a quiescent time during which the stimulus may become "imprinted" and evoke the quiescence via classical conditioning, but it is not clear what the US would be. Also against this hypothesis is the fact that some stimulus patterns are better for imprinting than others. Conceivably, these anxiety inhibitors and imprinting stimuli operate by evoking, on a more or less innate basis, an emotional response incompatible with anxiety. Such a response would be parasympathetic-like and, in replacing anxiety, would provide drive-stimulus reduction and thus explain the reinforcement value of social contact. Sullivan (1953) postulated such a response, calling it euphoria or security. Several learning theorists have used the concept of a relaxation, contentment, or dearousal response in connection with psychotherapy (Shoben, 1949; Dollard and Miller, 1950; Wolpe, 1958; and others). Whatever the exact nature of social contact, it functions as a primary reinforcement. Hill (1960) also takes this position and points out how difficult it is to distinguish between primary and secondary reinforcement in such cases—asking, for instance, whether food in the mouth is a primary or secondary reinforcement. It is also clear that increasing anxiety leads to the acquisition and performance of behavior to obtain social contact, as evidence from widely different sources indicates. Zoologists have observed that, in the presence of a predator, birds flock together, fish form a school, etc.—such grouping having survival value (Allee, 1958). Moltz (1960), in reviewing the literature on imprinting finds that, after the acquisition period, following behavior is increased by anxiety. With monkeys, Harlow (1958) found that fear increased the need for contact with the surrogate mother. College students, under anxiety-provoking conditions, choose to be with one another according to the research on affiliation need (Schachter, 1959). Furthermore, experimental procedures which arouse a need for affiliation, in subjects who are concerned about positive affective relationships, seem to evoke anxiety at the same time (Byrne, 1961). Anxiety is reduced by the appropriate set of social stimuli—often there is a visible change from an agitated state to a peaceful one. Who has not seen this in his own child?

On the other hand, removing or threatening to remove, a social object, once it has been established, results in anxiety. Köhler (1925) describes the violent reactions of young chimpanzees to solitude. Yarrow (1961) describes the immediate reactions to maternal separation as acute anxiety. This may be followed by withdrawal, apathy, and depression—the sequelae of prolonged stress. In order to maintain social contact, an individual may learn various avoidance reactions—the defense mechanisms or security operations.

One of the determinants of basic personality structure may be the reaction of the environment to the anxiety-motivated social response during the early critical period in maturation. The social response may be better conceptualized as an innate response tendency, not an inflexible reflex. The social response may be reinforced, extinguished, punished, or dealt with in a complex way. Thus, "normal" social development probably involves reinforcement which would consist of anxiety reduction through the parent's acceptance, protection, and affection. With emotional security comes imitation, identification, and mature socialization (Bandura, 1961). At the other extreme, social deprivation or total rejection during the early critical period may lead to an extinction of the response resulting in an asocial, autistic, or psychopathic personality (Yarrow, 1961).

Various forms of neuroses and reactive psychoses probably depend on more complex ways in which the environment reacts to the social response of the child. As Green (1946) points out, it is the degree to which the affection given a child is made contingent upon his fulfilling various role obligations, rather than pure rejection, that most likely determines neurosis. In these situations there is most likely a very strong initial reinforcement of the social response—perhaps too much so, to the exclusion of learning other ways of dealing with anxiety (Levy, 1943). Then, however, the child may be required to remain dependent, repress sexual needs, choose sides in a marital conflict, achieve great things, etc., in order to maintain a secure relationship with the parent.

The social learning situation may be so punitive in various ways, or the demands so incompatible, that the child withdraws. Social contact, while still desired, may increase, rather than decrease, anxiety; thus, it may be avoided, so as to reduce the possibility of rejection, humiliation, or provocation. The parental variables, here, may very well be largely unconscious. Thus, anxiety in the parent may provide cues which elicit anxiety in the child. This is sometimes referred to as empathy or emotional contagion (Sullivan, 1953). In air attacks, the anxiety of children depends largely on the emotional reactions of parents (Janis, 1951). In an experimental situation, very young children cried more if their mothers were anxious (E. Campbell, personal communication). This underscores the futility of training parents in child-rearing techniques on an intellectual level alone.

The main point is that anxiety is closely related to social relationships. Much social learning consists of ways of maintaining these relationships and thus avoiding anxiety. Reinforcement deficiency may lead to asociality while conflict may produce desocialization. The basic anxiety-social response hypothesis, proposed here, may serve as the base on which many of the higher order and differentiated social needs—for approval, power, prestige; for redheads, cooking like Mom's, the Republican Party, etc.—are acquired. Thus, the theory of learnable rewards and drives would apply here, except the anxiety-social contact phenomenon, rather than the usual physiological drives, is the foundation. Similarly, concepts of frustration, conflict, displacement, etc., would be applicable.

THE PSYCHOTHERAPY PATIENT

One cannot discuss psychotherapy meaningfully without some consideration of the patient himself—without, in essence, a theory of psychopathology. While a detailed consideration of such problems is beyond the scope of the present chapter, at least a few general statements can be made for purposes of orientation.

To begin with, it makes little sense, in terms of learning theory, to think of the patient as suffering from a "disease" in any sense analogous to physical disease. The "myth of mental illness" is under heavy attack from the more epistemologically sophisticated members of the medical profession itself (Szasz, 1960). Mental illness, using the term in its broadest sense, can better be described in terms of learned social behavior which is maladaptive in certain situations.

If psychotherapy is a new learning situation, then the patient must be motivated. Every psychotherapist has had a few "poorly motivated" patients— the hardened psychopath, the happy homosexual, or the extrapunitive marital partner. Many of these individuals do not want psychotherapy but are there simply because they were "brought in" by relatives, police, or other social agents (Hollingshead and Redlich, 1958). While other individuals, or society as a whole, are bothered by their behavior, they themselves are not disturbed—not anxious. They may desire help in handling the immediate situation, e.g., the threat of jail, but, generally speaking, they have little desire for increasing their self-understanding, changing their behavior, or playing the role of a mental patient. Therapy for such individuals might be more adequate in the future, probably relying on methods of mobilizing anxiety, but is generally agreed to be relatively ineffective now.

What, then, are more or less voluntary psychotherapy patients like? They tend to come from higher socioeconomic classes, to be more intelligent and verbal, and to be suffering emotionally. In general, these characteristics are associated with continuance in therapy and various kinds of improvement. These statements must be highly tentative, since much is still ambiguous in this complex area (Luborsky, 1959; Rotter, 1960; Seeman, 1961). Nevertheless, there is some evidence that anxiety, depression, feelings of inferiority, and other affective disturbances are critical factors in therapeutic outcome. A recent demonstration of this, in the Menninger psychotherapy research project, was that the single patient variable, of fourteen variables studied which predicted therapeutic change, was initial anxiety level (Luborsky, 1962). In Chapter 2, Byrne cites several studies in which anxiety, measured by the Taylor Manifest Anxiety scale, is reduced by psychotherapy.

Thus, it would seem that the patient who is most amenable to psychotherapy, as we know it today, comes to treatment with anxiety or related emotional disturbances. In other words, he is suffering enough to be motivated to change his behavior. Frequently, the anxiety is related to difficulties which threaten important social relationships, and, often, actual losses. In the cases to be mentioned later in this paper, anxiety was precipitated by: threats to the marital relationship, difficulty with a fiancée, ambivalence about leaving the parental nest, fear of rejection by girls, and similar problems in social living.

INITIAL ANXIETY REDUCTION

Ordinarily when a patient enters psychotherapy—the voluntary patient especially—his anxiety is high. This may be in the overt manifestation of anxiety or in prominent symptoms—physical symptoms, extreme activity or passivity, obsessive thoughts, hallucinations and delusions, defenses of various sorts, intense conflict in some life situation, etc. Typically, a discussion of these manifestations of anxiety dominates the first part of therapy.

In order to show this, a number of studies of psychotherapy using objective measures of verbal content will be mentioned (see the 1955 paper by Auld and Murray for a review of such methods). The discussion will be based mainly on the method devised by the author (Murray, 1956). In this content-analysis technique, typescripts of therapy interviews are first divided into scorable units—e.g., a single patient sentence. Then, each unit is scored in one of several content categories. Major categories, derived from learning theory, with a heavy emphasis on conflict, include approach, anxiety, and frustration responses related to drives such as sex, affection, dependence, and independence. Special categories for specific defenses, or symptoms, including physical symptoms, intellectualization, and psychotic manifestations are used for various cases. At times, simpler groupings of subcategories are used, such as hostility or family conflicts. The therapist's remarks are also scored, for example, as active and interpretive, or as passive and reflecting.

In one case studied with this method (Murray, 1954), a somewhat dependent young college graduate sought help because of a fear of dying while asleep. Initially, the therapy was dominated by two defenses, as they were called, intellectual discussion about psychology, philosophy, etc., and a variety of physical complaints. According to the theoretical analysis, these defenses and symptoms were motivated by anxiety. The anxiety, in turn, was attached to hostility—aggressive response tendencies, verbal responses, visceral reactions of a hostile sort—primarily directed toward his overprotective mother. There was a conflict between anxiety and hostility. The original symptom, fear of

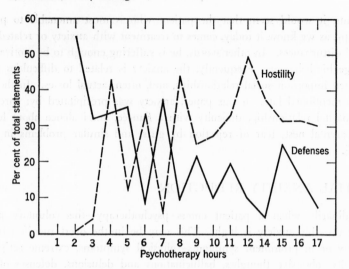

Figure 1. Percentage of hostility and defense statements throughout therapy—young college graduate (after Murray, 1954).

dying, was conceivably related to a fear of hostile material emerging more easily during dreams and leading to a loss of the social contact with the mother.

The content analysis reflects this conflict, as can be seen in Figure 1, where the percentage of patient statements in the hour which were in the two defense categories or in the hostility category (which included hostile statements about all persons) is shown. It can be seen that there is a strong reciprocal relationship; which, incidentally, is explained neither by the percentage measure used nor a ceiling effect forcing a correlation. Slowly the hostility wins out over the defensive material. Why? Possibly because of an extinction of anxiety in the therapeutic situation due to the permissive attitude of the therapist about the expression of hostility.

The patient described above was treated by a psychoanalytically oriented form of short-term psychotherapy. Other kinds of therapy tend to show somewhat similar changes, however. For example, in non-directive therapy there is often a shift from "problems," many of which are symptomatic, to "understanding" which would presumably include a closer examination of interpersonal feelings (e.g., Snyder, 1947).

Psychotic symptoms also appear to be motivated by anxiety and to show a reciprocal relationship with significant family material. This is shown in a study of Rosen's "direct analysis" approach to schizophrenics (Murray, 1962).

Rosen's idiosyncratic and controversial therapy is of some interest in itself, but here we are concerned mostly with changes which can also be shown in many other approaches to therapy with psychotics. Two cases were studied intensively.

In Case A, a nineteen-year-old girl, from a disturbed immigrant family, suffered an acute schizophrenic breakdown with psychotic symptoms including ideas of reference, peculiar physical sensations, generalized anxiety, and some delusional religiosity. As can be seen in Figure 2, discussion of, and manifestation of these symptoms dominated the first part of therapy. As the patient's obvious anxiety decreased, the content shifted from the psychotic material to affectional, dependency, and hostility conflicts in relation to parents, sibling, and boyfriend.

Between sessions five and six, the patient made a home visit which was quite upsetting. As can be seen in Figure 2, the result was an increase in psychotic symptoms, as manifested in the subsequent therapy session. Now, this is of great theoretical significance for the conflict interpretation. If the psychotic symptoms simply reflected one concern and the family conflicts another, with no dynamic connection between them, then the hour following the disturbing home visit should have been devoted to a discussion of family conflicts. This did not happen. Instead, the disturbance at home aroused anxiety about even thinking about family feelings, and the psychotic symptoms reappeared.

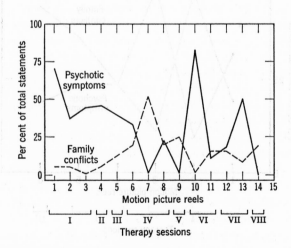

Figure 2. Percentage of total patient statements in the psychotic symptoms and family conflicts categories during the course of direct analysis with Case A.

In Case B treated by Rosen, a married man developed paranoid religious ideas including speaking in Biblical "tongues" and rolling around on the street. Figure 3 shows how these symptoms are reciprocally related to family conflicts. In both cases there was a trend toward greater concentration on family conflicts as therapy progressed, but not marked enough to warrant strong claims of therapeutic effectiveness.

By using a somewhat similar content scoring system, Dollard and Auld (1959) also found reciprocal relationships between several motivational categories, on the one hand, and categories of emotional disturbance on the other. In one case both sexual and hostile categories were negatively correlated with anxiety. In two others, hostility was inversely related to resistance —which in turn was probably motivated by anxiety in the therapy.

Symptom reduction during the initial stage of psychotherapy is a phenomenon found in nearly all approaches. It is an interesting and, possibly, important event, but it should not be taken too seriously as a criterion for therapeutic success, since the patient may not have solved very basic problems of marriage, occupation, and so on. The initial reduction in anxiety, and temporary symptom relief, can also be obtained by the use of a placebo (Shapiro, 1959). Such an effect is due to the doctor-patient relationship, according to Shapiro, and accounts for many general medical and psychiatric cures. In terms of our hypothesis, this would be due to the reduction of anxiety attendant upon

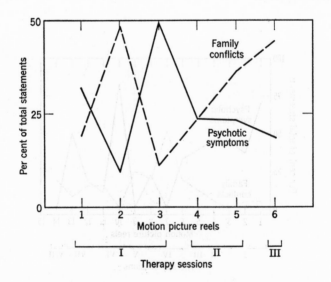

Figure 3. Percentage of statements in psychotic symptom and family conflict categories— Rosen's Case B (after Murray, 1962).

an insecure individual making a social contact with a protecting figure. This relationship may then enable the patient to continue in therapy, in the face of deeper anxieties, long enough for substantial anxiety extinction to occur.

APPROACH-AVOIDANCE WITH CONFLICT MATERIAL

After the initial decrease in anxiety, patients in psychotherapy typically begin to discuss more dynamically significant material concerning conflicts of various sorts with the significant individuals in their lives. This was shown in the three cases discussed, in the previous section, by the increase in hostility and family conflict categories.

The approach to significant material is anything but linear—it is characterized by conflict and reversal. In fact, the very approach to significant material may produce the reversal by arousing anxiety and forcing the individual to avoid the topic. This is called the negative therapeutic effect; Dollard and Miller (1950) deduce it from conflict theory. If the patient advances too close to a feared goal or action, he would experience increased fear, show symptoms, and retreat further away from the conflict point. Under these circumstances, patients often say that they are "right back where they started." Nevertheless, the patient may drop his symptoms and get back to his psychological problems faster than he did originally.

When a patient reaches the kind of conflict point just described, the increased anxiety may motivate a large variety of defensive maneuvers. These may include a concentration on physical symptomatology, intellectualization, long silences, missing appointments, and even leaving therapy. Auld and White (1959) have presented evidence showing that silence tends to follow resistant speech and vice versa, suggesting an equivalence in function. One other possibility is displacement—the patient continues to express important feelings (e.g., hostility) but shifts to less important individuals.

The young man in the first case presented (Murray, 1954), who had such deep resentment for his mother, began expressing his feelings but then shifted away from the mother to the aunt and others (Figure 4). Actually on the basis of conflict theory, one would expect a patient to express negative feelings, first about relatively unimportant people, then about persons of intermediate importance such as an aunt, and last toward the mother. The reverse happened—hostility was expressed first to the mother, then the aunt, and then others, although, later on, the patient returned to the mother with qualitatively stronger expressions of anger.

What seems to have happened is that the first expression of feeling was toward the basic, conflicted goal—the mother. As the patient expressed more hostility toward her (and approached the conflict point) anxiety increased and caused a displacement—first to the aunt and then to others. Later, with greater anxiety extinction in the therapy, the anger could be expressed more openly or, in other terms, the anxiety gradient was lowered and the conflict point shifted closer to the goal. A somewhat similar sequence was found in a case treated by non-directive therapy (Rogers, 1942). This is shown in Figure 5; there was a shift from all statements about parents, to those about girls, and to authority in general. Again there was a return to parental conflicts near the end of therapy.

These kinds of shifts are not easily explainable by conflict theory (Miller, 1944). However, it is possible to combine the conflict theory with the complementary theory of displacement (Miller, 1948; Miller and Kraeling, 1952; Murray and Miller, 1952; Miller and Murray, 1952). This was done by Murray and Berkun (1955) in a three-dimensional model. Predictions from this model were confirmed by animal experimentation. When rats were shocked in an alley in which they had been fed previously, they advanced only part way down, to the point of conflict, and then crossed over to a previously ignored "displacement" alley in which they made a goal response. In a later study, Berkun (1957) showed that there was no greater therapeutic affect of responding in the displacement alley than in the original alley. These studies illustrate how quantified data from psychotherapy can provide feedback for laboratory-based theories and suggest new areas for research.

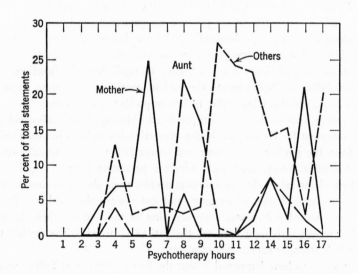

Figure 4. Hostile statements toward mother, aunt, and others—young college graduate (after Murray, 1954).

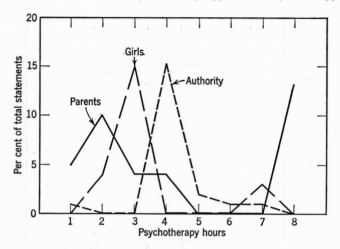

Figure 5. Statement about parents, girls, and authority—non-directive case (after Murray, 1956).

It should be kept in mind that displacement is only one of many defensive maneuvers occurring during psychotherapy. There are probably large individual differences in the presence or degree of this particular mechanism. The important thing is that approaching conflictful material arouses anxiety and motivates various responses to reduce that anxiety.

THE EXTINCTION OF ANXIETY

Once a patient has reached a therapeutic conflict point and manifests resistance, the major reason for his proceeding again is the extinction of anxiety, in the therapeutic situation, due to the permissive attitude of the therapist. Now, if anxiety extinction is taking place, should there not be a gradual decrease in the tension reflected in the interview? Several studies suggest just the opposite—that tension remains high during therapy until quite near the end. Mowrer and his associates (1953), for example, give numerous examples of increases of palmar sweating, the Discomfort-Relief Quotient, and other indices of tension during psychotherapy. Murray, Auld, and White (1954) have presented a case showing some therapeutic success, but no decrease in tension. Figure 6 shows the DRQ in six randomly selected hours and it will be noted that no downward trend is apparent.

How can this be explained? According to Miller's conflict theory one might predict that there would be little tension decrease during therapy, because as a patient advances nearer a feared goal, the absolute level of fear is

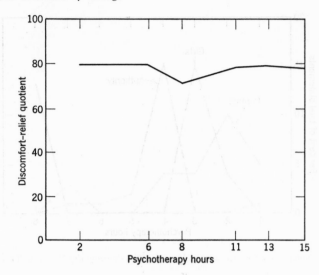

Figure 6. The DRQ in sample of hours—marital conflict case (after Murray, Auld, and White, 1954).

increased. Even with extinction occurring, the level would not necessarily decrease if the patient kept advancing to more and more difficult problems. A content study of the case in question offers support for this interpretation. Figure 7 shows all conflictful statements in the sample of hours and, like the DRQ, this shows no marked decline. One might conclude that nothing much was happening in the case. However, the subcategories of conflict show several striking changes. Figure 8 reflects a shift from a discussion about mother and daughter conflicts to those about the husband. Furthermore, as seen in Figure 9 the material dealing with the husband changed from generalized hostility to a discussion of sexual problems.

These content changes are in agreement with an exhaustive clinical analysis made of the same case (Dollard et al., 1953). The initial discussion of the problems of the woman with her mother appeared superficial and was described as a "cover story." The eventual explanation of the sexual difficulties with the husband, although painful, was judged more therapeutically valuable. If this case were consistent with the two neurotic cases mentioned above, we would expect an eventual return to problems related to mother, but at a deeper level. While this is not reflected in the content scores, there is some hint that continued treatment would show this, i.e., during the discussion of the sexual problems with the husband, Oedipal themes involving the mother were touched upon. In fact, one might suspect that in very pro-

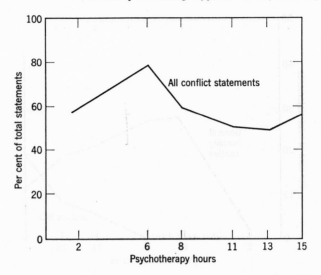

Figure 7. All conflict statements—marital conflict case (after Murray, Auld, and White, 1954).

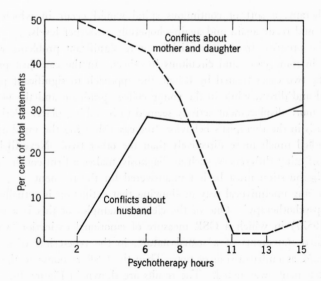

Figure 8. Conflicts about mother and daughter versus conflicts about husband—marital conflict case (after Murray, Auld, and White, 1954).

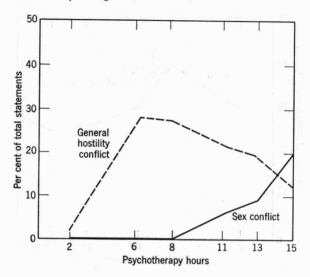

Figure 9. Hostility conflict versus sexual conflict—marital conflict case (after Murray, Auld, and White, 1954).

longed therapy, a sort of continuous spiral would occur in which certain themes would recur again and again—hopefully at deeper levels.

Still, the progress from superficial to more significant problems seems to be direct in some cases and circuitous in others. In the case just presented and in the two cases treated by Rosen, the approach to significant problems was rapid and direct, while in the young college graduate and the non-directive case, more displacement activity seemed to be taking place. Perhaps the difference is in the therapist's behavior—the cases showing the rapid approach were handled much more directively than the other two. Nevertheless, the existence of other differences, such as diagnosis, makes a firm conclusion difficult, so the question must be left unanswered for the moment.

Is there any unequivocal way of showing that extinction is actually taking place in psychotherapy? One of the clearest examples of this is a study by Dittes (1957a) in which a GSR measure of emotional extinction was used. Judges rated statements of a sexual nature, in the typescripts of a psychotherapy case, as embarrassing or not. Then the GSR response to the embarrassing statements was noted. The results are shown in Figure 10. During the course of therapy, the percentage of statements in which a strong emotional GSR response took place decreased. It is a classic extinction curve—reversals and all. Some of the reversals were related to visits to the patient's parents during which anxieties were aroused.

Wolpe (1958) has raised the very interesting question of whether extinction or reciprocal inhibition is involved in the reduction of anxiety during various forms of psychotherapy. He points to the greater efficiency of reciprocal inhibition in eliminating undesirable habits. However, it is very difficult to tell, from the data available, whether regular extinction or reciprocal inhibition is taking place in the cases we have presented. Is the anxiety reduced because the therapist does not disapprove or because he has a different reaction? Even here, the absence of disapproval may be a cue for relaxation—at least in some patients.

The question of extinction versus reciprocal inhibition is further complicated by the fact that, in experimental psychology itself, there is some controversy over the nature of extinction (see Deese, 1958, for a summary). Several theorists, notably Guthrie and Estes, explain extinction as the result of new, incompatible responses being attached to the old stimulus. Thus, extinction and reciprocal inhibition may be the same. The real question may be what therapeutic techniques achieve the best and most lasting new responses.

REINFORCEMENT BY THE THERAPIST

Up to this point, we have been discussing the changes in the patient's behavior as if they occurred in a vacuum. They certainly do not—they are strongly influenced by the behavior of the therapist. One way in which the

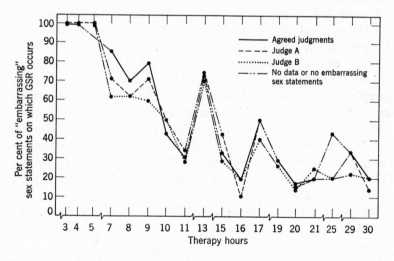

Figure 10. GSR response to embarrassing sex statements during psychotherapy (after Dittes, 1957a).

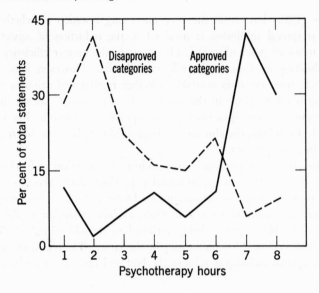

Figure 11.   Categories approved or disapproved by the therapist—non-directive case (after Murray, 1956).

therapist can influence behavior is by approval or disapproval—these social reactions may function as rewards and punishments.

A good deal of experimental and clinical observation has been brought together by Glad (1959) to show that the theoretical orientation of the therapist strongly influences the content of the verbal material during treatment and encourages an adoption of his own values. Thus, Freudian psychoanalysts selectively respond to sexual and transference material, client-centered therapists promote emotional understanding, Sullivanian analysts concentrate on social relations, and Rankians nurture pride in autonomy.

Very few therapists use grossly authoritarian methods of influencing patients and, in fact, are usually convinced that the content emerges spontaneously. How, then, is the content influenced? The demonstration by Greenspoon (1955) that simple sounds such as "good" and "Mm" can serve as reinforcements for classes of verbal responses, has provided an explanation. Krasner (1958, 1961) has reviewed the experimental evidence for the effectiveness of verbal reinforcement in laboratory and therapeutic situations. Often the patient is not fully aware that a topic is being reinforced.

In fact, the therapist also may not be fully aware that he is reinforcing certain topics. For example, in the case treated by non-directive psychotherapy the entire philosophy of treatment was based on the idea of trying not to influence the patient. Nevertheless, it is possible to demonstrate (Murray, 1956) that the therapist did approve, in a subtle way, certain categories and disapproved others. Independence was strongly approved, while sex, dependence, and intellectual defenses were disapproved. The approval and disapproval appeared to act as reward and punishment: the "rewarded" categories increased in frequency during therapy while the "punished" ones decreased. This relationship is shown in Figure 11.

Punitive techniques may have a dramatic but, basically, illusory effect on verbal content. In the first case presented in this paper, the young college graduate initially used two main defenses: intellectualization and physical complaints. These are shown in Figure 12. Intellectual defenses were not responded to, in any special way, and decreased consistently to hour six. In its place, the physical complaints increased but these were interpreted. It was pointed out that his problems were not physical and that concentrating on them avoided the real issues—kindly, but essentially punitive with respect to content. The punishment had its usual dramatic effect and on hour six a good deal of dynamic material about the mother came out. This had something of a negative therapeutic effect and on hour seven anxiety was high. Since the interpreted physical complaint defense was not permitted to emerge, the old intellectualization came back. In other words, punishing the one

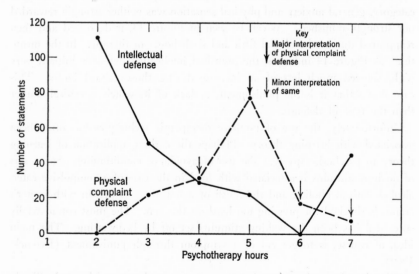

Figure 12. Intellectual and physical complaint defenses—young college graduate (after Murray, 1954).

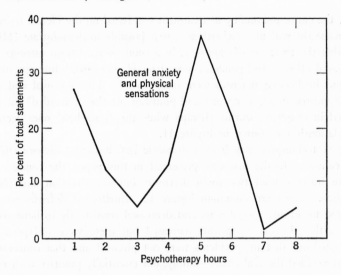

Figure 13.   Anxiety and physical complaints—non-directive case (after Murray, 1956).

symptom resulted in a return of an old one—just what a number of people have been saying about symptomatic treatment and substitution.

The non-directive case offers a complementary example. The analogous category, general anxiety and physical sensation was neither strongly rewarded nor strongly punished. As can be seen in Figure 13, it decreased and then reappeared during the crucial fifth and sixth hours of therapy. In the meantime, as Figure 14 indicates, the punished intellectual defenses, initially very high, showed much less of an increase during those critical hours. This case shows that it is the punishment, or lack of it, which is critical, rather than the type of defense.

Unfortunately, the use of punitive therapeutic techniques has often been associated with learning theory. Perhaps the earliest application of learning theory to psychotherapy was the use of avoidance conditioning. Some sort of noxious stimulus is associated with food in the case of a compulsive eater, alcohol with alcoholics, and the fetish of a fetishist. A person with writer's cramp is shocked for pressing too hard on the pen. The most commercially successful has been the waking stimulus set off by bed-wetting. The main idea, of course, is to get rid of a symptom through punishment (Eysenck, 1960).

What has the study of learning processes to say about punishment? Shock, or some other kind of punishment, serves as a drive-arousing operation and can thus motivate new learning (see Deese, 1958, for a summary). A more pertinent question, however, is how does it function to eliminate other behavior? The general finding seems to be that, at less than traumatic levels, punishment does not eliminate behavior, but merely suppresses it. Now, it is possible for a new response to be acquired during this period of suppression, but if we are dealing with a highly and complexly motivated subject then only a response which fulfills the motivational requirements would be expected to be learned and retained. Thus, the new response would be more or less equivalent to the old one. If the motivation for the original response still operates, then the response or its equivalent will reappear. In other words, a conflict has been set up and the behavior will depend on the relative strength of the opposing drives.

If the motivation for the symptom to be eliminated is low, then punishment may be quite effective. This would be especially true of what Lehner (1954) calls a "habit residual." If, however, the symptom is powerfully motivated, as it most likely is in cases of severe disturbance, then punishment may serve to create an intense conflict. Indeed, this is what has been found (Beech, 1960). Highly anxious sufferers of writer's cramp either did not improve or worsened with avoidance conditioning. Generalizing from this, one would conclude that avoidance conditioning is appropriate only for weakly moti-

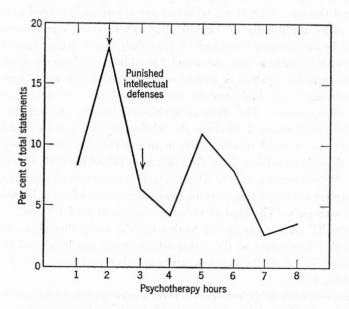

Figure 14. Disapproved intellectual defenses—non-directive case (after Murray, 1956).

vated, isolated symptomatic acts—hardly a description of the typical psycho-pathological problems faced by the mental health field today.

What are we to conclude from all this? The therapist, acting consciously or unconsciously, influences the content of the conflict areas and defenses. This is a serious limitation on the use of therapy protocols as evidence for any particular theory of personality. It also suggests that a pure non-directive approach is, probably, impossible. This does not mean that the evidence points to the therapist deciding what kind of a person the patient should be and then reinforcing that behavior. There are most likely restrictions on the effectiveness of the reinforcement, as we shall see. We may also conclude that negative reinforcement, or punishment, while sometimes producing dramatic results, operates mostly by suppression and, in highly motivated behavior patterns, it would not be expected to be therapeutically valuable.

REINFORCEMENT DEPENDENT ON RELATIONSHIP

The reinforcement value of social approval or disapproval depends on the two people involved and their relationship. Approval by one individual may be greatly rewarding, while the same sound uttered by someone else is meaningless. Some individuals seek approval more than others.

Earlier we saw that learning theory does not necessarily predict an impersonal therapy. First of all, reinforcement is intimately related to motivation—either intrinsically or extrinsically. What is the reinforcement dispensed by the therapist based on? It is unlikely that it derives from hunger or pain; it is unlikely that the sound "Mm-Hmm" is innately reinforcing. According to the analysis of anxiety presented earlier, we would expect the reinforcement to be based on the patient's need for a protective relationship, when anxious. The approval signifies continuance and security in the relationship; disapproval threatens the relationship and arouses anxiety.

The effect of social reinforcement, in an experimental situation with children, depends on who is doing the reinforcing (Gewirtz, 1954; Gewirtz and Baer, 1958; Stevenson, 1961). Depending to some extent on age, female experimenters are more successful in reinforcing boys and, to a lesser extent, males with girls. The kind of verbal reinforcement used ("Good," "You're doing well," etc.) seems similar to that used by many therapists. Furthermore, the effectiveness of the verbal reinforcement can be altered by prior experience in which the experimenter was either critical or complimentary (Simkins, 1961).

The personality of the subject also plays a role. Cairns (1961) used verbal reinforcement to condition the interview behavior of delinquent boys. Those who showed a high inhibition of dependency behavior conditioned less well than the more openly dependent boys.   Increasing the "dependency drive," by a brief period of social deprivation, increases the power of verbal rewards, according to some investigators (Gewirtz and Baer, 1958).   Recently, Crowne and Strickland (1961) have shown that the efficacy of verbal reinforcement is dependent on the subject's need for social approval, as independently assessed by a personality inventory.

Thus, verbal reinforcement depends on the personality of the subject and the personality of the experimenter.   Sapolsky (1960), in an important study, has gone further and demonstrated that the interaction of the personalities is crucial.   Pairs of E's and S's were matched, on the basis of a personality test, so that some had compatible needs and others incompatible ones.   The compatible E's and S's tended to like one another.   The often used verbal reinforcer "Mm-Hmm" worked, during the acquisition phase, only with the compatible pairs.   During the extinction phase the S's in the incompatible situation showed some delayed effect, indicating that the individuals were actively resisting the effects of the reinforcement.   Sapolsky concludes that, in psychotherapy, verbal reinforcement would be expected to be most effective when the relationship between the patient and therapist is positive or compatible.

Successful client-centered patients tend to like their counselor; they also tend to change their values in the direction of the counselor's (Rogers and Dymond, 1954).   By indirect reasoning, one might suspect that the influence of the therapist was through subtle reinforcement and this reinforcement was most effective when the patient liked the therapist.

In general, the outcome of psychotherapy is related to positive feelings for the therapist on the part of the patient.   Relevant therapist characteristics associated with favorable outcome include respect for the client, warmth, empathy, and attentiveness.   Therapists who moralize, who are disinterested, or who act superior are less successful (Snyder, 1961).   Snyder, himself, found that he established a better relationship with some patients than others, and that these were the ones who improved.   It is likely that the therapist's approval and disapproval was more effective when the relationship was good.

Some sort of relationship builds up in every therapeutic interaction, although the way in which this emerges probably depends on many factors. One way of showing the universality of therapeutic relationships, is by examining the number of statements made by the patient about the therapist. Murray (1956) found an increase in such statements in every one of seven cases studies.   This is shown in Figure 15, where, in spite of fluctuations, the slope was always positive.   In Table 2, it can be seen that specific content shifts include significant increases, for the group as a whole, in both positive

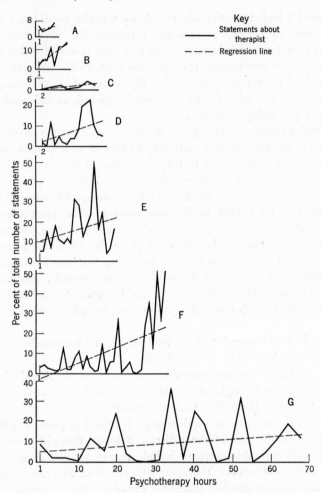

Figure 15. Statements about the therapist during psychotherapy (after Murray, 1956).

and negative feelings, hostility, independence, and other drives—in general, an increase in a complex human relationship.

Approval and disapproval may play an important role in the expression of transference material. There was some evidence, in the seven cases mentioned above, that the rate of increase of therapist-relevant statements is related to the degree to which the therapist is active in his remarks, although this breaks down in the Rosen cases. However, this should not be interpreted to mean that the therapist simply "reinforces transference." It is much more

ERRATA

p. 419, bottom

The reference to Arthur Cohen (1960) should read: Irving Sarnoff (1960, pp. 275–276)

Table 2.   The Mean Increase in the Average Percentage of Statements
in Individual Content Categories Related to the Therapist from the
First Half to the Second Half of Psychotherapy (after Murray, 1956)

Category	Average Increment	$p <$
Positive	2.2	.02
Negative	3.9	.05
Anxiety	1.9	.09
Hostility	2.0	.05
Sex	1.0	ns
Affection	2.0	.06
Dependence	−0.6	ns
Independence	1.1	.05

likely that the relationship comes first; if the patient relates favorably to the
therapist, then the therapist can use approval, etc., to get the patient to express all sorts of transference feelings—positive or negative.

This is shown dramatically in the cases treated by Rosen. In both cases
there was a clear increase in the therapist-relevant material (Figures 16 and
17). This was probably related to the fact that Rosen responded much

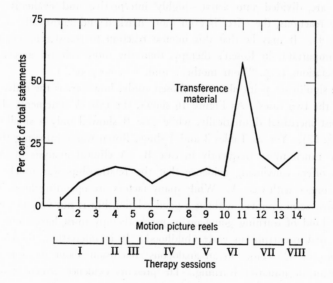

Figure 16.   Transference material—Rosen's Case A.

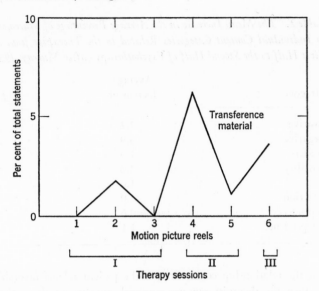

Figure 17. Transference material—Rosen's Case B.

more to the transference than to the other two major areas—psychotic symptoms and family conflicts (Table 3). Furthermore, if the therapeutic remarks are divided into active—highly interpretive and evaluative—versus
passive reactions, the effect is even more marked and statistically significant
(Table 4). It may be that this intense reaction to transference material is
more important, in Rosen's therapy, than the more colorful aspects of his
interpretations (e.g., "Your mother's milk was no good.").

The significant point about the Rosen study, however, is the difference between the two cases. As Figure 16 shows, the case A statements about the
therapist increased dramatically, while case B showed only a small increase
(Figure 17). Yet, as Tables 3 and 4 show, Rosen was reinforcing the transference much more frequently in case B. A clinical analysis of the typescripts offers convincing evidence that the relationship was much warmer
and stronger with case A. While many factors are operating here, it would
seem that reinforcement without a good relationship is not very powerful.

The kind of learning going on in psychotherapy must have some similarity to that occurring in early childhood. It is interesting, therefore, that
Bandura (1962) comes to an analogous conclusion about the role of reinforcement in imitative learning. He presents evidence which shows that,
while rewards facilitate imitation by focussing attention, they are not neces-

Table 3. Therapist Reaction to Patient Content
Categories (after Murray, 1962)

Patient Content Categories	Per Cent of Patient Statements to which Therapist Reacted	
	Case A	Case B
Psychotic symptoms	19	34
Family conflicts	16	44
Transference material	37	62

sary for imitative learning. Personality characteristics of the model and imitator are more powerful determinants. In addition, more identification with an adult model takes place in children when the relationship has been a nurturant one (Bandura, 1961).

The conclusion is inescapable: the verbal reinforcement used in psychotherapy is a secondary phenomenon dependent on the relationship between the patient and the therapist. The patient will modify his verbal behavior—and possibly his extrainterview behavior as well—in order to gain the approval of the therapist only to the extent that the relationship means something to him. Thus, the reinforcement has very real informational properties but is not the root of the process. Once given the relationship, different kinds of reinforcement techniques might have special advantages, so that research here may prove to be very important tactically.

Table 4. The Activity and Passivity of Therapist Remarks in Relation to Patient Content Categories (after Murray, 1962)

Patient Content Categories	Per Cent Active Remarks	
	Case A	Case B
Psychotic symptoms	33	39
Family conflicts	33	27
Transference material	42	100

THERAPEUTIC RELATIONSHIP AS EXTINCTION PROCESS

While there has been a convergence of opinion, recently, on the importance of the therapeutic relationship, the precise mechanisms through which it influences behavior are not well understood. First, there is the possibility that the relationship fulfills real gaps in the development of the person—a loving mother, a respected father, etc. Certainly some of these needs are fulfilled in therapy, along with the very basic social contact mentioned earlier. Nevertheless, it is difficult to see why these functions could not have been fulfilled by decent individuals on the outside—even granting that psychotherapists are exceptionally fine fellows.

The thing which differentiates therapeutic relationships from other social relationships is that thoughts and feelings ordinarily inhibited are purposely brought out and examined in a permissive atmosphere. This material, as we saw in an earlier section, may be the hostility which arouses anxiety or the positive feelings which are inhibited because of fear of rejection. In other words, therapy involves a social relationship in which the thoughts and feelings which have made for difficulty in social relationships are elicited and, since the therapist is not punitive, anxiety extinction takes place. The expression leads, not to rejection and an increase in anxiety, but to a continuation of the basic protective attitude engendering emotional security.

The importance of the *presence* of the therapist for anxiety extinction to take place—a factor doubted by some—has been nicely demonstrated by Martin, Lundy, and Lewin (1960). They had one group of patients speak into a tape recorder with no one present, another spoke to a therapist who did not respond verbally, while the last group had, more or less, normal psychotherapy. As the interviews progressed, the regular therapy group showed an increasing tendency to approach significant, anxiety-arousing material and consequently extinguished that anxiety, as shown by GSR recordings. The "tape-only" group, on the other hand, decreased their approach behavior, as the hours went on, and simultaneously increased in physiologically measured anxiety. The non-verbal therapy group showed intermediate results; conceivably more of a relationship is possible when the therapist talks. The results of this fine study show, then, that the therapist plays a critical role in the extinction of anxiety during psychotherapy. It does not, however, show that the anxiety extinction is about feelings specifically directed toward the therapist.

Let us take Rosen's treatment as a particularly dramatic example of the kind of extinction which may go on in the therapeutic relationship per se and which may hold the key to therapy in general. There is little doubt that direct analysis centers around the relationship between the patient and the therapist. Rosen actively imposes himself as a parental substitute who is all-wise, all-protective and all-loving. As a good parent, he will become angry with the patient, criticize him, etc., for the patient's long-range best interests. The results from the content analysis bear this out.

It should be pointed out that the transference relationship in direct analysis does not simply consist in Rosen's "giving love" to the patient—a popular misconception not only of direct analysis but of other types of psychotherapy with schizophrenics. Devereux (1959) is the one who has most clearly stated that, on the basis of his observations, Rosen's aim was to get the patient to express affection. True, Rosen does express love and approval but the crucial thing is to get the patient involved in the interaction. The therapist's expression of affections, however, are not made contingent upon the response by the patient. The therapist does not reject the patient for hostility or aggression toward him. In fact, the expression of the aggression is as important as the expression of love.

From the viewpoint of learning theory the stress on the transference is quite significant. In a previous section, it was suggested that extinction of anxiety connected with thoughts concerning family members took place. While important, this is all on the verbal level about people not present. The extinction effects might generalize to the family members themselves but with some decrement in effect. But by recreating the early family situation much more significant extinction might take place. By actively taking the role of the parent, usually the mother, Rosen further recreates the early family conflicts. Then by eliciting the patient's love and hate he appears to produce extinction of the anxiety which is attached to these two drives. This highly charged, life-like situation can be expected to produce extinction effects that will more readily generalize to family members and human beings in general.

If, indeed, anxiety extinction in the therapeutic relationship is a critical process in direct analysis one might ask is this the most efficient method of extinction. For one thing, the use of aggressive, punitive techniques for the initial reduction of psychotic symptoms may slow down learning to distinguish reality from fantasy. Garmezy (1952) found that schizophrenics had more difficulty learning a discrimination when the wrong choice was punished in addition to the correct choice being rewarded. Another thing is that direct analysis is a short, intensive therapy. This has certain advantages but the extinction of anxiety is probably more permanent when the treatment is spread out (Dollard and Miller, 1950, p. 73). While the experimental evidence is not conclusive, it seems that massed extinction will produce a greater immediate reduction in fear but the effects of distributed trials (or therapeutic contacts) would be expected to be more permanent. Perhaps this is why Rosen gets rapid, dramatic effects which do not seem to be long-lasting. Fromm-Reichmann's (1950) approach does not make use of puni-tive techniques and spreads treatment over a longer time period. Compara-tive data might show that her therapy results in more permanent anxiety extinction.

ANXIETY OF THERAPIST CAN SLOW DOWN EXTINCTION

So far, our analysis has pointed to the extinction of anxiety in the thera-peutic relationship as the central process in psychotherapy. Of particular im-portance here is the therapist's emotional reaction to the feelings expressed by the patient. Recall that in our hypothesis about the development of psycho-pathology it was the increasing anxiety of the parent—with its disruption of the relationship—which was responsible for repression, inhibition, and symp-tom learning. The same principle holds in psychotherapy; anxiety here may recreate the original pathological situation in the family. If the therapist be-comes anxious this will surely be communicated to the patient in some way. Then, instead of extinction of anxiety, the feelings may become further in-hibited.

In a previously mentioned study, Dittes (1957a) measured the extinction of anxiety with the GSR. In a further investigation, it was found that the GSR measure was inversely related to the permissiveness of the therapist (Dittes, 1957b). When the therapist was gentle and attentive, the patient could talk more easily about embarrassing topics. But when the therapist reacted in negative ways, the patient became anxious and resistant. The causes of non-therapeutic behavior on the part of the therapist, who was generally warm, were not determined, but they might include anxieties stemming from his personal life or aroused by the conflicts of the patient.

No one is free from anxiety—we vary only in degree and content areas. Let us take, as an illustration, Rosen's active elicitation of feelings toward himself. The reader can try to imagine the effects on his own feelings of actively arousing intense murderous wishes, perverse sexual desires, and all-engulfing dependency feelings toward himself on the part of a psychotic pa-tient not yet capable of clear thought. Apparently, Rosen does not get anx-ious with psychotics. Eisenbud has pointed to Rosen's lack of fear and hos-tility toward the patient as the critical factor in the treatment (Rosen, 1953, p. 85). From the viewpoint of learning theory, the anxieties of the patient could not be extinguished if the therapist was fearful or hostile. Both Rosen (1953) and Fromm-Reichmann (1950) point out the importance of the therapist's own analysis and his understanding of his own feelings. It may go beyond that; some individuals may have the life experiences, or temperament, which enable them to deal more easily with psychotic anxiety than others (Betz, 1961).

In two particularly significant studies, Bandura and his associates have related the anxiety of the therapist to therapeutic behavior. First, Bandura (1956) demonstrated that therapist anxiety, as rated by fellow students, was inversely related to therapeutic competence, as independently rated by supervisors. Therapists' insight into their own anxiety had no relationship with competence. Therefore, the critical factor is more emotional than intellectual. Other studies have also shown that therapist factors such as security, self-confidence, and a sense of personal adequacy are associated with favorable outcome, while a poor prognosis is indicated when a therapist is anxious, conflicted, etc. (see Snyder, 1961, for a summary).

Bandura et al. (1960) went on to show that actual interview behavior is related to therapist anxiety. Those therapists who had little anxiety about their own hostility encouraged the expression of general hostile feeling, while those with more anxiety avoided hostile themes. All of the therapists avoided hostility directed toward themselves, however, which may have been due to their lack of experience—they were students. These reactions on the part of the student therapists did, indeed, affect the behavior of the patient: "approach" reactions (reflection, explanation, approval, etc.) to hostility were followed by more expressions of that feeling, but "avoidance" reactions (ignoring, topical transition, etc.) led to fewer hostile statements.

A number of training experiences may be helpful in reducing the anxiety of a therapist. Strupp (1960) has shown the influence of professional training, personal analysis, and years of experience in interview behavior. Fiedler (1953) also points to the importance of experience. The influence of the personal analysis in reducing anxiety is obvious; the training and experience factor may provide situations in which anxiety about therapy is extinguished. Incidentally, this line of reasoning would suggest that supervision of student therapists should be oriented around anxiety reduction rather than, as is too often the case, the intellectual subtleties of interpretation.

These studies show how the discussion of the therapeutic relationship ties up with the earlier material on anxiety. The patient comes to therapy in an anxious state—the anxiety is bound up with basic social drives. These must be brought out, and the anxiety extinguished, especially in the therapeutic relationship, if therapy is to occur. However, if the therapist is anxious about this material, he will avoid it and so will the patient, so that extinction cannot take place. Conversely, warmth on the part of the therapist may enhance anxiety reduction.

SOCIAL LEARNING IN INDIVIDUAL PSYCHOTHERAPY

In addition to the reduction of anxiety in psychotherapy—largely in the therapeutic relationship—there may also be new social learning taking place. Some of this may be taught in a didactic fashion by some therapists. For example, Rosen once accompanied a schizophrenic man, who had never been able to select appropriate clothing, to the store to buy a suit. Much of this learning seems to have symbolic meaning in the relationship, rather than being a real attempt to provide all the social learning missed by the individual. It is incredible to think of an individual therapist attempting to teach a patient social patterns that ordinarily take twenty years or more to learn.

It is more likely that certain basic attitudes are learned by the patient on the same basis as a child learning from his parents—imitation and identification (Miller and Dollard, 1941; Kagan, 1958; Hill, 1960; Bandura, 1962). This is supported by the studies which show that patients tend to change their values in the direction of those of the therapist (Rosenthal, 1955). Here, too, the amount of social learning depends on the relationship.

The amount of social learning which can occur in an hour or so of treatment each week must, indeed, be limited. If neurotic and psychotic difficulties are the products of unfavorable learning experiences covering the life span of the individual and entering into his way of living in general, then a real change must require an extensive relearning experience. The usual hope is that what has been learned, or unlearned, in the therapy situation is generalized to the rest of the person's life. It is the behavior outside of therapy which must bring the person the real gratifications and security which constitute mental health.

Another kind of learning in psychotherapy is the development of intellectual insight; in fact, many readers will have wondered why this was ignored so far. Insight does occur and can be explained in terms of learning theory by such concepts as labeling, discriminating, etc. (Dollard and Miller, 1950). There are, nevertheless, several reasons for believing that insight learning plays a relatively minor role in therapeutic success.

First of all there are individuals with a great deal of insight—the classical obsessive—but poor adjustment. Similarly, it is not uncommon for a person to gain his own insights as anxiety is reduced. Finally, there is some direct evidence that insight is not necessary for therapeutic outcome. Coons (1957) found greater Rorschach and intelligence test changes in a non-insight group discussing everyday activities, than in either a low interaction, high insight group or a control group.

It is also apparent that the definition of insight depends on the therapist's theory of personality; insight to a Freudian is not the same as for a Sullivanian. Since all schools probably achieve therapeutic success, how can their cures be dependent on insight? Then, too, as we saw earlier, the insight is strongly influenced by the selective reinforcement of the therapist.

Another explanation of the role of insight in psychotherapy brings it closer to the anxiety extinction hypothesis: the interpretive behavior of the therapist designed to achieve insight may actually function to communicate the therapist's attitudes and feelings for the patient—this may relieve anxiety. For example, a sexual interpretation may be wide of the mark but lets the patient in on the therapist's permissive attitudes in this area—many of Rosen's "deep" interpretations may function in this way.

The more prolonged, detailed gaining of insight in intensive treatment may also involve anxiety extinction. The basic insight that one is afraid of one's father may be gained in an hour. Nevertheless, the patient may return again and again to the same topic, giving further examples, going over minutely separate facets of the problem—this is the well-known "working through" process. It may mean that anxiety attached to specific stimulus elements of the memory or actual behavior of the father must be individually extinguished—something which is implied by Estes' (1950) statistical learning theory.

SOCIAL FORMS OF THERAPY

In the analysis of individual therapy presented in the preceding sections of this chapter, the basic emotional relearning in the therapeutic relationship was stressed. Such a basic process as the extinction of anxiety about social relationships must be involved, to some extent, in all forms of therapy. However, other processes may also be important—specifically the learning of new social relationships, new cultural patterns, and new kinds of social problem solving. Some of this may take place in individual treatment but may be more efficient and practical in various kinds of multi-individual therapy. These new forms of sociotherapy are seen by many as holding out hope for the vast mental health problem. They seem very definitely to involve social learning and present a challenge to learning theory.

The best known of the social forms of treatment is group therapy. The unique feature of group therapy is that it consists of the creation of a small society of half a dozen or so individuals whose interactions are considerably more complex than the two-person group in individual therapy. Slavson (1950) has emphasized the importance of the selection of group members. A group composed mostly of similar people with similar problems leads to suppression; maximum stimulation is obtained from a group with contrasting problems; those with "indifferent" problems may turn more to the therapist, maximizing transference. The best groups may be those with a balance of similar, contrasting, and indifferent problems (Spotnitz, 1952). Group composition can be changed to increase or decrease stimulation; this may be the most important manipulation available to the therapist.

The kinds of social learning which can occur in a therapeutic group are numerous. Members who have never had an opportunity to socialize may acquire a basic social feeling for the first time. Shy and lonely people may particularly benefit. One special opportunity available in group therapy is to compare one's own problems with others and to gain some perspective on how other people feel behind their social facades. Much of the therapy consists of affective changes (Klapman, 1947).

Some of the same principles used in interpreting individual psychotherapy apply to groups. The initial anxiety reduction is found here, not just in connection with the therapist but in some feeling of group morale. Often, the patients help the therapist by interpreting the more superficial resistances of individual members. Since all forms of group therapy involve the discussion of problems and feelings, one would assume that anxiety extinction and new emotional learning are possible. There are some group techniques which appear to provide particularly good conditions for extinction; in Moreno's psychodrama therapy, a patient who feels an impulse which cannot be verbalized is encouraged to act it out in front of the group (Moreno, 1946). If this does involve extinction, then the effects should be more readily generalized to other social situations. Group therapy in general would be expected to provide more transfer of learning.

Another principle discussed in connection with individual therapy, which seems applicable to groups, is the importance of the relationship with the therapist. Here, too, a warm, understanding personality would be the basis for interpretive effectiveness, etc. The relationship with the therapist is, perhaps, not as intense as in individual therapy, except that competitive feelings might be brought out more readily. Group therapy may make extra demands on the social facility of the therapist. The group may be stronger than the individual therapist and show organized resistance (see Spotnitz, 1952, for a discussion of therapist factors).

Family therapy is a loose term to describe the treatment of children, parents, and marital partners in various combinations (Ackerman, 1958). Since the family is the social situation in which pathological behavior is most frequently learned and transmitted, it should be a good point for therapeutic intervention. Simultaneous treatment may have several advantages including the acquisition of vital knowledge by the therapist (Mittelmann, 1952). More basic, however, is the therapeutic benefit for all family members of positive changes in one individual.

According to the present theoretical analysis, the main point in family therapy is that anxiety on the part of the parent, either one or both, is interfering with the relationships in the family—usually in a complex way. The child may be drawn into a marital battle or expected to fulfill some needs of the parent which may interfere with the child's development. This produces anxiety and insecurity in the child. A therapist may establish a good relationship with the child and achieve some anxiety extinction. If, however, there is no change in the anxiety of the parent, the child's anxiety will be relearned. Reducing anxiety in the parent would prevent this undoing of the therapy with the child. Similar problems exist in therapy with marital couples.

Individual psychotherapy can be extended, and possibly made more effective, by creating a new family-like group for a patient in which fundamental new learning can take place. In the last decade, there has been a marked increase in interest in the social organization of the hospital, in therapeutic milieus, and in new forms of social therapy (Rioch, 1957). While it has not been emphasized, Rosen's therapy actually depends on a therapeutic milieu which is created by having the patient live in an ordinary house with two or three aides, who reiterate the interpretations and attitudes expressed in the formal therapy hours (Murray, 1962). A number of attempts to create milieu therapy groups, of family or ward size, have been made. We have some data on one such attempt at the Walter Reed Army Medical Center (Murray and Cohen, 1959).

An experimental milieu therapy ward was set up to study and treat soldiers who had had a schizophrenic breakdown during basic training. The ward was staffed with an unusually competent group of corpsmen, a nurse, several social workers, and a psychiatrist. No more than twelve patients were admitted to the ward at any one time. Group therapy sessions were held three mornings a week and patients could seek individual interviews with the psychiatrist. The treatment was not confined to the psychiatrist, however; everyone on the staff participated, creating a therapeutic milieu. The nurse was a particularly important variable, serving as a mother figure. The corpsmen may have functioned in something of a sibling role. The atmosphere was family-like. The entire staff met weekly, discussed each patient, and decided—democratically—how to handle each problem. Thus, the entire milieu might be quite permissive toward a patient during one period, and then gradually encourage him to socialize.

One way of examining this kind of therapy is to see what happens to social behavior. In order to measure social behavior, a sociometric technique was devised and a preliminary study done to assess its validity as a measure of social interaction. Patients in three wards, representing varying degrees of social cohesion, were given a sociometric questionnaire. The results are shown in Figure 18. Each circle represents a patient and a double arrow means a mutual sociometric choice. The control medical ward shows a complex social organization, the open psychiatric ward less, and the locked psychiatric ward practically none. The various differences are statistically significant. This reflects the social withdrawal and disorganization characteristic of mental illness. None of these wards used milieu therapy.

In order to evaluate milieu therapy, the sociometric questionnaire was given to the experimental ward and two control wards of approximately the same size: a metabolic disease research ward in which patients were restricted to the ward in much the same manner as psychiatric wards and a typical closed psychiatric ward emphasizing somatic therapy. The sociograms are presented in Figure 19 where it can be seen that the social organization of the milieu therapy ward is much closer to the non-psychiatric ward than to the typical closed ward. After a nearly complete patient turnover, the study was replicated with similar results (Figure 20). The increased social interaction was probably due to the reduction of anxiety in the permissive milieu.

The days when mental hospitals were thought of as neutral places in which to keep patients in between therapeutic contacts with a psychiatrist, or until they got well spontaneously, are gone forever. The mental hospital is a complex social organization with powerful effects on the lives and emotions of its inmates (Stanton and Schwartz, 1954; Rioch, 1957). Some aspects of the institution may even make the patient worse, causing further regression (Goffman, 1961). It is also possible that the social organization of the hospital may be set up and manipulated to produce therapeutic effects. This

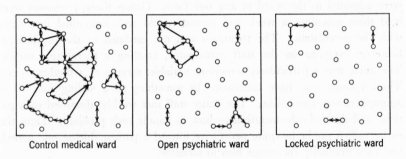

Control medical ward   Open psychiatric ward   Locked psychiatric ward

Figure 18. Social organization and mental illness. Sociograms of wards representing three degrees of mental illness (after Murray and Cohen, 1959).

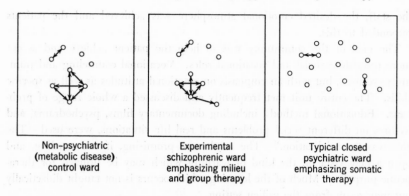

| Non-psychiatric (metabolic disease) control ward | Experimental schizophrenic ward emphasizing milieu and group therapy | Typical closed psychiatric ward emphasizing somatic therapy |

Figure 19. Psychotherapy and interpersonal relations. Sociograms showing effect of milieu therapy on social interaction (after Murray and Cohen, 1959).

would be similar to the milieu therapy on small wards, but on a larger scale involving the entire institution.

The experiments of Maxwell Jones (1953) offer an illustration of a therapeutic community. The patients treated here were about as difficult a lot as one would want to find: lower class, difficult to employ, criminally inclined character disorders, drug addicts, and psychotics. The method was to organize the entire unit—one hundred patients plus staff—into a community concentrating on the rehabilitation of the patients. Many staff problems had to be worked out, especially rivalry between different professional groups. With a basically constructive and democratic outlook on the part of

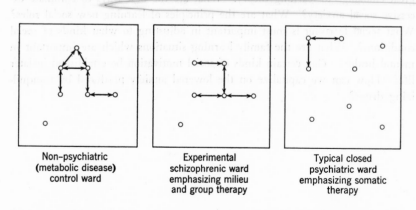

| Non-psychiatric (metabolic disease) control ward | Experimental schizophrenic ward emphasizing milieu and group therapy | Typical closed psychiatric ward emphasizing somatic therapy |

Figure 20. Replication of the study of psychotherapy and interpersonal relations. Sociograms showing replication of study of milieu therapy and social interaction (after Murray and Cohen, 1959).

the staff, the desired emotional atmosphere was achieved and the patients responded to this.

The goal of the community was to help the patient achieve and accept more rewarding social and vocational roles. Vocational counseling and training were used, but with an emphasis on emotional attitudes as well as specific skills. The entire unit met frequently and discussed a whole range of problems. Educational methods, including documentary films, psychodrama, and lectures on different social problems and real life situations, were used. The aim was "resocialization." The results are promising, if not startling, and open a new vista on the kind of learning which may be utilized for therapeutic purposes. Much of the learning which occurs is not taught didactically but may result from the milieu setting.

In one therapeutic community (Sivadon, 1957), weekly meetings are held and the staff waits for a legitimate gripe to come up—meals served too slowly, not enough evening activities, etc. If a natural griper does not initiate this, then the staff insidiously suggests it. A protest meeting is held and even quite regressed patients are found to get drawn into it. The staff becomes understanding but does not offer a solution with the frequent result that the patients organize and, with a little skillful channelizing on the part of the "sociotherapist," constructive improvement of the social situation is achieved, along with much increased social learning on the part of patients.

The reduction of social anxiety and the establishment of positive relationships with the staff and group members seem to be central factors in all forms of social therapy. The new social learning seems to be dependent on the emotional attachments. These new forms of social therapy present a great challenge to learning theory. What are the best ways to eliminate excessive social anxiety? What are the principles of learning new social roles? What social learning is most important in adjusting to what kinds of social conditions? What are the family learning situations which are important in mental health? Can certain kinds of social motivation be established in later life? How can we capitalize on the lowered anxiety produced by tranquilizing drugs?

chapter nine

Forcible Indoctrination and Personality Change

Robert R. Holt

Among the many contemporary methods for changing people, none is more spectacular than forcible indoctrination, and probably few are more generally misunderstood. In what follows, I shall first give a brief factual account of forcible indoctrination as practiced by the Russian and Chinese Communists. After an assessment of the effectiveness of these methods of inducing behavioral change, I shall essay a psychological explanation of the effects that are achieved. In a pair of concluding discussions, I want to take up the implications of these facts and theories for the general problem of changing personality, and finally to consider some of their social and political implications.

THE TECHNIQUES OF FORCIBLE INDOCTRINATION

In 1951, the newspaperman Edward Hunter published a book with the then novel title, *Brainwashing in Red China*. The term he introduced, as a rough translation of a Chinese phrase that has also been rendered as "thought reform," caught and held the public imagination. Seeming to imply a new, mysterious, and powerful method of affecting men's minds, it was first applied to the techniques that produced some collaborators with the enemy, false confessions, and even conversions to communism among prisoners of war held by the Chinese during the Korean conflict. After that it was quickly taken up and widely misused. A Southern senator declared to the

An earlier version of this paper, under the title "Brainwashing and Its Implications for Mental Health," was presented to the Duval County Mental Health Association in Jacksonville, Florida, on March 5, 1957.

press that the decision against segregation in the schools had occurred because the Supreme Court had been "brainwashed" by radicals; a woman in a civil suit charged that her mother-in-law had "brainwashed" her husband and turned him against her; and many other loose and reckless usages began to fly about the land. It is my impression that this furor has begun to die down, however, which may make it easier for us to make a dispassionate analysis of the unusual events that have been brought to light.

Forcible indoctrination has been used by the Communist nations to bring about two striking and widely publicized effects: false confessions and ideological conversion. To some extent, the techniques of extracting false confessions differ from those used to force a doctrine down people's throats, and the psychological processes are not entirely the same. The coercive manipulation of beliefs in Soviet Russia and her European satellites has concentrated mostly on the short-term effects that make people denounce themselves publicly for the most wildly implausible crimes, while Communist China has specialized in what they call "thought reform," a longer process aiming at a more thorough-going ideological reconstruction of the victim along Communist lines.

Perhaps the best way to get into the topic will be through an example. Consider first the case of Professor Dimitrov,[1] who was purged during the fantastic era of mass arrests and show trials in Russia during 1936–1938. Dimitrov was a rather non-political professor of history in one of the large Russian universities, a popular lecturer and a "good Communist" in that he always followed the party line as best as he could in his teaching and public utterances. His ordeal began with a critical article in a university magazine entitled "Intentionally or by Mistake?" written by one of his pupils. In a lecture on French history, the professor had remarked on the emotional instability of Joan of Arc. But she had just been declared a champion of the proletariat; the student seized on this alleged slur as a deviation from the party line. This touched off a series of equally absurd charges, accusations and a checking-up process at meetings in the university attended by both professors and students. Professor Dimitrov was upbraided for neglecting the classics of Marxism-Leninism, for espousing bourgeois ideology, and so forth, all on the flimsiest pretexts. Like a good Communist, he admitted as much of the charges as had any basis at all in truth and promised to observe the party line with utmost scrupulousness.

But he was a marked man. His friends began to avoid him; over a period of months he expected arrest any day. By the time it came, he was already haggard with the prolonged anxiety, and felt thoroughly like a criminal. He

[1] The name is false, but the case is true. The story is abridged and modified from F. Beck and W. Godin, 1951.

was taken from his home in the middle of the night by the NKVD, stripped, searched, told nothing, and put into solitary confinement. He knew that he had already been convicted in the eyes of the secret police, and that there was no way for his case to be closed without his signing a confession of some kind. Moreover, he had at times in the past expressed dissatisfaction with one or another little thing about the regime to friends. This alone was enough to give him a feeling of guilt, a knowledge that he was in the eyes of the law a criminal despite the fact that he had *done* nothing. The professor did not know exactly what he would be charged with, but he started out with the handicap of feeling guilty.

For the next few weeks, Professor Dimitrov was kept in isolation, in a small bare cell. He had already become anxious and preoccupied during the weeks of being under suspicion and surveillance and the expectation of arrest; now he rapidly became more disorganized as time dragged on interminably in his tiny windowless cell. He had no contact with friends, no counsel, not even any opportunity to converse with the silent guards who brought him his insufficient and unappetizing meals. The cell was always a little damp and cold, but he was allowed to do exercises only at stated hours of the day; the rest of the time he usually had to sit upright on his bunk. At night, he was forced to sleep on his back facing the bare bulb that always burned in the ceiling.

At first, he was bewildered and demanded explanations, or to be brought to trial. Getting no response from his jailors, he sank into a depressed and humiliated state of complete boredom and loneliness, always shot through with uncertainty about what might be done to him, and what might be happening to his family. At the end of three weeks, he had lost a good deal of weight, was desperately eager to talk to someone, and his joints constantly pained him from the rigid positions he had been forced to maintain. A less intelligent and resourceful man would have probably sunk even lower into despair, might have begun to soil himself, weep and pray constantly, see visions, and generally approach a psychotic condition. But Professor Dimitrov had tried to keep his mind occupied as best he could by thinking about historical topics, and to fill the day with repeated cleanings of his cell.

At the end of three weeks, he was suddenly taken out of his cell and into a room elsewhere in the prison, where he was faced by an interrogator. He was eager for human contact, but not as much softened up by the preceding period of isolation as many prisoners are; the interrogation, however, was more severe than is typical. He was subjected to almost continuous questioning, day and night, for fifty days. Professor Dimitrov estimated afterwards that he was never allowed to sleep more than two or three hours at a time, and then sitting up; on a number of days he was allowed no sleep at all. The examiners, of course, changed shifts, and further confused the prisoner by always starting over at the beginning with the same questions. During much of his ordeal, he was forced to stand, so that his feet and legs swelled badly.

Such an interrogation usually begins with a detailed review of the prisoner's entire life history. The interrogator goes into minute personal details that have no direct political implications as a part of a deliberate technique of getting close to the prisoner and cementing an intimate relationship like that of doctor and patient. Typically he tells the prisoner that he wants to help, that everything can be quickly wound up if the prisoner will only cooperate. The interrogator is demanding, never satisfied with answers, always pressing for more details; he tells the prisoner, "You might as well confess; we already know everything." Frequently he will reveal that he does in fact know the answers to questions the prisoner has evaded answering; or he will say, "Your associates have already told us all about it. You have nothing to gain by dragging this out—why don't you just confess so that we can close your case?"

All this time, the prisoner is subjected to drastic physical and psychological measures to weaken him; a state of extreme fatigue is always built up; he may be humiliated by having his face slapped, or by being forced to urinate and defecate in public; he may be subjected to intense lights in his eyes for hours on end. Often he is threatened in a non-specific way about what may happen to him; he may hear blood-curdling screams and sounds of savage beatings from the next room, but actual physical torture is seldom used. The prisoner will desperately search for some way out of this intolerable situation; he will rack his brains for something he can "confess" that may satisfy his interrogator. But his answers are usually unsatisfactory; the man he so much wants to placate is displeased, rejects and punishes him part of the time, at other times rewarding and approving of evidences that the prisoner is trying to cooperate. Bewildered and frustrated by this treatment, physically groggy, in constant fear for what may happen to himself and anyone he cares about, the prisoner gets into a frame of mind in which any suggestion offered by the interrogator may be adopted as the truth.

At this stage, when the prisoner is definitely cooperating in the production of a "confession," some of the pressure lightens. The attitude of the interrogator becomes more cordial and friendly; the prisoner may be allowed an occasional hour or two of rest in bed, but never enough to regroup his forces. The two of them settle down to the task of taking certain real events and associations that might have had a treasonable or counterrevolutionary implication, and reinterpreting them to produce as plausible a confession as possible.

In Professor Dimitrov's case, he expected to have to confess to "anti-Soviet propaganda," "ideological counterrevolution," and the like; instead, he soon discovered that the interrogators were not at all satisfied by confessions of this kind. Nothing less than an admission that he had been a spy for Japan would do! Since he had been a specialist in the ancient history of the Near East, it was an easy jump for the NKVD to equate Near and Far East, ancient and contemporary periods, but it was difficult for the prisoner to go along. His resistance was finally broken by being confronted by a couple of his colleagues, who were brought in to denounce him and declare that he had recruited them to help in his espionage.

There remained only the task of writing a more or less plausible "confession," which the interrogator and prisoner could both sign. Professor Dimitrov recalled that he had once met a distinguished Czech orientalist at a reception; this brief conversation became an occasion of his being recruited to spy for Japan. The professor had been invited to give a series of lectures on military history to officers of the Red Army—now reinterpreted as his opportunity to gather military information for transmission to Japan. And so forth, until the protocol was written and signed.

In this particular instance, which occurred in 1938, there was no public trial; it has been estimated that only about 1 per cent of Russian prisoners ever got to the point of the show trial (Hinkle and Wolff, 1956). But the experience of those who were brought to court and who denounced themselves publicly was quite similar. Whatever guilt lurked within them had been mobilized; the times when they had doubted the rightness of the Soviet cause, or the omniscience of Stalin, however briefly, had been revealed to them to have been just as treasonable as overt acts; they were humbled and broken, longing only for an end to their sufferings. They knew that if they repudiated a confession in court, it would only mean going through the whole thing again—and for what?

So much for the Russian system of extracting false confessions from their own people. Let us now look somewhat more abstractly at thought reform, as practiced in Communist China.

First, just a word about the varieties of treatment undergone by United Nations POW's in Korea. Those captured at the beginning received the most brutal treatment by the North Koreans, in clumsy and generally ineffective attempts to extract military information. After the Chinese entered the war, they took charge and used markedly less physical torture. They too interrogated some prisoners with the primary aim of getting military intelligence; others were exploited for phony confessions in the germ-warfare propaganda campaign; the great majority of prisoners were subjected to a variety of pressures and attempts at indoctrination, probably with the primary intent of making them less difficult to handle and of minimizing the military manpower needed to guard them. Certainly the Chinese were successful in the latter, and notably *un*successful in turning the men of the United Nations forces into Communists. A few key military and civilian prisoners were, however, exposed to prolonged and sometimes remarkably successful attempts not just to extort false confessions but to change their whole value systems and view of the world.

Thought reform has a direct history of at least thirty years in China, and its roots in classical Chinese Confucian and Taoist ways of thought go back many hundreds of years; so we learn from Robert J. Lifton's excellent recent book (1961).[2] In recent years, it has taken two main forms, varying slightly with the nature of the person being "reformed," whether a Western civilian or a Chinese intellectual.

The experience of the American or European missionary, doctor, or business-man who remained in China after the Communists succeeded in taking over the country and was interned in one of the special prisons used for thought re-form was similar in many ways to that of Professor Dimitrov. There was the period of anticipatory anxiety, followed by arrest, accusation of vague crimes against the state, and prolonged imprisonment without opportunity to communicate with anyone on the outside. The early phase of the treat-ment was typically aimed at breaking the prisoner down by fatigue, sleep deprivation, poor food, relentless and confusing interrogation, threats of physical abuse (sometimes actually carried out), pressure to confess, a search-ing out of all sources of guilt and exploiting them, humiliation, and frus-tration. In this first period of confusion, the prisoner would usually make a wild confession, which would be rejected; thereafter came a period of col-laborative work on an acceptable confession, with leniency rewarding co-operation.

In a number of respects, however, the Chinese methods differed from the Russian. In a smaller proportion of cases, there would be an initial period of solitary isolation. Sooner or later, however, and usually at once, the pris-oner was typically subjected to a superficially opposite condition: the steady presence of about half a dozen cellmates whenever he was not being interro-gated. These would almost invariably be prisoners (usually Chinese) in an advanced state of indoctrination who were eager to win credits with the Communist authorities by their zeal in assisting with the coercive process. The result was a steady, unrelenting pressure by a small group unanimously and vehemently lined up against the Westerner, and the omnipresence of informers to make reports on his "progress."

The Chinese also made more use of chains, frequently manacling a resis-

---

[2] The following account is based primarily on his book and papers (Lifton, 1954, 1956), but also on Schein (1956), Segal (1956), and Hinkle & Wolff (1956). See also Schein (1961).

tive prisoner's hands rigidly together behind his back until he should become less "reactionary." Thus handcuffed, the prisoner, helpless to feed himself or attend to his bodily needs, would become dependent on his cellmates and would be subjected to continuous and often excruciating pain. The Chinese interrogators in other ways seem to have been more likely to use physical brutality than their Russian colleagues (Hinkle and Wolff, 1956); Lifton (1961) reports on a prisoner whose back was fractured in a savage beating after a time of stubborn resistance.

When the prisoner's resistance has effectively been broken, he begins the writing of his confession, which may go through many revisions, just as the process may involve many cycles of increasing pressure up to the breaking point followed by sudden leniency and solicitude. At this time, the period of indoctrination proper begins. Here too the two Communist systems differ; the Russians have concentrated primarily on extorting confessions, following which comes the sentence, usually months or years of reform by labor in a Siberian camp. The Chinese use this method sometimes too, particularly in case of their own nationals, but almost always lay greater stress on ideological indoctrination. This process may go on for years, during which time the prisoner, now considered a "student," spends all his time reading, writing, and especially discussing Communist doctrine, in the context of the omnipresent group of cellmates. In the revolutionary universities, where much of the thought reform of the Chinese themselves is carried out, the total process is of this kind.

It is difficult to convey in a brief time the thoroughness and intensity of the educational phase of thought reform; for a fuller account, see Hinkle and Wolff (1956), Schein (1961), and Lifton (1956, 1961). A dozen features stand out.

1. Thought reform is *prolonged*. It may go on for years, though in some instances spectacular temporary effects have been achieved in a few months. The total number of hours devoted to the indoctrination of a Western prisoner, judging from Lifton's subjects, far exceeds the hours devoted to a college education or to the most prolonged of psychoanalyses.

2. It is *continuous,* as neither one of the above mentioned educative and therapeutic undertakings is. Every waking hour, when attention does not have to be concentrated on just enough eating, eliminating, and exercise to maintain life, is devoted to study, attending lectures, autobiographical confessional writing, or discussions with the group or with an interrogator (called a "judge").

3. It takes place in a *completely controlled environment*. No contradictory information is allowed to reach the prisoner, no escape is possible except

through submission to the inevitable, and the only persons he comes into contact with are part of the plan for inducing change.

4. There is a *two-fold social aspect* to this environmental control: on the one hand, the prisoner is *robbed of the usual social supports* of his beliefs and values; on the other, he is *subjected to a massive pressure to conform* to a new, unanimous society, that of his cellmates. The pressure of a social consensus can be overwhelming, as the experiments of Asch (1952) and Crutchfield (1955) have shown; but thought reform is one continuous, fantastically strengthened Asch experiment, with all of the others not only the stooges of the one in control, incessantly insisting that white is black, but doing so at the highest possible emotional pitch. The group's pressure takes the periodic form of the "struggle": the attention of the group is focused on the recalcitrant "reactionary"; they encircle him, take turns shouting insults, demanding confession and reform, reviling and denouncing all that he holds most precious, underlining all their points by spitting in his face, slapping him, or even beating him within an inch of his life.

5. Thought reform is *personalized*. Aside from the group lectures and rote learning of standard communist texts, the indoctrination is aimed at individualized reconstruction. No part of a man's life is exempt from scrutiny and public examination in light of "the people's standpoint." The immediate goal of the process is the writing of a confession that amounts to a complete autobiography, a total life re-evaluated in Communist terms. The pressure to confess all personal secrets, to the judge and to the group, is unrelenting.

6. There is a total *lack of privacy*. Except when being interrogated, the prisoner is never physically distant by more than a few inches from six to eight other people, who make it their business to find out everything about him. Details of everyone's life history, particularly the most shameful and humiliating parts, are known to all, being extorted in a confessional competition, and are relentlessly exploited in the group as well as in private sessions with the "judge." The individual never has a moment alone to pull himself together, to recover from the assaults of interrogation, to confront what he has been told with what he knows to be true, or to plan a strategy of resistance.

7. An integral part of thought reform is the *assault upon previous identity*. From an intuitive or empirical awareness that a man's value system is rooted in his underlying conception of who and what he is, the Communists attack that ego identity directly, attempting to destroy it so that a new person may be symbolically reborn. First, the prisoner is shown how his previous life was enmeshed with the capitalist imperialism of the nation in which he grew up, forcing upon him the negative identity of the exploiter of the poor

and enemy of the people. Then, many of his acts in China are reinterpreted to show how, under the Communist legal system, they constituted espionage, so that the identity of the spy is forced upon him too. Surrounded by people who continually denounce themselves as criminals, with his every susceptibility to guilt cleverly exploited, the Westerner can hardly resist coming to think of himself too as a guilty criminal whose former identity as a priest, scholar, or what not, was a fraudulent mask for a secret and evil self.

8. There is a systematic *application of rewards and punishments:* behavior expressing the old identity and ideology is severely and consistently punished, while movement in the desired direction is reinforced by means of social esteem, the friendship and praise of the judge (who grows to have great emotional importance to the prisoner via transference, which the prolonged contact encourages), even by prestige, as well as by modest comforts and amenities which seem by contrast to his usual lot to be luxuries.

9. Thought reform demands *sincerity and enthusiasm*—total emotional commitment to the new ideas. Members of the cell group are well acquainted with the many ploys of lip service, attempts to maintain inner reservations via external histrionics, and other devices used by resistive prisoners. The process is not infallible, so a clever actor can sometimes get away with emotional protestations, tearful self-denunciations, and outwardly earnest application of the ideology in the frequent sessions where group members examine their own and each others' "wrong thoughts," while still maintaining an inward set of contrary beliefs. To carry out such an act convincingly over a long period is most difficult, however, and it is well known that a person will tend to believe what he hears himself saying repeatedly even if he tries to maintain a secret denial. At any rate, thought reform aims at least as much at an emotional change as at a cognitive one. It wants converts, and it manages to get a person so emotionally entangled, so deeply compromised and contaminated, that he will have great difficulty in reverting to his earlier beliefs when the process is over.

10. Thought reform repeatedly pushes its victims to the breaking point, so that they reach a crisis in which all *sources of resistance to the new ideology are exhausted,* in the symbolic death of the old personality. In this way, it uses the phenomenon of "hitting bottom," which is so familiar in the treatment of alcoholics, psychotics, and other kinds of patients who resist psychotherapy until they have been convinced that their existing patterns of behavior lead to intolerable consequences. One of the main devices for bringing about this state is the alternation of encouraging acceptance and rejection with insatiable demands for more confessions.

11. Thought reform demands that its victims be *active in reforming others.* This is one of its shrewdest strokes: at one blow it gains useful allies and

catspaws, and forces the person to shift from a passively receptive to an actively involved role. Under the guise of what Christianity calls "salvation through works," it enforces what every teacher knows is the best way of learning—instructing someone else. By being forced to denounce his friends and associates, the prisoner reaches a point of no return in commitment to the regime; by persuading new prisoners who are struggling to defend values he himself has denounced and given up, he helps convince himself that he did the right thing.

12. In the final stage of *synthesis and reconstruction,* the rebirth of a new identity, a number of factors play a role. It is recognized by many theories and many therapies, from psychoanalysis through client-centered therapy to Alcoholics Anonymous, that personality tends to reconstitute itself after a period of regression. This is Rogers' basic actualizing tendency, Maslow's and Goldstein's self-realizing or self-actualizing tendency, and Freud's synthetic function of the ego. But thought reform puts tools into the hands of this force, among which is the fact that much of Communist ideology has a seductive similarity to most Western value systems. One does not need to give up the value of freedom, for example; one simply has to see that true Communist freedom of the press consists in having the newspapers controlled by the people through their instrument, the party, instead of the press's being controlled by the imperialist monopolies. In the hands of a skilled dialectician, with a wealth of "facts" at his fingertips, and confronted by a weary and broken defender of Christian or democratic ideology, the Communist value system can easily be shown to be a truer realization of human longing for decency, justice, and the equality of men than any other. Its ultimate commitment to such relatively universal values makes communism an acceptable basis for the reconstruction, then. This process is helped along by the judge, who has now become more and more human and supportive, sometimes by the help of "depth interpretations" of residual resistance in terms of important events in the subject's childhood.

EFFECTIVENESS

How successful have the Communists been with their several methods of forcible indoctrination? In seeking an answer, let us consider first the extortion of false confessions.

Viewed from the standpoint of this limited goal, both Russian and Chinese systems seem to have been highly successful when applied to their own people, and surprisingly so even when the victims have been foreigners. If we are to understand their ability to induce their nationals to confess, we have to be clear about several facts of Communist life (Hinkle and Wolff, 1956). To begin with, neither country has a legal system resembling the

Anglo-Saxon; in both Russia and Communist China the prisoner is presumed guilty unless he can prove his innocence. Moreover, the police of both countries follow the announced principle of never arresting an innocent person. This statement must be taken more seriously than one might think. It implies, first, that before he is arrested, a suspect is extensively investigated, and a great many incriminating facts are collected about him. The second implication is that almost everyone is actually guilty of "crimes against the state," since these are very broadly defined in the respective legal codes. Communist law judges conduct by its results, not its intent, so that failure to produce is defined as sabotage; and it defines ordinary grumbling against officials as treasonable. Few citizens can live for long in these "workers' paradises" without building up dissatisfactions and criticizing the regime occasionally to relatives or close friends, who may very well inform on them. Since such criticism is strictly forbidden, the man who is arrested is bound to feel guilty, or at least to recognize that he has in fact broken the laws of the state in which he lives.

A further peculiarity of the Russian legal system, borrowed by the Chinese, is that (with rare exceptions) no arrested person can be released until he has made a written statement of his guilt. Since the custom is not to bring *specific* charges, and since almost everyone is guilty of some "crimes against the state," almost no one is technically innocent. The alternative to confession, then, is indefinite imprisonment, with various unpleasant contingent consequences for the prisoner and his family.

When the prisoner is a foreigner, he is likely at first to be confused by expectations and demands which the Communist citizen takes as a matter of course. Eventually, however, the law is explained to him, and it is made clear that various innocent acts about which he had no previous reasons to feel guilty—which he thus may freely admit—are in fact explicitly considered criminal by the law of the country in which he finds himself. It is not difficult, then, to say, "When I wrote my friends back home about the inflation here, I had no intention of spying, but I can see that according to your laws, that is economic espionage." Once a prisoner has gone this far, not too much pressure is necessary to get him to drop the qualifications and simply say, "I committed economic espionage." The celebrated confession of Cardinal Mindszenty actually amounts to little more than this kind of thing; he admitted his opposition to the Communists, which was a matter of record, in the legal format of its having constituted espionage, treason, etc. "Confessions" that involve not the reinterpretation of real acts but the affirmation of obvious untruths, like the statement of a flyer that he engaged in germ warfare, are a good deal more difficult to rationalize, and the Chinese had less success with this type of attempt.

The best quantitative data on the effects of forcible indoctrination come from studies of United States prisoners of the Communists in Korea (Segal, 1956). Ten per cent of the POW's from the American Army informed on fellow prisoners; 27 per cent made at least a moderate contribution to enemy propaganda, about one in five making "confessions." Though 97 per cent of the prisoners were exposed to indoctrination in communism, about half of them to rather intensive efforts, 88 per cent showed absolutely no acceptance of communist ideology on repatriation, 7 per cent showing a little, 4 per cent a moderate amount, and only one man in a hundred much acceptance. Of a group of 59 Air Force personnel (mostly flying officers) who were selected for special pressure to "confess" germ warfare, about 64 per cent complied to some extent, and 39 per cent made statements the Communists considered satisfactory enough to use in propaganda (Sander, 1956). Out of approximately 4500 prisoners who were offered repatriation, only 21 initially decided to remain with the Communists, and even these began changing their minds as soon as possible thereafter. According to a news story in *The New York Times* on Sept. 8, 1963, 5 of these 21 still remained in Communist China, 1 had died, and the remaining 15 had all made their way back to this country.

Lifton (1961), who is probably as well informed as anyone, says that only one of the 25 Westerners he interviewed who had been subjected to prolonged, intensive indoctrination became lastingly converted to communism, and he knew of only one or two others in all. To be sure, a larger proportion praised their captors and avowed support for communism when first released, but most of them quickly reverted to their former beliefs when they returned to Western surroundings, only a few taking as long as a year to do so, and most of them ended up more strongly opposed to communism than they were before thought reform.

On the whole, forcible indoctrination as used by the Russians and Chinese seems to be a relatively effective technique of extorting false confessions, but quite ineffective in achieving lasting conversion. (No figures seem to be available on the effectiveness of thought reform in bringing about lasting conversion of the Chinese themselves to communism.) Nevertheless, it is the consensus of those who have studied victims of these coercive techniques that virtually no one can go through the full treatment and emerge with his beliefs and values wholly unchanged.

WHY DO PERSONALITY CHANGES OCCUR?

Before considering psychological explanations of the effects, let us look for a moment at some of the ways in which this so-called brainwashing does *not* work. Clearly, no direct manipulation of the brain is involved. Direct electrical stimulation of the brain by implanted electrodes had not yet been invented and, contrary to some rumors, not even drugs or hypnosis were used by either the Soviets or the Chinese. Nor were their methods simply a matter of torture and terror.

A more firmly established rumor has it that forcible indoctrination is a fiendish application of Pavlovian psychology. This statement has appeared in books by popular authors ranging from Hunter (1951) to Sargant (1961), and even by some psychiatrists who ought to know better and whom I shall not name. Any student of the psychology of learning who knows about the methods used in forcible indoctrination will be puzzled by such claims. Conditioned reflexes are notoriously unstable and evanescent, even in dogs, and are quite difficult to achieve in people. The attribution of brainwashing methods to Pavlov is apparently an indirect result of Russian propaganda, which presents him as the fountainhead of all that is profound in psychology. Pavlov was indeed a great physiologist, who made important contributions to the psychology of learning. As Russia's only figure of major world stature in psychology, he has been elevated to the position of a kind of infallible genius who must be quoted on all topics and given credit for all major psychological achievements; but there is no evidence that Russian prison interrogators were in the slightest influenced by his work. There is a great deal of evidence, on the other hand, that the Russian methods grow directly out of centuries-old traditions of a secret state police, which has had generations of trial and error to develop ways of breaking men for political reasons (Hinkle and Wolff, 1956; Hinkle, 1961).

Inducing Regression

Let us begin our psychological analysis of how forcible indoctrination works by asking what its aims are—what state it tries to achieve. The goal is to produce a person who will confess to and believe things that never happened, and who will give up his values, his ideology, his very identity, and become a new person. In order to bring about such effects, the brainwasher needs first to transform his victim into someone who is weak, who has no strong convictions of his own, who in fact does not have firm standards of what is logical and true but who can think in a magical or wishful way, spinning out fantasies which he cannot readily tell from what is real, someone who is extremely dependent on authoritative persons, suggestible and easy to influence and teach. In short, he needs to transform the adult in his power into a child. Psychologically, this is possible to an astonishingly large extent, for we all began as children and learned only after great difficulty and years of effort to become more or less mature. Moreover, we never leave the child entirely behind; he lingers inside, ready to take over when the grown-up gets tired, discouraged, anxious, or drunk. Anyone who has spent much time with young children knows how vivid their imaginations can be, how thoroughly they can disregard reality in favor of their own fantasies. We all shed our adult rationality and responsibility every night when we go to sleep; in our dreams, we use some types of thought processes that children use. Likewise, as we have known since Freud, a great part of the most serious mental illness can be understood as a return (or regression) to more or less childish ways of thinking and feeling.

A great many of the brainwashing techniques are primarily aimed at bringing about regression to a childish state, therefore. This is done mainly by six methods.

The first method of inducing regression is *anxiety and terror*. It is an old clinical observation that anxiety interferes with concentration, attention, and other aspects of adult, effective thinking, and that it causes a person to fall back on more primitive and infantile ways of thinking and acting; and recently we have had experimental demonstrations of these effects. But no experimenter would dare use the extreme methods employed by the Communists: literally putting a person in mortal terror, threatening everyone he loves, exposing him to danger or actuality of torture, and keeping him in ignorance of what may happen and how long he may be detained. In a way, the vague threats and the waiting in suspense, never knowing just what is happening or what will come next, are more unnerving and corroding to adult functions than anything else.

As we saw in the example of Dimitrov, anxiety begins to do its work before the victim is even arrested. As soon as the arrest occurs, however, the prisoner may be exposed to a second method of inducing regression: *isolation*. We have all heard that prisoners kept in solitary confinement sometimes go "stir crazy"; it has been known for centuries that complete solitude for long periods of time has strange effects on the functioning of the human mind. Man is a social animal; he is not made in such a way that he can live by himself and operate at a high level of effectiveness. We are not surprised to hear that a hermit sees visions. Solitary sailors or marooned Arctic explorers who have spent many weeks alone (of course, also subjected to various other extreme stresses) tell stories of weird states of mind in which they cannot tell whether what they experience is real or a dream (Lilly, 1956; Miller, 1962; Slocum, 1955; Lindemann, 1958).

Isolation is a relatively harmless component of forcible indoctrination, despite serious misapprehensions that have been caused by fragmentary reports of recent experiments on so-called sensory deprivation. Everyone "knows" that when a subject is kept in as unstimulated a condition as possible for a day or so, he begins to hallucinate, to have bizarre distortions of his body image, and in general to approach a psychotic-like condition. The only trouble is that the truth in all this is buried in exaggerations and misunderstandings to such an extent that it is difficult to set the record straight briefly. In a series of experiments[3] at the Research Center for Mental Health, Leo Goldberger and I have kept a total of nearly forty college students, Air Force officers and NCO's, and unemployed actors (plus ourselves) in a state of perceptual isolation for periods ranging from eight to seventy-two hours, and have been unable to replicate the most spectacular effects reportedly achieved by others. What have been called hallucinations often turn out to be ordinary hypnagogic images—which can be quite vivid and unexpected, to be sure—and the reported deterioration of thought seems to be little more than the familiar fact that when you lie down in the darkness at night before going to sleep, you tend to daydream and find it hard to think connectedly about serious topics. Yet this last is a real phenomenon of a regressive sort. I do not wish to deny that a day or so of isolation has effects; I just want to put them into perspective, and to show that they are mostly not bizarre nor outside the realm of usual experience. Most of the demonstrable effects, like the change from purposive and logical thinking to drifting, imagery-laden fantasy, constitute a kind of regression, and some subjects react to these experiments by emotional upset that constitutes a further regressive push.

A third, more immediately effective method of making a person regress into a receptive, child-like and dream-like state of mind is *preventing sleep.* One of man's most basic and insistent needs is to rest, sleep, and dream (Dement, 1961), and a person can be rapidly weakened by simply keeping him awake a few days and nights. If you have ever lost a few hours of your usual sleep you know how drowsy and dopey you can get, how sluggishly your mind will work, and how difficult it is to maintain concentration or directed thinking for long. In some recent experiments on the effects of preventing sleep, David Tyler (1955) found that 70 per cent of his subjects had auditory and visual near-hallucinations after a few days of going without sleep: they saw and heard things that were not there, like a psychotic or (we might add) like a dreamer, though most of them knew that these images were not real. Before five days and nights of sleeplessness were over, about 1 per cent of these normal volunteers (Marines and conscientious objectors) developed paranoid psychotic episodes: they had delusions that they were great and important persons who were being persecuted, and they started

[3] Supported by the Foundations Fund for Research in Psychiatry, and by contract AF 33(616)6103 from the Biomedical Laboratory, Aerospace Medical Laboratory, Aeronautical Systems Division, Air Force Systems Command, Wright-Patterson Air Force Base, Ohio. See Goldberger and Holt, 1958, 1960; Holt and Goldberger, 1960, 1961.

fights. Needless to say, they were at once allowed to sleep it off, after which they were all right. But such an experiment shows how readily the single device of preventing sleep can get adults into a remarkably regressed state, where the boundary between the real and the imaginary starts to waver and dissolve.

The fourth technique of inducing regression is *semi-starvation*. This is a much more complex matter than one might think at first. Obviously, if you can eat only poorly balanced, insufficient meals, you will lose weight and strength. In addition, however, there are less obvious effects. A few years ago at the University of Minnesota, a team of nutritionists, physiologists, psychologists, and others made a detailed experimental study of the effects of a concentration-camp diet on a group of volunteers over a six-month period (Keys et al., 1950). Besides various physiological changes, the subjects showed a marked increase in docility and apathy and a decrease in initiative. Four out of thirty-six developed severe personality disturbances, one of psychotic degree. All tended to be depressed and irritable, yet easy to manage and influence. This is reminiscent of observations in Russian famines of what is known as echopraxia and echolalia: starved people sometimes develop such a marked degree of suggestibility that they immediately and automatically repeat anything that is said to them and imitate any act performed in front of them. While pathological phenomena of this last sort have not been reported in any accounts of forcible indoctrination I have read, it seems likely that the semi-starvation that is practiced leads to increased suggestibility and tendency to take in uncritically what is placed before you.

Fifth, in a number of miscellaneous aspects, the interrogators treat prisoners in a *deliberately infantilizing* way. The helplessness of the prisoner, his ignorance and the relatively greater power and knowledge of the interrogator are emphasized; he is shamed and humiliated, scolded like a naughty child, and slapped in the face. Handcuffs make him as dependent on another person to help him take care of his most elementary needs as a child is on his mother; or he may be forced to soil himself like an infant. Then when the phase of leniency is reached, the interrogators deliberately assume the role of a kindly parent. One former prisoner of the Chinese remarked of this phase, "My mother could not have been much more good and kind than the judge was." Another told Dr. Lifton (1956), "You are not supposed to be pessimistic, but fully optimistic in prison and should throw yourself fully into the arms of the Government, like a child in the arms of its mother, and then be happy."

A sixth factor in inducing regression is oddly enough not usually alluded to, perhaps because it seems not to differentiate forcible indoctrination from other, more usual types of imprisonment: *heterosexual frustration*. It may nevertheless be important in interaction with some of the other influences, in two ways. First, prisoners of the Chinese were not only robbed of normal heterosexual gratification, they were put in a situation of continuous close physical proximity to other men which must have encouraged regression to a homosexual orientation. The lack of either physical or psychological privacy, plus the public nature of the group visit to an open latrine for a single daily defecation, undoubtedly contributed further to the stirring up of unwelcome homoerotic desires. Such impulses typically pose a severe problem of control, and would add to the already enormous psychological strain. Second, a happily married man who was suddenly arrested and separated from his wife, as happened to many in Russian and Chinese jails, would be robbed of the emotional support of intimacy with the person he loved most, who might in fact be endangered by his resistance. Such a man's need for affection and communication with another person, thus frustrated, could be channelled into a close and dependent relationship to his interrogator or judge.

These six techniques, then, are usually applied in the early phase of forcible indoctrination, most of them simultaneously, and they create a powerful pressure to slip back into an infantile condition: a state of emotional dependence on others, or suggestibility, and of dreamy inability to distinguish between reality and fantasy. It is truly remarkable that so many men have been able to fight these undertows successfully, and either remain silent or actively defy or deceive their captors. It should not be surprising that others, as weak as these are strong, succumb entirely and develop psychoses. But the indoctrinator fails if he drives his man crazy; he has to gauge his pressure carefully, and push the prisoner almost to the breaking point but not quite over it. Russian jails contained many psychotic prisoners who were the victims of clumsy interrogation until more refined methods were learned (Hinkle and Wolff, 1956).

The near-psychotic, extreme state cannot be maintained for many days, but is usually effective in cracking resistance, bringing about a preliminary "confession," and the development of an attitude of defeat and despair. After that, the pressures are lightened enough to allow the creation of a confession document that will appear sane enough for propaganda purposes.

Shame and Guilt

One theme that is vital to the understanding of forcible indoctrination runs throughout all the accounts: the importance of *shame and guilt*. In his valuable account of the growth and crises of the healthy personality, Erikson (1959) has written that shame, doubt, and guilt are the natural antagonists to and alternative developments in place of autonomy and initiative. Surely the qualities of autonomous initiative are central among those required if a person is to be able to resist the effects of forcible indoctrination. The destructive forces of shame and guilt strike at the heart of a person's confidence in himself, his sense of being a person of worth and substance. Erikson also writes that "only an ego identity safely anchored in the 'patrimony' of a cultural identity can balance the superego in order to produce a workable equilibrium" (1950, p. 368). This is to say that a sense of self rooted in continuity with an individual's origins is a bulwark against the erosive effects of guilt. Note that in coercive indoctrination, this constellation is attacked on all fronts: the prisoner's communication with his cultural patrimony is broken, the bases of his identity are reviled and assaulted, and every effort is made to search out and intensify the self-rejective, self-destructive emotion of guilt and shame. Everyone has done things he feels are wrong; everyone hides within himself the guilty knowledge that he has at times been mean, petty, destructive, or exploitative, and he operates most effectively when such memories are not stirred up. But the Communist prison official has enough intuition or experience to realize this and to build his attack on the person's own self-punishing tendencies. Any preexisting guilt is then diverted into channels the interrogator suggests. Moreover, feeling guilty puts a person on the defensive, makes it harder for him to be defiant and get angry at unjust treatment.

We should keep in mind the fact that the most natural reaction to much of the treatment received by prisoners of the Russians and Chinese is anger, resentment, and hatred of their persecutors. If these reactions were allowed to develop, however, they would work in the opposite direction to the desired effects. American troops captured by the Chinese in Korea were often surprised and thrown off guard by being greeted by beaming officers who would say: "Welcome and congratulations! You don't have to fight any more in this stupid war, but can now work for peace" (Schein, 1956). During all their mistreatment of our men, the Chinese claimed that they had the friendliest of feelings and were really sorry to have to punish them for not cooperating. As one POW put it,

> It is hard to explain, but everything that was done, regardless of whether it was good or bad, was done trying to give you the impression that it was either the best they had or you were very lucky, that they were really giving you a good deal. Little things—like evidently it was their policy to let the prisoners celebrate Thanksgiving, Christmas and New Years (Harris, 1956).

This kind of thing makes it harder to feel the hatred that is appropriate. It is significant that those men who overtly expressed their anger and hatred were most successful in withstanding the effects of even the most severe pressures. Moreover, the Chinese and Russians gave up reliance on physical brutality and torture because, contrary to popular impression, it simply *did not work*. Men who were subjected to severe beatings often became all the more bitterly determined not to give in—probably because it is so easy to hate someone who is physically cruel to you.

Many of the seemingly arbitrary details of interrogation may be seen to have the effect of turning the prisoner's aggressions against himself. Consider the torture of having to stand at attention for hours on end. This is reported to be as excruciating an experience as can be imagined; but who inflicts this pain? Actually, the prisoner hurts *himself*. Standing at attention is something that must be done by an act of will; it is a self-discipline. Prisoners would do it, of course, first of all because the kicks and blows they received if they refused were much more immediately painful than merely to stand, and also because it does not sound like a particularly cruel or unusual demand—especially to a military man. Thus, the communists could claim that they had stuck to their professed principles of legality and humaneness; they could avoid a showdown on their actual ability to inflict intolerable pain; and the prisoner's willpower was worn out in struggle with himself.

Active Participation

The use of self-inflicted punishment is also consistent with another general psychologically sound principle used by the Communists: getting the person to *participate* as much as possible in the total process. The prisoner has to figure out his own crime, to examine his own thoughts, to criticize himself; he must work on new captives, help with their "reform"; if he will do nothing else, he is required to write out answers that he had given orally, or to sit and copy Communist propaganda statements or other people's confessions. It is made extremely difficult, in the thought reform process, for a person to pretend to go along by lip service; fervor and enthusiasm are required, and a constantly repeated participation that makes it very difficult to keep yourself separated from what you are doing. Lectures were used in the thought reform procedure, but they were followed up by group discussions in which each individual had to participate and practice using the "people's standpoint."

The above account is by no means an exhaustive psychological explanation of the effects of forcible indoctrination. I have concentrated on bringing out various facets of two explanatory principles that seem to me both striking and illuminating: first, the ways in which the procedures of forcible indoctrination constitute powerful pressures towards regression, and second, the ways in which these attempts at coercive change enlist the person against his will by making use of his own tendencies to direct his aggression against himself rather than against external frustrations and assaults.

INDIVIDUAL DIFFERENCES IN RESPONSE TO FORCIBLE INDOCTRINATION

What kind of person has proved most resistive to forcible indoctrination, and what qualities are associated with being influenced? Let us consider first the findings of those who have studied the victims of thought reform. Lifton (1961, p. 150 ff.) reports that the most successful resisters resembled apparent converts in having "a significant amount of totalism; hence both extreme responses. But apparent resisters . . . possessed great strength of identity in contrast to the apparent converts . . . who tended to show identity diffusion." (By totalism is meant a proclivity towards sweeping, all-or-none emotional solutions.) Among his Chinese subjects, several features characterized those who were most resistive to thought reform: "tendencies towards rebelliousness and fear of domination . . . ; strong need for individual self-expression . . . ; binding family ties . . . ; previous patterns of anomie and of emotional escape . . . ; and a significant degree of Westernization, whether Christian or otherwise" (p. 359). By contrast, his two most nearly completely converted Western subjects (one of whom gradually turned against communism) had the following qualities in common:

> Both responded very strongly to the opportunity to merge with the Chinese people; both experienced an unusually strong sense of guilt, and a strong need to be *absolutely sincere* with their captors; both eventually achieved a greater harmony with their prison environment than with any they had previously known, and were loath to surrender it for the anticipated pain of 'freedom.'

They also shared "confusion of identity, and most important of all, a longstanding pattern of totalism . . . a tendency to embrace totally a series of influences" in an "unconditional surrender" (Lifton, 1961, p. 218 ff.).

From interviews with repatriated POW's after the Korean conflict, Schein (1956) reports four types of "resisters" (those who had collaborated the least): *obstructionists,* who had always been in conflict with authority, *idealistic martyrs,* who were strongly identified with a non-Communist ideology, *anxious guilt-ridden* persons who were so terrified of their strong tendencies to submit that they overreacted in the other direction, and *well-integrated resistance leaders,* who were generally used to authority and had good judgment. He describes six types of cooperators, who had collaborated to a significant extent with their indoctrinators: *the weakling,* unable to resist authority or bear any kind of suffering, *the opportunist,* swayed by immediate rewards, *the misguided leader* with bad judgment who thought collaboration a good stratagem for eventual resistance, *the bored or curious intellectual* who got interested in Communist literature, *the low-status person* who had not been rewarded by democratic society and was susceptible to the social rewards of collaboration, and the *Communist sympathizer* predisposed towards the content of the indoctrination.

In Segal's (1956) larger study of repatriated soldiers, based on a study of intelligence dossiers on 238 participators (who collaborated significantly with the enemy), 138 resisters, and 203 men in between, the general pattern is for the two extreme groups to resemble one another in contrast to the middle group. Both resisters and collaborators were better educated and more intelligent, less often married, more likely to be officers and with more military experience, and they had more talent in sports and entertaining. The main difference, then, Segal believes, is that the middle-group men (who "played it cool") had a general pattern of mediocrity and withdrawal, while the extremes were more predisposed to assert themselves in one direction or another. The most significant correlates of participation are not aspects of personality but ratings of "desire for preferential treatment" and "the need to avoid threat and abuse."

These data may be supplemented by laboratory studies of the kinds of persons who submit to social pressure, in situations like the celebrated Asch (1952) experiment on conformity pressure, which is too well known to need retelling here. Blake and Mouton (1961, p. 259) have summarized the findings of a couple of dozen of such studies as follows: "those who are more susceptible to conformity pressures are more likely to be submissive, low in self-confidence, less intelligent, less original, show less nervous tension, score higher on authoritarian scales, score on the simplicity end of the (Barron) complexity-simplicity scale, show greater dependence on the (visual) perceptual field, and comply with requests more frequently." In addition, Linton and Graham (1959) found their susceptible subjects to be high on anti-intraceptive items and on those reflecting admiration of power and toughness, from the California *F* Test; and to have immature and weak self-concepts as measured by projective tests—"to be unimaginative, and to have a limited range of interests. . . . [They] are likely to use repression as a characteristic defense. . . . Their actual reliance on external supports is seen in all the experimental situations where influence is exerted" (Witkin's tilting room and embedded figures, and in the autokinetic situation).

The one experiment that provides the richest data on personality correlates of resisting versus yielding to pressure of conformity is that of Crutchfield (1954) and Barron (1952), a variant of the Asch experiment. Crutchfield's ingenious apparatus tests four persons simultaneously; none can observe the behavior of the others directly, but each thinks he sees a record of their judgments in a panel of lights in front of him. The subject is given a variety of tasks, ranging from judging the relative length of lines, through choosing among answers to factual questions, to expressing tastes and preferences. To each of the four persons, the other three seem to answer first, and each one of them thinks he sees the others agreeing on what may be a clearly unrealistic choice before he has to indicate his answer which will be displayed to the whole group. Actually, the experience of all subjects is identical: each receives phony signals and all react at once, being told nothing about the real behavior of the other group members.

Subjects who had been through this experience were thoroughly assessed by means of self-ratings, objective tests, and situational and projective tests rated by an expert staff. Again, these who were most ready to yield to the apparent consensus were submissive, valued conformity, and were suggestible. But according to this study (Barron, 1952), yielders are also marked by rigid or excessive control of their emotions; they are conservative in their political and social attitudes, racially prejudiced, with a narrow range of interests, poor in making decisions, moralistic, and subject to strong feelings of guilt. They tend to submit to authority and respect any authority for its own sake, they have little insight into themselves, get confused and disorganized under stress, and agree to the statement: "I often think, 'I wish I were a child again'" (which probably indicates vulnerability to pressures towards regression). They view themselves as helpful, kind, obliging, and considerate—they are much more concerned with smoothing over difficulties than with honesty in relationships; they are sentimental, religious in a conventional way, and place a high value on getting along with other people.

By contrast, Barron and Crutchfield found that the people who stick to their guns and are least influenced by the majority value originality, fair-mindedness, and the intellect; indeed, they might well do so, because resisting majority pressure correlates more highly with intelligence than with anything else. They are efficient, capable, persuasive people, with leadership ability. They are more objective about themselves and less self-praising than yielders; they have strong emotional reactions and express their feelings in a more genuine, unaffected way. They are tolerant, responsible, and vigorous; they enjoy life, rely on themselves, and care more for self-respect than for the respect of others. Interestingly enough, they are much more likely to come from broken homes than the yielders are! And their values are more scientific and theoretical than religious and practical.

This is a great number of isolated bits of information, but it lends itself to the following approximate summary. In trying to draw together the threads of common meaning in the investigations just reported, I am going to add some additional findings from two studies by Leo Goldberger and myself (Holt and Goldberger, 1960; Goldberger and Holt, 1961) on personality correlates of an adaptive pattern of response to eight hours of experimental perceptual isolation in two separate and quite different samples of subjects.

The most consistent finding across studies is that people who are not adversely influenced by coercive manipulation show a pattern of *ego strength* (Holt and Goldberger) *and a firm sense of identity* (Lifton), while those who were most easily swayed were weak personalities in a variety of ways: weaklings and opportunists (Schein), people with diffuse identity (Lifton) or low self-confidence (Blake and Mouton; Linton and Graham). A second consistent theme characterizing adaptive reactors to isolation in our work was a dual one: *cognitive and emotional breadth, flexibility and richness;* compare the creativeness, broad interests, originality, intelligence and intellectual values of the non-influenced (Barron and Crutchfield; Linton and Graham), the need for individual self-expression (Lifton), the capacity to enjoy life and for genuine emotional expression (Barron and Crutchfield), versus opposite qualities among those easily influenced—low intelligence (Blake and Mouton), bad judgment (Schein), and little insight (Barron and Crutchfield; Linton and Graham). The positive qualities so far mentioned obviously connote *success and leadership ability,* so it is not surprising to find among the non-influenced well-integrated leaders (Schein), efficient, vigorous and responsible leaders (Barron and Crutchfield), while those influenced by the Chinese had had little success in the non-Communist world (Lifton) and had been able to achieve little status in it (Schein).

Many of the remaining qualities may be summarized under the broad rubric of Riesman (1950): *inner-direction versus other-direction* (cf. Linton and Graham, 1959). This is a concept generalized enough to include rebellion versus conformity (mentioned by all the above authors, in one way or another), idealistic devotion to one's own values versus authoritarian or totalistic submission to conventional values (Schein, Lifton, Barron and Crutchfield, Blake and Mouton), a primary need for self-respect versus a need to be liked, to get along, to be considered sincere, considerate, etc. (Barron and Crutchfield, Linton and Graham, Lifton). In addition, Linton (1955) found that subjects who were most easily influenced in the direction of conformity in a laboratory task were "field dependent" as measured by Witkin's measures of reliance on an external visual framework rather than inner bodily cues for spatial orientation. And Graham (Bell, 1955) developed a measure of inner-direction or other-direction which significantly discriminated between opinion changers and non-changers. Some of the more surprising and seemingly inconsistent characteristics of some resisters and the non-influenced—anxiety

(Schein), emotional anomie (Lifton), complexity and nervous tension (Blake and Mouton)—are understandable in terms of Linton's (1955) findings that field-independent subjects, of the kind who resisted social influence, were open in expressing anxiety and personal problems and were less rigidly defended against admissions of weakness than the field dependent.

GENERAL IMPLICATIONS FOR THEORY OF PERSONALITY CHANGE

Let us see, now, what we have learned of more general value for an understanding of personality change.

First, the most striking successes of forcible indoctrination have been temporary, short-run effects on behavior while the prisoner is under the total environmental control of the interrogators. This points towards a relatively obvious fact: behavior is a function, in part, of the environment and its stimuli or press; therefore, if you want to change behavior, manipulate the environment. Much therapy has concentrated on modifying the patient's environment: hospitalization itself is a major attempt to control behavior by massive manipulation of the stimulus situation. (By this last term I mean physical restraint along with the selective presence and absence of eliciting and enabling stimuli.)

Granted these facts, and considering the prevalence of S-R theories of behavior, the major problem seems to be to account for *stability* of behavior, not its change. Consider for a moment that an organism is by definition a constantly changing organization, at once growing and decaying, constantly accruing new experience that modifies its neural controls, embodying a ceaseless turmoil of physiochemical processes, turning over most of its stock of molecules and atoms in a few years, and vulnerable to a thousand jolts to its delicate homeostatic balances. Moreover, we exist in an environment of remarkably little constancy, even when we stay in one spot (which fewer of us seem to do every day); in addition to the profound changes of the seasons, there is the diurnal flood and ebb of light and heat, completely altering most of the sensory properties of man's surroundings. Even the relatively stable objects with which we buttress ourselves transmit to us patterns of stimuli that are almost never exactly repeated. In recent years, we have been learning what a slow and difficult matter it is to attain object constancy and the specific perceptual constancies; Hebb and Piaget have taught us what a tremendous advance it is in the life of the baby when he gradually begins to get through his little head that there are subtle invariances in the flux of stimuli, indicating reliable, recognizable, and vitally useful objects. The truly remarkable fact, therefore, would seem to be the continuities of behavior that we can observe in mobile people in a sea of fluctuating stimuli.

I do not mean to exaggerate the degree to which the environment is inconstant, but to point to the fact that much of its apparent constancy, which consistently evokes repeated patterns of behavior, is attributable to the development of structures within the person that accomplish invariance by establishing the functional equivalence of a factually diverse range of stimuli. Other structures within the person must be postulated to account for persisting traits, attitudes, styles, and abilities.

When I speak about inner structures, I do not wish to make you overlook the important contribution to stability made by the fact of our cyclical drives. Behavior is of course not simply a set of responses to stimuli, mediated by habits and similar structures. Man goes out and looks for stimulation, persistently strives after distant goals, repeatedly seeks the satisfaction of resurgent needs, all because he is constituted with a set of drives. Let me be explicit: when I talk generally about psychic structures, I am including both the enduring aspects of the human organism that give rise to the recurrent urges of the various drives *and* the structures that channel them into the particular interests, tastes, values, and other motivations that characterize an adult.

The immediate implication is that, as we have seen, people differ in the degree to which the structures mediating their responses to stimuli are well established and integrated into a mutually supportive organization. In any area where there is no pre-existing structure, it is easiest to bring about behavioral change and to set up a structure (via learning) that will ensure its continuity. People whose personalities were poorly integrated were generally easiest to influence; though it should be added that a rootless opportunist may be easily swayed at the moment but is not a good prospect for long-run behavioral consistency of any kind.

The logic of the structural viewpoint, further, is that where behavior of an undesired sort is produced by a structure, to change the behavior you must modify the structure: destroy or deactivate it. It is almost axiomatic that when you want to learn something, a certain amount of unlearning is necessary first. The necessity of a preliminary phase of destruction before constructive change is an elementary fact of political life, of cuisine (an omelette cannot be made without breaking eggs), and of physical construction, which always involves demolition of whatever occupies the space where a structure is to be built—unless it can simply be added on to what exists. In education, we hope to be able to add on without having first to destroy; but when the aim is not to supply an *additional,* new mode of behavior but to replace an existing one, thought undesirable for some reason, then destruction of some sort is inevitable. When psychic structure is put out of commission we speak of regression.[4]

Most ambitious forms of psychotherapy (prominently, psychoanalysis) and other treatments such as shock therapy of various sorts have an initial, deliberately regressive phase. The mere fact of hospitalization may bring about a regression, as the direct assaults on the brain of lobotomy and electric shock do, which can be part of a rational plan of treatment. Therapy with some drugs, notably LSD, operates in a similar way: by disrupting existing structures that maintain undesired patterns of behavior, all of these non-psychotherapies make an elementary effort at change. After the initial shake-up, most of them rely on a combination of environmental control and spontaneous reorganization of the person in a more satisfactory way, which naturally does not always happen; sometimes the result is a structural regrouping in ways considered even more pathological than before treatment.

The most sophisticated therapies, therefore, use a combination of regressive influences to break down existing structures and controlled, deliberate communication to facilitate the building of new structures. Such communication may consist of indoctrination, interpretation, reflection, or "corrective emotional experience" (in which the emphasis is on the interpersonal relationship rather than the content communicated). Deprivation of some kind is the usual press that produces regression and structural breakdown (hence the use of "sensory deprivation" in therapy; cf. Azima et al., 1961; Adams et al., 1960). As I have tried to bring out above, forcible indoctrinators rely heavily on an initial phase of regressive pressures to accomplish the necessary psychic bulldozing before they can begin to build their temporary or putatively more permanent ideological structures.

But something seems to be missing in the analysis so far presented. If personality can be changed by breaking down existing structures and fostering the development of new ones, did not the Chinese thought reformers try hard enough to induce regression and to enforce new learning? They cannot be accused of not having made intensive, fanatically strong, and persistent attempts. What was wrong, then? Why did they succeed in producing a negligible number of converts, and then only among people who lacked any stable, pre-existing identity and rootedness in Western democracy?

Two things, I think, worked against them. First, they were attempting nothing less than the total reconstruction of personality along lines directly opposed to many basic pre-existing structures, important among which were

---

[4] This statement does not constitute an adequate definition of regression, which need not involve permanent demolition of structures. It always connotes the *functional* removal of late-formed structures subserving mature behavior, but these may just be temporarily put out of operation, in certain kinds of benign regression.

the prisoner's identity and much of his inner world—his picture of social reality. Ingenious as they were in circumventing and even temporarily breaking the opposition of his will, much that they did inevitably reinforced that resentful opposition (cf. Lifton's [1961] "hostility of suffocation"). Second, and most important for the theory of personality change, they did not reckon with the fact that *psychic structures are almost indestructible* except through actual lesions of neural tissue. The very facts of regression teach us this: once formed, patterns of behavior produce permanent alterations of the organism; although superseded, outgrown, and apparently non-existent for many years, they can be revived by regression of the newer overlay. Think only of the facts of hypnotic age regression (Reiff and Scheerer, 1959), of psychopathology, of savings in relearning long-forgotten material.

The lesson for us is that regression can uncover dormant structures but only very rarely through the destruction of later ones, which are merely pushed aside and temporarily have no effect upon behavior. The more overlearned a structure and the more it is integrated into the core of the personality, the more it resists demolition or even temporary dismantling.

To alter personality and behavior lastingly and to any great extent, then, you must have the person's willing cooperation; the new behavior must be meaningfully related to important pre-existing aspects of the person's identity; environmental supports and reinforcements of the behavior one wants to eliminate must be altered, and such situational supports of the new behavior must be persistently supplied. If all of this can be assured, then regression-inducing procedures may help break the grip of the unwanted behavior patterns, and new structures which will help keep the old ones dormant may be built by education of some kind.

Again and again, in these pages, I have come back to the concept of identity (Erikson, 1954, 1959). I have been impressed by the extent to which thought reform concentrates on undermining a victim's previous identity, not merely on teaching him a set of Communist principles. What strikes me as the central fact about resisters versus yielders, the one characteristic that seems to illuminate all the other aspects of personality that are involved and to show their interrelatedness, is the strength versus diffuseness of identity.

I am led to conclude that a central organizing feature of personality, perhaps the most critical one for an understanding of attempts to induce change, is identity, a term that comprises all that is meant by self, self-concept, self-percept, and similar terms. A person's identity is a complex, a slowly changing, deeply rooted structure, with ramifications into his attitudes, ideology, beliefs, and knowledge; into his feelings of worth, security, belongingness or isolation, guilt, shame, and inferiority or superiority; into his patterns of relationship with other people, particularly the important figures in his family of orientation; into his widest social and cultural ties, with ancestors, fellow religionists, neighbors, people of common ethnic stock, and all other reference groups of any importance to him; into his personal standards of conduct, his goals, ideals and guiding images; into his defenses and controls over drives and anxiety; and into almost any other department of personality you can think of. I am referring to something much more than the general connectedness of a unified personality; I believe that its degree of implication in so many aspects of personality could be shown to be so great as to justify calling identity central. This is surely not a novel proposition in the history of personology, though the terms used have varied a good deal.

One reason that identity is so crucial for the problem of change is that an important constituent of it is a person's *feeling* of personal continuity, which—if strong—can itself be a bulwark against easy change in his behavior. Identity is also a link between the most intimate sense of self and enduring structures in the person's environment—his possessions, home, friends, relatives, countrymen, and so on. I believe that future research on psychotherapy will show identity to be strategic for an understanding of other aspects of personality change, just as work like Lifton's on thought control has taught us how intimately it is involved in values and ideologies.

ADDENDUM

I have come to the end of what I have to say about forcible indoctrination in relation to personality change. Yet I cannot resist the temptation to set forth a few further reflections that the problem of thought reform in Communist China has stirred up in me. The question presents itself most insistently: what is going to happen to this country, the largest and potentially most powerful on earth? The target of their most focused and manipulated hostility, we as Americans—and as fellow members of the human race, with the Chinese people—cannot be indifferent to the future of thought reform.

In his chilling novel, *1984,* George Orwell has portrayed all too convincingly one possible outcome: a war-oriented totalitarian society in which reality is sedulously and continually reshaped to fit a preconceived doctrine, where every act is controlled, and even thought is replaced by "doublethink." There is much in the new China that reminds one of this picture, much that is tending towards this horrible end point. Such a society is certainly conceivable, and Orwell tells us that it could work, perpetuating itself and destroying most of what is precious in life.

Since such a prospect is so repellent, we must exercise caution that we do not declare it impossible simply because we cannot tolerate the thought. Yet there is some rational basis for a judgment that the Chinese Communists will not continue in this direction but will become somewhat more human and humane.

First, there is the fact that the official ideology of communism has many positive values: "the ideals of self-sacrifice, equality, peace, freedom from want and freedom from fear, which are common to most of the major ethical systems of mankind" (Hinkle and Wolff, 1956). Much of the appeal of communism has always been its overt espousal of ideals of social justice, the pursuit of scientific truth, the abolition of exploitation and oppression, and the advocation of the broadest fellowship between men of all nations. Now it is factually true that in practice, most of these ideals have been flouted by the Russian and Chinese Communists, and that many aspects of their systems contrast glaringly with such values. To some degree, the same can be said, of course, about American democracy: in many ways, its practices are at wide variance with its professed values and goals. But that does not make the ideals any less important; on the contrary. As Myrdal (1944) has pointed out, the existence of an American creed of social justice, democracy, and fair play constitutes one of the most powerful forces working against segregation and ethnic prejudice. These values are built into the American character structure, and thus afford a fulcrum for persistently constructive leverage.

Another historical example can help sharpen the point: the Inquisition of the Catholic church. Here was an oppressive dictatorship of frightful extent and efficiency, which subjected many people to interrogations and tortures comparable to those of the Communists in their harrowing intensity if not always in their subtlety. They were effective enough to bring about many of the same types of effects: alongside Cardinal Mindszenty and General Dean we can put Galileo, and the self-denunciations of the Russian purge trials are easily equalled by the confessions of witches as late as the eighteenth century. Remember that these effects of forcible indoctrination were achieved in the services of Christian ideals. Surely the contrast between the words of Jesus of Galilee and the actions of Torquemada are as diametrically opposed as anything in the preachments and practices of modern communism.

The important thing about this example, however, is that *in the long run the inconsistency could not be tolerated*. One of the most hopeful things about the human makeup is what psychoanalysis calls the synthetic function of the ego, also called in sociology the strain towards consistency, and known by various other names. Whatever you call it, there is a powerful and intrinsic tendency in the human mind for ideas, facts, values, and other "presentations" to be brought into an internally consistent order. Many of the difficulties of thought reform are directly attributable to this fact: people find it difficult to accept the requirement that they make statements in conflict with their beliefs about reality.

The implications for the future of Chinese communism are twofold: The conflict between dogma and reality will tend, in the long run, to be resolved in favor of reality. Second, the existence of constructive values in Communist ideology will tend to work against the worst excesses of the system, particularly when it gets past its initial insecurity.

Another instructive historical parallel is provided by the Soviets. In its early days, when the USSR had just been established and was under constant attack from within (by remnants of the old order) and from without (by invading forces of the Whites, backed and accompanied by American and other Western troops), the Russian Communists were as extreme, rigid, and unrealistic as the Chinese are today. Subjected to the national equivalent of actual persecution, they produced the equivalent of a paranoid outlook, many aspects of which still exist. But the important fact is that with the consolidation of the government, its internal growth, the winning of World War II, and the death of Stalin, Russian communism has made real and important changes bringing its actions closer to agreement with its ideals. Even when the ideology itself has been changed, as in the momentous promulgation by Khrushchev of the doctrine of coexistence, there has not been a shift in the value premises but in some of the cognitive structure of communism that actually helps strengthen those values (Neal, 1961). One result is the widely publicized split between Moscow and Peiping, which remains "tougher," more Stalinist, more hostile to the West, and in greater conflict with its own value premises.

All of these considerations suggest, therefore, that the Chinese too will soften and begin to be affected by the decent aspects of their own ideology as their regime becomes more securely consolidated, as a new generation uncontaminated by the Kuomintang grows up and takes over—if external threats also subside. The very fact that the Mao Tse-tung government has more human beings under its control than any other has ever had anywhere makes it impossible to maintain the total control of thought reform over all of them continuously. No Communist apparatus is that efficient, and just to maintain life in China takes the major energies of most people quite aside from ideological considerations.

Therefore, I am hopeful that, if we can manage to avoid war—an *if* upon which everything that is dear to us depends—and coexist peacefully with communism, it will continue the gradual processes of positive political and social change that can be seen in the USSR today.

chapter ten

The Managerial Grid as a Framework for Inducing Change in Industrial Organizations

Robert R. Blake and Jane S. Mouton

Planned change involves applying behavioral science knowledge in concrete situations of organized human activity. The purpose is to develop a more productive and satisfying state of affairs among those who are mutually engaged in some definable effort and to do so in an orderly manner.

With tested theory and with effective techniques for introducing planned change it should be possible to avoid disruptive and demoralizing consequences from change impelled by crises, by crass manipulation, or through the exercise of naked power. It should also be possible to forestall the resistance to change, which so frequently results in the abandonment of efforts that meet stiff opposition. Development of theory and of professional skills for bringing about planned change, then, represents a key challenge confronting the behavioral sciences.

THE BLUEPRINT FOR PLANNED CHANGE INVOLVES
ANSWERING FOUR KEY QUESTIONS

One way to penetrate the issues surrounding a program of planned change is through asking and answering a number of questions. The general answers to these questions provide a broad framework for viewing any specific change activity. Concrete answers to these questions, tailored to fit an existing situation, sketch the outlines for any particular change program.

Preparation of this paper was partially supported by URI—Project No. r-414 entitled "Investigation of Behavioral Science Theory as a Basis for Organization Improvement," University of Texas, Austin, Texas, and by a grant from the Hogg Foundation for Mental Health, University of Texas, entitled, "Human Relations Research Monograph."

Identifying the Problem

Planned change is based on the notion that something is unacceptable about present circumstances. The term also implies that it would be desirable to correct, replace, shift, remove, or to change some aspect(s) of the existing situation in some direction. Diagnosing the problem as a problem is a first step.

Before a disturbance can be dealt with in an intelligent manner, however, it must be diagnosed in systematic or behavioral science terms, in contrast with a common sense description or in comparison with a more or less intuitive account of "what is wrong." A significant issue underlying planned change efforts then, is: "When described from a systematic or behavioral science point of view, what existing condition is a change effort intended to correct?"

Identifying the Unit of Change

A second and related question is this: "Change in what *unit* of behavior?" Is an individual the target of change, or is it a given group's performance, or is it an organization? The answer is linked closely with the systematic framework used in diagnosing the problem, but, there, too, the issue itself appears deceptively simple. For example, it is easy, in common sense terms, to see a group as little or nothing more than a number of separate individuals, when, in fact, its members may hold in common attitudes and codes of conduct that no single member would deviate from or relinquish if approached to do so, on a one-by-one basis. The same may be said for an organization, which may be seen as composed of many separate individuals or as many separate groups, as though there were no interplay either in terms of interpersonal, group, or intergroup influences. Yet, as is now well known, the concept of organization as a congregation of individuals is far too simple as the basic premise for organizational change induction. In spite of the fact, the primitive generalization that the unit of change must be accurately identified is violated in the efforts of many change specialists to bring about organizational improvement.

Differences between a common sense evaluation and a behavioral science view of the same *problem* or of the appropriate *unit* for change can be critical to the success of an effort to bring about planned change. If the common sense and the behavioral science approaches are not the same, and common sense dictates actions which contradict behavioral science formulations, a lessening of motivation to change may result, or resistance to change efforts which can ultimately lead to their failure may develop.

Establishing the Goals and Directions of Change

Another consideration in bringing planned change about involves identifying the direction toward which change is intended. It is not enough merely to diagnose the problem and define the unit of change. In addition, optimal conditions need to be specified in order that the change effort has character, direction and goals. Frequently it is necessary first to identify a number of alternative aims and then to select from among them the one toward which change is desired. Therefore, a third issue is: "What are the goals a given planned change effort is intended to achieve?" When this question can be answered satisfactorily, then the major conceptual dimensions of the planned change effort have been outlined—change of what, away from what present condition, and change toward what desired end? These three questions identify core issues of introducing planned change. They will be dealt with in detail in this chapter.

Other Issues

Related issues are: "By what techniques or methods are the desired changes to be brought to actuality?" and "How can the results of the change efforts be measured and evaluated?" These are engineering or technological questions which have important implications for any systematic program intended to bring about change.

THE BEHAVIORAL SCIENCE FORMULATION
OF THE PROBLEM

Recognition that something is wrong is a first step toward accomplishing change. The problem as described by those who have it may be little more than merely symptomatic that something more basic is out of kilter, however. Naïve acceptance of the problem as presented by those who have it, in contrast to the problem seen to exist when diagnosed in systematic terms, may define one of the strongest barriers that confront any effort at planned change. The problem here is that "common sense" descriptions frequently are grossly different from a "true," i.e. systematic, problem diagnosis.

An analogy here may help in giving sharper definition to this issue. Medicine is replete with examples of failure to correct or even to bring about improvement in physical health situations because of failure to diagnose the nature and the scope of a problem in a systematic manner. Only as common sense and mystical explanations have yielded to scientific analysis in biochemical terms has medicine made significant strides in understanding health problems and treating them effectively. Maintaining and restoring health has been accomplished by acting on physical conditions in terms consistent with scientific *laws* of physics, biology, and chemistry.

The same problem confronts behavioral health. Rule of thumb and mystical accounts of behavior frequently disregard the lawfulness of human contact. On occasion such interpretations have served to exaggerate the existing problem, to drive it underground, to generate defensiveness, or to produce resentment or other forms of resistance. Only as common sense and moralistic explanations of behavior have yielded to scientific analysis in psycho-social-cultural terms has it been possible to establish adequate problem diagnosis. As in the practice of medicine, so too here, the same basic assumption applies. Behavior is lawful in the scientific sense of lawfulness. When the lawfulness of human conduct is violated in the diagnosis of its determinants, efforts to bring about change are not very likely to meet with success. The point is that even at the present level of development the behavioral sciences constitute a framework of ideas for understanding concrete behavior situations in exactly the same manner (though not to the same degree) that the physical and biological sciences undergird diagnosis of physical conditions. Thus, in order to build a sound planned change program it is necessary to utilize a systematic framework as the basis for introducing the change effort. More will be said regarding this problem later on.

What Is the Behavioral Unit of Planned Change?

Given the necessity of applying a systematic, that is, a behavioral science framework for diagnosis, the next choice has been reached. Now the question to be discussed is that of the behavioral unit of a programmatic effort. There are several possibilities.

THE INDIVIDUAL IN ISOLATION. Much historical precedent identifies the individual "inside the skin" as the fundamental behavioral unit of change. Examination of the current status of psychiatry, clinical psychology, formal education, and management development leads to the conclusion that present practices emphasize the individual in isolation. The goal of planned change for an individual may be to help that *person* in a more or less general manner—in connection with given symptoms, or in a personal way—to become a better member of a group, an organization, a community, and so on. But whatever the *goal* of change may be, these definitions of the unit place the variables responsible for an individual's present actions *within* him, and potentially or actually subject to his control.

With the definition of the individual-in-isolation as the *unit* of change, it is seen as possible, with professional help, for the individual to change under his own initiative. In many of its applications, however, such an overgeneralized "common sense" conception has resulted in needless and wasteful effort. Convenient though it may be and accessible though he is, the individual in isolation is, rarely, a valid definition of a behavioral unit for the reason that too many critical influences outside his control condition his present behavior. Under such circumstances efforts to change only bring subtle counterpressures that return him to his old and established patterns of behavior and conduct. Needed, in other words, is a larger conception of the total situation, even when the object is to aid an individual to change. The question "What is the behavioral unit of change?" needs fundamental re-examination.

THE WHOLE SITUATION. An alternative to the too quick acceptance of the individual-in-isolation definition of the behavioral unit of change is obtained in the Lewinian treatment of this question (Lewin, 1951). Lewin's formula was $B = F(P, E)$. The formula indicates that behavior (B) is a function of the interdependence between a person (P) *and* his environment (E). Behavior, in other words, is a function of the *total situation*. According to this formulation a condition for the introduction of change involves the situation as a whole—the interactions of the behaving entity with its environment. If efforts at inducing planned change disregard significant factors that comprise the total situation, then the change program is likely to be ineffective, or to be piecemeal, or even to stimulate active resistance. A first answer for the question, what is the behavioral unit of change, then, is *the whole situation*.

It follows from Lewin's formula that the behavioral unit of change is likely to be not only an individual, but is likely to involve all members operating within the environmental properties of his situation. For example, a unit of change may be not only the alcoholic husband in isolation but it might also be the entire family membership. The whole situation in this example might include, among other variables, issues such as management of money, TV, school problems, and a host of other sources of tensions associated with the key problem, namely excessive drinking by the husband.

The same reasoning applies to a work situation within an industrial organization. A worker or an entire work group, for example, may be thought of as a more or less autonomous behavioral unit. Here, too, however, extremely strong sources of influence arise outside of the individual and outside of the group to control or to influence the units mode of operation. Efforts of a group of individuals to change in concert are equally likely to meet environmental counterpressures operating in the direction of forcing return to accustomed ways of behavior and conduct. Experience to date suggests that most groups, particularly work groups embedded in organizations, are too intimately linked into a network of organizational influences to be considered autonomous. Groups, then, frequently are too narrow in definition to constitute effective units of change. They too must be considered in terms of their interdependencies.

THE ORGANIZATION AS A FUNCTIONAL BEHAVIORAL UNIT. What is left? If we start from the same conceptual framework as above, a meaningful and realistic behavioral unit of change may be bounded by the environmental situation of an organization. Then, the behavioral unit becomes the *membership* organization, and it further includes significant variables encompassed by the organizational environment such as policies, rules, regulations, reward and punishment systems, production controls, informal social systems, etc.

The point emphasized in this section is that the locus of the problem, both from common sense and from the point of view of most individual-centered disciplines such as psychiatry and clinical psychology is that the individual-in-isolation or perhaps the group-in-isolation is the appropriate unit of change. When a disturbance arises, it is commonly attributed to individuals such as a few key people at the top or to ones at the bottom of the ladder, such as the shirker. Alternatively, the problem may be seen as located within a group-in-isolation, as for example, problems of labor-management conflict, which, from a managerial point of view, often are seen as stemming from deficiencies within the union officer group rather than being viewed from the standpoint of the relationship of union to management.

Whatever the entity, however, the same rule applies: behavior, whether of a person, a group, or an organization, etc., is a function of its total situation and of the interactions of all significant variables existing within that situation. Dealing with the parts on a one-by-one basis, without treatment of the total situation in which the parts are embedded and by which the behavior of the parts is conditioned, constitutes at best a partial definition of a behavioral unit of planned change.

Many organizational settings are, at least *relatively* speaking, total situations, particularly in *decentralized* organizations. Patterns of behavior of individuals and of groups appear to be conditioned quite completely by factors existing either within their own control or else by factors which are internal to the organization itself. The organization, in other words, is a functional environment within which individuals and groups perform and interrelate toward accomplishing organizational aims. In this sense, an organization is a functional behavioral unit. On the other hand, if the organization is not decentralized and relatively autonomous but does exist under a headquarters which exercises control, then other steps in the change process can be taken to bring about a closer integration between headquarters and the field installation (Blake and Mouton, 1961).

The answer for one of the questions above, namely, "Change of what behavioral unit?" is, then, "Planned change of a whole organization." Here again, however, the interaction between the unit of change and the motivation to change is critical. If key persons within the organization, from their intuitive, inside perspective, view the problem as being lodged in an isolated group, for example, in "lazy foremen who won't take responsibility for productivity," rather than in the total organization *including* themselves, the necessary motivation to change may not be present. Again, this potential resistance to change is dealt with in the methodological aspects of the change effort.

Change from What to What?

The next two questions are: "Change from what?" and "Change to accomplish what purpose, what end?" In any actual situation, these two questions may appear distinct and separate, but from the standpoint of planned change, they must be considered together. When answered, they define the systematic framework against which the concrete steps in the change effort can be specified. They also provide a basis for answering the question, "What problem?" and "What unit?"

The variables that define the existing situation or any desired one are, for the most part, the same. Differences between what exists and what is desired are a matter of degree or relative weighting of the interaction among these factors. Therefore, the first issue is: what variables undergird the definition of a total situation, when the unit of change is an industrial organization such as a factory?

VARIABLES IN A FACTORY. The purpose of a factory is to make an acceptable profit by manufacturing a needed product. Only with an adequate profit is the continuity of operations insured. Output or *production,* then, is one variable of a factory.

Production, however, often is not the result of individuals working one by one, in isolation from one another, with the degree of output attributable to factors "within the skin" of each employed person working on an individual in isolation basis. Rather, if a factory is of any size, output is accomplished through the coordinated efforts of many interacting individuals. The various individual contributions are interdependent and are organized so as to build one upon another, often in a quite complex manner. Thus, *human relationships* of those engaged in production is another significant variable in the behavioral unit of a factory.

For analytical purposes, these two variables—production and human relationships—can be treated as though they were independent of one another. In any concrete situation, however, they are truly interdependent variables. That is, the conditions of production influence relationships, and in turn the character of human relationships facilitates or hinders productive effort. Work and human relationships, then, are two important interdependent variables of a factory.

The next points to be considered have to do with the psychological aspects of production and human relations and the interdependence of one with the other.

PSYCHOLOGICAL ASPECTS OF PRODUCTION. Production, of course, does not happen in a haphazard manner. Rather, it requires intelligent mental effort from those concerned to achieve it. It is in the planning and execution of production where human capacity for mental effort finds expression in a factory.

What are the relevant characteristics of mental effort that appear in the context of production? From the person's point of view, it is the nature of mental effort to search for and to create conditions that are meaningful and purposeful. Thinking cannot be characterized as based on a sheer randomness nor can it be regarded as a process of mechanical trial and error. If entire situations of production, not just the parts concerned with the mechanics of work, disregard or violate human mental effort, then problems associated with production are likely to appear. The task, or the work itself, must provide participants with an outlet, a challenge to think toward psychologically purposeful goals regarding what they are doing. If it does not, then thinking that is purposeful is likely to take directions which detract from production. If the work activity fails to satisfy or violates its needs for meaningfulness, it can generate feelings of boredom, apathy, fatigue, dissatisfaction, resentment, and active resistance. On the other hand, if the total situation of production involves purposeful activities, then the associated reactions are likely to be ones of satisfaction, interest, excitement, challenge, and so on.

An important dimension of human mental experience as it finds application in a total situation of production, then, stems from engaging in meaningless, random, or repetitive activities to undertaking meaningful, purposeful, and goal-directed ones.

One goal of planned change within the setting of a factory is that of increasing the degree of meaningfulness in production effort. In this respect, the question "Away from what condition?" might be answered as "Away from situations which are repetitious, mechanical, arbitrary, or senseless, and toward ones which are meaningful, purposeful, and goal-oriented."

HUMAN RELATIONSHIPS. The other variable in the total situation of a factory involves interpersonal relations among those engaged in production. Again, from the psychological point of view, feelings of acceptance and rejection are a product of human interaction. Under circumstances of production, they can range from full acceptance or positive feelings toward people, to complete rejection, with negative, hostile, or antagonistic feelings toward others. Rejection tends to provoke distrust, tension, a sense of uneasiness, and withdrawal. Acceptance, on the other hand, is associated with trust, mutual support, involvement, and a sense of personal worth. The goal of human interaction triggered by production, again looked at from a psychological point of view, is to avoid situations that arouse negative emotions and to develop, maintain, and repeat situations that involve positive feelings. Thus, the direction of the change effort is change *away from* interactions that arouse distrust and disrespect and *toward* interpersonal relations that are based on mutual trust, support, and feelings of personal worth.

THE INTERACTION OF PRODUCTION AND RELATIONSHIPS. While productive effort in a factory may occur in social isolation, that is, independently of any human context, and while relations among people may occur in purely social terms without any connection to production, these pure conditions, pure production and pure relationships, certainly are exceptions rather than the rule. It is important that theory of planned change take into consideration the interaction of these variables.

Optimal interaction is obtained when requirements of production involve mental effort under conditions of relationships based on mutual support and trust. An observer might describe such a situation with phrases like, "People are talking through decisions about next steps," or "They are trying to break the production run record." Then, individual goals are blended with and fit the goals of the organization itself. People are not working against the organization; they are working with it. The atmosphere of the total situation, where something approaching optimal interaction between production and relationships has been achieved, is one in which members are described as participating, involved, and committed.

The operation of an industrial organization, such as a factory, then, is an expression of how the variables of production and human relationships interact in terms of concrete practices. It is now possible to describe various ways in which production and relationships interact either to the detriment or to the advantage of an industrial organization like a factory. Each of the points of interaction of these two variables described below, in a tentative manner, can be called a theory. A framework will be provided against which to assess the interaction of production and human relationships variables of an organization in terms of the state of affairs existing within it. Thus, it will be possible to provide an answer to the question "Change away from what?" by describing any given organization in terms of how these variables interact. The goal "Change to what?" will also be indicated by specifying the desired interaction between production and human relationships. Using these two descriptions as a basis, it becomes possible to design action strategies for achieving change.

THE MANAGERIAL GRID

The Managerial Grid, Figure 1, identifies a variety of theories of managerial behavior. These theories are based on two ingredients: *concern for production* and *concern for human relationships*.

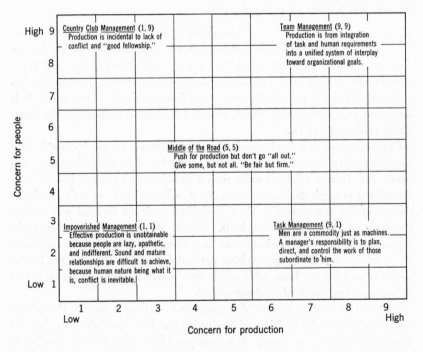

Figure 1. The Managerial Grid.

Before going on, a word is needed about "concern for." This is not meant to indicate *how much* production is obtained, nor is it intended to reflect the degree to which human relationship needs actually are met. Rather, emphasis here is placed on the *degree* of "concern for" because action is rooted in basic attitudes. Here, what is significant is how much a supervisor is *concerned* about *production* and how much about *human relationships.*

The words *production* or *human relationships* cover a range of considerations. Attitudes toward production, for example, may be assessed through a number of creative ideas that applied research turns into useful products, procedures, or processes, quality and thoroughness of staff services, workload and efficiency measurement, or units of output. Production is not limited to *things.* Its proper meaning covers whatever it is that people are engaged in accomplishing. In a similar fashion, human aspects of interaction cover a variety of different concerns. Included are concern for degree of personal commitment to completing a job for which one is responsible; accountability based on trust rather than force; self-esteem or the personal worth of an individual; desire for a sense of security in work; social relations or friendships with coworkers, etc. As will be seen, *concern for production* and *concern for people* are expressed in vastly different ways, depending on the specific manner in which these two concerns are joined together.

The Managerial Grid shows these two concerns and possible interactions between them.[1] The horizontal axis indicates concern for production, while the vertical axis indicates concern for people. Each is expressed as a nine-point scale of concern. The number 1 in each instance represents the minimum concern. The number 9 represents maximum concern.

There are eleven managerial theories which may be shown on this grid. Just now, however, emphasis will be placed on the corners and the midpoint. This will identify five theories. These extreme positions are seldom found in pure form, but they make clear-cut examples to discuss and then, too, there are situations that approach rather closely one or the other of these positions. The other six theories will be examined later.

At the lower left corner of the grid is the 1, 1 style. This has the minimum of both *concern for production* and *concern for people.* Going up the grid from the 1, 1 style to the upper left corner is found the 1, 9 style. Here there is maximum concern for people, but minimum for production. In the lower

---

[1] The line of thinking that leads to the generalized version of the Managerial Grid is consistent with work by Rensis Likert, *New Patterns in Management,* New York: McGraw-Hill, 1961; Edwin A. Fleishman, Edwin F. Harris, and Harold E. Burtt, *Leadership and Supervision in Industry,* Columbus: Bureau of Educational Research, Ohio State Univer., 1955; Chris Argyris, *Personality and Organization,* New York: McGraw-Hill, 1960; and K. D. Benne and P. Sheats, "Functional Roles of Group Members," *J. soc. Issues,* 1948, 2, 42–47.

right corner is 9, 1. This style has a maximum concern for production and a minimum concern for human relationships. In the upper right corner is the 9, 9 style, which has a maximum concern for both human relationships and production. Then, in the center, is the 5, 5 style, which is a middle-of-the-road style in both kinds of concern. Each of these five key managerial orientations is described in the following sections.

9, 1: TASK MANAGEMENT

The 9, 1 approach to the relationship between concerns for production and concerns for people is called "task management." Here, the chief concern is for production. People are viewed only in terms of their contribution to production. One assumption of a 9, 1 orientation is that the way to stay on top of production is to push people, even though this may be frustrating to them. Indeed, driving for production is sometimes thought to be essential because, as a 9, 1 manager might say, "At heart, people are lazy, apathetic and indifferent. If treated 'nicely,' they will take advantage of it, and the friendly sociable work situation which follows can't be tolerated." In other words, a 9, 1 attitude is based on the notion that *concern for production* and *concern for relationships* conflict with one another. The solution of the dilemma by the 9, 1 manager is to reduce or to sacrifice concern for people to whatever amount is necessary to insure production. The motto is "produce or perish."

How Management Views Its Responsibilities under 9, 1

Under a 9, 1 theory, a manager's main responsibilities are to plan, direct, and control the actions of his subordinates so as to obtain the highest output from them in order to reach the production objectives of the company. Subordinates are expected to carry out the various plans, directions, and controls placed upon them. The situation is one of authority on the part of the manager and obedience by the subordinate—all aimed at getting out production on schedule. Little thought or effort is given to helping those who do the work understand why it is to be done or to enable them to enter into planning. According to 9, 1, "a job is a job and someone has to do it." Like machines, people are seen as production tools. They must obey and do what they are told to do.

If a subordinate should question a 9, 1 supervisor about the advisability of the method by which work was performed, he would probably get an answer such as, "These are your instructions. Do them and don't give me any lip. If there's anything I don't like, it's insubordination."

Even at the middle management level, this attitude is seen. The following advice was given to managers in middle levels and is typical of the 9, 1 supervisor: "For an executive to challenge orders, directions, instructions, policies and procedures, rules and regulations, etc., smacks of insubordination, or lack of cooperation. It shows his failure to understand the need for decision at higher levels and for direction and control of operations."

At lower levels, concern for production is thought of in terms of actual *output*. At high managerial levels, concern for production is thought of in terms of decision making and policy formulation, and these are just as critical to high level people as are the units of output for non-supervisory employees. In this 9, 1 situation, there is some concern for people, but this concern is *low* on the Managerial Grid, because it is expressed in such a way as to prevent *people* from damaging the flow of *work,* rather than involving their skills in increasing total production. The goal is to design reliable systems of work flow and efficient physical facilities so as not to have to depend on unreliable people.

Under the 9, 1 theory, people should comply with job procedures, rules, and policies which are demanded of them. Heavy emphasis is placed on efforts and procedures that will get more output. One way of doing this is to measure the requirements of a job, simplify it to the greatest degree possible, and then train individuals to perform the job according to "scientific" standards. Here the concern for people is limited to that of designing the work and the work pace to minimize effort and fatigue so as to obtain maximum output.

The primary motivation for production is the exercise of power. The reward system is based on the concept of the economic man. These assumptions concerning motivation and reward come together in such statements as "All we ask of a man is that he do the work set before him." For this, a person is rewarded according to piece rate or, if that does not fit the situation, then, according to the best judgment of his supervisors.

Another important assumption of the 9, 1 theory is a sharp and definite division drawn between planning and execution of work. Planners *plan* and doers *do.* The relationships between planners and doers are along the strictest lines of authority and obedience. Management exercises authority, in the extreme, over the slightest motions of the doer. The person who performs the work is obligated to conform. He must do what and how he is told.

Because of the separation of planning and doing, very few provisions are made for the psychological need to find meaningfulness in work. If those who do a job are to find meaning in their work, there must be challenging mental effort. When the job is completely planned for a person, however, it becomes mechanical. The strict separation of planning and doing which occurs under 9, 1 managements fails to regard the need people have for finding meaningfulness in their work. Also, through the exercise of power by the authority and obedience model, mutual trust, which leads to a sense of personal worth, is essentially eliminated.

The 9, 1 theory further states that management can be so perfect that it can anticipate an individual's physical needs and can prescribe the best conditions for his work. All the worker needs to do is to submit to what management dictates. As a result of this, much resistance is generated. Rather than increasing productivity, which clearly is possible under this managerial approach, productivity may actually be decreased because people suspect management may be taking advantage of them.

A basic assumption of 9, 1 management is that the productive unit is, in a work situation, the working man and that the supreme relationship is that of the supervisor to the subordinate. In planning the placement of people in their work, the aim is to separate people so that they will not form social groups. Also, effort is made to prevent the interaction of human beings from interfering with the work. The results, however, have not always been what was hoped for, and there is ample evidence to show how many work groups operating under 9, 1 management have slowed down production instead of increasing it.

9,1 Approaches to Managing Conflict

In the course of operations, tensions often arise among people who interact with one another in deciding *how* to do work and in *doing* it. When people with ideas about how to get things done seek to get them listened to, and when their ideas go against the grain of those who are responsible, conflict is a common result. Conflict itself may be an indication that there is a faulty relationship between production needs and the way in which people are organized to achieve them.

Managing conflict under 9, 1 can be examined from two standpoints. One is how conflicts with one's boss and peers are adjusted. The other is how a supervisor deals with a subordinate who is in conflict with him.

When the disagreement producing conflict is with his peers or with his boss, the goal of the 9, 1 manager is to end the conflict by proving that he is right, through taking a win-lose approach in order to show the weaknesses in his opponent's point of view. While win-lose may lead to a "brick wall" or stalemate, it sometimes does solve the problem of open conflict. If open conflict is relieved through one person's demonstrating that he is right and that others are wrong, a victor and a vanquished are produced. Feelings based on victory and defeat are not a particularly good basis for establishing relationships between supervisors and subordinates that promote cooperation and mutually productive effort.

Conflict may also be viewed from the point of view of the boss looking at a subordinate who disagrees with him. Here, one approach to conflict is to deal with it by *suppressing* it. The expression of conflict is prevented by a supervisor applying the authority-obedience formula and saying, "That's it. Here's the way it's going to be." When the authority-obedience formula fails to suppress conflict, recourse frequently is available to a variety of punishments ranging from warning letters placed in an individual's file to time off without pay. Though discipline many times can be effective in ending open conflict, it fails to get at the core of the problem. It does not correct the causes that produced the conflict. Sources of conflict remain. The result is that unresolved but hidden conflicts many times appear in disguised ways (slowdowns, careless errors, misinterpretations of instructions, etc.) which can lower the quality of cooperation and reduce production effectiveness.

Impact of 9,1 on Creativity

Another symptom of difficulty associated with 9,1 management, particularly at the working level, is seen in the wealth of creative ideas by people who, denied an opportunity to participate actively in the planning process, use their talents to slow down production and to frustrate the goals of the organization.

Suggestion systems wither on the vine under 9,1 and much good grass-roots experience and thinking goes begging. However, the creative abilities of people in the middle and at the bottom of such organizations are not stifled. Rather, creative thinking goes into how to defeat the system and prevent it from working well. There are numerous examples available of ways of destroying machinery and equipment, hiding tools and so on, many of which are highly creative. When this happens, it is clear that the creativity of which people are capable is not being used for the good of the individual or the organization. The opposite is true. The capacity for creative thinking is being applied in ways which are harmful to the organization. The significant aspect is the direction in which creativity may be applied, namely, *away from,* rather than *toward,* achieving the goals of organizations.

Supervisory Style and Personal Characteristics

A 9,1 managerial outlook can be summarized in terms of how managerial responsibility for people is exercised to gain effective production. The following attitudes are typical:

Planning. "I do planning by setting goals and schedules to be followed by each subordinate. Then I work out procedures and ground rules and make individual assignments. I also establish check points so that I can assure myself that actions I have authorized are being taken as I intended them to be done."

Work execution. "I watch the work closely. I criticize as I see the necessity for it and authorize changes as needs for them arise."

Follow-up. "I have plans laid for the next assignments and move people on to them as operations dictate. Recognition and corrective action are extended to individuals on a one-by-one basis."

Managing mistakes by subordinates. "My immediate reaction is to find out who is responsible for the mistake and to mete out the appropriate disciplinary action in a swift and compelling manner."

When policies or procedures are violated. "Uniform policies are indispensable to orderly production. Policies and procedures should be well defined to cover all but emergency situations. They also should be continuously enforced whenever deviations from them arise."

The mental outlook of the manager who approaches situations in a 9, 1 way also can be summarized from a personal point of view. It should be emphasized that the 9, 1 manager does, in fact, place high value on making sound decisions. He is fully ready to stand up for his own ideas, opinions, and attitudes and to press forcefully their acceptance even when others are pushing for their own. Furthermore, he is willing to do so even if it results in stepping on toes.

From the standpoint of personal attitudes toward conflict, he finds little reason to shy away from it. Rather, he is more inclined to enjoy a fight. When dealing with subordinates, he is likely to cut off conflict. With peers or individuals above him in the managerial ladder, he is likely to try to win for his position. His temper can rise when things are not going according to his wishes, as his subordinates know, sometimes all too well. His humor is hard-hitting and tends to carry a sting.

9, 1, in a word, is "tough-minded," "hard" management.

1,9: COUNTRY CLUB MANAGEMENT

The country club, or "togetherness" approach to production, 1, 9, is found in the upper left corner of the grid. Here, 1, which is low concern for production, is coupled with 9, high concern for people.

In many respects, however, 1, 9 is the reverse of the 9, 1 style. 1, 9 thinking starts at the opposite end from 9, 1. Relationships among people are seen as all-important. Direct concern for production is minimal. The goal of 1, 9 is to achieve harmonious, positive relationships among people. While 9, 1 appears consistent with organizational goals of production, efficiency, and profit, the 1, 9 approach appears contradictory to the very purpose for which production or service organizations are created. A 1, 9 manager, in other words, is prepared to sacrifice production for people. Key emphasis is placed on relationships and little concern is given for accomplishing the organizational mission (Maier, 1955).

There are at least two situations in which the "country club" style can become a way of life in a company. One is that in which a company is operating on a cost plus basis. The other is one in which profits are so easy to make that operating efficiency is not important. In either instance, competition is not forcing the company to operate efficiently. In fact, the company can return a profit without being efficient. As a result, it becomes unattractive to make efficiency moves because these would spread anxiety and lead to conflict. It is simpler to take the easy way out and just let things go as they may. Of course, this is a negative decision and will not attain the maximum production or even relatively high production. People with a managerial orientation which is mainly 1, 9 are not really out to achieve production, but are concerned with maintaining what is believed to be good human relationships. The country club approach is not sound, however, for even though a profit may be realized, people are not really making a high contribution to production.

A 1, 9 supervisor might react to poor results in obtaining production goals by saying, "Don't take it too hard. We all make mistakes. Maybe we'll have better luck next time." Rather than calling attention to the poor work or the way in which it was done, the 1, 9 supervisor believes that if people are not crossed and if their happiness is not disturbed, they will produce as well as contented cows.

A dramatic example of 1, 9 as an organizational way of life is contained in the following situation. One of the larger manufacturing establishments, up to three years ago, maintained the practice built up over years of employing a special force of laborers during summer months to compensate for the absence of regular work force members on vacation. Vacations for permanent organizational members were *not* scheduled with production objectives in mind but, rather, the organization picked up the bill through the employment of substitutes. The result was that every member of the wage force had his vacation exactly when he wanted it. A dramatic conclusion from this 1, 9 mentality occurred, however. Because its product had become hopelessly noncompetitive, the plant was shut down. With this "luxury" style of management—not facing its real problem of involving people in solving the *real* problems of production—everyone then had fifty-two weeks of vacation per year!

Decisions against efficiency moves, such as the example above, that are motivated by a desire *not* to disturb people and in order to maintain personal security are negative. They do not accomplish the purposes of the organization. While such decisions *seem* to favor the development or maintenance of good relationships, such relationships are not sound in any basic sense. Looked at from a broad time perspective, they are built on a foundation of toothpicks. The reason is that in a profit-motivated economy, other organizations, which *are* responsive to economic pressures, can (and should) overtake a fat and happy organization. They should run it out of business because the *real* danger to cultural evolution of economic systems is that they *cease* to strive for change and improvement (Argyris, 1960). Under such circumstances, it can be seen why relationships motivated by "togetherness" are dangerous. They are dangerous, if for no other reason than that they contain the seeds of their own destruction; for example, the closing down of the plant above. More important, perhaps, is the threat they create toward the long-term erosion of a profit-motivated way of economic life.

In spite of the dangers involved, 1, 9 *is* common in business and industrial settings and in government and academic institutions. Therefore, its basic assumptions need to be examined in greater detail.

How Management Views Its Responsibilities under 1,9

When asked to describe his managerial responsibilities, a 1, 9 manager is likely to use the same *words* as a 9, 1 manager, i.e., to say that his job is to plan, direct, and control the activities of his subordinates.

His real attitude can be seen in more subtle ways, however. In commenting upon the importance of morale, for example, he is not likely to say that morale is associated with the opportunity for individuals to be productive and thereby to contribute to organizational goals. Rather, the subtle difference in his outlook is apparent in that he is more likely to say that high morale comes from having good working conditions and congenial coworkers (McNair, 1957). In a similar fashion, his implicit goal as a manager is to maintain production at a rate no higher than that which promotes satisfaction and security among organizational members, while avoiding the conflict that might arise from making needed production decisions that would disturb people. His deeper attitude is seen in the feeling that "You can't push people for production, because if you do, they balk and resist. When people have turned against you, you are in trouble."

The 1, 9 manager is anxious to be "nice" to people. If he should make a decision which his group did not like, he would probably withdraw it to keep harmony and then try to follow with a "soft sell." He would feel that he must keep making peace with people at all levels in order to win allies for this cause. Not only is the 1, 9 approach ineffective in achieving high output, but it is also ineffective in achieving any real gains in human relationships.

With respect to actual planning and work direction, the 1, 9 manager frequently adopts one of two ways of dealing with subordinates, who, of necessity, are looking to him to establish conditions of work. One way that the 1, 9 manager might adopt can be described in the phrase, "I try to lead rather than to push." The assumption here is that people should be shown rather than commanded. They should be supported and aided in their work efforts in the sense of a supervisor's doing for them those difficult parts of the job for which he (the supervisor) has more technical knowledge rather than for him to allow or expect his subordinates to struggle for themselves. Under these conditions, a 1, 9 manager expects people to be willing followers.

In contrast to the 9, 1 manager who demands accountability and responsibility from subordinates, the 1, 9 manager gives warmth, acceptance, and "understanding" in expectation of receiving devoted loyalty in return. Believing that devoted people will want to do what is needed without being directed, he is inclined to feel there is little reason to be concerned with accountability and responsibility. In this way, matters which are of such great concern to the 9, 1 manager appear of little significance under the 1, 9 orientation. Because the 1, 9 manager places little direct emphasis on productivity, it rarely becomes imperative for him, at least under his own initiative, to face up to whether or not subordinates are, in fact, discharging their work in a responsible and accountable manner.

The other way the 1, 9 manager adopts in dealing with his subordinates is the "soft sell." An order becomes either an apologetic request or the subordinate is supposedly led to see the error in his own thinking through gentle persuasion by the supervisor. These and other approaches typify the "be nice" school of thought.

Although work is likely to be planned without consulting subordinates, as is also true in 9, 1, if subordinates become unhappy with their work arrangements every effort is made by the 1, 9 supervisor to meet their complaints. Members of the work group get together with the main goal of providing good relations among people. True, they do share information of a noncritical nature and discuss, in a manner, issues which arise, and recommend action. They have family dinners and parties and use other such methods to achieve harmony and happiness—all in an attempt to get the people to think that management is interested in them as people.

1,9 Approaches to Managing Conflict

Perhaps the best way of understanding the 1,9 approach is to consider the concept of conflict. The 1,9 manager sees conflict between himself and others, or even conflicts in which he is not directly involved, except as an observer, as intolerable—something which must be avoided. The result is that a 1,9 supervisor tends to take whatever actions he can to maintain an appearance of harmony. He does all he can to prevent an eruption in relationships. The actions he takes are frequently harmful to production and are seen as "soft" by people who are more production-minded.

The 1,9 approach to conflict management can be viewed from two orientations. One is concerned with adjustments to situations of conflict with one's boss. The other deals with how conflicts with one's subordinates are managed.

A 1,9 manager places high value on avoiding conflict with his boss. His approach for insuring that conflict does not arise is simple. His aim is to stay in such close contact with his boss' thinking that he rarely "gets out on a limb." Under these circumstances, he is able to "parrot" his boss' thinking and, if he is effective in doing so, then occasions for dispute are few and far between. It has been truly surprising to see the ease with which bosses can be hoodwinked by head-nodding subordinates!

But another factor should be emphasized in connection with the 1,9 handling of conflict with the boss. It is that the 1,9 subordinate avoids reporting negative considerations or "bad news" that might place him in a position of criticism. In addition, when challenged by his boss to explain circumstances which, if accurately described might promote controversy, his inclination is to lie, or if not to lie outright, to shade the truth in such a way as to make it pleasing or acceptable. In this way, he avoids the conflict that he otherwise would be confronted with. A result is that the boss can be unaware, blinded, or fooled regarding situations that could lead to the serious loss of production, breakdown of interpersonal relations, or both. The above considerations should give the boss, who manages a subordinate with a 1,9 orientation to conflict, serious basis for concern. The kind of withholding, shading, or screening of negative information described here can easily result in a powder keg situation. When the explosion occurs, the boss does not know what produced it.

Management of conflict under 1,9 also needs to be considered from the standpoint of when the *boss* manages subordinates according to a 1,9 style. Here, his basic approach is to *smooth over* conflict. The meaning of "smoothing over" conflicts can be brought out by drawing distinctions between *smoothing over* conflict as in 1,9, and *suppressing* it, as in 9,1.

Conflict is *suppressed* when its expression is prevented, either by criticism or by the application of punishment. In comparison, conflict is *smoothed over* by "trying to talk people out of it." How can this be done? There is a variety of ways. One is to emphasize the positive factors in the situation in the hope that the factors causing conflict will appear trivial and unimportant in comparison. Another is to "jolly people along" through joking about it in order to put a light touch on the situation.

There are other ways in which the 1, 9 supervisor can keep an appearance of harmony on the surface and cover up any conflict which may exist. One way is to separate those who argue and disagree so that they do not have the opportunity to come into contact with one another. In this way conflict is avoided, though the group may lose the advantage that can come from different ideas. Another way is to pour oil on troubled waters. Conflict is smoothed over even though it remains beneath the surface. Or, the supervisor may treat these conditions in such general and loose fashion that the group never comes to grip with them and really identifies them. Thus, they are described in such general terms that everyone can agree with them and the problem is never actually faced. Also, it frequently is possible to table a decision until the tensions are reduced or until other issues become more pressing and the problem is forgotten. Alternatively, when issues become polarized, a committee can be appointed to look into the matter. By using a committee in this way a 1, 9 boss can avoid responsibility for a negative recommendation.

There are these and many other ways of smoothing over conflict without suppressing it as the 9, 1 manager would do, and yet without confronting the real cause of it, as, it will be seen, is the approach of the 9, 9 manager. The serious consideration here is that the underlying causes, the causes which generate the conflict, are not examined and cleared out of the way either by a smoothing approach or by an approach which suppresses the appearance of conflict. This means that many of the constructive contributions to problem solving that conflict can produce are automatically lost under both 9, 1 and 1, 9. A 1, 9 manager can, however, usually promote a spirit of friendly togetherness. This, it would seem, is a key motivating factor for the 1, 9 manager.

Impact of 1, 9 on Creativity

Little needs to be said regarding creativity under the 1, 9 orientation. The reason is that creativity, itself the product of strong mental independence or of clashes of opinion, or both, does not constitute a value toward which a 1, 9 manager strives. In addition, thinking in new, different, or strange ways or listening to others whose suggestions, ideas, or proposals might lead to change, cannot help but upset the status quo. Conditions that can produce disagreement tend to be avoided. Individuals who have been managed under several orientations report that 1, 9 is more stifling of creativity than any other style.

Supervisory Style and Personal Characteristics

In terms of managerial functions, a typical 1, 9 outlook can be expressed as follows:

Planning. "Little planning is done either by myself or with my subordinates. Rather, I tend to give broad assignments and to convey my confidence to subordinates by saying, 'I'm sure you know how to do this and that you will do it well.'"

Work execution. "I see my people frequently and encourage them to visit me as their work permits. My goal is to see that they are happy and that they are able to get the things they request. I rarely criticize but often compliment. That's the way to encourage people."

Follow-up. "I hold a meeting with those who are on the job where I place emphasis on congratulating the group as well as individuals. Our 'wrap up' sessions usually revolve around what did or did not cause friction on the job and how we can help things to go smoothly in the future. I try to minimize any mistakes and to smooth over conflicts so as to eliminate ill will. My people know that I feel I can only be helping myself when I am helping them."

Managing mistakes by subordinates. "My approach to errors is to avoid blaming or placing responsibility, but to support the person who was in the wrong by saying something like, 'Well, we all make mistakes, but I know you did the best you could. Maybe we'll have better luck next time.'"

When policies or procedures are violated. "Policies and procedures are intended as guidelines for action rather than as rigid requirements. When the deviation is slight or the policy not too important, it is best to wink. If the violation is more severe, the person will usually straighten up if he knows you want him to."

Whereas the 9, 1 manager was described as an individual who places high value on sound decisions in comparison with the value he places on good relationships, the 1, 9 manager places high value on good relationships in comparison with the value he places on sound decisions. He does so by accepting opinions, attitudes, and ideas of others in preference to pushing his own. He rarely generates conflict, but when it does appear, he tries to soothe bad feelings to keep people together. He is patient and his temper is not easily triggered. When tensions between people do arise, many times his humor has the effect of reducing them.

Then 1, 9 is the "soft," "togetherness," or "human relations" approach to management. Being soft, it rarely confronts or challenges an individual to grow. Being soft, it also rarely aids an organization to become the kind of responsible agency needed in a society that, quite properly, demands performance and achievement of its citizens.

The "be nice" approach, which smothers conflict and seeks to avoid the conditions that produce it, can lead to harmony in human relations, but it causes production to suffer severely. The 1, 9 manager may be seen as a likeable fellow, a good Joe, and a big brother who is prepared to make his subordinates happy and satisfied, regardless of production costs, yet he does not achieve a proper integration of the relationships among people and the requirements of production. Nor does he obtain the creative thinking from the people that is needed to accomplish the best in production. But not only is the 1, 9 approach ineffective in achieving high output, it is also unlikely to achieve any lasting human relationships, since conflict and frustration are not really dealt with and relieved, but are merely smoothed over or avoided.

It should be re-emphasized that the 1, 9 approach in which little or no emphasis is placed on getting production, but which achieves good human relationships by not "upsetting the applecart" and by not creating the conditions under which needed changes actually are effected, is no way to get a job done. Nevertheless, the 1, 9 approach is far more common than would be expected.

5, 5: MIDDLE-OF-THE-ROAD MANAGEMENT

In the center of the Managerial Grid, at 5, 5, is the middle-of-the-road theory. The 5, 5 theory is "middle of the road" because the manager pushes enough to get average production, yet he yields production enough to respond to the frustrations and dissatisfactions of people in order to avoid low morale or active hostility. Under 5, 5, it is assumed that by string pulling, management can prevent either of the two concerns from dominating the other completely. Thus, the dilemma faced by the 5, 5 manager between concern for people and concern for production is resolved by yielding some of the concern for each to get some concern for both.

How does a 5, 5 manager think? The answer lies in what a 5, 5 supervisor might say to a subordinate, such as, "Look, all we expect out of you is a fair day's work. You can expect a fair day's pay in return if you stay out of trouble. We know that the work is not always too interesting and that a man can get tired of it. Put out, but don't kill yourself. You can see what goes on around you. Do as much as the average, and we will be satisfied. In other words, be a regular guy. Maintain a steady pace that's fair to the company, but one that also treats you right."

How Management Views Its Responsibilities under 5,5

A 5,5 manager does not abandon his planning responsibility, as is more or less true of 1,9, nor is he thoughtless of the needs of those beneath him to be involved in planning to some degree, as is true of a 9,1 manager. Because he wants to keep people with him, he sets achievable production goals in terms of average ability of subordinates working under moderate pressures (Davis, 1951). In addition, he takes pains to explain the reasons why the work must be done according to his plan. Furthermore, he is "flexible" in that he listens to others and alters plans to meet unforeseen objections and to avoid undue resistances. In a word, a 5,5 manager wants his plans to be acceptable and to conform with the thinking of those around him, both above and below.

Yet, under 5,5, as under 9,1, people are treated as tools of production in relation to the job. For the 5,5 manager, however, people also are important to consider because, "You have more trouble in the long run if people are disregarded than if you take some of their needs into account as you go."

As a result of this line of thinking, a 5,5 manager does not *command* or *direct* so much as he *leads, motivates,* and *communicates* to get the job done. The 5,5 manager does not exert his formal authority in a strict authority-obedience way. He does not seek to obtain unquestioning obedience, as does a 9,1 manager. Rather, his approach to leadership is to *persuade, request,* and *sell.* He avoids the kind of conflict that criticism produces; he gets his point across by "questions."

In comparison with each of the managerial styles discussed up to this point, a unique feature of organizational life is recognized and given weight under the 5,5 managerial style. A 5,5 manager believes every *formal* organization should have its rules, regulations, policies, chains of command, span of control, job specializations, etc. However, he acknowledges that people being what they are, the formal organization also produces an *informal* organization which has its own norms, standards and rules of conduct, its leaders and followers, conformists and deviants, and channels of communication. He knows that the informal organization can either support the goals of the formal organization or, in a fantastically large number of ways, prevent their attainment. Recognizing the inevitability of the *informal* organization, his way of adjusting to it is to *use* it to keep in touch with what is going on. In this way he can keep organizational goals for production from frustrating people while preventing people from shirking reasonable organizational demands for production and efficiency placed upon them.

Toward his goal of maintaining a balance between the needs of the organization for production and the needs of individuals for having a stake or involvement in things, a 5, 5 manager concentrates his energies in two directions. On one side he listens intently to what the informal organization can tell him about the "pulse" of people—about how people are feeling and what they are saying. In this way he keeps informed as to any disturbing antiorganizational trends, as well as to individual pressure points. Thus, the 5, 5 manager is frequently able to recommend corrective actions concerning issues which, left unattended, might easily disrupt into disturbing organizational conflict that could push production below average attainment.

But the 5, 5 manager does far more than monitor the radar system of the informal organization in a passive way. He may take active steps to correct contrary or antiorganizational trends by "feeding" the informal system confidential information on a "not to be repeated" basis. In this way he is able to "correct" misguided rumors, to relieve tension and to calm troubled waters. At the same time, he is seen by influential members of the informal organization as a "regular guy" who will come through when the "chips are down" and let you in "on the know." By all of these and many other string-pulling strategies the 5, 5 manager seeks to keep the organization at least partly sympathetic to the individual needs of its members, and also to keep individual members at least somewhat tuned to the needs of the organization.

Whyte (1956), in his popular book, has offered a scorching, but accurate, analysis of 5, 5 as the "general" approach to management today, calling it *The Organization Man.* Serious debate needs to be given to his analysis and corrections made, as the ethics of the 5, 5 kind of string-pulling leaves much to be desired. In the absence of a truly sound managerial base, 5, 5 is seen as superior to a 9, 1 system, which can generate intense warfare that disrupts organizational and individual goals and to the 1, 9 approach of "sweetness and light" which results in people being contented and happy, but which, in the extreme, can produce a flat, fat, flabby, and ineffectual organization.

5, 5 Approach to Managing Conflict

To understand the 5, 5 approach, it is extremely important to recognize the underlying attitude toward managing conflict. Here the manager's attitude is: "Human nature being what it is, you can't expect to really go all out for either production or for people. If you go all out for production you lose the commitment and good will of people and may even generate their active resentment. If you go all out for people, production falls by the wayside. What you have to do is to yield and to trust, to turn and to bend in order to find a course down the middle that represents steady, even if not dramatic, progress. You've got to compromise, but there's nothing bad about that. People say compromise is bad, you know, but progress, in this world, is made by people who know how to give something to get something. By going this route you might not get a whole loaf, but on the other hand, you don't starve either."

These attitudes are basic for understanding a 5,5 manager's approach to conflict, which says, "Seldom is it wise to confront conflict head-on because someone always wins and someone loses. A lot of people don't know it, but a loser in a fight is a potential enemy when the next battle shapes up. Furthermore, many conflicts represent hot emotions of the moment. If you back off and let the situation cool a while, you can usually get a basis for pulling the warring parties together. Furthermore, a little breathing time gives you a chance to think of a middle ground. Frequently, it's possible to take some of one's idea and a little of another's and blend them together. The solution you come up with might not be the perfect one, but it will probably be acceptable in that some of the thinking of each of the contending factions is represented in it. Thus, everyone will win, at least a little bit, and be satisfied. On the other hand, another danger you run into in a conflict situation is to smooth it over. If you do that, you can become known as soft, someone who sinks into the quicksand rather than finding safe ground. People know then that you're not around to give support when the going gets rough."

The premium placed on compromise as the basis for getting workable solutions to problems often results in such solutions appearing to be quite acceptable to the 5,5 person. If a 5,5 manager's attitude toward conflict is looked at from the standpoint of either his supervisor or subordinates who are 9,1 or 1,9, a paradox or contradiction appears between his own perception of the problem and those of his boss or subordinates. The paradox is in the fact that when the 5,5 subordinate sees himself as *realistic,* by shifting into middle ground to reduce conflict, he is likely to be seen by both boss and subordinates as a person lacking in *character and integrity and internal strength.* From the other person's perspective, the 5,5 person frequently moves *away* from the position that was generating conflict, not in terms of his altered understanding of the problem, but rather by making proposals, which, being compromises, solve the surface problem, even though they may leave the depth problem unresolved. It is just this kind of thinking which comes through to a boss or subordinate, not as helpful, but as lacking in character and in intellectual strength.

Impact of 5,5 on Creativity

Because of the search for compromise as a way of dealing with conflict, creativity is *not* part and parcel of the work interaction. However, creativity itself is valued, at least in a superficial way, in a 5,5 organization.

How? In order to release the creative energies of people, various gimmicks and techniques are used. "Brainstorming" is one such example. Since *criticism* is suspended during the brainstorming period, conflict is avoided, and *compromise* is not needed as the basis for listening to new ideas. Alternatively, because supervisors do not listen very well to subordinates in either 9,1 or 5,5, the *administrative* solution to the creativity problem is likely to be a suggestion system which gets *around* the problem of the supervisor who cannot hear the creativity of subordinates to whom he refuses to listen.

Supervisory Styles and Personal Characteristics

Typical ways the 5,5 manager handles managerial functions can be described as follows:

Planning. "I plan the work for each subordinate. After explaining goals and schedules, I make individual assignments. I insure that subordinates understand what I expect of them and that they feel free to come back if they need help in carrying out the assignments that have been made."

Work execution. "I keep up with each man's job and review his progress with him from time to time, or when he asks for it. I am always there to lend support if he gets into trouble or to give positive suggestions if he is having difficulty."

Follow-up. "I hold a meeting with those involved in the job to point up the group's good points as well as mistakes and to indicate how they can improve. Each individual gets the opportunity to discuss any reasonable suggestions he might have for improvement as I give the next assignments."

When policies or procedures are violated. "It is essential that policies and procedures be followed, and it is my responsibility to 'sell' my people on following them. If they understand that rules are for the *good* of all, they generally will follow them willingly."

Managing mistakes by subordinates. "This is the kind of mistake that can't be overlooked more than once. Next time, I'll have to take some action."

The 5,5 manager takes pride in the fact that he does not work for *ideal* decisions, and he does not work for *ideal* relations; rather, his goal is to achieve workable solutions. As a result, when ideas, opinions or attitudes different from his own appear, he searches for compromise positions that will relieve the deadlock. When conflict does arise, however, he tries to be fair but firm to get a fair solution. His preferred approach to conflict is to find out what subordinates think the best course of action is, but then to make the decision himself as to what course of action should be taken. When he does introduce humor into a situation, it is the kind that either sells himself in terms of increasing his acceptance by others or the position he wants to see "bought."

5, 5 management is here to stay for a long time to come. It is entrenched. It is able, over long periods, to endure as a way of life in large, massive organizations. Many large organizations, whether industrial, government, military, or academic, have been unable to gear their membership to any greater accomplishment or commitment than that represented by 5, 5.

Yet, the challenge confronting modern management *is* to set higher goals than 5, 5 as the basis for future accomplishment.

1, 1: IMPOVERISHED MANAGEMENT

The lower left-hand corner is entitled "impoverished management." It is "do-nothing" management. The reason is that neither the attainment of work objectives nor of sound human relationships is a positive value that the 1, 1 manager strives after. 1, 1 is an "ostrich" situation where the goal is that of "staying out of trouble" and of avoiding getting involved in problems of work or in interpersonal feelings. In terms of job requirements, the individual stays busy enough to give an appearance of effort, but his actual contribution is little.

How 1, 1 Management Views Its Responsibilities

The managerial philosophy of work under 1, 1 is to assign people jobs and to leave them alone. "Don't put your hand in a hornet's nest," is a motto of a 1, 1 manager. He does this by letting people do their work and by not pestering them. Since the 1, 1 manager only does enough to keep from being a sitting target, he is not likely to be found exercising power, as is the 9, 1 manager, nor is he concerned with the "happiness" of his people, as is the 1, 9 person. In comparison with a 5, 5 person, his goal cannot be described as finding an intermediate ground. His approach is that of minimum exposure. He sticks by the rules so as not to stand out from the crowd. In a sense, he is a specialist in the psychology of non-self-involvement. When he does get pushed, his reaction is *not* that of yielding, as is that in a 1, 9 solution, or of pushing back, as in the 9, 1 solution, or trying to find a safe middle ground, which is the 5, 5 solution. His responses are of minimum movement, enough to get the pressure off his back, but no more.

Under the 1, 1 orientation, the following remarks are typical of a person in the lower levels of an organization:

"My goal is to keep my nose clean. The best way to do it is to stay out of sight. I do enough to get by and to keep people off my back."

Sometimes, in both industry and government, a 1, 1 orientation can be found under the circumstances in which a person has been repeatedly bypassed for promotions and seems stuck in his position. Rather than looking elsewhere, he adjusts in the work setting by doing as little as possible, seeking satisfaction elsewhere.

"The work isn't too bad. We like the town. We have a comfortable house. I'm *marking time* until my retirement. I hope my chair doesn't break down."

Certainly the 1, 1 style of managing is not the most common. A business operated under 1, 1 concepts would be unable to continue very long. On the other hand, many individuals may perform in the 1, 1 manner and be able to survive for long periods of time. This is true especially in production situations that have become bureaucratic in nature and where "no one is ever fired." It also appears that there is a tendency for 1, 1 as well as 1, 9 managers to gravitate away from positions of line responsibility and into staff assignments where little positive contribution is expected, where damage from inactivity is only slight, or where the staff functions carry little prestige in the organization as a whole.

1,1 Approaches to Managing Conflict

With respect to dealing with conflict, rather than suppressing conflict as in the 9, 1 situation, smoothing it over as in the 1, 9, or seeking for compromise as in 5, 5, the 1, 1 manager's solution is to avoid it. This is accomplished in any of several ways. One way is literally to withdraw from situations of conflict if physical flight is possible. By getting out of the situation, the dangers it contains of getting an individual in trouble can be pretty well avoided. The way to deal with a disturbing memo, for example, is to file it and forget where you filed it. An alternative, which is often available when withdrawal is not possible, is to maintain strict neutrality. This not taking of sides ought not be confused with searching for compromise, as the 5, 5 manager might do. Instead, the 1, 1 manager is more likely not to voice any opinion at all. If compelled to do so, he might deflect the pressure in some way such as by saying, "I haven't had time to solve the problem," or "I would need more facts before making a judgment." If pressured still more, the 1, 1 manager's final appeal is to tradition and past practices. "Perhaps the best way to proceed is as we have done in the past."

Impact of 1,1 on Creativity

In a similar way, the 1, 1 person's creativity is likely to be evident only in his superior ability to appear uncreative and to blend invisibly into the background like a chameleon. It should be commented here, however, that a striking observation points to the fact that many individuals whose organizational adjustment is 1, 1 actively pursue interests in community life, at home through hobbies, or in their families. One manager we know, who might truly be characterized as having a 1, 1 orientation in his work setting, is an active member of the city council in the town where his plant is located.

Supervisory Styles and Personal Characteristics

1, 1 attitudes toward managerial functions can be described as follows:

Planning. "I give broad assignments but I don't tend to think in terms of goals or schedules. I do little planning. A way that you might describe my job is that I'm a message carrier. I carry the story from those above me to those below me and put as little embroidery or interpretation on it as possible."

Work execution. "I make the rounds, but take little on the spot action. I leave people to solve their own problems. They like it best that way and I do too."

Follow-up. "I talk to my boss to find out what is to be done next and to find out how he wants to do it."

Managing mistakes by subordinates. "Oh! *They* are always causing trouble, but what can you do?"

When policies or procedures are violated. "When policies and procedures are violated it's better to turn your head than to cause a furor unless the situation is one which is actually dangerous. Many rules are made to be broken, and most people use good judgment when they do so."

The 1, 1 supervisor is likely to say that he accepts the decisions of others without disagreement. He goes along with opinions, attitudes, and ideas of others or avoids taking sides. He is likely to be described as the kind of person for whom it is difficult to know where he stands. When conflict does arise, he tends to remain neutral and, if at all possible, to stay out of it, for, as he says, "Bullets that fly over you don't hurt." By remaining neutral he also is able to avoid getting stirred up. If he does provoke humor, it is only to keep things from getting too serious.

In some ways the 1, 1 behavior is an unnatural behavior. It is a situation of personal defeat that an individual "comes to" instead of "begins with." The 1, 1 behavior is really an indication of failure for the individual and for the organization. It is failure for the organization in that individual productive efforts are not integrated with sound human relationships. It is failure for the individual in that he has accepted defeat and has withdrawn from participation to the degree that even criticism no longer carries a sting.

9, 9: TEAM MANAGEMENT

The final position to be considered is "team management." The team concept is based on recognizing the interdependence of people engaged in productive activities. The production unit is rarely an individual working alone where the output of each is added to get the overall total output. Rather, the building block of a 9, 9 situation is the team (Blake and Mouton, 1962). The concept of team emphasizes the unity of effort of individuals in the work group, the interdependence among members, "team play," and "moving together." Team leadership avoids the task-centeredness of 9, 1, with its concept of people as tools of production. It also avoids the 1, 9 person-centeredness, with its minimum concern for obtaining organization performance goals. It also avoids yielding production to keep people satisfied, so characteristic of 5, 5. "Team management" recognizes and deals with relationships of members to one another, since all are embedded in a situation of "common fate" where success comes from accomplishing the mission of the organization. As a result, attitudes toward achieving production and toward people in the 9, 9 situation are different from those under any of the other theories mentioned above.

How Management Views Its Responsibilities under 9, 9

A 9, 9 manager views his responsibility as that of attaining effective production through participation and involvement of people and their ideas. Understanding and agreement as to what the organizational goals are and the means by which they are to be attained is the core of work direction. In a real sense people and work *are* interconnected. For example, personal satisfaction is seen to result from successful work performance through team effort under conditions of confidence and respect. Mutual understanding and agreement are the bases for planning, directing, and controlling.

An important point needs to be emphasized here. Control is no less and, indeed, may be more under 9, 9 than under other organizational systems. The critical issue is *how* control is achieved. Self-control, where an individual is regulating his own performance in terms of understanding the purpose of and agreement with the objectives introduced, is far more rigorous than the kind of control that is exercised when the man does not see the larger issues and has to be guided and goaded to see distortions in his own behavior which, from the standpoint of the organization, are detrimental to the organizational goals.

Certain distinctions for gaining an appreciation of 9, 9 team effort can be made by drawing comparisons between 9, 1 and 9, 9 concepts. Planning of work is one area in which contrasts can be drawn. In the 9, 1 situation, planning tends to be centralized, and the responsibility of those who execute the work consists of following the instructions they receive. Here the attitude is that there is 100 per cent responsibility for getting the task done and to the degree that one member of the pair feels responsible, the other person does not. Subordinates under a 9, 1 system say, "That's my supervisor's responsibility. If he is responsible, then I'm not." The goal of 9, 9 management is to arouse participation and to get involvement in planning so that *all* who share concern for production can find the opportunity to think through and to develop a basis of effort which reflects the best thinking. In this way, each of the members of the team feels responsible for getting the job done.

Getting team work is not for the purpose of "maintaining morale," as is likely to be true under 5, 5. The team concept does not provide a hiding place for inadequate performance as frequently occurs under 1, 9. The key to team management is that sound interpersonal relations are seen as the best way to achieve and to maintain production at peak levels.

9, 9 Approach to Managing Conflict

Of course, as people think together and work together in the planning and performance of work, feelings and emotions arise. Conflict is one result. When a number of people are working problems, planning work, etc., it is almost certain that there will be different points of view. People have intense feelings about their own positions. Conflict, then, is certain to appear.

The manner in which the 9, 9 manager deals with conflict shows an important distinction between the 9, 9 theory and the others discussed. Instead of attempting to suppress, smother, deny, or avoid conflict, the 9, 9 theory offers an opportunity for conflict to be relieved or "worked through." As a result, the 9, 9 manager would purposely bring together those with different points of view so that they could work through their differences. This is in contrast to that of separating people, as in 1, 9, punishing them, as in 9, 1, or compromising, as in 5, 5, or avoiding them, as in 1, 1.

Without really giving the matter serious thought, 9, 1 managers are likely to see 9, 9 managers as soft because they treat conflict in this way. However, it takes great effort and a high quality of leadership to get people to participate in the solution of problems and to do serious and original thinking when confronted with difficulties. This involvement and participation is what a 9, 1 manager may see as weak.

On the other hand, a 1, 9 manager is likely to see a 9, 9 manager as too hard, since he places key emphasis on production. The point is that the reason people work together in an industrial situation is to reach the goal of that organization, which is production. This is what the 9, 9 manager accomplishes. A 5, 5 person is likely to look upon 9, 9 as idealistic and, for that reason, wholly unattainable.

Impact of 9, 9 on Creativity

Creativity is high under 9, 9 for several reasons. Because of the emphasis on participation and involvement of people in work activities, innovation in the work setting itself is likely to arise. As conflict is tolerated, and even encouraged relative to task aspects, interplay of ideas which stimulate creativity is likely to be present.

An attribute of 9, 9 associated with creativity, which is not likely to be present under other managerial systems, is that of experimentation. Looking for alternative ways of operating invites experimentation for a person whose managerial outlook is 9, 9 in comparison with tried and true methods which are frequently relied on in 9, 1. Concern for what the boss wants or wishing to avoid the anxieties that might be aroused in subordinates if an alternative course were experimented with is the 1, 9 approach. Putting a wet finger into the wind to test for acceptance to an alternative course would be typical of the 5, 5 orientation. What is being said, in other words, is that one of the critical ways of inducing change under a 9, 9 system is by experimentation.

Supervisory Style and Personal Characteristics

The 9, 9 attitudes toward managerial functions can be summarized as follows:

Planning. "I get the people together who have relevant facts and/or stakes in the outcome to review the whole picture, get reactions and ideas. Then, my subordinates and I establish goals and flexible schedules, as well as procedures and ground rules, and set up individual responsibilities."

Work execution. "I keep familiar with major points of progress and exert influence on subordinates through identifying problems and revising goals and schedules with them as necessary. I lend assistance when needed by re moving road blocks."

Follow-up. "I conduct a 'wrap-up' to evaluate how a job went and to find out what can be learned from it. If appropriate, I give recognition on a team basis as well as recognizing outstanding individual contributions."

Managing mistakes by subordinates. "Tough luck. It's embarrassing, but the thing is to study the problem and to learn from it. When can we get together?"

When policies or procedures are violated. "I discuss violations with those involved in order to diagnose what the problem is. If the procedure or policy is inappropriate, steps are taken to change it. If misconduct, what motivated it needs understanding before corrective action is taken."

A 9, 9 manager places high value on getting sound creative decisions that result in understanding and agreement. In doing so, he listens for and seeks out ideas, opinions, and attitudes different from his own. Although he is likely to have clear convictions, he responds to sound ideas by changing his mind. When conflict arises, he tries to identify the reasons for it and to re- solve underlying causes by working it through. He rarely loses his temper, even when stirred up, and his humor gives perspective to things.

Finally, there is a basic psychological need of people that is satisfied by the 9, 9 theory but is not satisfied by either 9, 1 or 9, 9. This need is the need to apply mental effort in production work. People are not like machines. Their jobs need to involve more than just physical effort. This basic psy- chological need must also be considered with another equally important need. This is the need for establishing sound and mature relationships among people, which are ones of mutual trust, mutual support, pleasure, and satis- factions. People can work together in the solutions of problems and reach production goals as a team better when there is trust and mutual support rather than distrust, suspicion and tension.

Thus, the situation where we have the 9, 9 concerns for production and human relationships is one in which the capacities of individuals to think creatively—to come up with new ideas—are utilized. The 9, 9 manager creates conditions under which the relationships among people are centered on and conditioned by their needs for solving problems of production.

Summary

Finally, it may be possible to give further clarification to the concept of 9, 9 management by returning to the introduction in which the psychological needs of people for the opportunity to apply mental effort in the attainment of production is seen as central. This basic psychological need must also be considered in the context of the other equally important need, namely, that of establishing sound and mature relationships among people, which can be characterized as one of mutual trust, mutual support, pleasure, and satisfaction. The answer to the question, "Change to achieve what end or goal?" can now be given. The position stated here is that thinking through problems of production is most possible when individuals are related in such a manner that there is trust and mutual support, rather than distrust, suspicion, and tension. The interaction of production and people under 9, 9 is one which takes advantage of the capacities of individuals to think creatively and innovatively by creating the conditions under which the relationships among people are centered on and conditioned by the need for solving problems of production.

DO BEHAVIORAL SCIENCE CONCEPTS
AND METHODS HAVE UTILITY FOR
INDUCING ORGANIZATIONAL CHANGE?

Efforts to construct a science of behavior were begun by pioneers such as Pavlov, Freud, Durkheim, Pareto, Radcliffe-Brown, Malinowski, and others. They have continued, with almost constantly gathering momentum, to the present. But after 75 to 100 years of effort, it is appropriate to ask, "Have the behavioral sciences become sufficiently strong in concept and method so that, in concrete application, they have utility for dealing with problems such as those typified in the factory situation described above?"

The general question can be made more pointed. How would a Hullian theorist apply the insights from learning theory regarding the acquisition of new behavior to correcting an ongoing problem of industrial intergroup warfare between a union and a management? How would the psychoanalyst, an industrial psychiatrist, or a clinical psychologist insert his clinical skills into the top management of a company in such a way as to help them develop the problem-solving ability needed to make sound decisions that do not have to be reversed? Alternatively, how would a sociologist proceed in assisting foremen to develop a culture within which they could act in a positive and concerted manner, rather than trying to provide supervision under conditions where they frequently are pitted, not only against upper management, and against the wage man, but also against each other? How would an anthropologist intervene in the life of a factory so as to shift its entire culture away from conflict and mutual suspicion toward problem-solving and mutual support? Answers to such questions remain exceedingly difficult to find in the behavioral science disciplines.

In formulations of these kinds of issues, a serious contradiction can be sensed between what *is* known about behavior and what would *need* to be known in order to change an industrial organization. As far as can be determined, none of the disciplines has been able to cope adequately with problems of bringing about change in multiperson, organized situations of work and production. This is not to say that organizational changes have not been documented and analyzed according to behavioral science concepts, for they have (Lawrence, 1958; Mann, 1960; Guest, 1962). For the most part, however, the few organizational studies which are available are ones in which the changes came about by actions from upper management, with changes put into effect through policy positions and procedural decisions or by "clearing out" deadwood at the top and bringing in a new regime. The behavioral scientist came into the situation before, during, and after the changes took place in order to describe, to analyze, and to measure the shifts that occurred. However, instances in which there has been a deliberate attempt to bring about the kinds of planned changes needed, which have been based on behavioral science theory and concepts, are extremely few and limited in scope (Holmberg, 1960; Jacques, 1951; Trist, 1951; Sofer, 1961; Pages, 1959; Argyris, 1962). This statement appears to be true, even though the notion of planned change has come to be of more interest to behavioral scientists in the recent past (Lippit, Watson, and Westley, 1958; Bennis, Benne, and Chin, 1961).

One answer to the question asked in this section, then, is that the behavioral sciences have accomplished little of systematic character in the direction of achieving change in situations of organized human activity.

CLINICAL EFFORTS TO DEVELOP TECHNIQUES FOR INDUCING PLANNED CHANGES INTO ORGANIZED SITUATIONS

Over the past decade, intensive effort has been devoted, from a systematic point of view, to identifying the conditions necessary for bringing about change in an organized situation of production. During this time, behavioral scientists have been asked to aid in inducing change in a number of factory situations. These factories were faced with a wide range of problems of varying seriousness which were pertinent to their survival. Thus, the opportunity has been afforded to evaluate various approaches and procedures in the effort to resolve human problems of production encountered in a factory *without* replacing organizational leadership and *without* achieving change through the callous use of edict.

The Dilemma

One statement of the dilemma that might be faced by a behavioral scientist who enters a factory for the purpose of inducing change is this:

First, he is presented with quite open and challenging opportunities to apply behavioral science concepts and methods as the basis for inducing change. That is to say, the situation is receptive to his suggestions. Casting about for concepts and techniques of demonstrated or of potential value for application under these circumstances, he finds himself confronted with a body of rather highly elaborate behavioral science knowledge. For the most part, however, he is not likely to find that this knowledge will prove useful in dealing concretely with the factory situation at hand. To add to his perplexity, often tried procedures for teaching effective managerial behavior in the classroom, ranging from the more tradition-based academic approaches such as lectures and case method to the opposite extreme of action procedures such as role playing and psychodrama, appear, on the basis of a decade of experience with their use, to have little demonstrated impact in aiding organizational members to solve their difficulties of integrating people into a sound production effort. He will find consulting firms that employ testing techniques, that offer human engineering services, and that provide quasi-clinical assistance to individuals. He is, however, unlikely to find examples in which such firms have achieved change in basic aspects of the production-people problem.

Faced with this dilemma, which consists of an opportunity to test the utility of his concepts and methods for inducing change, he can take any of several paths, from trial and error to engaging in an effort to find out how to induce change by conducting a series of pilot project experiments.

It is with a description of our own approach to inducing planned change, when confronted with the dilemma presented above, that we want to deal in this presentation.

Under such circumstances, one casts about for anchorages and guidelines to direct his thinking and effort. By way of perspective, then, from our own point of view, we can answer the question, "What ideas and experiments from the behavioral sciences have proven useful in diagnosing factory situations and in designing change strategies?" The answer is, "None, directly, but some have offered suggestions regarding important organizational problems and possible approaches for exerting change influences on them." Some *examples* follow.

In a broad way, Gestalt psychology, particularly Lewinian formulations, has provided us the most meaningful background orientation for analyzing an organization as the unit of change and for providing a framework for viewing and evaluating change process (Lewin, 1951). Of great usefulness in understanding such concrete situations as interdepartmental conflict and union and management warfare have been Sherif's (1953) penetrating analyses of the conditions and consequences of intergroup tension and harmony. Insights into the dynamics of the work group which stem directly from Homan's (1950) work and such experimental studies as Lewin, Lippitt, and White's (1939) leadership climate study. Sherif's (1936) work on norm formation, Back's (1951) work on cohesion, Schachter's (1951) on communication, deviation, and rejection, Asch's on conformity (1940), and Horwitz's (1958) on power reduction, as well as studies of reference group phenomena from *The American Soldier* (Stouffer et al., 1949) and *The Organization Man* (Whyte, 1956) all gave important leads. These studies and many others were helpful in a general way. Such studies, coupled with early experimental work by Lewin (1951), Coch and French (1948), Levine and Butler (1952), and others, on conditions of change, were directly applicable to thinking through problems of improving communication, control, and decision making within work groups at various levels within the organization. Insight into issues connected with vertical and horizontal linking within the organizational structure were derived from such sources as Roethlisberger's (1945) description of the plight of foremen and Likert's (1961) concepts of linkpinning. In addition to the examples of theory and experimental work referred to above, sources of insight into the methodologies of change included Freud's (1938) concept of interpretation, laboratory training techniques pioneered by National Training Laboratories (1953), Moreno's work with sociometry and role-playing (1953), and Korzybski's concepts of time binding, the nature of abstraction, and language structure (1948).

Yet it would be inappropriate to conclude that any of these sources supplied the concepts or methods needed to induce organizational change. What they did offer were useful background concepts and methods in terms of which thinking about change variables and processes could be oriented.

Our approach has been that of conducting a series of pilot projects for evaluating a given approach in one factory and a second methodology in another, and so on, until we felt some sense of assurance that at least one orderly approach to organizational change induction could be described.

Organizational Change Efforts Should Be Viewed as Clinical Studies

A major difficulty that has confronted behavioral scientists in attempts to study planned change is that it has been very difficult, up to the very recent past, for them to gain access to ongoing organizations for change induction purposes. This has been particularly true of profit-based organizations which frequently regard themselves as "hard headed" and see behavioral scientists as little more than "headshrinkers." As a result, change specialists have had relatively impoverished opportunities to test out, to evaluate, and to compare the impact of one approach to change with an alternative.

But the past decade has provided opportunities of the kind needed in order to learn something regarding the character of organization change processes.[2] The remarks below are based on experiences of the authors with fifteen different factories, ranging in size from five hundred to over five thousand employees.

Various combinations of change strategies and other types of interventions have been utilized in different situations. The particular approach applied was based on our understandings of organizational change dynamics at any particular point in time. Taking the fifteen factories as a sample, in other words, our efforts to induce organizational change have not been the same in any but two. Rather, different types of efforts have been applied in each. Thus, it might be said that the pilot project approach has been that of the clinical experiment. The goal has been to employ a different change methodology or a combination of procedures in each factory location until we could get a sense of what seemed fundamental and had effects, and what appeared trivial and did not.

The remarks here reflect our present understanding regarding the conditions and consequences of organizational change efforts.[3] While we feel that the basic strategy to be described has been quite well established by now, much further work will be required before our assertions can be accepted or rejected in probabilistic terms.

How, then, should our generalizations be evaluted? While we started with the idea of measuring organizational change in a systematic and rigorous manner, this attempt was abandoned as we came to understand better the more basic dimensions of the problem. Factories are as individualistic as are

[2] Appreciation is expressed to the following people whose interest and aid made these projects possible: A. C. Bidwell, Frank Cassens, Charles Draughn, John Farrell, Harry Kolb, and Ross Murrell, Humble Oil and Refining Co.; Gerry Bassler, Continental Oil Co.; Drew Daly, International Business Machines; Richard Forrest, Lever Brothers, Ltd.; M. L. Goeglin, Pacific Finance; Gordon Harrison, Dominion Tar and Chemical Co., Ltd.; Carl Johnson, Shell Oil Co.; Richard Knopf, General Aniline and Film; Dwight Meader and William Davidson, General Electric Co.; Arn Penner, Trans Canada Airlines; Paul Reichertz, Socony Mobil Oil Co.; Nelson Tulley, E. I. du Pont de Nemours.

[3] Many behavioral scientists have contributed in one way or another to various parts of the approach outline. Included are: Chris Argyris, Yale University; Michael Blansfield, Pacific Finance; Leland P. Bradford, National Training Laboratories; Rensis Likert, University of Michigan; Douglas McGregor, Massachusetts Institute of Technology; and Herbert Shepard, Case Institute of Technology.

people. After coming to know factory after factory, it has become evident that the paramount problems of one factory may not even be present in another. Under such conditions, research efforts to test systematically stated hypotheses regarding organizational change seemed to us to be premature. Needed in the beginning stages was a more basic understanding of the underlying characteristics of *many* factories and of the results from many different kinds of efforts to apply change strategies. Such efforts could then serve as the basis for decisions regarding significant variables that should be subjected to measurement for the purpose of coordinating change efforts. It seemed to us that the kind of effort vitally needed over the near term was precise clinical work supported by quantitative measurement wherever possible as the basis for critical experiments in the next phase of organization change effort. Only now is this phase at hand, and an organizational change project in a five-thousand-man factory is now being launched under conditions approximating a critical experiment, with measurements of a sociological, economic, and psychological character being made on a prepost basis and with similar measurements available in a control factory.

The remarks below, then, are expressed with tentativeness. They are not intended to be interpreted as a final formulation of an approach to organizational change. They should be read, we think, as defining an important point of departure from which continuous changes, improvements, and refinements may prove possible.

A SIX-PHASE APPROACH TO ORGANIZATIONAL CHANGE

The approach to organizational improvement is *not* based on treating symptoms, such as union and management antagonism or low production. Rather, it seeks to treat and to correct underlying *causes* of problems.

The primary focus has been on changing *patterns* of relationships at interpersonal, group, intergroup, and organizational levels so that more effective and integrated organizational problem solving can occur. Then *actual* operations of the factory, such as detecting and correcting technical failures, or making better economic or business decisions, or doing a better job of conducting union and management affairs, or getting greater commitment to production, are predicted to improve as a result.

The six-phase approach considers within a single longitudinal effort the achievement of production requirements through mature interpersonal relationships which are integrated around the production purposes of the organization. While the six phases were not applied in every situation, they do represent our most thorough and systematic approach to date, one that has been applied in a more or less standard way in two main factory change experiments. Since descriptions of all but one phase are available in the literature, they are summarized below. The phase concerned with direct intervention of the behavioral scientist is described more fully in the next section.

The first intervention is a laboratory training program, conducted as a series of learning sessions, in which factory members are afforded the opportunity to examine behavioral science theory, to participate in controlled experiments, and to engage in face-to-face feedback of the training group variety (Blake and Mouton, 1961). This step provides background from which an increased number of alternative possibilities for dealing with people in connection with production can be evaluated for concrete use with greater deliberateness than is possible without a background of behavioral science concepts. Recent experimental work has verified that such training does in fact increase the number of alternatives from which individuals can select a course of action.

The second phase, team training, involves direct interpersonal feedback among actual work group members who have boss-subordinate and peer relationships with one another (Blake, Mouton, and Blansfield, 1962). The target here is to examine and to resolve relationship problems of communication, control, and decision making among those whose work involves close integration of effort among interdependent members. Horizontal linking across groups, including members at the same level but from different groups who are in contact in day-by-day activities, is the focus of the third phase.

Setting broad organizational improvement goals in a manner that involves the entire managerial force takes place as the fourth phase.

The fifth phase is designed to bring about, in a concrete way, the organizational improvement goals outlined in phase four, with on-the-job training aspects supplied by a behavioral scientist who intervenes in the day-to-day problem-solving activities of the organization.[4] A period of stabilization is a final phase. Its aim is to insure that changes already achieved are maintained and that they become firmly meshed into organizational operations.[5]

[4] An alternative, and in some respects a better approach in this and other phases, is to train organization members in the skills necessary to guide the change effort. In doing so, they function as does the behavioral scientist, i.e., by aiding groups other than those in which they hold no direct membership to face and to solve their problems of communication, control, and decision making.

[5] Both of us have participated in overall design work and in conducting the various phases. In the larger-scale projects, Robert R. Blake has assumed primary responsibility. During this phase, the other author, Jane S. Mouton, through evaluating dictated reports by Professor Blake, served as a control in the psychoanalytic sense by evaluating the style and content of interventions that were being introduced by him. In a developing field of

In an industrial organization of a substantial size, say as many as two thousand or more employees, these phases outlined may require three to five years, or even longer, to complete, with the length depending on the intensity of the effort which is applied, the seriousness of the problems confronting the organization, and the degree of improvement sought.

FACILITATING ORGANIZATIONAL CHANGE THROUGH BEHAVIORAL SCIENTIST INTERVENTION

A critical need in the organization change sequence summarized above is for intervention by a behavioral scientist into the day-by-day activities of the organization. The question, however, can be legitimately asked as to why this is so.

Need for Interventions

There are several reasons. Among the most important is the great difficulty for individuals, or teams, to make an appropriate separation between the *content* of a problem that is being solved and the processes of relationship and operations by which it is being approached. This distinction is subtle and very difficult to maintain in focus. Training of the kind described in phase one, where *process* problems are examined in detail and content or operating problems are pushed into the background, is designed as one way to remedy this lack of skill. But presuming that this orientation can be maintained after team training and horizontal linking phases are completed is an unwarranted assumption. Needed continuously, and over an extended period of time, are interventions which keep content-process distinctions in focus and which permit the continuous examination of process problems in order to improve the strategies involved in gaining solutions for content problems.

Breaking up old habits and traditional ways of thinking is one of the critical problems of inducing planned change. Interactions which focus the implicit assumptions and conventional behavior for examination and evaluation aid the organization and its members to become more flexible, innovative, and creative. Extending the range of alternatives in any situations, rather than

specialization such as is characterized here, the concept of the behavioral science control has proved to be a most useful one.

In addition to these arrangements for control of the interventions, we have held weekly conferences throughout the period when these clinical experiments were under way in order to evaluate the background and present state of affairs in greater detail and to develop plans for next steps as indicated.

coming down impulsively on one and using it as the basis for judgment, is another reason why interventions are needed. Thorough knowledge of behavioral science theory and concepts on the part of an interventionist makes it possible for him to confront the traditional patterns of relationship and of managerial assumptions. This again is difficult for members embedded within the organizational framework to do.

A third reason that an outsider is frequently indispensable is that much organizational effort *is* impulsive and actions are taken before they are really thought through. By intervening in the problem-solving activities of an organization in such a way as to suspend action, prior to decision, deliberateness can be increased and impulsiveness reduced. Once this has happened, it becomes possible actually to move in the direction of achieving the organizational goals set in phase four.

Relationship to the Organization

Without going into detail, several criteria governing this relationship of the behavioral scientist to the organization can be stated. One is that, while he works in the organization, he is not a member of it. He does not have line or staff responsibility in the conventional sense. Furthermore, he does not accept a direct reporting relationship to *anyone* in the organization except in terms of organizational mechanics such as administration of personal affairs. The situation is somewhat like that of an industrial medical officer whose assignment makes it difficult for line or staff management to give professional direction to or to exercise performance control over his efforts. Rather, as is true for medical specialists who deal with personal health in an industrial setting, it is the behavioral scientist's responsibility to define, within broad and agreed-upon general limits, the way in which he will apply his effort toward the development and maintenance of organizational health. He remains the specialist responsible for the sound application of his technical knowledge.

A behavioral scientist can exert many influences on individual, team, and organizational behavior to bring about the kinds of actions required to achieve the goals of this phase. From a most general point of view he gains access for training purposes to a variety of working situations within the organization in order to aid members to solve their own problems rather than to make specific recommendations regarding operational details. Access is achieved, not by edict from the top, but rather by discussion and agreement within each of the working teams. This procedure, though much more difficult than access through authority, reduces resistance and increases the quality of the joint effort between the behavioral scientist and the work team.

Before proceeding to describe how some behavioral scientists have worked to insure the implementation of these relationships, operations, and performance goals, it becomes necessary to answer some key questions regarding the character of his relationship to the organization. It should be recognized that the following statements are not intended as other than standards of conduct.

Kinds of Interventions

Given arrangements which permit him to work freely with various groups but without becoming a part of the power structure of the organization, the question is: "What does a behavioral scientist do?" or "How does he work?"

The behavioral scientist can intervene in day-by-day organizational life at critical points of here-and-now action where actual difficulties of interaction are being experienced. There are at least eight major kinds of behavioral science interventions which can aid in bringing about the concrete changes in behavior requisite for organizational improvement to take place. These kinds of interventions are described below.

DISCREPANCY INTERVENTION. A discrepancy intervention calls attention to a contradiction in action or attitudes. The most frequently noted discrepancy is one where a course of action is agreed upon at some time, and then, at a later period, the behavior in the situation is incongruent with the initial direction without an explicit agreement to change the goal occurring during the interim. In addition, there may be discrepancies between what people say they want to do and what actually is done. The adage, "practice what you preach," is a sample in everyday occurrences of a discrepancy intervention.

A frequent area for discrepancy intervention by the behavioral scientist occurs when a course of action being planned in this phase is contradictory to the statements of goals and purposes previously set. The identification of such a contradiction can do much to bring about an examination of present or proposed actions and to bring these actions into line with the requirements stated in phase four. This kind of confrontation is useful for keeping the organization on its new course, rather than allowing it to shift unwittingly into old and less satisfactory behavior patterns, due to momentary pressures.

THEORY INTERVENTION. Because organization members are not so likely to be thinking in terms of behavioral science concepts as they are to be applying common sense notions, needed theory interventions frequently are absent unless supplied by the behavioral scientist.

A theory intervention is where a confrontation draws on behavioral science concepts and theory to throw into bold relief the connection between under-lying assumptions and present behavior. In addition, theory sometimes can be useful in predicting the consequences likely to follow from embarking on any specialized course of action.

A theory intervention is made whenever behavioral science theory is avail-able from which alternative courses of action can be evaluated or when pre-dictions as to probable consequences of a given course of action can be made. Many times the untested assumptions of individuals and teams, as they think about and plan for the solution of a problem, are quite different from the kinds of assumptions that would be more valid if based on behavioral science theory. Frequently, improved consequences can be attained by shifting from "common sense" to behavioral science theory. Insofar as intuition and experi-ence correspond with theoretical generalizations, a specific theory intervention need not be made by an outsider. There are, however, enough points at which theory and intuitive basis of action differ so that these kinds of con-frontations are relatively frequent and highly useful.

PROCEDURAL INTERVENTION. A procedural intervention invites a critique of how various steps of effort may or may not aid problem solving.

The questions: "How should we proceed?" or "Is this the best way to move?" or even "Is this the appropriate group or unit to tackle the issue?" are ones that may need to be made explicit and opened to public discussion. This is particularly true in groups or among people who have a long history of interaction and where problem-solving procedures have become rather fixed and ritualistic. After a period of time working together, patterns of deliber-ation tend to become stabilized with meetings following a relatively predict-able, though not necessarily a functionally adequate, pattern. Informal or-ganization and implicit procedure rather than problem-solving requirements govern endeavors. It is, however, possible to gain new perspective on a problem or to engage in more effective decision making by examining the procedural assumptions upon which interactions are based. The procedural intervention is designed for this purpose.

RELATIONSHIP, "SENSITIVITY," OR PROCESS INTERVENTION. Another kind of in-tervention focuses attention of participants on their own *relationships*. This is one of the kinds of confrontations most likely to be utilized by the behavioral scientist during phase two, where team training is taking place, or in phase three, during the early stages of horizontal linking. Feelings and attitudes which arise between people as they work together are unlikely to be examined in face-to-face intervention by those affected. With the aid of a behavioral scientist to focus attention on personal feelings, particularly strong negative emotions which can only hinder coordinated effort, emotions connected with work can be examined and worked through to resolution. Unless this step is taken, emotions are likely to be suppressed with resulting negative effects on subsequent efforts at problem solving. Interventions, then, which focus on relationships are as indispensable as are procedural confrontations in bringing about improved problem solving among team members.

EXPERIMENTATION INTERVENTION. Another intervention involves experimentation. The experiments that are outlined are not necessarily of the highly controlled or technical variety of the psychology laboratory, but are often ones which permit testing and comparing two or more courses of action *before* a final decision is taken as to which one to follow. Many times problems exist for which either one of two or more courses of action look equally attractive. Under circumstances in which individuals cannot agree on the better course, there are at least three options available for the final determination. One is to shift the problem to a higher level of organization, where one individual of greater authority than others can make a choice from among a series of alternatives. Another is to go the way of the "stronger" faction. A third alternative, which can break an *impasse,* is to conduct a simple experiment which evaluates, from among several possibilities, which is the best way to go. This is the "pilot" project concept as used in applied research settings.

Another critical point at which an intervention for considering an experiment frequently is indicated occurs when the way to proceed has become institutionalized or tradition-bound. Under these conditions, behavior is "frozen" in the sense that it is necessary to jar people into looking for new or alternative ways of solving the problem. If the situation is one in which traditional solutions are only marginally adequate, but perhaps not optimal, it is all the more difficult to seek for innovation. It is here that an outsider, by proposing an experiment, can provoke a re-examination of old solutions.

DILEMMA INTERVENTION. An intervention which aids in accurately identifying a choice point in managerial actions often can help members to re-examine outworn assumptions and to search for alternatives other than those under consideration. The situation calling for a dilemma intervention frequently is one in which managers are unaware that a choice point has been reached, and are prepared to follow a course of action which has been successful in the past, without even testing the implicit assumption that it is the way to proceed. It is at this point that an outsider can step in to focus the issue of whether the choice point or dilemma *is* recognized as such and whether the alternatives could profitably be examined before actions predicated on past practices are somewhat automatically set in motion. The goal of the intervention, in other words, is to present the dilemma in order to provoke a more thorough examination of it.

PERSPECTIVE INTERVENTION. Many times in the intensity of the effort applied in production settings, it seems almost inevitable that individuals or teams lose their sense of direction. Thereafter, it is increasingly difficult to re-establish a course of action which can move the situation away from momentary problem solving toward larger issues. A perspective intervention permits present actions to be evaluated by providing a background of a broader historical orientation in terms of which to view present actions.

Another point at which a sense of direction can be regained through a perspective intervention is when actions are saturated with emotions. A heightened feeling level surrounding the circumstances under which decisions must be made can seem to blind participants to more objective issues. The most prominent example of high emotions which can block effective organizational change or movement is that of win-lose conflict or competitiveness at interpersonal and more particularly at intergroup levels. Under those circumstances, stepping back away from the situation to trace the events leading up to the present competitiveness can aid in reducing emotional tension and wasted efforts. By interventions which set perspective, it becomes possible for individuals and teams to re-establish a sense of direction.

ORGANIZATIONAL INTERVENTION. It is possible to think of many organizational improvement efforts which leave the very structure of the organization unevaluated and unexamined. Students of organizational change are correct in pointing out that many causes of organizational effectiveness are not to be found in the areas of procedures or team effectiveness or even in the absence of performance goals. Rather, the fabric of the organization itself can prevent communication, decision making, and the application of effort from being as effective as it might be under organizational arrangements different from those presently being employed.

An organizational intervention focuses issues which confront the total membership of an organization. Such a confrontation may focus on organizational structure, its ways of working, its reward systems, and so on. For people who work and live every day within the boundaries of a given organizational framework, the organization itself tends to become a "given." Challenging the appropriateness of structure is difficult. Overseeing the organization as a whole and its problems is only seen as a requirement of one or at most a limited number of people at the top. Yet it can be that the deliberate re-examination of the properties of the organizational fabric itself may be required if problems of lesser scope are to be resolved. Thus, organizational interventions that place the focus of a problem on organization *structure* or organizational *function* can be useful in bringing about or implementing changes.

OVERVIEW

This chapter confronted three fundamental questions regarding the induction of change. The first matter treated dealt with: "What is the *unit* of change?" The answer given was that the unit of change is the whole situation. When planned change is considered, the whole situation is unlikely to be defined by the individual in isolation or even as a group in isolation. More likely, it will be found to be the entire organization, such as a factory.

The second issue treated was: "Change *from what* to *accomplish what purpose?*" The Managerial Grid, which defines a variety of theories of how to achieve production through people, was presented.

The third question examined was concerned with how a planned change program is executed. Here a six-phase approach was described, with emphasis placed upon the manner in which the behavioral scientist, acting on the organization as the agent of change, functions to aid the attainment of planned change goals.

It was suggested that planned change efforts only will be effective when the problem of change is accurately and adequately conceived.

chapter eleven

Psychopharmacology and Personality

Joseph Zubin and Martin M. Katz

Drugs occupy a unique place among the various factors which bring about changes in behavior. Relief from intractable pain, operative pain, psychotic and neurotic symptoms, seasickness, headaches, fatigue, boredom, the induction of moods, and the facilitation of learning and sleep are but a few of the alterations which psychopharmacological agents attempt to bring about.

The implications of these various drug effects on the physiology, biochemistry, and overt behavior of the organism have drawn research workers from many diverse disciplines to the field of psychopharmacology. The research literature, in the general area of drugs and personality, reflects interests in (1) behavior theory and personality measurement, (2) the nature of drug action, and (3) the interaction between these two, i.e., the influence of personality factors on reaction to drugs and the effects of drugs on personality.

The general approach of this chapter will involve reviewing and assessing the interaction of drug effects and personality factors. The main intention will be to search for the more promising channels along which work in this area might be directed. The study of psychopharmacology and personality change is very much in its infancy and suffers from a lack of sound, testable theory and adequate methodology to apply to its problems. The theory and recommendations which will be presented here will hopefully contribute toward clarification of some of the basic issues in the field.

The preparation of this report was supported in part by NIMH Grant 1541. The authors are grateful to Miss Jean Andersen for her assistance in the preparation of this manuscript.

Personality Measurement

In a discussion of the effects of drugs on personality—or indeed a discussion of whether or not there is, or can be, any experimental evidence for such effects—the present vague status of the concept of "personality" has to be dealt with. Obviously, only a concept which is relevant to experimental investigation can be accepted for our purposes. Such a concept of personality must permit change and its detection. As everyone would agree, the concept of personality, as representing the unique pattern of behavior of the individual, is no more than a scientific model. If it has ceased being a useful model, we ought to discard it. If it is still useful in the study of behavior, it ought to be retained.

Traditionally, measurement in personality has been introduced at two different levels, depending upon the model of personality adhered to by the investigators. A review of the various scientific models proposed for personality (Zubin, 1954) indicates the following models: (1) differential, (2) clinical, (3) personalistic, and (4) neurophysiological. In the differential model, an analysis of behavior into traits is made first and then techniques are chosen for assessing these traits. The trait theorists have approached measurement by assembling independent but additive factors of personality which they sought to identify and then measure. Their primary statistical tool is factor analysis. In the clinical model, normal personality is regarded as the central portion of behavior which in the extremes are psychopathological. The basic approach here is the identification of types of behavior over many dimensions and the attempt then to isolate the measures which characterize these types. These holistically oriented investigators begin with a totality and try to analyze it through measurement. The personalistic approach is geared to the single individual, considering each person as a separate universe. The neurophysiological approach is more like the differential, except that it deals with behavior reflecting brain function rather than with behavior reflecting organized traits. For the purpose of this chapter, measurement in the field of personality can be thought of as the attempt, first to isolate, but then to synthesize the dimensions on which the behavioral uniqueness of the individual rests.

No matter what organizational principles may be postulated (needs, traits, etc.), personality is inferred from behavior. It might be interesting to classify observable behavior into its parts in order to recognize that sector for which a concept of personality is useful. Behavior includes parts which are overdetermined by biology and hence highly predictable, e.g., reflex action, imprinting, and other natively endowed behaviors. It also is composed of parts that are overdetermined culturally, e.g., language, food habits, dress, etc. While these two types of overdetermined behavior are highly consistent and characteristic, they do not differentiate among individuals in the same social-cultural and biological subgroup, and hence are not useful in predicting individual systematic behavior. There is a third class of behaviors, which may be regarded as accidental or erratic and unsystematic, which are not useful in prediction. The rest of behavior may be sampled for its usefulness as measures of personality.

It seems that personality is here to stay no matter how much objectively minded psychologists may disdain it. Our problem is to find a suitable model or structure for it, which can be examined scientifically and from which testable hypotheses can be drawn. An evaluation of the present status of the concept of personality in drug research will be gained from the section of this chapter which reviews the methods now in use in attempts to measure the influence of personality on drug response and the changes in personality brought about by drugs.

Nature of Drug Action

Pharmacology is the study of the interaction of exogenous chemical agents (drugs) with the endogenous chemical substances of a living organism. Within the general body of pharmacology, the study of chemical interactions which involve the central nervous system is designated as psychopharmacology if those chemical interactions lead to changes in behavior, or, neuropharmacology if they lead to merely local neural changes.

Since the nervous system is itself composed of chemical substances, and is characterized by ongoing chemical processes, one can readily see why a knowledge of neurochemistry is so essential for the understanding of psychopharmacology. Unfortunately, the science of neurochemistry is also in its infancy, and the knowledge that is available requires a high degree of specialization for its understanding. Consequently, many behavioral scientists are reduced to the status of watching a "black-box" from the outside to note the effects of the exogenous factors that are added to it. Hopefully, this is only a temporary state in the preparation of research workers in this field.

In considering the variety of techniques which may be useful in gauging the effect of drugs on the behaviors which reflect personality, it is necessary to bear in mind that the drugs bring about their physiological effects through alterations in the biochemical milieu of the nervous system. Since we are not concerned with peripheral or segmental aspects of the central nervous system but with its higher centers—those which presumably are concerned with personality—we must look for techniques which measure behaviors altered by alterations in brain function.

REVIEW OF THE LITERATURE

The question of whether drugs are capable of producing changes of an enduring nature in the personality is still very much an open one. A definitive answer to the question will require less ambiguous evidence than is so far available. Most of what is known in this area is derived from studies in which drugs are administered on an acute basis (single dose) and the methodology which would be appropriate for assessing changes of any depth has usually been lacking. Methods of measurement developed in the field of personality have, however, made a contribution to our understanding of the mechanisms of drug action. Before reviewing some of these general findings it will be worth while to indicate several restrictive characteristics of the research in this area.

Studies with normals are characterized by an avoidance, for the most part, of the more potent tranquilizers, despite the fact that this class of drugs has had the greatest impact in the clinical area. This restriction is based partly on practical considerations. These drugs are more potent, can have more disturbing side effects, and their general effects are not as well understood as those of the older stimulants and sedatives. This is especially troublesome to the non-clinical investigator who may be using drugs to study other phenomena and prefers to confine himself to those drugs on which a good deal of information is already available. On the other hand, chronic studies, i.e., drugs administered over extended periods of time, have usually been carried out by clinical investigators. Here it would seem that the opportunity for exploring the more profound effects on personality would be greater. Unfortunately, methods which would be appropriate for the investigation of such changes are usually not included in these studies because of the following: (1) the investigator's assumption that profound changes will not occur; (2) the lack of adequate methodology for dealing with the problem; and (3) the lack of training in experimental methodology of clinical investigators.

Results from clinical investigations of the tranquilizers and the work with the psychotomimetics, would lead one to think that basic changes are certainly possible, and that there is a great need for the application of more appropriate methods. The problem is somewhat like that encountered in the investigations of the effects of psychotherapy. The field of personality suffers, in general, from a lack of adequate methodology for studying basic change. Inventories are influenced by factors which have nothing to do with the aims of these studies, e.g., social desirability. The record of projective techniques in formal research is still not very laudable despite some of the newer promising approaches to quantification (Katz, 1960), and the relating of performance measures to personality factors is still in a very early stage of development.

These techniques have managed to contribute to our understanding of drug effects and the influence of personality factors on drug response, despite their limitations. Inventories, i.e., self-reports, rating scales, projectives, and performance tests have provided some dependable information in this field and it will be of value to review the more consistent of these findings.

Influence of Personality on Drug Action

One relatively consistent finding is that atypicality of drug response and increased reactivity to drugs are related to "personality maladjustment." This stems from the work of von Felsinger, Lasagna, and Beecher (1955, 1956) in which maladjustment as measured with the Rorschach was related to atypical or unusual patterns of response to different drugs, from Kornetsky and Humphries' (1957) finding that extent of deviance as measured by several MMPI scales was positively related to the amount of subjective effect derived from a given drug, and that the factor of "neuroticism" on the Maudsley Personality Inventory is related to the likelihood of a toxic reaction to methylpentynol (Bartholomew and Marly, 1959). With regard to the problem of predicting response to drugs from personality type, van Ree (1960) was able to demonstrate a relationship between introversion-extroversion as measured by the Maudsley Medical Questionnaire, to type of reaction to LSD, though the data analysis is somewhat sketchy in this research. Introversion was more likely to lead to a "schizophreniform" (withdrawal) reaction under LSD; extroverts tended to react to LSD with a "maniform" (manic) reaction. Klerman and DiMascio (1959) are using MMPI patterns along with several other indices to separate out two contrasting somatotypes, and have been successful to some extent in predicting differential reactions to drugs.

Individual "atypicality" of response to drugs is apparently almost as common as typicality. Von Felsinger, Lasagna, and Beecher (1955) found approximately 50 per cent of subjects on such drugs as morphine, amphetamine, and phenobarbital produced atypical responses. The relating of personality factors to individual differences in drug response would seem to be, then, a natural direction for research in this area to take. For the most part, the techniques for classifying subjects into personality types have not been highly refined and the unresolved conflict between the holistic and the trait approaches tends to inhibit this kind of research. General traits such as neuroticism, deviance, introversion-extroversion look promising as predictors, but other more specific traits have not been experimented with to any great extent. The work of the Michigan group (Kelly et al., 1958), which employed a large number of specific personality variables from the MMPI, CPI, EPPS, and Cattell's 16-PFT, was very discouraging in this respect. Despite some limited findings, careful analysis failed to relate any of the measures to drug effects.

When one is attempting to link up a single trait with drug response he has, however, to contend with the fact that his subjects, though having one personality trait in common, are also likely to differ in other traits and thus make it impossible to relate the trait in question to the drug. This, in addition to the impreciseness of our measures of traits makes this particular predictive approach highly tenuous. On the other hand, the holistic approach introduces another set of methodological problems. A personality type implies a pattern of characteristics. It becomes difficult to find subjects who match all of the required characteristics and difficult to set up objective criteria for determining whether they do. The holistic approach is usually forced to settle for less precision in the typing of people than it would like, which then makes it difficult adequately to test the predictive hypotheses. The more general traits such as introversion-extroversion and neuroticism seem to represent a compromise here and have in fact worked reasonably well as noted. The Klerman-DiMascio work and the patterning approach to the MMPI used by Heartzen and Hill (1959) and by Belleville (1956) with several types of psychopaths demonstrates, though, some real promise for the patterning approach.

Effects of Drugs on Personality

If work in the predictor area is still very much in an exploratory stage, results from research on the effects of drugs on personality are probably even less definitive. If we accept the assumptions that personality structure is highly stable and that drugs produce only temporary effects, one should not then expect drugs to produce any profound effects on personality. Most investigators in this area have learned to operate with these assumptions and consequently, attention has been focused on the measurement of those aspects of personality which also have a somewhat temporary quality. These are the aspects of "mood" or "affect." It should be noted also that the field is influenced by the pharmacological and clinical nomenclature of drugs which tend to emphasize the effect on mood as against other possible effects. The majority of psychotropic drugs are classified, for example, as sedatives, stimulants, tranquilizers, and antidepressants. Where the major interest is in the concept of mood, these drugs have become highly useful tools in its study.

Nowlis and the group at Rochester (with the study of mood as a prime concern) have contributed to the methodology in this field by constructing an inventory to assess the various mood factors (Nowlis and Nowlis, 1956). The Clyde Mood Scale (Clyde, 1961) as another instrument of this type was developed specifically for the measurement of drug effects and has been used in a wide variety of studies. These inventories, because they offer added refinement to the measurement of subjective effects, tend to supplement older symptom questionnaires in studying drugs and, in many cases, replace them. In the long run, their promise would seem to lie in their ability to provide data on differential mood patterns in reactions to various drugs, which should also help in refining the nomenclature (Lindemann and von Felsinger, 1961). At present, there are little data of this type available.

Other promising approaches to the measurement of affect under drugs come from the field of verbal behavior. Gottschalk and Gleser have developed and partially validated measures of anxiety and hostility with the verbal sampling method (Gottschalk and Hambidge, 1955) and have demonstrated its sensitivity to the effects of perphenazine in reducing the hostility of patients (Gottschalk et al., 1960). It has the advantage of avoiding some of the methodological difficulties of inventories and may provide some sort of bridge toward more objective methods in this area. Other work on verbal behavior is particularly relevant to problems in this area and will be gone into in greater detail later in the chapter.

As far as the concept of mood is concerned, we will probably always want to ask the patient how he feels after the administration of a drug, but given the difficulties with inventories, i.e., halo effects, response sets, etc., we would prefer to have other more objective indices of his affect state.

Mood as Nowlis (1956) and Kubie (1960) point out, however, is not always so temporary. We sometimes use the concept to denote a fairly stable characteristic of temperament. Kubie conceives of this more enduring mood concept as a basic emotional attitude, e.g., pessimism or optimism. Do drugs have any effect on this aspect of personality? From what has been learned through acute (single) dosage studies, the likelihood, as previously noted, is small. To determine whether changes of this type will occur under chronic administration, one would have to apply methodology from the personality area which is aimed at assessing durable change in the basic structure. This has not been done and the reasons as previously noted may, for the most part, be tied to our lack of adequate methods.

Basic emotional attitudes, perceptions of and attitudes toward self and others, and mechanisms for dealing with anxiety are some of the fundamental characteristics of the concept of personality structure, and the available methods for measuring these phenomena have not turned out to be wholly reliable or satisfactory. This, of course, only becomes a problem if we think that drugs are presently capable of promoting such changes or that new drugs will appear which will force these issues. Clinical experience with chronic administration of tranquilizers has certainly raised these questions, and the psychotomimetics have produced profound effects in people, which we must continue to admit are not fully understood. These questions as noted, for all intents and purposes, remain open.

The Testing of Theory

With regard to either of the central problems, the personality factors which influence drug response or the effects of drugs on personality, it is evident that we are presently forced to work with a great many unknowns. It may be that the technical problems of objective measurement in this field are less of an obstacle where the research is guided by an explicit and testable theory.

In this respect, Eysenck's work (1957) represents one of the few attempts to follow a program of research on drugs and personality which is aimed at systematic testing of hypotheses within an explicit theoretical framework. His theories of drug action, which are based on those of McDougall and Hull, have to do with the differential effects of stimulants and depressants on cortical excitation, and have resulted in a series of discrete hypotheses and experiments. There is broad and selective application of experimental psychological methods and the results have been very helpful in providing information on the effects of standard drugs on a wide variety of behaviors. Some of the predictions and results are summarized in Table 1.

It is worth noting that the testing of his predictions failed as often as it succeeded in giving significant support to the predictions. It is difficult to attribute this lack of consistency in confirmation to any specific aspects of Eysenck's theory, but he seems to be operating with several questionable assumptions. For example, he oversimplifies the action of d-amphetamine and sodium amytal when he designates one a "standard stimulant" and the other a "standard depressant." As demonstrated in previous work with these drugs, they are not as consistent in their effects as he proposes (see previous discussion). His tendency to work with very few subjects in most of these experiments only helps to exaggerate this problem. There is little sound information on the effects of these drugs on cortical excitation, and his assumptions in this area are again of a highly speculative nature and represent a somewhat oversimplified picture of neurophysiological processes. Nonetheless, the data add to our general knowledge about the effects of contrasting drugs on psychological functions and the systematic nature of the research program contributes to the needed theoretical stimulation in this field.

Table 1. Experimental Tests of Predictions Based on Eysenck's Theory [a]

Effects of Stimulant (d-Amphetamine)		Effects of Depressant (Amytal)	
Prediction	Result [b]	Prediction	Result
1. Long visual after-effects (rotating spiral).	+(31) −(36)	1. Short visual after-effects (rotating spiral).	−(36) +(31)
2. Slow perspective reversals.	−(35)	2. Fast perspective reversals.	−(35)
3. Lower threshold for suppression of primary visual stimulus.	+(27)	3. Higher threshold for suppression of primary visual stimulus.	+(27)
4. Decreased static ataxia.	−(29)	4. Increased static ataxia.	+(29)
5. Continuous work facilitated.	+(28)	5. Continuous work impeded.	+(28)
6. Less visual figural after-effects.	−(32)	6. Greater visual figural after-effects.	−(32)
7. Less kinaesthetic after-effects.	−(33)	7. Greater kinaesthetic after-effects.	−(33)
8. Higher auditory flutter-fusion threshold.	−(34)	8. Lower auditory flutter-fusion threshold.	−(34)
9. Fast pupil contractions.*	+(30)	9. Slow pupil contractions.*	+(30)

[a] Eysenck has, upon our request, made the following comments concerning this table and the evaluation of his work presented here. We were unable to implement these suggestions, due to time considerations, but include them so that the interested reader may be made aware of Eysenck's views and pursue the problem further on his own, if he wishes.

"Table 1 deals only with experiments I have done myself, and is incomplete even as regards these; for a tally of successful and unsuccessful predictions I think it would be necessary to include the many studies made by other people in my department and elsewhere as well. Upon quick inspection of a random 100 articles from my list, I found that the number of successful predictions is well above the 80 per cent level. It is natural that the proportion in my own experiments would be smaller because in the natural way of things I would give the more obvious and certain researches to students and do the more unlikely and novel ones myself.

"Failure in confirmation of a prediction is often an indication, not of any fault in the theory, but rather of a defect in the connecting link between general experimental psychology and my prediction. I have discussed in *Experiments in Personality*, H. J. Eysenck, London: Routledge & Kegan Paul, 1960, one such case in detail, i.e., that of the bowing of the serial learning curve. The argument used there applies to other apparent failures as well.

"I don't think it is true to say that I over-simplify the action of certain drugs; at least I have made a systematic attempt to provide a methodology for testing the assumption I make (in *Experiments in Personality*). We have found the drugs to have consistent effects in experiments relevant to my hypothesis, clearly related to the excitation-inhibition balance. Inconsistencies outside that framework are not relevant to my hypothesis.

"I agree with what is said about our lack of knowledge regarding the effects of drugs on cortical excitation, but I am making no assumptions on the physiological level; the processes I am talking about are explicitly defined in behavioural terms."

[b] + Confirmation of prediction.
    − No significant confirmation.
    * No predictions made from theory, simply a finding.
    Numbers indicate references.

Summary

On the basis of previous findings then, the question of the durability of the effects of drugs on personality still appears to be an open one. Drugs administered acutely, as far as we can tell, produce only short term changes. There is a need for more chronic dosage studies and a need for the inclusion in such studies of methods which are appropriate to measuring the long term effects on personality. Personality measures so far have been more helpful on the predictive side than they have in the assessment of drug effects. This applies particularly to research in which general rather than specific traits have been related to drug response. More refined techniques are now available for measuring the effects on subjective mood, and objective measures of affect are becoming available. These techniques will assist in the specification of mood patterns for various classes of drugs and contribute to improvements in the precision of nomenclature in this area. The available data, then, do not provide definitive answers concerning personality change, but from this brief review of findings and methodological problems, it would seem that research which is guided by explicit theory can contribute a more systematic base for the gathering of this information.

A MODEL FOR STUDYING DRUG EFFECTS ON PERSONALITY

The Variables

The study of personality, concerned as it is with such phenomena as motivations, feeling, organizing principles of experience and behavior, suffers greatly from a lack of adequate criteria with which to measure its characteristics. The history of personality measurement has involved a continuing search for those external behaviors which are most relevant to the understanding of the intervening internal phenomena. In seeking appropriate techniques of investigation in this field, the following elements require attention: (1) the behavior to be measured; (2) the environmental situation in which the behavior takes place; (3) the individual under observation, and (4) the chemical agent.

In a previous study (Burdock, Sutton, and Zubin, 1958) a classification of the types of measurable behavior that can be observed under controlled conditions and which presumably reflect brain function as discussed earlier has been provided. By utilizing the classical categories of physiological, sensory, perceptual, psychomotor, and conceptual responses as the basic types of responses of which human beings are capable, it is shown that each of these types of responses can be found under each of the classes of stimulation, ranging from the idling state, in which no stimulus is applied, through energy stimuli and signal stimuli as shown in Table 2. (For the definitions of these terms see Burdock, Sutton, and Zubin, 1958).

The idling state is merely the initial state of activation present when the stimulus is applied—and can vary the entire gamut from drowsiness to extreme alertness. Energy stimuli refer to those stimuli whose physical energy is in some way related to the intensity of the response, while in signal stimuli no such relationship exists, the stimulus merely serving to trigger the response.

This table, however, deals only with two aspects of experimentation—the stimulus and the response. In order to deal with the total spectrum of possibilities, not only the stimulus but all the parameters of the various facets which determine a response would have to be included. The variety of facets on which a response may depend are shown in the following equation based on Graham (1951): $R = f (S, Rc, I, O, H, . . . , Xi)$, where R represents the response as a function of S, the stimulus characteristics; Rc, the receptor organ(s) on which the stimulus impinges; I, the possible instructions for carrying out the task to be performed; O, the possible states of the organism at the time the stimulus is applied; H, the varieties of histories which may characterize the organism with reference to the task under consideration; and Xi, possible facets which have, so far, gone unrecognized but which are needed to explain the residual but systematic variation.

Each of the facets consists of many possible parameters—e.g., the stimulus facet consists of intensity, spatial extent, temporal duration, wavelength of energy, etc. Each experiment represents a selection from the Cartesian product of the multiplicity of possible parameters in each facet (Zubin, 1957a). If these parameters are sufficient to predict the response in a sample of individuals, we can end the equation with H. However, if a systematic residual variance appears which is not attributable to variations in the parameters of the facets, it may be necessary to introduce an additional facet of parameters, the X's, to take up the slack.

It may eventually be discovered that these X parameters correspond to personality traits such as impulsiveness, anxiety proneness, etc. If we eventually find endogenous factors such as components of body fluids, or exogenous factors such as past traumas which are the underpinnings of such personality traits, we would attribute them to the state of the organism (O) or to history (H), where they would rightfully belong.

It should be noted that only the first three facets—S, the stimulus properties; Rc, the receptor organ; and I, the instructional variables—are subject to direct manipulation by the experimenter. The state of the organism, O, is

Table 2.   *Examples of Measures Used at Each Behavior Level for Each Class of Stimulus Under the Load of Drugs*

Level of Observed Behavior	Idling State	Energy Variables		Signal Variables		
		Appropriate	Inappropriate	Configuration	Sign	Symbol
Conceptual	Hallucinations—Rinkel, De-Shon, Hyde, & Solomon, 1952 Ostfeld, Visotsky, & Lebovits, 1958 Isbelle, 1959	*Fantasy to uniformly diffused light**		Estimation of quantities—Brengelmann, 1958 Time estimation—Aronson, Silverstein, & Klee, 1959	*Stroop Test II*	Personality inventories—Kelly, Miller, Marquis, Gerard, & Uhr, 1958 Claridge & Herrington, 1960 Kornetsky & Humphries, 1957 Word association tests—Oh & Evans, 1960 Symptom questionnaires—Trimble, 1959 Smith & Becher, 1960 Joyce, 1959 Conditioning of affect statements—Salzinger, Pisoni, Feldman & Bacon, 1961
Psychomotor	Static ataxia test—Barendregt, 1960 Eysenck & Easterbrook, 1960a Preferred tapping rate—Kelly, Miller, Marquis, Gerard, & Uhr, 1958	*Reaction time*	*Limb movements to electroshock*	Figure reconstruction test—Brengelmann, Parc, & Sandler, 1958 Pursuit rotor—Eysenck, Casey, & Trouton, 1957 Kornetsky, Humphries, & Evarts, 1957	Driving skills on autotrainer—Kelly, Miller, Marquis, Gerard, & Uhr, 1958 Marquis, Kelly, Miller, Gerard, & Rapoport, 1957 Eyeblink conditioning—Bartholomew, Franks, & Marley, 1958 Franks & Trouton, 1958 Manual RT—Hill, Belleville, & Wikler, 1957	Speed of copying numbers—Kornetsky, Humphries, & Evarts, 1957

Perceptual	*Spatial orientation*—Temporal orientation—Ostfeld, Visotsky, & Lebovits, 1958; Benda & Orsini, 1959; Wapner & Krus, 1959	*Orientation to direction of white noise*	*Phosphenes to pressure on eye*	Necker cube reversals—Eysenck, Holland, & Trouton, 1957a; Archimedes spiral—Eysenck, Holland, & Trouton, 1957b; CFF—Holland, 1960; Shagass & Lipowski, 1958; Cranston, Zubin, & Landis, 1952; Matching block widths by palpation—Eysenck & Easterbrook, 1960e	Visual acuity—Marquis, Kelly, Miller, Gerard, & Rapoport, 1957; Tachistoscopic discrimination of circle size—Kornetsky, Humphries, & Evarts, 1957	*Pitch discrimination*
Sensory	*Cortical grey*	Tactual threshold—Kornetsky, Humphries, & Evarts, 1957; Threshold for colored lights—Eysenck & Aiba, 1957	*Temperature sensation to electrical stimulation of thermal receptors*		
Physiological	Temperature—Masserman, 1959; EEG—Nymgaard, 1959; Boudreau, 1958; Shagass & Jones, 1958; PGR—Kelly, Miller, Marquis, Gerard, & Uhr, 1958; Blood tests—Johnson, Fordyce, Masuda, & Darpat, 1960	Pupilography—Eysenck & Easterbrook, 1960b	*Heart rate during pressure on carotid sinus*	*EEG during photic driving*	*Conditioning of salivary response to a bell*	*GR after instructions to prevaricate*

Measures in italics are examples for categories where no appropriate measures were found in the literature reviewed.

only partly under the control of the experimenter. Such factors as age, sex, and psychopathology cannot be manipulated, but subjects can be selected according to these parameters. The same holds true of H, the previous history of the organism with reference to the task at hand.

One of the valuable assets of the facet equation stems from the fact that we can titrate changes brought about through the drugs by means of alterations in values of some of the parameters in the three manipulatable facets— S, Rc, and I. Suppose a drug raises the threshold for perception of light; the increase in the intensity of light necessary to attain threshold value is in a sense a measure of the effect of the drug in terms of illumination units. Thus, the effect of the drug can be titrated by increases in intensity, or temporal duration, or area of stimulation, etc. This titration may lead to an understanding of how and where the drug brings about its effects. By triangulating the drug effect against changes in intensity across modalities, or with temporal duration or spatial extent, deeper understanding of the biochemical nature of the drug and how and where it interacts with the neurochemistry of the organism may eventuate. When the response of the organism to various stimuli is examined while the organism is under the influence of a drug, some consideration of the new idling state produced by the drug must be undertaken. To distinguish such states from the unrestricted free idling state, the drug can be designated as a load and the new idling state under the influence of the drug can be referred to as being under a load. Thus, a load is a constraint imposed on the organism prior to measurement of the behavior being investigated.

If the drug is considered to be a stimulus and is the only stimulus used, no special problem is encountered, since a measure of a particular ongoing activity, such as blood pressure in the idling state, can be readily obtained and the change produced by the drug noted. A direct approach to the discovery of changes in behavior attributable to drug effects utilizes the idling state itself as the vehicle for detecting the change, and no new stimuli except the drug need to be introduced.

The introduction of a chemical agent may alter the idling state and also bring about changes in ongoing behavior. If these behaviors are to be measured, in the spirit of this direct approach, they must be of a variety that does not need a controlled external stimulus for elicitation. Physiological activities fall into this category as do highly practiced behaviors such as conversation, writing, reading, walking, and swimming.

Physiological measures like blood pressure, heart rate, and similar vegetative functions have long been used as measures of drug effect, because severe changes in these functions are a threat to survival, and also because they yield good quantitative indices. In searching for conceptual changes induced by drugs, speech or verbal behavior can serve a similar purpose in tapping the conceptual level as do blood pressure and heart rate in tapping the physiological level. For this reason, studies of verbal behavior before, during, and after drug administration can yield meaningful data.

A Measure of the Conceptual Response

The utilization of verbal behavior as a measure of drug effects already has an extensive literature, although most of it deals with uncontrolled clinical observation. The parameters of verbal behavior which have been measured under drug effects are (1) fluency, (2) intelligibility, (3) grammatical structure, and (4) conditionability.

These, however, do not exhaust the possible parameters that could be employed. Frieda Goldman-Eisler (1956) has proposed additional variables concerning relative rates of speech and respiration, and the predictability of words in a given context. She has related changes in speech rate, breathing, and muscle tension to interview content. Certain relationships seem to have been found between the objective measures and stages of "catharsis or abreaction through talking." These relationships might be studied with respect to certain personality factors as well as with respect to the course of the psychotherapeutic process.

The parameters described above can be utilized in the evaluation of drug effects. An example of the application of some of these methods to the investigation of chlorpromazine is afforded by the work of Salzinger and his coworkers (Salzinger, Pisoni, Feldman, and Bacon, 1961), in the Biometrics Research Laboratory.

It was possible to demonstrate a lawful reduction in rate of speech with increase in dosage in 25 mg steps in one normal subject. A comparison of the control conditions and the largest dosage condition (125 mg) in three other normal individuals corroborated this finding. On the other hand, a schizophrenic subject who had been reinforced for self-referred affect statements rather than speech in general (as had the normals mentioned above) did not show a decrease in speech rate but rather in affect statements. This suggested the hypothesis that chlorpromazine influences behavior only through its effect on the reinforcement which controls the behavior. A further effect of the drugs consisted of interference with the extent to which context controls the emission of words. Thus, the "intelligibility" of speech under the influence of chlorpromazine was lowered as measured by the Cloze Technique.[1]

As far as the general conclusions of the study are concerned, it is reasonable

[1] The Cloze Technique was introduced by Taylor (1953).

to say that it demonstrates that greater stimulus control over behavior produces more lawful results in response to drugs.

The extent of control over the behavior is revealed by the fact that the normal subject who was reinforced for speech received the maximum number of reinforcements over all dosages despite changes in speech rate. There were relatively few degrees of freedom left for him to vary in and, therefore, little chance that variables, other than those applied systematically, would have any effect.

Further evidence for the point that more stimulus control allows the drug effect to reveal itself more lawfully has been found in weight judgment experiments. The time required for judging heaviness of weights varied more lawfully under conditions where a heavy weight had been introduced before each standard weight than when this anchor was not introduced.

A Measure of the Physiological Response

In the previous examples we dealt with the effect of chlorpromazine on an ongoing conceptual function—speech. Here the effect of increasing dosage is to interfere with the ongoing conceptual activity and presumably, if the dosage became large enough, greater and greater conceptual distortion would occur until finally the physiological component would overwhelm the individual and put him to sleep. Let us now examine the influence of the drug on an ongoing physiological function—pupil dilation and contraction. Ordinarily, the pupil diameter waxes and wanes to changes in light intensity (a sensory-physiological response), but it also responds to conceptual stimulation accompanying fear, anxiety, etc. To the latter it dilates, but only light can cause it to contract. The contraction has been related to parasympathetic innervation while the dilation has been related to sympathetic activity. When a low dosage (50 mgs) of chlorpromazine is injected in a normal individual, as Hakerem and Sutton (1962) have done in the Biometrics Research Laboratory, the diameter of the dark adapted pupil remains unchanged as compared to the predrug state. However, repeated stimulation with brief light stimuli (1 millisecond in duration) prevents the pupil from recovering to its initial size during the interpulse periods of darkness. The undrugged pupil, on the other hand, can readily accomplish this recovery during the several seconds of the interpulse period. Otherwise, the pupillary response to the light pulse shows no differential between the drug and control states. Thus, even the small 50 mgs dosage of chlorpromazine, which requires fine biochemical tests for its detection, shows its effect on an ongoing physiological response.

A single, relatively high dosage of chlorpromazine used in the normal individual (125 mgs) causes profound sleepiness, slight ptosis, and other reportable side effects. From the point of view of pupillary measurement, the diameter of the pupil after thirty minutes in darkness is more contracted, or smaller, than in the predrug or idling state. However, the response to light stimulation seems to be the same as for the lower dosage. This would be consistent with a reduced sympathetic tonus which would tend to reduce the dilation of the pupil. Incidentally, the findings for *acute* schizophrenics, not under drugs, was that they are characterized by a smaller dark adapted pupil diameter than normals. In other words, schizophrenics seem to show a reduced sympathetic tonus.

The Integration of Response Levels

The Mendelejeff-like table giving the relationship between responses and their stimuli represents the results of a theoretical analysis of experimentally elicited human behavior. In actual experience these heuristic elements do not occur in isolation any more than the chemical elements occur in the pure state in nature, although certain underlying dimensions tend to separate the five levels.

Before considering the interdependence of the response levels in a total behavioral event, it may be well to clarify some basic assumptions regarding the two extreme ends of the spectrum—physiological and conceptual responses. The physiological response is elicited by any stimulus which excites the central peripheral or autonomic nervous system. Physiological responsiveness underlies all levels of responses, but there is no reason to assume an identity between the physiological aspects and the total response. By conceptual responses, we mean responses based on previous experience—on the stored memories of the organism. This conceptual response must, to be sure, have neurophysiological concomitants, but its primary essence is its dependence upon prior experience. As one goes from physiological to sensory, perceptual, psychomotor, and conceptual responses, the importance of prior experience and reinforcement increases. Regardless of whether the stimulus is an external object or event, or an internal spontaneously occurring event, the conceptual response is highly dependent upon memory storage which, in turn, may depend on intricate neural or protein organization.

To understand the interdependence of response levels first let us consider the threshold response. Determination of absolute thresholds is usually regarded as belonging to the category of sensory response. The determination of the presence or absence of light or sound stimulation is a psychophysical process which has a long history and in practiced hands is said to yield results which reflect the sensitivity of the organism to such a high degree that variations in threshold determination have been attributed to fluctuations in the stimulus, rather than fluctuations in the response (Hecht, 1934). More recently, however, Swets (1961) has pointed out that the absolute nature of the threshold is very much in doubt, and the very existence of thresholds has been questioned.

The redesigning of the classical threshold experiment to include "catch" trials during which the experimenter actually does not present a stimulus, provides a new perspective on threshold determination. Apparently, the number of times a subject gives an inappropriate response (i.e., reports presence of stimulus when there is none, and vice versa) depends on the proportion of trials during which the stimulus really *is* or *is not* presented. For example, if the stimulus is presented in 90 per cent of the trials, the expectancy created by the induced set is such that during the catch trials (when the stimulus is *not* presented) the subject will report it as present (false alarm) 62 per cent of the time; but, when it is *present,* he will report it absent (misses) only 3 per cent of the time. On the other hand, in a series of trials in which the stimulus is presented in only 10 per cent of the trials, the comparable figures are 4 per cent false alarms and 72 per cent misses. The introduction of rewards for correct responses (saying yes when the stimulus is on and no when the stimulus is off) and of punishments for incorrect responses is another method for manipulating the results (Galanter, 1962).

Apparently the expectancies experienced by the subject and his system of values regarding monetary or other rewards and punishments, loom large in determining sensory responses. These are definitely conceptual components (based on memory storage), and hence sensory responses can no longer be regarded as independent of the other systems of response.

Now let us examine one situation where the conceptual and physiological responses have to coexist in order to bring about a given pattern of behavior, and where it seems possible to prevent this pattern from occurring if one or the other component meets interference. The reaction of a subject to a frightening object involves the entire spectrum of responses from the conceptual to the physiological. Thus, following the usual analysis (Arnold, 1960) the sighting (sensation and/or perception) of a fear-inducing object leads to an immediate appraisal of its dangerous character (conceptual—based upon prior experience) and is accompanied by visceral (physiological) excitation and leads to flight (psychomotor). The initiating sensory or perceptual response and the final psychomotor response [2] seem to have been taken for granted by

---

[2] Some disagreement regarding the psychomotor aspects of emotional behavior is raised by Bull (1945, p. 51) in which the perception of an emotion producing stimulus gives rise immediately (through some organismic linkage such as neural predisposition) to a motor attitude which then leads to the emotional state and to action (see Arnold, 1960, Vol. I, p. 150). This has not been verified experimentally.

most theoreticians, but the relative importance and temporal sequence of the conceptual and physiological components have given rise to one of the classic controversies in psychology (James and Lange, 1922; Cannon, 1927, 1929, and 1931; Duffy, 1934, 1948; Arnold, 1960). Attempts have been made to demonstrate the relative importance of these two components experimentally. Experiments by Maranon (1924) confirmed later by Cantril and Hunt (1932) and Landis and Hunt (1932) demonstrated that the physiological response induced by an injection of adrenalin does not by itself yield a genuine experience of fear in which all the components are activated. Though the sympathetic discharge (physiological) common to strong emotional states was present (palpitation, tremor, face flushing, etc.) a full-blown emotional state did not develop (no psychomotor response), because conceptually there was no basis for it. The subjects knew the source of their physiological reactivity and did not have to "fear" it (conceptual) or run away (psychomotor).

A subject, however, can sometimes experience a genuine emotion after the injection of adrenalin if he spontaneously generates a conceptual response suitable to the occasion. Thus, one of the subjects reported "I seemed oppressed with a vague fear of something—feeling much the same as when I'd lain awake all night, frightened that Bill might die" (Cantril and Hunt, 1932, p. 303). In her case, a genuine full-blown fear seemed to have taken place.

An example of how the elimination or reduction in the physiological component will interfere with an expected response is the experiment of Schachter and Wheeler (1962). They induced the conceptual component (evoking of stored memories) by a comic film which elicited laughter and euphoria in most people. They blocked the physiological response in one group by administering 25 mgs of chlorpromazine and contrasted the behavior of this group with another which had been given ½ cc of epinephrine solution (1:1000 solution of Suprarenin) and with a third group given a placebo.

The group which received adrenalin showed the highest degree of overt amusement or euphoria, the placebo group was second, and the chlorpromazine group showed the least amount of euphoria. Apparently, the sympathetic pattern elicited by adrenalin seems to be able to enhance the expressions of emotional states while the blocking agent (chlorpromazine) reduces it considerably. Thus, emotional expression can be brought under the control of chemical agents.

The contrast between the physiological and conceptual component has occurred in several other experiments, though the experimenters were not always aware that their work was focused on this problem. It has been known for a long time that such techniques as psychosurgery reduce the conceptual aspects of pain (anticipation, fear, anxiety), while the sensory threshold for pain remains unchanged (Mettler, 1949). More recently, Beecher has concluded (1960) that both placebo and active drug treatments are more effective in bringing about relief when conceptual components (stress and anxiety) are present, and are not as effective in relieving the simple sensory pain responses. Similarly, Wikler and his colleagues have shown (Hill, Kornetsky, Flanary, and Wikler, 1952) that morphine is more effective in reducing the tendency to overestimate pain induced by electric shock when considerable anticipation (through induction of anxiety or fear) of the pain is promoted by the experimenter. When no anticipation of pain is introduced, morphine does not interfere with the accurate subjective estimate of pain as gauged objectively by the intensity of an electrical current. Here again, the conceptual component is the one which morphine seems to influence most, leaving the sensory aspects untouched.

The role of the conceptual or cognitive component is further stressed by Beecher and his coworkers (1959). He found that 10 mgs of morphine increased subjective responses of friendliness in one test environment (in which the needs of the subjects were supported) and decreased it in another environment in which their needs were frustrated.

We can subsume the facts of social facilitation in drug studies under the conceptual component, since a subject's awareness of his colleagues and their mood is probably based more on conceptual than on physiological factors (Hyde, 1958; Schacter and Singer, 1962a). Whether the presence of others alters directly the biochemical balance within the organism and thus brings about a different interaction between the chemical agent and the endogenous chemicals within the organism, or whether the presence of others serves indirectly to distract the individual from paying as much attention to his inner-goings-on, or to orient the expression of his feelings regardless of his physiological responses, remains a question for further examination.

Some animal experiments also throw light on the relative importance of the conceptual and physiological components. An example of the importance of the conceptual or stored memory component is afforded by Harlow's (1962) experiments with the mothering behavior of monkeys who are themselves raised on surrogate mothers. Though these mothers experienced the entire physiological cycle of gestation, they do not have the conceptual or stored memories of their own mother's behavior nor of play experience with their siblings. Without this conceptual component, they fail to care for their offspring. On the other hand in Birch's (1956) rats, the mothers who possess the conceptual component fail to mother their offspring if the chain in the physiological component is broken by interfering with the self-licking sequence mechanically. This was accomplished by placing a collar about their necks to prevent them from licking the fluids emanating from their vaginal areas during the gestation period. In their next pregnancy, when no such interference occurred with the physiological cycle, normal mothering behavior ensued.

Following the same pattern of analysis, Seymour Fisher (1962) has manipulated the conceptual component directly by varying the instructional variable or set in drug studies. He has shown that dextroamphetamine, compared with placebo, has its greatest effect in elevating mood and facilitating psychomotor performance when subjects expect to be aroused by the drug. When the same drug is given to subjects who think they are being given a depressant, there are no differences in effect between drug and placebo. Here again arousal of the conceptual component acts to make certain the appearance of the mood or the emotional state, and the arousal of a contrary conceptual component tends to reduce it.

Perhaps the waning of sexual arousal with age can be placed in this framework. While the conceptual component provided by visual, auditory, tactual, and olfactory stimulation may still operate, the absence of physiological reinforcement through depletion of endocrine supplies may eventually extinguish even the conceptual arousal. One wonders whether the rise in threshold for anxiety and other psychopathological feelings in psychosis after ECT, lobotomy, and some drugs may not reflect the same type of process—i.e., reduction in the involvement of the sympathetic nervous system, with subsequent extinction of the conceptual component of anxiety, depression, etc. If we assume that the emotion of anxiety permeates the conceptual behavior of the patient, and that this conceptual anxiety produces reverberations in the physiological responses of the patient and sets up a vicious circle of mutual reinforcement between the conceptual and physiological component, it becomes possible to understand how interference with the physiological component may bring about a reduction in anxiety. If the conceptual response of anxiety continues, but the physiological component is reduced by therapy, the conceptual anxiety will eventually be extinguished for lack of physiological reinforcement. This, then, represents a direct attack on the physiological component in order to eliminate the conceptual component.

An example of a direct interference with the physiological component preventing a full-fledged emotion from arising may be inferred from the work of Steinberg et al. They

. . . found that an amphetamine/barbiturate mixture markedly increased the exploratory behaviour in a Y-maze of rats which had not been in the maze before, but that the drug mixture had no such effect on rats which had had repeated previous experience of the Y-maze. It is possible that these differential effects could largely be accounted for in terms of fear reduction by means of the drug mixture: "inexperienced" rats were afraid of the new environment and, therefore, responsive to fear-reducing medication; "experienced" rats had presumably already overcome their fear of the environment, and so the drug mixture had no effect. Amphetamine/barbiturate mixtures are often used in psychiatry in the treatment of anxiety states.[3]

From the point of view of the paradigm that we have presented for the interaction between the conceptual and physiological components, we may regard the failure of the "inexperienced" rats to show fear as the effect of an interference with the sympathetic arousal. The drug mixture prevented this arousal, and hence only the conceptual component (perception of the environment as strange and "potentially dangerous") was operative. Since the conceptual component alone is insufficient to evoke a full-fledged emotion of fear, the competing drive of curiosity took over, leading to the uninhibited exploratory behavior which is normally expected in a rat in a non-fearful new environment.

If we utilize the same paradigm it becomes possible to explain the extinction of the conditioned emotional response in rats (Howard Hunt et al., 1952, 1956), by postulating that chlorpromazine prevents the sympathetic arousal when the conditioned tone is heard. The conceptual experience which the tone induces is insufficient to arouse a full-fledged experience of fear, and therefore the rat blithely keeps on pressing the bar as if it heard nothing. Similarly, the patient under chlorpromazine can experience episodes which ordinarily would arouse his anxiety but which fail to do so because the chlorpromazine prevents sympathetic arousal. It would, of course, be extremely enlightening if it could be demonstrated experimentally that chlorpromazine actually interferes with sympathetic arousal by direct recording of electric potentials.

By the same token, one may view psychotherapy as a direct attack on the conceptual component in emotional disorder. Once the conceptual component is reduced, it will in turn gradually bring about the extinction of the sympathetic component because of the reduction in the interaction between the two. Behavior therapy perhaps is explicable on this basis. For example, the reduction of tics may be accomplished by separating the psychomotor response from its conceptual (anxiety) substrate. By repeatedly practicing the tic without the anxiety accompaniment, the link between the two can be eventually extinguished (Dunlap, 1932). Similarly, hysterical blindness can be eliminated by conditioning to light and thus breaking the link between the sensory-perceptual component and the conceptual fear or anxiety (Brady and Lind, 1961).

To summarize, both the conceptual component of a given pattern of behavior or emotion as well as the physiological are necessary for the existence

---

[3] Personal communication.

of the pattern. Thus, our analysis of behavior into the five components of physiological, sensory, perceptual, psychomotor, and conceptual responses seems useful, since it permits experimentation with each of these components so that the nature of the total response can be better understood.

Earlier in this chapter, it was indicated that four basic elements must be considered in a discussion of research in the field of drugs and personality. The first two, the behavior to be measured and the environmental situation in which the behavior takes place, have received the most attention so far. The last two, the individual under observation and the chemical agent, must now be considered more fully.

The Individual Under Observation

The individual under observation is sometimes naïvely regarded as representative of all other individuals who might be selected at random. This is a tenuous assumption. First, the subject usually is a person who has volunteered for the experiment, and there is considerable evidence that volunteers may not represent the general population (Esecover, Malitz, and Wilkens, 1961; Pollin and Perlin, 1958). Secondly, there is a tremendous difference among individuals in response to drugs.

One important source of variation in response to drugs is the subject's own body chemistry. While drugs may bring about certain expected changes in most people, it should be remembered that the enzyme systems of individual subjects are quite distinct and may respond quite deviantly to certain ingested chemicals. For example, while most individuals will respond within given limits of tolerance to insulin, a diabetic may not show the same response. In this chapter, we are not considering deviant body chemistry. But even normal body chemistry shows considerable variation, as Roger Williams has shown (1960). Just how these deviations affect behavior still remains to be determined.

In considering the individual under observation, one might liken the relationship between personality and drugs to the relationship that exists between personality and disease. It has been pointed out elsewhere (Zubin, 1958) that the most tenable hypothesis today regarding mental disorder and personality is the hypothesis of independence, i.e., that there is no relationship between premorbid personality and the occurrence of psychopathology. Once the disease occurs, however, the personality of the patient may determine the direction the disease will take. Similarly, the effect of the drug may correlate with the kind of personality the subject possesses.

Because of the difficulties presented by present day typological approaches, it might be useful to eliminate them entirely and substitute more empirically determined subgroupings utilizing some new statistical developments along the lines indicated by Mahalonobis' distance function (Rao, 1952). Since the Mahalonobis distance function is applicable only when the subgroups or types that exist in the population are already known, we cannot make use of this method. Instead, the test profiles of each possible pair of individuals in a given group can be compared and the standardized distances between these profiles computed over each of the tests in the profile. These distances may then be decomposed into discrepancies in shape and in level. On the basis of these two kinds of discrepancies, the whole population can be fractionated into homogeneous subgroups or types (Zubin, Fleiss, and Burdock, 1962).

The Chemical Agent

The drug itself presents a series of problems with regard to measuring its effects on behavior. One of the stumbling blocks to research in this area is the lack of a universally accepted general system of drug classification. Tentative classifications have been based on either the chemical structure of the drug, the site of the drug action (acting on heart, thyroid, etc.), or its mode of action (antidepressant, sedative, etc.).

Isolated knowledge of the chemical structure of a drug has been of little relevance for the psychopharmacologist, at least, until now. He has been more concerned with the site and mode of action, but, especially the latter. Unfortunately, research on the mode of action has, so far, revealed considerable variability among subjects, and such classifications are decidedly tentative and occasionally misleading.

One of the most serious drug problems is that of dosage. What may be a "load" for one person may be no load at all for another. The characteristic differences between individuals with regard to minimally effective dosage and maximally effective dosage may be likened to the effects of a snowfall on the landscape. If the snow is heavy enough (maximum dosage) it will cover the whole landscape uniformly and hide any individual differences in its parts. If the snow is not sufficiently heavy, though it falls on all parts alike, the forms it assumes are, to paraphrase Thoreau, "as various as those of the twigs and the leaves which receive it." In submaximal dosages, the personality of the subject may be a more important predictor of the behavioral change than the drug itself (Kornetsky and Humphries, 1957).

Perhaps the effects observed in the middle range of dosage, between little or no drug and maximum dosage, is the resultant of the two contending forces which we have described earlier—the conceptual and physiological. In the lower dosages, the conceptual factor, induced either by the instructional variable, or by spontaneously generated expectancy, may be the prepotent factor. As the dosage increases, the physiological and sensory responses begin to play more and more important roles. Finally, when the maximum dosage takes effect, the role of physiological and sensory responses are fully in command. Perhaps, we will some day find that the point of inflection in the dosage curve indicates some sort of balance between the two factors contending for control of behavior, the conceptual and the physiological components. This conceptual component especially when triggered systematically from within, may be the personality characteristic with which this chapter is concerned. For low dosages, personality is in command regardless of the nature of the drug. For the maximum dosage, the physiological component takes over regardless of personality.

Dosage curves have to be developed for each individual to determine the range of change in behavior characterizing a given individual. These dosage curves may differ from person to person in level of dose necessary to bring about a given change in performance and in the shape of the dosage curve. It is necessary to find a way of grouping people into homogeneous groups with regard to these dosage curves and the distance method suggested previously may prove suitable (Zubin, Fleiss, and Burdock, 1962).

At the present time, because of the lack of knowledge about drugs and because of the lack of knowledge about personality, drug investigations are limited to a specific type of behavior investigated with regard to a specific type of drug, without the scope necessary to transcend individual function and individual drugs. As our knowledge increases, greater scope can be given to these investigations. Apparently dosage curves are superior to single measurements with single dosages.

But dosage is only one of the factors to be taken into consideration in producing a given effect. Leake (1961), suggests the following formula:

$$I = f\left(D\frac{r_A}{r_E}, P, S\right)$$

Where I = intensity of the action of a chemical on biological material

D = dosage expressed in terms of mass of chemical per mass of living material

r_A = rate of absorption and distribution of the chemical through the living matter

r_E = rate of detoxification or excretion of the chemical from the living matter

P = physical chemical properties of the chemical which really determines the activity of the chemical on living material

S = the specific and peculiar characteristics of the living material concerned, including its organizational status (in terms of macromolecules or ecological milieus), its age, its metabolic state, its "allergic" sensitivity, its pathological status, and such integrating factors as enzyme systems and sex.

All of these factors are capable of precise scientific study and the expression $D(r_A/r_E)$, the product of the dosage by the ratio of the rate of absorption and distribution to the rate of detoxification and excretion, gives the concentration of the drug in the living tissues at any time after administration. It is this concentration, with its mass action effect, according to Leake, which is a predominant factor in drug action.

NEW DIRECTIONS AND PROSPECTS IN PSYCHOPHARMACOLOGY

In contrast with the rather continuous progress made in pharmacology under the impetus of the sudden appearance of the tranquilizers and energizers, the progress in psychopathology has been rather meager. The psychopathologist has apparently been caught off guard. While pharmacology and psychopharmacology have made great practical strides forward, the strides in personality measurement, for example, are notably absent.

Why has there been so little progress in the development of the relationship between pharmacology and personality? Pharmacology is undergoing a revolution according to Wooley (1958). Until recently progress in the discovery of new drugs depended on chance only. While this is still true, certain principles have been developing as guide lines for the synthesizing of new compounds that are predicted to have certain properties. One of these principles is the antimetabolite principle which may be briefly stated as follows. There are a certain number of chemical substances which are vitally essential to metabolism. If any of these vital compounds is missing or in short supply, normal processes fail to occur. Sometimes an excess of the vital substance also interferes with normal processes. It has been found that if the chemical structure of one of these metabolites is changed in any one of several defined ways, the molecule which results is not able to substitute for the metabolite in living processes. Instead this new substance has the capacity to evoke in the organism the specific signs of deficiency of the metabolite which it resembles. It is as if it serves as an inadequate key in the lock of the metabolic process. It gets stuck in the lock and prevents the genuine metabolite from entering and opening the door to the progress of the metabolic process. Such antagonists, or antimetabolites, as they are called, can be used to control an excessive amount of the metabolite, e.g., antithyroxine for the control of excess thyroxine.

Another principle is that of biochemical individuality proposed by Roger Williams at the University of Texas (1960). In brief, this principle states that an examination of the biochemistry of each individual would reveal reliable and consistent differences between individuals which could be found useful in the classification of people into relatively homogeneous subgroups. Another emerging principle is that of regional organization of the neurochemistry of the nervous system. In contrast with the earlier studies of brain function in which the brain tissues were macerated and chemical tests applied to the resulting mass, the newer approach rests on the hypothesis that the brain is compartmentalized, and that the particular site of a chemical reaction in the brain is equal in importance to substrate and enzyme activity in determining outcome.

While these new principles seem to keep the field of pharmacology stirring, the field of personality measurement has reached a static plateau cushioned by factor analysis on the one hand and by psychodynamics on the other. In contrast with the revolution in pharmacology, personality is in the doldrums. Results from research on the effects of drugs on personality are, therefore, not very definitive.

It seems that we may have gone as far as we can go with the present methods of investigating personality through psychometric methods (inventories and rating scales) and perhaps also through psychophysical and other experimental methods. Perhaps our stimuli penetrate the web of personality only superficially and not with sufficient reliability. The individuality of the person is lost in a maelstrom of insufficiently reliable indicators produced by tickling his epidermis. New methods are required. It might be possible to replace, at least temporarily, psychophysics, on the basis of which much of our testing is done, and clinical methods, through which most of our classification is done, by psychochemistry. If we could begin to cluster people into subgroups in accordance with the changes that occur in their ongoing behavior under various dosages of specific chemical substances, we might strike at a deeper layer of personality. These new subgroups, obtained through the clustering on the basis of similarities in shape and level of dosage curves for a variety of selected chemical agents, on a variety of ongoing naturally occurring activities like conversing, writing, walking, or engaging in other highly practiced activities, might serve as new starting points for the investigation of like-structured homogeneous subgroups.

With the similarity of response to drugs in these basic activities established, we could begin looking for other variables which a given like-minded group of individuals may possess in common and thus provide a new typology to replace the present unsatisfactory personality variables by means of which we attempt to classify people or predict change. The kinds of stimuli which we utilize now in our experimental approaches to assessing personality are evanescent. Intermittent light for flicker fusion, tachistoscopic exposures for concept elicitation, inkblots for mental content, etc., merely touch the surface of behavior. They can hardly evoke as much response as a drug which influences the total nervous system. Perhaps after we have discovered the natural lines of cleavage in human populations through psychochemical methods we can return to a study of the psychophysical and psychometric functions that now hold the field.

CONCLUSIONS

Our survey of the relation between psychopharmacology and personality change has forced us to realize that neither of these two fields is sufficiently defined to enable us to make definitive conclusions regarding their interaction at the present time. Both fields are themselves at a low level of articulation and any attempt at studying their interaction is very hazardous.

We have not yet reached an integrative state in psychopharmacology, nor in personality or in their interaction. Perhaps we never will. As the Abbé Galiani said without discouragement (as quoted by Thompson, 1961) "Science is *plutôt destiné à étudier qu'à connaître, à chercher qu'à trouver la ve-rité"* (p. 14).

On the positive side, however, we have drawn up a model based on some of the assumptions and definitions arising from the observations that the literature and our own work have provided which may have heuristic value. Let us regard the behavioral change accompanying any drug dosage as an interaction between the ongoing brain activity present when the drug enters and the effect of the drug. We can relate the former, the ongoing brain activity, to the conceptual or cognitive component, i.e., memory storage, which, if it is systematically characteristic of the individual, may be designated as personality. The immediate drug effect on the brain may be equated to the physiological sensory and perceptual aspects of behavior. As the dosage rises from 0 to a maximum the role of the conceptual component declines and the role of the other components rises. That is why it is so important in drug research to specify the state of the organism, its environment, and the ongoing conceptual trend as well as the dosage. When these factors are specified, it becomes possible to integrate observed results that now seem contradictory under one model. This includes such events as the contradictory effects under various instructional and situational variables, placebo effects, and drug effects which will elicit hostility in one situation, friendliness in another, elation in still another, and apathy in still another.

The model of the interaction between the conceptual and other components permits a systematic investigation of testable hypotheses which may accomplish for our generation what psychophysics accomplished for the gay 90's. But we must not dally too long. Let us hurry up and develop psychochemistry while the drugs still work!

chapter twelve

Attitude Change and the
Reduction of International Tensions

Ross Stagner

This chapter is from a series of papers dealing with problems of change within the individual, first as a theoretical question in psychology, and second, as a practical issue having major implications for our survival as a race. My remarks will touch upon both of these facets of the problem of personality change. We shall discuss theory and research in attitude change, and then try to apply the ideas so generated to the problem of reducing international tensions.

To say that this is an alarmingly complicated assignment is truly an understatement. We must take at least a brief look at different ways of conceptualizing attitudes, because theories of attitude change are obviously dependent upon the concept of attitude which has been adopted. I must also consider the kinds of attitudes which affect our international relations. Then I shall explore the literature on attitude change, and finally offer some comments about changing the attitudes which seem crucial to tensions between nations. All of this involves some assumptions about the role of the individual in determining the course of international affairs—a topic, I regret to note, on which historians and political scientists show as much disagreement as we psychologists show about the theory of psychotherapy.

In the interests of clarity, let me delimit my field somewhat. The term "international tensions" inevitably brings to mind such problems as the Cold War, the Marshall Plan, the Cuban question, the dollar gap, and other controversial matters. These will enter into the discussion only casually, in the form of illustrations. And obviously I shall not be attempting to analyze the actual operations of NATO or the United Nations. My concern is with *the representation of such large-scale phenomena in the minds of individuals.* To the leader of an underdeveloped nation, a steel mill may have tremendous symbolic significance, regardless of the fact that his country has no iron ore, coal, or oil. To people who sell raw materials to the United States, a change in our buying habits may be perceived as a hostile act, a blow to their nation.

The analysis, then, will deal with attitudes, values, and decisions, *not* with the presumed *realities* behind these psychological processes. When Khrushchev makes a decision about our activities in Laos, he is guided by what he perceives to be real, not by what *we* assert to be real. Not surprisingly, too, the decision makers in this country operate on the basis of reality as they perceive it, not on what is claimed by Khrushchev, Adenauer, or de Gaulle to be the fact. It is, as all of you know, a fruitless task to try to define "reality" even in the physical world; reality in social affairs is as slippery as a snake soaked in crude oil.

To avoid certain verbal complications, I shall use the term "image" to identify this subjective or perceived reality. Thus I shall discuss, not Russian strategy, but the American image of Russian strategy; not the revolution in Cuba, but various images of that revolution, and so on. This tactic is essential in order to make it clear that my analysis is solely psychological and lays no claim to being an economic or political document.

While an image normally has a verbal label attached to it, we must not identify the image with the label. The image includes a whole array of perceptual-cognitive-affective content, much of which may be partly or wholly unverbalized. Actions are determined by the image content, not by the verbal label.

Let me turn now to the concept of attitude. We can accept in a preliminary way the traditional view of attitude as a disposition to respond favorably or unfavorably to an object or class of objects. We may consider the term image, as used above, to identify an object as a member of a class of objects. However, in addition to the image, which constitutes the cognitive facet of the attitude, we must recognize the importance of motivational and behavioral components in all attitudes.

Consider the case of a group of "Freedom Riders" entering a segregated bus station in Alabama. This can be perceived by one observer as a violation of state law, by another observer as an assertion of rights guaranteed by the federal government. The attitude is defined by the *perceptual* categorization of the event. Secondly, it is obvious that *motives* become involved—aggression and hostility, anxiety, self-assertion, idealism, and so on. These motives are likely to be so mixed that a detailed analysis would have to be made for each observer. And third, there is the question of *response,* and responses may take the form of words, the use of baseball bats, contributions of money, legal actions, and so forth. Now my point is chiefly this: the same motives may operate on both sides of the attitudinal continuum, hence motivational analysis does not help us in this phase of attitude study. Secondly, the same individual may shift from one response to another, according to the nature of the situation, the presence of police, and related factors. But we would not call this a change of attitude. It seems to me, therefore, that, from the point of view of psychological analysis, the process of perceiving has outstanding importance. "Attitude" depends on the situation as it appears to each observer. (It must be conceded that the attitude, once established, modifies incoming perceptions. This is no more than the common phenomena of perceptual constancy, context, apperceptive mass, and assimilation, familiar to us from the perception laboratory.)

I could as easily use an example from the area of international tensions. A Cuban does not perceive Fidel Castro in the same way as most citizens of this country do. A Russian does not perceive our soldiers in West Berlin as we do. Perceptual differences, I shall allege, are crucial to the study of attitudes in international tensions.

It should not be surprising that different experts have built their theories of attitude change, and their research designs, by emphasizing the cognitive, the motivational, or the response components of attitude. I shall contrast these views in later pages.

One value of adopting a given conceptualization of attitude is that it makes available a whole array of related formulations and concepts. A response definition of attitude, for example, carries with it, at least by implication, the facts and generalizations about conditioning, extinction, repetition, reward, punishment, and so on. It seems probable that concepts of stimulus generalization and response generalization will be useful in dealing with problems of attitude change.

If, on the other hand, we adopt a perceptual formulation, we find readier access to principles of closure, *Prägnanz,* assimilation, perceptual constancy, perceptual defense, and affective distortion of percepts. Finally, a definition of attitude in motivational terms is likely to lend itself most efficiently to the utilization of the extensive psychoanalytic literature, involving cathexis, object fixation, overdetermination, condensation, symbolism, and the like.

CONCEPTUALIZATION OF ATTITUDE CHANGE

Response Theory

In terms of traditional behavioristic (i.e., Hullian) theory, attitude change must needs be related to the process of reinforcement because reinforcement is the only agent directly modifying habit strength. The difficulty with relating reinforcement, in any customary sense, to attitudes toward the United Nations, toward Russia, or toward other key international objects, seems obvious. We can plausibly relate the studies by Brophy (1946) and those reported by Stouffer et al. (1950) to reinforcement theory, because both deal with attitude change in situations where concrete behavior and real rewards were involved. In symbolic situations this is not so clear.

The conceptualization of attitudes as responses can best be illustrated by Hovland, Janis, and Kelley (1953), who say (p. 7), "the term 'attitude' will be used exclusively for those implicit responses which are oriented toward approaching or avoiding a given object, person, group, or symbol." This ties in, of course, with the customary tendency to treat all attitudes as "being for or against something." The authors, in their ingenious experiments on the role of anxiety in attitude change, attempt to demonstrate the rewarding function of anxiety-reduction as the decisive factor, but the reasoning seems rather strained. I shall return to this problem later.

Like Hovland et al., Osgood (1957) uses the concept of an implicit or mediating response to bridge the gap between attitude and traditional behavior theory. He says (p. 6), "Whenever some stimulus other than the significate is contiguous with the significate, it will acquire an increment of association with some portion of the total behavior elicited by the significate as a representational mediation process."[1] In this view, the attitude is a fractional, implicit response, part of the original total response to the object, and attitude change is a matter of response modification.

In the Osgood formulation, attitude change seems to be a consequence of response conflict and interaction: "Whenever two signs are related by an assertion, the mediating reaction characteristic of each shifts toward congruence with that characteristic of the other, the magnitude of the shift being inversely proportional to intensities of the interaction reactions" (pp. 200–201). On close examination, this hardly differs from a cognitive analysis of change; Osgood is treating these mediating processes as if they somehow reproduced the effective environment; "The total representational process is assumed to be coordinate with a point in the semantic space . . ." (p. 200).

Cognitive Theories

In contrast to behavioristic theories which attempt to maintain an emphasis on some kind of response, cognitive theories of attitude and attitude change emphasize the perceptual or input side of the behavioral cycle. The approach

---

[1] It is not clear whether this phrasing implies abandonment of reinforcement as an explanatory principle; but see page 424.

which I find most congenial starts with very simple assumptions about the organism recording external and internal cues, establishing expectancies based on the probability that cue A will be followed by cue B, and organizing these expectancies in accordance with a gestalt approach to perception. Every percept is assumed to be determined in part by scanning the immediately present stimulus and in part by residues of past stimulation. Objects are here conceived in Egon Brunswik's manner, as "the most probable source" from which certain cues would have been emitted. The percept, then, carries certain attributes which pertain to this probable object, and which are experienced as a consequence of scanning the residues of past events.[2]

Translating this formulation now to the topic of attitude, I would define an attitude as a percept of an object or class of objects which is phenomenally endowed with certain attributes. Theoretically these attributes may differ extensively both as to quality and as to intensity; in practice, the work of Osgood with his semantic differential (1957) makes it appear that there may be not more than three qualitatively different dimensions, the other differences being quantitative. Osgood finds that most of the judgmental variance derives from his *evaluative* dimension, and this is of course identical with the good-bad or favorable-unfavorable dimension traditionally used in attitude studies.

I would suggest, therefore, that the position assigned by a person to a specified object on the evaluative dimension is the weighted probability,[3] based on past direct and indirect experiences with the object, that contact with it will be followed by phenomenally pleasant or unpleasant experiences. These attributes are conceived as the intervening variables which determine the kind of response—approaching or avoiding—given by the person in the presence of the stimulus object.

Attitude change, in this conceptualization, is a process of inducing expectancies different from those earlier established. Concretely, if the goal of the experimenter is to change an attitude from one favoring complete, undiluted national sovereignty to one favoring the yielding of some national power to a world government, stimulation must be applied which will change the expectancies regarding independent sovereignty, or world government, or both.

This is closely similar to the theory of *cognitive dissonance* expounded by Festinger (1957). Without quoting his formal definition of dissonance, let me note that he says (p. 15), "the relation between the two elements is disso-

---

[2] A fuller statement of these assumptions will be found in the 1961 edition of my *Psychology of Personality*, New York: McGraw-Hill, pp. 74–83.

[3] I use this expression as substantially equivalent to Helson's (1948) concept of adaptation level. The similarity will become more apparent in later pages.

nant if, the one does not, or *would not be expected to,* follow from the other." Such a situation would arise if a person viewed Khrushchev as a power-mad megalomaniac and also a trustworthy cooperator on international problems. When such dissonance occurs, one facet of the image must be modified. Festinger states that "The presence of dissonance gives rise to pressures to reduce or eliminate the dissonance. The strength of the pressures to reduce the dissonance is a function of the magnitude of the dissonance" (p. 18). While Festinger is not very explicit about what he means by *pressures,* it is clear that he predicts a modification of perception when mutually contradictory cues are present. It will be noted that, while the formal terms are different, this approach differs only slightly from that of Osgood (*supra*). It is also compatible with the notion that percepts become modified as new information is received regarding attributes of an object.

I am assuming (as does Festinger) that the percept tends, over the long run, to conform to *reality.* Veridical perception is, as Gibson has argued, much more the rule than the exception. In the field of attitudinal objects, as contrasted to physical objects, however, it is not always simple to decide what is veridical. Reality testing is often difficult. The child acquires his percepts of many socially defined objects by contact with his culture, not with the object referred to; e.g., the southern white child's percept of a Negro is weighted heavily with cultural reality, only slightly with the reality of personal experience. Thus, when I say that the percept tends to be veridical, I mean only that each of us moves toward expectancies which are reinforced by our experiences. These experiences may be only encounters with the prejudices of our associates.

Motivational Theories

In the attitude area, psychoanalysts have attempted to apply their motivational analysis. Unfortunately, this necessarily gets involved in a cognitive or perceptual approach as well, because motives cannot become cathected without being cathected to something—an object, a person, a symbol, or an ideology. Psychoanalysts have, therefore, been more interested in phenomena of attitude change, in which a change in the dynamics of energy distribution within the organism can be related to modifications of behavior relative to some attitudinal object. This is observed in the phenomena of displacement, rationalization, etc. It is not, unfortunately, very helpful in the area of international relations, where manipulation of motive states is extraordinarily difficult.

Katz and Stotland (1959) have recently emphasized the importance of treating attitude as a motivational phenomenon. They say, "Our own insistence upon affect as a major component of an attitude places us in the latter camp (i.e., holding that attitudes are dynamic), since we assume an affective process has energizing properties" (p. 434). Yet they seem to be reluctant to identify the attitude with the motive, since they speak of "the motivational support available to the attitude" (p. 435).

In the light of these conflicting views, it may seem preferable to deal with attitude as a *function of the total organism,* having cognitive, motivational, and behavioral components. In certain contexts, and for certain purposes, we may find it necessary to stress one or another aspect, but the complete attitude structure always involves all three factors to some extent.

"Finding the Facts"

The perceptual approach to attitude research warns us about a danger which is often ignored—especially by response theorists. It can be identified by citing the frequent concern for finding out "the real facts" about India, about Laos, about Communist infiltration in Ghana, and so on. The response theorist, with his emphasis on stimuli in the physical sense, tends to assume that we can somehow find these external stimuli and define them in objective terms. The perceptionist, if I may coin a term, promptly replies that the phrase, "the real facts," is an illusion. Every fact depends upon an observer, and in a complex, ambiguous field, the "facts" reported by one individual may diverge sharply from those reported by another. Even where we get a consensus among observers, there is still room for doubt—consider the case of Christopher Columbus. The consensus of qualified observers, in his day, was all wrong. It may be just as wrong today, with regard to Cuba, or Egypt, or Chiang-Kai-Shek.

But the Columbus example also serves to point out one *desirable* feature of a response definition. *Action* based upon a given percept may be successful. We may, therefore, approach the problem of "the real facts" indirectly by stating that one view of the facts is to be preferred to another when the first provides a more dependable guide to action. Thus, in the period 1919–1939 one view widely held in the USA was that the oceans provided a safe barrier behind which we could relax and ignore foreign quarrels. Action based on this approach, however, led to some unpleasant consequences, and we now have a majority if not unanimous agreement that we may be threatened by changes as far as 10,000 miles away. We are even coming around to consider the possibility that events at a distance of 250,000 miles, or 25 million miles, may be relevant to our safety and freedom. The success of this approach remains to be tested by events.

Operationism has pointed to another respect in which we can narrow the range of disagreement about "the real facts." By defining particular concepts in terms of responses, i.e., in terms of operations, we increase chances for agreement. Let me give an example. We could hardly arrive at agreement that wealth is "fairly distributed" within this nation or between nations. The concept of "fair" in this context has no response referent. It is, on the other hand, quite easy to arrive at agreement that in 1959 the per capita income in New York was $2350, in Texas $1696, in Mississippi $1067, and in India $70. The use of such operational definitions does not solve our problems; we may still argue about the reasons for the backwardness of Texas, Mississippi, or India, but at least communication is greatly improved by the use of quantitative measures.

Operational definitions could reduce the misunderstandings and disappointments which follow international conferences. At Yalta the Russians promised "free democratic elections" in the regions being freed from Nazi domination. But by this they meant only freedom to choose among candidates chosen by the Communist party, not a free choice among parties. This is a definition we could have understood; most elections in the South are limited to a choice among Democratic party candidates, and in Vermont they are limited to a choice among Republican candidates. The disappointment after Yalta, then, when the Russians permitted no opposition parties to offer candidates, could have been avoided by a better labeling of the kind of elections which would be held.

Does our inability to obtain "the real facts" about international affairs mean that we can take no action? Obviously not. We must act; we cannot delay interminably in search of more reliable information. We must, however, set some minimum standards of reliability. This means avoiding personal prejudices and group stereotypes as far as possible. It means using operational terms instead of glittering labels such as "peace-loving nations" or "subversive agitators." It means using numerical observations where possible, instead of ambiguous, value-loaded, qualitative terms. It means pooling observations, preferably among observers of differing prejudices, to increase the probability of getting reliable cues for action. Some suggested applications of these ideas will be offered in later pages.

ATTITUDE CHANGE AND PSYCHOTHERAPY

Let me comment briefly on the similarity between the problem attacked in this paper and those discussed earlier under the heading of psychotherapy. Consider the task of the propagandist as an example. In every bit of propaganda issued, either to the home nation or to an unfriendly nation, it is necessary to distinguish between *manifest content* and *latent thought*. The propagandist rarely reveals his intention overtly; the decoding of propaganda is thus parallel in many respects to that of the therapist seeking to identify unconscious behavior tendencies as these are revealed in acts and conscious verbalizations. This approach is also useful in examining diplomatic history, memoirs, official documents, etc.

Similarly, from the point of view of the recipient, it seems correct to assert that the impact of the communication may occur on more than one level. In semantic terms we might say that there is both a denotative, or factual, impact and a connotative, or emotional, influence. To use Osgood's phrase, which is also relevant to psychotherapy, the major intent of the communication is to produce a change on the *evaluative dimension* as regards a certain concept, person, institution, or policy. In phenomenal terms, we may say that the intent is to change the *perceived attributes* of the object.

Finally, we have noted earlier that every percept is a synthesis of the present stimulus and the residues of past experience. In psychotherapy, one is constantly faced with the fact that significant figures (parents, spouse, authority figures, etc.) are perceived primarily as representatives of past experiences, not in terms of their present attributes. This is the very essence of any psychological approach to the problem of international attitudes. Our attitude toward Russia is (properly) influenced in a major degree by our past experiences with that great power. But what becomes crucial is this question: Is Khrushchev's Russia the same as Stalin's Russia? Psychology does not answer this question; but it does point up the necessity of answering this question as part of any planned foreign policy.

In treating attitude as a cognitive function, I have spoken of dissonance, or the tension created by contradictory, incongruous information about a given object. Looked at in motivational terms, this resembles Freud's concept of ambivalence. Specifically, if a respected leader (+ valence) endorses an unpopular policy (− valence), a condition of dynamic conflict is created. Therapists are familiar with this problem, and with the need for resolving the ambivalence to some kind of steady state. A more significant problem, in terms of the scope of this chapter, is the relevance of psychotherapy to attitude change. Would the proposal of the psychoanalysts (cf. Strachey, 1957) that all statesmen undergo therapy have any significance? In the present atmosphere in Washington, of course, anyone who has seen a psychiatrist or a clinical psychologist is likely to find himself an *ex*-diplomat rather than being given decision-making authority. If we suppose the existence of a different state of affairs, we can speculate on the lessened amount of perceptual distortion that might follow.

No systematic studies have been done on the attitudes of persons who have been successfully analyzed. There are, however, some data on attitude modifications associated with arousal of self-insight and reduction of ego defensiveness (Stotland et al., 1959; Katz et al., 1956) which support the alleged value of such steps. If the defensiveness is directly related to the prejudiced attitude, and if the reduction of defensiveness occurs in this context, prejudice is reduced. This does not, unfortunately, indicate whether generalized therapy related to personal and familial problems would have any value whatever in reducing hostility displaced onto foreign symbols. And in any case, one has difficulty in imagining that a Khrushchev or a de Gaulle will take time off to be analyzed.

SOURCES OF INTERNATIONAL TENSION

Let me turn now to the second major facet of my paper: the concept of international tension. I shall assume that we all agree that the kind of tension with which we are concerned is the kind which potentially leads to war between nations; this assumption permits me to draw on the vast literature on the causes of war for principles and data.

Waltz (1959) has categorized the various theories about the causes of war into three groups: those which focus on the nature of man; those which focus on the nature of the state; and those which focus on the *system* of states. To be more explicit, some writers hold that war is due to man's instinct of aggressiveness or pugnacity; some ascribe war to properties inherent in any government imposed upon man; and yet others find the significant source of war to be the kinds of interactions which result from the existing system (or lack of system) of sovereign nation-states.

Manifestly, it is not my purpose to attempt to explore the validity of all three of these. It is important, none the less, to consider what light can be thrown on each by considering it as a psychological problem.

The first view needs no recasting to put it in a psychological frame of reference. It is purely and simply an assertion of the priority of human motives over other potential determinants of war; in effect, it suggests that war will occur irrespective of political and economic conditions.

The second approach requires modest reshaping to cast it in a psychological mold. Essentially it alleges that life under social controls induces certain impulses and attitudes which make war inevitable. Sigmund Freud has been quoted as asserting that "Foreign wars are the price of internal stability," thus aligning himself with Aristotle, Macchiavelli, and others who have advised princes to avert revolution by pointing to foreign enemies. This approach is also compatible with frustration-aggression theory, since socialization of the individual necessarily involves some frustration of primary drives.

The third class of theories, stressing interactions among states, is more remote from any simple psychological conception. These theories, however, can be restated in terms of images, attitudes, and motives. The general thesis runs as follows: Individuals necessarily acquire images of their own nation and of other nations. Because of the unity of the nation, in foreign policy actions, each national image has a unitary quality. Since acts of our own nation and of other nations may have need-satisfying or threatening attributes for the individual, he develops attitudes with respect to nations. Under appropriate environmental conditions, then, he will endorse war as a policy to remove frustrations and threats perceived as inhering in some foreign nation or nations.

This is not intended to imply that the "real" cause of war is always to be found at the level of the individual human being. All social phenomena, wars included, require the involvement of individual human beings. But certain complex relations are also necessary. Perhaps an example will help. Presumably all matter is made up of electrons, protons, neutrons, etc. But it makes a great deal of difference to us whether a particular neutron is organized into an atom of oxygen or an atom of plutonium. It is even more important, for all of us, whether this atom of plutonium is isolated, or is brought together with others to reach critical mass.

Nuclear physics does not pretend to offer us specific explanations for chemistry, biology, and psychology, although all of these sciences deal with organized units made up of electrons, protons, etc. The physicist acknowledges (at least for the present) that some phenomena are best studied at the more complex levels, ignoring the subatomic particles. He would, none the less, be justified in demanding that theories on these other levels must not imply phenomena on the subatomic level which are contrary to known data at this level.

In the same way we can concede the necessity of theories about economics and government, without abandoning all psychological analysis. Essentially I would assert that the economist, or the historian, must not make assumptions about human nature which are clearly contrary to reliable data. And conversely, if we seek to change any of these large-scale institutions, we can insist that the techniques employed must be compatible with advanced scientific knowledge of human behavior. Specifically, we are going to be concerned with the questions: What images and attitudes contribute to international tension? Can these be changed to reduce tension, and if so, in what manner?

The Image of the Enemy

What, then, are the images and attitudes which guide men's behaviors leading to international tension and hostility? The easiest to identify is the image of an enemy nation. To an American the chief cause of tension is the greedy, expansionist, ruthless Russian (or Communist) empire. To the Russian the chief cause is the greedy, imperialistic, ruthless capitalist world.

We can break these down into more specific aspects if we wish. Westerners in general (even those who own little property) share an unfavorable attitude toward the Communist technique of expropriation of private property. We have protested this in Russia, in China, and most recently in Cuba. (Surprisingly few Americans know that in 1776 the revolutionary government in this country expropriated Loyalist property without compensation; the Loyalists were eventually given some compensation by the British government.)

We also express unfavorable attitudes toward the Communist techniques of the police state, the use of informers, fostering distrust between children and parents, and so on. The dictatorial structure of the Communist governments, with their high concentration of power in a few hands, also elicits unfavorable attitudes. And their readiness to resort to violence, to supply arms to revolutionary groups in other nations, and even to send in their own forces, as in Hungary and Tibet, sets off hostile feelings.

Behind all of these specific dislikes, and perhaps basic to them, is our image of the Communist movement as completely self-centered, ruthless in relation to non-Communists, expansionist, violent, fanatical, ready to resort to espionage and revolution. The dedicated Communist strives to expand the movement and to increase its power. He derives personal gratification from the strength and achievements of the party.

The In-group Image

But is this so different from other forms of nationalism? Sovereignty is by its very definition self-centered, disdainful of the rights of other nations. Most nations are, or have been expansionist. All nations resort to espionage, and most have been willing to finance rebellions within unfriendly neighbor countries, as well as to resort to war, the ultimate in violence.

Religious wars have been characterized by the same glorification of the in-group, and vilification of the out-group, which now characterizes the Cold War between the East and the West. The anthropologists tell us that primitive tribal wars also show these psychological attributes.

Thus the nucleus of these tension-arousing attitudes, as I and many other scholars see it, is the phenomenon of nationalism or ethnocentrism. Essentially this means the glorification of one's own nation or in-group, and vilification of other nations (out-groups), perceived as bad, cruel, dangerous, and untrustworthy. Buchanan and Cantril (1953) have documented the marked differences in "how nations view each other." But other images are also important. Let me cite only a single study to illustrate how any program for reducing international tensions must be founded on a wide range of psychological data. I refer to a simple little investigation by Rosen (1959), comparing Americans with Italians. Here are some of the differences: Italians view socialism as more kind, more successful, more wise, and more beautiful. The Italians perceive the United Nations as more cruel, more feminine, more untimely, more foolish, and bad.

How can we expect active cooperation on a program which attempts to strengthen the United Nations, from people with such an image of the United Nations? Or, putting the issue another way, if we hope to build international cooperation, is it not essential that we initiate activities which will change this image of the UN? Similarly, considering the Italian image of socialism, which is far more favorable than ours, can we expect cooperation if we are openly antagonistic to socialism? May it not be wiser to try to show the Italians how many of the values they associate with socialism have already been attained in this country without a resort to a socialist government?

The study of international images, consequently, cannot be limited to our own population. We need to understand how people, and especially leaders, in other nations view the Great Powers, the United Nations, and the ideologies which get intricately involved in, if they do not cause, Cold War conflicts. This is another facet of the research program which is desperately needed if we are to learn what is needed for survival.

Nationalism versus Militarism

The foregoing paragraphs stress the decisive role of nationalistic attitudes rather than of militarism as such, in evoking tension. This conclusion was arrived at by the SPSSI Committee on Psychology of War and Peace over twenty years ago (cf. Stagner, Brown, Gundlach, and White, 1942). A careful study of historical documents, as well as a lengthy questionnaire submitted to a large number of nationally known social scientists, supported this conclusion. The role of armament races as such was considered not very important; as one respondent wrote, "fire does not cause the conflagration."

The importance of nationalism as opposed to militarism is also indicated in the longitudinal study by Stagner and Osgood (1946), which covered the period May, 1940–March, 1942. The American groups surveyed switched to a very nationalistic position long before they began approving of militaristic concepts.

At the heart of the nationalist attitude-complex is the phenomenon of sovereignty. It is this attribute—which most of us find essential to our nation-image—that prevents peaceful settlement of international disputes. Sovereignty has qualities which psychoanalysts find in their concept of the infantile ego: infantile omnipotence, utter disregard of the welfare of others, unlimited violence, complete independence of action. Belief in sovereignty has been expressed by such slogans as "My country, right or wrong." It carries implicitly the notion that we shall submit to no one else any decision affecting our national welfare.

The nationalist attitude-complex becomes more dangerous because of another psychological phenomenon. As Franz Alexander (1951) wrote, "at present conscience officially stops at national boundaries" (p. 277). Even the restraints of the adult superego on violence do not apply when the act is committed in the name of the nation. Thus, while we are shocked at an Eichmann giving orders for the murder of six million Jews, we are not particularly affected by an American military commander giving orders for the death of a hundred thousand Japanese by means of an A-bomb.

The lack of superego restraints is exaggerated by the operation of what we may call the "principle of agency." We are told that Lord Grey burst into tears when, in 1914, he felt impelled to recommend a declaration of war against Germany. But his personal feelings could not (according to the idea of agency) interfere with his duty to the English nation. This means that, even if we were so fortunate as to have diplomats who had been psychoanalyzed, their behavior would probably conform to the established patterns of violence and destruction. A government official is required by his *social role* to be suspicious of foreign countries, to be hypersensitive to threats, to maintain the nation's position even when this is contrary to ordinary moral standards. These are some of the factors which make nationalist attitudes the core of the problem of maintaining world peace.

Since the nation has a monopoly of violence, and since sovereignty implies that the nation can do no wrong, it follows that the nation is completely justified in using violence against its enemies. To the extent that this view is shared widely over the earth's surface, we are all in imminent danger of violent death.

PROBLEMS OF ATTITUDE CHANGE

It would be most appropriate if I could now turn to an extensive literature dealing with efforts to reduce nationalism and to build a less infantile, more tolerant set of international attitudes. Unfortunately, this literature does not exist. There is, however, a substantial body of material dealing with changes of attitudes less firmly established and less intensely held. Since principles established in these studies will undoubtedly apply also in the realm of nationalism and internationalism, I shall first briefly review the literature on relevant phases of the attitude change problem, and then offer certain applications in the area of international tensions.

The position I shall adopt is that attitude change is most effectively induced by modifying the *image* of the object toward which the attitude is directed. By this I mean that, if we wish to reduce conflict-increasing attitudes as between the United States and Russia, the most hopeful method is to modify the image held by each population of the other nation. There are many ways of inducing such changes; while communications from the government are especially important, individual citizens may also affect this process. The following comments pick out only a few of the major variables indicated by theory or by empirical research to be relevant. The listing is highly selective; for example, I shall have little to say about research dealing with the attributes of the *recipient* of propaganda as determinants of change, except in the respect that we must be aware of the phenomenon of audience self-selection and the corollary that much of the time we may only be talking to ourselves.

Within the more delimited field of communications which seek to modify attitudes of random samples of people, we are concerned largely with studies relating to the attributes of the communication, including, to some extent, the perceived attributes of the communicator. In the former group we may include studies which deal with the relative realism of the communication, its emotional value, its personal or impersonal quality, and so on. In the latter category we find studies dealing mainly with the variable of credibility of the communicator. In an additional group we find studies which manipulate the degree of discrepancy or dissonance, i.e., the extent to which the communication diverges from the pre-existing attitudes of the recipient.

DISCREPANCY OF COMMUNICATION FROM PRIOR ATTITUDE

Let me begin with the problem of discrepancy. It is apparent that no attitude change will occur if there is no discrepancy between prior attitude and the attitude urged in the communication. Festinger originally developed his concept of dissonance to identify the fact that incoming information may not agree with residues of past experience, and that a percept must be modified to harmonize all the evidence. Brunswik (1943) pointed out that a percept corresponds to the pooled probability derived from various contacts with a stimulus source. This is related to the formulation by Helson (1948) of adaptation level as a determinant of perception. Festinger's dissonance supplies a label for the tension which presumably occurs when a new sensory input fails to correspond to the expectancy based on prior experience.

This problem has also been dealt with by Osgood in his studies on the principle of "congruity" (cf. Osgood and Tannenbaum, 1955) and is very close to the situation analyzed by Newcomb (1953). The similarity of these three approaches has been well analyzed by Zajonc (1960). Because of the relatively non-committal quality of the term "dissonance" in relation to perceptual versus response theories, it is used in this discussion.

If a communication is received which disagrees in some degree with attitudes already established, dissonance, or incongruity, or response conflict will be induced. The Festinger hypothesis is that dissonance induces tension, and that efforts will be made to eliminate the dissonance. He says, "The existence of dissonance, being psychologically uncomfortable, will motivate the person to try to reduce the dissonance" (p. 3). It would follow from this that a message highly discrepant from prior attitude will induce greater attitude change than one of less discrepancy. Data to support this prediction have been offered by Helson, Blake, and Mouton (1958). In this case a fictitious majority gave judgments two, four, or six scale steps away from the modal judgment of a group of subjects. Individuals responded by accepting scale positions shifted more or less proportionately in the direction of the presented majority opinion.

It must be noted that according to this view a Goldwater Republican should be influenced more by Communist propaganda than a New Frontier Democrat. Since this manifestly is not true, Festinger modifies his theory to note that the person may seek additional information consonant with prior attitudes, may reject the total propaganda message as invalid, may get social support for his prior attitudes, etc. The dissonance theory, in short, accounts fairly well for changes of moderate discrepancy on issues which do not involve major ego identifications or intense emotional conviction; what happens in the latter cases must be arrived at ex post facto, by looking at the data. It may be, of course, that amplifications of the theory will be able to embrace such instances.

Another study on magnitude of discrepancy is that of Cohen, Terry, and Jones (1959). In this case the attitude object was "men should marry by the age of 23," a topic which had been much discussed in the local college paper. Those reporting a given attitude favorable or unfavorable received contrary propaganda. It appeared that whether the discrepancy of propaganda from prior attitude was large or small made little difference; both groups showed about the same attitude change. If, however, an individual were allowed a *choice* of listening or not listening to the propaganda, this made a marked difference. In the low choice group, more attitude change resulted from low discrepancy propaganda. In the high choice group, more change occurred if the propaganda differed sharply from the prior attitude. (Since only three subjects dropped out in the high choice group, the effects are not due to resistant subjects eliminating themselves.)

Osgood's studies of discrepancy (or incongruity) have generally involved three variables, the communicator, the object of the communication, and the prior attitude of the recipient. Under these conditions he finds that he can predict with a high degree of accuracy the amount of change which will be induced by a given type of communication. Thus if a *positive* source (e.g., Dwight D. Eisenhower) makes a *positive* statement about a *disliked* object, the amount of change will be a function of the intensity of liking Eisenhower as opposed to the intensity of disliking the object, e.g., Cuba.

Osgood's analysis may help us to understand one of the patterns of change reported in the Festinger studies. If discrepancy of attitude and communication is great, the consequence may be that *the recipient rejects the communicator.* He may deny that Eisenhower could have said this, or may—if the evidence is convincing—decide that he dislikes Eisenhower. Hence, in Festinger's terms, dissonance may affect the attitude toward the communicator as well as toward the object.

Let us briefly consider the problem of applying these observations to international attitudes. The principle of discrepancy would seem to suggest that statement of an extreme attitude (e.g., that a World Government should be established now) will induce more shift toward internationalism than a moderate position (e.g., strengthen the United Nations). But the person who adopts the extreme view runs the *risk* of being rejected, of losing any prestige status he may have enjoyed.

From the point of view of world peace, it would appear that we need people who will speak up for the extremes of international cooperation and world government, to foster perception of these policies as somewhat tolerable. And these people, in turn, must be masochistic enough to be willing to suffer the personal discomfort which is likely to be their lot. They must be able to take some satisfaction in the fact that conservatives (as most of us are) like to worship *dead* radicals.

REALISM OF THE COMMUNICATION

Let me turn now to another dimension along which communications can vary: the dimension of realism. I shall contrast here primarily studies using purely symbolic stimuli, i.e., verbal messages, with communications which involve goal-oriented, effortful activity on the part of the person to be changed.

The most dramatic instances in the latter category are those accumulated during World War II, where it was found, for example, that anti-Negro prejudice in soldiers was most rapidly diminished by participating in integrated combat units. Where the white soldier worked and fought side by side with the Negro, he lost his distorted percept of the Negro much more rapidly than by listening to lectures about tolerance (Stouffer et al., 1950). Similarly, Brophy (1946) observed that merchant seamen lost anti-Negro attitudes in direct proportion to the number of voyages made in mixed-crew ships.

Efforts to take advantage of this kind of realistic pressure toward attitude change have been reported by various investigators (cf. Iisager, 1949; Bjerstedt, 1958). In general, they report that situations involving close contact with people of other nations (as in a Danish folk school, a summer camp) and discussion of international ideas, seem to be more effective in changing attitudes than lectures alone. Lectures, even when given in a series by well-known experts (Stagner, 1942) on crucial issues of international political and economic cooperation, to a very attentive audience, have been shown to produce only slight changes in opinions.

This point should not be overstressed. We know that many tourists come back from Europe more nationalistic rather than more international-minded. Some white tenants of integrated housing projects become more prejudiced against Negroes. If the realistic experience is to produce specified attitudinal effects, the nature of the experience and the kind of interpretation placed upon it need to be in some degree controlled.

A situation in which such control is possible is that of role-playing. Industrial training programs make use of role-playing in inducing attitudinal changes in supervisors. The supervisor, taking the role of an aggrieved worker or a union steward, acquires more information than he does by listening to lectures on the feelings of others; and he perceives conflict situations differently after such training.

The effectiveness of role-playing in modifying attitudes appears to depend primarily upon the amount of active effort involved (Hovland et al., 1953, pp. 218–228). It is not clear, however, whether this is chiefly due to the making of appropriate responses, or whether it is due to a changed perception of the situation. In those conditions of maximal effectiveness, the subject had to *search for cues* to guide his responses. Role-playing had little value when all the cues were easily available (reading a script) even though the words were in general the same for both groups.

A similar conclusion may be justified with respect to the other studies cited in this section. Fighting alongside Negro soldiers, or shipping with Negro sailors, does not lead to rehearsal of favorable verbal responses; but it may very well lead to a modified perception of the *attributes* of Negroes, and this in turn guides a new set of verbal responses when the attitude scale is presented.

Further evidence that realistic communications are much more effective than those which appear artificial is found in the observation that the propaganda of deeds is more potent than that of words. Our attitudes toward Khrushchev, for example, are influenced more by his antics in the United Nations than by his speeches on peaceful coexistence. The extent to which our image of Russia was changed between June 1941 and March 1942 was studied quantitatively by Stagner and Osgood (1946); the data showed that Russians were judged to be far more strong, fair, and noble (and indeed, even more kind and more Christian) subsequent to the stubborn resistance they showed to the Nazi invaders during that winter.

It must be remembered, none the less, that most of us are dependent upon mass media of communication for the accounts of these deeds, and consequently that substantial distortions often enter. It is not so easy to detect these in reports from abroad, because in such instances American reporters share a common attitudinal bias; but on domestic issues the distortions are pretty obvious. To take just a single example, the account of a union-management dispute that one gets from the *Chicago Tribune* differs so radically from that in *The New York Times* that he could be pardoned for doubting that the event referred to was actually the same.

The molding of attitudes by the deeds of foreign governments, therefore, depends to a considerable extent on how much gets included in the communication. Most of us, for example, feel indignation at the Communist guerrillas in Laos, forgetting—because it has hardly been mentioned—that the neutralist regime of Souvanna Phouma was overthrown by military force, and allegedly this coup was financed by our own CIA. It is easy not to mention our own violence; thus we can express more indignation when the enemy resorts to it.

Proponents of psychological warfare are now, much more than twenty years ago, inclined to the view that effective psychological warfare is carried out by actions, not by words. Dyer (1959) has presented effectively the arguments for this tactic. Consequently, policy proposals for lessening tensions, such as those by Osgood which I will discuss later, fall in this category of actions selected primarily for their value in communicating something to the opponent.

EMOTIONAL VALUE OF THE COMMUNICATION

A third dimension along which communications vary is emotional value. A famous but limited study is that of Hartmann (1936), who ran as a Socialist candidate for Congress and used his campaign leaflets as material for the experiment. Matched wards received voting appeals, one form quite rational, the other using strong emotional appeals. Statistically, the emotional approach was more effective, although the number of Socialist votes was not large enough in either sample to give very solid support to the conclusion.

In recent years interest has centered on the effect of anxiety-arousing communications. The classic study is that of Janis and Feshbach (1953). The authors presented material to high-school students on the importance of dental hygiene. One presentation was filled with "atrocity stories," gruesome illustrations, in full color, and threats of what would happen to the listener personally if he did not adopt the correct methods. A second version used mild threats of discomfort, in a less personal context. The third was quite detached, with little mention of unpleasant consequences of tooth neglect. It was clear from subjects' reports that the fear-arousing communication was really disturbing. Yet, in a follow-up after a week, it was found that the order of change in actual *behavior* (tooth care) *and attitude* was partly independent of the intensity of emotional arousal. Most change was induced by the mild anxiety presentation, least by the very frightening approach.

This study has obvious implications for the propaganda devices so often utilized by pacifists, in which they stress the fact that seventy million persons would be killed in the United States by an all-out nuclear war—that so many would be hospitalized, so many abnormal children result from genetic damage, and so on. The statistics are certainly frightening, yet this kind of appeal seems to have little effect on behavior.

What may be the explanation of such ineffectiveness? Hovland, Janis, and Kelley (1953), reflecting on the Janis-Feshbach study, propose three hypotheses about the result obtained.

1. *Inattentiveness to the communication.* It may be that people are distracted by the emotion-arousing content and simply do not receive the positive suggestions for change of behavior. (The data disprove this hypothesis.)

2. *Aggressiveness toward the communicator.* It may be that the chief effect was to induce hostility toward the person making the presentation and hence to show unwillingness to follow his advice. Certainly those who have campaigned vigorously against nationalism have encountered this reaction.

3. *Defensive avoidance.* The most plausible interpretation of the data seems to be that the anxiety aroused by part of the message induced avoidance responses, so that the individual failed to follow through a sequence of ideas and remember the positive suggestions for action.

If the Janis-Feshbach study had dealt with attempts to change strong attitudes, a fourth hypothesis would be relevant: namely, that the habit strength of the practiced responses was so great that they remained at the top of the response hierarchy, even though some learning of the new responses had occurred. This is the characteristic situation with regard to strong attitudes such as nationalism and militarism.

Reward and Attitude Change

Implicit in the fear-arousing study was the notion that reduction of anxiety (by changing attitude) would reinforce responses in the process of being established. A related device has been used by Festinger and Carlsmith (1959) and by Brehm (cited by Cohen, 1960). In this case, role-playing under slight reward conditions is contrasted with role-playing with a large reward. Response theory would seem to predict that a large reward would be more reinforcing, hence would establish the new attitude being practiced more rapidly. Festinger, on the other hand, predicted that a large reward would produce less change in private attitude.

The data in both studies support the Festinger prediction. People (whose private attitudes were obtained some weeks earlier) were offered a chance to earn prizes (one dollar or twenty dollars) for taking a public position contrary to this private belief (about which the experimenter was supposed to be ignorant). In each case the group with high incentive showed less change on a post-test of private attitude. Though Sarbin in Chapter 7 offers an alternate explanation, Festinger interprets the situation as follows: expressing publicly an attitude contrary to private belief creates dissonance. But in the high-reward situation, so much consonance (getting this money, in relation to personal need) is created that there is no tension to reduce dissonance by modifying the attitude. In the small-reward group, the dissonance induced by public expression was greater relative to the total situation, and hence the subject tended to modify his private attitude as a way of *escaping the feeling* that he was *saying something he did not believe*. Festinger seems to endorse a formula like the following:

$$D = \frac{D}{D + C}$$

in which D represents all dissonances, C all consonances, and D the net effective dissonance. This is faintly amusing, if only because it resembles so closely the "hedonic calculus" of the classical economists, which we psychologists have been quick to denounce on many occasions.

Let me digress here for a moment to comment on the implications for international affairs of the studies by Janis and Feshbach on anxiety, and those of Festinger and his collaborators on rewards. It would seem to be a legitimate inference that, when national welfare is at stake, learning and intelligent decision making are blocked by the sheer magnitude of the goals involved.

As I suggested earlier in commenting on the principle of agency, the diplomat may perceive his own personal beliefs and values to be so trivial, in relation to the magnitude of the national gain or disaster impending, that he simply cannot function as an intelligent person. The dissonance between personal ethics and national policy is not observed. He acts out his social role without making use of his personal code of morality, or his knowledge of the unsatisfactory character of violent solutions. There is room for valuable research here on ways to train people to deal with such tremendous stakes without losing their analytical ability.

CREDIBILITY OF THE COMMUNICATOR

Let us turn, now, to a variable which is not an aspect of the communication but is a part of the interaction situation, viz., the credibility of the communicator. Osgood et al. (1957) cite a study by Kerrick in which communications were ascribed to plausible communicators or to an irrelevant communicator. For example, John Foster Dulles was quoted on what our attitude should be toward Red China, for one group, while another received the same communication ascribed to a circular issued by the Museum of Modern Art. Few will be surprised to hear that an irrelevant source has relatively little effect, although even here the changes obtained were in the direction of shifting attitudes to agree with the communication.

Kelman and Hovland (1953) presented a message urging lenient treatment of juvenile delinquents to three groups. In one case, the "speaker" (over a public address system) was alleged to be a judge in a juvenile court; in the second, a member of the studio audience; and in the third, a former juvenile delinquent currently involved in some shady activities. Although the three groups had been equal before the message, group I favored lenient treatment much more than group III after the message.

It will be recalled that one possible explanation of the ineffective nature of strong fear appeals (Janis and Feshbach, 1953) was hostility to the communicator. We must recognize that strongly threatening messages may be so disturbing that the recipient protects his equilibrium by denouncing the communicator. The ancient Hebrews reacted in this manner to some of their prophets who foresaw disaster. Such a fate can easily befall the exponent of a pessimistic or frightening world-view today.

PRESTIGE OF THE COMMUNICATOR

In the studies just cited, prestige as well as area of competence may have been unintentionally varied. It is of interest, therefore, to consider an instance in which prestige effect is measured independently of area of competence. In an early study (Stagner, 1941) I selected ten opinion statements on political, military, and economic nationalism. These were given to groups of college students; then three weeks later, the same statements were presented, ascribed to a general in the United States Army, to a prominent religious leader, to a big business executive, to a trade union official, and to a high government official (no names were used). The shift to agree with the statement was positive and significant for business men, negative and significant for trade-union leaders, non-significant for the other leaders. Since the statements were rotated across sources, this effect shows the generalized prestige value of the occupational categories utilized, and indicates that, as the labor unions are now beginning to endorse nationalism, our task of getting college students away from nationalism may be simplified.

The prestige data foreshadow a particular difficulty with the reduction of nationalistic attitudes. People who have achieved prestige status in our society are in preferred positions within the institutional structure. A change in our ideology—as regards national sovereignty, economic nationalism, militarism, or in any other respect relevant to international tensions—would tend to undermine their preferential status. We can thus hardly expect much help from prestige figures at this time.

It is also worth noting that prestige figures are often persons who are in a position to hand out rewards and punishments. Whether or not we accept the Freudian thesis that the first prestige figures are the parents, it is clear that the boss, the commanding officer, or the government official may be in a position to give or to withhold favors. The great effectiveness of attitude change programs in the army and in business may be due to the fact that motivational as well as information pressures are involved. It does not seem probable, at present, that internationalists will be able to dispose of important rewards or punishments.

VALUE OF MOTIVATIONAL STUDIES

Let me now say a little more about this question of motivation. I have stated that attitudes are total-organism functions, but I have stressed the basic role of perceptual organizations and suggested that attitude change derives principally from adding perceptual elements, deleting elements, or restructuring the situation to form a new gestalt. In this frame of reference motivational theory and experiments on the effects of motivation tend to play a minor role.

Let me first indicate how this framework can make room for motivational studies and then comment on the utility of some of the research done within a motivational frame. My view is that dynamic states, quite unrelated, in terms of content, to the attitude under study, may influence the *effective representation* of the attitude in two ways: (1) by modifying the process of perceiving, dynamic influences favor polarized, extreme, and intensely affective percepts of classes of objects; and (2) dynamic states may affect the intensity of an overt *response* to an attitudinal object in some fashion such as Hull proposed with his multiplicative function of drive.

Studies using the technique of manipulating motivational states do not provide good models for the purposes of this paper, since so few opportunities are likely to occur in everyday life to utilize these methods in changing attitudes. For the sake of validating the theoretical proposition just stated, however, I shall review briefly a few studies which demonstrate that dynamic states, lacking any relation at the content level to the attitudinal object, may modify opinions and attitudes.

Displacement of Aggression

The classical study on the effects of aggression is, of course, that by Miller and Bugelski (1948). In this case frustration (imposed by preventing camp boys from seeing a much desired movie) induced aggression; the attitudinal change observed was an increase in hostility toward minority groups. While this effect was not duplicated by Stagner and Congdon (1955), it has been confirmed by Cowen, Landes, and Schaet (1959). It seems clear that an irrelevant frustration can, under certain circumstances, elevate the level of aggression and that this can be expressed as added hostility toward convenient scapegoat objects. There is, however, little evidence as to the permanence of such changes; furthermore, it seems obvious that the irrelevant frustration did not induce the prejudice but only intensified it. Thus the argument that economic depressions induce wars is only partly supported here; if hostile attitudes have already been established, then domestic frustrations may evoke aggression which is then channeled into foreign pathways. But it seems that the negative images must have been already present for this effect to appear.

Affiliation and Cynicism

Some of the studies on motivational effects require a more devious logic. Arthur Cohen (1960) has proposed that cynical attitudes about human behavior may be a reaction formation used by some individuals as a defense against a motive of affiliation which is perceived as too strong. Cohen selected individuals who showed evidence of using reaction formation as a defense mechanism, and stimulated the affiliation motive by a dramatic presentation. As predicted, those who were high on reaction formation responded to this presentation by becoming more cynical, while those who were low on reaction formation reacted by becoming more sympathetic. Such research may throw light on the curious and contradictory ways in which individuals respond to the horrors and hardships of war.

ATTITUDE AND ITS INFORMATIONAL SUPPORT

The presentation of information relating to specific supports of an attitude may lead to changes in the attitude itself, as is illustrated by many of the studies cited in the preceding pages. It is, however, important to consider a different kind of investigation, in which it appears that the individual will gather for himself information and similar supporting material appropriate to an attitude change.

The technical problem here is to induce an attitude change without supplying new information or arguments. Rosenberg (1960) solved this problem by hypnotizing his subjects and commanding them to adopt an attitude the reverse of that formerly held (e.g., a person favoring our foreign economic aid policy is told that he opposes it). Posthypnotic amnesia is, of course, induced. A week later the subject is asked to give the arguments pro and con on foreign aid; he can recall facts and opinions against the program, but blocks when asked for material favoring it. At the same time, he may say, "I can't understand this, because I know I used to be in favor of the aid policy."

This kind of study has not been explored sufficiently for us to provide a sound theoretical analysis. Freud, of course, stressed the motivational interpretation: "We are not used to feeling strong affects without their having any ideational content, and therefore, if the content is missing, we seize as a substitute upon another content which is in some way or other suitable . . ." (Collected Papers, Vol. 3, 1946, p. 314). On the other hand, it might be a function of response set; once the individual adopts (under instructions) a certain set, only those responses which are compatible will get through into action. Conversely, we may note that this finding resembles the studies of perceptual defense, in which material contrary to firmly held opinions simply is not recognized. As Cooper and Jahoda (1947) noted of some prejudiced individuals exposed to propaganda for tolerance, "the prejudiced person's perception is so colored by his prejudices that issues presented in a frame of reference different from his own are transformed so as to become compatible with his view. Quite unaware of the violation of facts he commits, he imposes on the propaganda item his own frame of reference" (p. 20). This distortion may or may not be preceded by initial understanding; if the recipient does get the point at first, he quickly loses it in a thicket of rationalization.

Audience Self-selection

We must, therefore, consider a problem which was largely ignored in the propaganda studies, which dealt with captive audiences. Studies of the mass media confirm the importance of *audience self-selection;* Republicans read newspapers of Republican orientation, and so for people of other political persuasions. Few Protestants read the arguments favoring Catholicism (and, since the penalties are greater, even fewer Catholics read about Protestant views). Wall Street bankers are not likely to peruse the *Daily Worker*. Hyman and Sheatsley (1947) discuss some of the devices used by people to shut out information contrary to their views. And Schramm and Carter (1959) describe a particular instance (a marathon television performance by Senator Knowland, seeking the governorship of California) in detail. In this case persons friendly to Knowland watched much of the program, whereas those hostile to his candidacy saw little or none of it. Both unconsciously and consciously we defend ourselves against dissonance, against any challenge to our established beliefs.

The classic study by Levine and Murphy (1943) showed that, even if people are coerced into memorizing passages contrary to their attitudes, such material is learned less effectively than material consonant with established views. A novel twist is given to this finding by Jones and Kohler (1958), who found that a subject could learn without difficulty a set of arguments contrary to his beliefs if these arguments were quite *implausible*. Such arguments apparently create no dissonance; they are at once perceived as no threat to the established attitudinal structure.

WHAT CAN BE DONE?

If we assume—as seems justified by the analysis—that the crucial attitude change that can reduce international tensions is one which reduces nationalism or ethnocentrism, and simultaneously strengthens favorable attitudes toward international organization, the question then becomes focal: how can this be achieved? This question can be covered only very sketchily here.

In terms of the data, it seems clear that we must somehow manage to get more information to citizens of all nations about the dangers involved in *nationalism* and the values of *cooperation* through the United Nations. This will be difficult enough in this country, where many "lunatic fringe" groups oppose the United Nations; it will be almost impossible in Russia, where the government has aligned itself with our Daughters of the American Revolution to get the United Nations out of the United States and the United States out of the United Nations.

One proposal along this line is, of course, simply to publicize the activities of the United Nations over the "Voice of America" and through other channels. At a policy level, however, the argument above implies a deliberate expansion of American participation in the United Nations. Even if the Russian role is chiefly one of opposition, this must involve publicity for United Nations' programs which will reach the population of the Soviet Union, and may be expected to stimulate thoughtful Russians to develop a changed attitude more favorable to United Nations' programs. Such a policy might also develop an image of a stronger United Nations among neutrals.

Communication, of course, implies a two-way street. The American government tries to communicate with the Russians, by way of the Voice of America and a few publications which are allowed to circulate. The Russians try to communicate with us via the Communist party and by official spokesmen. But both governments try to prevent their citizens from *receiving* the alien communications. Each wishes to present a point of view, but is unwilling to receive statements of divergent views.

An even more serious complication, in this country, is the fact that our policy decisions seem not to be made with an eye on the image of America abroad; and indeed, the people who make policy do not always inform those who issue communications, as witness the deplorable confusion when our U-2 was shot down. Despite such bungling, returning visitors report that the image of America inside Russia is not so negative as might have been expected.

Our communications with the Western and neutral nations have, of course, included much more than mere words—military aid, economic development, technical assistance, and so on. There is a good deal of evidence that the image of America in Western Europe is favorable, and that we will receive support on crucial Cold War issues. But the essential problem is communication beyond the Iron Curtain. I shall speak briefly of some proposals in this area, with reference to the theories and research data already cited.

Would an exchange of visitors help? Hayakawa (1960) asserts that merely listening to Russian speakers (if they would listen to ours) would have beneficial results. I see little reason to be optimistic about this. The familiar phenomena of selective perception, learning, and forgetting, represent important obstacles. The attitudes involved are too powerful to be modified by purely verbal appeals.

Would widespread tourist exchange be of value? Perhaps we could benefit by learning that the Russians look quite human, and similarly they should know that we are not born with hoof and horn. But I hardly need to point out the fallacy of assuming that mere day-to-day contact with members of an out-group will result in better understanding of that out-group. Southern whites have, on the average, many more interactions with Negroes than do Northern whites; yet it is doubtful that they have better understanding, and it is manifest that their attitudes are not made more favorable by such interaction.

We must not, therefore, place too much emphasis on sending Americans abroad, nor on bringing foreigners here. Such cultural interchanges seem, on the average, to lead to better—i.e., more international—attitudes. But it is just as possible that increased hostility may result; most of us can think of at least one or two Americans whose overseas travel has made them isolationistic, not sympathetic to closer international ties.

I think that the factor which accounts for the apparent incongruity of the foregoing observation and the well-known data from military service, merchant seamen, and similar groups, is this: in the studies of soldiers and sailors, in which prejudice was markedly reduced by contact with Negroes, the situation required cooperative effort by both races toward the goal of mutual survival. This is not the kind of situation encountered by tourists or even by Fulbright scholars. They are just as likely to get involved in competitive situations, e.g., arguing about the high price of meals or souvenirs, attempts to follow American norms instead of local laws, and the like. Such incidents may increase antagonism rather than decreasing it. For such reasons I think it unlikely that efforts to "make every American tourist an Ambassador of his country" will ever pay dividends.

On the other hand, projects conducted jointly by scholars or professional people from both sides of the Curtain may be of great value. A relevant example may be cited from a recent issue of the *Bulletin of Atomic Scientists:* "The Soviet participants (in the Sixth Pugwash Conference, held in Moscow, Nov. 26–Dec. 5, 1960) must consider as the *main success* of the Moscow discussion, from their point of view, the fact that Western participants left the conference with a *changed attitude* towards the importance of the Soviet proposals for total disarmament, and with an at least open-minded attitude towards the Soviet assertion of a willingness to accept effective methods of disarmament control . . ." (1961, April, p. 123). This example fits our needs for two reasons: first, it indicates that a change of attitude may be considered a major goal in an exchange of communications; and second, it confirms the suggestion that cooperative efforts to solve a problem (disarmament and arms control) may induce changes of images more effectively than straightforward communications. The American participants in the conference had no doubt read statements of the Russian position many times. But to work directly with the Russian scientists on details of problem solving can be far more convincing than such reading. It seems likely that the *credibility of the communicator* is also involved in such attitude changes.

The Pugwash Conference is of course privately sponsored. It would be desirable also to have governmentally arranged conferences in which small groups worked together on concrete tasks. The image of a nation, however, is probably shaped more by perceived national policies than by percepts of the citizens of that nation. We need, therefore, to be more inventive in developing new policies for the purpose of communicating the desired image. Let me examine just one example in this category.

Osgood's "Graduated Reciprocation" Proposal

One of the more elaborate proposals for communication with the Soviets, aimed at tension reduction, is that offered by Osgood (1959). His approach is based on the assumption that deeds speak louder than words—hence it is a policy proposal, not simply a propaganda device—but that deeds must be well-advertised if they are to communicate optimally.

Essentially the idea is that we should choose certain gestures which we can make unilaterally, and which will reduce our threat value vis-à-vis the Soviets without rendering ourselves helpless. Such gestures might include opening up certain nuclear arms locations to inspection by neutrals, closing overseas bases one at a time, declassifying certain scientific data, and so on. Each gesture would be carefully publicized, and each would be accompanied by an open invitation to the communists to reciprocate. This invitation, however, should not be specific; i.e., we should not define the reciprocal concession expected, but should point out the urgency of withdrawing threatening salients which increase tension.

The immediate and major obstacle to a communicative experiment of this sort is, of course, the presence of strongly opposed attitudes among American leaders and citizens. The general preference is for deeds which *increase* our threat-value to the Russians. This, not surprisingly, stimulates them to new efforts which enable them to threaten *us* more effectively. Osgood suggests that we must take the initiative in trying, even if on a very small scale, to reverse this vicious cycle.

Let us examine Osgood's "graduated reciprocation" proposal in terms of the theoretical frameworks discussed earlier.

In terms of S-R reinforcement theory, Osgood's proposal does not seem to make sense at all. Our first gesture in effect rewards the Soviets for their belligerence and obstinacy. The behavior elicited would probably be still more aggressive demands, applying pressure to us at another sensitive spot. This is the criticism of such policies offered by those who cry that such measures constitute "appeasement." With Hitler, it must be conceded, our gestures of conciliation led only to more aggression.

In terms of orthodox psychoanalytic theory, it would be predicted that Osgood's proposal would make no difference. If the dynamic of aggressive nationalism (or aggressive ethnocentrism, to take account of communism as an ideology) derives from infantile libidinal and aggressive cathexes, such gestures become unimportant. The leaders of the opposing party are driven by their own unconscious motivations, and our actions will be interpreted as tricks to deceive them into disarming so that we can launch a surprise attack.

An ego-oriented psychoanalyst might, of course, argue that Osgood's proposal is sound. In his view the hostility of the leaders is based upon perceived threats; for these, some basis exists in reality. The unilateral disarming gesture thus serves to reduce the need for ego defensiveness; and it follows plausibly that energy will be diverted to other pressing needs, thus inducing the reciprocity on which Osgood relies for success.

Finally, we may note that the cognitive theory supports Osgood's prediction. According to this view, mutual hostility derives from a cognitive structure in which certain traits are ascribed to the image of the opponent; and these views are supported by realistic percepts of policies and actions. The occurrence of the unilateral disarmament step creates cognitive dissonance in the opponent; the most likely mode of reduction of this dissonance will be a modification of the perceived attributes of the United States. Attitude change will, therefore, result. After a sufficient degree of tension reduction has been achieved, the perceptions by the parties of each other should make possible a more rational settlement of issues which do realistically pose conflicting demands.

The survey of research already presented does not help us decide whether the Osgood technique will work.[4] It seems clear, however, that we must quickly develop methods of communication which will have a favorable effect on international tensions.

CONCLUDING COMMENTS

In closing, I must make some regretful comments about the difficulties inherent in applying these theoretical and empirical studies to the reduction of international tension. Perhaps the most important derives from the fact that attitude change may be relatively unimportant or very important, depending on the social role of the person influenced. If we could change some percepts held by Nikita Khrushchev, the significance would be great; the same changes in the attitudes of Ivan Krylenko, a farmer in the Ukraine, would be of

---

[4] It is, however, encouraging to find that one simulation study using the Osgood strategy did in fact result in diminution of "tension" between "nations." See W. J. Crow and L. N. Solomon, *A simulation study of strategic doctrines.* LaJolla, Calif.: Western Behavioral Sciences Institute, 1962.

little import. Similarly, a change in the beliefs of Dean Rusk, the American Secretary of State, will have greater impact than a change in the views of John Smith, an assembly-line worker in Detroit.

Unfortunately, some of the factors we have enumerated as militating against attitude change are intense in the case of such key leaders as Khrushchev and Rusk. The images involved have a high level of phenomenal reality. They are embedded in a context having a marked degree of consistency. Messages which are dissonant with these beliefs elicit strong negative emotions and, in general, will not be received clearly. Misperceptions of such materials will be frequent. In fact, it will probably be futile to try to modify the attitudes of such individuals by purely verbal techniques. "Communications" will have to take the form of deeds, and even these must be carefully chosen, or their significance too will be distorted to confirm the pre-existing picture of reality.

Difficulties also arise, as regards modifying attitudes of leaders, by the fact that their views receive strong support from their immediate associates. Each national leader is likely to be surrounded by a group of persons who not only reinforce his misperceptions, but have their own reasons for clinging to these beliefs. President Eisenhower, in his "farewell address" to the nation early in 1961, called attention to the potent combination of military officers and big business executives which has been extremely influential in Washington. Sociologists like C. Wright Mills have spoken of a "power elite" which tends to have vested interests in nationalist attitudes. We can scarcely question that similar groups in the Soviet Union play important roles in governmental decisions.

Messages calling for a change in policy of another nation are further likely to be rejected because they constitute an attack on the ego of the foreign leader. When the Russians tell us that we should change our policy on West Berlin, they are in effect attacking all governmental officials who have had a hand in formulating or implementing that policy. And our calls for a change in their policy in Cuba are likely to produce a similarly ego-involved hostility.

Finally, let us consider the alternative of attempting to modify the attitudes of the rank-and-file citizens of a foreign nation. Here the crucial percepts are at a lower level of reality and are not embedded in the network of emotion and ego involvement as in the case of leaders. Verbal techniques, therefore, might be effective. But it is extraordinarily difficult to get any messages to the population in such nations as Russia, Hungary, and Communist China. Their newspapers and television networks are most unlikely to carry our messages. Conversely, one is not likely to find any paeans of praise for Soviet ideology in the American press or on our airwaves, for all our boasts about freedom of discussion. So, while changing attitudes of the rank and file might be of some value by modifying pressures upon leaders, the prospects do not look very good for this tactic either.

As a kind of summary to this wide-ranging chapter, let me offer the following resumé which may help to identify the linkages of various topics which I have discussed in rather rapid succession:

1. Policies which seek to aggrandize one group at the expense of another exacerbate group tensions.

2. Where members of these conflicting groups recognize a superior authority (as in the case of groups *within* a nation), it is possible to limit violence and foster peaceful accommodation.

3. In the case of nations as conflicting groups, no such superior authority is recognized, and violence in the service of the nation is judged to be good.

4. The prospects of peaceful settlements of international conflict are decreased to the extent that images of foreign nations involve attributes such as cruel, threatening, and untrustworthy. Such images reduce the effectiveness of communications from the foreign nation, and facilitate displacement of hostility onto the foreign group.

5. It would appear, therefore, that: (*a*) procedures for modifying images of other nations to make them more realistic would facilitate international communication and peaceful settlement of international disputes; and (*b*) steps to modify the image of the United Nations in the direction of attributes such as strength and justice would facilitate acceptance of an international authority to mediate and arbitrate such disputes.

6. Verbal communications have some (but limited) value in modifying such images. Prestige figures may induce modifications through suggestion and conformity effects. Logic appears to be somewhat less effective than direct appeals to emotion. The most effective communications seem to be on a non-verbal level, i.e., actions as opposed to purely symbolic messages.

7. In the interest of survival it appears that we should all be devising and testing methods for modifying conflict-exacerbating attitudes both within our own population and among citizens of other nations.

8. There are powerful psychological forces which operate to support nationalistic attitudes both here and in Russia. Research on, or even advocacy of, policies likely to reduce international tensions may encounter vigorous criticism.

It does not follow that psychologists should not engage in efforts aimed at reducing international tensions. The necessity of such efforts is clear, and the useful tactics have been fairly well delineated. We should work at this difficult task as if our lives depended on it—because they do.

PART FOUR

UNPLANNED CHANGE

It is a truism to state that individuals are constantly subjected to forces which tend to bring about changes in their characteristic modes of responding to their environments. Personality change, then, is not only a function of deliberate manipulations such as psychotherapy and training in human relations laboratories; there are also changes which happen as unplanned and often uncontrolled consequences of other events. For example, when inexpensive labor is imported from a neighboring country, no one is deliberately planning to bring about fundamental changes in the personality characteristics of the workers, their families, and their descendants. Nevertheless, these changes do occur. In this final portion of our symposium several such situations and their effects on personality are discussed. Two major facts stand out in the presentations given in these final four chapters. First, the effects of these "real-life" situations are probably more powerful and far-reaching than any psychological technique yet devised to influence personality. Second, our knowledge of such effects is quite limited, and the field is in need of an increased amount of systematic research.

As a bridge between studies of planned and unplanned changes in personality, Haggard presents material on isolation which encompasses both experimental manipulation of isolation conditions and the effects of naturally occurring isolation experiences. Haggard suggests that the crucial factor in changing personality is a change in environmental conditions for which preexisting habits, etc., are inappropriate. If the changed conditions endure for a sufficient period of time, changes in personality variables are to be expected. As a specific example of such altered conditions, he discusses isolation with respect to its effect on behavior and with respect to individual differences in response to such situations. In addition, he presents a schematic formulation in which changes in environment, in adaptive mechanisms, and in motivation may be conceptualized.

The history of the United States is a history of the blending of cultures from all parts of the world. As wave after wave of immigrants have attempted to settle in a new land, there have been inevitable conflicts in terms of the confrontation of different languages, different customs, and perhaps most important, different value systems. To some extent, both the existing majority culture and the incoming minority culture are affected by this clash. The eventual result in succeeding generations is a homogeneous culture somewhat different from either original group. In the meantime, what of the effect on individuals involved in the value conflicts? Madsen brings the approach of an anthropologist to this question and explores some of the facets of value conflicts as revealed in his own work with Mexican-Americans in South Texas. After summarizing a number of the specific differences in values held by the Anglo and the Latin groups, Madsen discusses the effects of these value conflicts on those caught between two cultures. The pressures from the Anglo culture for change in the Mexican-American culture are exerted in a variety of forms with the public schools, the church, and the public health services predominating. Madsen indicates the general results stemming from this situation and exemplifies one type of outcome with a description of the problem faced by one individual trying to move across cultures.

Of obvious importance in investigations of personality development is the influence of experiences within the family setting. It is also true that various events within the family may occur which bring about both temporary and long-lasting changes in the developing individuals. The Yarrows discuss this problem and point out that such studies must reject the classical psychoanalytic notion that personality structure is irreversibly fixed by the end of infancy. They examine both normal changes that occur within most families (birth of siblings, differing expectations for different aged children) and more unusual changes in the form of crises and traumatic events that can disrupt the family. It is clear that the family environment changes during the development of a child—in feelings, attitudes, and child-rearing practices. However, more data are badly needed to assess the effects of these changes. The Yarrows discuss the available evidence dealing with personality consistency, and conclude that the degree of consistency depends on the specificity of the variable studied and on the points in the developmental sequence which are sampled. They summarize the literature on normal changes in the family environment and the more voluminous data on the effects of severe disruptions following crises. They indicate that one of the greatest needs in this area of research is a more precise conceptualization of the way in which such variables as "broken homes" are mediated to the family members.

While only a relatively limited number of individuals undergo psychotherapy or brainwashing or the confrontation of different cultures, everyone is influenced by the processes associated with aging throughout his life span. Kuhlen discusses both some of the methodological problems involved in research on aging and a portion of the substantive findings in this type of developmental research. Among the topics considered are motivational changes with specific data concerning a group of motives broadly conceived as needs for growth and expansion along with the reverse process of disengagement. Increases in anxiety and symptoms of maladjustment also seem to be a function of aging. In addition, particular patterns of anxiety-reducing behavior become more common in later years. Aging does not involve only change, however, and Kuhlen also presents evidence pertinent to stability of traits. He concludes with a suggestion that future research should concentrate on the identification of those independent variables which account for the relationships between age and various dependent variables.

chapter thirteen

Isolation and Personality

Ernest A. Haggard

The question of personality change can be approached in different ways. We are all familiar with the fact that personality changes as the result of development over time and that innumerable experiential factors tend to shape and modify it. This approach to personality change has been highly fruitful. In fact, most of what we know today about personality—its development, vicissitudes, and characteristics—can be credited to the genetic approach. However, it is also possible to speculate about a hypothetical state of personality stability and the conditions under which personality would be expected to change. From this point of view, we would expect that as long as the person (including his motives, attitudes, habits, and so on) and his environment do not change appreciably, his "personality" would remain unchanged. Correspondingly, we would expect "personality changes" to occur when there are appreciable changes in the person and/or in his environmental context.

In this discussion I will refer to several types and conditions of isolation specifically to emphasize that significant changes in the environmental context can effect marked personality changes and, more generally, to suggest a schema for conceptualizing some of the major determinants of personality. In terms of general content, my discussion will be divided into two main sections. In the first section I will review some of the more consistent conditions and effects of short-term isolation under more or less rigorous experimental conditions—that is, the *experimental isolation* [1] of subjects for periods

[1] Various terms have been used in connection with studies involving marked decreases of sensory stimulation of one sort or another. The general term "experimental isolation"

This investigation was supported in part by a Public Health Service research career program award (MH-K6-9415) from the National Institute of Mental Health.

up to about a week. In the second section I will review some of the accounts, usually anecdotal or autobiographical, of the *extreme or extended isolation* of individuals, often for periods lasting from several weeks to over a year. Following each of these sections I will discuss some of the theoretical considerations which bear upon questions of personality and personality change.

EXPERIMENTAL ISOLATION

The now famous "perceptual isolation" studies were begun about a decade ago by several investigators in Hebb's laboratory at McGill. The initial experiments of Bexton, Doane, Heron, and Scott at McGill have been followed by many studies in which various types of individuals have been subjected to a variety of experimental conditions for varying lengths of time. I will not attempt to review all of these studies—partly because there are too many of them and partly because several excellent summaries of this literature have recently appeared, such as those by Scott (1957), Solomon et al. (1957, 1961), Wheaton (1959), Rosenzsweig (1959), Fiske (1961), Freedman et al. (1961), Kubzansky (1961), Miller (1962), Zuckerman and Cohen (1964), and various chapters in West (1962).

The reported experiments can be divided into two main groups: those emphasizing the characteristic reactions of subjects to the specified conditions of experimental isolation and those emphasizing the individual differences among the subjects in their reactions to such conditions.

Studies Emphasizing Effects of Experimental Conditions

Because of the many procedural variations among this group of studies, it is not possible to summarize here all of the experimental conditions and their effects on the experiences and behavior of the subjects. However, in most cases normal adults were placed in some sort of confining "isolation chamber" in which they experienced a marked reduction in sensory input, either in the overall amount or in the degree of patterning of visual, auditory, tactual, and kinesthetic cues, and involving a general restriction of bodily movement and contact with other persons. Thus, in some experiments the subjects were in darkness and in others they saw light through translucent goggles; some

will be used to designate the many types of studies involving such reduced sensory stimulation and other activity under more or less controlled or experimental conditions. Such terms as "interference with reality contact," "afferent isolation," "reduced level of sensory input," "reduced sensory patterning," "perceptual isolation," "sensory isolation," "perceptual deprivation," and "sensory deprivation" have frequently been used to refer to this type of experimental situation.

subjects were in cubicles and others were in tank-type respirators; in some experiments the subjects were in relative quiet and in others they heard "white noise" of random frequencies through earphones; in some experiments the subjects were restrained or had their arms in cardboard cuffs and hands gloved to minimize movement and tactual stimulation; in others they were unrestrained physically but asked to move about as little as possible. Although in most of the experiments the subjects were alone in the isolation chamber, they nevertheless knew that they were not really cut off from others but, rather, were being watched or monitored and that they could terminate the experiment on demand.

The dramatic effects of "just doing nothing and having nothing happen," even for short periods of time, have been reported by the subjects both during and after isolation. In most cases, the subjects reported a variety of sensory, sensory-motor, affective, and cognitive changes during the experiment. Although the reported disturbances are not the same in all cases, there appears to be a general deterioration and lability (and often unpredictability) of the usual mental processes and functions. More specifically, reported changes include such perceptual disturbances as the spontaneous appearance of partial or full-blown visual, auditory, and somatic illusions, hallucinations, or delusions, color anomalies and distortions of tactual experience, body image, and the time sense. Affective disturbances, including spontaneous bursts of such affects as fear, anxiety, and anger, or reactions involving restlessness, boredom, agitation, and a sense of depersonalization were frequently reported. As for cognitive processes, some subjects reported a rapid disintegration of their ability to attend, concentrate, or think in a directed and sustained manner, to solve abstract problems or even to carry out such simple tasks as serial counting. Instead, they reported that their minds often went blank or, if active, were involuntarily filled with emotionally toned and highly personalized thoughts and images (cf. Bexton et al., 1954; Lilly, 1956). The range and intensity of such perceptual, cognitive, affective, and other behavioral changes have led several writers to infer that the conditions of experimental isolation may induce a temporary traumatic neurosis (e.g., Bressler et al., 1959), or that the subjects in these experiments may show any or virtually all of the "symptoms" which characterize mentally ill patients such as schizophrenics (e.g., Rosenzsweig, 1959).

In contrast to the usual "symptoms" which develop under the impact of experimental isolation, performance on some tasks either did not show marked deterioration or improved moderately in the case of some relatively simple functions, such as mirror drawing (e.g., Heron, 1961), sensory acuity and discrimination (e.g., Doane et al., 1959; Shurley, 1960), perception of apparent

movement (e.g., Ormiston, 1958), digit span (e.g., Cohen et al., 1961) and
rote learning (e.g., Vernon and Hoffman, 1956; Vernon and McGill, 1957).
It appears that experimental isolation resulted in such facilitation only when
the tasks were not self-initiated, were externally structured, and did not
require the subject to engage in complex integrative functions (see also Zuckerman et al., 1962).

Following isolation, subjects have also reported corollary disturbances lasting
for periods ranging from a few minutes to several days or longer after the
isolation experience had ended.   Many of the reported post isolation effects
were visual, perhaps because in most cases the subjects had been in darkness
or had been deprived of pattern vision as a result of having worn translucent
goggles while in isolation.   These visual disturbances include the apparent
movement of objects, changes in the size and shape of persons and objects,
pronounced negative afterimages, luminescence, shimmering or subjective
colors, instability and fluctuations of lines, contours, and surfaces, and the disruption of habitual visual-motor coordinations.   These disturbances generally
were dissipated within the first half-hour or so after isolation (cf. Heron et al.,
1956; Doane et al., 1959).   Frequently, however, subjects reported that certain
reactions persisted a good deal longer, such as feelings of fatigue, dizziness,
drowsiness, loss of motivation, feelings of being confused or disoriented; and
some reported continued preoccupation with various thoughts and feelings,
such as the fears and anxieties or suggestions which occurred during isolation.

Although the variability among the reported effects during and following
isolation can presumably be attributed to the wide differences among both the
experimental conditions used and the individuals who were subjected to them,
the effects themselves appear to be due, at least in part, to the marked reduc-
tions in the basic aspects of sensory stimulation and the duration of the experience.   That is to say, the major experimental variables—or at least those which
can be controlled experimentally—are the degree of reduction of: (a) the overall level of external stimulation involving one or more modalities—i.e., reduced sensory input, (b) the temporal and spatial patterning of such stimuli—
i.e., reduced information, (c) the overall level of proprioceptive stimulation because of restricted bodily movement, and (d) the duration of these conditions.

The experiments which best demonstrate the extent to which the reduction
of sensory stimulation will produce the classical effects of experimental isolation were initiated by Lilly (1956).   He attempted to reduce all physical
stimuli to the lowest possible level by having the subject immersed in a tank
of slowly flowing water of near-body temperature (94.5°F.), with his only
contact a light-proof face mask for breathing.   Thus the subject, who was supposed to inhibit all movements as far as possible, could feel only slight tactual

stimulation from the face mask and could hear only his own breathing and the muted gurgling of water in the pipe. Lilly, who was one of the subjects, reported the following characteristic sequence of experiences. The first hour was taken up with a review of recent experiences and events and a developing relaxed enjoyment of feeling isolated in space. During the second hour, acute tensions involving a pervasive "stimulus-action" hunger or craving developed, and he found intense satisfaction in such self-stimulation as rubbing his fingers together or making slow movements to feel the flow of water over the skin. The inhibition of such maneuvers might result in a build-up of tensions which, in turn, could force him to leave the tank. If he inhibited all voluntary movements, he was able to attend only to any available stimuli, such as the slight pressure of the face mask; the awareness of such stimuli became the whole content of his consciousness. During the third hour, Lilly observed a shift from directed thinking to reveries and fantasies which were so highly personal and emotionally charged that he never reported them; he also experienced full three-dimensional hallucinations, including forms like those sometimes seen in hypnogogic states. After leaving the tank, he reported the illusion that the day started anew after immersion and that he found it was necessary to readjust to social intercourse in subtle ways.[2]

In addition to the more obvious experimental variables, several other and less manifest variables also may modify the subject's experiences and behavior during experimental isolation. One such variable is the degree of social isolation and its meaning to the subject. Although social isolation per se does not result in the usual behavioral changes (e.g., Steinkamp et al., 1959; Freedman et al., 1961) the immediate or remote presence of other persons—i.e., a relative decrease in the degree of social isolation—tends to alleviate the severity of the isolation symptoms (e.g., Linn et al., 1953; Davis et al., 1961). Furthermore, although in most experiments the subjects were isolated from vis-à-vis contact with other persons during the experiment, they were nevertheless aware that the experimenters were "out there" observing and monitoring them. In none of the experiments were the subjects led to believe that they would be aban-

---

[2] At the time of his reports, Lilly (1956) had not remained in the tank longer than three hours, although subjects in similar experiments have remained as long as 400 minutes (cf. Shurley, 1960), and Graveline and Balke (1960), who kept subjects immersed under somewhat different conditions most of the time for periods up to seven days, did not discuss psychological effects of immersion but did report marked changes in cardiovascular reflexes, diminished muscle tone and disruption of psychomotor effectiveness, and a sharp decrease in need for sleep. It should also be noted that although Camberari (1958) carried out experiments similar to Lilly's, he did not report similar findings, perhaps indicating the great importance of individual differences among subjects in such experiments.

doned (even though some feared they might be); on the contrary, they had been told that they could terminate the experiment at will and on demand. As a consequence of this fact, the reported range, type, and intensity of the symptoms generated under conditions of experimental isolation may not be fully generalizable to situations in which individuals actually are isolated from other persons, regardless of the surroundings. It is to be expected that if the subjects had been deprived of the means of controlling the duration of the isolation, they would have been under substantially greater stress and experienced more pronounced disturbances (cf. Haggard, 1949).

A second possible variable is the degree of physical and psychological passivity imposed on the subjects in experimental isolation. In most cases, and for most of the time in isolation, the subjects either were not called upon to do, or were prevented from doing, much of anything that corresponded to their usual adaptive behaviors. Since the effects of such enforced passivity have not been studied apart from isolation, it is not possible to determine the extent that enforced passivity contributed to the various disturbances which were reported. It is possible that hallucinations and other phenomena often associated with inhibited bodily movement may have been due as much to the backwash of being unable to "work off" or express in normal fashions aroused energies or tensions as to the decreased kinesthetic or proprioceptive stimulation which normally supports the functions of the higher centers.

A third possible variable is the degree of unfamiliarity of the isolation situation, including its monotonous aspects, and the fact that in the normal course of events the subjects had not experienced or had occasion to develop cognitive structures and adaptive behaviors to cope with such situations in the waking state.[3] Furthermore, during longer periods, isolation almost necessarily involves a major disruption of usual routines to the extent that the subject will tend to lose the time referents or other cognitive structures which he had used to orient his thoughts and behaviors so that, for example, he becomes "lost in time." The absence or loss of appropriate cognitive structures may significantly increase the stressful aspects of such situations (cf. Haggard, 1949; Levy et al., 1959).

[3] There are indications that in cases where an individual has repeatedly experienced the conditions of experimental isolation, adaptive mechanisms develop which tend to reduce the disturbing aspects of the experience and, in fact, may result in integrative and lasting personality changes (cf. Lilly 1956 and his discussion of Shurley's paper, 1960, p. 545; Pollard et al., 1962; Ruff et al., 1961). Or, to state the point differently, it would be expected that persons who had become accustomed to such sensorially restricted and monotonous surroundings while awake would have developed adaptive means for dealing with such situations, hence would not tend to experience the usual reported disturbances with the same frequency and intensity.

Studies Emphasizing Individual Differences Among Subjects

In almost every report of the effects of experimental isolation, the point has been emphasized that subjects vary widely in their reactions to such conditions. Although a few general tendencies hold for most subjects, the range of individuals' reactions to isolation is almost as striking as are the reactions themselves. For example, some subjects were able to "take" isolation for at least a week without undue strain whereas others were able to endure comparable conditions for less than an hour; some subjects rather enjoyed the experience whereas others reacted with paranoid-type fantasies and became almost panic-stricken—and similar differences occurred with respect to the various sensory, cognitive, and related corollaries of isolation. The differences in how individuals react to isolation have been reported for normal subjects, mental patients, such as schizophrenics, and persons in "non-experimental" situations, such as solitary confinement in prison.[4]

In the studies which have focused attention on individual differences among normal subjects, it was found that their reactions to the stress of isolation are, as is the case in ordinary life, related to their personality structure (e.g., Wexler et al., 1958; Levy et al., 1959; Shurley, 1960) and tend to involve an exaggeration of their characteristic adaptive and defense mechanisms (e.g., Mendelson et al., 1961; Ruff et al., 1961). Reactions to isolation are related to the ways the individual habitually relates to other persons and objects and his dependence on them to maintain his own orientation and adjustment (e.g., Cohen et al., 1961). The central factor relating to tolerance for isolation apparently has to do with how much the individual tends to be oriented primarily toward his inner life and experiences or toward the external world. Individuals with self-concepts, egos (or whatever) strong enough so that they could "withdraw into themselves" and be passive toward the external environment seemed to fare much better in the isolation situation than those who could not. Although there have been relatively few studies of individual differences, the ones which have appeared are compatible with the above proposition. For example, both satiability and tolerance for pain [5] were negatively related to tolerance for isolation (Petrie et al., 1960) and such characteristics as suggestibility (Camberari, 1958) and a tendency to be "body dependent" rather

[4] For example, Meltzer (1956) observed that "there were some inmates who were inclined to use solitary as a retreat and catalyst for a regressive experience of the mystical union type. This was the fellow who instead of being shoved into solitary, would dive into solitary in the way some people dive into bed at the end of a hard day" (p. 99).

[5] Since a large component of experienced pain depends upon prior experience (cf. Melzack, 1961), it is reasonable to expect that satiability and pain tolerance should be positively related insofar as both imply heavy reliance on external factors.

than "field dependent," as measured by figure-drawing and the rod-and-frame tests, were positively related to ability to tolerate isolation (Silverman et al., 1961).

In investigating individual differences among subjects, Goldberger and Holt (1961) designed studies to test several hypotheses regarding the subject's personality structure and his reactions during an eight-hour period of isolation. Their studies were based on the general psychoanalytic theory of primary and secondary thought processes [6] and Rapaport's (1958) theory of the ego's relative autonomy from id and environmental forces. On the basis of preisolation Rorschach scores (cf. Holt and Havel, 1960), the subjects were divided into those who could, and those who could not, deal with their primary processes in a mature, flexible fashion. In comparing the reactions of these two groups of subjects, Goldberger and Holt found several significant differences between them on the behavioral measures collected during the period of isolation. They found, for example, that the subjects who could handle with maturity and flexibility their primary process thoughts were, when in isolation, better able to control or engage freely in daydreaming and fantasy or, if they chose, also engage freely in secondary process thought; they were better able to amuse themselves by singing or talking, welcomed and enjoyed more vivid visual and auditory imagery, and experienced little negative affect but rather were able to relax and tended to enjoy themselves in the situation. On the other hand, the subjects scored as having difficulty in handling primary process thoughts were, when in isolation, unable to control intrusions of bizarre or non-rational thoughts and were made anxious by them, had more difficulty controlling their rational thoughts, tended to quit earlier or be preoccupied with the idea of quitting the experiment early (see also Goldberger and Holt, 1958; Holt and Goldberger, 1959, 1961; and Goldberger, 1961). Thus, although isolation resulted in a variety of visual and other disturbances for all the subjects, certain aspects of their character structure appear to have determined in large measure both the nature of their experiences and how they dealt with them.

The relatively few studies in which psychiatric patients have been sub-

[6] Primary process thought refers to the more primitive, prelogical, irrational, drive-dominated, and unrealistic thought processes whereas secondary process thought refers to the more mature, logical, rational, orderly, and realistic thought processes. These two types of thought processes are assumed to be on a continuum. (In terms of the conceptual scheme presented in a later section, one might say that, within the *A-B-C* system, in primary process thinking the *A-B* component relationships predominate whereas in secondary process thinking the *B-C* component relationships predominate, where *C* exists in reality or is a memory representation of it.) See also Hilgard's (1962) discussion of primary-secondary process thinking.

jected to experimental isolation have not only shown the usual variations in their reactions to such conditions but, in general, their reactions to the isolation experience have been markedly different from those of normals.[7] That is to say, psychiatric patients have tended not to experience the typical visual, etc., disturbances reported by normal subjects but, instead, the period of isolation characteristically appears to have had a negligible or even a therapeutic effect. For example, B. Cohen et al. (1959) reported that schizophrenic subjects responded positively and without anxiety to isolation, and Harris (1959) reported that, in contrast to normal subjects, the intensity of schizophrenics' psychotic hallucinatory activity frequently was reduced or absent during isolation and that some subjects were reluctant to leave the situation. Other investigators have suggested that for various types of psychiatric patients isolation may provide substantial therapeutic gains, either by itself or as a therapeutic tool in conjunction with other approaches or techniques (cf. Azima et al., 1961).

The possibly beneficial therapeutic effects that partial or brief periods of isolation may have for psychiatric patients were indicated in a study by Azima and Cramer (1956). They found that such patients, after being subjected to partial sensory and expressive isolation, tended to show an initial phase of disorganization, which frequently was followed by a partial personality reorganization involving constructive aggression and increased responsiveness to other persons in their environment. Similarly, Gibby et al. (1960) reported that periods of isolation lasting up to six hours resulted in a variety of positive changes for most of the psychiatric patients in their study. Some of the characteristic changes include a relaxing of the patients' customary defenses—which frequently led to a recall and verbalization of previously forgotten experiences, a temporary increase in anxiety or expression of hostility, an increased awareness of their inner conflicts and anxieties, and insight into the fact that their difficulties often arose from inner more than outer factors—which in turn led to increased efforts to relate to and communicate with others and to seek therapeutic help from the professional staff. Systematic ratings of the patients' behavior also showed a number of significant positive changes, such as their being less apathetic, withdrawn, suspicious, evasive and guarded, showing and reporting less anxiety and signs of disorganized thinking, and

---

[7] For example, Smith et al. (1961), who subjected both normals and schizophrenics to comparable isolation conditions, observed that "normal subjects find great difficulty in adapting to or tolerating the stress of sensory isolation but schizophrenics find no difficulty. It appears to be their normal habitat" (p. 843). This observation suggests that schizophrenics have developed waking-state mechanisms which are more adaptive to the conditions of experimental isolation than to (what is for most individuals) the normal physical-social environment.

making fewer somatic complaints.[8]   Although some negative changes were reported, most of the subjects showed positive changes on most of the behavior rating scales shortly after isolation.   Furthermore, when the subjects were again rated a week later, it was found that the positive changes were more numerous and more lasting than the negative, disruptive changes, and that the individuals who did improve tended to hold virtually all of their improvement.   In a corollary study, Cooper et al.   (1962) reported that the patients showed a marked tendency for improvement on such Rorschach measures as form level and Cartwright's (1958) ego strength scores, with the patients who functioned least well before the isolation experience showing the greatest gain.

In summary, a comparison of the reactions of normal and psychiatric patients to experimental isolation can be viewed as illustrating the adage, "one man's meat is another man's poison."   That is to say, many normals apparently react to the experience of isolation with the same range of disturbances that many psychiatric patients show in their reactions to ordinary life situations, and vice versa.   Thus, it appears that, in contrast to normal subjects, psychiatric patients such as schizophrenics have somehow negated the cue value of many of the normal environmental stimuli, so that they have come to react to the usual physical and social realities of most persons as though they did not exist.

Situations Related to Experimental Isolation

Although many of the effects of the recent isolation experiments are dramatic, they are not qualitatively different from those reported by individuals in many other situations involving the restraint of habitual bodily movement in restricted, monotonous, or otherwise unfamiliar environments.   Representative situations in which individuals have reported such phenomena include interstate truck drivers (cf. McFarland et al., 1942) and pilots flying missions alone at night (cf. Rosenzsweig, 1959) or at high altitudes (cf. Bennett, 1961), orthopedic patients suffering prolonged immobilization or poliomyelitic pa-

---

[8] However, not all of the studies using psychiatric patients have reported positive therapeutic effects following experimental isolation.   Smith et al. (1961) reported that their subjects did show an initial period of disorganization (almost catatonic stupor) without any following increase in motivation or socialization, and Azima and Cramer-Azima (1957) reported that an obsessive-compulsive patient developed what appeared to be a paranoid psychotic episode during five days of isolation.   In order to generalize about the role of isolation as a therapeutic agent with psychiatric patients, it will be necessary first to investigate the effects of such subject variables as age, type, degree, and duration of the illness and such experimental variables as the type, duration, etc. of the isolation conditions.

tients in tank-type respirators (cf. Mendelson et al., 1961), and hypnosis (cf. Gill and Brenman, 1959). In all these situations, individuals have reported such sensory phenomena as hallucinations, a sense of unreality, and various affective disturbances. Pronounced effects also have been reported when individuals have been separated by one means or another from their usual social or physical environments, with resulting reports of "culture shock" (cf. Muller-Hagemann, 1958), the psychoses of language-isolated refugees (Allers, 1920; Pedersen, 1949) and prisoners in solitary confinement (Nitsche and Wilmanns, 1912), "arctic" or "desert madness" of persons in bleak environments, "black patch delerium" or related disturbances of persons recently deafened or undergoing surgery for cataracts or patients with detached retinas (cf. Greenwood, 1928; Bartlet, 1951; Leiderman et al., 1958; Weisman and Hackett, 1958; Arbit, 1960; Ziskind et al., 1960; Davis et al., 1961). All of these reports indicate that normal functioning depends in part on the existence of an environment with which the individual is familiar and can act effectively.

There have also been reports of isolation-type disturbances in connection with various experimental situations involving atypical sensory experience. These situations include, for example, sensory overload, as when two or more sense modalities are subjected to stimuli of greater than normal intensity, sensory distortion, as when an individual experiences delayed auditory feedback (cf. Lindsley, 1961) or wears distortion lenses, the visual rearrangement experiments of Kohler, Stratton, and Held, which involve a vertically inverted or laterally reversed or displaced visual field (cf. Held, 1961), distortions of afterimages (cf. Ferree, 1908), and the autokinetic effect—the apparent movement of a stationary pin-point light in a dark visual field. Incidentally, the autokinetic effect (which involves the minimal remnant of the usual visual field) bears several similarities to experimental isolation: its onset and extent are increased by the restraint of bodily movement (Goldman, 1953), it is made more persistent by isolation (Doane et al., 1959), the effect occurs much more often in normal than in schizophrenic subjects (Kline, in Lilly, 1956, p. 22) with large variation among psychiatric groups (Voth, 1947), and the nature of the visual distortion is similar to some of those observed following isolation.[9] Although the autokinetic effect usually occurs within a matter of seconds or minutes, it appears to be due to active central processes which "take over" in the absence of the regulating and structuring function of the normal visual field (cf. Haggard and Rose, 1944; Haggard and Babin, 1948). In any case, experimental isolation and these various clinical or experimental situations have in common the fact that they involve conditions which deviate in

---

[9] Freedman (1961) reports that, following eight hours of isolation, "shapes seemed to flow in a direction away from the fixation point" (p. 18)—the typical apparent movement of the stationary pin-point light which is the autokinetic effect.

one way or another from the usual modes of sensory experience and environmental adaptation.

Theoretical Considerations

The explanations which have been proposed to account for the phenomena associated with experimental isolation vary widely: some pertain to a single modality such as vision whereas others pertain to the total adaptive behavior of the individual, and some are in neurophysiological terms whereas others are in psychological terms. A representative sample of the proposed explanations range from: deviations from the customary activity patterns—such as level and phasing—in the reticular system (e.g., Lindsley, 1961); the decrease in sensory stimulation below the level necessary for normal mental functioning (e.g., Lilly, 1956); the incorporation of "non-order" into the spatial schemata necessary for normal adaptive behavior, which results in the deterioration of those schemata (e.g., Freedman et al., 1961); the existence of stimulus conditions which are atypical in terms of the exposure-history of the individual (e.g., Held, 1961); the decrease in the relevance of the stimuli, or the amount of "information," necessary for adaptive behavior (e.g., Rosenzsweig, 1959); and the removal of the normal external reality reduces the ego's relative autonomy from the id forces, so that primary process and related phenomena predominate (e.g., Rapaport, 1958). Although such explanations may be complementary and all of them may be valid, they vary in their relevance to the central interest of this symposium, viz., personality and personality change.

In line with this interest, I would like to sketch out parts of a behavioral system which will, I believe, be useful in conceptualizing personality and personality change as well as the phenomena associated with experimental isolation. This system has three major components: [10] *A,* the energetics of behavior; *B,* the structures and schemata, innate or acquired, that organize and regulate behavior, overt or covert; [11] and *C,* the environmental context in which the behavior occurs.

[10] This term is used in a sense analogous to the "components of variance" in an analysis of variance model—i.e., the definable sources of variation and their interactions which together make up the scores or units (or here, the behaviors) which are of interest to the investigator.

[11] Although it may be sufficient for our purposes here to think of the *B* component in such global terms, its characteristics will need to be defined more specifically to deal effectively with such psychoanalytic concepts as: the ego and superego, primary and secondary thought processes or primary and secondary ego autonomies, or with such related concepts as: the first and second signaling systems, concrete and abstract thinking, or sensory-motor and conceptual intelligence (cf. Bridger, 1960).

The *A, B,* and *C* components are, of course, familiar constructs. For example, the *A* component corresponds in general to what has been called primary or basic drive, id, impulse, urge, or motivational state. The *B* component, which involves the means by which the individual interacts with his environment (e.g., perception, learning, memory, thinking, and overt response) has been referred to by such terms as mind, self, and ego, and various constructs (e.g., associations, central integrations, cell assemblies, engrams, memory traces, psychic structures, and schemata) have been inferred to account for the development and nature of the *B* component. The *C* component refers to parts or all of the total environmental stimuli, reality, field or context, including the cultural, social, and physical aspects of it, and to which the "individual" (i.e., the *A* and *B* components) must relate in one way or another. Although these three components are not quite coordinate and the boundaries between them are not quite clear, it is essential to keep in mind that the properties of the three components must be considered in concert and as aspects of a conceptual unity.[12]

The behavioral system involving the *A, B,* and *C* components rests on certain general assumptions or propositions, such as:

1. At birth the normal infant possesses the constitutional structures necessary for survival in a benign and supportive environment. This assumption implies the existence of those primitive *B* structures and/or schemata which permit at least minimal articulation (or adaptation) between the *A* and *C* components which are normal for neonates.

2. Along with the rapidly developing neurophysiological structures, new schemata develop to facilitate new *ABC* articulations under increasingly complex but relatively specifiable *A* and *C* conditions. In the human being, the system initially is dominated primarily by the *A* component (i.e., the infant is "practically all id"), but with time the *B* component develops in relation to an increasingly complex *C* component, so that (relative to *A*) *B* and *C* come to play increasingly important roles in determining behavior. Along with the intrinsic differences in the properties of individuals' *A, B,* and *C* components, with time increased definition develops between the *A* and *B* and the *B* and *C* components and the relationships among them, so that in-

[12] The proposition that, in appraising any particular behavior, two or more of the components must be considered in concert is not new. For example, Klein and Krech (1952) emphasized the indivisibility of motivation and cognition and Werner and Wapner (1952, 1956) have emphasized the indivisibility of the person and his perceptual world. Furthermore, the general outlines of this behavioral system are similar in many respects to those discussed by such psychoanalytically oriented theorists as Hartmann (1939), Gill and Rapaport (cf. Rapaport, 1958; Gill and Brenman, 1959; Gill, 1959; Rapaport and Gill, 1959) and Miller, 1962.

dividuals will differ with respect to their AB, BC, and ABC definitions and relationships.

3. Particular B schemata "have their roots" in both the particular A and C components existing at the time such B schemata are developed. Subsequently, particular B schemata will be activated if the associated A's and C's exist and are sufficiently imperative. Using the subscript (e) to indicate existing or familiar conditions and the subscript (i) to indicate new or unfamiliar conditions (e.g., isolation), then if schemata B_e were developed under conditions which define components A_e and C_e, given A_e and C_e the existing B_e schemata will be activated. If, on the other hand, A_i and C_i differ significantly from A_e and C_e, then given A_i and/or C_i, the B_e schemata will not be activated. (In discussing the effects of isolation we will consider primarily changes in the B component which result from changes in C. It is also to be expected that any marked changes in the A component will result in changes in the B component under unchanged C conditions. Examples of changes in A include short-term shifts from one drive state to another and such long-term shifts as are involved in the preadolescent to postadolescent changes. The fact that henceforth the A component will not be specified by a subscript does not mean that it could not be—e.g., as sex or aggression—but rather that such specification is not essential for the purposes of this discussion.)

With respect to greater than usual changes in the C component—as for example, in the experimental isolation and related situations—individuals will be expected to vary in their types and patterns of response insofar as they differ in terms of their A and B components. But, generally speaking, let us assume: first, that the individual enters isolation with a range of existing B schemata (B_e's) which are appropriate for the range of C_e's familiar to him and, second, that the isolation condition involves a change of the C component from C_e to C_i, for which appropriate B_i have not yet been developed. In experimental isolation, C_i typically involves a marked decrease in the strength (or "input") and/or definition (or "information") of the C component. Then, under the C_i conditions, and in the absence of appropriate B_i:

4. If the change from C_e to C_i is relatively moderate, of short duration, or readily terminable:

  (a) The total system will attempt to maintain its customary $A_e B_e C_e$ relationships. If this is not possible,

  (b) The definition of the B component will change, with the change determined in part by the characteristics of C_i and in part by the nature of A and the general relations between the A and B components. Under these conditions,

  (c) New B schemata and AB relationships which are appropriate to C_i will tend to develop. If appropriate B_i schemata do not become available—

i.e., if the A, B, and C components remain inarticulate—the system may be described as being under "stress," with an eventual change of the A component also. Under these conditions,

(d) The system will attempt various maneuvers to make the three components articulate, as by terminating the experiment in order to reinstate C_e, for which appropriate B schemata do exist.

5. If the change from C_e to C_i is sufficiently great and/or persistent, and if appropriate B_i are not available, the total system can be characterized as being under severe stress, especially if associated stress factors are present. If, under conditions of extreme or extended isolation, the system is not able to maintain its customary $A_eB_eC_e$ relationships, develop appropriate B_i or reinstate C_e, the behavioral integrity of the system will be lost.

In order to relate the above propositions to questions of personality change as a result of experimental isolation, it is necessary first to specify what we mean by "personality." Although there are no clear, concise, and generally accepted definitions of personality, the term generally refers to "what a person is like," especially his individuality as he habitually relates to and is seen by other persons. However, in the more sophisticated attempts to define the concept of personality, its development and its functions, it is difficult to distinguish between the phenomena of learning and of personality. This difficulty raises the question of whether the presumed differences between these two orientations are fundamental or only superficial.

In terms of the A, B, and C components, "learning theorists" traditionally have been concerned primarily with the specifiable conditions which, over time, facilitate the development and maintenance of new B schemata. Such conditions involve, for example, the nature and strength of the A component, the nature and stability of existing B schemata, and various intensity and spaciotemporal patternings of the C component, and the relationships among these conditions. In addition, learning theorists generally have studied primarily verbal and motor behaviors and often have used animals as subjects, partly as a matter of methodological convenience. "Personality theorists," on the other hand, traditionally have been concerned primarily with the overall functioning of the individual at a given time in definable C situations, especially with respect to the motivational, affective, attitudinal, and interpersonal aspects of the behavior of human subjects. Some of them (e.g., most psychoanalysts) have emphasized the relationships between the A and B components whereas others (e.g., most psychologists) have emphasized the relationships between the B (or AB) and C components. But although learning and personality theorists—and hence the facts and theories which have interested them—have emphasized different aspects of behavior, such artifacts as differential substantive interests, historical emphasis, or methodological approaches in no way means that there need be any fundamental difference between learning theory and personality theory. Our purpose here is to outline a behavioral system which appears to permit an integration of "learning" and "personality" phenomena.[13]

If we consider that personality involves relationships among the existing A, B, and C components, then personality change involves a significant modification of one or more of these components, and hence of their overall relationships. In the experimental isolation studies we have seen that marked changes in the environmental context have resulted in a variety of dramatic changes in overt and covert behavior. Without attempting to rereview this literature, the above propositions can be used to draw general conclusions which relate, directly or indirectly, to the phenomena associated with experimental isolation. For example:

If any one generalization applies to all the findings from the experimental isolation and related situations, it is that otherwise normal individuals suffer a variety of cognitive, affective, sensory, or other functional disturbances when confronted with an environmental context which is significantly different from those to which they are accustomed. Or, in other words, when C_e changes to C_i, and B_i which could articulate effectively between the existing A and C components are not available, "normal" behavior deteriorates. This conclusion suggests that the previously developed B_e schemata (and the established ABC relationships) are rather restricted in the extent to which they generalize effectively to the unfamiliar C_i conditions. This line of reasoning also suggests that if an individual were subjected to completely foreign environmental conditions, he would, so to speak, be "without an ego," unless he could project a C_e context and/or develop B_i schemata appropriate to that context. Also, the fact that subjects showed an apparent "passivity, weakness, or defenselessness of the ego" during and shortly following experimental isolation does not mean that they would do so under the normal range of C_e conditions for which they have developed adequate B_e schemata.

When faced with such unfamiliar C_i conditions, individuals initially try to act as though the change from C_e to C_i had not occurred. This attempt usually involves behaviors which are more relevant to C_e than to C_i, such as searching for any aspects of C_i which are familiar, attempting to establish customary time referents, reviewing prior events and experiences, talking, singing, or humming, doing exercises, counting or making more elaborate mental

---

[13] An analysis of data from classical conditioning and instrumental act learning situations in terms of such constructs as motivational states, central integrations, and stimulus conditions—i.e., the A, B, and C components—is given in Haggard (1946).

manipulations. When such C_e related activities can be maintained, the characteristic disturbances otherwise associated with C_i are minimized.

Other things equal, the onset and severity of the behavioral disturbances are proportional to the extent and duration of the disparity between C_e and C_i. However, since large differences exist in the manner in which individuals react to the same physical or objective changes of C_e to C_i, it may be assumed that such variations are due to differences in the nature of and relationships between the individuals' A and B components, and in their combined relation to the C component, including any changes in it. Although the variation in response to isolation is marked in samples of normal subjects, it is also seen in a comparison of the reactions of normals and psychiatric patients, e.g., schizophrenics. A number of possible differences between such patients and normals may account for the observed differences in their reaction to isolation, such as significant differences in: (a) the B schemata which have been developed in connection with C conditions in general (e.g., schizophrenics' apparently having learned to reject or negate the normal physical-social environment) [14] and (b) the overall relations among the A, B, and C components (e.g., in schizophrenics the role of the A and B components and of the AB relationships appear to be maximized and that of the C component minimized as determinants of behavior).

In almost all of the isolation studies reported, individuals have been subjected to C_i conditions on only one occasion and, lacking appropriate B_i, it may be expected that the initial exposure to the C_i conditions should result in maximal behavior disturbances. In only a few studies have subjects repeatedly experienced the C_i conditions, in which case it appeared that new and adaptive B_i began to develop and that the usual "symptoms" tended to disappear. Although all individuals characteristically showed increasing signs of disturbance the longer they remained in isolation, they varied dramatically in the extent of disturbance and the length of time they were able to tolerate the isolation conditions. Some individuals reported near-panic states in less than an hour whereas others were relatively undisturbed after several days in isolation. Or, in terms of the propositions stated earlier, some individuals moved from stages $4a$ to $4d$, involving marked changes in the A component in a short time, whereas others appear to have remained at stages $4a$ or $4b$ for periods up to a week.

[14] In this connection, Winder (1960), in comparing the learning patterns of normals and schizophrenics, observed that "The findings of the punishment-reward studies suggest that in some way these patients either have not developed or have lost the expectation that rewards and satisfactions can be attained. The further implication is that escape from noxious conditions focuses the pattern of living, and it is tempting to believe that rewards have come to provoke anxieties" (p. 240).

Since the individuals subjected to experimental isolation were able to terminate the experiment at will (i.e., reinstate C_e conditions), it may be assumed that the various "personality changes" which occurred were relatively short-lived and superficial. If, however, the individuals had been forced to remain under C_i conditions after marked changes occurred in the A and B components of the system, involving a redefinition of these components and their relationships, it would be expected that such personality changes would be substantially more profound and enduring. But in any case, the stability of "personality" and other forms of behavior rests upon the stability of the A, B, and C components and their interrelationships. In other words, behavioral stability, like a clothesline, must be supported at both ends by stable A and C conditions.

EXTREME OR EXTENDED ISOLATION

The accounts of individuals who have survived partial or complete isolation for weeks or months under traumatic or otherwise precarious conditions are always dramatic—perhaps because in them man is pushed to the limits of his courage, resourcefulness, and endurance. There are hundreds of such accounts by solitary or shipwrecked sailors, frontiersmen, or explorers of the wilderness, the desert, or polar ice cap, prisoners in solitary confinement, and other persons or groups exposed to the hazards of isolation for long periods of time. These anecdotal or autobiographical accounts, while providing vivid descriptions of how individuals have struggled successfully to survive in isolation, contain little approaching the objective, systematic observations which characterize the studies of experimental isolation. Many accounts of extreme or extended isolation have been summarized and discussed by such writers as Doyle (1953), Lilly (1956), Merrien (1954), Wheaton (1959), Miller (1962), and others cited by them.

Although the conditions and consequences of extended isolation are in some ways similar to those of the experimental isolation studies, there are crucial differences associated with the psychological and environmental parameters of these two types of isolation. By comparison, extended isolation not only is of much longer duration but also the individuals exposed to it are not able to terminate the isolation at will, regardless of whether they subjected themselves to it voluntarily or had it thrust upon them. Under these conditions, individuals are characteristically faced with various immediate or potential dangers to their physical and mental well-being—and to their survival, for that matter. Also, even though both types of isolation involve an unfamiliar environmental context, with a corresponding reduction in the level of "information" provided by such conditions, the nature of the changes in that context are substantially different. Experimental isolation usually involves an interference with the normal modes of sensory stimulation and reaction, as by a marked reduction in the level and/or meaningfulness of sensory input and the inhibition of normal activity. In cases of extended isolation, as a sailor on the open sea or an explorer on the polar ice cap, the individual usually is not artificially constrained to inhibit normal physical activity, and it can hardly be said that he experiences a reduction in the level of sensory stimulation (especially if he is suffering from thirst, hunger, cold, sunburn, or exposure) although such stimulation may be relatively unvaried and unpatterned.

The accounts of extended isolation may be grouped roughly into four types: individuals whose isolation was voluntary or involuntary and groups whose isolation was voluntary or involuntary. Because of the many factors involved in these types of isolation, no two accounts are strictly comparable. They vary along several dimensions, such as differences in the physical environment in which the isolation occurs, the presence or absence of other persons, individual differences among the persons experiencing the isolation, and differences in such associated stress factors as hunger, pain, and illness. However, these accounts have in common the fact that the individuals experiencing isolation, regardless of its form, are faced with environmental conditions which involve personal risk and which differ significantly from those to which they are normally accustomed.

Individual Isolation (Voluntary or Involuntary)

In some cases, individuals have voluntarily subjected themselves to isolation for long periods, as by going to sea alone (e.g., Slocum, 1943; Bernicot, 1953; Bombard, 1953; and Lindemann, H., 1958), or by spending long periods alone in the Arctic or Antarctic (e.g., Ritter, 1900; Byrd, 1938; Courtald, 1932). In these cases, careful preparations are made beforehand to insure survival and the eventual return to normal living, barring serious mishap, and the individual's time tends to be filled with the many day-to-day chores necessary for survival. However, for prisoners of war or political prisoners in solitary confinement (e.g., Burney, 1952; Bone, 1957; Ignotus, 1959; Dean, 1954), isolated castaways (e.g., Tiira, 1955), or persons who became isolates to avoid capture (e.g., Howarth, 1958), the isolation is by definition involuntary and usually is unexpected and unplanned. Under these conditions, the individual either has little if anything to do or is faced with enforced passivity (so that if his time and thoughts are structured, he has to do so on his own, even if in fantasy) and the outcome of the isolation—including the likelihood of survival—is in large part unpredictable and beyond his control.

In appraising reports of the extended isolation of individuals, it should be kept in mind that only a small fraction of such experiences are reported—namely, those of persons who have survived to tell the tale, who were not too shattered by their experiences, and who could and did write about them. It should also be kept in mind that the reports of such persons are probably subject to unconscious distortions and conscious decisions not to reveal very much of what they considered too bizarre or severely abnormal. Furthermore, it may be assumed that, by virtue of their survival, the reactions of persons who have reported their experiences are, if anything, less extreme than those of persons who did not survive their ordeal.

Regardless of the widely divergent conditions under which individuals have suffered extreme or extended isolation, they report strikingly similar phases or patterns of reactions to these conditions. Briefly, during the first phase, the individual usually responds adaptively and realistically, such as by carrying out routine chores, escaping a sinking ship, or getting used to solitary confinement. (Some persons, of course, panic at the time of a shipwreck or other catastrophe—but they characteristically have no opportunity to adjust to the additional stress of isolation.) This first phase may last for a few hours or a few days. Then comes the crisis of isolation: this second phase involves the gradual or sudden awareness (usually accompanied by emotional shock) that one is indeed alone, and that the recently familiar world is gone, be it the land, the sunken ship, family, friends, duties, routines, or whatever. The aftermath of this undeniable realization of being alone is critical to survival, and is soon followed by one of two modes of reacting: by giving up or by attempting to adapt to the isolation. Giving up, which is accompanied by rapid ego disintegration, may result in extreme withdrawal, despair, psychosis with hallucinations and delusions, and violent emotional reactions such as uncontrollable self-pity or rage. Persons who react in these ways soon die—from their inability to cope with the fact of isolation as much as (or more than) from physical dangers or threats.[15] The other mode of reacting to the crisis of isolation involves an attempt at gradual adaptation to the conditions of the isolation situation.

[15] According to Bombard (1953), "statistics show that ninety per cent of the survivors of shipwreck die within three days, yet it takes longer than that to perish of hunger and thirst." He goes on to ask, "How many castaways through the ages have become stiff and sudden corpses, killed, not by the sea, not by hunger or thirst, but by their own terror?" Also, in commenting on the aftermath of the sinking of the Titanic, he observed that "When the first relief ships arrived, three hours after the liner had disappeared, a number of people had either died or gone mad in the lifeboats. Significantly, no child under the age of ten was included among those who had paid for their terror with madness and for their madness with death. The children were still at the age of reason" (p. x).

Adaptation to extreme or extended isolation is not achieved without some symptoms which typically characterize the mentally ill. In all the reports, one or more of these side effects of having to adjust to isolation have been mentioned by otherwise normal individuals: periods of severe anxiety, hallucinations and delusions, superstitiousness, at least partial distrust of sensory experience and concern for loss of rationality, the development of compulsive rituals, engaging in imaginary conversations, and marked withdrawal. Some writers have tended to emphasize these aspects of individuals' reactions to isolation. But of equal interest, and of greater importance, is the manner in which those who did survive achieved their new adaptation to the isolation. After realizing the undeniable fact of being alone and the penetrating sense of loneliness (and perhaps also humility, awe, fear, anger, anxiety, or terror), these individuals have reported a gradual withdrawing into themselves while at the same time seeking out remnants of their former world or acting as if it were still there.

The attempt of isolated individuals to maintain contact with their former world was done in several ways, as by calling on their memory, by reading and rereading everything available, by keeping a log or diary, by engaging in mental exercise (as by counting words or posing and solving mathematical problems), by conversing with non-human or imaginary companions, by working, doing calisthenics—or just anything to organize their time, thoughts, and activities. Thus, they constructed an "as if" environment which had familiar properties as a psychological crutch while they also turned inward to make up for the unfamiliarity and barrenness of their alien but "real" current environment. This crutch served a variety of purposes: it structured their attention and thoughts, thus avoiding the mental vacuum which would have left them at the mercy of their otherwise unchecked impulses, anxieties, and fantasies and, in the absence of established adaptations to the external world, enabled them to rely on the "as if" environment while they turned inward for hope and to retain their sense of identity. In turning inward, these individuals found it necessary to avoid as much as possible all unpleasant and disturbing thoughts and impulses in order to maintain the new and delicate balance between their "inner" and their "outer" life—a balance which was necessary to maintain if they were to keep their sanity and to survive.

The achievement of a new inner-outer balance, which involves a basic personality change, has several consequences. One is that, psychologically, the individual is no longer so much at the mercy of the monotony or whims of the isolation environment. Another consequence is that the individual's view of his current environment tends to become laden with his projections of his inner life to the point that he may hallucinate his hopes or fears, or may come to feel himself "at one with the universe." In the latter case, individuals also spoke of achieving a new sense of integration or tranquility. But after having thus achieved a viable adjustment to the isolation, they often experienced difficulty in readjusting to society on emerging from extended isolation. This difficulty was apparent, for example, in their initial refusal to mingle with or even talk to others, for fear they might not be able to converse properly or might be thought to be insane.

Two characteristics help to tip the balance between the disintegration and death or the adaptation and survival of individuals in extended isolation: their character structure and their prior experience. By and large, emotionally healthy and mature individuals with active, imaginative minds who can become absorbed in such pastimes as reading and who can structure their thoughts and activities adapt best to isolation. The personal characteristics which facilitate survival in extended isolation are, in fact, essentially those which facilitated adaptation to experimental isolation, as reported by Goldberger and Holt (1961). In extended isolation, however, two additional and related characteristics are crucial for survival. One is the ability to appraise the situation realistically and to adapt to it, as by becoming passive in the face of starvation or remaining active if there is danger of freezing. The other is the unshakable belief that one will survive—in spite of hunger, illness, exposure, etc., even in the absence of any apparent external justification for this belief.

The importance of prior experience in similar situations is seen in two ways. One is that the first few days of isolation are the most difficult to tolerate; if one can survive, say, the first week, he is well on the way to making a reasonably good adjustment to extended isolation. The importance of prior experience is also seen in the fact that having lived through similar situations in the past serves to buffer the stress of isolation. In this connection Lilly (1956), who reviewed twenty reports of individuals who survived extended isolation, states that "in all cases of survivors of isolation, at sea or in the polar night, it was the first exposure which caused the greatest fears and hence the greatest danger of giving way to symptoms; previous experience is a powerful aid in going ahead, despite the symptoms" (p. 2).

Group Isolation (Involuntary)

The situations involving groups of individuals that have been isolated as a result of some catastrophe, whether it be a shipwreck at sea (e.g., Gibson, 1953) or a similar misfortune on land, such as befell the ill-fated Donner party (e.g., Stewart, 1960), are not strictly comparable to those of isolated individuals. The stress of being literally alone is not present when two or more persons are involved and, in addition, the latter situation is complicated by the introduction of various interpersonal factors and reactions. These include, for example, the presence or absence of group leadership and morale and the emergence of behaviors which range from altruistic heroism and self-sacrifice to murder and cannibalism.

In several respects, however, these group situations are similar to those in which single individuals are isolated. In both types of cases the individuals are cut off from their familiar world, and it is possible for each person in the group to view himself as being isolated, even though others are physically present. This view tends to develop under duress and lack of group morale so that individuals come to think of survival in terms of "every man for himself." Under these conditions former companions may be viewed with a jaundiced eye as being part of the hostile and threatening environment—as, for example, an enemy who consumes precious food and water. Another set of similarities between individual and group isolation is that practically all the emotional, cognitive, and other behavioral disturbances of isolation; the personal characteristics which make for disintegration or adaptation; and the modes of achieving adaptation in the face of isolation and associated stresses are essentially the same, whether the individuals are alone or in groups.

Group Isolation (Voluntary)

Groups, like some individuals, have voluntarily entered "isolation" for extended periods. In both types of voluntary isolation, provisions are made ahead of time to maximize the chances of survival with at least adequate comfort and convenience; consequently, the individuals involved are provided with day-to-day duties which serve to organize their time, thoughts, and activities. In the absence of extraordinary misfortunes, then, these situations differ in important ways from those involving involuntary isolation. Examples of voluntary group isolation for extended periods include members of crews of whaling ships or others sailing before the mast for the first time or in parties of explorers of the frontier, the deserts, and the polar regions.

Until recently, reports of groups in voluntary isolation have been autobiographical and subject to the usual omissions and distortions which are typical of such accounts. However, structured interviews with men who had just spent almost a year wintering over in the small stations in Antarctica (which were set up in connection with the International Geophysical Year) provide relatively systematic and objective data on the characteristic patterns of adaptation to isolation under these circumstances (cf. Mullin, 1960; Rohrer,

1960).[16]   All the men interviewed (in Rohrer's study, 163 officers, enlisted men and civilians from seven stations) reported a common phasic reaction to the year; anxiety during the first month or two, depression during the dark winter months, and increased agitation with expectations of and preparations for leaving.[17]   These three phases can be characterized as follows:

Since provision had been made for the men's comfort and safety, the anxiety during the initial phase stemmed primarily from their concern over how well they would be able to adapt to and perform adequately during their stay in the Antarctic. This initial phase of anxiety, then, was not really an adaptation to the isolation as such, but was adaptive insofar as it spurred the men to settle down to the work of preparing to "winter over."

The basic pattern of adaptation to being isolated in the Antarctic IGY stations occurred during the second phase. After the monotony of winter set in, all the men showed changes in their impulse life, activity patterns, mental habits, and interpersonal roles, and some of them developed unusual symptoms during this period of isolation. More specifically, the men came to ignore the irritating habits of others and to inhibit the expression of their own hostile feelings (and were deeply disturbed when others did not do so). They developed increased interest in and appetite for food (gains of 20 to 30 pounds were not uncommon among the men), and they also lost interest in sex. This general tendency to find their adaptation in a regressive and repressive-passive direction was matched in their behavior by an increased listlessness, a slowing down of activity, and a decreased involvement in their work and other duties. This adjustment in a low key also found expression in their mental life: the men showed an increased tendency to have lapses of memory, difficulty in concentrating, and a general intellectual inertia, including great difficulty in carrying out their "self-improvement programs" and other preset goals. A representative comment to Rohrer (1960) was, "I brought along some correspondence courses but I didn't have time to work on them while I was down here. Seems like all we did down here was to work, eat, go to the movies, drink a couple of beers, and then go to bed. This went on for months" (p. 12). Similar reactions have been reported by many others, including Byrd (1938) who said, "There was no end to the books that I was forever

---

[16] Wintering over in the Antarctic differs from many similar group situations currently being studied in that once the last boat or airplane has left, the only contact with the outside world is by radio and there is no possibility of leaving until the following summer—and the men know it.

[17] Similar phasic reactions have been reported for various other "group isolation" situations, such as one week in a simulated shelter, in which "agitation and tension were greatest immediately following shelter entry and prior to anticipated release. Mild depression was common toward the middle of the shelter stay" (Altman et al., 1960, pp. iii–iv).

promising myself to read; but, when it came to reading them, I seemed never to have the time or the patience. With music, too, it was the same way; the love for it—and I suppose the indefinable need—was also there, but not the will or opportunity to interrupt for it more than momentarily the routine which most of us come to cherish as existence" (p. 6).

In their interpersonal roles, rank and other status differences lost importance and were replaced by increased group cohesion and a working assumption that everyone was equal—with one exception: the men jealously guarded their work role, as though it defined their identity. Thus, it appears that the men tended to structure their activities and define their identities on the level of a stimulus-activity-bound existence. There were, of course, individual differences but the general pattern of adaptation was more or less true for all the men.

Typical symptoms which tended to develop during the winter phase of the year included moodiness, headaches, and sleep disturbances (occasionally oversleeping but more often insomnia, called the "Big Eye"). Two symptoms were reported which appear to be almost unique to this type of isolation. One symptom was hypersensitivity to and disturbance by various auditory stimuli.[18] The other symptom was called the "Long Eye"; in this case the afflicted individual would sit and stare at the others (without "seeing" them), or would just go off by himself in silence. One man described this symptom as "a twelve-foot stare in a ten-foot room." Usually, this condition was preceded by a period of sleeplessness and always followed the individual's either voluntarily isolating himself from the group or being isolated by the group, and was accompanied by such associated symptoms as hallucinations (light flashes and apparent movement), breaking down in tears, loss of appetite, loss of skin color, prolonged silence, suspiciousness, and reduction of work role. The symptom disappeared when the individual began to interact again with the other members of the group.

During the third phase, when it became clear that the year of isolation was coming to an end, the adjustment pattern of the second phase began to break up. At this time, the men started to express their pent-up hostilities verbally, develop sexual fantasies, and some experienced an increase in such symptoms as headaches, sleeplessness, and inability to concentrate. There was also a general tendency to "let go" (on the rationalization that they were about to leave anyway), which was reflected in doing less work and drinking more beer, in petulance, pranks, and occasional refusal to do chores or take orders,

[18] With respect to this symptom, Rohrer (1960) hypothesized that "given a reduction (because of repressive processes) in the intra-psychic sources of stimulation there should develop an increased awareness of external stimulus configurations, particularly if they are unrelated to the repressed material" (p. 17). See also Giaever (1954).

and in bragging of how much they had accomplished. Such types of behavior, which are more typical of eight- to sixteen-year-olds, suggests that during this final phase the men behaved in terms of the level of emotional maturity which they had adopted during the long winter phase of isolation.

Theoretical Considerations

In appraising the effects of isolation, it is possible to select from among a variety of factors which seem to be related to the deterioration of individuals' customary behavior. Some factors rest in environmental conditions, so that they are more or less observable and objective; others have to do with inferences regarding hypothesized intraindividual conditions, and hence are not directly amenable to objective description and quantification. We have already seen that the behavioral changes observed in the experimental isolation studies have been attributed to the relative or absolute reduction of the level of sensory input, information, and kinesthetic or proprioceptive stimulation, and to the duration of these conditions. (These factors are derived simply by observing the manifest characteristics of the isolation situation, and then attributing the effects of isolation to those characteristics.) However, other factors may account for the effects of isolation, such as the extent to which the individual loses his customary spacio-temporal referents for organizing behavior, his inhibition of normal activities and expressive outlets because of enforced passivity or social isolation, and how he feels about and evaluates his experiences. Although the more objective "explanations" have obvious advantages, they are not sufficient by themselves to account for the effects of experimental isolation—primarily because of the very large differences among individuals in the onset, type, extent, and duration of their reactions to otherwise comparable isolation conditions.

It seems reasonable to speculate that a common set of conditions underlie the behavioral disturbances associated with all types of isolation. If so, the one common denominator is the fact that when otherwise normal individuals are faced with environmental conditions which are radically different from those to which they have become accustomed, they typically show a marked deterioration of their habitual patterns of behavior. But this fact, by itself, is hardly a theoretical explanation of those behavioral changes. And, while it seems safe to assume that the extreme conditions under which a man may experience extended isolation no doubt play a significant role in determining his reactions and adjustments, it should not be forgotten that he leaves a familiar world as he enters the unfamiliar one involving isolation. Thus, one can ask the following question: Does the individual's behavior deteriorate in isolation primarily because he is removed from, or loses, his familiar environment or because he is faced with an unfamiliar environment?

The relevance of this question lies in the fact that it highlights the theoretical consequences of an emphasis on the role played by the more objective or the more intraindividual corollaries of the environmental change. Using the terminology introduced earlier, a strong environmental emphasis would be that an individual faced with a change of C_e to C_i and, not possessing adequate B_i, would soon experience behavioral disturbances as a result of the impact of the C_i conditions. This position assumes the sequence of events to be essentially that the new and unfamiliar C_i effects changes in the B and eventually in the A components, with the implication that B and A are relatively passive with respect to the changes in C. The alternate position assumes that over time significant aspects of C_e serve to support the B_e which, in turn, normally "bind" or channelize the A component in relation to those aspects of the C component. From this point of view, given the change from C_e to C_i and the absence of adequate B_i, the customary B_e schemata become unstable and deteriorate initially because of the absence of the previously supportive C_e more than from the presence of C_i.

As a lead to answering the above question, it is instructive to recall the experiences and responses of persons shortly after they enter isolation. Such persons characteristically report some degree of anxiety and thought disturbance and frequently report hallucinations or more bizarre symptoms.[19] These symptoms imply the emergence of uncontrolled and disturbing impulses or affects. In response, isolated individuals typically cling to any available remnants of their preisolation world and attempt to engage in those activities, thoughts, or fantasies which had their roots in and were appropriate to it— even if they have to project an "as if" world to do so. Indeed, under the circumstances, what else could they do but rely upon the mechanisms and modes of adjustment which they had developed in preisolation contexts? The process of projecting an "as if" world and engaging in activities appropriate to it serves several purposes: to buffer the shock of fully realizing the raw fact of isolation, to ward off or to mitigate the behavioral disturbances, and to give time to develop B_i schemata appropriate to cope with the isolation conditions. Thus the experiences and responses of isolates suggest that it is the absence of the familiar (at least as much as the presence of the unfamiliar) environmental context that leads to the disturbances associated with isolation.

In the examples of isolation which we have discussed thus far, individuals have experienced a loss of many or most of the familiar aspects of their pre-

---

[19] The most severe disturbances occur during periods when, for one reason or another, the projected "as if" C_e world ceases to be tenable and before new B_i schemata are fully developed.

isolation world. But in the normal course of living individuals continually lose or leave—without any disturbance whatever—parts of their familiar world. In some instances, though, the loss of a quantitatively small, but personally significant, part of the environmental context is followed by phenomena which are quite similar to those reported by persons experiencing isolation. For example, the loss of loved persons, objects, or locales gives rise to such phenomena as mourning (e.g., Freud, 1917; Lindemann, 1944; Volkart and Michael, 1957; Bowlby, 1961; Pollock, 1961) or homesickness (e.g., Abse, in Lilly, 1956, pp. 19–20). In these cases individuals typically experience emotional shock on realizing the reality of the environment change, with accompanying loneliness, anxiety, depression, despair, or other uncontrolled emotions, and a sense of disorientation or depersonalization, and many of them experience various perceptual distortions (e.g., hallucinations) or cognitive disturbances (e.g., inability to concentrate). Such individuals also tend at times to act as if the loss had not occurred or may attempt to reinstate what is lost by one means or another or, if that is not possible, to do so symbolically or in fantasy until they can adjust to the loss. The inference to be drawn from the conditions which lead to mourning and homesickness is— less equivocally than in the case of isolation—that the disturbances arise from the loss of familiar (rather than from being faced with unfamiliar) aspects of the environment.[20]

Mourning and homesickness further indicate that it is not how much of the familiar environmental context is lost but rather how much is lost of what matters most to the individual. That is to say, it is the loss of cathected objects and relationships that is disturbing. But if this is so, then it follows that it is the presence of cathected objects in the environment, and relationships with them, which stabilize the B schemata and so help the individual to "bind" his impulses and energies. In other words, the presence of previously cathected aspects of the C_e support the B_e which serve to bind or direct the associated aspects of the A component in relation to such C_e. Ideally, if the cathected aspects of C_e exist, we would expect the A, B, and C components to be articulate and the individual to function normally. If, however, the cathected aspects of C_e are not present, we would expect that the system would cease to be articulate, that the impulses of the A component would "overwhelm" the unsupported B schemata, and that the individual would manifest what we have called "behavioral disturbances."

[20] Although the process of adaptation to a new, stress laden environment also may engender behavioral disturbances (Haggard, 1949), they may well differ from those resulting from loss of the familiar, even though frequently the two will be confounded if, as in the case of isolation, the individual moves rapidly from the familiar to the unfamiliar.

We have thus hypothesized that the existence of the cathected aspects of C_e serve to support or reinforce the B_e which, in turn, serve to bind or direct the individual's impulses or energies in relation to his environment. But this is only another way of speaking of what is usually called the "socialization of the individual" or, from the genetic view, the "socialization process" which involves the development of those adaptive mechanisms which enable one to utilize and direct his energies in relation to his environment. In these terms, the individual confronted with extended isolation is faced with the task of becoming "resocialized." If he is to survive in isolation, he must quickly develop new adaptive mechanisms which will serve both to control his partially unchecked and disturbing impulses and to cope effectively with an unfamiliar environment. This process will be facilitated if the isolated individual can maintain his cathexis of some remnants of his C_e (or his "as if" C_e) world and at the same time can cathect at least some aspects of the C_i environment. We have seen that this is essentially what isolated individuals do —at least according to the reports of those who have adapted to and survived extended isolation.

In analyzing the factors involved in adaptation to isolation, it is not possible to equate experimental isolation with extended isolation, even though they are similar in some respects. Experimental isolation is limited and relatively benign and, as we saw in our earlier analysis (cf. proposition 4a–d, p. 446 ff.), the subject is not forced to adapt to it since he can reinstate C_e at will by terminating the experiment. In extended isolation, the individual must continue to endure the isolation and may be forced to tolerate such additional stresses as pain and hunger—but if he is to survive at all he must do so in the C_i context.

It should also be noted that the process of adaptation to any given isolation situation cannot be defined only in terms of the properties of that situation: the individual must be considered in relation to it. For example, persons reared essentially in social isolation or those who, like hermits, have long since chosen isolation as a way of life, should have little if any difficulty "adapting" to similar types of (what we would call) extreme or extended isolation.[21] For such persons, however, adaptation to life in an urban society might be at least as stressful as it is for an urbanite to adapt to isolation. The central issue thus involves the discrepancy between C_i and C_e and the

[21] In connection with the importance of cultural or other individual differences, Gladwin (1958, and in Lilly, 1956, p. 18) reports that the Trukese not infrequently are becalmed on the open sea in small sailing canoes for extended periods. Although they suffer prolonged exposure, they apparently do not experience the perceptual, affective, etc. disturbances usually associated with such extended isolation and exposure.

demands of adaptation (or resocialization) required of the individual—which is the reason why we have heretofore implicitly equated "isolation" with "a new and unfamiliar" environmental context.

In appraising the factors which influence adaptation to extended isolation, we will consider: how the isolate relates to himself, how he relates to his environment, and some of the consequences of adapting to isolation.

How the Isolate Relates to Himself

In this section we will consider some of the ways in which the individual's *A* and *B* components and characteristic *AB* relationships influence his ability to adapt to isolation. It is to be expected that the extent of his available free energy to develop new *B* schemata and the range of his existing *B* schemata will facilitate or interfere with any new adaptations he might be required to make. Thus, ample energies and successful prior adaptations, or depleted energies and disabling experiences in similar situations on previous occasions will affect the likelihood of successful adaptation. In this connection, Gibson (1953) credited his ability to survive in an open boat in part to the fact that he had for some years lived out of doors in the tropics. It is to be expected that one could become so accustomed to (what was once) "isolation" that adaptation ceases to be involved. It is also to be expected that, in general, the larger one's repertoire of appropriate *B* schemata which represent his range of knowledges and skills, the more likely will he be able to adapt to new and unfamiliar situations.

The individual's experience history determines in part the new *B* schemata which can be developed as well as those which have been. In recent years it has become increasingly clear that unless the individual has been exposed to "normal" ranges of stimuli and other forms of experience, he may be unable at a later date to perceive, experience, or respond in a "normal" fashion. For example, the withholding of visual stimulation for sufficiently long periods during early life will have irreversible effects on neural growth and metabolism and, correspondingly, the ability later to integrate complex visual perceptions and relationships (e.g., Senden, 1932; Chow et al., 1957; Hess, 1958; Riesen, 1960). Studies with primates involving early social deprivations similarly have shown profound irreversible effects on later social behavior, including mating (e.g., Harlow and Harlow, 1962) and, following Freud, clinicians have investigated the extent to which early experiences have shaped the mental, emotional, and other adaptive functions of children (e.g., Spitz, 1945, 1946). The literature on early and prolonged experience deprivation indicates that the structures and schemata which comprise the *B* component may be so affected that the development of appropriate B schemata at a later date is seriously interfered with or even precluded.[22]

The characteristic relationships between the A and B components usually are referred to as "character structure." The properties of these relationships —such as relative plasticity (or lack of rigidity), articulation (or lack of conflict), and autonomy (or lack of dependence on the environmental context)— are important determinants of the individual's adaptive capabilities. We have seen, for example, that those who fare best in isolation tend to be not only accepting of their impulse life but also able to maintain contact with and enjoy psychic derivatives of it (cf. Courtald, 1932; Goldberger and Holt, 1961). On the other hand, they may at times need to "isolate" (in the psychoanalytic usage of the term, e.g., Eissler, 1959; Marasse, 1959) certain aspects of A to maintain the functional integrity of the B component. It was in this sense that Byrd (1938) found it necessary to "put out of his mind" those thoughts and feelings which he believed would have led to his undoing if he had permitted himself to entertain them.

Another important aspect of the relationships between the A and B components has to do with the development and stability of the B schemata. If we assume that some B schemata articulate only with the A component whereas others articulate with both the A and C components, we would expect, first, that every individual could develop both types of B schemata and, second, that individuals would vary in terms of some tendency toward one type or the other. Individuals vary greatly in the extent to which they can function relatively autonomously with respect to their environmental context or are dependent upon it for "support." It is a commonplace observation that individuals tend to become more autonomous as they mature and also that the behavior of some individuals is relatively uninfluenced by environmental factors whereas the behavior of others is much more dependent upon them. Parenthetically, in terms of the value systems in our society, we believe that it is "good" for the individual to develop sufficient autonomy (so that he is "stable," "independent," and has "good ego strength") but not too much of it (so that he is "out of touch with reality").

With respect to the task of adapting to isolation, we saw that isolates typically rely on remnants of their C_e (or "as if" C_e) world until they can develop adaptive mechanisms, B_i, that enable them to cope with the isolation situation, C_i. But although the maintenance of cathexes relevant to C_e may be necessary to retain personal integration or even sanity, such cathexes need not be directly relevant to C_i so that, with respect to C_i, the AB_e relationships may be equivalent to B schemata which involve only

[22] For reviews and theoretical discussions of this literature see: Hebb, 1949; Bowlby, 1951; Beach and Jaynes, 1954; Thompson, 1955; Riesen, 1961; and Yarrow, 1961.

the A and B components. The isolate confronted with what he considers to be a too hostile C_i may (via his "as if" C_e) develop B schemata which articulate only with aspects of the A component to "escape from" the unpleasant realities of C_i. It would be expected that the personality changes accompanying the development of such B schemata would be quite durable since their maintenance is no longer dependent upon changes in the C component (i.e., they are not subject to extinction by external events). To paraphrase, then, it appears that isolates may become partially "schizophrenic" with respect to C_i—or, in their terms, to "withdraw into themselves"—in order to retain their sanity as they adapt to isolation. In order to survive, however, the isolate must also be able to relate to and cope with at least some of the realities of the C_i—that is, he must develop at least some B schemata that are articulate with both the A component and his C_i context. It is for this reason that adaptation is greatly facilitated if the isolate is able to cathect some aspects of C_i (or activities related to his survival in it) in order to develop the B_i necessary for him to relate adaptively to the C_i.

How the Isolate Relates to His Environment

We have already reviewed how isolates tend to perceive the situation in which they find themselves and some of their many ingenious ways of working out their adaptation to and survival in isolation. We have also suggested that isolates tend to distort their perception of C_i, especially during the early phases of their adaptation to it. The distortion of C_i may take various forms, such as by fusing an "as if" C_e with the current C_i or by attempting to deny those aspects of C_i which would otherwise be intolerable. But if, as we have assumed, all behavior is a function of the total ABC system, then perception is determined by the properties of the C component in concert with the existing A (e.g., motivational state) and B (e.g., prior learning) components. Perceptual distortions of C_i, then, involve attempts within the system to define aspects of the C component so that they will be congruent with the existing A and B definitions and relationships. In other words, C_i is perceived (or misperceived) so as to be articulate with the A and B components.[23]

Isolates also tend to distort the temporal dimension, as by pretending they are still in some past C_e world or by believing that they will find relief from C_i by being rescued or by returning to C_e. In addition to the primitive wish to survive, such factors as religious faith or the desire to return to loved ones

---

[23] From this point of view, the meaning of such terms as "perception," "projection," "projected imagery," and "hallucination"—or "transference" in the interpersonal area—lies in the extent of the disparity between the definition of particular aspects of the C component offered by the individual in question and other (judging) persons or groups.

enable the isolate to look to the future and thus help him to avoid giving up to the stress of isolation. In order to survive, however, the isolate must not distort C_i too much and runs a serious risk if he distorts those aspects of C_i which pertain to his moment-to-moment physical survival.

It is not possible to generalize in any tidy fashion regarding uniformities in how isolates have reacted to their isolation environment successfully, primarily because individuals and the conditions which are concomitant with isolation vary so greatly. In summarizing instances of extended isolation we have, however, enumerated many of the techniques which isolates have used in the process of achieving a viable adjustment to their isolation. But, of course, the isolate's response to the stress of isolation depends upon more than his adaptive techniques. For example, the presence of such associated stress factors as hunger and exposure serve to speed up the onset and increase the frequency and intensity of the behavioral disturbances that generally accompany isolation, thus decreasing the likelihood of adaptation and survival. On the other hand, if the isolate is able to engage in activities that structure his time and thoughts and, if possible, also contribute to his physical well-being, the likelihood of his adaptation and survival will be increased. But in any particular case the ways in which the isolate relates to himself and to his environment may depend in large measure on conditions which are beyond his control. The techniques of adaptation which we have discussed will aid in his psychological and physical survival if the situational odds against him are not too great.

Some Consequences of Adaptation to Isolation

We have seen that shortly after entering isolation and before adapting to it, the isolate finds himself faced with both his uncontrolled impulses and affects on the one hand and an unfamiliar and precarious environment on the other. If he is to survive in isolation, he must learn rather quickly to control his impulses and affects and to deal effectively with the realities of his environment. We have also seen that whether or how he survives depends not only on environmental factors but also on the kind of person he is and how he relates to himself and to his environment. If he does adapt to and survive such an extreme situation as extended isolation, it would not be surprising to find, as a consequence of such adaptation, basic changes in his personality and mental life.

In discussing the factors involved in adapting to extended isolation we concluded that the isolate must become at least partially "resocialized" and theorized as to how this is accomplished. Resocialization thus implies that, insofar as C_i differs from C_e, the isolate must develop new B schemata for controlling and utilizing his basic impulses and energies in ways that are appropriate in the C_i context. But since how the individual customarily utilizes his energies is essentially a definition of "personality," any change in this respect would amount to a "personality change" as a corollary of his adaptation to isolation. It would also be expected that, other things equal, the extent of the personality change would be proportional to the discrepancy between C_i and C_e.

As an aspect of personality change, the development of B schemata which are appropriate to the C_i conditions protect the isolate from disturbing affects and impulses which, if uncontrolled, could result in his destruction by making him unable to act realistically in relation to C_i. Furthermore, many isolates have reported that, eventually, they came to experience both a deep sense of inner tranquility and, at the same time, an "oceanic feeling" or of "being at one with the universe." Thus, the world of isolation ceased to be alien and became very real to them, and instead of fearing and hating it they came to love it, and later looked back upon their experiences with nostalgia (as in "I must go down to the seas again"). These individuals were usually among those who, for one reason or another, had entered isolation voluntarily and had been able to cathect important aspects of the isolation environment. Needless to say, not all isolates reacted in this manner, especially those who were thrust into isolation involuntarily and suffered such additional stresses as illness, injury, exposure, or near starvation. After rescue, individuals in this latter group preferred not to think about their experiences or, if they did, to look upon them as a "bad dream" or as an alien experience.

Finally, some individuals found it difficult to reenter their former world after a prolonged period of isolation, often for fear that they would be considered insane. It appears that after having adjusted to the isolation they were aware of the profound changes within themselves and dreaded the difficulty (or even questioned the possibility) of readjusting to the way of life they had previously known. This type of reaction emphasizes the extent to which adaptation to isolation can change personality in basic ways, and indicates the durability and possible irreversibility of some of these changes. (Relatively systematic observations have, however, been made in connection with the resocialization of men from a related situation, namely, repatriated prisoners of war, e.g., Newman, 1944; Curle, 1947.)

Concluding Remarks

One of the most salient features of isolation is the fact that it is relatively rare, at least for urbanized man; hence his experiences in and methods of responding to it have an air of the unusual—if not the bizarre. But this very feature brings into question the possible generalizability of conclusions drawn from an analysis of behavior in response to isolation. One can argue that, because extended isolation is an atypical experience, any conclusions drawn from it are thereby restricted to such situations. Or, one can argue that, since isolation is unusual and often involves extreme reactions, it thereby serves to highlight some of the basic aspects of behavior modification and adaptation to new environmental contexts which may not be so apparent in man's day-to-day experiences. From time to time we have implied that some of the factors involved in the process of adapting to isolation are fundamentally the same as those at work in a variety of other situations. And, although our central purpose has not been to emphasize such implications and relevancies, in concluding this discussion we will merely note what appear to be meaningful parallels with three related situations. These include the concentration camp as a situation frequently marked by extreme isolation and stress, the adaptation patterns of individuals who chronically isolate themselves from others, and individuals reared essentially in social isolation.

If adaptation to extreme or extended isolation is thought of as a function of the discrepancy between C_i and C_e and the extent to which concomitant stress factors exist in C_i, it seems plausible to expect that the basic processes and consequences of adaptation to isolation should be similar to those found in other extreme situations. In discussing one such situation, the concentration camp, Bettelheim (1943) indicated, for example, the prisoners' initial dependence upon the stability of their previous (but now current "as if") C_e world and their characteristic adaptations to C_i which eventually resulted in basic changes of character structure. But even though the mechanisms of adaptation which are utilized in extended isolation and in the concentration camp may be similar, there are fundamental differences in the consequences of adaptation to these two situations. These differences in outcome appear to be determined not only by the fact that the C_i was more punitive and often more stressful in the concentration camp but also by other more substantive aspects of the C_i to which the individuals in the two situations were forced to adapt. For example, in the IGY stations (Rohrer, 1960) some of the distinctive aspects of the C_i were the relative physical comfort, the dull monotony of the long winter months, and the absence of women; after adapting to life in the station, the men's behavior was characterized by listlessness, mental inertia, and the absence of sexual impulses and fantasies. In the concentration camp, however, dominant aspects of the C_i included almost constant physical threat and the Gestapo's attitude and value systems as expressed in their verbal and physical treatment of the prisoners; of those who survived and adapted to life in the camp, many of the prisoners adopted the Gestapo's attitude and value systems with a vengeance in relating both to themselves and their fellow prisoners. Thus, it seems reasonable to conclude that, by taking into account differences in the definition of the C_i, the factors involved in adaptation to isolation are relevant to a variety of other "extreme" situations. The process of adapting to extended isolation appears to be related also to the schizophrenic process. In adapting to isolation, individuals frequently withdraw into themselves or, as we have hypothesized, develop B schemata which articulate with and hence can be activated by the A component. (Theoretically, the B schemata normally serve to articulate between the A and C components.) In the schizophrenic process, individuals appear either to develop B schemata which do not articulate, or which articulate negatively, with the C component, so that schizophrenics come to "live in their own private world." Insofar as this mechanism is used, the individual is shielded from many disappointments and frustrations from the environment; he is also beyond the reach of "reality" so that his behavior is essentially unmodifiable by those aspects of the environment which normally serve to control and regulate behavior in socially acceptable ways. Although this schizophrenic-like technique of adaptation may have been temporarily expedient in adapting to isolation, some isolates carried it to extremes. According to reports of persons who survived group isolation, the maladaptive behavior of those individuals who withdrew excessively could not be distinguished from some forms of schizophrenia.

Although urbanized man often finds even short periods of isolation to be stressful, some individuals are reared under conditions of extended small-group isolation. Almost by definition, since such persons seldom have contact with organized society, relatively little is known about them or their way of life. However, preliminary findings based on a study of individuals reared in isolated families [24] indicate that they differ significantly from urbanized man in a variety of ways (e.g., character structure), that they develop adaptive mechanisms similar to those of urbanized persons forced to endure extended isolation, and that they experience emotional stress and the corresponding behavioral disturbances when they are thrust into complex social structures. For persons reared as social isolates, then, the shift from their familiar world, C_e, into a complex social structure, C_i, is roughly analogous in effect to urbanized man's entering extended isolation.

In this discussion of isolation and adaptations to it, we have tended to stress its disturbing effects upon those who experienced it. But there are degrees of isolation and, if the discrepancy between C_i and C_e is not too great, exposure to isolation need not be disturbing or detrimental to the individual. On the contrary, it could hardly be coincidental that all of the great religious leaders

[24] This research, conducted in remote areas of Norway, was begun by the author in 1960 under Grant M-4019-A from the National Institute of Mental Health, USPHS, and currently is supported by a Grant 62-259 from the Foundations' Fund for Research in Psychiatry.

have subjected themselves to periods of self-imposed isolation, and that generally the most creative and productive writers, artists, scientists, and other scholars have done their best work under such conditions. Moderate isolation may serve to clear away much of the "noise" emanating from the environmental context, thus permitting the individual better to integrate his thoughts, feelings, and behavior.

chapter fourteen

Value Conflicts in Cultural Transfer

William Madsen

In a world dedicated to massive culture change and secular missionizing on a global scale, we know remarkably little about the psychological effects of these developments on the individual. A microcosm of the total picture can be seen in our own country where a large number of distinct ethnic groups are constantly changing in the direction of the national norm or moving away from it in a process that affects group behavior and the norm itself.

The tolerated range of cultural variation for minority groups in this country fluctuates between two poles. In one of these polar trends, the goal is massive assimilation resulting in common behavior and common values as expressed in the "melting pot" ideal. The other trend encourages cultural variation among different ethnic groups. Generally speaking, our tolerance of cultural variation is greatest during periods when there is a strong feeling of national security. In the interim between World Wars I and II, popular publications frequently described with enthusiasm the different ways of life found among the minority groups in the United States and indicated that we could take pride in the richness and variety of our cultural makeup. After Pearl Harbor, deviation from the national norm was viewed as a threat to American survival. The mass evacuation and internment of the Japanese-Americans at the beginning of World War II is an example of our fear of those who are different.

The "melting pot" ideal has generally triumphed in regard to material culture and observable behavior in America. Despite the multiple national origins of our population, there is probably less regional and group variation in the material culture of America than in any other large nation of the world. Any foreigner traveling across the United States will be struck by the similarity of towns, homes, machines, and behavior.

Despite the outward appearance of uniformity in America, our culture has a high degree of value competition and value conflict. There is no general agreement as to whether Americans should strive for integration or segregation, support or oppose foreign aid, and seek better living conditions through individual endeavor or through group action. Although the goal of "progress" permeates most segments of our society, there is no universally accepted definition of progress. The majority of our population regards technological advancement as one goal in the concept of progress but there is no general agreement on the direction of desired change in social organization, education, the arts, and other aspects of non-material culture. Progress means different things to the New York business executive, the Detroit union member, and the southern share cropper.

EFFECTS OF VALUE CONFLICT

Internalization of competing or conflicting values reduces the psychological security of the individual and the integration of a culture. In a primitive culture or a folk culture, the value system is composed almost entirely of universals shared by all members of the society. In a civilized society, values may be either universals or alternatives (Linton, 271–287). At the official level, the value systems of ancient Rome, Nazi Germany, Fascist Italy, and Communist Russia are composed entirely of universals. Most civilized societies, however, have more alternative values and less universal values than are found in primitive societies. When two or more alternative values come into conflict, two opposing value systems may develop in a single society resulting in secessionist movements or civil war. There can be no doubt that an increase in the number of a culture's alternative values reduces the individual's feeling of security within his society. When this psychological insecurity becomes intense and widespread in a society, there may be a conscious or unconscious drive to return to an integrated system of universal values which makes the individual feel more comfortable. The value conflicts in Germany, Italy, and Russia played an important role in the origin of the totalitarian systems of Europe in the period between World Wars I and II. In the United States a number of groups are currently trying to simplify the value confusion in our society. The Un-American Activities Committee and the John Birch Society are examples. The popular appeal of Billy Graham is partly due to the integrated system of universal values which he persuasively advocates.

ETHNIC VALUES IN SOUTH TEXAS

The central problem to be discussed in this paper is the effect of value conflict on the individual who is caught between two cultures. This situation exists in South Texas where there is increasing pressure on the Mexican-American to abandon his folk culture and adopt Anglo-American culture. The distinct cultures of two ethnic groups have been intensively studied during the last five years by the Hidalgo Project on Differential Culture Change and Mental Health.[1]

The culture of Hidalgo County in South Texas was predominantly Mexican from the time the Rio Grande Valley was permanently settled by immigrants from Mexico in the middle of the eighteenth century until the early part of the twentieth century when large land investment companies bought up all available land, improved it with irrigation, and sold it to migrants from the Midwestern states for the establishment of truck-farming and citrus-raising enterprises. These Midwesterners constitute a large part of the county's Anglo-American population, commonly called "Anglos." A heavy migration of Mexicans took place at about the same time due to new employment opportunities and the flight of refugees from the Mexican Revolution. Today, the Anglos maintain economic control of Hidalgo County while Mexican-Americans constitute the bulk of the labor force. A small Mexican-American élite is descended from the Mexicans who first settled the area under land grants issued by the Spaniards. The members of this upper class include important land holders and professionals in the fields of law and medicine. A rapidly growing middle class is composed of white-collar workers, small store owners, and technicians. The data presented below refer only to the lower- and middle-class Mexican-Americans.

The settlement pattern in Hidalgo County is a clear expression of the social distance maintained between the Anglo and the Mexican-American. Although a few small villages are inhabited exclusively by Mexican-Americans, the typical community embraces both ethnic groups which are separated from each other by railroad tracks or a highway. The Mexican-American side of town is clearly recognizable by the inferiority of living quarters, the smallness of the yard area, and the absence of first class stores and restaurants. Until recently, Mexican-Americans were expected to keep out of the Anglo side of town after dark except when gainfully employed at night. The Anglos likewise avoided the Mexican-American side of town at night except for "slumming" trips to the *cantinas* (saloons) found there.

The Mexican-American population of Hidalgo County is divided into two groups distinguished by different patterns of culture. The primary group consists of conservative Mexican-Americans who adhere to the traditional folk

[1] Sponsor: The Hogg Foundation for Mental Health; director: William Madsen; field director: Mrs. Antonieta Espejo; research associates: Albino Fantini, Octavio Romano, and Arthur Rubel; research assistants: Mrs. Marian Emerson, Mrs. Thomasine Gyetvai, and Mrs. Maria L. Raynes.

culture derived from Mexico. They have no admiration for the Anglo value system or behavior pattern but they envy the Anglo for his higher economic status and associated material benefits. The second group consists of Mexican-Americans who are trying to emulate Anglo behavior and abandon their mother culture. Members of this group are contemptuously called *inglesados* or *agringados* by the conservatives. These terms are the equivalent of the word *pocho* used in Mexico for a Mexican who emulates *gringo* ways.

The psychological stress involved in transferring from one culture to another must be understood in terms of the value conflict between Mexican-American and Anglo cultures.

WORLD VIEW

The Mexican-American views the universe as an integrated totality of God, man, and nature. The dominant component of this complex is God. Both man and nature must adjust to the preconceived patterns that He has established for the world. The Mexican-American finds satisfaction in the daily fulfillment of the fate that God has planned for him. For this reason, the Mexican-American lives for today, rather than for an unknown tomorrow over which he has no control. The individual fulfills his destiny by living up to his obligations and carrying out his roles according to the ideal behavior patterns of his people. Since the blueprint for society and the destiny of the individual are both products of God's will, any violation of His directives may bring punishment in the form of illness for the individual or misfortune for an entire group.

Although the Anglo usually believes in a Creator, he sees man's role on earth in an entirely different fashion. He believes that man can exercise his own free will to achieve the fullest development of his individual potential. His success in this process of development is measured primarily by economic advancement and vertical social mobility. Perhaps, the highest reward visualized by the Anglo is that which is to come tomorrow as the result of his dedicated work today. The time orientation of both the individual and the group is focused on a better tomorrow. For the Anglo-American of South Texas, progress is the highest value.

LA RAZA

The Mexican-American value system is embodied in the concept of *La Raza* (the race) which conveys a feeling of unity within the group. This concept comes from Mexico and refers to the spiritual bond between all persons of Mexican descent. In Mexico, the term carries a belief that the Mexican people are destined to greatness because of their spiritual strength. In the United States, the Mexican-American concept of La Raza includes the idea that "The Race" will never achieve the glorious destiny intended for it by God because of the weakness of a few individuals who behave in ways contrary to God's wishes. It is generally held that the group must move forward together or not move at all. Each individual should devote himself to helping La Raza attain greatness. One of the worst sins that a Mexican-American can commit is to abandon La Raza and transfer his loyalties to another ethnic group with a different philosophy and a different destiny. Since the spiritual bond holding the members of La Raza together was intended by God to be binding, such cultural transfer greatly weakens the potential strength of the group. Each "inglesado" is regarded as a traitor to La Raza.

Because the Mexican-American takes pride in his United States citizenship and the technical achievements of his country, his attitude toward Mexico differs from that of the Mexican national. The Mexican-American looks upon Mexico as the fountainhead of philosophical truth and artistic achievement but at the same time he believes that Mexicans are incapable of turning out efficient tools or machinery. Mutual suspicion and hostility often exists between the Mexican and the Mexican-American in the border area. Mexican-Americans describe Mexican nationals as unreliable and dishonest. Part of this antagonism stems from economic competition for agricultural labor.

MALE AND FEMALE ROLES

Mexican-American and Anglo value systems show a marked contrast in role behavior prescribed for the male and the female. Among the Mexican-Americans there is a strong belief in male superiority. The male plays the leading role in both family life and community life. The values associated with respected male behavior are defined in the concept of *machismo* or manliness. Dignity is the main attribute of machismo. A male must at all times be aloof, maintain social distance, and avoid putting himself in a ridiculous or humiliating situation. He must not express his opinions freely, for once he has taken an open stand on any subject he must defend his position regardless of the consequences. He must avenge any reflection on his honor. Revenge may be achieved by direct physical action or by hiring the services of a witch. Never will the offended male seek revenge by a personality attack upon his antagonist. Indulgence in gossip lowers the dignity of the male and may force the target of gossip to retaliate. An offense is never completely forgiven and an enemy remains an enemy for life. Reconciliation with an antagonist is regarded as evidence of weakness on the part of a man.

Drinking patterns play an important role in male status. A true male drinks in the company of his fellows. His capacity to hold his liquor while keeping his wits and humor contributes to his prestige in male society. Sexual prowess and conquests constitute further proof of machismo. The male concentrates his sexual activities on seduction rather than purchase due to the prestige associated with conquest and the economic expense of a prostitute. After marriage, the ability of a male to hold the affection and sexual privileges of more than one woman enhances his reputation. If it is economically feasible, a married man may keep a mistress in a second house called a *casa chica*. Male society has high regard for such an arrangement which is accepted as normal by female society. The relationship of a man and his mistress is not supposed to interfere with his family obligations. A mistress may expect financial support as long as the relationship continues, but the male is free to break it off at any time. Illegitimate offspring have no claim on their father's purse but he is expected to see to their needs if this expense does not interfere with the support of his legal family.

The Anglo male of South Texas demonstrates his worth as a male in a different way. The respected man has successfully demonstrated strong aggressive drives channeled in the spheres of economic activity, social mobility, civic activity, church allegiance, and marital fidelity. The male who openly violates the monogamous ideal is condemned. Drinking is frowned upon in a large part of Anglo society due to the strong influence of the Bible Belt. Public drunkenness may result in social ostracism. Some Anglo males outwardly conform to the role expectations of society while playing secondary (and they hope secret) roles in the context of purely male society. The proximity of Mexican border towns provides facilities for a male to "go out on the town" in areas forbidden to females of his own society. Outside of his circle of close male associates, the Anglo male must never discuss the drinking or whoring activities of another Anglo in one of the "boy's town" sections across the border. Due to the need for concealment and the limited time factor, many Anglo males conduct their extramarital activities through the media of prostitution.

Female roles also differ between the two ethnic groups. The Mexican-American woman is expected to be subservient in her relationships with elder males of her family or those respected by the community. A "good" woman is highly respected and receives deference from her family and neighbors.

Above everything else, a woman is expected to be sexually and spiritually pure. There is a strong belief that women are inherently weak in a moral sense so they must be secluded and protected not only from men but also from their own weak will. Some of the lowest class families relax the usual precautions with their daughters whose only hope of achieving social mobility or economic advancement lies in becoming the mistress of a man who has a higher social status. The Mexican-American male also finds mistresses among the *inglesadas*—Mexican-American girls who have adopted the Anglo way of life. It is believed that inglesadas and Anglo girls are morally weak in behavior as well as in spirit. The Anglo teenager freely associates with males and the association is frequently conducted without adult supervision. No female could resist the temptation of sex under these circumstances, according to the Mexican-American point of view. The popular Anglo girl is one who responds in some degree to the sexual advances of the male.

MARRIAGE AND THE FAMILY

Anglo marriage is primarily the concern of the individuals who "fall in love" and form the nuclear family. After marriage, the ideal relationship between man and wife is one of partnership. Instead of dedicating herself to the will and well-being of her husband, the Anglo wife is expected to help mold his plans and promote his social advancement. She also expects rights which are undreamed of in the conservative Mexican-American world.

The Anglo concept that love is the main prerequisite for marriage is not found among conservative Mexican-Americans. Marriage in the Spanish-speaking community is always an alliance of families. No wedding is fully sanctioned unless it meets with the approval of the families of the bride and groom. A match may be suggested by the couple but it must be formally arranged by the respective families with the object of maintaining social position or improving it. No good son or daughter would think of ignoring his parents' opinions on his plans for marriage. After marriage, the couple usually takes up residence in or near the home of the groom's father.

Marriage does not end the Mexican-American son's obligation to his parents. A son abides by his father's dictates until the father dies. Before and after marriage, a young man tries to repay his family for the love, protection, and material benefits they have given him. The Mexican-American regards the Anglo nuclear family as a degeneration of that institution as planned by God. The Mexican-American family is an extended, bilateral family including uncles, aunts, grandparents, and cousins. The family is the unit of primary social allegiance which must stand together at all times, especially when it is threatened with danger. The custom of divorce, which is gaining increased acceptance among the Anglos, is regarded as a major sin among the Mexican-Americans.

Godparenthood is found in both ethnic groups but it is comparatively unimportant among the Anglos. Among the Mexican-Americans, godparents constitute an extension of the family. Godparents are chosen for a child by his parents at the time of baptism, confirmation, and marriage. The godparents of a child become the *compadres* or coparents of the parents. The compadre relationship is highly formalized. It dictates a rigid pattern of interpersonal relationships as well as a set of rights and responsibilities. A man must defend and respect his family, including his compadres, under any conditions. Outside of his own biological family, a man first turns to his compadre for aid. Compadres rarely address each other in the familiar form and avoid joking relationships.

CHILD REARING

Child rearing practices heighten the contrast between the Mexican-American and the Anglo family. The Spanish-speaking child must begin contributing to the family earnings at an earlier age than the Anglo child due to the lower wage scale maintained for Mexican-American workers in the Rio Grande Valley. Inadequate family income is a major reason for the Mexican-American child's early withdrawal from school. The Anglo child is ideally supported by his parents until he has obtained the maximum education possible.

The concept of education is also different in the two groups. To the Anglo, education is formal schooling which endows the individual with prestige and techniques for economic and social advancement. Informal education in the home is not nearly so important for the Anglo as it is for the Mexican-American. An "educated person" in the Mexican-American community is one who has learned how to behave with grace and dignity in any social situation. He must know how to react to equals, superiors, and inferiors, as well as to Anglos and inglesados. In his relations with these people, he must not only remain loyal to his family and La Raza but also prove himself to be an intelligent individual with a mind of his own. He must be self-reliant and indebted to no one outside of the extended family.

Among the lower class Mexican-Americans, a minimum of formal education is considered necessary for the purpose of learning English so that the child can "defend" himself in a world dominated by Anglos. The middle-class Mexican-American puts a high premium on the value of formal education beyond the primary level. He sees education as a means of improving his economic position within his own class and maintaining his superiority to members of the lower class. It is in the realm of technical education that he thinks he can obtain the most for his children from the Anglo-dominated educational system. In contrast, the upper-class Mexican-American focuses his education on philosophy, religion, the humanities, and the fine arts in addition to professional training for profitable and respected positions.

The pattern of interpersonal relations within the Mexican-American family invests the father with ultimate and final authority. The Mexican-American child obeys his father without hesitation, whereas the Anglo child soon learns that a paternal command may be altered by means of persuasion or argument. The "buddy" role played by the Anglo father and son is unknown in the Mexican-American home. Mexican-American children are expected to show the highest respect for their father. Beyond the age of early childhood, they rarely engage in verbal or physical play with the father. The mother is often equated to the Virgin of Guadalupe because she is pure, retiring, loving, and an ever-present source of comfort in time of trouble or strife. It is considered almost sinful for a Mexican-American child to sadden his mother with behavior that reflects on the family honor and dignity.

On reaching the age of puberty, the Mexican-American girl is pulled tightly into the protective confines of her family. She is permitted to play only with a few girls of her own age and never allowed to associate with boys except under strict adult supervision. During this period, the girl receives instruction from her mother and older female relatives about the duties of a good wife. She learns the fundamentals of housework, child care, curing techniques, and marital etiquette. She is taught that she must never disagree with her future husband, cause him worry, or criticize his behavior. A mother continually reminds her growing daughter that she must accept her subservient position with grace and contentment for it is the will of God.

The Anglo girl, on the other hand, frequently learns by example that the position of authority in the family is contested. She may be instructed by her mother in the techniques of preserving her female rights in marriage. The declining authority of the father in the Anglo family is reflected in the rapid disappearance of the phrase "to love, honor, and obey" in the Anglo marriage ceremony.

ETIQUETTE

Etiquette is highly formalized in the Mexican-American community where the informal give-and-take of Anglo society is missing. A visitor must not cross the doorway, sit down, or express an opinion in a Mexican-American home unless he is asked to do so by his host. A guest must avoid contradicting his host or verbally questioning his opinions.

Visitors who fail to observe these rules are looked down upon as contemptible individuals who are unworthy of association. They are never invited to make a return visit. Anglo public health nurses and physicians are rarely asked to return.

GROUP AFFILIATION

The emphasis on club, lodge, church, and political affiliation which dominates Anglo society is absent in Mexican-American society. The conservative Mexican-American is not a joiner. Mutual aid organizations, unions, religious groups, and political parties have trouble in recruiting and holding Mexican-American membership. Affiliation with such groups would lower the individual's loyalty to his family in the Mexican-American view.

Furthermore, everybody outside of the family is regarded with suspicion. In dealing with members of La Raza, the Mexican-American can never be sure which individuals belong to the immoral group holding back its people from their glorious destiny. In dealing with Anglos and inglesados, he is aware of the contempt they hold for his ways of life. He can easily see the economic discrimination that the Anglos have forced upon him by paying an Anglo more than a Mexican-American for exactly the same work. He also observes the preferential treatment given the Anglo and the inglesado in employment opportunities, promotions, and social relations. Therefore, the conservative Mexican-American usually believes that he would expose himself to exploitation and possible loss of honor by joining any formal association outside of the family.

SOCIAL STATUS

Opposite means of achieving social status distinguish the Mexican-American and Anglo value systems. The conservative Mexican-American follows a policy of inconspicuous consumption in order to avoid arousing the envy and suspicion of his friends. The individual who tries to outdo his fellows through social and economic advancement may be suspected of violating the mores of La Raza and abandoning the group for his own self-interest. The person who arouses the envy of others by possessing a better house, better clothes, and a better job than his neighbors places himself in a dangerous position. Those who envy him become his enemies and they may hire a witch to hex him. The Mexican-American who can afford to buy some luxury items may deliberately limit them to things that can be kept in the home where they will not be observed by a passerby. The individual who is on the road to economic advancement constantly fears arousing the envy of others and suspects the motives of his acquaintances. The Mexican-American pattern of inconspicuous consumption conflicts directly with the Anglo pattern of conspicuous consumption and the philosophy of "keeping up with the Joneses" as a means of obtaining status and community approval.

The expense of the medical treatment that an Anglo can afford is a reflection and a re-enforcement of his social status whereas this is not the case in Mexican-American society. The conservative Mexican-American is reluctant to let his ailments be known in the community because of the belief that any disease may be a punishment from God or the saints for immoral behavior.

THEORIES OF DISEASE

The supernatural orientation of Mexican-American folk medicine conflicts with the scientific basis of Anglo medicine. Many of the diseases recognized by Mexican-American folk medicine seem to involve psychosomatic reactions to blocked emotions. Living in a hostile world believed to be filled with individuals who become suspicious or envious of any small success, the Mexican-American is inwardly often in a highly emotional state. As the outward expression of emotion is considered in bad form, there are very few ways to channelize hostility and fear. These emotions may be made manifest in diseases such as bewitchment, evil eye, fright, and anger.

Witchcraft is said to be responsible for the illness called *demencia* (insanity) which comes from an evil element put into the atmosphere and directed at the intended victim by a witch. The bewitched person may suffer from amnesia, hallucinations, and feelings of guilt and persecution. *Miedo* (fear), another witch-sent disease, causes unreasonable fears and hideous hallucinations.

Mexican-Americans realize that an extreme emotional experience can be a source of illness. Natural fright causes the sickness called *susto* which is accompanied by nightmares and a feeling of impending tragedy. *Espanto,* a fright disease caused by seeing ghosts, brings on extreme nervousness, instability, moroseness, and difficulty in reasoning out the small problems of everyday life. Unreleased anger is believed to upset the balance of the humors causing the sickness called *bilis* (bile). A person suffering from bilis experiences diarrhea and vomiting.

One of the most common diseases, particularly among children, is caused by the evil eye. It is believed that certain individuals are born with powerful psychic forces which are directed through their eyes at people they like or admire. Since young children are weak, they are most likely to be harmed by the power of the evil eye. Individuals possessing the evil eye are not resented or hated because the harm they do is unintentional. However, care is taken to protect children from them. The symptoms of evil eye sickness include nervousness, insomnia, and irrational weeping. The person who caused the illness can cure it by touching the afflicted one on the head to remove the evil from him.

No member of the Mexican-American family is officially "sick" until so defined by the head of the household whereas in Anglo society a state of illness is usually a matter of self-definition. In the case of children who may be suspected of trying to avoid school, the Anglo mother or father makes the ultimate decision which is commonly based upon the confirming evidence of a thermometer.

MEDICAL REFERRAL SYSTEMS

Medical referral systems differ between the two groups. The Anglos refer virtually all cases of illness to physicians. The Mexican-Americans also consult physicians in case of ailments recognized to be of natural causation such as fractures, serious bleeding, or appendicitis. Diseases believed to be of supernatural origin are referred to a folk curer called a *curandero*. The curandero operates within a system of folk beliefs accepted by the conservative Mexican-Americans. He carefully explains the reasons for his diagnosis and treatment. From the beginning of his treatment, he establishes a close, affective relationship with the patient and his family. The curandero uses herbs, massage, and cleansings (*limpias*) accompanied by appeals to God and the saints for divine aid. If treatments by more than one curandero prove unsuccessful, the family of the patient may consult a physician as a last resort. In this case, no attempt is made to understand the scientific nature of the diagnosis or the treatment recommended by the physician.

As the Mexican-American rises in the class system, he shows an increasing reliance on modern medical facilities. While a member of the lower-lower class seeks the services of both physicians and curanderos, the middle-class individual relies more on physicians. A member of the upper class follows the Anglo pattern of modern medical care.

CLASS DIFFERENCES IN ACCULTURATION

A differential degree of acculturation in the lower, middle, and upper classes is observable in other aspects of Mexican-American culture. Generally speaking, the lowest class is the most resistant to change. The upper-lower class and the upper-middle class are the most susceptible to Anglo acculturation. Both of these subclasses have accepted the Anglo goal of economic gain as one of the prime motives in life.

A member of the upper-lower class who is determined to advance his social and economic position may try to enter the lower-middle class or directly transfer to Anglo culture. A member of the lower-middle class usually finds institutional means to facilitate his elevation to the upper-middle class so that he is not likely to make a transfer to the Anglo way of life. A member of the upper-middle class who is still seeking social and economic mobility encounters strong resistance blocking his acceptance in the upper class. Hence, he is likely to emulate Anglo roles and seek identification with Anglo society. Throughout the class structure, Anglo influence is noticeable in the realm of material culture.

PRESSURES FOR CHANGE

Today the Anglo society is exerting organized pressure for change on the Mexican-American. The schools of South Texas are making a concerted effort to anglicize the Mexican-American child. School authorities generally feel that the subject matter taught in the schools will convince the Mexican-American of the superiority of Anglo culture and cause him to abandon the conservative traditions of his parents.

One symbol of Latin culture which arouses antagonism in Anglo society is the Mexican-American's insistence on using the Spanish language. Most Anglos want a monolingual, English-speaking society although some educated individuals express the opinion that bilingualism would be more desirable. It is obviously essential for the Mexican-American child to speak English in the public schools. A large number of Mexican-American children have done failing work in the primary grades because they did not understand English. In order to cope with this problem, school authorities have instituted accelerated programs of English instruction for preschool children from Spanish-speaking families. Other means of enforcing the use of English have frequently aroused hostility. In some schools the use of Spanish is forbidden on the school grounds, as well as in the class rooms, on threat of punishment or expulsion. The use of Spanish is discouraged in conversations between staff members of the public health clinics for consultation. Anglo school teachers sometimes visit the homes of their Mexican-American pupils to urge the parents to speak English instead of Spanish in the home.

The Anglo beliefs that the Mexican-American child of a conservative family learns in school are in conflict with the traditions he has been taught at home. He soon learns not to inform his family of new values and ideas to which he has been exposed at school. Vocalized cultural heresies are reprimanded by the father and the child is exposed to ridicule by the whole family.

There is intensive Anglo pressure to re-educate the Mexican-Americans in the subject of health because their resistance to modern medicine is viewed as a threat to the entire community. School hygiene courses instruct the Mexican-American child in the importance of clean utensils, daily needs in nutrition and excretion, and the basis of contagion. Public health clinics give inoculations, chest X-rays, and instruction in the theory of preventive medicine as well as courses in prenatal and postnatal care. Health education programs focused on the germ theory of disease seem to have made very little impression on the conservative Mexican-American. He rationalizes that bacteria which cannot be seen cannot exist. Sometimes he expresses the suspicion that the germ theory is a fabrication invented by doctors to exploit the Mexican-Americans. In addition to the fundamental conflict in the disease theories of Mexican-American folk medicine and Anglo medicine, there are a number of other reasons for the resistance to Anglo re-education programs. The Mexican-American is reluctant to seek aid and advice from Anglo doctors and public health personnel, because they frequently assume an unconscious air of superiority and ridicule his medical beliefs as "superstitions." The Anglo doctor's ignorance of folk disease theory may convince the conservative Mexican-American that the curandero is indeed a superior medical practitioner. As most public health workers do not speak Spanish, the language barrier constitutes another major obstacle to the establishment of a harmonious interpersonal relationship between the Mexican-American patient and the Anglo public health worker or doctor.

Both Catholic and Protestant churches exert pressure on the Mexican-American to accept Anglo religious and medical beliefs and to conform to Anglo behavior patterns. Priests and ministers bombard the Mexican-American with sermons attacking his religious and medical "superstitions" and "lax" moral behavior. They also distribute printed material designed to make the Mexican-American conform to Anglo ideals. These pressures have little effect on the conservative members of the lower class who assume that great realms of supernatural phenomena, including the supernatural power of the curandero, are not understood by the priest. Protestant churches rarely have the opportunity of approaching the Mexican-American who is not an inglesado.

The individual most likely to adopt Anglo culture is a member of a middle-class family who has been exposed to Anglo ideas in schools and employment situations for several decades. The exposure of the lower-class family to Anglo culture is far more limited because their children are taken out of school after a few years and they are not qualified for jobs which would bring them into contact with Anglos. The middle-class individual has accepted the Anglo goals of economic and social advancement, but he finds social advancement virtually impossible within his own society because the upper class will not accept him. Hence, he turns to Anglo society. Quite frequently, the individual begins adopting Anglo ways without any conscious desire to change his group affiliation. However, his changed behavior immediately affects his social relations within the conservative group. When the individual becomes aware of the hostility of his friends or family, he may abandon his Anglo ways and retreat back into the conservative group, or he may try to affiliate with the Anglo population.

IMPACT OF CULTURAL TRANSFER
ON SOCIAL RELATIONSHIPS

The partly anglicized Mexican-American finds himself in an exceedingly uncomfortable position. His friends may reject him and his family relationships become strained. Moreover, he does not find full acceptance among the Anglos whom he is emulating. The Anglo group will not accept the inglesado until his behavior completely reflects Anglo values. At best, the partly acculturated inglesado finds his close friendships limited to other Mexican-Americans who also are in an incompleted stage of anglicization.

Decision making becomes difficult and complicated because of the conflict between the individual's Anglo and Mexican-American values. The highest degree of anxiety, fear, and guilt is found in this group of partly anglicized individuals. A few of them react by rebelling against society and committing overt acts of violence resulting in arrest. Cognitive dissonance between Anglo and Mexican-American values usually causes the individual to readjust his goals. He may retreat into Mexican-American society where he becomes more conservative than before, or he may make a physical retreat by moving to California or another part of Texas. The other alternative is to seek clear identification and affiliation with groups operating within the framework of Anglo culture.

If the individual decides to transfer from Mexican-American to Anglo culture, he may join some organization such as a political action group, a service club, lodge, a union, or more typically a Protestant church. In renouncing Catholicism for Protestantism, the inglesado is placing an unbreachable gap between himself and the conservative group of Mexican-Americans. Moreover, in the Protestant church he finds that he is not associated with Anglos but assigned to a mission church composed almost entirely of Mexican-Americans in his own position between two cultures.

Protestantism offers the inglesado a simplified value system with a clear-cut distinction between "right" and "wrong." If the individual can force himself to accept the new religious concepts, decision-making is greatly simplified. However, the behavior demanded of him by the carefully supervised mission churches subjects him to the scorn of the conservative Mexican-Americans and often fails to bring him any closer to the Anglos. Not only do his new church-defined roles alienate him from his former friends but they may lead to extreme self-doubts about his own worth, particularly his masculinity.

Most Protestant sects in South Texas expect a convert to stop smoking, drinking, and pursuing women. He is taught to forgive his enemies and accept any offense without thought of protecting his honor through revenge. Some of the more emotional sects, known as *aleluyas*, demand behavior which lacks dignity in terms of conservative Mexican-American values. The convert often feels that church handouts of clothing and food reflect on his traditional concept of self-reliance. His position subjects him to increasing ridicule from conservative Mexican-Americans. As a defense mechanism, the convert may begin to gossip about the religious "superstitions" of folk Catholicism, and about the individuals who adhere to Mexican-American culture. By indulging in such gossip, he violates the traditions of *machismo*. At this point in the process of cultural transfer, many individuals again try to retreat to conservative Mexican-American culture or to migrate to other parts of the nation.

A CASE HISTORY OF CULTURAL TRANSFER

A case history from Hidalgo County clearly demonstrates the psychological hazards of cultural transfer. This is the story of a Mexican-American whom I will call Juan Gallo because that is not his real name. In a general way, Juan was a typical son of a typical middle-class family belonging to the conservative Mexican-American group. He grew up learning the ideals of La Raza which he tried to fulfill in his everyday behavior. He enjoyed the approval of his family, his neighbors, and the conservative society.

As a youth, he succeeded in proving his worth to the members of his own age group except in regard to his sexual prowess. On two occasions he established sexual relationships with girls whose affections were stolen by his male friends. The third girl to take his fancy was an inglesada. Highly desirable physically, she defied his attempts at seduction. Juan defended himself against the taunts of his friends by stating that he intended to marry the girl and could not insult her sense of purity by an immoral proposition. He finally did propose to her and she accepted, much to his surprise.

Because Juan made a promise of marriage without consulting his parents, he was criticized by his father. His mother grieved over his filial disobedience. Juan denied his family obligations and his church when he married the inglesada in the Protestant revivalist church to which she belonged. Shortly after the marriage, he was baptized in his wife's church. He then found himself labeled as an inglesado by his former friends and the conservative society as a whole.

His reaction was a conscious effort to become an economic success within the framework of Anglo society and culture. He and his wife spoke English at home and he avoided using the Spanish language whenever possible. He avoided Spanish language movies and began to ridicule the amusements of his former friends. He adopted the dress and mannerisms of the inglesados.

In his search for group identification, Juan tried to follow the way of life advocated by the minister of his new church. He stopped drinking and avoided the cantinas in which he had previously spent his free time. This step cut him off from further contact with his former friends who now ridiculed him. He stayed true to his wife and refrained from engaging in the exchange of dirty jokes. He attempted to quit smoking but found this ordeal too difficult. However, he did not smoke in his home or near the church grounds.

Juan obtained a job in a grocery store where he set out to achieve economic success and thus justify his denial of his cultural heritage. By working overtime and making a great effort to please his customers, he soon received a pay raise and a better position in the grocery store. His advancement helped compensate for the uneasiness he felt about his machismo. He found further satisfaction in his star role on the church baseball team composed entirely of inglesados. In game after game, his team defeated all comers including several teams of conservative Mexican-Americans. To all outward appearances, he had made a successful transfer to Anglo culture. He radiated confidence, boasted of his happy home life, and dedicated himself to becoming a progressing member of his new society. He joined LULAC (League of United Latin American Citizens) and worked for the betterment of Mexican-Americans. He found a sympathetic audience at the LULAC meetings and among his newly cultivated inglesado friends.

Beneath the surface, however, Juan did not find his new life comfortable. He acquiesced to his wife's desire for a completely anglicized household which caused him distress. Juan helped his wife with the dishes and household chores following the Anglo pattern that they had learned from the movies and comics. On one occasion, he was ashamed to find himself with a towel tied around his waist like an apron when an unexpected guest arrived. Even more serious was his doubt about his masculinity because his wife had not conceived a child during the two years of their marriage. He also missed the happy evenings he used to spend with his old friends.

One day all of his anxieties culminated in a mental breakdown. Juan had worked himself up to the point of being considered for the position of manager of the store in which he was employed. He expected to receive this promotion and thereby achieve what he believed to be his highest goal in life. On this day he was informed by his employer that an Anglo had been hired as store manager. After work, he joined his baseball team for a game against a conservative Mexican-American team. Upset by his experience at the store, Juan made a series of errors during the game, and his team lost. He assumed personal responsibility for the defeat.

He returned home in a state of semi-shock and told his wife about losing the promotion at the store. She immediately attacked him with loud and cutting remarks to the effect that he would have certainly gotten the job if he had "acted like a man." She accused him of being a "sissy" unable to defend his rights. Then she served him a chicken dinner. Juan recalled the Anglo connotation of the word "chicken," and he also remembered a magical formula prescribing the use of chicken parts by women who wanted to increase their sexual allure. At this point, he exploded with a series of illogical accusations against his wife. He accused her of using magic to make him lose the last vestige of his manhood so that she would be free to devote herself to a lover. He began to beat her, and her screams aroused a neighbor who called the police. When a policeman knocked on the door, Juan shouted to his wife that he would fix her lover for good. Grabbing a revolver, he threw open the door and shot the policeman between the legs. Following his arrest, Juan was committed to a mental institution.

The case of Juan Gallo is an extreme case. Few Mexican-Americans reach the point of arrest and institutionalization during the process of anglicization. However, the doubt and anxiety that led to Juan's breakdown are present in a smaller degree among most Mexican-Americans who attempt to make a rapid transfer to Anglo culture.

MULTIGENERATIONAL TRANSFER

A constantly increasing number of Mexican-Americans have succeeded in making the cultural transfer. They include prominent professional men and political leaders who are accepted as English-speaking members of Anglo society. These men have moved "above" their Mexican-American heritage and today they live on the Anglo side of the tracks.

Successful identification with Anglo culture is not often possible within the lifetime of the individual. Rather it is a multigenerational process that usually begins in the upper-lower class. From this class, the family moves into the lower-middle class and advances to the upper-middle class. Identification with Anglo individuals and exposure to Anglo culture frequently occurs in the middle class resulting in the acceptance of some Anglo goals. The family may then move into a marginal culture whose value system incorporates both Anglo and Mexican-American goals. Children raised in this marginal culture may complete the internalization of Anglo values and transfer to Anglo culture. As more and more of these cultural transfers are being made, the general pattern of behavior for Mexican-Americans is also moving closer to Anglo behavior. However, complete integration of the two ethnic groups based on a common value system does not lie within the foreseeable future.

chapter fifteen

Personality Continuity
and Change in the Family Context

Leon J. Yarrow and Marian Radke Yarrow

Until very recently much of personality theory has focused on the significance for personality development of experiences during infancy and early childhood. This preoccupation with one aspect of psychoanalytic theory has led rather subtly to an orientation which assumes that little of significance for personality development occurs *after* the Oedipal period. By a peculiar process of logic, this highly deterministic view is often thought to be the only position consistent with the theorem that experiences in infancy and early childhood play a significant role in personality development. Belief in the importance of early experiences and belief in the modifiability of the organism are incompatible only on a very superficial level. The more differentiated our questions become with regard to both the impact of early experiences and the modifiability of the organism, the more clearly we see these problems as different aspects of common theoretical issues.

The extent to which response patterns and behavioral predispositions developed in infancy are susceptible to modification by later influences is an open theoretical issue, and certainly a ripe question for research. Eminent psychoanalytic theorists equivocate on this question but suggest the possibilities of modification and change in personality beyond the preschool period. Hartmann, Kris, and Lowenstein (1946) state, "We assume that the essential elements in the structure of personality exist in children of our civilization at the age of five or six. Developmental processes occurring after that age can be described as modifications, as enrichment, or in pathological cases, as restriction of the then existing structure" (p. 19). Later in the same article, they note,

The development of personality is not concluded at this point (end of preschool period) and we feel that the potentialities for its transformation throughout latency

489

and adolescence have for some time been underrated in psychoanalytic writings. But it seems that the basic structure of the personality and the basic functional interrelations of the systems have been fixed to some extent. The child does not stop growing and developing, but after that age both growth and development modify existing structure (p. 34).

In examining the question of personality change in the family, one is implicitly rejecting the notion of fixed, irreversible patterns laid down by the end of infancy and opening up the question of the impact of experiences in middle childhood and in adolescence. From a developmental perspective, personality formation is a process of personality change. At each developmental stage, the child's relationship to his environment changes. He becomes part of increasingly complex interactional systems, and he takes on new roles which dictate changes in goals, motives, and behavior. With changes both in the social environment and in the child's capacities come alterations in many aspects of personality—in ways of coping with the environment, in self-concept, and in the hierarchy of needs, motives, and defenses. From this perspective, the question of the role of the family environment in personality change is almost indistinguishable from the problem of family influences on personality development. The concepts and theoretical principles underlying personality growth undoubtedly are applicable to questions of personality changes in the family.

Although there is a voluminous literature on the personality correlates of many parental and family characteristics, research directly concerned with personality change as a consequence of identifiable changes in family variables is almost non-existent. In attempting to clarify the theoretical questions and research problems related to personality change in the family environment, we have examined the following issues: (*a*) continuity and change in the family environment; (*b*) personality continuity and change through the developmental cycle; (*c*) the relationship between changes in the family environment and personality changes, considering both normal changes that occur in the developmental history of most families, and crises and traumatic events leading to major disruptions in family roles and relationships. The relevant data come from several sources: longitudinal and follow-up studies of personality continuity; cross-sectional studies of continuity and change in child-rearing practices; studies of family structural characteristics in relation to personality development; and studies of the impact on personality of deviant conditions in the family, such as parental pathology, death of a parent, maternal separation, and disordered parent-child relationships.

As one attempts to integrate the diverse studies, with their immensely varied orientations, many methodological difficulties become apparent. Most of the studies are limited to the immediate reactions to an event, without follow-up study of the persistence of these reactions over long periods of time. Some research is based on clinic or court populations with sparse retrospective data on the earlier events. The antecedent variables are on many different levels; some studies deal with surface manifestations, others with more basic personality dispositions. Most of the studies are atheoretical; the research questions have usually not been formulated within any systematic framework; the problems represent a random assortment of issues. Most of the variables are empirically derived. Frequently they are broad phenotypic ones, such as "broken homes" or "divorce."

In considering these data within the framework of personality change, we have often had to refocus the research questions and impose conceptual perspectives. To arrive at even suggestive conclusions concerning personality change, much extrapolation has been necessary. The available data are small blocks that only begin to build an empirical base for an expanded theory of personality development and personality change.

CONTINUITY AND CHANGE IN THE FAMILY ENVIRONMENT

In the absence of unanticipated traumatic events, can we assume that the normal family environment is essentially unchanging throughout the course of development? It is obvious that the family is not static; for a given child there are repeated changes in the structural and dynamic characteristics of his family environment throughout his developmental history. We have, however, very meager knowledge of family environments viewed developmentally, and very few data on the kinds of changes that occur normally in the family's life history. The limited data on continuity and change come from varied research contexts: a few longitudinal and follow-up studies of child-rearing practices, several clinical reports on the correlates of maternal behavior at different developmental stages, and some less direct data on cultural determinants of parental roles and attitudes at different age levels. Conclusions regarding the consistency of the parental environment depend, in part, on the particular variables which have been chosen for study and, in part, on the level of correlation which one accepts as evidence of continuity.

One of the few studies that have dealt directly with the question of consistency over time in parents' relationships to the child is that of Schaefer and Bayley (1960). Data based on descriptions of mother-infant interactions in a testing situation were compared with interview data obtained from the same mothers when the children were between nine and fourteen years of age. On one dimension of the parental relationship—hostility-love—they found high correlations between ratings in infancy and in middle childhood, correlations of $+.73$ for boys and +.61 for girls. On the dimension of autonomy control, correlations were insignificant, indicating little consistency over time on this aspect of child rearing.

Other studies have found significant changes in parental behavior with the changing structure of the family and with the changing age of the child. In a comparison of parental behavior towards three-year-old and nine-year-old children, Baldwin (1946) found parents of nine-year-olds are less warm, less intellectually stimulating, less indulgent, and more restrictive than parents of three-year-olds. Changes in the mother's relationship with the existing children in a family have also been found during pregnancy and after the birth of the new child (Baldwin, 1947; Lasko, 1954). During pregnancy mothers became more "understanding" and were less directive with their children. Following the birth of a child, there was a shift in maternal behavior. Mothers not only gave less time to the older children, but they showed less warmth, and became more restrictive and more severe in discipline. The greatest changes occurred following the birth of the second child.

The findings of several studies might lead one to hypothesize that there are systematic differences in the degree of environmental continuity for children of different ordinal positions. First-born children are likely to experience more changes in parental handling and parental attitudes than children in other ordinal positions (Lasko, 1954; Baldwin, 1947). In contrast, later-born children presumably experience greater consistency in parental behavior. (The effects of these changes are considered later in the discussion of personality correlates of ordinal position.)

Fragmentary clinical data indicate that there are discontinuities in maternal behavior at different periods of the child's development which seem to be related to the mother's individual personality dynamics. Coleman et al. (1953) present case material on mothers who were able to establish close and mutually gratifying relationships with completely dependent infants but who had difficulty in relating to older children who were more autonomous and self-sufficient. Other mothers were able to relate better to the autonomous older child than to the dependent infant. Fries (1944) discusses the extent to which the mothers' feelings and behavior are influenced by the degree of gratification she derives from the child's characteristics. Both sex and age-related characteristics of the child may influence the mother's behavior. The sex of the child may have special significance in relation to the mother's feelings about her own sex role. As the child grows older, his sex may become increasingly salient for the mother and, thus, may be associated with significant changes in her behavior.

Other "regularized" discontinuities in parental behavior are related to cultural prescriptions and norms for child rearing. Anthropological accounts of other cultures (Whiting and Child, 1953) describe distinct age-linked patterns of parental handling as a result of which marked and abrupt changes occur in the child's experiences in his family. In the Kwoma, for example, a pattern of complete indulgence in infancy is followed by sudden and severe independence training. Within our own culture there are similar, perhaps less extreme, sequential changes in rearing practices; Davis and Havighurst (1946) found among lower-class urban Negro parents sudden changes from permissive and indulgent practices in infancy and very early childhood to harshness in the management of aggression and hostility at the school ages. Specific age-grading and age-sex-typing pressures in the middle-class American family have been pointed out by the Murphys (1937) who describe differences in the "social situations" of boys and girls of different ages associated with changes in the parents' handling of aggression and independence, in their standards and pressures for achievement, etc. One might speculate on the extent to which Gesell's (1943) descriptions of characteristic personalities and motivations for each age level have helped to create different family environments for different ages by determining parental expectations and standards.

The relative dominance of the maternal and paternal roles in child rearing at different developmental periods seems to be culturally prescribed. Such changes are probably associated with some degree of discontinuity in the family environment. The amount of change may differ for boys and girls, insofar as the father's techniques and basic relationship with a boy and a girl may differ.

As the child passes from one developmental stage to another, the changes in his abilities, needs, and ways of interacting with his environment affect the delicate balance of interaction patterns in the family. Psychoanalytic theory postulates rather marked shifts in the child's relationship with each parent at different developmental stages, almost as a biologically determined fact—during infancy, at the Oedipal period, during adolescence. Although it is likely that these developmental alterations in family relationships represent significant changes for the child, to the extent that they are in keeping with his developing capacities and needs, they may provide psychological continuity rather than change in the environment.

In general, research on the family in the American and Western cultures has not given much attention to patterned successive consistencies or changes in the kinds of family influences to which the developing personality is exposed. We certainly do not have a very differentiated view of our culture and the subcultures within it in terms of *phasing* of different rearing practices during the childhood period. The impact of individually or culturally determined changes and the child's perception of them may depend on the abruptness or gradualness with which they are introduced. Some parents and cultures decide quite precipitously at a given age that the child is no longer an infant and, therefore, should learn to accept delays in gratification, should acquire appropriate impulse controls and should show greater sensitivity to the parents' needs; other parents and cultures introduce such changes gradually and manage a smoother course of family environmental change. A readying, stepwise procedure of change in rearing practices, in fostering independence and impulse control may have a very different impact on personality than sudden and radical shifts in rearing procedures.

To evaluate the effects of individual and culturally monitored changes in parents' behavior towards their children, we need detailed longitudinal data on parents and on children from several subcultures. It is clear that the data on the parents should include not only their overt behavior but the meaning of the behavioral changes to them. We also need measures of the child's perception of these changes and their meaning in relation to his developmental stage and sex role identity, as well as data on the salience of these changes in terms of the child's vulnerabilities and idiosyncratic motives and conflicts.

From the available data we can draw only limited conclusions about developmental changes in the family environment. Moreover, since the research does not deal simultaneously with both antecedent and consequent variables—with family environment and child personality—we know little about the effects of changes in normal family environments. The data to be considered on personality consistency are similarly limited to one set of variables. In only an indirect way do they offer some leads on the impact of the changing family environment on personality development.

PERSONALITY CONSISTENCY

In the context of a life history, personality change becomes a rather elusive entity. If one attempts to relate a given family event to specific personality consequences, one must make some assumptions about the course of personality development had the given event not occurred. A base line from which to measure change is needed. In a sense, data on personality continuity through the developmental cycle provide such a base line. For purposes of measurement, personality change can be conceptualized on a scale ranging from no change, i.e., continuity, to much change. The data on continuity, then, are part of the data on change.

In examining the research it becomes clear that conclusions regarding personality continuity and change are very much dependent on one's criteria, which, in turn, are based on one's theoretical orientation regarding personality. Two rather different concepts of personality continuity can be distinguished: a phenotypic consistency and a dynamic consistency. Phenotypic consistency assumes complete congruence or identity in a given characteristic from time one to time two. Such isomorphic identity is not part of the concept of dynamic continuity. Rather, changes in overt behavior or personality characteristics may be seen as developmental transformations which are dynamically related to earlier behavior patterns or functions. For example, either tense hyperactivity or passive withdrawal at the preschool age may be seen as predictable expressions of hypersensitivity in early infancy.

It is difficult to arrive at any simple conclusions about personality consistency, because the studies have varied in many significant respects: on the level at which personality is conceptualized, in the time span covered by the research, and in the specific developmental points at which the data have been obtained. Some studies have dealt with relatively simple behavioral variables, others with more basic personality functions; some have dealt with very specific traits, others with global functions or personality style. The time interval during which consistency has been measured has ranged from several months during infancy to almost the total life span. Some research has compared personality characteristics between infancy and five years of age, other studies have compared two points in middle childhood. One would anticipate differing degrees of stability over such varied time intervals and between such different developmental periods.

Evidence from Infancy Studies

In spite of the methodological difficulties in assessing infant characteristics and in spite of the known variability of infant behavior, a number of studies suggest that there is a high degree of consistency between early infancy characteristics and characteristics at the end of the preschool period. Escalona and Heider (1959) were able to predict with moderate success personality characteristics during the preschool years (ages two-eight to five-six) from infancy data. Their predictions were not of specific traits but were predictions based on dynamic theoretical hypotheses. For example, it was hypothesized that "high activity level in conjunction with other factors reflects either an unusual intensity of impulse or unusually weak mechanism for impulse control and modulation." They also hypothesized a relationship between sensory reactivity in infancy and intensity and quality of fantasy life, and social sensitivity in later childhood. Moderately high consistency was found in measures related to physiological functions, e.g., sensory threshold, activity level, and in overall "personality style." The findings are interpreted as evidence of dynamic consistency, "As one notes behavioral alterations from infancy to later preschool ages, one knows that not a single behavior has remained the same, yet one is struck with the inherent continuity of behavioral style and of the child's pattern of adaptation." The investigators also conclude that "characteristics of behavior which refer to overall style or pattern may prove more stable than those which refer to intensity or magnitude and also than those characteristics which pertain to a single function rather than to the whole of behavior."

Similar kinds of personality consistencies between infancy and the early preschool years have been reported by Shirley (1933), by Gesell and Ames (1937), and more recently by Chess, Thomas, and Birch (1959). Shirley found that characteristics such as irritability and activity level noted in infancy tend to persist as distinctive characteristics of children at three years of age. Gesell and Ames reported a high degree of "internal consistency" between one and five years of age in such characteristics as energy output, motor coordination, emotional expressiveness, and exploitation of the environment. Chess, Thomas, and Birch found continuity during the first two years in characteristics such as quality of response to new stimuli and tenacity of involvement. On the whole, the findings of these studies are interpreted as evidence of intrinsic reaction types based on biological and constitutional factors. Gesell and Ames conclude, "Our findings must not be over-generalized but they strongly indicate that certain fundamental traits of individuality, whatever their origin, exist early, persist late and assert themselves under varying environmental conditions."

Evidence from Preschool to Middle-Childhood Years

Studies of personality continuity from the preschool years to middle childhood tend to be less definite in their conclusions than are the infancy studies. Several investigators point to both continuity and change. In contrast to the emphasis on constitutional factors in the infancy studies, no direct discussion of the role of such factors appears in studies of this age group. Lois Murphy (1960), on the basis of longitudinal data obtained during the preschool and middle childhood years concludes,

While persistent characteristics are extremely important, we also find dramatic changes in overt coping style in certain children who blossom with new developmental resources or new environmental opportunities or supports, and in children who fade or lose their grip under new environmental stress or external intensification of inner problems they managed comfortably before the new stress (p. 257).

McKinnon (1942) came to somewhat similar conclusions on the basis of study of sixteen children from three to nine years of age:

Persistence or change in behavior seems to be largely a matter of degree. No children studied remained absolutely constant with respect to the predominant forms of behavior. Similarly, in no case was there a revolutionary change, but the shift in dominant behavior trends was always in the direction of a form of behavior that has been evident, but less pronounced, at an earlier age.

When studies of elementary school age children have used the social stimulus characteristics of children (their popularity and reputations with peers and adults) as measures of personality, consistency over the years is emphasized (Bonney, 1943*a*; Bonney, 1943*b*; Tuddenham, 1959). These findings may be interpreted as reflections of consistency in personal characteristics or in quality of social interaction, or they may reflect the consistency with which a person is perceived, after a reputation is established. It is likely that consistencies in expectations of others play a significant role in maintaining personality continuity. This problem has not been extensively studied although it lends itself to experimental manipulation. It may also be highly relevant in interpreting the effects of family experiences upon personality, for, undoubtedly, there is considerable constancy in the expectations of family members for one another.

Evidence from Early Childhood to Adolescence and Adulthood

Fewer studies on personality consistency encompass a long time span. Among those that do, the findings differ. Several studies document the persistence of some broad personality characteristics from early childhood through adolescence. Neilon (1948) was able to match, with a high degree of efficiency, well above chance expectancy, personality sketches of a group of seventeen-year-olds with sketches made of these same individuals in infancy by Shirley. Stott (1957) found that the child's patterns of interaction with other children in school (dominance, leadership, ascendance, conformity) showed a high degree of persistence from preschool through high school. Stott considered this persistence particularly significant in view of the fact that considerable effort had been made by the nursery school staff to bring about changes.

Kagan's and Moss' (1960) report on the stability of measures of passive and dependent behavior from preschool to middle childhood (at ten years) and also to early adulthood brings up several additional issues regarding personality continuity. They found considerably lower correlations between ratings of these variables at three years and at ten years than between ratings at ten years and at adulthood and considered this indicative of more significant changes in dependency characteristics during early and middle childhood than in later childhood. These data suggest the importance of considering the interaction between the specific personality characteristics and the developmental period. Certainly marked changes in overt manifestations of dependency would be expected between three and ten years of age. Their finding that girls showed much greater stability than boys in passive and dependent behavior between early childhood and adulthood suggests the possibility of differential reinforcements for boys and girls in this kind of behavior. The implication for the larger issue of personality continuity is that there may be different orders of stability over time for the two sexes.

The longitudinal data of MacFarlane, Allen, and Honzik (1954) on behavior problems, e.g., restlessness in sleep, food finickiness, and personality characteristics (shyness, dependency, irritability), between 21 months and 14 years also demonstrate the difficulties in attempting to arrive at simple conclusions regarding continuity over long time intervals. Correlations for any single problem or characteristic vary greatly even between adjacent age levels. For example, correlations on ratings of severity of destructiveness at adjacent ages range from +.25 to +.64. Over long time intervals, the correlation coefficients on some characteristics tend to be negligible; on others they are moderately high. Thus, ratings of emotional dependence and shyness at 5 and 6 years show little relation to ratings of these characteristics at later ages, whereas ratings of irritability at 6 years correlate fairly highly with ratings at 11 years, r = +.74 for boys and r = +.55 for girls. In general there seems to be increasing consistency with increasing age: correlations between 5 and 6 years range from +.12 to +.43 compared to correlations of +.56 to +.86 between 13 and 14 years. Findings that correlations on several characteristics were greater between 7 and 14 years than between 7 and 12 years (e.g. for shyness r = +.22 between 7 and 12 years and r = +.60 between 7 and 14 years), are interpreted as indicative of temporary changes in behavior associated with the beginning of adolescence, after which there is a reversion to the individual's more characteristic behavior patterns. In summing up, MacFarlane, Allen, and Honzik comment,

> Our findings show that, although there is a tendency for problems to be present for varying lengths of time, change rather than persistency is of the greater significance. Not only are changes occurring all the time in these behaviors, but there are certain epochs in the child's life when the problem patterns tend to be disrupted. A year after the "epoch," the old pattern may be resumed, but not with the same intensity that was prevalent before. These pivotal points or epochs seem to coincide with the ages at which children are called upon to make major adjustments in their school life, the year of kindergarten entrance, the last year of elementary school, and the year of entrance to junior high school.

To what extent are personality deviations in childhood predictive of disturbances in later life? On this question there is a limited literature. Bergman and Escalona (1949) have hypothesized that hypersensitivity in infancy may be prognostic of significant personality disturbances in later life. Clinical follow-up studies by Bender (1953) of schizophrenic children, by Eisenberg (1956) of autistic children, and by Morris (1956) of hyperaggressive children indicate that these types of personality disturbances tend to be predictive of similar disorders in adult life. Even when there has been therapeutic intervention, there is a tendency for the persistence of these disturbed behavior patterns (O'Neal and Robins, 1958). The research only suggests some of the factors which may be involved in the persistence of maladaptive behavior patterns. In some cases, the initial damage is so severe that there is little possibility of reversing the pattern; in others, the continuation of an unfavorable environment tends to reinforce the disturbed behavior patterns; in still other cases, it seems likely that the maladaptive behavior tends to maintain an unfavorable environment, e.g., it stimulates parental rejection or recurrent changes in foster homes.

From the studies dealing with continuity in specific personality traits over the span of years from middle childhood or early adolescence to adulthood (Anderson, 1959; Beilin, 1957; Cantoni, 1955; Hertz, 1951; Jayaswal and Stott, 1955) no definitive conclusions emerge; low or moderate associations are found in some traits, marked changes in others.

Several reports from the California Adolescent Study on the relationship between personality characteristics rated during adolescence (around 15 years) and other presumably similar characteristics measured in adulthood (around 30 years of age) point to consistency in some personality characteristics and inconsistency in others. McKee and Turner (1961), comparing clinical ratings on strength of drives during midadolescence with scores on the California Psychological Inventory fifteen years later, found a fair degree of behavioral consistency over this time interval. On the whole, a greater degree of stability was found for women than men.

Mussen's (1961) analysis of data from the Adolescent Growth Study on masculine sex typing suggests some additional issues which complicate the evaluation of personality consistency over time. The data point to a basic continuity between adolescence and early adulthood in attitudes, beliefs, and behavior patterns considered indicative of high or low masculinity. However, there was a change in the evaluation of these cases on overall adjustment and adequacy of functioning in adult roles. In adolescence, the highly masculine boys were rated as making a better adjustment than the boys who were low on masculine characteristics. In adulthood this trend was reversed; the men who had been rated low on masculinity during adolescence were evaluated as functioning better in their adult roles than the men who had been highly masculine in adolescence. Mussen indicates that these findings may be dependent on the criteria used for evaluating adjustment. He suggests that the bases for evaluating good adjustment may shift between adolescence and adulthood, and that the characteristics required for successful functioning in adult roles may differ from those required in adolescence.

From the same study H. E. Jones et al. (1958) conclude that adolescent ratings are not highly predictive of adult characteristics. However, significant relationships were found between a few adolescent ratings and adult personality test scores. Ratings on "impulsivity" and degree of socialization in adolescence were highly related to adult measures of "drive for aggression." "Drive for achievement" in adolescence correlated significantly with social responsibility in adults. Jones concludes

> . . . in spite of these apparent consistencies it can be noted that overall measures of adult adjustment show little relation to adolescent drives. Although strong drives and incompatible drives are often associated with adolescent maladjustment, they are not clearly predictive of adult maladjustment. . . . The problem here may lie partly in the fact that over a long period, behavioral consistency, when it occurs, may be countered by changes in the environment. The adaptive significance of a given behavior pattern can thus be interpreted only with reference to changing demands in the life situation (pp. 49–50).

Clearly no simple conclusions about personality consistency are possible from the existing research. There is some evidence of continuity in personality characteristics, and there are also data which point to changes over time. On the whole, the research which has dealt with global personality characteristics, personality style, indicates a moderately high degree of consistency over time, whereas the research which has focused on more specific traits shows little consistency. Although the findings are not precise or clear-cut, the periods of greatest stability appear to be between infancy and the early preschool period and between late adolescence and adulthood; the greatest degree of variability seems to occur between middle childhood and adolescence. The findings on sex differences indicate different degrees of stability over time for boys and girls in different characteristics, e.g., girls show greater consistency in dependent behavior and social prestige, boys in drive aggression. On the whole, there seems to be a greater degree of stability for girls than for boys.

The infancy studies have many implications for our basic assumptions about personality development and change. The data on personality continuity in infancy might lead one to question the assumption that early infancy is the most fluid developmental period, the period during which sensitivity to environmental influences is greatest. These studies also raise many questions regarding the role of constitutional factors in determining the degree of vulnerability to early experiences. It is likely that there are individual differences which determine the particular class of events to which the organism is most sensitive, resulting in a selective impact of environmental events. There may also be constitutional differences in the plasticity of the organism leading to differences in degree of susceptibility to changing environments and to traumatic stimulation. Data from psychophysiological research on the behavioral correlates of different stimulus thresholds and mechanisms mediating different response intensities to similar stimulus intensities would be relevant.

The conviction persists among many theorists, particularly those who take a global, clinical approach, that there is a core of continuity underlying diverse behavioral expressions at different developmental points and under different circumstances. The limitations in attempting "trait" comparisons from one age to a later age—either as evaluations of constancy or of change—are apparent. This is particularly true in predictions from infancy or early childhood to later periods.

With regard to research on the issue of dynamic continuity, there are very subtle conceptual problems and very difficult methodological problems. We are far from any clear systematic theory from which we can formulate the rules which govern personality transformations. Further prediction studies on a dynamic level are likely to contribute to the development of a systematic theory of personality consistency and personality transformations. Such research should add to our understanding of the role of biologically determined sensitivities in persistence and change. It is clear that we need more precise specification of the theoretical rationale for predictions (Benjamin, 1959) and the testing of dynamic predictions on larger populations.

PERSONALITY CHANGE AND THE FAMILY ENVIRONMENT

There are a few studies that deal with the effects on personality of specific conditions within the family. They are not easily cast into a theoretical framework relevant to issues of personality continuity and change. We have classified them in terms of the antecedent variables under two broad headings: changes within the intact family which occur as part of the normal life cycle (such as the changing sibling group, the adult roles of parents, the aging family) and changes in which the family itself is disrupted or destroyed as a result of illness, disaster, or death of a family member.

Sibling Variables

The research findings on the reactions of older children to the birth of a sibling and the data on the relationship between ordinal position and personality characteristics can be interpreted in the framework of normal changes in the family environment which bring about alterations in interpersonal and role relationships among family members. The studies on sibling rivalry (Levy, 1936; MacFarlane, 1938; Sewall, 1930; Orr, 1960) attest to the strong immediate impact of the arrival of a sibling on young children's behavior. A variety of behavior changes has been observed: increased aggression towards parents and peers, and often towards the new sibling; increased dependency on the mother, and various kinds of regressive behavior—in language, in feeding and toilet habits; as well as an increased level of anxiety. Despite these sometimes severe reactions, this experience is not generally considered traumatic. The research data are only on the immediate effects; we have no follow-up data specifically directed to the question of whether these behavior changes are the precursors of significant personality changes in the child. The impact of this event undoubtedly varies with the age of the child and is modified by the context of interpersonal relationships in the family. There has been no systematic research in which these variables have been considered. The arrival of a sibling may have no lasting effects as a traumatic event, but its effects on personality development are probably related to the changes it creates in the total family environment. The research questions might be formulated in terms of effects of a change in the role of the child, from being an only child to becoming an older brother, or from being the youngest of four daughters to one of the four older daughters with a single young brother.

The data on child-rearing practices and parental relationships with children of different ordinal status referred to previously (Baldwin, 1947; Lasko, 1954; Sears, Maccoby, and Levin, 1957) suggest that there are significant changes in the family environment for older children following the birth of a sibling. By far the most significant changes occur for the first born, toward whom there is increased parental restrictiveness. Those born later, on the other hand, receive more consistent handling, with fewer extremes, either positive or negative; the parents show less enthusiasm about their arrival and are less severe in discipline. From these findings, a simple prediction might be that the first-born child would show less consistency in personality over time; however, it is clear that the relationships between environmental consistency and personality consistency are not so direct.

The data on personality correlates of ordinal position probably can be accounted for, in part at least, in terms of different degrees of consistency in the family environment for children of different ordinal status. A large number of consequent variables—achievement, aggressiveness, dominance, neuroticism, psychosis—have been studied in relation to ordinal position (Cobb, 1943; Murphy, Murphy, and Newcomb, 1937; Roberts, 1938), with far less than complete accord from study to study. There are some consistencies. Some studies find that first-born children tend to have more difficulties in social relationships and show a higher incidence of problem behavior, e.g., oversensitivity, mood swings, fears (MacFarlane, Allen, and Honzik, 1954). The most consistent finding with regard to ordinal position is that first-born children are likely to be more dependent than later-born children (Sears, 1950; Sears, Maccoby, and Levin, 1957). Schacter's data (1959) on college students are interpreted as supporting these findings. He found that first-born subjects show a higher level of anxiety in experimental anxiety-provoking situations and are more likely to express a wish to be with other people than later-born subjects.

An attempt to deal on a theoretical level with the effects on personality development of changing parental practices (applicable to the findings on ordinal position) is the theory of the origins of the dependency drive (Sears et al., 1953; Whiting and Child, 1953). The basic hypothesis is that the strength of the dependency drive is positively related to the amount of nurturance during infancy, a critical period for the development of this drive. After the dependency drive is established, its strength will vary directly with the degree of frustration experienced by the child. Thus, if the first-born child receives a high degree of nurturance from the mother during infancy, and then experiences severe frustration following the arrival of a sibling, he should develop a very strong dependency drive.

In addition to changes in parental practices there are other changes in the family associated with the addition of a new member to the family group. There are changes in family structure and changes resulting from the addition of a new identification object. After the infancy period, the sibling subgroup constitutes another affectional system within the family with its own sources of gratification and tension, a subgroup which provides its own identification models and socializing agents. As the child grows older, the influence of the sibling group is likely to become stronger. A given child's role in a sibling group—as the youngest or oldest of the group, or as the one possessing or lacking particular qualities or skills—is undoubtedly significant for personality development. Since the child's role in the sibling group is not a transient one, as are many other roles, but is one which continues over a long period of time, one should expect continuing effects. The self-concept which develops and is reinforced in the sibling context probably carries over to other contexts. The data on these issues are almost non-existent.

Brim (1958) offers some data on the specific contributions of the sibling subgroup to personality development. His analyses are based on Koch's data (1955) on personality characteristics of children in two-child families. Comparing children from sibling groups of varied age-sex combinations: two boys, two girls, older girl and a younger boy, and an older boy and a younger girl, Brim found more traits of the opposite sex in children from cross-sex sibling pairs than from same-sex sibling pairs. The younger child seemed to be more susceptible to the influence of the opposite sex sibling.

The research on sibling order and the sibling influence reinforces the image of the family as a changing environment for each member. The alterations in the family environment associated with the addition of a sibling have been considered primarily in terms of traumatic implications; the potential constructive and growth-stimulating aspects of these changes in a long-term perspective might be given more consideration. The simple category of the child's position in the family group has led to some provocative correlations with some limited aspects of personality functioning. At this point, we should be ready to go beyond correlation to more dynamic hypotheses concerning the links between structural family variables and personality variables, and to formulate hypotheses in terms of more differentiated antecedent and consequent variables. The role of such modifying variables as the age of the child at the time of arrival of the new sibling, his sex, and his relationship with each of the parents need to be considered. We might hypothesize that the impact of changes in child-rearing patterns and changes in relationships with the parents following the birth of a sibling would vary with the developmental stage of the child and with the relative strength or significance of particular drives at the time the change occurs. Thus, for example, the child may be most vulnerable to a change in parental handling of dependency needs during early infancy when these needs are strongest or during adolescence when they are in a transitional stage. Similarly, the point in development that the child has reached with respect to sex identity may influence his response to a change in the father's or mother's degree of participation in child rearing.

Other changes happen within the normal family to alter its character, thereby changing the family experiences of the child. The addition of the grandparent generation to the family group is not an infrequent occurrence. For the children this change may signify the presence of additional socializing agents or may be the condition for a diffusion of the mother image or the introduction of conflicting patterns of reinforcements. The age of the child again would be significant in predicting consequences of this kind of multiple parenting. The composition of the family undergoes normal changes as older siblings leave home for college, employment, or marriage. The relationships between parents and the children remaining in the family group are likely to change following one child's detachment from the immediate family environment.

If one views the family as a continuing life-long environment, the effects of family changes upon adult members cannot be ignored. Kelly's (1959) follow-up data on adults, after an interval of sixteen to eighteen years, emphasize the fact that such personality changes do occur. He concludes that, "significant changes in the human personality may continue to occur during the years of adulthood. Such changes . . . are potentially of sufficient magnitude to offer a basis of fact for those who hope for continued psychological growth during the adult years." However, there are few empirical data on the impact on the adult personality of significant events such as marriage, pregnancy, and the assumption of the parental role.

Pregnancy and Parenthood

There has been a good deal of theoretical discussion of personality changes during pregnancy and following the assumption of the mother role. Pregnancy is regarded as a developmental crisis in the woman's life; it is assumed that the adequacy of her resolution of this crisis will have a major impact upon subsequent development of her personality (Bibring et al., 1961; Caplan, 1960). Benedek (1959) postulates that the effects of motherhood on the woman's personality will depend on her relationship with the child. There are "reciprocal ego developments." If the relationship with the infant is a good one, and the infant is thriving, in essence the mother achieves a new integration of her personality, and her own feelings of adequacy and positive self-image are strengthened. On the other hand, if the infant is not progressing well, and if the relationship (partly determined by the infant) is not a satisfying one, there are destructive effects on the personality of the mother, regressive and aggressive components of the personality are intensified. "Just as the positive balance of the transactional processes leads to confidence in the child and to self-confidence in the mother, so we can recognize the effects of negative balance of the transactional processes in the mother and in the child. The frustrated infant frustrates his mother; by this he induces a regression in the mother which intensifies the aggressive components of her receptive needs . . ." (p. 396).

Benedek also hypothesizes the possibilities of personality change in the parent at each developmental phase of the child. This concept is similar to Erikson's (1950) concept of focal conflicts for the child at each developmental phase. At each "critical period" the child reactivates in the parent his own related developmental conflicts. If the conflict is resolved, it may bring about a "new level of integration" in the parent, or it may lead to pathological developments. She speculates that similar dynamic processes may be operating with regard to men in assuming a father role.

Research on the effects of the role change to parenthood where clear personality disturbances are not involved is almost non-existent. A longitudinal study of the transition to parenthood which should contribute data on this problem is currently in progress at the National Institute of Mental Health (Goodrich et al., 1961). In this study (begun in 1959) initial stages of family formation are being investigated; data are being obtained on the interpersonal adaptation of newly married couples and their reactions to pregnancy and to initial parenthood.

Aging

Transitions occur in later stages of family life that are potentially of great importance to the individual, as discussed in more detail by Kuhlen in Chapter 16. Thus, the adolescent's psychological emancipation and subsequent physical departure from home has its complement in the "loss" suffered by the parent, and the necessary readjustment of the parent to a new phase of parent-child relationships. The critical role of family factors in the adjustment of the aged parent is emphasized in data on physically healthy men in their seventies and eighties (Perlin and Butler, 1963; M. Yarrow et al., 1963). These reports show the close relation between good mental health of the aged parent and the presence of significant family ties. Where extensive disintegration of the family group, through deaths, had taken place, the elderly parent showed up poorly on a diverse set of assessments (behavioral, cognitive, and motivational). One might hypothesize that in advanced age, as in early infancy, the nurturant and sustaining relationships with immediate family members are the most crucial environmental factors for the individual's psychological well-being. Conceivably, the older person becomes increasingly dependent upon the family for his gratifications, much more dependent than he has been through the years of middle adulthood when social motivations and rewards have been of greater importance. Hence he is more vulnerable to family changes.

Changing Adult Roles of Parents

As parents change in the process of maturing and as they acquire new roles in society, their parental roles change, not only with regard to child-rearing practices but also with respect to the adult role models they represent for their children. For the father, life in the nuclear family begins in an occupational role, and there are likely to be many kinds of changes in this role over time: the occupational content itself may change; the status and security provided by the job may change; the father is likely to become increasingly socialized into the role characteristics or role stereotypes of his job or profession. Curiously, the carryover into family life of these various and changing ways of life of fathers is rarely explored in psychological research.

The mother's employee role has been given more consideration as a possible influence upon the personality development of children. The fact that 40 per cent of mothers of school-age children are employed outside the home

(National Manpower Commission, 1957) has recently spurred research on this problem. Two comprehensive reviews of the effects of mother's employment on child personality (Stolz, 1960; Hoffman, 1963) reach rather similar conclusions. They agree that many of the older views concerning the detrimental effects of mothers' employment upon child personality (such as employment being a major contributor to juvenile delinquency) are unwarranted. When comparative studies of families of working and non-working mothers are designed with adequate controls, differences disappear. These authors agree, too, on the necessity of analyzing mothers' occupations in terms of more carefully specified subgroups (social class, full-time versus part-time employment, age of child when mother begins to work, sex of child, attitudes of mother, etc.). It appears that a mother's employment may and probably does affect the child, but the distinction of mother's working or not working is too gross a classification to permit adequate evaluation of the nature of effects upon family functioning and child personality.

The mother's going to work may result from, as well as result in, varied psychological changes in the family. Hence, the predicted consequences for the child differ. Some of the changed family conditions represented by maternal employment are: decreased contact between mother and child, new supplemental mother figures, conflicting socialization practices from various child caretakers, intensification or change in critical relationships between husband and wife (e.g., shared fulfillment of family goals through wife's employment, conflict between husband and wife, weakened husband-father image). Going to work may be an expression of widely differing motivations and feelings. It may express the mother's rejection of familial and maternal roles; it may be a personally enriching experience; it may be a means of providing the rewards of better income to the family; it may result in anxiety and guilt feelings over leaving her children. Future research in this field needs to be pointed towards evaluation of the effects upon the child of each of these varied psychological conditions, singly and in complex interaction. The existing research data, although not definitive, suggest a number of significant psychological and social factors which modify the effects of maternal employment on the child's personality. The mother's feelings about her work role appear to influence significantly the kind of relationship she has with her child (M. Yarrow et al., 1962; Hoffman, 1961), anxiety and guilt-feelings, dissatisfaction with her role, all contribute to less favorable relationships. The effects of mothers' working appear to be different for boys and girls (Hoffman, 1962; Siegel et al., 1959; Hartley, 1961). For girls, the mother's employment may result in greater admiration and emulation of the mother. For boys in families of working mothers the findings suggest a higher incidence of negative and "problem" behaviors. Scott's (1962) data on preschool-age children of working and non-working mothers point to a shortcoming in research dealing with behavioral correlates of maternal employment. The child's personality tends to be evaluated either in very global terms (delinquent versus nondelinquent) or there is a concentration on a few variables (dominance-submission, succorance-nurturance, sociability-aggression). When Scott compared Australian children of working and nonworking mothers on these variables, she found no significant differences, findings consistent with American studies (Siegel et al., 1959). However, after examination of other dependent variables, she found impressive differences. She concluded that a young child's "progress towards socialization is not retarded when mothers work. But working status significantly affects the cost at which socialization is achieved." In the preschool age children of working mothers, Scott found more frequent evidences of displaced aggression, tension-relieving symptoms such as nail biting and the like, avoidance of competition, fantasy nurturance, and succorance. She suggests the importance of looking more closely at mother-child sequential interactions, looking particularly for sequences of alternating gratification and frustration in the-being-with and the-being-away-from the child. One might hypothesize the development of ambivalence as well as the intensification of needs that are intermittently frustrated and gratified.

The occupational experience of adults is one non-parental role variable which has an influence on parental behavior. There are undoubtedly other adult roles and experiences which influence parents' values and child-rearing behavior. This area of research on the margins of social psychology and personality theory is relatively unexplored territory.

The Family as Part of Society

In a number of ways the position of the family in society—its social class status, its national, religious, or ethnic background, its rural or urban character, etc.—affects the behavior of parents and children. These cultural factors contribute to variations in family and individual behavior in very fundamental and widely differing respects (Bronfenbrenner, 1958; Zbrowski, 1952; Miller and Swanson, 1960). It is well known that ways of rearing children, the nature of individual goals and goal striving behavior, attitudes toward life and death, health and illness, patterns of defense, and many other behavioral characteristics vary by class and culture.

The individual family articulates with society or culture generally in a stable way, that is, it is likely to maintain a more or less stable class position or cultural identity, at least within a single generation. These social identifications of the family can be expected, therefore, to contribute to the continuity and predictability of personality and behavior. However, they also have relevance for personality *change*. The social and cultural background of the family in many ways *patterns* the kinds of changes, both normal and disruptive, that are likely to occur in family life, and to some degree the social group memberships of the family dictate family and individual reactions to the changes that occur.

Particular kinds of changes in family environment are more likely in some social groups than in others. Thus, absence of the father is linked with certain occupations (Lynn and Sawrey, 1959). Broken homes, in general, are more apt to be found in lower economic groups. The incidence of changing "parents" or serial monogamy is undoubtedly higher in the Hollywood culture and in certain lower class urban groups (Miller, 1958; Rohrer and Edmonson, 1960) than in rural Kansas towns. Since these conditions are likely to be significant for personality development, their differential occurrence in families of various subcultures leads to expectations of differential influences upon personality development in these families.

Class and cultural differences in ways of handling the crises that occur in the family may also be anticipated. Variations in handling critical experiences (loss of parent, change in surroundings, etc.) have not been the object of extensive research, yet such variations (in giving support, in supplying understanding, in providing substitutes) may be powerful modifiers of the effects of the experience. One might hazard the guess that families deal with crises (preparation of the child for a new sibling, explanations of divorce, or death, etc.) in ways that are consistent with other family patterns, some of individual and some of cultural origins, and that there are tremendous variations in the therapeutic adequacy of the handling. When, for example, a family member becomes mentally ill, the anticipated impact upon the other members, particularly the children, will most certainly be affected by the interpretation given to the illness and by the kinds of reactions and feelings toward the ill member (M. Yarrow et al., 1955). If the family's interpretations stress the strange and frightening and shameful, or if they emphasize the illness aspect and the expected recovery, the child's relation to a mentally ill parent will surely vary. The conceptions of mental illness as well as its treatment are known to vary with social class and cultural background (Hollingshead and Redlich, 1958). Similar cultural variations exist in relation to the family's response to physical illness. Zbrowski's (1952) study of reactions to pain illustrates this association. He found differences among the three groups studied—old-American, Italian-American, and Jewish-American—in the degree of support and sympathy given to family members who were ill, in the amount of stoicism or complaint shown by the sick person, and in his expectations regarding family support.

The usual cultural continuity of family life may lead one to overlook the possibility of major changes in the family's relation to society. These changes may be sudden, severe, and acute. For example, there are cultural disloca-tions that come about as the aftermath of economic and political events, as in the refugee family. The family's voluntary migration from one culture to an-other may represent a similar drastic change. A family may experience a sudden downward plunge in socioeconomic level in the event of severe eco-nomic depression, or its relation to the culture may be markedly altered by a parent's sudden rise to fame or by his sudden loss of status following political defeat or loss of job. Even a move from a rural to an urban environment may find the family shaken internally by its changed external position. The family need not be socially transplanted so abruptly to experience considerable change. For example, gradual changes in ground occur for the family living within a racially segregated environment which gradually becomes a racially integrated one. Through social mobility, upward or downward, the family also experiences gradual change.

One may regard all of these conditions as remote from individual personality dynamics. In a sense, of course they are; but in another sense they are cer-tain to affect the family as much psychologically as physically or economically and thereby bring about changes in family conditions theoretically significant in personality development. Again few studies are specifically designed to study personality change as a consequence of changes in cultural or social status. However, from the descriptive studies relating social variables to fam-ily variables, we can arrive at some hypotheses. Thus, to the extent that fam-ily practices in child rearing are associated with social class (Bronfenbrenner, 1958), changes in the family's class status may be expected to influence child behavior and personality. There is some evidence of such parental changes in studies of socially mobile mothers. Bishop (1951) observing mothers in inter-action with their children in experimental situations found that those mothers designated as upwardly mobile showed more directive behavior and more severe control techniques than mothers in stable class positions.

The concept of "marginal man" can fruitfully be extended to the marginal family. The dual loyalties, incompatible motives and uncertainties in the be-havior of the individual in a marginal position (Lewin, 1948) may influence the structural characteristics and permeate the interrelationships within the marginal family. Within a given cultural framework, family properties such as the roles of father and mother, the parent-child status differential, and the accepted codes of behavior tend to be quite stable. However, the family in the midst of two classes or cultures, or the family passing from one group identity to another may experience conflicting pressures in regard to parental roles, family values, child-rearing procedures, and many other aspects of family functioning. There may be inconsistencies in parental behavior during the period of transition, and subtle changes over a long-time period.

Studies of immigrant families illustrate some consequences of marginality for the individual, although they do not describe in detail the changes taking place within the families. In immigrant families of past generations, adaptive defenses of the first generation typically involved isolation and insulation within little urban islands of their own nationals (Little Italy, Chinatown, etc.). For the second generation, conflict was high as movement back and forth between the old culture and new culture increased. Child (1943), in analyzing patterns of coping with marginality, found a number of types of solutions among young Italian-American men of the second generation. Some tried to remain predominantly within the ties and values of the old group, others tried to establish themselves within the new culture, actively rejecting the old, still others avoided identity with either group. Clearly, as Child indicates, these are not pure reaction types, but they indicate grossly the modal defenses used by the individual. We do not know how antecedent intrafamilial factors and personality characteristics relate to the kinds of individual coping that take place in these situations and eventual effects upon the personality. Nor do we know in any detail what happens to the relationships among family members in these cultural transplantations. As already indicated, we would expect the parental role to reflect uncertainties in practices of child rearing and in the inculcation of values, but these uncertainties could have various manifestations. We would anticipate, too, varied disturbances within the group life of the family as any one of its members brings back into the family some of the acquisitions from his experience in the new culture. For example the child going to school may bring home "foreign" expectations or the father's experiences relating to his work may initiate changes within the family.

Within our culture there are families of quite different social class levels that experience frequent changes of social context as part of the normal history of the family. For example, in the case of the professional military (Gabower, 1959) and the diplomatic corps, the family moves periodically from one national group to another. The rural migrant worker has only a succession of moves to anticipate. For both the children and the adults in these families this way of life includes frequent losses in significant object relations. It requires repeated adaptations to new peer groups. May there not result characteristic protective defenses? If an individual is going to lose significant persons frequently, perhaps he learns not to form relationships that are too close and too involved. Perhaps he learns to relate to others in a more superficial manner. He might perceive his own family as the only group to be counted on and as the only source of security, thus leading to exaggerated dependency. In the absence of research data we can only speculate on the possible impact of these kinds of family experiences.

Some of the behavioral and personality implications of moving from one culture or subculture to another might be examined fruitfully in terms of the new behavior setting requirements which confront the individual. Barker and Wright (1954) have pointed out the importance of the nature of available and permitted behavior settings in determining action patterns of individuals at every age. In a comparison of the child's position in his family and community in an English village and in a Midwestern American town, Barker (1963) found striking differences in what the children of the two cultures do *not* do as well as in what they do. The behavior settings for the English child tend to be separate and distinct from the behavior settings of adults; whereas in the Midwest many settings (even such as running the town newspaper, carrying out community projects) are shared by children and adults. Barker makes it vividly clear that in a family's transplantation from one culture to another a whole new system of discrete environmental demands takes hold, and behavior reflects accommodations to the new situational requirements. Whether a family's change from one cultural setting to another, with consequent modification in behavior, results in personality changes probably depends on the depth of the changed behavior patterns and their significance in the individual's psychological economy.

To deal more directly with the issues of interpersonal family changes as part of social changes, it is necessary for two rather separate lines of inquiry to come closer together: research with a clinical approach to problems of family change and its effects upon personality needs to be integrated with research that deals with critical social stimuli in the family environment in terms of epidemiological and demographic variables.

Family Crises

Beyond the normal changes which occur in the course of the family's development, there are unanticipated events which precipitate drastic changes in the family environment. Among the family crises which have been studied are crises due to social causes, such as unemployment or war; crises associated with individual tragedy, such as illness or death of a family member; and crises associated with interpersonal tensions in the family which may be reflected in marital discord or divorce. By far the greatest share of literature on family influences on personality deals with the effects of severe disruptions in the ongoing patterns of family living following family crises. This research represents a convergence of many disciplines: sociology, anthropology, clinical and social psychology, and psychiatry. No attempt will be made to review in detail the correlational findings between grossly deviant family environments and personality development. The varied studies do not add up easily; even the general conclusions are not consistent from study to study. This is due, in part, to the differing antecedent conditions encompassed under such broad labels as "broken homes" or "divorce"; and, in part, to the different dependent variables which have been measured. Some studies have focused on consequent variables, e.g., delinquency, which are as broad and ill-defined as the antecedent variables. Many of the studies deal only with retrospective data on the family background of clinic cases with behavior deviations, or hospitalized psychotic patients, or "juvenile delinquents." On the whole, the research that has studied cases of a given diagnostic category, such as schizophrenics from clinic or hospital populations, has found bases for relating these disturbances to disturbances in parental attitudes and child-rearing behavior. From these findings it has been concluded that specific psychological disturbances are associated with disturbed parental relationships. On the other hand, studies of parental attitudes have less frequently found significant differences in attitudes between parents of disturbed cases and "normal" controls. As Spiegel and Bell (1959) note ". . . the review of the trait studies produces the impression that none of the parental traits held up for investigation can be correlated with a distinct and predictable pathological outcome, and that, while they may constitute a necessary condition, they certainly do not constitute a sufficient condition for the appearance of a specific form of psychological disorder in the child" (see p. 124).

The category of "broken homes" appears with almost monotonous regularity in the literature on family deviation. Simply on the basis of frequency of occurrence in the literature, it might be assumed that this is a significant antecedent of personality change or personality disorder. The findings on broken homes per se (Oltman, McGarry, and Friedman, 1952; Goode, 1956; Koos, 1946; Altus, 1958; Toby, 1957; Madow and Hardy, 1947; Nye, 1957) are inconsistent. They suggest that insofar as this variable is associated with family disorganization, it may be related to personality disturbances in the family members. It seems clear that the experiences associated with family disorganization which end in divorce or separation can have a variety of meanings to the child. Their significance is probably modified by the larger experiential context in which they occur, as well as by the child's age and his individual strengths and vulnerabilities. It may be that for some children the loss of daily contact with a parent as a result of divorce may be less severe than the stresses associated with constant interparental tension. On the other hand, for boys, the loss of a father may be especially destructive at certain periods of development, e.g., the end of the Oedipal period or during early adolescence. Toby (1957), in reviewing studies on the differential impact of family disorganization, presents some support for the view that a broken home may have a different impact on boys and girls and on different age groups. Clearly, broken homes and divorce are phenotypic variables which in themselves cannot be considered antecedents of personality change. If we can conceptualize more precisely the ways in which these events are mediated to the family members—through changes in interpersonal relationships, changes in role relationships among family members, and through changes in the family status in the community, etc.—we may be able to design more definitive studies of the significant dynamic variables.

Other studies have considered family crises precipitated by alcoholism in the father (Jackson, 1956); unemployment (Bakke, 1940); mental illness of the father (Clausen and M. Yarrow, 1955); prolonged illness and death of a child (Cobb, 1946); and the presence of a mentally deficient child in the family (Farber, 1957). Koos (1946, 1948) has dealt with a range of family problems which change the usual patterns of family functioning. He suggests that there are different effects on family solidarity dependent on whether the crisis is seen as precipitated by outside forces or as coming from within the family. In all of these studies, it seems clear that these crises are associated with changes in dominance and authority relations in the family. The father's illness, alcoholism, or loss of employment may result in weakening his authority. To the extent that the family is disorganized by crises, inconsistencies in socialization practices may occur. There is increased interpersonal conflict among family members, and ambivalent feelings toward the member who is perceived as responsible for the crisis. Many compensatory relationships develop in the wake of absence or impairment of a family member. The mother's overprotectiveness towards remaining siblings, the assumption of a substitute mother role by the oldest daughter, or the mother's turning to the son to meet her own dependency needs following the loss of a husband are all examples. In the studies by Cobb (1946) and by Farber (1957), after the death of a sibling the remaining siblings showed heightened dependency upon the parents and assumed some of the characteristics and interests of the dead sibling. Farber notes a decline or an impairment in the maturity level of the entire family in which there is a mentally deficient child. The relationship of the family to other families and to the community is strongly influenced by the requirements of the deficient child or by the reaction to the child which the family anticipates.

Some clinically oriented reports have looked at the effects on the child and on the relationships within the family of the immediate crisis resulting from the death of a parent (Eliot, 1948; J. Hilgard et al., 1960). Hilgard, studying adults whose fathers had died during their childhood, found significant differences in life experiences between the cases who were functioning adequately and those who had personality breakdowns sufficiently severe to require hospitalization. Two main factors differentiated the healthy from the disturbed adults: the character of the family environment prior to the death of the father and the degree of disruption consequent to the father's death. The well-functioning adults came from families which provided healthy experiences prior to the death of the father. Following the father's death, the families of the healthy adults remained intact whereas, in the disturbed group, there was a high incidence of family breakup.

When the mother or father becomes mentally ill and is institutionalized, the effects are similar to those associated with the loss of a parent—shifts in roles and responsibilities of the remaining family members (Clausen and Yarrow, 1955). There may be intensified dependency between a child and the remaining parent. Social attitudes toward mental illness may lead to a loss in social status for the family, with possible effects on the child's sense of self-worth similar to those sometimes associated with minority status. For the individual family members, depending on their knowledge and feelings about mental illness, this event may engender anxieties and fears and even feelings of guilt concerning their own responsibility for the illness of the parent or sibling.

The effects of crises and disorganization of the family group are problems which are not easily amenable to precise formulation and measurement. On the whole, existing research does not demonstrate specific relationships between the trauma associated with such crises as the loss or illness of a parent and later personality characteristics. It is apparent that the effects on personality are related to the complex interactions of the absence of one parent, the personality pathology of the remaining parent, and the distorted family relationships consequent to the loss or illness of the parent (Neubauer, 1960).

Unfortunately, in most of these studies the data are limited to responses in the midst of the crisis or immediately thereafter. We do not know the extent to which the effects are lasting or the conditions under which they may be reversible. How long the disruptive events go on, when they occur in a child's life, and the severity of the immediate impact may be important in relation to recovery. The research has concentrated on the destructive effects of family crises. Caplan (1961) has suggested that there may be constructive outcomes following a successful resolution of disruptive crises. Studies are needed on the factors which determine the kinds of reorganizations and readjustments following acute family crises. Research in progress (Caplan et al., 1961) on families who have experienced crises associated with grave illness or institutionalization of a parent, or the birth of a premature infant should give more adequate data than are currently available on the long-term effects, and on the differential determinants of constructive and destructive outcomes.

Loss of a Parent: Maternal Separation and Father Absence

The effects on personality development of the loss of a parent as an aftermath of a severe family crisis have been studied rather extensively and have been the subject of much theoretical speculation. Studies of maternal separation and father absence have had a somewhat different perspective than the research on other family crises. The research on maternal separation has been concerned with such dependent variables as the development of interpersonal relationships and the acquisition of superego controls; studies of father absence have been concerned almost exclusively with sex-role identification.

The extensive literature on maternal separation has resulted in broad and sweeping conclusions about the impact of separation experiences on personality development. It has been concluded that separation from the mother during infancy or early childhood is a severely traumatic experience, one which may have enduring consequences for personality development. As has been pointed out in a recent review (L. Yarrow, 1961) the concept of maternal separation, as used in the research, is not a simple one, and the findings of these studies cannot be interpreted as showing a simple relationship between loss of the mother-figure and personality disturbance. The personality consequences are undoubtedly related to other significant changes in the child's environment which often occur following maternal separation. Not only is the continuity of relationship with a mother-figure disturbed, but there are losses of other significant object relationships—with the father, with siblings, etc.; and there are often major disruptions in the physical environment involving significant changes in learning conditions, e.g., changes in patterns of gratification, in types of rewards and punishments, and in reinforcement schedules. Maternal separation may occur in association with other significant events, such as the child's illness, with the concomitant traumata of hospitalization and surgery. Separation from the parents may be followed by long-term institutional placement in which, in addition to the loss of the mother, there may be other important environmental alterations, such as a decrease in amount of social and intellectual stimulation, changed patterns of child-rearing, the absence of any consistent mothering person.

Several studies of the immediate reactions to separation of infants and young children are in substantial agreement. Some infants and young children show very severe reactions. After an initial period of protest, infants and children under two years characteristically show a depressive reaction. Regressive behavior is also sometimes found. Finally, marked disturbances in interpersonal relationships are noted, a development which Bowlby hypothesized might be a precursor of a psychopathic character formation (Robertson and Bowlby, 1952; Roundinesco, David, and Nicolas, 1952; Spitz and Wolf, 1956).

Schaffer's (1958) study provides clear evidence that young infants' reactions to separation vary with age. Infants who were separated from their mothers under seven months of age showed global disturbances which might be associated with a total change in the environment, whereas infants over seven months showed more specifically social and emotional disturbances, such as excessive crying, fear of strangers, and clinging to the mother.

Data from a longitudinal study now in progress (L. Yarrow, 1962) on the effects of a change in mother figures during infancy indicate that the developmental level of the infant is extremely important in determining the immediate impact of separation and is likely to be significant for the long-term consequences. Although there are some reactions to change in the mother figure before there is evidence of the existence of a focused relationship with her, reactions are much more severe after the development of a relationship. The type of disturbance varies with age, with severe disturbances in relationship to the new mother figure common among infants after 6 months of age. Analysis of the long-term effects are not complete. These overt disturbances in functioning may be of only short-term significance. We have hypothesized that serious long-term damage to the personality is much less likely where maternal separation has been followed by the provision of an adequate mother substitute. Children separated under these conditions, however, give indications of greater vulnerability to subsequent separation experiences. Whether or not serious personality disturbances occur later in these separation-vulnerable children probably will depend on the degree to which the later environment is reinforcing of separation trauma.

There has been much theoretical speculation about the long-term effects of separation on personality, but the data are tenuous. Whether such experiences are the antecedents of personality change or adult personality disturbance is not well established. Bowlby (1944, 1951), Bender (1947), and Goldfarb (1955) have suggested a relationship between early separation from the mother and the development of psychopathic character disorders. The retrospective studies of adults and older children who have been brought to clinics because of psychopathic character disorders, sometimes diagnosed as schizophrenia, have found in the histories of these cases significant separation experiences following the death, illness, or divorce of the parents.

Although the data on the intervening history tend to be sparse, there are indications that significant changes in the child's environment occur subsequent to separation; the event often initiates a series of destructive experiences, such as institutionalization, repeated changes in foster parents, etc. Goldfarb's pioneer studies (1944, 1945, 1947), Bowlby's (1944) study of juvenile thieves, and more recent studies by Lewis (1954) and by Pringle and Bossio (1960) are consistent in their findings that repeated traumatic experiences in early life tend to be associated with personality disturbances in adult life. Other studies report less severe long-term effects of early separation experiences. On the basis of a follow-up study of sixty children between six and thirteen years of age, who had been in a sanitarium for tuberculosis for varying periods of time before their fourth birthday, Bowlby et al. (1956) found great variation in personality outcomes. Although many of the children showed personality disturbances, they concluded, "only a small minority develop those very serious disabilities of personality which first drew attention to the pathogenic nature of the experience" (see p. 240).

A recent study (Maas, 1963) of twenty adults who as children had been separated from their parents during World War II in England and then returned to their parents, found no serious psychological disturbance in this group. These adults were functioning well. There was a tendency toward less adequate functioning, particularly in the capacity for interpersonal relationships, among the cases who had been separated from their parents in early infancy (under six months of age) than among those separated after one year. One might interpret these data in terms of the critical period hypothesis. During the period critical for the development of significant interpersonal relationships, these infants were deprived of the learning conditions which are normally provided by a single mother figure.

With regard to the long-term effects of the loss of a love object in infancy and childhood, several psychoanalytically oriented reports (Beres and Obers, 1950; J. Hilgard, 1960) suggest that although personality development may appear to be normal, traumatic losses suffered in childhood "may leave scars that can be opened again at a later time" (Hilgard, p. 797). It is their contention that events at a later time may reactivate the earlier trauma, insofar as these events pose problems similar to the initial experience, concretely or symbolically. In essence, they are hypothesizing that an early traumatic loss results in a permanent change in the organism which leads to increased vulnerability to later similar experiences.

In spite of the inconclusive nature of the data, there has been a tendency to overextend the findings from retrospective studies, which often are based on biased samples and deal with very severe conditions of repeated trauma and subsequent severe sensory, emotional, and affectional deprivation. It has been assumed that destructive personality changes result from simple separation experiences which tend to occur with some frequency in the lives of many children, e.g., temporary absences of the mother, a single hospital experience for operation or illness. Although the immediate reactions to such separations may be severe, it does not necessarily follow that permanent personality changes occur. There have been no adequate long-term follow-up studies, and the findings of the retrospective studies cannot be accepted as conclusive evidence of the permanent effects of these simpler kinds of experiences (L. Yarrow, 1964).

Conclusions that severe personality disturbances in later life are usually an aftermath of early separation experiences are not supported by the research findings. The data suggest strongly that the effects are modified by many variables. The age at which the trauma occurs is likely to be highly significant. Although the findings are not definitive, they indicate that there may be a critical period during infancy when maternal separation may be most severe in its impact on the child. They also suggest that the kinds of deprivation experiences that commonly occur following separation—particularly decreased amount of sensory, language, and social stimulation—are likely to have more severe long-term effects if they occur during the first two years than if they occur later.

We can conclude that significant personality change may occur subsequent to traumatic separation experiences, particularly if they are followed by a series of reinforcing life events, but personality changes and deviations are not the inevitable outcome of traumatic events in the family. We are at a point where specific research questions regarding long-term effects and reversibility can be formulated in terms of specific variables. The data on maternal separation and deprivation have implications for other kinds of traumatic events in relation to personality change. They point up some of the modifying variables that need to be studied: constitutional differences in vulnerability to specific trauma, age-linked or developmental stage differences in vulnerability, the intensity of the trauma, the duration of the initial traumatic conditions, and perhaps constitutional differences in resiliency.

The concentration on the significance of the infant's relationship with the mother during the early months of life has resulted in a relative neglect in theory and research on the father's role in personality development. During World War II, some research (Bach, 1946; Sears et al., 1946) was initiated on the effects of father's absence on children's development. As distinguished from the research on maternal separation, the studies on father absence have dealt with situations in which the father's departure from the family is not a result of sudden, severe crisis but often is a consequence of occupational necessity or is due to the fulfillment of a culturally defined obligation, such as joining the military service.

It has been generally assumed that the absence of the father during early infancy is not likely to have direct effects upon the child; rather the father's absence has been considered in relation to its influence on the mother's relationship to the infant. There is no research specifically relevant to this point, but it is assumed that the early absence of the father will be associated with a more intense relationship of the mother with the child, or with distortions in this relationship.

In the psychoanalytic literature, the loss or absence of the father is related to later difficulties in sex identification. Freud (1938) notes that, "The early loss of one of the parents, whether by death, divorce, or separation, with the result that the remaining parent absorbs the whole of the child's love, determines the sex of the person who is later to be chosen as a sexual object and may thus open the way to permanent inversion." Ferenczi (1950) suggests that a fixation on the lost father develops in the absence of "unavoidable conflict between father and son." Fenichel (1954) theorizes regarding the "guilt engendered by fantasy fulfillment of Oedipal wishes when the same-sex parent dies, and the fantasy idealization, based on the unsatisfied Oedipal longing, when the opposite-sex parent dies."

A number of studies on the effects of continued absence of the father or periodic absence throughout childhood tend to support these clinical speculations. Burton and Whiting (1961) in examining cross-cultural data find support for the hypothesis of conflicts in sex identity for boys in societies in which the father is absent during infancy and the mother is the exclusive relationship object available for the infant. Several studies on preschool children (Sears, Pintler, and Sears, 1946; Bach, 1946; Stolz, 1954) find a more feminine orientation in doll play behavior among boys in father-absent families. Stolz found more feminine overt as well as fantasy behavior in boys during the father's absence and after his return. Burton and Whiting (1961) interpret these findings as consistent with their hypothesis that the assumption by an adult male of a significant role in child-rearing after an absence in the early years will be associated with the male child's conflict over sex identification.

In a study of children in families of Norwegian sailors who are absent from the home for extended periods of time, Lynn and Sawrey (1959) found a number of personality differences between these children and children from intact families. Boys from father-absent homes were found to be more immature and more insecure in their identification with the father. They showed a tendency toward compensatory, overly masculine behavior, and poor peer adjustment. The girls in these families developed greater dependence on the mother. There are some indications that the mothers in the father-absent families were more protective and somewhat more oriented toward authoritarian rearing practices than were mothers in the control families.

From the vast and conflicting literature on the origins of delinquent behavior come data on the father role (Toby, 1957). The findings, although inconclusive, recurrently suggest that antisocial behavior and failure to develop adequate impulse control and behavior reflecting poor superego integration are more likely to occur in boys who have grown up without adequate identification models, i.e., in homes where the father was absent because of divorce, desertion, or death or where the father was weak and ineffectual and failed to perform adequately in work or family roles.

The conflicting findings on the effects of the many different kinds of family crises described above cannot be interpreted simply in terms of validation or invalidation of the thesis that traumatic events in the family may precipitate personality change. Changes in the family initiated by abrupt, severe crisis situations may be the antecedents of significant personality changes; however, these experiences do not inevitably lead to severe personality or behavior disorders. The immediate impact of a family crisis will undoubtedly depend upon a variety of conditions antecedent to the crisis; it will be influenced by the concurrent family situation—the interpersonal relationships existing among family members and the parental handling and interpretation of the crisis to the children. The long-term effects of crises undoubtedly will depend upon the aggravating or ameliorating experiences subsequent to the event. In addition to the modifying effects of antecedent events and later experiences, undoubtedly individual differences in vulnerability to stress will modify the impact of any given type of crisis.

CONCLUSIONS

The family is the environmental context in which personality development begins, and throughout the life cycle the family remains the core context for the individual. During early infancy the child's world is the mother; his major learning experiences, gratifications, and frustrations occur in relationship to the mother. After early infancy, the child's family environment expands; he becomes part of other configurations of relationships, child-father, child-sibling, child-parents, husband-wife-child, as well as part of a total family group with its unique differentiation of roles and functions. Because of the emotional bonds and identifications among family members, the learning which takes place in the family is likely to be much more significant and resistant to extinction than that which occurs in other situations.

Personality development in the family can be viewed as a process of constant change, changes associated with biological growth, changes associated with the child's capacity to handle and manipulate his environment, changes associated with new focal problems at successive developmental stages, and changes associated with altered demands and expectations in the environment. There are good theoretical bases and some empirical evidence for assuming that at particular developmental points there is an increased probability of change in specific personality functions; the organism may be particularly vulnerable to destructive experiences or more receptive to growth-stimulating experiences. The concepts of critical periods and learning readiness converge. These developmental points of vulnerability or receptivity correspond to Erikson's (1950) growth crises or to the psychosexual stages in psychoanalytic theory. From a social-psychological perspective, certain life history events overlap these crises or stages to some extent. They are events which are coordinated with significant role changes for the individual, e.g., becoming a member of a sibling group, extending his group membership beyond the family to a school peer group, or becoming a parent or grandparent. Each of these developmental "crises" is associated with special demands on the individual. Some changes in the individual's functioning are inevitable outcomes of the resolution of these crises. New ways of responding to the environment and of coping with these demands, as well as changes in the self-concept occur in response to these changed situations. The successful resolution of these crises may lead to personality growth; inadequate resolution may be the precursor of personality disturbance (Erikson, 1950).

During these developmental crises, the interactional patterns within the family and the quality of relationships among family members are likely to show some changes, alterations which might be considered adaptive responses. It is undoubtedly important whether a basic consistency in relationship patterns is maintained or whether there are radical changes in the family environment associated with the growth crises. Through the course of the developmental cycle, a number of factors tend to support or maintain continuity in the family environment. The personalities of the family members and the field-defined characteristics of the family are sources of consistent reinforcements or pressures. To some extent, the continuity of the family environment may be maintained through the selective impact of the individual on his environment, e.g., the socially active child elicits a high level of social response from the people around him. After the family is stabilized in size, the role relationships and associated interactional patterns among siblings and between parent and child are likely to achieve some degree of equilibrium.

Beyond the changes in the family environment which accompany normal developmental changes there are "abnormal" events which give rise to special stresses for the individual members of the family and which may be disruptive of the family unit. How these are handled and resolved, and whether they lead to temporary or to permanent changes in the structural properties and interaction patterns of the family group may be decisive for personality change. A given family crisis does not have a predictable personality outcome. Although some family crises may in themselves be traumatic events, probably more significant in long-term perspective are the marked changes in the child's life which occur subsequent to these events; the death or illness of a parent may be followed by the child's removal from the familiar family environment and placement in a foster home or in institutional care. It is important in conceptualizing the impact of such events to distinguish between the emotional concomitants of the immediate experience and the sequelae of the event, i.e., the effects on personality resulting from the continuing impact of changed patterns of living which follow from the event. In much of the research, this distinction has not been clearly made. We must also consider the sequence in which events occur. A crisis which has been preceded by a long period of stable supportive family experiences may have an entirely different impact from that of a crisis which is one in a series of recurrent destructive experiences. In addition to the modifying effects of antecedent events and later experiences, undoubtedly organismic differences and phase differences in vulnerability to stress will modify the impact of any given type of crisis.

It is not very meaningful to consider personality change in a global sense, as an either/or phenomenon, as something which does or does not occur. Consistency and change are not incompatible concepts if we conceptualize personality in terms of many differentiated functions, some of which are central and others peripheral. There may be some characteristics which show a high degree of continuity in an individual's life history and others which change significantly. Perhaps one can think of a principle of selective action of environmental events. Just as certain chemical agents may selectively attack certain kinds of cells or tissues, given environmental events may have a selective action on specific personality functions at given periods of development.

chapter sixteen

Personality Change with Age

Raymond G. Kuhlen

A number of the other chapters in this book have been concerned primarily with changes in personality that have come about as a result of contrived situations or influences or which have been produced by rather catastrophic social events, such as war or depression. The present discussion will focus upon those changes in personality that presumably represent the consequences of the normal interaction of the individual with his environment over time, his adjustment to the typical transitions and crises that punctuate the adult life span, and the biological and other changes he is experiencing.

Within the space available, it will be impossible to do more than present a somewhat cursory overview of the literature in this field. Fortunately, for those who wish more extensive treatments, reasonably definitive summaries of the literature are available (Birren, 1959; Tibbetts, 1960) and up-to-date continuing bibliographies are maintained in the *Journal of Gerontology*. In the Birren volume, the chapters by Riegel (1959) and Kuhlen (1959) [1] are most relevant to the present discussion.

In the pages that follow, we turn first to a brief comment regarding methodological difficulties in aging research and then successively to consideration of descriptive data depicting age changes in motivation, in anxiety and symptoms of maladjustment, and in adjustive predispositions (personality traits), and conclude with data specifying the degree of stability of and range of individual variation in personality characteristics over time rather than change.

---

[1] The present chapter, though including some data not summarized in the chapter in Birren (1959), is essentially a briefer statement of the ideas and evidence there presented; however, certain findings (such as those from Rorschach studies) have been omitted.

METHODOLOGICAL PROBLEMS IN AGING RESEARCH

As a caution to those not accustomed to dealing with aging data, it may be useful at the outset to call attention to certain methodological difficulties which beset developmental psychologists who are concerned with personality change over broad age ranges. A first and persistent problem is that of partialing out the effects of cultural change. In view of the general direction of cultural trends over the past several decades—e.g., enriched verbal environments, a more liberal opinion milieu—cross-sectional studies have the effect of putting the older individual at a disadvantage compared to his younger contemporary (e.g., more conservative), whereas the longitudinal study tends to reveal him as having made gains compared to himself when younger (e.g., more liberal).

It is probable that this circumstance is responsible for some of the inconsistencies that have appeared in the past decade between longitudinal and cross-sectional data describing the growth and decline of intelligence. In the area of personality, contradictory trends also exist. For example, Terman and Miles (1936) found age trends in the direction of increased femininity on the part of women, whereas Kelly (1955) found greater masculinity with increasing age. The latter was a longitudinal study, and it is not unlikely that this trend reflected, at least in part, the general reduction of differences between sex roles in the American society during recent decades. By exercising appropriate controls, Nelson (1954) and Bender (1955) have been able to show that what seemed to be increases in liberality of opinion and in favorable attitude toward religion, respectively, during the fourteen or fifteen years of young adulthood following college were in fact due to cultural change.

A second major problem involves sampling. Because of the extreme difficulty of obtaining random or comparable samples of successive age groups, the subjects actually employed are likely to be progressively selected as their age increases, with the result that available research may either overestimate or underestimate the extent of age differences. Jones and Conrad (1933) have shown that curves of intellectual decline based on volunteers are likely to underestimate the amount of decrement. In contrast, the use of institutionalized populations at older ages (as is often done) is likely to yield curves overestimating the amount of decrement. These two illustrations will serve to suggest the complexity of the sampling problem, and the caution necessary in interpretation of age differences.

Finally, there are very special problems in the area of measurement. On one hand, it is difficult to devise a test which has common meaning *as a stimulus* for the various age groups tested. Obviously, a test of intelligence is not the same test for a group of young adults with good vision and a group of adults of advanced age with markedly impaired vision. Similarly, a projective test picture depicting, for example, a scene typical of a particular developmental task does not carry the same psychological stimulus to members of widely disparate age groups. Nor is the interpretation of *responses* to the stimulus material an easy matter across a broad age range. Because of various changes that occur with age, the diagnostic significance of responses to personality type tests may change greatly between young adulthood and old age. These problems characterize not only verbal tests but laboratory type procedures as well, and are especially critical when it is recognized that many tests used in adult life research are built, keyed, and normed on groups in their late teens or early twenties.

In short, anyone not accustomed to interpreting aging data should be wary of the methodological pitfalls which have in one way or another contaminated much of the available data.

CHANGES IN MOTIVATION

Motivation not only represents an intrinsic aspect of personality (and often is the dependent variable in aging studies) but in turn constitutes one of the more important age-related *independent* variables which influence other aspects of personality and behavior change. This is especially true of growth-expansion motives which will be considered next and of age trends in anxiety to be noted later.

A few illustrations will serve to suggest some of the factors that may produce adult age changes in motivation. For example, changing roles bring new patterns of arousal cues, of environmental stimulation and expectation, and perhaps, a failure of certain environmental support (reinforcement) for already existing motives. Since motivational tendencies are largely learned (and unlearned), it is reasonable to expect that motives will be changed as new sustained patterns of punishment, reward, or neutrality are encountered. Also, as Maslow's (1943) notion of a hierarchy of needs would suggest, certain psychological needs may be important at one phase of life only to fade and give way to others as the years pass, simply because they have been relatively satisfied or chronically frustrated. Thus, for a man who is successful in his career, or persistently unsuccessful, need for achievement may become less important. There are, in addition, a variety of organic changes—slowing down, loss of vigor, endocrine change—which may be of major importance in altering the motivational picture. And, it might be anticipated that critical age periods introduced by factors such as changing time perspectives may result in reorientations of such magnitude as to represent a change in motivational pattern, not simply in goal object, or cause heightened motivation at particular ages as time begins to run out or other sources of frustration or threat are encountered.

Evidence Describing Changing Motivation

Our prime example of changing motivation will be an array of needs which have in common the promotion of growth and expansion. They include those commonly assigned such labels as *achievement, power,* and *self-actualization,* as well as broader orientations suggested by such phrases as need to attain and maintain a significant role, need for expansion and ongoingness, generative needs. Buhler (1951, 1957), who has written extensively on changing needs as major explanatory variables in the life cycle, tends to subsume such motives as just listed under the general category of *expansion,* and to urge that there is a continuing need for expansion throughout the life span.

A number of studies have demonstrated the greater importance of achievement needs in early adult years, especially for men (Kuhlen and Johnson, 1952; McClelland, 1953). And a study by means of projective pictures of a nationwide sample of adults showed high points in young adulthood and middle age followed by a decrease in need achievement, but an increase in need power (Veroff, Atkinson, Feld, and Gurin, 1960). This finding recalls Strong's early (1931) item analysis by ages of the Strong Vocational Interest Blank. Liking for opportunities for promotion declined with age but increasingly with age his subjects were of the opinion that they could inspire ambition in others.

In another study Neugarten and Gutmann (1958) asked subjects aged forty through seventy to tell a story and to characterize each of the figures in a four-figure TAT card—a young man, an old man, a young woman, and an old woman. The investigators assumed that the stories told probably reflected Ss' own experiences with and their expectations regarding people of these varying ages. The young men were described as actively striving toward goals. As a group they were self-propelled and achievement oriented. In contrast the older men were inactive, submissive, and introspective. Interestingly enough, while the female subjects did not give responses that could be categorized in the same way, they did portray the older female in the picture as characterized by a marked increase in dominance and assertion.

The data are not entirely consistent, however. Gheselli (1960) has reported that initiative tended to drop off for lower level workers and to increase somewhat for those in management roles with age, but that there was no significant overall change. And he also noted that the differential trends between the groups may well have been caused by selective factors influencing the character of the sample. This suggestion of the long-term maintenance of initiative, though not in line with research summarized above, is consistent with an investigation by Reissman (1953) who reported that older high achievers were more willing than young high achievers to undergo the inconvenience of moving to a new city and to accept limitations upon freedom of religious and political expression for the sake of a better position.

Affiliation needs and social interests play a prominent role in life, and are here classified under growth and "expansion" needs since it is through expanding social relationships with individuals and groups that many individuals are able to achieve a sense of significance. Although it is difficult to infer whether there are marked changes in strength of affiliation and related social needs with age (the data of Veroff et al. [1960] suggest a decline in the case of women), certainly there are important shifts in ways in which such needs are satisfied. There is, as is well known, an upsurge of social interest during the course of adolescence and into the early twenties. But from that point on there seems to be less interest in extensive social interaction with large numbers of individuals, and a shift to a greater liking for closer relationships with fewer people.

Strong's analysis of changing interests with age (Strong, 1931, 1943) has provided the most extensive array of evidence depicting this trend. Although revealed in individual item analysis, the overall change is best illustrated in the interest-maturity scores. A single interest-maturity scale encompassing the total range of his subjects (15–60 years of age) did not prove possible; instead two scales were necessary, one based on trends from 15 to 25, the other on trends from 25 to 55. Items relating to social relationships were prominent among the items that forced the development of two scales and the fact that there was a reversal after an initial upsurge in such interests was reflected in a correlation of −.41 between the two scales. The developing phase showed relative rapid change, with the rate of change slowing substantially after the shift in direction occurred.

Bendig (1960) has offered further evidence suggesting a decline in social activity with age, in a factor analysis of scores on the Guilford-Zimmerman Temperament Survey for separate groups in the twenties, the thirties, the forties, and the fifties. One of the factors that emerged was labeled social activity, and all three of the scales loading on this factor showed decreasing scores with increasing age. However, another facet of the "orientation to others" pattern showed little change. Two of the three scales defining a friendliness factor remained relatively constant with age whereas scores on the third tended to increase.

Changing Goals and Interests

The postulation of a need or set of needs for continuing growth and expansion serves to relate in a meaningful way the goals and interests of people of different ages. As Buhler points out, family and work constitute major avenues of expansion, until these no longer offer possibility of continued satisfaction, whereupon interests shift to other kinds of activity. This shift from one orientation to another as a result of continued frustration of the possibility of "expanding" along the lines of marriage and family on the part of single women is illustrated in a study from which Figure 1 is taken (Kuhlen and Johnson, 1952). When asked what they most wanted to be doing ten years hence, the vast majority of young single women gave marriage and family as a goal. This response dropped off rapidly by 30 or 35 and was succeeded by desire to get a new or better job, a shift not apparent among married women. Other studies suggest that this process of forced reorientation in major goals is likely to be accompanied by considerable stressfulness. The increasing participation of married women [2] in organizational activities at around 50 years of age may be interpreted as an effort to achieve a sense of significance in a new setting once children have left home.

In total, an analysis of changes in interests, activities, and orientations with increasing years reveals a shift from active direct gratification of needs to gratifications obtained indirectly and vicariously. An illustration of this trend is found in the study earlier referred to (Kuhlen, 1948) in which an age sequence emerged in reasons given for major happy episodes in life. Starting with the late teens or early twenties, the following sequence was evident: romance, marriage, birth of children, satisfaction with children's success. Presumably, through identification with one's own children, one achieves a sense of continuing expansion when one's own life becomes stagnant. It is of further interest, though not well documented in research, that people of older ages seem to evidence a greater interest in genealogy and in religion,[3] particularly in a belief in immortality. These orientations may well represent efforts, albeit unconscious, to maintain a sense of ongoingness even when it is recognized that one's own years are short.

Presumably, if Buhler is correct that needs for expansion are continuing, such shifts may reflect not so much a decrease in need strength (at least over a wide range of years) as a change in method of gratification necessitated by

[2] Data were unavailable for single women.
[3] There is considerable disagreement regarding this trend. Despite a drop in other out-of-home activities, church-going holds up well until very old age, whereas sedentary religious activities increase steadily. Differences in definition of religiousness are probably at least partially responsible for different interpretation of trends.

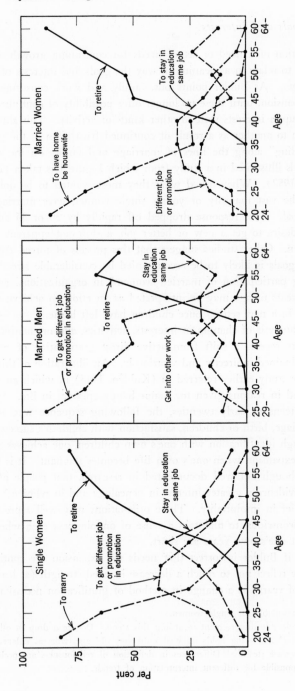

Figure 1. Changes in goals with increasing adult age as reflected in the responses of public schoolteachers to the question, "What would you most like to be doing 10 years from now?" (*From Kuhlen and Johnson, 1952.*)

decreasing capacity or opportunity to obtain the gratifications as actively and directly as was possible at an earlier age.

Disengagement

Paralleling the shifts just described is a general pattern of expansion and restriction in a variety of life activities. This is evident in age curves relating to income, family size, participation in organizations (Kuhlen, 1951), and the social life space as reflected in the relative number of psychological settings penetrated in the community (Barker, 1961). Similar to these patterns of expansion restriction are the curves obtained by Schaie (1959) for scores on a social responsibility test. These scores increased until the mid-fifties and then decreased among a sample of five hundred subjects ranging in age from 20 to 70.

Presumably data such as the foregoing, but more especially data from the Kansas City study of middle and old age, led to the proposal of a theory of aging to which was given the label "disengagement," an interpretation first presented in 1960 by Cumming and her associates, and later given more formal form and elaboration in a book (Cumming and Henry, 1961). In a sense, this hypothesis asserts a reversal of a need for expansion, i.e., in later years the individual is motivated to disengagement. Though the point is not made as explicitly as might be wished, the implication is that the disengaged state of affairs is something desired for its own sake and not a second-best role adopted as a means of avoiding the threat developing in more significant participation or as a result of societal rejection from more significant roles.

This "theory" has not yet been subjected to extensive independent test, but some data are beginning to appear. Thus, one study bears on the hypothesis implied by those proposing the disengagement theory that in old age psychological equilibrium accompanies passivity whereas at younger ages active participation is necessary for equilibrium. The data reported by Tobin and Neugarten (1961) do not support this view. They found that an index of life satisfaction was correlated *more* highly with participation in older years than in middle age. Although the supporters of the disengagement theory hypothesize that there would be no loss in morale with increased age or with retirement, available data seem not to support this view. Kutner and his associates (1956) have shown morale to decrease with age, and Phillips (1957) has reported more maladjustment among old people who have moved into less favored roles. Another study, by Filer and O'Connell (1962), is especially noteworthy in that it involved an *experimental* manipulation of environmental conditions. A special attempt was made to modify for an experimental group the environmental demands and expectancies in a VA domiciliary so as to provide a "useful-contribution" climate. Care was taken to avoid the appearance of a "special project" and the participants were probably not aware of the group they were in. Nor was the rater who evaluated their later adjustment. Significant gains in adjustment characterized the experimental group.

A report by Dean (1960), one of the collaborators in an early statement of the disengagement theory, has presented data on the decline of "instrumentality" in support of the theory. The present writer is inclined to place an opposite interpretation upon these findings, concluding that the data show oldsters to be quite unhappy about their lot because of their loss in instrumentality. For example, in answer to the question "What are the worst things about being the age you are now?" there was a decided increase with age in responses classified as "frustrated output," e.g., loss of ability to do, to achieve, to assume responsibility; loss of respect from others. In the two oldest age groups (70–79, 80+), this category of response was the *most frequently* employed category, suggesting very real unhappiness at their inability to remain "engaged." One may also interpret Simmons's earlier findings (1946) based on a survey of the treatment of older people in primitive societies as contradictory to the disengagement hypothesis. He emphasized that *protection* and *conservation* of gains made earlier seem to characterize the motivational pattern of old people the world over.

Despite the contradictory lines of evidence summarized in the foregoing paragraphs, it is already evident that the disengagement concept has considerable heuristic value. Already it appears to have stimulated a variety of studies which have added to the store of empirical data on aging.

Drive Level and Degree of Involvement in Life

Although available evidence does not particularly favor the view that older people seek a disengaged state of affairs as a desirable circumstance in its own right, it does appear that degree of psychological involvement in life becomes less. This might well be anticipated on the part of people who are experiencing declining energy and other organic decrements, who have lived long enough to have achieved what they want or to have become reconciled to their failure to do so, and who less frequently find genuinely new experiences or new opportunities to stimulate them. For such reasons, and possibly others, they "invest" less in life, are less vigorously motivated.

This decreased investment in living with increasing age has already been suggested by the less direct, more vicarious methods of achieving gratification characterizing the later years. In total, there seems to be a reduction in "drive level," a decrease in ego-involvement in life. The latter is reflected in analyses of TAT stories obtained in the Kansas City study of middle and old age. Older people told less complex stories, introduced less conflict and peopled their stories with fewer inhabitants. Also a reduction in ego energy seems to occur, as reflected in a count of the number of assertive rather than passive activities described and in ratings of the emotional intensity of stories. The relevant data, reported in a paper by Rosen and Neugarten (1960), are summarized in Table 1. Gurin et al. (1960) reported older people to worry less than younger individuals, a finding which they also interpret as reflecting less investment in life.

Somewhat related to the foregoing are two studies of the decline of affect in old age. A recent paper by Dean (1962) reports a decline in frequency of becoming "irritated" from 50 years of age to over 80, but little change from 60 to over 80 in frequency of becoming angry, and no change in frequency of reported boredom. However, in the latter instance those younger (50–59) tended to define boredom in terms of absence of interaction whereas those older (80+) defined it in terms of absence of activity. Lakin and Eisdorfer (1962) contrasted two groups (mean ages of 24 and 73) with respect to the degree to which their responses to a stick-figure projective test revealed differences in number of affects, intensity of affect, somatic comments, and activity. Only in the instance of number of affects and activity did these two groups differ reliably, with the oldsters evidencing decrement.

Table 1. Mean Ego Involvement and Ego Energy Scores of Men and Women Combined, Derived From TAT Data (Adapted from Rosen and Neugarten, 1960)

Age	Number Interviewed	Ego Involvement		Ego Energy	
		Introduced Figures	Introduced Conflict	Assertive Energy	Emotional Intensity
40–49	48	2.23 [a]	3.02 [a]	13.19 [a]	5.75
50–59	48	1.67 [b]	2.38	12.27 [b]	5.17 [b]
64–71	48	.94 [c]	2.35 [c]	11.54 [c]	4.08 [c]

[a] Applying Tukey's test to the Studentized Range (Snedecor, 1956, pp. 251–252), the difference between means for the youngest and middle age groups is significant at or beyond the .05 level.

[b] The difference between means for the middle and oldest age groups is significant at or beyond the .05 level.

[c] The difference between means for the youngest and oldest age groups is significant at or beyond the .01 level.

Although in both instances these investigators interpret their results as indicating a paucity of affective energy in old age and a disengagement of the aged from life outside themselves, it is evident that substantially more research is needed to establish both the generality and the meaning of these trends. Do we have here a "preferred" state of affairs or an apathy generated by rejection, organic losses, and/or lack of external stimulation?

ANXIETY AND MALADJUSTMENT

Anxiety is an important motivator whether it is translated into achievement-type drives or into defensive mechanisms utilized for its control. There is reason to believe that anxiety, especially susceptibility to threat, increases with age. Certainly such would be expected as social and physical losses are experienced, as the individual moves into less favored age groups in a youth-oriented society and experiences loss of status and opportunity, as physical losses make it increasingly difficult to master or maintain mastery over his environment and to achieve gratifications in the ways and to the degree previously possible, as he finds it increasingly difficult to get out of threatening situations in which he may be "locked" by the commitments (marriage, children, seniority of position, specialization of work interest) that come with age.

Various types of evidence will be presented to describe adult age changes in anxiety and maladjustment—facts regarding happiness, self-concept, and self-confidence. (These types of symptoms overlap several of the major dimensions of adult adjustment identified by Veroff, Feld, and Gurin, 1962.) If it is hypothesized that such symptoms are generated primarily by *losses* (whether actual or perceived), then it would be further hypothesized that they would bear a curvilinear relationship to adult age, showing improvement during those adult years when evidences of growth and competence are clear (bringing a sense of security) and increasing anxiety and maladjustment as increments give way to decrements and the restrictive phases of life take over. There may, of course, be "critical periods" of heightened anxiety, as earlier suggested or special age trends in sources of anxiety (Powell and Ferraro, 1960).

Changes in Subjective Happiness

One would anticipate that happiness would increase with age as important previously frustrated needs are satisfied. Thus in young adulthood, in contrast to adolescence, sex needs and needs for autonomy are more likely to be satisfied, and important life developments in the area of family and work probably bring a sense of achievement and security, and presumably happiness. Later, as losses are encountered, and fewer opportunities for need gratification present themselves, one would anticipate a reduction in happiness. That a curvilinear relationship between adult age and estimates of happiness does exist is suggested in an unpublished study by the writer (Kuhlen, 1948). In this investigation, adults of different ages were asked to rate in retrospect the degree of happiness which characterized their lives year by year up to the present time. There was an increase of happiness to the late twenties and a fairly steady decrease thereafter. In view of our expectation that ratings of happiness would reflect the individual's sense of progress (expansion), it is of interest that for married women the curve of "happiness" reaches a peak earlier than in the case of single women, who must wait (we speculate) until they begin to find intrinsic satisfactions in occupational achievement, a circumstance that does not occur until occupation becomes a primary goal for them, probably in the thirties.

Other data are consistent with these findings, though in no other study was the age breakdown fine enough to permit the curvilinear pattern evident in the Kuhlen study. Morgan (1937), Landis (1942), and Gurin and his associates (1960) all have reported decreasing proportions of subjects reporting happiness as adult age increased. A continuation of these trends into very old age, the oldest group being over 100, indicates that the downward trend continues (Cavan et al., 1949).

Changes in Self-Concept

It is apparent that the well-adjusted individual will have positive self-regarding attitudes, whereas the individual who is maladjusted and insecure—and hence more susceptible to anxiety and threat—will tend to have a low regard of himself and be lacking in self-confidence. Again, one would anticipate that the character of the self-concept will vary curvilinearly with age, becoming more favorable during the periods of gains and increased status, and less favorable in the years beyond when losses are being experienced. Although there have been some interesting theoretical considerations of developmental changes in self-concept during the adult years (see particularly Erikson, 1959; and Buhler, 1962), relatively few developmental *data* are available. One of the few arrays of data with which this writer is acquainted that shows the expected curvilinear relationship of self-concept to age was assembled by Lehner and Gunderson (1953), utilizing a draw-a-person test. It was found that men tended to draw larger figures the older they got up to about age thirty, and thereafter they drew smaller pictures, whereas women drew larger pictures up to age 40 and then smaller pictures. Since it is often assumed that in such picture drawing the individual projects his self-image, it possibly may be inferred that these trends reflect trends in self-evaluation, and that the picture is drawn larger until the individual senses that he has passed the prime of life.

Some of the data bearing on the self-concept in later years are on the amusing side, though nonetheless revealing. For example, when taking intelligence tests in the course of an experiment, older college professors made twice as many self-belittling comments as did those younger (Sward, 1945). And older women, particularly older single women, have a strong tendency to omit their ages from autobiographical sketches in such places as *Who's Who* and *American Men of Science* (Norman, 1949). Presumably this is done because such admission is painful to themselves or viewed as self-damaging in the eyes of others. More systematic is the study by Mason (1954) who administered a number of measures of self-concept to several groups from different backgrounds. A group of institutionalized indigent old people had more negative self-concepts than did a group of independent, middle-class oldsters, and both, in turn, had more negative self-concepts than did a more youthful, low economic group. However, individual differences among the old groups were greater than among the young, suggesting that reactions to the aging process vary substantially among individuals.

Still a further line of evidence is of interest here, particularly since it is often said that a person is as young—or as old—as he feels. Although there are certain methodological difficulties in current research (Jeffers, Eisdorfer, and Busse, 1962), how one classifies one's self age-wise may be construed as reflecting his self-concept. The surprising finding from several studies (Tuckman and Lorge, 1954; Phillips, 1957; Kutner et al., 1956) is that many people of quite advanced years describe themselves as "middle-aged"—half of over three hundred individuals over 70 years of age in one of the studies and about a third of those over 75 in another. That one's subjective age has significant implications is suggested by the fact that, with actual age controlled, those oldsters who rated themselves as middle-aged in one study (Havighurst and Albrecht, 1953) were better adjusted on other measures, and that in another study (Kogan and Wallach, 1961) a relationship was found between subjective age and indices of caution, when chronological age was held constant. Curiously, however, this relationship was attributable almost entirely to a rather high relationship to subjective age and caution in that portion of the group that was low in measured anxiety. The investigators considered the lack of relationship between subjective age and "decision caution" in the high anxiety group to stem from the greater heterogeneity of this group, a circumstance they thought due to the different possible meanings of high anxiety for older people. For the low anxiety subjects, the theoretical interpretation stressed the importance of "image maintenance" in bringing about behavioral consistency.

This relationship between self-concept or self-image and "decision confidence" brings us to another major line of evidence relating to self-concept, namely, that bearing on the self-confidence of individuals of different ages. As suggested above, one would expect that individuals with positive self-concepts would be more self-confident, whereas those with negative self-concepts would be less self-confident. Following our expectation that self-concept would improve during those phases of the life span where there are pronounced gains and evidences of accomplishment, Brozek (1952) has shown that men around 50 were more self-confident on a questionnaire than those younger. Wallach and Kogan (1961) have compared younger adults (college age) and a group of older adults (between 47 and 85 years of age) on a number of measures of caution and self-confidence. They found a number of interesting relationships, one of which involved the fact that the older group was more cautious than the younger group, and, in the case of men, less self-confident. The basic facts are presented in Table 2, where it is also shown that a reliable relationship between caution and age exists among the older group of women, but not among the men. These data suggest that aging experiences in the Amer-

Table 2. Age Differences in Mean Indexes of Self-confidence and Caution (Adapted from Wallach and Kogan, 1961)

	Young	Old	p	r * (older group)
Confidence index (Low scores indicate confidence)				
Men	2.83	3.19	<.01	...
Women	3.11	3.08	ns	
p	<.01	ns		
Deterrence of failure (Caution) (High scores indicate caution)				
Men	5.82	6.38	<.01	.05 (ns)
Women	5.88	6.36	<.02	.33 (p <.01)
p	ns	ns		

* Correlation is between "deterrence of failure" score and age in the older group. "Older men" averaged 70.2 years (SD = 7.3); women 69.5 years (SD = 7.7). Number of subjects: 132 young women, 89 older women; 225 younger men, 65 older men. Young people were college students.

ican culture affect the sexes differentially with respect to decline of confidence and caution, with respect to both timing and degree.

Another, possibly very significant, finding was the fact that the odd-even reliability of the test involving degree of caution (a dozen verbally described situations in which the subjects were asked to recommend action) was higher for the older group (*r:* males, .80; females, .80) than for the younger group (*r:* males, .53; females, .63). This finding may be interpreted as indicating a greater *generality* of caution, i.e., less dependence upon specific situational factors, among the old than among the young. This particular finding, if confirmed, can have substantial theoretical significance. The fruitfulness of a theoretical interpretation of aging in terms of anxiety and threat depends in part upon the degree to which anxiety is shown to be generalized and not highly situational in origin.

Still another study (Kogan and Wallach, 1961) is of interest here, partly because it utilized a different technique, but also because it compared the values placed upon different phases of the life span by a younger and older group of subjects. With respect to "self-concept," the concepts of "myself" and "ideal person" were included among those studied by means of the semantic differential, with special reference to the evaluative factor score. Here again a decline in the favorability of the self-concept in old age appeared. The difference between the old and young was especially significant in the case of the "ideal person." This was interpreted by the authors as suggesting "that older individuals are either more willing to admit unfavorable elements into their image of their ideal or that the very connotation of the concept evokes a more negative reaction in an older person whose age status renders unrealistic any aspirations toward an unrealized ideal self. . . . However, such devaluation may have ego defensive properties for both old and young individuals."

Table 3 contains scores on the "evaluative factor" for those concepts relating to developmental stages in life. It will be noted that both young and old age groups of both sexes assign negative valuations to such concepts as elderly, old age, and death. However, the older individuals were reliably less negative toward old age and death than were the younger. Thus, while older people place a negative valuation upon their phase of life, they seem to achieve a certain adaptation to old age, and do not view it nearly as negatively as do young adults.

Changes in Incidence of Anxiety Symptoms

Evidence presented thus far in this section indicates rather clearly that as people get older, they are as a group less happy, have more negative self-

Table 3. Age Differences in Mean Evaluative Scores (Semantic Differential) for Several Life Stage Concepts (Adapted from Kogan and Wallach, 1961)

			Concept			
	Baby	Youth	Middle Age	Elderly	Old Age	Death
Men						
Young	2.24	.99	.61	−.77	−.97	−3.02
Old	1.75	1.05	.29	−.69	−.11	−2.25
p	ns	ns	ns	ns	.02	ns
Women						
Young	2.32	1.17	.22	−1.02	−1.79	−4.28
Old	2.09	1.35	.20	−1.14	−.30	−2.33
p	ns	ns	ns	ns	.001	.001

concepts, and evidence less self-confidence. One would expect increases in anxiety symptoms to parallel these changes. Trends should be examined under two conditions: first, under what might be considered "normal" circumstances of living, and second, under stressful or threatening conditions. Study in these two settings is desirable because, as is the case in the instance of physiological functioning, the effects of aging are not likely to be so noticeable under normal conditions as under conditions of stress. Thus, we might anticipate that people would not show much in the way of trends in anxiety symptoms with age under normal conditions of living, but would under conditions of environmental or organic stress.

The bulk of the data obtained under ordinary conditions of living, seem to be consistent with the expectation noted in the preceding paragraph. Despite the expectation that "nervousness" would increase with age or be particularly noticeable at certain critical points, such as menopause, Hamilton (1942) found no particular age trends. Nor was an increase with age in the frequency of nervous symptoms evident among a large number of individuals taking health examinations in another study (Britten, 1931). No age trends or a trend toward decreased anxiety might well be expected, in view of the fact that people tend to seek out those circumstances in life which are positively rewarding and non-threatening. To the degree that one is successful in this, as he is likely to be as time (age) passes, and as long as this state of affairs is maintained, no increase with age in anxiety would be anticipated. And this seems to be the finding of a number of early studies.

However, certain facts emanating from a more *recent* national mental health survey appear to be contrary to earlier findings and warrant particular attention because of the size and representativeness of the sample. The interview schedule utilized in this survey contained questions dealing with some twenty symptoms of psychological distress. A factor analysis suggested four factors which were labeled "psychological anxiety," "physical health," "immobilization," and "physical anxiety." Table 4 carries the percentage of subjects in various age groups who evidenced high scores in three of these factors. It will be noted that there is a substantially greater incidence of anxiety symptoms among older people than among younger except in the instance of the factor dealing with immobilization. These investigators offer the following interpretation (an interpretation not unlike Erikson's, 1959) of the greater incidence of immobilization symptoms in young adulthood:

Immobilization, ennui, and lack of energy are all psychological states that suggest lack of integration, rather than insurmountable, immediate psychological difficulty. In a life situation, where one is caught among different pressures for integration of the self—pressures that may operate at cross-purposes (such as the "achievement versus housewife" conflict for some women) or pressures that are so varied that they are not all attainable at the same time—one may frequently experience a lack of integration. Such pressures are more likely to occur early in life and then gradually diminish as patterns of integration are chosen. Until such

Table 4. Percentage of Subjects of Various Ages Who Received High Score (6, 7, or 8) on "Psychological Anxiety," "Immobilization," and "Physical Anxiety" (Adapted from Gurin, Veroff, and Feld, 1960)

	Age					
	21–24	25–34	35–44	45–54	55–64	65+
Psychological Anxiety						
Men	5	6	8	11	14	17
Women	10	14	17	20	29	34
Immobilization						
Men	22	10	10	3	1	2
Women	14	15	12	6	5	4
Physical Anxiety						
Men	3	4	4	8	13	17
Women	8	9	10	14	17	28
No. of Subjects						
Men	65	252	241	209	146	161
Women	98	344	307	250	183	191

integration occurs, however, one might expect that a common reaction to these cross-pressures which are too divergent or too numerous to handle would be with-drawal, with its concomitant restlessness and disruption. Since this problem is more often encountered by the young adults, perhaps this is one reason that young people are prone to symptoms of the immobilization type (Gurin, Veroff, and Feld, 1960, pp. 191–192).

Adequate explanations of the contrast between this recent study and earlier findings are not readily apparent. Differences in methodology or in sample may be responsible, or it may be that current times are particularly stressful compared to the social-political context of earlier research. As will be de-veloped next, older individuals seem particularly susceptible to stress, and thus it is possible that under current "normal" conditions they may reflect more anxiety.

For more definitive evidence regarding reactions of people of different ages to stressful situations, we turn now to reports of observations in "naturalistic settings" and to studies which were specifically designed to check this phe-nomenon. A first line of evidence, usually not quantified in reports of investi-gations, is the common experience that investigators have of difficulty in ob-taining cooperation of older individuals (e.g., Welford, 1951). One explana-tion of this reluctance is their unwillingness to expose themselves to threat. Data on the incidence of mental illness and suicides also suggest greater sus-ceptibility to stress in older years. Another study of younger adult years, done by the present writer (Kuhlen, 1951) during World War II, revealed a greater relationship between age and anxiety symptoms among enlisted naval personnel who were presumably in a more stressful situation than were others.

Two other studies, utilizing different procedures, suggest an increase in anxiety with age. In these studies, reaction time to stimulus words was utilized as a measure of threat or stress. Here we are especially concerned with reaction time to words such as "worry, afraid, unhappy, restless, anx-ious." Such words might be considered generalized anxiety "stimuli" in con-trast to "church" which might be viewed as representing the religious area of life. Powell and Ferraro (1960) found reaction time to these words to increase from the twenties through the fifties for both married and single women elementary school teachers, and Olsen and Elder (1958) reported the same result for a group of older (60 to 80 age group) compared to a younger group of women. Since these generalized anxiety words were interspersed with words from potentially stressful areas of living, it is not clear whether the results should be construed as bearing on changes under "normal" cir-cumstances of living or under "stressful" circumstances.

Although the data are by no means as extensive as one might wish, either with respect to the range of symptoms sampled or the range of ages, the evidence does seem to suggest that increasing age brings increasing susceptibility to stress and threat. Presumably this threat is engendered by cultural and physical losses that are experienced with increasing age and by various and sundry commitments which are more binding as age increases and which make threats more serious. Certainly more careful studies should be undertaken of this variable, not only for the purpose of marking out the age relationships under different conditions, but also with respect to determining the degree to which increasing age brings with it a *generalized* type of anxiety which might be reflected in a whole array of behaviors, in contrast to anxiety which is fairly specific to certain situational changes that occur with age. In view of the theoretical importance of anxiety as a variable influencing personality and performance changes with age such studies assume great importance.

CHANGES IN PERSONALITY TRAITS: ADJUSTIVE PREDISPOSITIONS

Perhaps as convincing as any line of evidence regarding the increasing incidence with age of anxiety and its importance as a motivating force is the fact that a variety of behaviors which serve to reduce anxiety tend also to increase with age. Typically, for example, people avoid and/or get out of anxiety-producing situations. This may be one of the reasons why people tend to elect to live in an increasingly restricted social matrix as they get older and to develop sundry personality characteristics which have anxiety-reducing value. Quite independently of age the types of traits to be discussed in this section are those which reliably differentiate the anxious and the non-anxious person. Rokeach (1961) asserts that "closed-mindedness" is a means of controlling anxiety; Brim (1955) interprets the use of extreme responses on an attitude scale as motivated by insecurity; conservatism may be interpreted as a clinging to the old and familiar as a means of avoiding the threat of the new. Indeed, when one surveys the types of differences that have been noted between anxious and non-anxious individuals, one is struck by the similarity of these differences to those observed between the old and the young.

Such interpretations as the foregoing have been put together with particular reference to aging by such theoretical writers as Kaufman (1940), Atkin (1940), and Schuster (1952), all writing from a psychoanalytic point of view. They interpret many of the personality changes with age, particularly those to be described, as representing ego defenses against the anxiety generated by the physical and cultural losses experienced with increased age.

Conservatism-Liberalism

One needs only to examine the details of the opinion poll data presented in the monumental volume by Cantril (1951) to document the fact that wherever age trends are presented older adults typically favor practices which are essentially "old-fashioned." Thus is their conservatism, their tendency to support the "status quo" (of yesterday), revealed. A number of studies have been summarized by the present writer elsewhere (Kuhlen, 1945; Pressey and Kuhlen, 1957) which generally, but not with perfect consistency, support this generalization. On the other hand, the tendency for people to dislike change as they get older has been documented consistently in investigations. This was noted by Bean (1933) in an early study, and also by Strong (1931) in a study which he confirmed later (1943), and by Pollack (1943) who studied attitudes toward changes of packages of retail commodities.

Rigidity-Dogmatism

A substantial body of evidence is accumulating indicating that as people get older they become more rigid. We turn first to evidence that illustrates the variety of rigidity measures and the possible inconsistency of age trends, and then to studies which support the view of increasing rigidity. The variety and inconsistency have been emphasized particularly by Chown. She points out that there are many types of rigidity (Chown, 1959) and several types of personality rigidity (Chown, 1960), and that they show different age trends (Chown, 1961). Although there seems to be a general decline in flexibility, especially in the very late years, the curves presented in Figure 2 from her research reveal striking differences. Spontaneous flexibility, for example (see Figure 2*a*), which is largely cognitive in nature, does not appear to decline until after 50. Of the three subscales relating to "personality rigidity," only one (liking for habit) provides evidence for increasing rigidity over the greater portion of adult years. In contrast, the trends based on a substantially larger sample studied by Schaie (50 in each of ten semi-decade groups) were consistently in the direction of greater rigidity with age. Because of the practical as well as theoretical importance of rigidity his findings are also presented (Figure 3). Riegel and Riegel (1960) have reported regular trends in the direction of greater rigidity with age, and other studies to be summarized next also support the view that rigidity increases with age.

A number of studies, for example, reveal a tendency for people to see things in more highly structured terms as they get older, findings that might be expected in view of the low positive relationship of .19 reported by Adorno

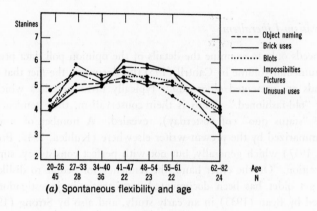

(a) Spontaneous flexibility and age

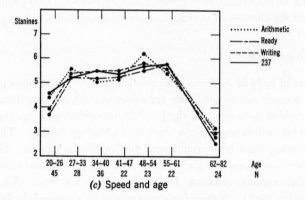

(c) Speed and age

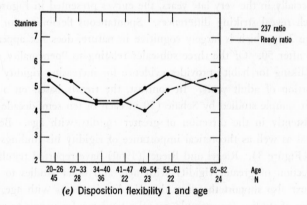

(e) Disposition flexibility 1 and age

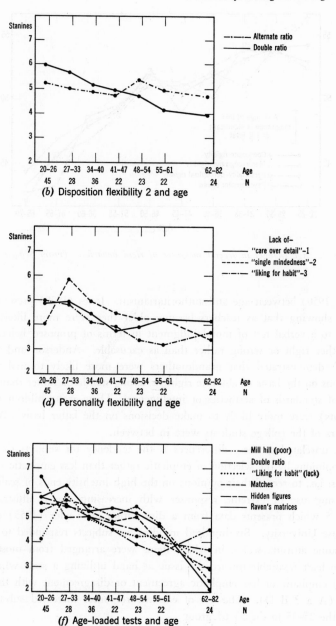

Figure 2. Age trends in various types of rigidity. All the tests except the Mill Hill Vocabulary have been scored for these graphs so that a high stanine means a flexible performance. In the case of the Mill Hill test, a high stanine here means a poor performance. (From Chown, 1961.)

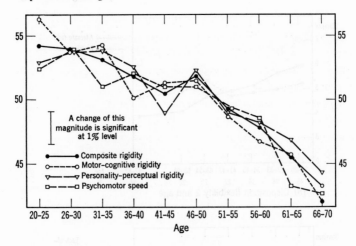

Figure 3. Age changes in several measures of rigid behavior. (From Schaeie, 1958.)

et al. (1950) between age and authoritarianism. Jones (1929) presented evidence showing that as teachers became older they were more likely to respond to a verbal test of moral judgment in terms of proposed behavior being either right or wrong rather than as excusable. Anderson and Dvorak (1928) demonstrated that grandmothers were more likely to make moral decisions on the basis of absolute right or wrong standards rather than on the basis of standards of aesthetics or intelligence. Their grandchildren (college students) were more likely to make decisions on the latter basis. And the mothers of the college students were in between.

Not unrelated to these differences is the tendency for subjects to express their opinions by the selection of emphatic rather than less emphatic response choices, i.e., to record their opinions on the high intensity ends of scales. An increasing use of extreme responses with increasing age is illustrated by Table 5 which presents data from a dissertation by Taylor (1955) done at Syracuse University. Six hundred middle-class subjects responded to several Thurstone attitude scales, in which items were arranged from most favorable to least favorable toward the issue at hand utilizing a scale which permitted emphatic or less emphatic agreement or disagreement with the statement (A a ? d D). The use of extreme responses increased substantially from the 25–35 to the 55–65 group.

One may argue, in interpretation of these changes, that as people get older they *should* have firmer opinions on the matters about which they were questioned, having had longer time to reach judgments and more experience on which to base them. In this connection, it is of special interest that the "range of agreement" scores (number of items separating the most and least favorable item endorsed) also increased with age, suggesting that instead of becoming more integrated, opinions actually became more inconsistent. This finding suggests the influence of emotional rather than cognitive determinants of the increased intensity of response. Perhaps the need to structure the environment becomes sufficiently strong that inconsistent and other unrelated elements are increasingly incorporated into that structure.

The Taylor study is presented in some detail because it provided evidence bearing on a number of dimensions of the response patterns of older and younger people to attitude items. However, it is by no means unique in demonstrating the increased tendency for older individuals to give more highly structured emphatic responses. For example, this same tendency, somewhat stronger for women but increasing for both sexes with age, was reported by Riegel and Riegel (1960) and earlier studies are in the same general direction.

Table 5. Age Contrasts in Mean Scores Indicative of Various Patterns of Responses to a Scale of Attitudes Toward War (Adapted from Taylor, 1955)

	Age Group			$t,$*
	A 25–35	B 40–50	C 55–65	A-C Difference
"Range of agreement" scores	12.07	13.20	13.42	3.3
"Length of sequence" scores	4.48	4.79	5.12	4.2
"Use of extremes" scores	5.98	8.38	10.36	9.0
"Use of question mark response" scores	4.34	2.55	1.92	8.7
Attitude scale scores	2.57	2.53	2.52	
N	200	200	200	

* Value of 2.27 significant at the .01 level.

Caution and Avoidance

A few pages earlier note was made of the fact that people seem to be less self-confident as they get older, as this trait is measured on paper-and-pencil tests. It has become apparent in aging studies that this is a trait worth investigating in its own right, a significant dimension of personality which may reveal itself in a wide variety of situations. For example, one of the most consistent trends observed by Kuhlen (1955) in an unpublished study of attitude changes, was the increasing omission of responses with age. Although the differences were sometimes small, there was not a single item of all of those analyzed in which this did not occur. Basowitz and Korchin (1957) have also observed this tendency not only in studies of verbal learning but also in studies involving the perception of ambiguous materials. Even under instructions to guess if they did not know the answer, there was a strong tendency to inhibit responses with increasing age, a tendency which was interpreted as reflecting increased caution, i.e., defensive reluctance to venture response for fear of recognizing their own inadequacy. Somewhat related is the observation by Botwinick, Brinley, and Robbin (1958) that with increasing age there may be an increase in "response reviewing or confidence level required before responding" and a similar interpretation may be put upon the results of Arnoff (1959) who observed in a stimulus generalization study that older adults were substantially slower but more accurate than younger adults in some of their responses. Griew (1959) obtained evidence supporting similar interpretations of some of his results of an earlier study of age and performance.

STABILITY OF TRAITS AND INDIVIDUAL VARIABILITY

Since we have focused in preceding pages upon changes in personality commonly observed with the passing of years and evident in trends in means and medians, we will now examine the other side of the coin, that of relative stability and individual variability.

Stability of Traits. Information regarding the long-term stability of traits, of course, can be obtained only from longitudinal studies in which the same individuals are tested and retested. Fortunately, some of the subjects of carefully planned longitudinal studies beginning in childhood and adolescence are reaching their thirties and even forties. Findings from such investigations indicate that some traits are quite stable, whereas other relationships over time approach zero (Jones, 1958). However interesting and revealing, such correlations are only tangential to the present discussion, since in addition to early adulthood they bridge a substantial portion of adolescence, suspected by some to be a period of instability. In addition to systematic longitudinal studies, such as those conducted at Berkeley, certain investigators (e.g., Kelly, 1955) were farsighted enough to lay the early groundwork for later follow-up checks, and others (e.g., Owens, 1953) have discovered old data in storage files and have undertaken to follow-up the same individuals. The result is that we now know something about the relative stability of various traits over substantial periods of time.

As Table 6 shows, some human traits and behavior patterns are remarkably stable. Owens (1953) reported a correlation of .77 for total score of the Army Alpha Test administered at age 19 and again at 50, a span of 31 years. Dennis (1954) has shown a high degree of constancy to characterize publication rates

Table 6. Correlations Showing Relative Status of Adults with Respect to Selected Traits Measured at Widely Separated Points in Time

Trait and Measure	Approximate Age			Correlation Coefficient	Investigator
	1st Test	2nd Test	Age Span		
Intelligence (Army Alpha)	19	50	31	.77	Owens, 1953
Written sentence length (direct count)	25	75	50	.78	Dennis, 1960
Masculinity-femininity (Strong)	25	45	20	.65	Kelly, 1955
Self-confidence (Bernreuter)	25	45	20	.61	Kelly, 1955
Theoretical values (Allport-Vernon)	25	45	20	.51	Kelly, 1955
Social values (Allport-Vernon)	25	45	20	.32	Kelly, 1955
Religious values (Allport-Vernon)	25	45	20	.60	Kelly, 1955
Breadth of interest (self-ratings)	25	45	20	.37	Kelly, 1955
Conventionality (self-ratings)	25	45	20	.43	Kelly, 1955
Vocational interest profiles (Strong)	22	44	22	.75	Strong, 1955
Liberalism-conservatism (Lentz)	20	34	14	.57	Nelson, 1954

of most scientists, and the length of sentences written over the adult life span in published correspondence by a group of fourteen well-known individuals (Dennis, 1960). In view of the span of years covered, the magnitude of these correlations may come as a surprise to many readers. It will be noted in Table 6 that correlations relating to traits more typically classified under the rubric of personality are somewhat lower though the time span is less than in the above two illustrations, ranging from .32 in self ratings of breadth of interest to .75 for interest profiles. The correlations are nonetheless substantial, even when the measures were self ratings. Other studies, beyond those cited in the table, confirm these findings with other groups and other traits. For example, stability of personality is reflected in the study by Lorge (1939) showing higher reliability of attitude scales over a two week interval in the case of older compared to younger adults. And Marple (1933) demonstrated greater stability of the attitudes of older adults even when specific attempts were made to change them.

It should be noted in passing that correlations of this type, even when quite high, do not necessarily mean high stability of a trait. They describe only relative position in the group. Thus a correlation between physical size (height) at age 8 and at 18 is about .75, but obviously there has been notable growth and change over this age interval.

Although the correlations cited suggest a substantial stability of relative position within the group, they are in the main sufficiently low to suggest also that considerable shifts in position have nonetheless occurred on the part of many individuals. Thus far no investigator has sorted the individual records into significant subgroups for the purpose of relating long-term adult personality change to significant events in the intervening life history, though Owens (1962) is making some effort in this direction in the instance of mental abilities.

Though overlapping adolescence, the interdisciplinary character of Jones's investigation (1958) revealed the complexity of the interrelationships among personal traits, biological factors, and institutional and situational factors in the determination of stability or change from the teens to the thirties. Thus, for males, early maturing was correlated around .40–.50 with later measures of social activity and of occupational status. On the other hand, traits associated with adolescent maladjustment were not clearly predictive of adult maladjustment, suggesting that "the adaptive significance of a given behavior pattern can thus be interpreted only with reference to changing demands in the life situation" (Jones, 1958). In a paper reporting a long-term prediction study from the school years into very early adulthood, Anderson (1959) noted that different factors apparently influenced the later adjustment of the two sexes, and similarly stressed the importance of studying the specific situational factors and the nature of the criteria (of adjustment, for example) as they differ for significant subgroups of the population and at various stages in life. Obviously studies of this type, extending into the adult years, will provide important information as to the types of influences that operate to shape lives and personalities as people grow older.

Individual Differences and Age

There are two facets to the problem of "individual differences" in aging. One has to do with the range of differences found in various age bands, the other relates to patterns of aging that characterize different individuals or significant subgroups of the population. Defined either way, the data give rise to significant questions: Do selective perception, selective learning, and selective forgetting result in people becoming more like themselves as they get older thus accentuating individual differences? Is there differential maintenance and/or deterioration of personality with age as a function of initial status or other variables? Does culture tend to form people to a common mold as time and age passes? Do generalizations about old people have broader application than those concerning young adults?

To turn first to age differences in variation among individuals, it should be pointed out that though the differences in central tendencies (which have served to bolster most of the generalizations and discussions thus far in this chapter) are found to be reliable, the correlations of the several variables with adult age are relatively low. This, of course, is due to the wide range of individual differences at all ages, a circumstance which should serve to caution the reader against overgeneralizing from slight age trends in means or medians.[4]

Such facts as are available [5] seem to point to a reduction of interindividual differences or, at best, little change. Although Mason (1954) found greater variability among the self-concepts of the old compared to the young, relatively little published evidence supports the frequently encountered assertion

---

[4] Actually, when age is viewed as one of the many variables producing individual differences, it turns out to be much less significant over a broad age range than variables associated with sex, education, and social class.

[5] It perhaps should be noted that available data must be interpreted with extreme caution. Sampling problems are especially likely to influence SD's. The selective death rate, for example, will restrict the range in even representative samples of living oldsters. It is likely that the use of volunteers will progressively, with increased age, restrict the range whereas the use of institutional groups to supply additional subjects to older samples collected in other ways may overemphasize extremes and increase standard deviations. On the other hand, resort to institutional populations for the total old-age sample may restrict the range when compared with younger groups obtained in other ways.

that individual differences in personality are greater among older people, though admittedly data for *very* old groups are sparse. Illustrative of findings suggesting a possible reduction in individual differences is the study by Kelly (1955) covering the twenty-year age range from the mid-twenties to the mid-forties. He found evidence for a general phenomenon of "maturational regression," i.e., a tendency for the retest scores of extreme scoring subjects to regress toward the mean of the group, to a much greater degree than expected on the basis of statistical regression alone. Kelly interpreted this change as likely being a function of the social forces operating on the individual, causing the deviant person to shift toward the norm as he grows older. A similar decline in the magnitude of the SD's with increasing age was reported by Terman and Miles (1936), a trend marred only by a slight increase in the SD of the 70 to 89-year-old males (likely due to a single outlying case). Schaie (1958) reported practically no change in the standard deviations of his semi-decade groups, ranging in age from 20 to 70, in any of his measures of rigidity. Nor did Bendig (1960) find an age trend in SD's in Guilford-Zimmerman scale data. The Wallach and Kogan (1961) and Kogan and Wallach (1961) studies reveal no consistent differences.

There is no reason, of course, to believe that all traits will show the same trends. Instead of a linear trend in SD's over age, it is probable that individual differences in certain traits may increase or decrease up to a particular age, perhaps mid-life, with the trend reversed thereafter, or other "cycles" may exist. Data presented earlier in Figure 1, for example, suggest that young people are much alike in their major goals, as are old people, whereas those in the mid-years are quite heterogenous. Similar mid-life heterogeneity compared to relative homogeneity at the beginning and end of the adult life span is also suggested in the work area in a study of job satisfaction (Johnson, 1951).

It is unfortunate that more definitive information is not available on this issue. Although there seems to be some ego involvement on the part of gerontologists in the question of individual differences in mental ability (perhaps because such facts presumably bear on the question of differential decline), investigators have generally failed to comment upon interindividual variation in personality, indeed often have not even presented appropriate descriptive data in published reports.

One type of example will serve to call to the reader's attention the probability that the pattern and direction of personality change will differ greatly among individuals and various subgroups in society, namely, the degree to which different subgroups are likely to experience *threat* at various points during the course of the adult life span. This is a particularly pertinent illustration in view of the possible significance of anxiety as a generator of a number of personality changes.

While facts are not available for all subcultures, the point can be made by selected sample data. Incidence of suicide varies greatly between the sexes and between Negroes and whites. Whereas the rate constantly climbs for males with age, for females it is a relatively level smoothly rounded curve, with an actual decline in the advanced years. These differences may be interpreted as reflecting the more stressful environment in which males live, and the greater difficulty they experience in maintaining their role. Geared as men are to the work life, career frustrations and inability to find useful employment presumably would be a serious blow to self-concept and the generator of much unhappiness and anxiety. Women occupying quite a different role are not exposed to this source of anxiety and particularly not with increasing age.

Illustrations of social class differences are to be found in the ways people perceive the prime of life and aging. Among the interesting difference observed in a University of Chicago [6] 1959 study were in answers to the question of when is a man "mature," "at the prime of life," "most confident." The lower-lower class individuals gave 25 years of age and those in successively higher social classes regularly raised the age until those in the upper middle gave a mean age of 40. Similarly, upper-middle individuals defined "middle age" and "old age" as notably older than did those in lower-lower class groups. When women were asked at what age a woman was most "good looking," "most confident," "in her prime," or "old," again the lower-lower class groups gave younger ages than did those in the upper-middle classes.

Other significant subgroups of the population can very readily be identified. Buhler (1935), for example, has contrasted a "psychological curve" with the "biological" curve of life, and has pointed out that those individuals who are most dependent upon physical status—either strength or attractiveness—will have psychological curves closely approximating the biological curve of life, whereas those engaged in mental pursuits will have a psychological curve lagging the physical curve. One would expect, for example, a narcissistic person, a chorus girl, or a prize fighter to feel the threat of age much earlier than a non-narcissistic person, a university professor, or a physician. It remains for further research to demonstrate whether such predictions are correct.

In order to conclude these comments regarding individual differences on an optimistic note, it perhaps should be noted that readers of this volume are

[6] Aging and the aged, *The University of Chicago Reports,* **12**, No. 2, Nov. 1961.

likely to be in a more favored position as regards the impact of aging. To the degree that life unfolds with continuing gains, to that degree the psychological impact of aging should be delayed. And, of course, what constitutes a "gain" is subject to highly personal interpretations.

SOME CONCLUDING COMMENTS

Although age has been the primary means of ordering the data described in these pages, it is almost self-evident that age in itself is not a particularly meaningful psychological variable. Age is *time* in which other things of importance happen. Among these important "other things" are: biological changes; changes in cognitive abilities; changes in habit strengths (flexibilities, rigidities); changes in patterns of reward, threat, punishment, opportunity, deprivation, training schedules, the latter tending to be culturally age-graded; and changes in motivation. Most research thus far has been aimed at determining the degree to which variables such as these are age-related. Few studies have been designed to examine the significance of these variables as *independent* variables producing age-relatedness in other characteristics.

The fruitfulness of conceptualizing the aging process in terms of variables such as the foregoing is evident in studies by Lansing and Kish (1957), who employed stages in the family life cycle as an independent variable, and by Phillips (1957), who conceptualized aging in terms of role theory. In these studies the important thing seemed not being 45 years old, but being 45 *and* single, or 45 *and* married with *young* children, or 45 with grown children. Nor was being 70 so important as being 70 and employed *or* retired, 70 and married *or* widowed. The psychology of aging (or better, the developmental psychology of adult years) has much to gain from attempts to conceptualize aging in terms suggested by theories generated in other areas of psychology. For example, Murray's (1938) need-press concept would seem especially to have much to offer, and Helson's (1959) adaptation level theory has intriguing possibilities of application to certain aging phenomena. If a variety of psychological theorists could be attracted to the task of interpreting various segments of aging data in their own terms and applying their concepts more broadly to the process of aging, more rapid advance in psychological gerontology might be anticipated.

Although "outside" help would undoubtedly accelerate our efforts to fathom the nature and causes of personality change with age, it is significant that there is growing awareness among those doing research in aging of the multidimensionality of the problem and the inadequacy of any "theory" that does not incorporate within itself features which will predict and explain different outcomes for different categories of individuals. Sands and Rothschild (1952) have described the interaction of organic deficit, premorbid personality, and environmental stress in determining different reactions to aging. Buhler (1961) and Filer and O'Connell (1962) have called attention to the different outcomes of "normal" aging and of experimental environmental manipulation, respectively, with the implication that "disengagement theory" (discussed earlier) is a satisfactory explanation for only a portion of the subjects. Maddox and Eisdorfer (1962) concluded a report on morale among the elderly with this observation: "The common notion that 'busy people are happy people' would have to be qualified by specification of what kind of busyness would be most likely to produce or maintain morale and what structural contexts rather than assuming that interpersonal activity invariably has high morale as a concomitant." These are healthy signs in a field that in two and a half decades has advanced from purely descriptive studies to relatively simple theoretical conceptualizations to an awareness of need for much more sophisticated theory.

have described the interaction of organic defect, premorbid personality, and environmental stress in determining different reactions to aging. Bühler (1961) and Pillel and O'Connell (1962) have called attention to the different outcomes of "normal" aging and of experimental environmental manipulation, respectively, with the implication that disengagement theory (discussed earlier) is a satisfactory explanation for only a portion of the subjects. Maddox and Eisdorfer (1962) concluded a report on morale among the elderly with this observation: "The common notion that busy people are happy people" would have to be qualified by specification of what kind of busyness would be most likely to produce or maintain morale and what strategies... rather than assuming that interpersonal activity invariably has high morale as a concomitant." These are healthy signs in a field that in two and a half decades has advanced from purely descriptive studies to relatively simple theoretical considerations to an awareness of need for much more sophisticated theory.

Bibliography

Ackerman, N. W. *Psychodynamics of family life.* New York: Basic Books, 1958.

Adler, A. Individual psychology. In C. Murchison (Ed.), *Psychologies of 1930.* Worcester, Mass.: Clark University Press, 1930. Pp. 395–405.

Adorno, T. W., Frenkel-Brunswik, Else, Levinson, D. J., & Sanford, R. N. *The authoritarian personality.* New York: Harper & Bros., 1950.

Alexander, F. *Our age of unreason.* Philadelphia: J. B. Lippincott, 1951.

Allee, W. C. *The social life of animals.* Boston: Beacon, 1958.

Allers, R. Über psychogene Störungen in sprachfremder Umgebung. (Der Verfolgungswahn der sprachlich Isolierten) *Ztschr. f. d. ges. neurol. u. Psychiat.,* 1920, Berl., Orig., LX, 287–289.

Allport, G. W. *Personality.* New York: Henry Holt, 1937.

Allport, G. W. *Pattern and growth in personality.* New York: Holt, Rinehart, & Winston, 1961.

Altman, J. W., Smith, R. W., Meyers, R. L., McKenna, F. S., & Bryson, S. *Psychological and social adjustment in a simulated shelter: a research report.* Pittsburgh, Pa.: American Institute for Research, 1960.

Altus, W. D. The broken home and factors of adjustment. *Psychol. Rep.,* 1958, **4**, 477.

American Psychological Association, Committee on Psychological Tests. *Technical recommendations for psychological tests and diagnostic techniques.* Washington, D.C.: APA, 1954.

Amsel, A. Frustrative nonreward in partial reinforcement and discrimination learning: Some recent history and a theoretical extension. *Psychol. Rev.,* 1962, **69**, 306–328.

Anderson, J. E. *A survey of children's adjustment over time: a report to the people of Nobles County.* Minneapolis: University of Minnesota Press, 1959.

Anderson, J. E. The prediction of adjustment over time. In I. Iscoe and H. W. Stevenson (Eds.), *Personality development in children.* Austin: University of Texas Press, 1960. Pp. 28–72.

Anderson, A., & Dvorak, B. Differences between college students and their elders in standards of conduct. *J. abnorm. soc. Psychol.,* 1928–29, **23**, 286–292.

Arbit, J. Two early reports on the effects of sensory deprivation. *Amer. J. Psychiat.,* 1960, **117**, 467–468.

Argyris, C. *Personality and organization.* New York: Harper & Bros., 1956.

Argyris, C. Organizational effectiveness under stress. *Harvard Bus. Rev.,* May–June, 1960.

Argyris, C. *Interpersonal competence and organizational effectiveness.* Homewood, Ill.: Dorsey Press, 1962.

557

Arnhoff, F.　Adult age difference in performance on a visual-spatial task of stimulus generalization. *J. educ. Psychol.,* 1959, **50,** 259.

Arnold, M. B.　*Emotion and personality.* New York: Columbia University Press, 1960.

Aronson, E., & Carlsmith, J. M.　The effect of the severity of threat on the devaluation of forbidden behavior. *J. abnorm. soc. Psychol.,* 1963, **66,** 584–588.

Aronson, E., & Mills, J.　The effect of severity of initiation on liking for a group. *J. abnorm. soc. Psychol.,* 1959, **59,** 177–181.

Aronson, Harriet, Silverstein, A. B., & Klee, G. D.　The influences of lysergic acid diethylamide (LSD-25) on subjective time. *Amer. Med. Ass. Arch. Neurol. Psychiat.,* 1959, **1,** 469–472.

Ås, A.　Hypnotizability as a function of nonhypnotic experiences. *J. abnorm. soc. Psychol.,* 1963, **66,** 142–150.

Asch, S. E.　Studies in the principles of judgments and attitudes: II. Determination of judgments by groups and by ego standards. *J. soc. Psychol., SPSSI Bulletin,* 1940, **12,** 433–465.

Asch, S. E.　*Social psychology.* New York: Prentice-Hall, 1952.

Asratyan, E. A.　The initiation and localization of cortical inhibition in the conditioned reflex arc. *Ann. N. Y. Acad. Sci.,* 1961, **92,** 1141–1159.

Atkin, S.　Discussion of the paper by M. R. Kaufman, "Old age and aging: the psychoanalytic point of view." *Amer. J. Orthopsychiat.,* 1940, **10,** 79–83.

Atkinson, J. W., & Litwin, G. H.　Achievement motive and test anxiety conceived as motive to approach success and motive to avoid failure. *J. abnorm. soc. Psychol.,* 1960, **60,** 52–63.

Auld, F., & Murray, E. J.　Content-analysis studies of psychotherapy. *Psychol. Bull.,* 1955, **52,** 377–395.

Auld, F., & White, A. M.　Sequential dependencies in psychotherapy. *J. abnorm. soc. Psychol.,* 1959, **58,** 100–104.

Azima, H., & Cramer-Azima, Fern J.　Studies on perceptual isolation. *Dis. nerv. Syst.* (Monogr. Suppl.), 1957, **18,** 80–86.

Azima, H., & Cramer, Fern J.　Effects of partial perceptual isolation in mentally disturbed individuals. *Dis. nerv. Syst.,* 1956, **17,** 117.

Azima, H., Vispo, R., & Azima, Fern J.　Observations on anaclitic therapy during sensory deprivation. In P. Solomon et al. (Eds.), *Sensory deprivation.* Cambridge, Mass.: Harvard University Press, 1961. Pp. 143–160.

Bach, G. R.　Father-fantasies and father-typing in father separated children. *Child. Develpm.,* 1946, **17,** 63–79.

Back, K.　Influence through social communication. *J. abnorm. soc. Psychol.,* 1951, **46,** 9–23.

Baker, B. O., & Sarbin, T. R.　Differential mediation of social perception as a correlate of social adjustment. *Sociometry,* 1956, **19,** 69–83.

Bakke, E.　*Citizens without work.* New Haven, Conn.: Yale University Press, 1940.

Baldwin, A. L.　Differences in parent behavior toward three- and nine-year-old children. *J. Pers.,* 1946, **15,** 143–165.

Baldwin, A. L.　Changes in parent behavior during pregnancy: an experiment in longitudinal analysis. *Child Develpm.,* 1947, **18,** 29–39.

Bandura, A.　Psychotherapist's anxiety level, self-insight, and psychotherapeutic competence. *J. abnorm. soc. Psychol.,* 1956, **52,** 333–337.

Bandura, A.　Psychotherapy as a learning process. *Psychol. Bull.,* 1961, **58,** 143–159.

Bandura, A. Social learning through imitation. In M. R. Jones (Ed.), *Nebraska symposium on motivation.* Lincoln: University of Nebraska Press, 1962.

Bandura, A., Lipsher, D. H., & Miller, P. E. Psychotherapists' approach-avoidance reactions to patients' expressions of hostility. *J. consult. Psychol.,* 1960, **24,** 1–8.

Barber, T. X. Toward a theory of pain: Relief of chronic pain by prefrontal leucotomy, opiates, placebos, and hypnosis. *Psychol. Bull.,* 1959, **56,** 430–460.

Barber, T. X. "Hypnosis," analgesia, and the placebo effect. *J. Amer. Med. Ass.,* 1960, **172,** 680–683.

Barber, T. X. Physiological effects of "hypnosis." *Psychol. Bull.,* 1961, **58,** 390–419.

Barendregt, J. T. Performance on some objective tests under LSD-25. *Fortschritte der Psychosomatischen Medizen,* 1960, **1,** 217–219.

Barker, R. *The stream of behavior: Explorations of its structure and content.* New York: Appleton-Century-Crofts, 1963.

Barker, R., & Barker, L. S. The psychological ecology of old people in Midwest, Kansas, and Toredale, Yorkshire. *J. Geront.,* 1961, **16,** 144–149.

Barker, R., & Wright, H. *Midwest and its children: The psychological ecology of an American town.* Evanston, Ill.: Row, Peterson, 1954.

Barron, F. Some personality correlates of independence of judgment. *J. Pers.,* 1952, **21,** 287–297.

Barron, F. Threshold for the perception of human movement in inkblots. *J. consult. Psychol.,* 1955, **49,** 33–38.

Bartholomew, A. A., Franks, C. M., & Marley, E. Susceptibility to methylpentynol: Eyelid conditioning and P.G.R. response. *J. ment. Sci.,* 1958, **104,** 1167–1173.

Bartholomew, A. A., & Marley, E. Susceptibility to methylpentynol: Personality and other variables. *J. ment. Sci.,* 1959, **105,** 957–970.

Bartlet, J. E. A. A case of organized visual hallucinations in an old man with cataract, and their relation to the phenomena of the phantom limb. *Brain,* 1951, **74,** 363–373.

Basowitz, H., & Korchin, S. J. Age differences in perception of closure. *J. abnorm. soc. Psychol.,* 1957, **54,** 93–97.

Bates, A. P., & Cloyd, J. S. Toward the development of operations for defining group norms and member roles. *Sociometry,* 1956, **19,** 26–39.

Bateson, G., Jackson, D. D., Haley, J., & Weakland, J. Toward a theory of schizophrenia. *Beh. Sci.,* 1956, **1,** 251–264.

Baughman, E. E., & Welsh, G. S. *Personality: A behavioral science.* Englewood Cliffs, N.J.: Prentice-Hall, 1962.

Beach, F. A., & Jaynes, J. Effects of early experience upon the behavior of animals. *Psychol. Bull.,* 1954, **54,** 239–263.

Bean, C. H. The psychology of adherence to the old and acceptance of the new. *J. soc. Psychol.,* 1933, **4,** 340–352.

Bechtoldt, H. P. Response defined anxiety and MMPI variables. *Iowa Acad. Sci.,* 1953, **60,** 495–499.

Bechtoldt, H. P. Construct validity: A critique. *Amer. Psychologist,* 1959, **14,** 619–629.

Beck, F., & Godin, W. *Russian purge and the extraction of confession.* New York: Viking, 1951.

Beech, H. R. The symptomatic treatment of writer's cramp. In H. J. Eysenck (Ed.), *Behaviour therapy and the neuroses.* New York: Pergamon, 1960.

Beecher, H. K. Increased stress and effectiveness of placebos and "active" drugs. *Science,* 1960, **132,** 91–92.

Beilin, H. The prediction of adjustment over a four-year interval. *J. clin. Psychol.*, 1957, **13**, 270–274.

Bell, Elaine G. Inner-directed and other-directed attitudes. Unpublished doctoral dissertation, Yale University, 1955.

Belleville, R. E. MMPI score changes induced by lysergic acid diethylamide (LSD-25). *J. clin. Psychol.*, 1956, **12**, 279–282.

Benda, P., & Orsini, F. Apropos of temporo-spatial strangeness under LSD-25. *Annales Medico-Psychologiques*, 1959, **117**, 525–533.

Bender, I. E. Changes in religious interest: A retest after 15 years. *J. abnorm. soc. Psychol.*, 1958, **57**, 41–46.

Bender, Lauretta. Psychopathic behavior disorders in children. In R. M. Lindner (Ed.), *Handbook of correctional psychology.* New York: Philosophical Library, 1947. Pp. 360–377.

Bender, Lauretta. Childhood schizophrenia. *Psychiat. Quart.*, 1953, **27**, 663–679.

Bendig, A. W. Age differences in the interscale factor structure of the Guilford-Zimmerman Temperament Survey. *J. consult. Psychol.*, 1960, **24**, 134–138.

Benedek, Therese. Parenthood as a developmental phase. *Amer. J. Psychoanal.*, 1959, **7**, 389–417.

Benjamin, J. D. Prediction and psychopathological theory. In Lucy Jessner & Eleanor Pavenstedt (Eds.), *Dynamic psychopathology in childhood.* New York: Grune & Stratton, 1959. Pp. 6–77.

Benjamin, J. D. Some developmental observations relating to the theory of anxiety. *Amer. J. Psychoanal.*, 1961, **9**, 652–668.

Bennett, A. M. H. Sensory deprivation in aviation. In Solomon et al. (Eds.), *Sensory deprivation.* Cambridge, Mass.: Harvard University Press, 1961. Pp. 161–173.

Bergmann, G. Psychoanalysis and experimental psychology: A review from the standpoint of scientific empiricism. *Mind*, 1943, **52**, 122–140.

Bergmann, G. The logic of psychological concepts. *Phil. Sci.*, 1951, **18**, 93–110.

Bergmann, G. Theoretical psychology. In C. P. Stone (Ed.), *Annual review of psychology.* Stanford, Calif.: Annual Reviews, 1953. Pp. 435–458.

Bergmann, G. The contribution of John B. Watson. *Psychol. Rev.*, 1956, **63**, 265–276.

Bergmann, G., & Spence, K. W. Operationism and theory in psychology. *Psychol. Rev.*, 1941, **48**, 1–14.

Bergmann, G., & Spence, K. W. The logic of psychophysical measurement. *Psychol. Rev.*, 1944, **51**, 1–24.

Bergman, P., & Escalona, Sibylle. Unusual sensitivities in very young children. In Anna Freud et al. (Eds.), *Psychoanalytic study of the child.* New York: International Universities Press, 1949. Vols. 3–4. Pp. 333–352.

Berkun, M. M. Factors in the recovery from approach-avoidance conflict. *J. exp. Psychol.*, 1957, **54**, 64–73.

Bernicot, L. *The voyage of Anakita.* London: Rupert Hart-Davis, 1953.

Berry, J. L., & Martin, B. GSR reactivity as a function of anxiety, instructions, and sex. *J. abnorm. soc. Psychol.*, 1957, **54**, 9–12.

Bettelheim, B. Individual and mass behavior in extreme situations. *J. abnorm. soc. Psychol.*, 1943, **38**, 417–452.

Betz, B. J. Experiences in research in psychotherapy with schizophrenic patients. In H. H. Strupp (Ed.), *Second research conference on psychotherapy.* Chapel Hill, N.C.: American Psychological Association, 1961.

Bexton, W. H., Heron, W., & Scott, T. H. Effects of decreased variation in the sensory environment. *Canad. J. Psychol.*, 1954, **8**, 70–76.

Bibring, E. Psychoanalysis and the dynamic psychotherapies. *J. Amer. psychoanal. Ass.*, 1954, **2**, 745–770.

Bibring, G., Dwyer, T., Huntington, D., & Valensteen, A. A study of the psychological processes in pregnancy and of the earliest mother-child relationship. I. Some propositions and comments. In R. Eissler et al. (Eds.), *Psychoanalytic study of the child.* New York: International Universities Press, 1961, Vol. 16. Pp. 9–24.

Bindra, D., & Scheier, I. H. The relation between psychometric and experimental research in psychology. *Amer. Psychologist,* 1954, **9**, 69–71.

Binswanger, L. Über die Daseinsanalytische Forschungsrichtung in der Psychiatrie. *Ausgewahlte Vortrage und Aufsatze.* Bern: I. A. Francke A. G. Verlag, 1947.

Birch, H. G. Sources of order in the maternal behavior of animals. *Amer. J. Orthopsychiat.,* 1956, **26**, 279–284.

Birren, J. E. *Handbook of aging and the individual.* Chicago: University of Chicago Press, 1959.

Bjerstedt, Ake. Reduction of "barrier tendencies" during experience of international co-living. *Acta psychol.,* 1958, **14**, 329–346.

Blake, R. R., & Mouton, Jane S. *Group dynamics: Key to decision making.* Houston: Gulf, 1961.

Blake, R. R., & Mouton, Jane S. The experimental investigation of interpersonal influences. In A. D. Biderman & H. Zimmer (Eds.), *The manipulation of human behavior.* New York: Wiley, 1961. Pp. 216–276.

Blake, R. R., & Mouton, Jane S. The developing revolution in management practices. *ASTD Journal,* 1962, **16**, 29–50.

Blake, R. R., Mouton, Jane S., & Blansfield, M. How executive team training can help you. *ASTD Journal,* 1962, **16**, 3–11.

Blum, G. S. *A model of the mind.* New York: Wiley, 1961.

Blum, R. H. The choice of American heroes and its relationship to personality structure in an elite. *J. soc. Psychol.,* 1958, **48**, 235–246.

Bombard, A. *The voyage of the heretique.* New York: Simon & Shuster, 1953.

Bone, Edith. *Seven years solitary.* London: Hamish Hamilton, 1957.

Bonney, M. E. The relative stability of social, intellectual and academic status in grade II to IV, and the interrelationships between these various forms of growth. *J. educ. Psychol.,* 1943, **34**, 88–102. (*a*)

Bonney, M. E. The constancy of sociometric scores and their relationship to teacher judgments of social success, to personality self-ratings. *Sociometry,* 1943, **6**, 409–424. (*b*)

Botwinick, J., Brinley, J. F., & Robbin, J. S. The interaction effects of perceptual difficulty and stimulus exposure time on age differences in speed and accuracy of response. *Gerontologia,* 1958, **2**, 1–10.

Boudreau, D. Evaluation of the sedation threshold test. *Amer. Med. Ass. Arch. neurol. Psychiat.,* 1958, **80**, 771–775.

Bovard, E. W. The effects of social stimuli on response to stress. *Psychol. Rev.,* 1959, **66**, 267–277.

Bowlby, J. Forty-four juvenile thieves. *Int. J. Psychoanal.,* 1944, **25**, 1–57.

Bowlby, J. *Maternal care and mental health.* Geneva: World Health Organization, 1951.

Bowlby, J. Processes of mourning. *Int. J. Psychoanal.,* 1961, **42**, 317–340.

Bowlby, J. et al. The effects of mother-child separation: A follow-up study. *Brit. J. Med. Psychol.,* 1956, **29**, 211–247.

Brackbill, G., & Little, K. B.   MMPI correlates of the Taylor scale of manifest anxiety. *J. consult. Psychol.,* 1954, **18,** 433–436.

Brady, J. P., & Lind, D. L.   Experimental analysis of hysterical blindness.   *Arch. gen. Psychiat.,* 1961, **4,** 331–339.

Brehm, J.   Post-decision changes in desirability of alternatives.   *J. abnorm. soc. Psychol.,* 1956, **52,** 384–389.

Brengelmann, J. C.   Effects of LSD-25 on tests of personality.   *J. ment. Sci.,* 1958, **104,** 1226–1236.

Brengelmann, J. C.   Problems of measurement in objective personality evaluation.   In H. P. David and J. C. Brengelmann (Eds.), *Perspectives in personality research.* New York: Springer, 1960. Pp. 294–315.

Brengelmann, J. C., Pare, C. M. B., & Sandler, M.   Alleviation of the psychological effects of LSD in man by 5-hydroxytryptophan.   *J. ment. Sci.,* 1958, **104,** 1237–1244.

Brenman, M.   On teasing and being teased and the problem of "moral masochism." *Psychoanalytic study of the child.* New York: International Universities Press, 1952. Vol. 7.   Pp. 264–285.   (Also in R. P. Knight and C. R. Friedman (Eds.), *Psychoanalytic psychiatry and psychology.* New York: International Universities Press, 1954.)

Bressler, B., Silverman, A. J., Cohen, S. I., & Shmavonian, B.   Research in human subjects and the artificial traumatic neurosis: Where does our responsibility lie?   *Amer. J. Psychiat.,* 1959, **116,** 522–526.

Breuer, J., & Freud, S.   *Studies in hysteria* (1895).   New York: Nervous and Mental Disease Publications, 1937.

Bridger, W. H.   Signaling systems in the development of cognitive functions.   In Mary Brazier (Ed.), *The central nervous system and behavior.*   Transactions of Third Conference Josiah Macy Foundation.   Madison, N.J.: Madison Printing Co., 1960.

Brim, O. G.   Attitude content intensity and probability expectation.   *Amer. soc. Rev.,* 1955, **20,** 68–76.

Brim, O. G.   Family structure and sex role learning by children.   A further analysis of Helen Koch's data.   *Sociometry,* 1958, **21,** 1–16.

Britten, R. H.   Sex differences in physical impairment in adult life.   *Amer. J. Hygiene,* 1931, **13,** 741–770.

Bronfenbrenner, U.   Socialization and social class through time and space.   In Eleanor Maccoby, T. Newcomb, and E. Hartley (Eds.), *Readings in social psychology.*   New York: Holt, 1958.   Pp. 400–425.

Brophy, I. N.   Luxury of anti-Negro prejudice.   *Publ. Opin. Quart.,* 1946, **9,** 456–466.

Brown, J. S.   *The motivation of behavior.*   New York: McGraw-Hill, 1961.

Brown, J. S., & Farber, I. E.   Emotions conceptualized as intervening variables—with suggestions toward a theory of frustration.   *Psychol. Bull.,* 1951, **48,** 465–495.

Brozek, J.   Personality of young and middle-aged normal men: Item analysis of a psychosomatic inventory.   *J. Geront.,* 1952, **7,** 410–418.

Bruner, E. M.   Cultural transmission and cultural change.   *Southwestern J. Anthrop.,* 1959, **12,** No. 2.

Brunswik, E.   Organismic achievement and environmental probability.   *Psychol. Rev.,* 1943, **50,** 255–272.

Buchanan, W., & Cantril, H.   *How nations see each other.*   Urbana, Ill.: University of Illinois Press, 1953.

Bugenthal, D. E., & Lehner, G. F.   Accuracy of self-perception and group-perception as related to two leadership roles.   *J. abnorm. soc. Psychol.,* 1958, **56,** 396–398.

Buhler, Charlotte. The curve of life as studied in biographies. *J. appl. Psychol.*, 1935, 19, 405–409.

Buhler, Charlotte. Maturation and motivation. *Pers.*, 1951, 1, 184–211.

Buhler, Charlotte. Zur Psychologie des menschlichen Lebenslaufes. *Psychol. Rdsch.*, 1957, 8, 1–15.

Buhler, Charlotte. Old age and fulfillment of life with considerations of the use of time in old age. *Vita Humana*, 1961, 4, 129–133.

Buhler, Charlotte. Genetic aspects of the self. *Ann. N. Y. Acad. Sci.*, 1962, 96, 730–764.

Burdick, H. A., Ekartsberg, R. von, & Ono, H. Two experiments in social power. *Psychol. Rep.*, 1959, 5, 781–789.

Burdock, E. I., Sutton, S., & Zubin, J. Personality and psychopathology. *J. abnorm. soc. Psychol.*, 1958, 56, 18–30.

Burney, C. *Solitary confinement.* New York: Coward-McCann, 1952.

Burri, Clara. The influence of an audience upon recall. *J. educ. Psychol.*, 1931, 22, 683–690.

Burton, R. V., & Whiting, J. W. M. The absent father and cross-sex identity. *Merrill Palmer Quart.*, 1961, 7, 85–95.

Buss, A. H., Wiener, M., Durkee, Ann, & Baer, M. The measurement of anxiety in clinical situations. *J. consult. Psychol.*, 1955, 19, 125–129.

Byrd, R. E. *Alone.* New York: Putnam's, 1938.

Byrne, D. The relationship between humor and the expression of hostility. *J. abnorm. soc. Psychol.*, 1956, 53, 84–89.

Byrne, D. Anxiety and the experimental arousal of affiliation need. *J. abnorm. soc. Psychol.*, 1961, 63, 660–662.

Byrne, D., & Holcomb, Joan. The reliability of a response measure: Differential recognition-threshold scores. *Psychol. Bull.*, 1962, 59, 70–73.

Cairns, R. B. The influence of dependency inhibition on the effectiveness of social reinforcement. *J. Pers.*, 1961, 29, 466–488.

Camberari, J. The effects of sensory isolation on suggestible and nonsuggestible psychology graduate students. Unpublished doctoral dissertation, University of Utah, 1958.

Cameron, N. *The psychology of behavior disorders.* Boston: Houghton Mifflin, 1947.

Campbell, D. T. Lectures in social psychology. Unpublished manuscript, 1959.

Campbell, D. T. Blind variation and selective retention in creative thought as in other knowledge processes. *Psychol. Rev.*, 1960, 67, 380–400.

Campbell, D. T. Recommendations for APA test standards regarding construct, trait, or discriminant validity. *Amer. Psychologist*, 1960, 15, 546–553.

Cannon, W. B. The James-Lange theory of emotions: A critical examination and an alternative theory. *Amer. J. Psychol.*, 1927, 39, 106–124.

Cannon, W. B. *Bodily changes in pain, hunger, fear and rage.* (2nd ed.) New York: Appleton-Century, 1929.

Cannon, W. B. The James-Lange and the thalamic theories of emotion. *Psychol. Rev.*, 1931, 38, 281–295.

Cantoni, L. A study in emotional adjustment: The correlation of student and adult forms of the Bell Adjustment Inventory over a period of thirteen years. *Educ. Psychol. Measmt.*, 1955, 15, 137–143.

Cantril, H. (Ed.) *Public Opinion, 1935–1946.* Princeton, N.J.: Princeton University Press, 1951.

Cantril, H., & Hunt, W. A. Emotional effects produced by injection of adrenalin. *Amer. J. Psychol.*, 1932, 44, 300–307.

Caplan, G. Patterns of parental response to the crisis of premature birth. *Psychiatry,* 1960, **23**, 365–374.

Caplan, G. (Ed.), *Prevention of mental disorders in children.* New York: Basic Books, 1961.

Carey, G. L. Sex differences in problem-solving performance as a function of attitude differences. *J. abnorm. soc. Psychol.,* 1958, **56**, 256–260.

Carlson, E. R. Attitude change through modification of attitude structure. *J. abnorm. soc. Psychol.,* 1956, **52**, 256–261.

Cartwright, Rosalind D. Predicting responses to client-centered therapy with the Rorschach prognostic rating scale. *J. counsel. Psychol.,* 1958, **5**, 11–15.

Cattell, R. B. Personality theory growing from multi-variate quantitative research. In S. Koch (Ed.), *Psychology: a study of a science. Vol. 3. Formulations of the person and the social context.* New York: McGraw-Hill, 1959. Pp. 257–327.

Cavan, R. S., Burgess, E. W., Havighurst, R. J., & Goldhamer, H. *Personal adjustment in old age.* Chicago: Science Research Associates, 1949.

Chess, Stella, Thomas, A., & Birch, H. Characteristics of the individual child's responses to the environment. *Amer. J. Orthopsychiat.,* 1959, **29**, 791–802.

Child, I. L. *Italian or American? The second generation in conflict.* New Haven, Conn.: Yale University Press, 1943.

Child, I. L. Socialization. In G. Lindzey (Ed.), *Handbook of social psychology.* Reading, Mass.: Addison-Wesley, 1954.

Chow, K. L., Riesen, A. H., & Newell, F. W. Degeneration of retinal ganglion cells in infant chimpanzees reared in darkness. *J. comp. Neurol.,* 1957, **107**, 27–42.

Chown, S. M. Rigidity—a flexible concept. *Psychol. Bull.,* 1959, **56**, 195–223.

Chown, S. M. A factor analysis of the Wesley Rigidity Inventory. *J. abnorm. soc. Psychol.,* 1960, **61**, 491–494.

Chown, S. M. Age and the rigidities. *J. Geront.,* 1961, **16**, 353–362.

Chun, K. T., & Sarbin, T. R. Role-demands as a central variable in perceptual defense experiments (ms.), 1961.

Claridge, G. S., & Herrington, R. N. Sedation threshold, personality and the theory of neurosis, *J. ment. Sci.,* 1960, **106**, 1568–1583.

Clausen, J. A., & Yarrow, Marian Radke (Issue Eds.), The impact of mental illness on the family. *J. soc. Issues,* 1955, **11**, 3–65.

Cline, V. B., & Richards, J. M. Accuracy of interpersonal perception—a general trait? *J. abnorm. soc. Psychol.,* 1960, **60**, 1–7.

Clyde, D. J. *Clyde Mood Scale.* Washington, D.C.: George Washington University, 1961.

Cobb, B. Psychological impact of long illness and death of a child on the family circle. *J. Pediatrics,* 1946, **49**, 746–751.

Cobb, Elizabeth. Family press variables. In N. Sanford et al., Physique, personality and scholarship: a cooperative study of school children. *Monogr. Soc. Res. Child Develpm.,* 1943, **8**, No. 1. Pp. 327–361.

Coch, L., & French, R. P., Jr. Overcoming resistance to change. *Hum. Relat.,* 1948, **1**, 512–532.

Cohen, A. R. Attitudinal consequences of induced discrepancies between cognitions and behavior. *Publ. Opin. Quart.,* 1960, **24**, 297–318.

Cohen, A. R., Terry, H. I., & Jones, C. B. Attitudinal effects of choice in exposure to counterpropaganda. *J. abnorm. soc. Psychol.,* 1959, **58**, 388–391.

Cohen, B. D., Rosenbaum, G., Dobie, S. I., & Gottlieb, J. S. Sensory isolation: Hallucinogenic effects of a brief procedure. *J. nerv. ment. Dis.,* 1959, **129**, 486–491.

Cohen, S. I., Silverman, A. J., Bressler, B., & Shmavonian, B. Problems in isolation studies. In Solomon et al. (Eds.), *Sensory deprivation*. Cambridge, Mass.: Harvard University Press, 1961. Pp. 114–129.

Coleman, Rose W., Kris, E., & Provence, Sally. The study of variations in early parental attitudes. In R. Eissler et al. (Eds.), *Psychoanalytic study of the child*. New York: International Universities Press, 1953, Vol. 8. Pp. 20–47.

Condon, E. V. Physics. In J. R. Newman (Ed.), *What is science?* New York: Simon and Shuster, 1955. Pp. 102–149.

Coons, W. H. Interaction and insight in group psychotherapy. *Canad. J. Psychol.*, 1957, **11**, 1–8.

Cooper, E., & Jahoda, Marie. The evasion of propaganda: How prejudiced people respond to anti-prejudice propaganda. *J. Psychol.*, 1947, **23**, 15–25.

Cooper, G. D., Adams, H. B., & Gibby, R. G. Changes in ego strength following perceptual deprivation: Report on a pilot study. *Amer. Med. Ass. Arch. gen. Psychiat.*, 1962, **7**, 213–217.

Coue, E., & Brooks, C. H. *Better and better every day*. New York: Barnes and Noble, 1961.

Courtald, A. Living alone under polar conditions. *The polar record*, No. 4. Cambridge: Harvard University Press, 1932.

Cranston, R. E., Zubin, J., & Landis, C. The effect of small doses of thonzylamine, dexedrine, and phenobarbital on test performance and self-ratings of subjective states. *J. Psychol.*, 1952, **33**, 209–215.

Cronbach, L. J. The two disciplines of scientific psychology. *Amer. Psychologist*, 1957, **12**, 671–684.

Cronbach, L. J., & Meehl, P. E. Construct validity in psychological tests. *Psychol. Bull.*. 1955, **52**, 281–302.

Crowne, D. P., & Strickland, B. R. The conditioning of verbal behavior as a function of the need for social approval. *J. abnorm. soc. Psychol.*, 1961, **63**, 395–401.

Crutchfield, R. S. Conformity and character. *Amer. Psychologist*, 1955, **10**, 191–198.

Cumming, E., Dean, L. R., Newell, D. S., & McCaffrey, I. Disengagement—a tentative theory of aging. *Sociometry*, 1960, **23**, 23–35.

Cumming, E., & Henry, W. *Growing old*. New York: Basic Books, 1961.

Curle, A. Transitional communities and social re-connection: A follow-up study of the civil resettlement of British prisoners of war. Part I. *Hum. Relat.*, 1947, **1**, 42–68.

Davids, A. Relations among several objective measures of anxiety under different conditions of motivation. *J. consult. Psychol.*, 1955, **19**, 275–279.

Davids, A., DeVault, S., & Talmadge, M. Anxiety, pregnancy, and childbirth abnormalities. *J. consult. Psychol.*, 1961, **25**, 74–77.

Davids, A., & Eriksen, C. W. The relation of manifest anxiety to association productivity and intellectual attainment. *J. consult. Psychol.*, 1955, **19**, 219–222.

Davis, A., & Havighurst, R. J. Social class and color differences in child rearing. *Amer. sociol. Rev.*, 1946, **11**, 698–710. .

Davis, J. M., McCourt, W. F., Courtney, J., & Solomon, P. Sensory deprivation: The role of social isolation. *Arch. gen. Psychiat.*, 1961, **5**, 106–112.

Davis, J. M., McCourt, W. F., & Solomon, P. The effect of visual stimulation on hallucinations and other mental experiences during sensory deprivation. *Amer. J. Psychiat.*, 1960, **116**, 889–892.

Davis, R. C. *The fundamentals of top management*. New York: Harper & Bros., 1951.

Dean, Lois R. Aging and the decline of instrumentality. *J. Geront.*, 1960, **15**, 403–407.

Dean, Lois R.   Aging and the decline of affect.   *J. Geront.*, 1962, **17**, 440–446.

Dean, W. F.   *General Dean's story.*   New York: Viking, 1954.

Deese, J.   *The psychology of learning.*   New York: McGraw-Hill, 1958.

Dement, W.   The effect of dream deprivation.   *Science*, 1960, **131**, 1705–1707.

Dennis, W.   Predicting scientific productivity in later maturity from records of earlier decades.   *J. Geront.*, 1954, **9**, 465–467.

Dennis, W.   The long-term constancy of behavior: Sentence length.   *J. Geront.*, 1960, **15**, 155–196.

Devereux, G.   A psychoanalytic scrutiny of certain techniques of direct analysis.   *Psychoanal. Rev.*, 1959, **46**, 45–65.

Dittes, J. E.   Extinction during psychotherapy of GSR accompanying "embarrassing" statements.   *J. abnorm. soc. Psychol.*, 1957, **54**, 187–191.   (*a*)

Dittes, J. E.   Galvanic skin response as a measure of patient's reaction to therapist's permissiveness.   *J. abnorm. soc. Psychol.*, 1957, **55**, 295–303.   (*b*)

Doane, B. K., Mahatoo, W., Heron, W., & Scott, T. H.   Changes in perceptual function after isolation.   *Canad. J. Psychol.*, 1959, **13**, 210–219.

Dollard, J., & Auld, F.   *Scoring human motives: A manual.*   New Haven, Conn.: Yale University Press, 1959.

Dollard, J., Auld, F., & White, M. A.   *Steps in psychotherapy.*   New York: Macmillan, 1953.

Dollard, J., & Miller, N. E.   *Personality and psychotherapy.*   New York: McGraw-Hill, 1950.

Doob, L. W.   The behavior of attitudes.   *Psychol. Rev.*, 1947, **54**, 135–156.

Dorcus, R. M., Brintnall, H. K., & Case, H. W.   Control experiments and their relation to theories of hypnotism.   *J. gen. Psychol.*, 1941, **24**, 217–221.

Doris, J., & Fierman, Ella.   Humor and anxiety.   *J. abnorm. soc. Psychol.*, 1956, **53**, 59–62.

Doyle, W., & O'Dell, S.   *Man alone.*   New York: Bobbs-Merrill, 1953.

Duffy, E.   Emotion: An example of the need for reorientation in psychology.   *Psychol. Rev.*, 1934, **41**, 184–198.

Duffy, E.   Leeper's motivational theory of emotions.   *Psychol. Rev.*, 1948, **55**, 324–328.

Dunlap, K.   *Habits: Their making and unmaking.*   New York: Liveright, 1932.

Dyer, M.   *The weapon on the wall: Rethinking psychological warfare.*   Baltimore, Md.: Johns Hopkins Press, 1959.

Ebel, R. L.   Must all tests be valid?   *Amer. Psychologist*, 1961, **16**, 640–647.

Edwards, A. L.   *Manual. Personal Preference Schedule.*   New York: Psychological Corp., 1954.

Edwards, A. L.   *The social desirability variable in personality assessment and research.*   New York: Dryden, 1957.

Eisenberg, L.   The autistic child in adolescence.   *Amer. J. Psychiat.*, 1956, **112**, 607–612.

Eissler, K. R.   The Chicago Institute of Psychoanalysis and the sixth period of development of psychoanalytic technique.   *J. gen. Psychol.*, 1950, **42**, 103–157.

Eissler, K. R.   The effect of the structure of the ego on psychoanalytic technique.   *J. Amer. psychoanal. Ass.*, 1953, **1**, 104–143.

Eissler, K. R.   On isolation.   *The psychoanalytic study of the child.*   New York: International Universities Press, 1959, Vol. 14.   Pp. 29–60.

Ekstein, R.   Psychoanalytic techniques.   In D. Brower & L. Abt (Eds.), *Progress in clinical psychology.*   New York: Grune & Stratton, 1956, Vol. 2.   Pp. 79–97.

Eliot, T. H.   Classification of efforts to relieve family crises.   In H. Becker & R. Hill (Eds.), *Family, marriage and parenthood.*   Boston: Heath, 1948.

Ellis, A. *Reason and emotion in psychotherapy.* New York: L. Stuart, 1962.

Eriksen, C. W., & Davids, A. The meaning and clinical validity of the Taylor Anxiety Scale and the Hysteria-Psychasthenia scales from the MMPI. *J. abnorm. soc. Psychol.,* 1955, **50**, 135–137.

Erikson, E. H. *Childhood and society.* New York: Norton, 1950.

Erikson, E. H. On the sense of inner identity. In R. P. Knight & C. R. Friedman (Eds.), *Psychoanalytic psychiatry and psychology.* New York: International Universities Press, 1954.

Erikson, E. H. Identity and the life cycle: Selected papers. *Psychol. Issues,* 1959, **1**, 1–165.

Escalona, Sibylle, & Heider, Grace M. *Prediction and outcome.* New York: Basic Books, 1959.

Esecover, H., Malitz, S., & Wikens, B. Clinical profiles of paid normal subjects volunteering for hallucinogen drug studies. *Amer. J. Psychiat.,* 1961, **117**, 910–915.

Estes, W. K. Towards a statistical theory of learning. *Psychol. Rev.,* 1950, **57**, 94–107.

Estes, W. K. Stimulus-response theory of drive. In M. R. Jones (Ed.), *Nebraska symposium on motivation.* Lincoln, Neb.: University of Nebraska Press, 1958. Pp. 35–69.

Eysenck, H. J. *The scientific study of personality.* London: Routledge & Kegan Paul, 1952.

Eysenck, H. J. Drugs and personality—I. Theory and methodology. *J. ment. Sci.,* 1957, **103**, 119–131.

Eysenck, H. J. (Ed.), *Behavior, therapy and the neuroses.* New York: Pergamon, 1960.

Eysenck, H. J. *Experiments in personality.* London: Routledge and Kegan Paul, 1960. Vol. 10.

Eysenck, H. J., & Aiba, S. Drugs and personality. V. The effects of stimulant and depressant drugs on the suppression of the primary visual stimulus. *J. ment. Sci.,* 1957, **103**, 661–665.

Eysenck, H. J., Casey, S., & Trouton, D. S. Drugs and personality. II. The effect of stimulant and depressant drugs on continuous work. *J. ment. Sci.,* 1957, **103**, 645–649.

Eysenck, H. J., & Claridge, G. The position of hysterics and dysthymics in a two-dimensional framework of personality description. *J. abnorm. soc. Psychol.,* 1962, **64**, 46–55.

Eysenck, H. J., & Easterbrook, J. A. Drugs and personality. VI. The effects of stimulant and depressant drugs upon body sway (static ataxia). *J. ment. Sci.,* 1960, **106**, 831–834. (*a*)

Eysenck, H. J., & Easterbrook, J. A. Drugs and personality. VII. The effects of stimulant and depressant drugs on pupillary reactions. *J. ment. Sci.,* 1960, **106**, 835–841. (*b*)

Eysenck, H. J., & Easterbrook, J. A. Drugs and personality. VIII. The effects of stimulant and depressant drugs on visual after-effects of a rotating spiral. *J. ment. Sci.,* 1960, **106**, 842–844. (*c*)

Eysenck, H. J., & Easterbrook, J. A. Drugs and personality. IX. The effects of stimulant and depressant drugs upon visual after-effects. *J. ment. Sci.,* 1960, **106**, 845–851. (*d*)

Eysenck, H. J., & Easterbrook, J. A. Drugs and personality. X. The effects of stimulant and depressant drugs upon kinaesthetic figural after-effects. *J. ment. Sci.,* 1960, **106**, 852–854. (*e*)

Eysenck, H. J., & Easterbrook, J. A. Drugs and personality. XI. The effects of stimulant and depressant drugs upon auditory flutter fusion. *J. ment. Sci.,* 1960, **106**, 855–857. (*f*)

Eysenck, H. J., Holland, H., & Trouton, D. S. Drugs and personality. III. The effects of stimulant and depressant drugs on visual after-effects. *J. ment. Sci.,* 1957, **103**, 650–655.

Eysenck, H. J., Holland, H., & Trouton, D. S. Drugs and personality. IV. The effects of stimulant and depressant drugs on the rate of fluctuation of a reversible perspective figure. *J. ment. Sci.*, 1957, **103**, 656–660.

Farber, B. Effects of a severely retarded child on family integration. *Monogr. Soc. Res. Child Develpm.*, 1959, **24**, No. 2.

Farber, I. E. Anxiety as a drive state. In M. R. Jones (Ed.), *Nebraska symposium on motivation.* Lincoln, Neb.: University of Nebraska Press, 1954. Pp. 1–46.

Farber, I. E. The role of motivation in verbal learning and performance. *Psychol. Bull.*, 1955, **52**, 311–327.

Farber, I. E. The things people say to themselves. *Amer. Psychologist,* 1963, **18**, 185–197.

Farber, I. E., Harlow, H. F., & West, L. J. Brainwashing, conditioning and *DDD* (debility, dependency, and dread). *Sociometry,* 1957, **20**, 271–285.

Fantini, A. E. Illness and curing among the Mexican-Americans of Mission, Texas. Unpublished master's thesis, University of Texas, 1962.

Feigl, H. Operationism and scientific method. *Psychol. Rev.,* 1945, **52**, 250–259.

Fenichel, O. *Problems of psychoanalytic technique.* New York: Psychoanalytic Quarterly, Inc., 1934.

Fenichel, O. *The psychoanalytic theory of neuroses.* New York: Norton, 1945.

Fenichel, O. Specific forms of the Oedipus complex. In *The collected papers of Otto Fenichel.* New York: Norton, 1954.

Ferenczi, S. *Sex in psychoanalysis.* New York: Basic Books, 1950.

Ferree, C. E. The streaming phenomenon. *Amer. J. Psychol.,* 1908, **19**, 484–503.

Festinger, L. *A theory of cognitive dissonance.* Stanford, Calif.: Stanford University Press, 1957.

Festinger, L., & Carlsmith, J. M. Cognitive consequences of forced compliance. *J. abnorm. soc. Psychol.,* 1959, **58**, 203–210.

Festinger, L., & Kelley, H. H. *Changing attitudes through social contact.* Ann Arbor, Mich.: Institute of Social Research, 1951.

Fiedler, F. E. Quantitative studies on the role of therapists' feelings toward their patients. In O. H. Mowrer (Ed.), *Psychotherapy: theory and research.* New York: Ronald, 1953.

Filer, R. N., & O'Connell, D. D. A useful contribution climate for the aging. *J. Geront.,* 1962, **17**, 51–57.

Fisher, S. The role of expectancy in the performance of posthypnotic behavior. *J. abnorm. soc. Psychol.,* 1954, **49**, 503–507.

Fisher, S. On the relationship between expectations and drug response. *Clin. Pharm. exp. Therapeutics,* 1962, **3**, 125–126.

Fiske, D. W. Effects of monotonous and restricted stimulation. In D. W. Fiske and S. R. Maddi, *Functions of varied experience.* Homewood, Ill.: Dorsey, 1961. Pp. 106–144.

Franks, C. M., & Trouton, D. Effects of amobarbital sodium and dexamphetamine sulfate on the conditioning of the eyeblink response. *J. comp. physiol. Psychol.,* 1958, **51**, 220–222.

Freedman, J. L. Attitudinal effects of inadequate justification. *J. Pers.,* 1963, **31**, 371–385.

Freedman, S. J. Perceptual changes in sensory deprivation: Suggestions for a conative theory. *J. nerv. ment. Dis.,* 1961, **132**, 17–21.

Freedman, S. J., Grunebaum, H. U., & Greenblatt, M. Perceptual and cognitive changes in sensory deprivation. In P. Solomon et al. (Eds.), *Sensory deprivation.* Cambridge, Mass.: Harvard University Press, 1961. Pp. 58–71.

French, Elizabeth G. Development of a measure of complex motivation. In J. W. Atkinson (Ed.), *Motives in fantasy, action, and society.* Princeton: Van Nostrand, 1958.

French, J. R. P. Role playing as a method of training foremen. In J. L. Moreno (Ed.), *Group psychotherapy.* New York: Beacon, 1945.

Freud, Anna. *The ego and the mechanisms of defense* (1936). New York: International Universities Press, 1946.

Freud, Anna. Special experiences of young children, particularly in times of social disturbances. In K. Soddy (Ed.), *Mental health and infant development.* New York: Basic Books, 1956. Vol. I. Pp. 141–160.

Freud, S. Papers on technique (1910–1919). *Collected papers.* London: Hogarth, 1948. Vol. 2. Pp. 285–402.

Freud, S. Recollection, repetition and working through (1914). In *Collected papers,* Vol. II. New York: Basic Books, 1959. Vol. 2. Pp. 375–376.

Freud, S. Instincts and their vicissitudes (1915). *Standard edition.* London: Hogarth and Institute for Psychoanalysis, 1957. Vol. 14. Pp. 117–140.

Freud, S. Mourning and melancholia (1917). In *Collected papers.* London: Hogarth, 1950, Vol. 4. Pp. 152–170.

Freud, S. Lines of advance in psycho-analytic therapy (1919). *Standard edition.* London: Hogarth and Institute for Psychoanalysis, 1955. Vol. 17. Pp. 159–168.

Freud, S. *A general introduction to psychoanalysis* (1916–17). New York: Garden City Publishing Co., 1920.

Freud, S. Jenseits des Lustprinzips (1920). In *Gesammelte Werke,* Vol. XIII. London: Imago Publishing Co., 1940.

Freud, S. *The problem of anxiety* (1926). New York: Psychoanalytic Quarterly and Norton, 1936.

Freud, S. Analysis terminable and interminable (1937). *Collected papers.* London: Hogarth and Institute of Psychoanalysis, 1950. Vol. 5. Pp. 316–357.

Freud, S. *An outline of psychoanalysis* (1938). New York: Norton, 1949.

Freud, S. The interpretation of dreams. In *The basic writings of Sigmund Freud.* New York: Random House, 1938.

Freud, S. Three essays on the theory of sexuality. In *The Basic writings of Sigmund Freud.* New York: Modern Library, 1958. Pp. 553–629.

Freud, S. *An outline of psychoanalysis* (1940). New York: W. W. Norton, 1949 (Abriss der psycho-analyse. In *Gesammelte Werke,* vol. XVII. London: Imago Publishing Co., 1940).

Freud, S. *Collected papers.* New York: Basic Books, 1959.

Friedlander, J. W., & Sarbin, T. R. The depth of hypnosis. *J. abnorm. soc. Psychol.,* 1938, **33,** 453–475.

Fries, Margaret E. The psychosomatic relationship between mother and infant. *Psychosomat. Med.,* 1944, **6,** 159–162.

Fromm-Reichmann, F. *Principles of intensive psychotherapy.* Chicago: University of Chicago Press, 1950.

Fuller, J. Personal communication, 1962.

Gabower, Genevieve. *Behavior problems of children in Navy officer's families: as related to social conditions of Navy family life.* Washington, D.C.: Catholic University of America Press, 1959.

Gage, N. L. Accuracy of social perception and effectiveness in interpersonal relationships. *J. Pers.,* 1953, **22,** 128–141.

Galanter, E. Contemporary psychophysics. In *New directions in psychology*. New York: Holt, Rinehart, & Winston, 1962.

Gallagher, J. J. Manifest anxiety changes concomitant with client-centered therapy. *J. consult. Psychol*, 1953, **17**, 443–446.

Garmezy, N. Stimulus differentiation by schizophrenic and normal subjects under conditions of reward and punishment. *J. Pers.*, 1952, **21**, 253–276.

Gendlin, E. T. A process concept of relationship. *Counseling center discussion papers, III*, 2. Chicago: University of Chicago Library, 1957.

Gendlin, E. T. Experiencing: a variable in the process of therapeutic change. *Amer. J. Psychotherapy*, 1961, **15**, 233–245. (*a*).

Gendlin, E. T. Initiating psychotherapy with "unmotivated" patients. *Psychiat. Quart.*, 1961, **35**, 134–139. (*b*).

Gendlin, E. T. Client-centered developments in psychotherapy with schizophrenics. *J. counsel. Psychol.*, 1962. (*a*)

Gendlin, E. T. *Experiencing and the creation of meaning*. New York: The Free Press of Glencoe, 1962. (*b*)

Gendlin, E. T. Need for a new type of concept: current trends and needs in psychotherapy research on schizophrenia. *Rev. existential Psychol. Psychiat.*, 1962, **2**, 37–46. (*c*)

Gendlin, E. T., & Berlin, J. I. Galvanic skin response correlates of different modes of experiencing. *J. clin. Psychol.*, 1961, **17**, 73–77.

Gendlin, E. T., Jenny, R. H., & Shlien, J. M. Counselor ratings of process and outcome in client-centered therapy. *J. clin. Psychol.*, 1960, **16**, 210–213.

Gendlin, E. T., & Shlien, J. M. Immediacy in time attitudes before and after time-limited psychotherapy. *J. clin. Psychol.*, 1961, **17**, 69–72.

Gendlin, E. T., & Zimring, F. M. The qualities or dimensions of experiencing and their change. *Counseling center discussion papers*, **1**, 3. Chicago: University of Chicago Library, 1955.

Gesell, A. L., & Ames, Louise B. Early evidence of individualization in the human infant. *Scientific Mon.*, 1937, **45**, 217–225.

Gesell, A. et al. *Infant and child in the culture of today*. New York: Harper, 1943.

Gewirtz, J. L. Three determinants of attention-seeking in young children. *Monogr. Soc. Res. Child Develpm.*, 1954, **19**, No. 59.

Gewirtz, J. L., & Baer, D. M. The effect of brief social deprivation on behaviors for a social reinforcer. *J. abnorm. soc. Psychol.*, 1958, **56**, 49–56.

Ghiselli, E. E. Correlates of initiative. *Personnel Psychol.*, 1956, **9**, 311–320.

Giaever, J. *The white desert: The official account of the Norwegian-British-Swedish Antarctic expedition*. London: Chatto and Windus, 1954. Pp. 112–128.

Gibby, R. G., Adams, H. B., & Carrera, R. N. Therapeutic changes in psychiatric patients following partial sensory deprivation. *Amer. Med. Ass. Arch. gen. Psychiat.*, 1960, **3**, 33–42.

Gibson, W. *The boat*. Boston: Houghton Mifflin, 1953.

Gill, M. M. Ego psychology and psychotherapy. *Psychoanal. Quart.*, 1951, **20**, 62–71.

Gill, M. M. Psychoanalysis and exploratory psychotherapy. *J. Amer. Psychoanal. Ass.*, 1954, **2**, 771–797.

Gill, M. M. The present state of psychoanalytic theory. *J. abnorm. soc. Psychol.*, 1959, **58**, 1–8.

Gill, M. M., & Brenman, Margaret. *Hypnosis and related states: psychoanalytic studies in regression*. New York: International Universities Press, 1959.

Glad, D. D. *Operational values in psychotherapy.* New York: Oxford University Press, 1959.

Gladstone, A. I., & Taylor, Martha A. Threat-related attitudes and reactions to communications about international events. *J. conflict Resolution,* 1958, **2,** 17–28.

Gladwin, T. Canoe travel in the Truk area: Technology and its psychological correlates. *Amer. Anthrop.,* 1958, **60,** 893–899.

Gleser, G., & Ulett, G. The Saslow screening test as a measure of anxiety-proneness. *J. clin. Psychol.,* 1952, **8,** 279–283.

Glover, E. *War, sadism, and pacifism.* London: G. Allen & Unwin, 1946.

Glover, E. *The technique of psycho-analysis* (1928), rev. ed. New York: International Universities Press, 1955.

Goffman, E. *Asylums: Essays on the social situation of mental patients and other inmates.* Garden City, New York: Doubleday, 1961.

Goffman, E. *Encounters.* Indianapolis: Bobbs-Merrill, 1961.

Goldberger, L. Reactions to perceptual isolation and Rorschach manifestations of the primary process. *J. proj. Tech.,* 1961, **25,** 287–302.

Goldberger, L., & Holt, R. R. Experimental interference with reality contact (perceptual isolation): Method and group results. *J. nerv. ment. Dis.,* 1958, **127,** 99–112.

Goldberger, L., & Holt, R. R. Experimental interference with reality contact: Individual differences. In P. Solomon et al. (Eds.), *Sensory deprivation.* Cambridge, Mass.: Harvard University Press, 1961. Pp. 130–142.

Goldberger, L., & Holt, R. R. Studies on the effects of perceptual alteration. *USAF ASD tech. Rep.,* 1961, No. 61-416.

Goldfarb, W. Effects of early institutional care on adolescent personality: Rorschach data. *Amer. J. Orthopsychiat.,* 1944, **14,** 441–447.

Goldfarb, W. Psychological privation in infancy and subsequent adjustment. *Amer. J. Orthopsychiat.,* 1945, **15,** 247–255.

Goldfarb, W. Variations in adolescent adjustment of institutionally reared children. *Amer. J. Orthopsychiat.,* 1947, **17,** 449–457.

Goldfarb, W. Emotional and intellectual consequences of psychologic deprivation in infancy: A re-evaluation. In P. W. Hoch & J. Zubin (Eds.), *Psychopathology of childhood.* New York: Grune & Stratton, 1955. Pp. 105–119.

Goldman, A. E. Studies in vicariousness: Degree of motor activity and the autokinetic phenomenon. *Amer. J. Psychol.,* 1953, **66,** 613–617.

Goldman-Eisler, F. Speech-breathing activity and content in psychiatric interviews. *Brit. J. Med. Psychol.,* 1956, **29,** 35–48.

Goldstein, K. Methodological approach to the study of schizophrenic thought disorder. In Kasanin & Lewis (Eds.), *Language and thought in schizophrenia.* Berkeley, Calif.: University of California Press, 1951. Pp. 17–41.

Goode, W. J. *After divorce.* Glencoe, Ill.: Free Press, 1956.

Goodrich, D. W. *Developmental patterns in the infant and in the young family.* Bethesda, Md.: Annual Report, Child Research Branch, National Institute of Mental Health, 1961.

Goodstein, L. D. Interrelationships among several measures of anxiety and hostility. *J. consult. Psychol.,* 1954, **18,** 35–39.

Gorska, T., & Jankowska, E. The effect of differentiation on the instrumental conditioned reflexes established in dogs by reinforcing passive movements. *Bulletin de L'Academie Polonaise des Sciences,* Cl. II. 1960, 8. Presented by J. Konorski on July 9, 1960.

Goss, A. E. Early behaviorism and verbal mediating responses. *Amer. Psychologist,* 1961, **16,** 285–298.

Gottschalk, L. A., Goldine, G. C., Springer, K. J., Kaplan, S. M., Shanon, J., & Ross, W. D. Effects of perphenazine on verbal behavior patterns: A contribution to the problem of measuring the psychologic effects of psychoactive drugs. *Amer. Med. Ass. Arch. gen. Psychiat.,* 1960, **2,** 632–639.

Gottschalk, L. A., & Hambridge, G., Jr. Verbal behavior analysis: A systematic approach to the problem of quantifying psychologic processes. *J. proj. Tech.,* 1955, **19,** 387–409.

Gough, H. G. A sociological theory of psychopathy. *Amer. J. Sociol.,* 1943, **53,** 366–395.

Gough, H. G. *Manual for the California Psychological Inventory.* Palo Alto, California: Consulting Psychologists Press, 1957.

Grace, H. A. Effects of different degrees of knowledge about an audience on the content of communication. *J. soc. Psychol.,* 1951, **34,** 111–124.

Graham, C. H. Visual perception. In S. S. Stevens (Ed.), *Handbook of experimental psychology.* New York: Wiley, 1951.

Graveline, D. E., & Balke, B. *The physiologic effects of hypodynamics induced by water immersion.* School of Aviation Medicine USAF Aerospace Medical Center, Brooks Air Force Base, Texas, 1960. Pp. 60–88.

Green, A. W. The middle-class male child and neurosis. *Amer. sociol. Rev.,* 1946, **11,** 31–41.

Greenspoon, J. The reinforcing effect of two spoken sounds on the frequency of two responses. *Amer. J. Psychol.,* 1955, **68,** 409–416.

Greenwood, A. Mental disturbances following operation for cataract. *J. Amer. Med Ass.,* 1928, **91,** 1713–1716.

Griew, S. A further note on uncertainty in relation to age. *Gerontologia,* 1959, **6,** 335–339.

Gross, M. L. *The brain watchers.* New York: Random House, 1962.

Grosz, H. J., & Levitt, E. E. The effects of hypnotically induced anxiety on the Manifest Anxiety Scale and the Barron Ego-Strength Scale. *J. abnorm. soc. Psychol.,* 1959, **59,** 281–283.

Guest, R. *Organizational change.* Homewood, Ill.: Dorsey Press, Richard E. Irwin, 1962.

Gumpert, P., & Festinger, L. Affective reactions toward people who violate rules. Unpublished manuscript.

Gurin, G., Veroff, J., & Feld, Sheila. *Americans view their mental health: A nationwide interview survey.* New York: Basic Books, 1960.

Haertzen, C. A., & Hill, H. E. Effects of morphine and pentobarbital on differential MMPI profiles. *J. clin. Psychol.,* 1959, **15,** 434–437.

Haggard, E. A. An evaluation of certain concepts in learning theory. Unpublished doctoral dissertation, Harvard University, 1946.

Haggard, E. A. Psychological causes and results of stress. *Human factors in undersea warfare.* National Research Council, 1949. Pp. 441–461.

Haggard, E. A., & Babin, Rachel. On the problem of 'reinforcement' in conditioning the autokinetic phenomenon. *J. exp. Psychol.,* 1948, **38,** 511–525.

Haggard, E. A., & Rose, G. J. Some effects of mental set and active participation in the conditioning of the autokinetic phenomenon. *J. exp. Psychol.,* 1944, **32,** 45–59.

Hakerem, G., & Sutton, S. The effect of chlorpromazine on the pupillary reflex. Final report, USPHS Grant MY 4759. Unpublished. 1962.

Hall, C. S., & Lindzey, G. *Theories of personality.* New York: Wiley, 1957.

Hall, E. T. *The silent language.* Garden City, New York: Doubleday, 1957.

Hallowell, A. I. Ojibwa personality and acculturation. *International Congress of Americanists, 29th Proceedings,* 1952.

Hamilton, G. V. Changes in personality and psychosexual phenomena with age. In E. V. Cowdry (Ed.), *Problems of aging.* (2nd ed.) Baltimore: Williams & Wilkins Co., 1942. Pp. 810–831.

Harlow, H. F. The nature of love. *Amer. Psychologist,* 1958, **13**, 673–685.

Harlow, H. F. The heterosexual affectional system in monkeys. *Amer. Psychologist,* 1962, **17**, 1–9.

Harlow, H. F., & Harlow, Margaret K. Social deprivation in monkeys. *Sci. Amer.,* 1962, **207**, 136–146.

Harlow, H. F., & Zimmerman, R. R. Affectional responses in the infant monkey. *Science,* 1959, **130**, 421–432.

Harris, A. Sensory deprivation and schizophrenia. *J. ment. Sci.,* 1959, **105**, 235–237.

Harris, T. T. In *Communist interrogation, indoctrination and exploitation of American military and political prisoners.* Hearings before the Permanent Subcommittee on Investigations of the Committee on Government Operations, U.S. Senate, June 19–27, 1956. Washington, D.C.: U.S. Government Printing Office, 1956.

Hartmann, G. W. A field experiment on the comparative effectiveness of "emotional" and "rational" political leaflets in determining election results. *J. abnorm. soc. Psychol.,* 1936, **31**, 99–114.

Hartmann, H. *Ego psychology and the problem of adaptation* (1939). Translated by David Rapaport. New York: *J. Amer. Psychoanal. Ass.,* Monograph Series, No. 1. International Universities Press, 1958.

Hartmann, H. Comments on the psychoanalytic theory of the ego. *Psychoanalytic study of the child,* 1950. Vol. 5. Pp. 74–96.

Hartmann, H., Kris, E., & Lowenstein, R. Comments on the formation of psychic structure. *Psychoanalytic study of the child.* New York: International Universities Press, 1946. Vol. 2. Pp. 11–38.

Hartshorne, H., & May, M. A. *Studies in deceit,* Book I in *Studies in the nature of character.* New York: Macmillan, 1928.

Hathaway, S. R., & McKinley, J. C. A multiphasic personality schedule (Minnesota): I. Construction of the schedule. *J. Psychol.,* 1940, **10**, 249–254.

Havighurst, R. J., & Albrecht, R. *Older people.* New York: Longmans, Green, 1953.

Hayakawa, S. I. On communication with the Soviet Union. *Etc., Rev. gen. Semant.,* 1960, **17**, 389–400.

Hebb, D. O. *The organization of behavior.* New York: Wiley, 1949.

Hecht, S. Vision II: The nature of the photoreceptor process. In C. Murchison (Ed.), *Handbook of general experimental psychology.* Worcester, Mass.: Clark University Press, 1934.

Held, R. Exposure-history as a factor in maintaining stability of perception and coordination. *J. nerv. ment. Dis.,* 1961, **132**, 26–32.

Helfand, I. Role taking in schizophrenia. *J. consult. Psychol.,* 1956, **20**, 37–41.

Helson, H. Adaptation-level as a basis for a quantitative theory of frames of reference. *Psychol. Rev.,* 1948, **55**, 297–313.

Helson, H. Adaptation level theory. In S. Koch (Ed.), *Psychology: A study of a science,* Vol. 1. *Sensory, perceptual and physiological foundations,* McGraw-Hill, 1959. Pp. 565–621.

Helson, H., Blake, R. R., & Mouton, Jane S. An experimental investigation of the effectiveness of the "big lie" in shifting attitudes. *J. soc. Psychol.,* 1958, **48**, 51–60. (*a*)

Helson, H., Blake, R. R., & Mouton, Jane S.   Petition-signing as adjustment to situational and personal factors. *J. soc. Psychol.,* 1958, **48**, 3–10. (*b*)

Henry, Edith M., & Rotter, J. B.   Situational influences on Rorschach responses. *J. consult. Psychol.,* 1956, **20**, 457–462.

Heron, W.   Cognitive and physiological effects of perceptual isolation. In Solomon et al. (Eds.), *Sensory deprivation.* Cambridge, Mass.: Harvard University Press, 1961. Pp. 16–27.

Heron, W., Doane, B. K., & Scott, T. H.   Visual disturbances after prolonged perceptual isolation. *Canad. J. Psychol.,* 1956, **10**, 13–18.

Hertz, Margaret R., & Baker, E.   Personality changes in adolescence. *Rorschach Res. Exch.,* 1941, **5**, 30 (abstract).

Hess, A.   Optic centers and pathways after eye removal in fetal guinea pigs. *J. comp. Neurol.,* 1958, **109**, 91–115.

Hess, E. H.   Effects of meprobamate on imprinting in waterfowl. *Ann. N.Y. Acad. Sci.,* 1957, **67**, 724–732.

Hilgard, E. R.   Impulsive versus realistic thinking: An examination of the distinction between primary and secondary processes of thought. *Psychol. Bull.,* 1962, **59**, 477–488.

Hilgard, E. R., Jones, L. V., & Kaplan, S. J.   Conditioned discrimination as related to anxiety. *J. exp. Psychol.,* 1951, **42**, 94–99.

Hilgard, Josephine, Newman, Martha F., & Fisk, Fern.   Strength of adult ego following childhood bereavement. *Amer. J. Orthopsychiat.,* 1960, **30**, 788–798.

Hill, H. E., Belleville, R. E., & Wikler, A.   Motivational determinants in modification of behavior by morphine and pentobarbital. *Amer. Med. Ass. Arch. Neurol. Psychiat.,* 1957, **77**, 28–35.

Hill, H. E., Kornetsky, C. H., Flanary, H. G., & Wikler, A.   Effects of anxiety and morphine on discrimination of intensities of painful stimuli. *J. clin. Invest.,* 1952, **31**, 473–480.

Hill, R.   *Families under stress.* New York: Harper Bros., 1949.

Hill, R.   Generic features of families under stress. *Soc. Casework,* 1958, **39**, 139–150.

Hill, W.   Learning theory and the acquisition of values. *Psychol. Rev.,* 1960, **67**, 317–331.

Himelstein, P., Eschenbach, A. E., & Carp, A.   Interrelationships among three measures of need achievement. *J. consult. Psychol.,* 1958, **22**, 451–452.

Hinde, R. A.   The modifiability of instinctive behavior. *Advanc. Sci. Lond.,* 1955, **12**, 19–24.

Hinkle, L. E., Jr.   Communist manipulation of behavior. *Science,* 1961, **133**, 1912–1914.

Hinkle, L. E., Jr., & Wolff, H. G.   Communist interrogation and indoctrination of "Enemies of the State." Analysis of methods used by the Communist State Police. (Special report.) *Amer. Med. Ass. Arch. Neurol. Psychiat.,* 1956, **76**, 115–174.

Hoffman, Lois.   Effects of maternal employment on the child. *Child Develpm.,* 1961, **32**, 187–197.

Hoffman, Lois.   Research findings on the effects of maternal employment on the child: Summary and discussion. In Lois Hoffman & F. I. Nye (Eds.), *The employed mother in America.* New York: Rand McNally, in press.

Holland, H. C.   Drugs and personality, XII. A comparison of several drugs by the flicker-fusion method. *J. ment. Sci.,* 1960, **106**, 858–861.

Hollingshead, A. B., & Redlich, F. C.   *Social class and mental illness.* New York: Wiley, 1958.

Holmberg, A. R.   The search-and-development approach to change: Participant intervention in the field. In R. N. Adams and J. J. Preiss (Eds.), *Human organization research.* Homewood, Ill.: Dorsey Press, 1960.

Holt, R. R. Personality growth in psychiatric residents. *Amer. Med. Ass. Arch. neurol. Psychiat.,* 1958, **81**, 203–215.

Holt, R. R., & Goldberger, L. Personological correlates of reactions to perceptual isolation. *USAF WADC tech. Rep.,* 1959, No. 59-735.

Holt, R. R., & Goldberger, L. Research on the effect of isolation on cognitive functioning. *USAF WADC tech. Rep.,* 1960, No. 60-260.

Holt, R. R., & Goldberger, L. Assessment of individual resistance to sensory alteration. In B. E. Flaherty (Ed.), *Psychophysiological aspects of space flight.* New York: Columbia University Press, 1961. Pp. 248–262.

Holt, R. R., & Havel, Joan. A method for assessing primary and secondary process in the Rorschach. In Maria A. Rickers-Ovsiankina (Ed.), *Rorschach psychology.* New York: Wiley, 1960.

Holt, R. R., & Luborsky, L. *Personality patterns of psychiatrists.* New York: Basic Books, 1958. 2 vols.

Holtzman, W. H., Calvin, A. D., & Bitterman, M. E. New evidence for the validity of Taylor's manifest anxiety scale. *J. abnorm. soc. Psychol.,* 1952, **47**, 853–854.

Homans, G. C. *The human group.* New York: Harcourt, Brace, 1950.

Honzik, Marjorie P. A developmental study of persistence, change, and recurrence of behavior over certain age periods. Paper presented at Western Psychological Ass. Meeting, 1954.

Hopkins, P. *The psychology of social movements.* London: G. Allen & Unwin, 1938.

Horwitz, M. The veridicality of liking and disliking. In R. Tagiuri & L. Petrullo (Eds.), *Person perception and interpersonal behavior.* Stanford, Calif.: Stanford University Press, 1958. Pp. 191–209.

Hovland, C. I., Janis, I. L., & Kelley H. H. *Communication and persuasion.* New Haven, Conn.: Yale University Press, 1953.

Howarth, D. *Escape alone.* London: Collins (Fontana Books), 1958.

Hoyt, D. P., & Magoon, T. M. A validation study of the Taylor Manifest Anxiety Scale. *J. clin. Psychol.,* 1954, **10**, 357–361.

Hubel, D. H., & Wiesel, T. N. Receptive fields, binocular interaction and functional architecture in the cat's visual cortex. *J. Physiol.,* 1962, **160**, 106–154.

Humphreys, L. G. The organization of human abilities. *Amer. Psychologist,* 1962, **17**, 475–483.

Hunt, H. et al. The effect of electroconvulsive shock (ECS) on a conditioned emotional response: The effect of post-ecs extinction on the reappearance of the response. *J. comp. physiol. Psychol.,* 1952, **45.**

Hunt, H. Some effects of drugs on classical (type S) conditioning. *N.Y. Acad. Sci.,* 1956, **65**, 258–267.

Hunter, E. *Brainwashing in Red China.* New York: Vanguard, 1951.

Hyde, R. W. Psychological and social determinants of drug action. In G. J. Sarwer-Foner (Ed.), *The dynamics of psychiatric drug therapy.* Springfield: Charles C Thomas, 1960. Pp. 297–315.

Hyman, H. H., & Sheatsley, P. B. Some reasons why information campaigns fail. *Publ. Opin. Quart.,* 1947, **11**, 413–423.

Igel, G. J., & Calvin, A. P. The development of affectional responses in infant dogs. *J. comp. physiol. Psychol.,* 1960, **53**, 302–305.

Ignotus, P. *Political prisoner.* London: Routledge & Kegan Paul, 1959.

Iisager, H. An evaluation of an attempt to form international attitudes. *J. soc. Psychol.*, 1949, **30**, 207–216.

Isbelle, H. Comparison of the reactions induced by psilocybin and LSD-25 in man. *Psychopharmacologia*, 1959, **1**, 29–38.

Jackson, D. N., & Bloomberg, R. Anxiety: Unitas or multiplex? *J. consult. Psychol.*, 1958, **22**, 225–227.

Jackson, Joan K. The adjustment of the family to alcoholism. *Marriage Fam. Living*, 1956, **18**, 361–369.

Jacques, E. *The changing culture of a factory*. London: Tavistock Publications, 1951.

James, W., & Lange, G. C. *The emotions*. Baltimore: Williams and Wilkins, 1922.

Janis, I. L. *Air war and emotional stress*. New York: McGraw-Hill, 1951.

Janis, I. L., & Feshbach, S. Effects of fear-arousing communications. *J. abnorm. soc. Psychol.*, 1953, **48**, 78–92.

Janis, I. L., & King, B. T. The influence of role playing on opinion change. *J. abnorm. soc. Psychol.*, 1954, **49**, 211–218.

Janis, I. L., Lumsdaine, A. A., & Gladstone, A. I. Effects of preparatory communications on reactions to a subsequent news event. *Publ. Opin. Quart.*, 1951, **15**, 487–518.

Jayaswal, S. R., & Stott, L. H. Persistence and change in personality from childhood to adulthood. *Merrill Palmer Quart.*, 1955, **1**, 47–56.

Jeffers, F. C., Eisdorfer, C., & Gusse, E. W. Measurement of age identification: a methodological note. *J. Geront.*, 1962, **17**, 437–439.

Johnson, G. H. Differences in the job satisfaction of urban teachers as related to age and other factors. Unpublished doctoral dissertation, Syracuse University, 1951.

Johnson, M. H., Fordyce, W. E., Masuda, M., & Darpat, T. L. The Abood and Akerfeldt Tests: Assessment of their reliability, predictive efficiency, and relationship to the MMPI. *J. Neuropsychiat.*, 1960, **2**, 24–30.

Jones, D. S., Livson, N. H., & Sarbin, T. R. Perceptual completion behavior in juvenile delinquents. *Percept. mot. Skills*, 1956, **5**, 141–146.

Jones, E. E., & Kohler, R. The effects of plausibility on the learning of controversial statements. *J. abnorm. soc. Psychol.*, 1958, **57**, 315–320.

Jones, H. E. Consistency and change in early maturity. *Vita Humana*, 1958, **1**, 43–51.

Jones, H. E., & Conrad, H. S. The growth and decline of intelligence: A study of a homogeneous group between ages of 10 and 60. *Genet. Psychol. Monogr.*, 1933, **13**, 223–298.

Jones, H. E., MacFarlane, Jean W., & Eichorn, Dorothy H. A progress report of growth studies at the University of California. *Vita Humana*, 1960, **3**, 17–31.

Jones, M. *The therapeutic community*. New York: Basic Books, 1953.

Jones, V. Ideas on right and wrong among teachers and children. *Teachers College Record*, Columbia University, 1929, **30**, 529–541.

Joyce, C. R. B. Consistent differences in individual reactions to drugs and dummies. *Brit. J. Pharmacol. Chemother.*, 1959, **14**, 512–521.

Kagan, J. The concept of identification. *Psychol. Rev.*, 1958, **65**, 296–305.

Kagan, J., & Moss, H. A. The stability of passive and dependent behavior from childhood through adulthood. *Child Develpm.*, 1960, **31**, 577–591.

Kagan, J., & Moss, H. *From birth to maturity*. New York: Wiley, 1963.

Kahn, H. *On thermonuclear war*. Princeton, N. J.: Princeton University Press, 1960.

Katz, D., Sarnoff, I., & McClintock, C. Ego defense and attitude change. *Hum. Relat.*, 1956, **9**, 27–46.

Katz, D., Sarnoff, I., & McClintock, C. Measurement of ego defense as related to attitude change. *J. Pers.,* 1957, **25**, 465–474.

Katz, D., & Stotland, E. A preliminary statement to a theory of attitude structure and change. In S. Koch (Ed.), *Psychology: A study of a science,* Vol. 3, New York: Mc-Graw-Hill, 1959.

Katz, M. M. Projective techniques and drug research. In L. Uhr and J. G. Miller (Eds.), *Drugs and behavior.* New York: Wiley, 1960. Pp. 501–514.

Kaufman, M. R. Old age and aging: The psychoanalytic point of view. *Amer. J. Orthopsychiat.,* 1940, **10**, 73–79.

Kelly, E. L. Consistency of the adult personality. *Amer. Psychologist,* 1955, **10**, 659–681.

Kelly, E. L., Miller, J. G., Marquis, D. G., Gerard, R. W., & Uhr, L. Personality differences and continued meprobamate and prochlorperazine administration. *Amer. Med. Ass. Arch. Neurol. Psychiat.,* 1958, **80**, 241–246.

Kelly, E. L., Miller, J. G., Marquis, D. G., Gerard, R. W., & Uhr, L. Continued meprobamate and prochlorperazine administration and behavior. *Amer. Med. Ass. Arch. Neurol. Psychiat.* 1958, **80**, 247–252.

Kelman, H. C., & Hovland, C. I. "Reinstatement" of the communicator in delayed measurement of opinion change. *J. abnorm. soc. Psychol.,* 1953, **48**, 327–335.

Kendler, H. H., & Kendler, Tracy S. Vertical and horizontal processes in problem solving. *Psychol. Rev.,* 1962, **69**, 1–16.

Kerrick, Jean S. Some correlates of the Taylor Manifest Anxiety Scale. *J. abnorm. soc. Psychol.,* 1955, **50**, 75–77.

Kessen, W., & Mandler, G. Anxiety, pain, and the inhibition of distress. *Psychol. Rev.,* 1961, **68**, 396–404.

Keys, A., Brozek, J., Hershel, A., Mickelson, O., & Taylor, H. L. *The biology of human starvation.* Vol. 2. Minneapolis: University of Minnesota Press, 1950. (See also Vernon et al., 1956.)

Kimble, G. A. Social influence on Rorschach records. *J. abnorm. soc. Psychol.,* 1945, **40**, 89–93.

Kipnis, D. The effects of leadership style and leadership power upon the inducement of an attitude change. *J. abnorm. soc. Psychol.,* 1958, **57**, 173–180.

Kirtner, W., & Cartwright, D. Success and failure in client-centered therapy as a function of initial in-therapy behavior. *J. consult. Psychol.,* 1958, **22**, 329–333.

Kissel, S., & Litting, L. W. Test anxiety and skin conductance. *J. abnorm. soc. Psychol.,* 1962, **65**, 276–278.

Klapman, J. W. *Group psychotherapy: Theory and practice.* New York: Grune & Stratton, 1947.

Klein, G., & Krech, D. The problem of personality and its theory. In D. Krech and G. Klein (Eds.), *Theoretical models and personality theory.* Durham: Duke University Press, 1952. Pp. 2–23.

Klein, Henriette R. A study of changes occurring in patients during and after psychoanalytic treatment. In *Current approaches to psychoanalysis.* New York: Grune & Stratton, 1960.

Klerman, G. L., Dimascio, A., Greenblatt, M., & Rinkel, M. The influence of specific personality patterns on the reactions to phenotropic agents. In J. Masserman (Ed.), *Biological psychiatry.* New York: Grune & Stratton, 1959. Pp. 224–237.

Koch, Helen L. Some personality correlates of sex, sibling position, and sex of sibling among five- and six-year-old children. *Genet. Psychol. Monogr.,* 1955, **52**, 3–50.

Koch, S. Behavior as "intrinsically" regulated: Work notes towards a pretheory of phenomena called "motivational." In M. R. Jones (Ed.), *Nebraska symposium on motivation.* Lincoln, Neb.: University of Nebraska Press, 1956. Pp. 42–86.

Koch, S. Epilogue. In S. Koch (Ed.), *Psychology: A study of a science.* Vol. 3. *Formulations of the person and the social context.* New York: McGraw-Hill, 1959. Pp. 729–788.

Kogan, N., & Wallach, M. A. Age changes in values and attitudes. *J. Geront.,* 1961, **16,** 272–280.

Köhler, W. *The mentality of apes.* New York: Harcourt, Brace, 1925.

Koos, E. L. *Families in trouble.* New York: Columbia University Press, 1946.

Koos, E. L. Middle-class family crises. *Marriage Fam. Living,* 1948, **10,** 40–48.

Kornetsky, C., & Humphries, O. Relationship between effects of a number of centrally acting drugs and personality. *Amer. Med. Ass. Arch. Neurol. Psychiat.,* 1957, **77,** 325–327.

Kornetsky, C., Humphries, O., & Evarts, E. V. Comparison of psychological effects of certain centrally acting drugs in man. *Amer. Med. Ass. Arch. Neurol. Psychiat.,* 1957, **77,** 318–323.

Korzybski, A. *Science and sanity* (rev. ed.). Lakeville, Conn.: International Non-Aristotelian Library, 1948.

Krasner, L. Studies of the conditioning of verbal behavior. *Psychol. Bull.,* 1958, **55,** 148–170.

Krasner, L. The therapist as a social reinforcement machine. In H. H. Strupp (Ed.), *Second research conference on psychotherapy.* Chapel Hill, N.C.: American Psychological Association, 1961.

Krasner, L., Ullman, L. P., & Weiss, R. L. Distribution and validation of modal perceptual responses of normal and psychiatric subjects. Paper presented to Annual Meeting, A.P.A., New York, September, 1961.

Kris, E. On preconscious mental processes. In D. Rapaport, *Organization and pathology of thought.* New York: Columbia University Press, 1951. Pp. 474–493.

Kris, E. *Psychoanalytic explorations in art.* New York: International Universities Press, 1955.

Kris, Marianne. The use of prediction in longitudinal study. In R. Eissler et al. (Eds.), *Psychoanalytic study of the child.* New York: International Universities Press, 1957, Vol. 12. Pp. 175–189.

Kroger, R. O. "Operant verbal conditioning" as problem solving and interpersonal influence. Paper presented at Calif. Psychol. Ass., San Francisco, 1961.

Kubie, L. S. A psychoanalytic approach to the pharmacology of psychological processes. In L. Uhr and J. G. Miller (Eds.), *Drugs and behavior.* New York: Wiley, 1960. Pp. 209–224.

Kubzansky, P. E. The effects of reduced environmental stimulation on human behavior: A review. In A. D. Biderman and H. Zimmer (Eds.), *The manipulation of human behavior.* New York: Wiley, 1961. Pp. 51–95.

Kubzansky, P. E., & Leiderman, P. H. Sensory deprivation: An overview. In P. Solomon et al. (Eds.), *Sensory deprivation.* Cambridge, Mass.: Harvard University Press, 1961. Pp. 221–238.

Kuhlen, R. G. Age differences in personality during adult years. *Psychol. Bull.,* 1945, **42,** 333–357.

Kuhlen, R. G. Age trends in adjustment during the adult years as reflected in happiness ratings. Paper read at a meeting of the American Psychological Association. Boston, 1948.

Kuhlen, R. G. Expansion and constriction of activities during the adult years as reflected in organizational, civic, and political participation. Paper read at Second International Gerontological Congress, St. Louis, 1951.

Kuhlen, R. G. Nervous symptoms among military personnel as related to age, combat experience, and marital status. *J. consult. Psychol.,* 1951, **15**, 320–324.

Kuhlen, R. G. Adult age trends in attitudes. Unpublished paper presented at the Baltimore meeting of the Gerontological Society, 1955.

Kuhlen, R. G. Changing personal adjustment during the adult years. In J. E. Anderson (Ed.), *Psychological aspects of aging.* Washington, D. C.: American Psychological Association, 1956. Pp. 21–29.

Kuhlen, R. G. Aging and life adjustment. In J. E. Birren (Ed.), *Handbook of aging and the individual.* Chicago: University of Chicago Press, 1959. Pp. 852–900.

Kuhlen, R. G., & Johnson, G. H. Changes in goals with increasing adult age. *J. consult. Psychol.,* 1952, **16**, 1–4.

Kutner, B., Fanshel, D. Togo, Alice M., & Langner, T. S. *Five hundred over sixty: A community survey of aging.* New York: Russell Sage Foundation, 1956.

Lakin, M., & Eisdorfer, C. A study of affective expression among the aged. In C. Tibbitts and Wilma Donahue (Eds.), *Social and psychological aspects of aging.* New York: Columbia University Press, 1962. Pp. 650–654.

Landis, C., & Hunt, W. A. Adrenalin and emotion. *Psychol. Rev.,* 1932, **39**, 467–485.

Landis, J. T. What is the happiest period of life? *School and Society,* 1942, **55**, 643–645.

Lansing, J. B., & Kish, L. Family life cycle as an independent variable. *Amer. Sociol. Rev.,* 1957, **22**, 512–519.

Lasko, Joan K. Parent behavior toward first and second children. *Genet. Psychol. Monogr.,* 1954, **49**, 97–137.

Lauterbach, C. G. The Taylor *A* Scale and clinical measures of anxiety. *J. consult. Psychol.,* 1958, **22**, 314.

Lawrence, P. R. *Changing of organizational behavior patterns: A case study of decentralization.* Boston: Harvard Graduate School of Business, 1958.

Lebo, D., & Applegate, W. S. The MAS and the DRQ. *J. gen. Psychol.,* 1959, **61**, 275–279.

Lebo, D., Toal, R. A., & Brick, H. Manifest anxiety in prisoners before and after CO_2. *J. consult. Psychol.,* 1958, **22**, 51–55.

Lehner, G. F. J. Negative practice as a psychotherapeutic technique. *J. gen. Psychol.,* 1954, **51**, 69–82.

Lehner, G. F. J., & Gunderson, E. K. Height relationships on the Draw-a-Person Test. *J. Pers.,* 1953, **21**, 392–399.

Leiderman, P. H., Mendelson, J., Wexler, D., & Solomon, P. Sensory deprivation: Clinical aspects. *Amer. Med. Ass. Arch. Int. Med.,* 1958, **101**, 389–396.

Leighton, A. H. *My name is legion.* New York: Basic Books, 1959.

Lenke, C. D. The scientific status of pharmacology. *Science,* 1961, **134**, 2069–2079.

Levine, J. M., & Murphy, G. Learning and forgetting controversial material. *J. abnorm. soc. Psychol.,* 1943, **38**, 507–517.

Levy, D. M. Hostility patterns in sibling rivalry experiments. *Amer. J. Orthopsychiat.,* 1936, **6**, 183–257.

Levy, D. M. *Maternal overprotection.* New York: Columbia University Press, 1943.

Levy, E. Z., Ruff, G. E., & Thaler, V. H. Studies in human isolation. *J. Amer. med. Ass.,* 1959, **169**, 236–239.

Levy, L. H.   Anxiety and behavior scientist's behavior.   *Amer. Psychologist,* 1961, **16,** 66–68.

Lewin, K.   Inter-group conflicts and group belongingness.   Part III.   In G. K. Lewin (Ed.), *Resolving social conflicts.*   New York: Harper & Bros., 1948.   Pp. 145–216.

Lewin, K.   Frontiers in social science.   In D. Cartwright (Ed.), *Group dynamics.*   New York: Harper & Bros., 1951.

Lewin, K., & Butler, J.   Lecture vs. group decision in changing behavior.   *J. appl. Psychol.,* 1952, **36,** 29–33.

Lewin, K., Lippitt, R., & White, R. L.   Patterns of aggressive behavior in experimentally created "social climates."   *J. soc. Psychol.,* 1939, **10,** 271–300.

Lewis, H.   *Deprived children.*   London: Oxford University Press, 1954.

Lewis, J. H., & Sarbin, T. R.   Studies in psychosomatics: The influence of hypnotic stimulation on gastric hunger contractions.   *Psychosom. Med.,* 1943, **5,** 125–131.

Lieberman, S.   The effects of changes in roles on the attitudes of role occupants.   *Hum. Relat.,* 1956, **9,** 385–402.

Lifton, R. J.   Home by ship: Reaction patterns of American prisoners of war repatriated from North Korea.   *Amer. J. Psychiat.,* 1954, **110,** 732–739.

Lifton, R. J.   "Thought reform" of western civilians in Chinese Communist prisons.   *Psychiat.,* 1956, **19,** 173–195.

Lifton, R. J.   *Thought reform and the psychology of totalism.*   New York: Norton, 1961.

Likert, R.   *New patterns of management.*   New York: McGraw-Hill, 1961.

Lilly, J. C.   Mental effects of reduction of ordinary levels of physical stimuli on intact, healthy persons.   *Psychiat. res. Rep. Amer. Psychiat. Ass.,* 1956, **5,** 1–28.

Lindemann, E.   Symptomatology and management of acute grief.   *Amer. J. Psychiat.,* 1944, **101,** 141–148.

Lindemann, H.   *Alone at sea.*   New York: Random House, 1958.

Lindemann, H., & von Felsinger, J. M.   *Psychopharmacol.,* 1961, **2,** 69–92.

Lindsley, D. B.   Common factors in sensory deprivation, sensory distortion, and sensory overload.   In P. Solomon et al. (Eds.), *Sensory deprivation.*   Cambridge, Mass.: Harvard University Press, 1961.   Pp. 174–194.

Lindsley, O. R.   Operant conditioning methods applied to research in chronic schizophrenia.   *Psychiat. Res. Rep.,* 1956, **5,** 118–139.

Linn, L., Kahn, R. L., Coles, R., Cohen, Janice, Marshall, Dorothy, & Weinstein, D.   Patterns of behavior disturbances following cataract extraction.   *Amer. J. Psychiat.,* 1953, **110,** 281–289.

Linton, Harriet B.   Dependence on external influence: Correlates in perception, attitudes, and adjustment.   *J. abnorm. soc. Psychol.,* 1955, **51,** 502–507.

Linton, Harriet B., & Graham, Elaine.   Personality correlates of persuasibility.   Ch. 4.   In I. L. Janis and C. I. Hovland (Eds.), *Personality and persuasibility.*   New Haven: Yale University Press, 1959.   (See also Bell, 1955.)

Linton, R.   *The study of man.*   New York: Appleton-Century, 1936.

Lippitt, R., Watson, J., & Westley, B.   *The dynamics of planned change.*   New York: Harcourt, Brace, 1958.

Logan, F. A.   *Incentive.*   New Haven: Yale Universtiy Press, 1960.

Lorand, S.   *Technique of psychoanalytic therapy.*   New York: International Universities Press, 1946.

Lorge, I.   The Thurstone Attitude Scales II: The reliability and consistency of younger and older intellectual peers.   *J. soc. Psychol.,* 1939, **10,** 199–208.

Lorr, M., McNair, D. M., Michaux, W. W., & Raskin, A. Frequency of treatment and change in psychotherapy. *J. abnorm. soc. Psychol.*, 1962, **64**, 281–292.

Luborsky, L. Psychotherapy. In P. R. Farnsworth (Ed.), *Annual review of psychology*. Palto Alto, Calif.: Annual Reviews, 1959.

Luborsky, L. Clinicians' judgments of mental health: A proposed scale. *Arch. Gen. Psychiat.*, 1962, **7**, 407–417.

Luborsky, L. The patient's personality and psychotherapeutic change. In H. Strupp and L. Luborsky (Eds.), Vol. II. *Research in psychotherapy*. Washington, D.C.: American Psychological Association, 1962.

Luborsky, L., Fabian, M., Hall, B., Ticho, E., & Ticho, G. Treatment variables. *Bull. Menn. Clin.*, 1953, **22**, 126–147.

Luborsky, L., & Strupp, H. Research in psychotherapy: A three-year follow-up. In H. Strupp & L. Luborsky (Eds.), Vol. II. *Research in psychotherapy*. Washington, D.C.: American Psychological Association, 1963.

Lynn, D. B., & Sawrey, W. L. The effects of father absence on Norwegian boys and girls. *J. abnorm. soc. Psychol.*, 1959, **59**, 258–262.

Maas, H. The young adult adjustment of war-time residential nursery children. *Child Welfare*, 1963, **42**, 57–72.

Macfarlane, Jean. Studies in child guidance: I. Methodology of data collection and organization. *Monogr. Soc. Res. Child Develpm.*, 1938, **3**, No. 6.

Macfarlane, Jean, Allen, Lucille, & Honzik, Marjorie. *A developmental study of the behavior problems of normal children between 21 months and 14 years*. Berkeley, Calif.: University of California Press, 1954.

Maddox, G., & Eisdorfer, C. Some correlates of activity and morale among the elderly. *Soc. Forces*, 1962, **40**, 254–260.

Madow, L., & Hardy, S. E. Incidence and analysis of broken family in the background of neurosis. *Amer. J. Orthopsychiat.*, 1947, **17**, 521.

Madsen, W. *Society and health in the Lower Rio Grande Valley*. Hogg Foundation for Mental Health, University of Texas, 1961.

Maier, N. R. F. *Psychology in industry* (2nd ed.). Boston: Houghton Mifflin, 1955.

Mann, F. *Managing major change in organizations*. Ann Arbor, Mich.: Foundation for Research on Human Behavior, 1960.

Mann, J. H., & Mann, C. H. The effect of role playing experience on self-ratings of interpersonal adjustment. *Group Psychother.*, 1958, **11**, 27–32.

Maranon, G. Contribution à l'etude de l'action emotive de l'adrenaline. *Revue Francaise D'endocrinologia*, 1924, **2**, 301–325.

Marasse, H. F. Isolation. *J. Amer. Psychoanal. Ass.*, 1959, **7**, 163–172.

Marlowe, D. Relationships among direct and indirect measures of the achievement motive and overt behavior. *J. consult. Psychol.*, 1959, **23**, 329–332.

Marple, C. H. The comparative susceptibility of three age levels to the suggestion of group versus expert opinion. *J. soc. Psychol.*, 1933, **4**, 176–186.

Marquis, D. G., Kelly, E. L., Miller, J. G., Gerard, R. W., & Rapoport, A. Experimental studies of behavioral effects of meprobamate on normal subjects. *Ann. N.Y. Acad. Sci.*, 1957, **67**, 701–710.

Martin, B., Lundy, R. M., & Lewin, M. H. Verbal and GSR responses in experimental interviews as a function of three degrees of "therapist" communication. *J. abnorm. soc. Psychol.*, 1960, **60**, 234–240.

Maslow, A. H. A theory of human motivation. *Psychol. Rev.*, 1943, **50**, 370–396.

Maslow, A. H., & Mintz, N. L. Effects of esthetic surroundings: I. Initial effects of three esthetic conditions upon perceiving "energy" and "well-being" in faces. *J. Psychol.,* 1956, **41,** 247–254.

Mason, E. P. Some correlates of self-judgments of the aged. *J. Geront.,* 1954, **9,** 324–337.

Masserman, J. H. (Ed.), *Biological psychiatry.* New York: Grune & Stratton, 1959.

McClelland, D. C. *Personality.* New York: Holt-Dryden, 1951.

McClelland, D. C. The psychology of mental content reconsidered. *Psychol. Rev.,* 1955, **62,** 297–302.

McClelland, D. C., Atkinson, J. W., Clark, R. A., & Lowell, E. L. *The achievement motive.* New York: Appleton-Century-Crofts, 1953.

McClintock, C. G. Personality syndromes and attitude change. *J. Pers.,* 1958, **26,** 479–493.

McClintock, C. G., & Davis, J. Changes in the attribute of "nationality" in the self-percept of the "stranger." *J. soc. Psychol.,* 1958, **48,** 183–193.

McFarland, R. A., Holway, A. H., & Hurvich, L. M. *Studies in visual fatigue.* Boston: Harvard Graduate School of Business Administration, 1942.

McGinnies, E. Emotionality and perceptual defense. *Psychol. Rev.,* 1949, **56,** 244–251.

McKee, J. P., & Turner, W. S. The relation of "drive" ratings in adolescence to CPI and EPPS scores in adulthood. *Vita Humana,* 1961, **4,** 1–14.

McKinnon, K. M. Consistency and change in behavior manifestations as observed in a group of sixteen children during a five-year period. *Child Develpm. Monogr.,* Teachers College, Columbia University, 1942.

McNair, M. P. Thinking ahead: What price human relations? *Harvard Bus. Rev.,* March–April, 1957.

Mead, G. H. *Mind, self, and society.* Chicago: University of Chicago Press, 1934.

Mead, G. H. *The philosophy of the act.* Chicago: University of Chicago Press, 1938.

Meehl, P. E. *Clinical vs. statistical prediction.* Minneapolis: University of Minnesota Press, 1954.

Meehl, P. E. Structured and projective tests: Some common problems in validation. *J. proj. Tech.,* 1959, **23,** 268–272.

Meili, R. Research in personality assessment: A commentary. In H. P. David and J. C. Brengelmann (Eds.), *Perspectives in personality research.* New York: Springer, 1960. Pp. 342–357.

Meltzer, M. Report on solitary confinement. Factors used to increase the susceptibility of individuals to forceful indoctrination: Observations and experiments. *GAP Symposium No. 3.* New York. (Group for the Advancement of Psychiatry), 1956.

Melzack, P. The perception of pain, *Sci. Amer.,* 1961, **204,** 41–49.

Mendelson, J. H., Kubzansky, P. E., Leiderman, P. H., Wexler, D., & Solomon, P. Physiological and psychological aspects of sensory deprivation—a case analysis. In P. Solomon et al. (Eds.), *Sensory deprivation.* Cambridge, Mass.: Harvard University Press, 1961. Pp. 91–113.

Menefee, S. C., & Granneberg, Audrey G. Propaganda and opinions on foreign policy. *J. soc. Psychol.,* 1940, **11,** 393–404.

Menninger, K. *Theory of psychoanalytic technique.* New York: Basic Books, 1958.

Merrien, J. *Lonely voyagers.* New York: Putnam's, 1954.

Merton, R. K. Bureaucratic structure and personality. *Soc. Forces,* 1940, **18,** 560–568.

Merton, R. K. *Social theory and social structure.* Glencoe, Ill.: Free Press, 1957.

Mettler, F. (Ed.), *Selective partial ablation of the frontal cortex.* New York: Paul B. Hoeber, 1949.

Miller, D., & Swanson, G. *Inner conflict and defense.* New York: Holt, 1960.

Miller, N. E. Experimental studies of conflict behavior. In J. McV. Hunt (Ed.), *Personality and behavior disorders.* New York: Ronald Press, 1944. Pp. 431–465.

Miller, N. E. Theory and experiment relating psychoanalytic displacement to stimulus response generalization. *J. abnorm. soc. Psychol.,* 1948, **43**, 155–178.

Miller, N. E. Learnable drives and rewards. In S. Stevens (Ed.), *Handbook of experimental psychology.* New York: Wiley, 1951. Pp. 435–472.

Miller, N. E. Liberalization of basic S-R concepts: Extensions to conflict behavior, motivation, and social learning. In S. Koch (Ed.), Vol. 2. *Psychology: A study of a science.* New York: McGraw-Hill, 1959. Pp. 196–292.

Miller, N. E. Learning resistance to pain and fear: Effects of overlearning, exposure, and rewarded exposure in context. *J. exp. Psychol.,* 1960, **60**, 137–145.

Miller, N. E. Some recent studies of conflict behavior and drugs. *Amer. Psychologist,* 1961, **16**, 12–24.

Miller, N. E. Some reflections on the law of effect produce a new alternative to drive reduction. In M. R. Jones (Ed.), *Nebraska symposium on motivation.* Lincoln, Neb.: University of Nebraska Press, 1963. Pp. 65–112.

Miller, N. E., & Barry, H. Motivational effects of drugs: Methods which illustrate some general problems in psychopharmacology. *Psychopharmacologia,* 1960, **1**, 169–199.

Miller, N. E., & Dollard, J. *Social learning and imitation.* New Haven: Yale University Press, 1941.

Miller, N. E. et al. Strengthening the behavioral sciences, Statement by the Behavioral Sciences Subpanel of the Life Sciences Panel, President's Science Advisory Committee, The White House, Washington, D.C. *Science,* 1962, **136**, 233–241.

Miller, N. E., & Kraeling, D. Displacement: Greater generalization of approach than avoidance in a generalized approach-avoidance conflict. *J. exp. Psychol.,* 1953, **43**, 217–221.

Miller, N. E., & Murray, E. J. Displacement and conflict: Learnable drive as a basis for the steeper gradient of avoidance than of approach. *J. exp. Psychol.,* 1952, **43**, 227–231.

Miller, N. E., & Stevens, S. S. Agitated behavior of rats during experimental extinction and a curve of spontaneous recovery. *J. comp. Psychol.,* 1936, **21**, 205–231.

Miller, S. C. Ego-autonomy in sensory deprivation, isolation, and stress. *Int. J. Psychoanal.,* 1962, **43**, 1–20.

Miller, W. B. Lower class culture as a generating milieu of gang delinquency. *J. soc. Issues,* 1958, **14**, 5–19.

Mills, C. W. Further notes on the strategic causes of World War III. *Nation,* June 18, 1960.

Mills, J. Changes in moral attitudes following temptation. *J. Pers.,* 1958, **26**, 517–531.

Milton, G. A. The effects of sex-role identification upon problem-solving skill. *J. abnorm. soc. Psychol.,* 1957, **55**, 208–212.

Mittelmann, B. Simultaneous treatment of both parents and their child. In G. Bychowski and J. L. Despert (Eds.), *Specialized techniques in psychotherapy.* New York: Grove, 1952.

Moltz, H. Imprinting: Empirical basis and theoretical significance. *Psychol. Bull.,* 1960, **57**, 291–314.

Moran, L. J., Kimble, J. P., Jr., & Meffard, R. B., Jr. Repetitive psychometric measures: Memory-for-Faces. *Psychol. Rep.,* 1960, **7**, 407–413.

Moreno, J. L. *Who shall survive?* Washington, D.C.: Nervous and Mental Disease Publishing Co., 1934; New York: Beacon, 1953.

Moreno, J. L. *Psychodrama.* New York: Beacon, 1946.

Morison, R. S. "Gradualness, gradualness, gradualness" (I. P. Pavlov). *Amer. Psychologist,* 1960, **15,** 187–197.

Morgan, C. M. The attitudes and adjustments of recipients of old age assistance in upstate and metropolitan New York. *Arch. Psychol.,* 1937, No. 214.

Morris, H. H. et al. Aggressive behavior disorders of childhood: A follow-up study. *Amer. J. Psychiat.,* 1956, **112,** 991–996.

Mowrer, O. H. *Learning theory and personality dynamics.* New York: Ronald Press Co., 1950.

Mowrer, O. H. Neurosis, psychotherapy, and two-factor learning theory. In O. H. Mowrer (Ed.), *Psychotherapy: Theory and research.* New York: Ronald, 1953. *(a)*

Mowrer, O. H. *Psychotherapy: Theory and research.* New York: Ronald, 1953. *(b)*

Mowrer, O. H. *Learning theory and behavior.* New York: Wiley, 1960. *(a)*

Mowrer, O. H. *Learning theory and the symbolic processes.* New York: Wiley, 1960. *(b)*

Mowrer, O. H., Light, B. H., Luria, Z., & Zeleny, M. P. Tension changes during psychotherapy, with special reference to resistance. In O. H. Mowrer (Ed.), *Psychotherapy: Theory and research.* New York: Ronald, 1953.

Muller-Hegemann, D. Beitrag zur psychopathologie der sozialen isolierung. (Contribution to the psychopathology of social isolation.) *Psychiat. neurol, med. Psychol.,* Leipzig, 1958, **10,** 347–355.

Mullin, C. S. Some psychological aspects of isolated antarctic living. *Amer. J. Psychiat.,* 1960, **117,** 323–325.

Murdock, G. P. *Social structure.* New York: Macmillan, 1949.

Murphy, G. *Personality.* New York: Harper & Bros., 1947.

Murphy, G., Murphy, Lois B., & Newcomb, T. M. *Experimental social psychology.* (Rev. ed.) New York: Harper & Bros., 1937.

Murphy, Lois B. Coping methods. In H. David and J. Brengelmann (Eds.), *Perspectives in personality research.* New York: Springer, 1960. Pp. 254–257.

Murray, E. J. A case study in a behavioral analysis of psychotherapy. *J. abnorm. soc. Psychol.,* 1954, **49,** 305–310.

Murray, E. J. A content-analysis method for studying psychotherapy. *Psychol. Monogr.,* 1956, **70** (Whole No. 420).

Murray, E. J. Direct analysis from the viewpoint of learning theory. *J. consult. Psychol.,* 1962, **26,** 226–231.

Murray, E. J. Learning theory and psychotherapy: Biotropic versus sociotropic approaches. *J. counsel. Psychol.,* 1963, **10,** 250–255.

Murray, E. J., Auld, F., & White, A. M. A psychotherapy case showing progress but no decrease in the discomfort-relief quotient. *J. consult. Psychol.,* 1954, **18,** 349–353.

Murray, E. J., & Berkun, M. M. Displacement as a function of conflict. *J. abnorm. soc. Psychol.,* 1955, **51,** 47–56.

Murray, E. J., & Cohen, M. Mental illness, milieu therapy, and social organization in ward groups. *J. abnorm. soc. Psychol.,* 1959, **58,** 48–54.

Murray, E. J., & Miller, N. E. Displacement: Steeper gradient of generalization of avoidance than approach and age of habit controlled. *J. exp. Psychol.,* 1952, **43,** 222–226.

Murray, H. A. *Explorations in personality.* New York: Oxford University Press, 1938.

Murray, H. A., Skinner, B. F., Maslow, A. H., Rogers, L. R., Frank, L. K., Rapaport, A., & Hoffman, H. Cultural evolution as viewed by psychologists. *Daedalus,* 1961, **90,** 570–586.

Mussen, P. Some antecedents and consequents of masculine sex-typing in adolescent boys. *Psychol. Monogr.*, 1961, **75**, No. 2.

Mussen, P. H., & Scodel, A. The effects of sexual stimulation under varying conditions on TAT sexual responsiveness. *J. consult. Psychol.*, 1955, **19**, 90.

Myers, J. K., & Roberts, B. H. *Family and class dynamics in mental illness.* New York: Wiley, 1959.

Myrdal, G. *An American dilemma.* New York: Harper & Bros., 1944.

National Manpower Council, *Womanpower.* New York: Columbia University Press, 1957.

National Training Laboratories in Group Development. *A report of the first six years.* Washington, D.C.: National Training Laboratories, 1953.

Neal, F. W. *U.S. foreign policy and the Soviet Union.* Santa Barbara, Calif.: Fund for the Republic, 1961.

Neilon, Patricia. Shirley's babies after fifteen years. *J. genet. Psychol.*, 1948, **73**, 175–186.

Nelson, E. N. P. Persistence of attitudes of college students fourteen years later. *Psychol. Monogr.*, 1954, **68**.

Neubauer, P. The one parent child and his Oedipal development. In R. Eissler et al. (Eds.), *Psychoanalytic study of the child.* New York: International Univ. Press, 1960. Vol. 15. Pp. 286–309.

Neugarten, B. L., & Gutmann, D. L. Age-sex roles and personality in middle age: A thematic apperception study. *Psychol. Monogr.*, 1958, **72**, No. 17 (Whole No. 470).

Newcomb, T. M. *Personality and social change.* New York: Dryden, 1943.

Newcomb, T. M. *Social psychology.* New York: Dryden, 1950.

Newcomb, T. M. An approach to the study of communicative acts. *Psychol. Rev.*, 1953, **60**, 393–404.

Newman, P. H. The prisoner-of-war mentality: Its effect after repatriation. *Brit. med. J.*, 1944, **1**, 8–10.

Nitsche, P., & Wilmanns, K. The history of the prison psychoses. Trans. by F. M. Barnes, Jr. and B. Glueck. *Nerv. & ment. Dis. Monogr.*, 1912, No. 13, 1–84.

Norman, R. D. Concealment of age among psychologists: evidence for a popular stereotype. *J. soc. Psychol.*, 1949, **30**, 127–135.

Nowlis, V., & Nowlis, Helen H. The description and analysis of mood. *Ann. N.Y. Acad. Sci.*, 1956, **65**, 345–355.

Nye, F. I. Child adjustment in broken and in unhappy unbroken homes. *Marriage Fam. Living*, 1957, **19**, 356–361.

Nymgaard, K. Studies on the sedation threshold: Reproducibility and effect of drugs; sedation threshold in neurotic and psychotic depression. *Amer. Med. Ass. Arch. Gen. Psychiat.*, 1959, **1**, 530–536.

Oh, J. O., & Evans, C. A. Suppressive effects of pyrilamine maleate and d-lysergic acid diethylamide (LSD-25) on early corneal lesions produced in vitro by Newcastle disease virus (NDV) and compound 48/80. *Virology*, 1960, **10**, 127–143.

Olsen, I. A., & Elder, J. H. A word-association test of emotional disturbance in older women. *J. Geront.*, 1958, **13**, 305–308.

Oltman, J. E., McGarry, J. J., & Friedman, S. Parental deprivation and the broken home in dementia praecox and other mental disorders. *Amer. J. Psychiat.*, 1952, **108**, 685–694.

Ormiston, D. W. The effects of sensory deprivation and sensory bombardment on apparent movement thresholds. Unpublished doctoral dissertation, Purdue University, 1958.

Orne, M. T. The nature of hypnosis: Artifact and essence. *J. abnorm. soc. Psychol.*, 1959, **58**, 277–299.

Orne, M. T., & Schiebe, K. The effect of demand characteristics on the elicitation of sensory deprivation-like effects. Unpublished manuscript, 1961.

Osgood, C. E. Suggestions for winning the real war with communism. *J. Conflict Resolution*, 1959, **3**, 295–325.

Osgood, C. E., Suci, G. J., & Tannenbaum, P. H. *The measurement of meaning*. Urbana, Ill.: University of Illinois Press, 1957.

Osgood, C. E., & Tannenbaum, P. H. The principle of congruity in the prediction of attitude change. *Psychol. Rev.*, 1955, **62**, 42–55.

Ostfeld, A. M., Visotsky, H. M., & Lebovits, B. Z. A comparison of the psychotomimetic effects of acopolamine, lysergic acid diethylamide and *n*-ethyl-3-piperidyl benzylate (JB 318). *Clin. Res.*, 1958, **6**, 416 (abstract).

Owens, W. A. Age and mental abilities: A longitudinal study. *Genet. Psychol. Monogr.*, 1953, **48**, 3–54.

Owens, W. A. Age and mental abilities: A second phase of a longitudinal study. *J. Geront.*, 1962, **17**, 472 (abstract).

Pavlov, I. P. *Experimental psychology and other essays*. New York: Philosophical Library, 1957.

Pedersen, S. Psychopathological reactions to extreme social displacement (Refugee neuroses). *Psychoanal. Rev.*, 1949, **36**, 344–354.

Perlin, S., & Butler, R. The psychiatric study of an aged population. In J. Birren et al. (Eds.), *Human aging: A biological and behavioral study*. Public Health Service publication #986. Washington, D.C.: U.S. Government Printing Office, 1963.

Petrie, A., Collins, W., & Solomon, P. The tolerance for pain and for sensory deprivation. *Amer. J. Psychol.*, 1960, **73**, 80–90.

Phillips, B. S. A role theory approach to adjustment in old age. *Amer. sociol. Rev.*, 1957, **22**, 212–217.

Pollak, O. Conservatism in later maturity and old age. *Amer. sociol. Rev.*, 1943, **8**, 175–179.

Pollard, J. C., Uhr, L., & Jackson, C. W., Jr. Studies in sensory deprivation. *Arch. Gen. Psychiat.*, 1963, **8**, 435–454.

Pollin, W., & Perlin, S. Psychiatric evaluation of "normal control" volunteers. *Amer. J. Psychiat.*, 1958, **115**, 129–133.

Pollock, G. H. Mourning and adaptation. *Int. J. Psychoanal.*, 1961, **42**, 341–361.

Postman, L. Comments on papers by Professors Brown and Harlow. In *Current theory and research in motivation: A symposium*. Lincoln, Neb.: University of Nebraska Press, 1953. Pp. 55–58.

Postman, L., Bronson, W. C., & Gropper, G. L. Is there a mechanism of perceptual defense? *J. abnorm. soc. Psychol.*, 1953, **48**, 215–225.

Powell, M., & Ferraro, C. D. Sources of tension in married and single women teachers of different ages. *J. educ. Psychol.*, 1960, **51**, 92–101.

Pressey, S. L., & Kuhlen, R. G. *Psychological development through the life span*. New York: Harper & Bros., 1957.

Pringle, M. L. K., & Bossio, V. Early prolonged separation and emotional maladjustment. *Child Psychiat. & Psychol.*, 1960, **1**, 37–48.

Rankin, R. E., & Campbell, D. T. The galvanic skin response to Negro and white experimenters. *J. abnorm. soc. Psychol.*, 1955, **51**, 30–33.

Rao, C. R. *Advanced statistical methods in biometric research*. New York: Wiley, 1952.

Rapaport, D. Interpersonal relations, communication, and psychodynamics. Paper presented at the Menninger Foundation General Seminar, 1949 (Unpublished manuscript).

Rapaport, D. Discussion in H. Powdermaker (Ed.), *Mass communications seminar: Proceedings of an interdisciplinary seminar.* New York: Wenner-Grenn Foundation, 1953. Pp. 121–128.

Rapaport, D. The theory of ego autonomy: A generalization. *Bull. Menn. Clin.,* 1958, **22,** 13–35.

Rapaport, D. The structure of psychoanalytic theory—a systematizing attempt. *Psychol. Issues,* 1960, **2,** 1–158. (*a*)

Rapaport, D. On the psychoanalytic theory of motivation. In M. R. Jones (Ed.), *Nebraska symposium on motivation.* Lincoln, Neb.: University of Nebraska Press, 1960. Pp. 173–246. (*b*)

Rapaport, D., & Gill, M. The points of view and assumptions of metapsychology. *Int. J. Psychoanal.,* 1959, **40,** 1–10.

Raphelson, A. C. The relationships among imaginative, direct verbal, and physiological measures of anxiety in an achievement situation. *J. abnorm. soc. Psychol.,* 1957, **54,** 13–18.

Ratliff, F. Inhibitory interaction and the detection and enhancement of contours. In W. A. Rosenblith (Ed.), *Sensory communication.* New York: Wiley, 1961. Pp. 183–203.

Reichenbach, H. *Experience and prediction.* Chicago: University of Chicago Press, 1938.

Reiff, R., & Scheerer, M. *Memory and hypnotic age regression.* New York: International Universities Press, 1959.

Reigrotski, E., & Anderson, N. National stereotypes and foreign contacts. *Publ. Opin. Quart.,* 1959, **23,** 515–528.

Reissman, L. Levels of aspiration and social class. *Amer. sociol. Rev.,* 1953, **18,** 233–242.

Riegel, K. F. Personality theory and aging. In J. E. Birren (Ed.), *Handbook of aging and the individual.* Chicago: University of Chicago Press, 1959. Pp. 797–851.

Riegel, K. F., & Riegel, R. M. A study of changes of attitudes and interests during later years of life. *Vita Humana,* 1960, **3,** 177–206.

Riesen, A. H. Effects of stimulus deprivation on the development and atrophy of the visual sensory system. *Amer. J. Orthopsychiat.,* 1960, **30,** 23–36.

Riesen, A. H. Stimulation as a requirement for growth and function in behavioral development. In D. W. Fiske and S. R. Maddi (Eds.), *Functions of varied experience.* Homewood, Ill.: Dorsey, 1961. Pp. 57–80.

Riesman, D. *The lonely crowd.* New Haven: Yale University Press, 1950.

Rinkel, M., DeShon, H. J., Hyde, R. W., & Solomon, H. C. Experimental schizophrenialike symptoms. *Amer. J. Psychiat.,* 1952, **108,** 572–578.

Rioch, D. McK. (Ed.), *Symposium on preventive and social psychiatry.* Washington: U.S. Government Printing Office, 1957.

Ritter, C. *A woman in the polar night.* New York: Century, 1900.

Roberts, C. Ordinal position and its relation to some aspects of personality. *J. genet. Psychol.,* 1938, **53,** 173–213.

Roberts, W. W. Fear-like behavior elicited from dorsomedial thalamus of cat. *J. comp. physiol. Psychol.,* 1962, **55,** 191–197.

Robertson, J., & Bowlby, J. Responses of young children to separation from their mothers: II. Observation of sequences of response of children aged 18–24 months during course of separation. *Cour. Cent. Int. l'Enfance,* 1952, **2,** 131–139.

Roethlisberger, F. J. The foreman: Master and victim of double talk. *Harvard Bus. Rev.,* 1945, **23,** 285–294.

Rogers, C. R. *Counseling and psychotherapy.* Boston: Houghton Mifflin, 1942.

Rogers, C. R. The necessary and sufficient conditions for therapeutic personality change. *J. consult. Psychol.*, 1957, **21**, 95–103.

Rogers, C. R. A process conception of psychotherapy. *Amer. Psychologist*, 1958, **13**, 142–149. Reprinted in W. G. Bennis, K. D. Benne, and R. Chin (Eds.), *The planning of change*. New York: Holt, Rinehart, & Winston, 1961. Pp. 361–372.

Rogers, C. R. A tentative scale for the measurement of process in psychotherapy. In E. Rubinstein (Ed.), *Research in psychotherapy*. Washington, D.C.: American Psychological Association, 1959. Pp. 96–107. (*a*)

Rogers, C. R. A theory of therapy, personality, and interpersonal relationships as developed in the client-centered framework. In S. Koch (Ed.), *Psychology: A study of a science*, Vol. III. *Formulations of the person and the social context*. New York: McGraw-Hill, 1959. Pp. 184–256. (*b*)

Rogers, C. R. Significant trends in the client-centered orientation. In D. Brower and L. E. Abt (Eds.), *Progress in clinical psychology*, Vol. IV. New York: Grune & Stratton, 1960. Pp. 85–99.

Rogers, C. R. The process equation of psychotherapy. *Amer. J. Psychother.*, 1961, **15**, 27–45.

Rogers, C. R. Toward becoming a fully functioning person. In A. W. Combs (Ed.), *Perceiving, behaving, becoming*. 1962 Yearbook, Ass. for Supervision and Curriculum Development. Washington, D.C., 1962. Pp. 22–31.

Rogers, C. R., & Dymond, R. F. *Psychotherapy and personality change*. Chicago: University of Chicago Press, 1954.

Rohrer, J. H. Human adjustment to antarctic isolation. Armed Services Technical Information Agency. Publication AD 246610, Arlington Hall Station, Arlington, Va., 1960.

Rohrer, J. H., & Edmonson, M. S. *The eighth generation*. New York: Harper & Bros., 1960.

Romano, V., *The social factors of donship in a Mexican-American community*. Berkeley, Calif.: Kroeber Anthropological Society, 1960.

Romano, V., Octavio Ignacio, Donship in a Mexican-American community in Texas. *Amer. Anthrop.*, 1960, **62** (6).

Rosen, E. A cross-cultural study of semantic profiles and attitude differences (Italy). *J. soc. Psychol.*, 1959, **49**, 137–144.

Rosen, J. L., & Neugarten, B. L. Ego functions in the middle and later years: thematic apperception study of normal adults. *J. Geront.*, 1960, **15**, 62–67.

Rosen, J. N. *Direct analysis*. New York: Grune and Stratton, 1953.

Rosenberg, M. J. Cognitive reorganization in response to the hypnotic reversal of attitudinal affect. *J. Pers.*, 1960, **28**, 39–63.

Rosenberg, M. J. A structural theory of attitude dynamics. *Publ. Opin. Quart.*, 1960, **24**, 319–340.

Rosenow, C., & Whyte, A. The ordinal position of problem children. *Amer. J. Orthopsychiat.*, 1931, **1**, 430–434.

Rosenthal, D. Changes in some moral values following psychotherapy. *J. consult. Psychol.*, 1955, **19**, 431–436.

Rosenzweig, N. Sensory deprivation and schizophrenia: Some clinical and theoretical similarities. *Amer. J. Psychiat.*, 1959, **116**, 326–329.

Rotter, J. B. Psychotherapy. In P. R. Farnsworth (Ed.), *Annual review of psychology*. Palo Alto: Annual Reviews, 1960.

Roudinesco, Jenny, David, Miriam, & Nicolas, J. Responses of young children to separation from their mothers. I. Observations of children ages 12–17 months recently separated from their families and living in an institution. *Cour. Cent. Int. l'Enfance,* 1952, **2,** 66–78.

Rubel, A. J. Concepts of disease in Mexican-American culture. *Amer. Anthrop.,* 1960, **62** (5).

Ruff, G. E., Levy, E. Z., & Thaler, V. H. Factors influencing reactions to reduced sensory input. In P. Solomon et al. (Eds.), *Sensory deprivation.* Cambridge, Mass.: Harvard University Press, 1961. Pp. 72–90.

Salter, A. *Conditioned reflex therapy.* New York: Capricorn, 1961.

Salzinger, K., Pisoni, Stephanie, Feldman, R. S., & Bacon, Pauline M. The effects of drugs on verbal behavior. Paper presented at the symposium, Control of Verbal Behavior, A.A.A.S., Denver, Colorado, 1961.

Sander, H. J. Testimony. In *Communist interrogation, indoctrination and exploitation of American military and political prisoners.* Washington: U.S. Government Printing Office, 1956.

Sanders, R., & Cleveland, S. E. The relationship between certain examiner personality variables and subjects' Rorschach scores. *J. proj. Tech.,* 1953, **17,** 34–50.

Sands, S. L., & Rothschild, D. Sociopsychiatric foundations for a theory of reactions to aging. *J. Nerv. Ment. Disorders,* 1952, **116,** 233–241.

Sapolsky, A. Effect of interpersonal relationships upon verbal conditioning. *J. abnorm. soc. Psychol.,* 1960, **60,** 241–246.

Sarason, I. G. Empirical findings and theoretical problems in the use of anxiety scales. *Psychol. Bull.,* 1960, **57,** 403–415.

Sarason, I. G. Characteristics of three measures of anxiety. *J. clin. Psychol.,* 1961, **17,** 196–197.

Sarason, S. B., & Gladwin, T. *Psychological problems in mental deficiency: Part II.* New York: Harper & Bros., 1959.

Sarbin, T. R. The concept of role-taking. *Sociometry,* 1943, **6,** 273–285.

Sarbin, T. R. Contributions to role-taking theory. I. Hypnotic behavior. *Psychol. Rev.,* 1950, **57,** 255–270.

Sarbin, T. R. Contributions to role-taking theory. III. A preface to a psychological analysis of the self. *Psychol. Rev.,* 1952, **59,** 11–22.

Sarbin, T. R. Role theory. In G. Lindzey (Ed.), *Handbook of social psychology.* Cambridge, Mass.: Addison-Wesley, 1954.

Sarbin, T. R. Delinquency research project working paper. No. 3. June, 1955. (ms.).

Sarbin, T. R., & Allen, V. L. Role enactment, audience feedback, and attitude change. *Sociometry,* in press.

Sarbin, T. R., & Andersen, M. L. Correlates of "group suggestibility." Unpublished manuscript, 1961.

Sarbin, T. R., & Andersen, M. L. Base-rate expectancies and perceptual alterations in hypnosis. *Brit. J. soc. clin. Psychol.,* 1963, **2,** 112–121.

Sarbin, T. R., & Baker, B. Psychological predisposition and/or subcultural participation. *Sociometry,* 1957, **20,** 161–164.

Sarbin, T. R., & Hardyck, C. D. Conformance in role perception as a personality variable. *J. consult. Psychol.,* 1955, **19,** 109–111.

Sarbin, T. R., & Jones, D. S. Intra-personal factors in delinquency: A preliminary report. *Nerv. Child,* 1955, **11,** 23–27. (*a*)

Sarbin, T. R., & Jones, D. S. The assessment of role-expectations in the selection of supervisory personnel. *Educ. psychol. Measmt.,* 1955, **15,** 236–239. (*b*)

Sarbin, T. R., & Jones, D. S.   An experimental analysis of role behavior.   *J. abnorm. soc. Psychol.,* 1956, **60,** 236–241.

Sarbin, T. R., & Jones, D. S.   Intrapersonal characteristics of juvenile delinquents.   Unpublished.   1958.

Sarbin, T. R., & Lim, D. T.   Some evidence in support of the role-taking hypothesis in hypnosis.   *Int. J. clin. & exp. Hypnosis,* 1963, **11,** 98–103.

Sargant, W.   *Battle for the mind.*   Baltimore, Md.: Penguin Books, 1961.

Sargent, H., Modlin, H., Paris, M. F., & Voth, H. M.   Situational variables.   *Bull. Menn. Clin.,* 1958, **22,** 148–166.

Sarnoff, I.   Psychoanalytic theory and social attitudes.   *Publ. Opin. Quart.,* 1960, **24,** 251–279.

Schachter, S.   Deviation, rejection and communication.   *J. abnorm. soc. Psychol.,* 1951, **46,** 190–207.

Schachter, S.   *The psychology of affiliation.*   Stanford, Calif.: Stanford University Press, 1959.

Schachter, S., & Singer, J.   Cognitive, social and physiological determinants of emotional state.   *Psychol. Rev.,* 1962, **69,** 379–399.

Schachter, S., & Wheeler, L.   Epinephrine, chlorpromazine and amusement.   *J. abnorm. soc. Psychol.,* 1962, **65,** 121–128.

Schaefer, E. S., & Bayley, Nancy.   Consistency of maternal behavior from infancy to preadolescence.   *J. abnorm. soc. Psychol.,* 1960, **61,** 1–6.

Schafer, R.   On the psychoanalytic study of retest results.   *J. proj. Tech.,* 1958, **22,** 102–109. (*a*)

Schafer, R.   Regression in the service of the ego: The relevance of a psychoanalytic concept for personality assessment.   In G. Lindzey (Ed.), *Assessment of human motives.* New York: Rinehart, 1958.   Pp. 119–148. (*b*)

Schaie, K. W.   Rigidity-flexibility and intelligence: A cross-sectional study of the adult life span from 20–70 years.   *Psychol. Monogr.,* 1958, **72** (Whole No. 462).

Schaie, K. W.   The effect of age on a scale of social responsibility.   *J. soc. Psychol.,* 1959, **5,** 221–224.

Scheier, I. H., & Cattell, R. B.   *Temporary handbook for the IPAT 8-Parallel-Form Anxiety Battery.*   Institute for Personality and Ability Testing, Champaign, Ill., 1960.

Schein, E. H.   The Chinese indoctrination program for prisoners of war; a study of attempted brainwashing.   *Psychiatry,* 1956, **19,** 149–172.

Schein, E. H. (with Inge Schneier & C. H. Barker).   *Coercive persuasion, a socio-psychological analysis of the "brainwashing" of American civilian prisoners by the Chinese Communists.*   New York: Norton, 1961.

Schutz, W. C.   *FIRO: A three-dimensional theory of interpersonal behavior.*   New York: Rinehart, 1958.

Schuster, D. B.   A psychological study of a 106-year-old man: A contribution to dynamic concepts of aging and dementia.   *Amer. J. Psychiat.,* 1952, **109,** 112–119.

Schramm, W., & Carter, R. F.   The effectiveness of a political telethon.   *Publ. Opin. Quart.,* 1959, **23,** 121–127.

Scott, A.   Attitude change through reward of verbal behavior.   *J. abnorm. soc. Psychol.,* 1957, **55,** 72–75.

Scott, T. H.   Literature review of the intellectual effects of perceptual isolation.   *Dept. Nat. Def. Rep.,* Canada, 1957, No. HR 66.

Scott, T. H., Bexton, W. H., Heron, W., & Doane, B. K.   Cognitive effects of perceptual isolation.   *Canad. J. Psychol.,* 1959, **13,** 200–209.

Sears, R. R., Hovland, C. I., & Miller, N. E. Minor studies of aggression: I. Measurement of aggressive behavior. *J. Psychol.*, 1940, **9**, 275–294.

Sears, R. R., Maccoby, E. E., & Levin, H. *Patterns of child rearing.* Evanston, Ill.: Row, Peterson, 1957.

Seeman, J. Counselor judgments of therapeutic process and outcome. In C. Rogers and R. F. Dymond (Eds.), *Psychotherapy and personality change.* Chicago: University of Chicago Press, 1954. Pp. 99–108.

Seeman, J. Psychotherapy. In P. R. Farnsworth, O. McNamar, and Q. McNamar (Eds.), *Annual review of psychology.* Palo Alto, Calif.: Annual Reviews, 1961. Pp. 157–194.

Segal, J. Testimony. In *Communist interrogation, indoctrination and exploitation of American military and political prisoners.* Washington, D.C.: U.S. Government Printing Office, 1956.

Shagass, C., & Jones, A. L. A neurophysiological test for psychiatric diagnosis: results in 750 patients. *Amer. J. Psychiat.*, 1958, **114**, 1002–1009.

Shagass, C., & Lipowski, Z. J. Effects of methedrine on critical flicker fusion and its relation to personality and affect. *J. nerv. ment. Disease*, 1958, **127**, 407–416.

Shapiro, A. K. A contribution to a history of the placebo effect. *Behav. Sci.*, 1960, **5**, 109–135.

Shatin, L. A clinical correlative study of the Manifest Anxiety Scale. *J. clin. Psychol.*, 1961, **17**, 198.

Sheehan, J. G., Handley, R. G., & Gould, E. Authority role as a variable in stuttering. *J. Speech and Hearing Disorders*, in press.

Sherif, M. *The psychology of social norms.* New York: Harper & Bros., 1936.

Sherif, M., & Sherif, Carolyn. *Groups in harmony and tension.* New York: Harper & Bros., 1953.

Shipley, T. W., & Veroff, J. A projective measure of need for affiliation. *J. exp. Psychol.*, 1952, **43**, 349–356.

Shlien, J. M. A client-centered approach to schizophrenia: first approximation. In A. Burton (Ed.), *Psychotherapy of the psychoses.* New York: Basic Books, Inc., 1960. Chapter II.

Shoben, E. J. Psychotherapy as a problem in learning theory. *Psychol. Bull.*, 1949, **46**, 366–392.

Shoben, E. J. Some observations on psychotherapy and the learning process. In O. H. Mowrer (Ed.), *Psychotherapy: Theory and research.* New York: Ronald, 1953.

Shurley, J. T. Profound experimental sensory isolation. *Amer. J. Psychiat.*, 1960, **117**, 539–545.

Siegal, R. S., & Rosen, I. C. Character style and anxiety tolerance: A study of intrapsychic change. In H. Strupp & L. Luborsky (Eds.), Vol. II. *Research in psychotherapy.* Washington, D.C.: American Psychological Association, 1962.

Siegman, A. W. Cognitive, affective, and psychopathological correlates of the Taylor Manifest Anxiety Scale. *J. consult. Psychol.*, 1956, **20**, 137–141.

Silverman, A. J., Cohen, S. I., Shmavonian, B. M., & Greenberg, G. Psychophysiological investigations in sensory deprivation, the body-field dimension. *Psychosom. Med.*, 1961, **23**, 48–61.

Simkins, L. Effects of examiner attitudes and type of reinforcement on the conditioning of hostile verbs. *J. Pers.*, 1961, **29**, 380–395.

Simmons, L. W. Attitudes toward aging and the aged: Primitive societies. *J. Geront.*, 1946, **1**, 72–95.

Simpson, G. G. *The meaning of evolution.* New Haven: Yale University Press, 1950.

Sivadon, P. Technics of sociotherapy. In D. McK. Rioch (Ed.), *Symposium on preventive and social psychiatry.* Washington: U.S. Government Printing Office, 1957.

Skinner, B. F. *The behavior of organisms.* New York: Appleton-Century, 1938.

Skinner, B. F. *Science and human behavior.* New York: Macmillan, 1953.

Skinner, B. F. Freedom and the control of men. *Amer. Scholar,* 1955–56, **25,** 47–65.

Skinner, B. F. The design of cultures. *Daedalus,* 1961, **90,** 534–546.

Skinner, B. F., & Ferster, C. B. *Schedules of reinforcement.* New York: Appleton-Century-Crofts, 1957.

Slavson, S. R. *Analytic group psychotherapy.* New York: Columbia University Press, 1950.

Slocum, J. *Sailing alone around the world.* New York: Blue Ribbon Books, 1943.

Smelser, W. T. Dominance as a factor in achievement and perception in cooperative problem solving interactions. *J. abnorm. soc. Psychol.,* 1961, **62,** 535–542.

Smith, E. E. The effects of clear and unclear role expectations on group productivity and defensiveness. *J. abnorm. soc. Psychol.,* 1957, **55,** 213–217.

Smith, G. M., & Beecher, H. K. Measurement of "mental clouding" and other subjective effects of morphine. *J. pharm. exper. Therapeutics,* 1959, **126,** 50–62.

Smith, G. M., & Beecher, H. K. Amphetamine, secobarbital, and athletic performance. II. Subjective evaluations of performances, mood states, and physical states. *J. Amer. Med. Ass.,* 1960, **172,** 1502–1514.

Smith, S., Thakurdas, H., & Lawes, T. G. G. Perceptual isolation and schizophrenia. *J. ment. Sci.,* 1961, **107,** 839–844.

Snyder, W. U. A comparison of one unsuccessful with four successful non-directive counseled cases. *J. consult. Psychol.,* 1947, **11,** 38–42.

Snyder, W. U. *The psychotherapy relationship.* New York: Macmillan, 1961.

Sofer, C. *The organization from within: A comparative study of social institutions based on a sociotherapeutic approach.* London: Tavistock, 1961.

Solomon, P., Kubzansky, P. E., Leiderman, P. H., Mendelson, J. H., Trumbull, R., & Wexler, D. (Eds.), *Sensory deprivation.* Cambridge: Harvard University Press, 1961.

Solomon, P., Leiderman, P. H., Mendelson, J., & Wexler, D. Sensory deprivation: A review. *Amer. J. Psychiat.,* 1957, **114,** 357–363.

Spence, K. W. The nature of theory construction in contemporary psychology. *Psychol. Rev.,* 1944, **51,** 47–68.

Spence, K. W. The postulates and methods of behaviorism. *Psychol. Rev.,* 1948, **55,** 67–78.

Spence, K. W. Clark Leonard Hull: 1884–1952. *Amer. J. Psychol.,* 1952, **65,** 639–646.

Spence, K. W. *Behavior theory and conditioning.* New Haven: Yale University Press, 1956.

Spence, K. W. The empirical basis and theoretical structure of psychology. *Philos. Sci.,* 1957, **24,** 97–108.

Spence, K. W. A theory of emotionally based drive (D) and its relation to performance in simple learning situations. *Amer. Psychologist,* 1958, **13,** 131–141.

Spiker, C. C. Verbal factors in the discrimination learning of children. *Child Develpm. Monogr.,* 1962, **28,** 53–71.

Spitz, R. A. Hospitalism: An inquiry into the genesis of psychiatric conditions in early childhood. In *Psychoanalytic study of the child.* New York: International Universities Press, 1945, Vol. 1. Pp. 53–74.

Spitz, R. A. Hospitalism: A follow-up report. In *Psychoanalytic study of the child.* New York: International Universities Press, 1946. Vol. 2. Pp. 113–117.

Spitz, R., & Wolf, Katherine. Anaclitic depression. In Anna Freud et al. (Eds.), *Psychoanalytic study of the child*. New York: International Universities Press, 1949. Vols. 3–4. Pp. 85–120.

Spotnitz, H. Group therapy as a specialized psychotherapeutic technique. In G. Bychowski & J. L. Despert (Eds.), *Specialized techniques in psychotherapy*. New York: Grove, 1952.

Srole, L., et al. *Mental health in the metropolis: Midtown Manhattan study*. New York: McGraw-Hill, 1962.

Stagner, R. Prestige value of different types of leadership. *Sociology and soc. Res.*, 1941, **25**, 403–413.

Stagner, R. A note on education and international attitudes. *J. soc. Psychol.*, 1942, **16**, 341–346.

Stagner, R. Peace planning as a problem in the psychology of learning. *J. abnorm. soc. Psychol.*, 1943, **38**, 183–192.

Stagner, R. Opinions of psychologists on peace planning. *J. Psychol.*, 1945, **19**, 3–16.

Stagner, R. Perception and personality: Notes for a theory. *Ontario Psychol. Ass. Quart.*, 1960, **13**, 85–91.

Stagner, R. *Psychology of personality* (3rd ed.). New York: McGraw-Hill, 1961.

Stagner, R., & Britton, R. H. Conditioning technique applied to a public opinion problem. *J. soc. Psychol.*, 1949, **29**, 103–111.

Stagner, R., Brown, J. F., Gundlach, R. H., & White, R. K. An analysis of social scientists' opinions on the prevention of war. *J. soc. Psychol.*, 1942, **15**, 381–394. (*a*)

Stagner, R., Brown, J. F., Gundlach, R. H., & White, R. K. Survey of public opinion on the prevention of war. *J. soc. Psychol.*, 1942, **16**, 109–130. (*b*)

Stagner, R., & Osgood, C. E. Experimental analysis of a nationalistic frame of reference. *J. soc. Psychol.*, 1941, **14**, 389–401.

Stagner, R., & Osgood, C. E. Impact of war on a nationalistic frame of reference. *J. soc. Psychol.*, 1946, **24**, 187–215.

Stanton, A., & Schwartz, M. *The mental hospital*. New York: Basic Books, 1954.

Steinberg, Hannah, Rushton, Ruth, & Tinson, Christine. Modification of the effects of an amphetamine-barbiturate mixture by the past experience of rats. *Nature*, 1961, **192**, 533–535.

Steinkamp, G. R., Hawkins, W. R., Hauty, G. T., Burwell, R. R., & Ward, J. E. Human experimentation in the space cabin simulator. *USAF School of Aviation Medicine*, 1959, 59–101.

Stevenson, H. W. Social reinforcement with children as a function of CA, sex of E, and sex of S. *J. abnorm. soc. Psychol.*, 1961, **63**, 147–154.

Stewart, G. R., Jr. *Ordeal by hunger, the story of the Donner Party*. Boston: Houghton Mifflin, 1960.

Stolz, Lois M. Effects of maternal employment on children: evidence from research. *Child Develpm.*, 1960, **31**, 749–782.

Stolz, Lois M., et al. *Father relations of war-born children*. Stanford, Calif.: Stanford University Press, 1954.

Stotland, E., Katz, D., & Patchen, M. Reduction of prejudice through arousal of self-insight. *J. Pers.*, 1959, **27**, 507–531.

Stott, L. H. The persisting effects of early family experiences upon personality development. *Merrill Palmer Quart.*, 1957, **3**, 145–159.

Stouffer, S. A., et al. *The American soldier: Combat and its aftermath*. Princeton: Princeton University Press, 1949.

Stouffer, S. A., et al. *The American soldier.* Princeton: Princeton University Press, 1950.

Strachey, A. *The unconscious motives of war.* New York: International Universities Press, 1957.

Strong, E. K., Jr. *Change of interests with age.* Stanford: Stanford University Press, 1931.

Strong, E. K., Jr. *Vocational interests of men and women.* Stanford: Stanford University Press, 1943.

Strong, E. K., Jr. *Vocational interests 18 years after college.* Minneapolis: University of Minnesota Press, 1955.

Strupp, H. M. *Psychotherapists in action.* New York: Grune & Stratton, 1960.

Strupp, H., & Luborsky, L. (Eds.), Vol. II. *Rorschach in psychotherapy.* Washington: American Psychological Association, 1962.

Sullivan, H. S. *Conceptions of modern psychiatry.* New York: Norton, 1940.

Sullivan, H. S. *The interpersonal theory of psychiatry.* New York: Norton, 1953.

Summer, W. G. *Folkways.* Boston: Ginn, 1906.

Sutcliffe, J. P. "Credulous" and "sceptical" views of hypnotic phenomena: A review of certain evidence and methodology. *Int. J. clin. exp. Hypnosis,* 1960, **8**, 73–101.

Sutcliffe, J. P. "Credulous" and "skeptical" views of hypnotic phenomena: Experiments on esthesia, hallucination, and delusion. *J. abnorm. soc. Psychol.,* 1961, **62**, 189–200.

Sward, K. Age and mental ability in superior men. *Amer. J. Psychol.,* 1945, **58**, 443–470.

Swets, J. A. Is there a sensory threshold? *Science,* 1961, **134**, 168–177.

Szasz, T. The myth of mental illness. *Amer. Psychologist,* 1960, **15**, 113–118.

Taylor, C. Age differences in rigidity as revealed in attitude scale responses. Unpublished doctoral dissertation, Syracuse University, 1955.

Taylor, Janet A. A personality scale of manifest anxiety. *J. abnorm. soc. Psychol.,* 1953, **48**, 285–290.

Taylor, W. L., "Cloze Procedure": A new tool for measuring readability. *Journ. Quart.,* 1953, Fall, 415–433.

Terman, L. M., & Miles, C. C. *Sex and personality: Studies in masculinity and femininity.* New York: McGraw-Hill, 1936.

Thomas, E., Polansky, N., & Kounin, J. The expected behavior of a potentially helpful person. *Hum. Relat.,* 1955, **8**, 165–174.

Thompson, D. W. *On growth and form.* J. T. Bonner (Ed.), abrgd. ed. Cambridge: Cambridge University Press, 1961.

Thompson, W. R. Early environment—its importance for later behavior. In P. H. Hoch and J. Zubin (Eds.), *Psychopathology of childhood.* New York: Grune & Stratton, 1955. Pp. 120–131.

Tibbitts, C. *Handbook of social gerontology.* Chicago: University of Chicago Press, 1960.

Tiira, E. *Raft of despair.* New York: Dutton, 1955.

Tinbergen, N. *The study of instinct.* Oxford: Clarendon, 1951.

Tobin, S. S., & Neugarten, Bernice L. Life satisfaction and social interaction in the aging. *J. Geront.,* 1961, **16**, 344–346.

Toby, J. The differential impact of family disorganization. *Amer. Soc. Rev.,* 1957, **22**, 502–512.

Tolman, E. C. Operational behaviorism and current trends in psychology. *Proc. 25th Anniv. Celebration Inaug. Grad. Stud.* Los Angeles: University of Southern California, 1936. Pp. 89–103.

Tomlinson, T., & Hart, J. A validation study of the process scale. *J. consult. Psychol.,* 1962, **26**, 74–78.

Toulmin, S. *The philosophy of science.* London: Hutchinson University Library, 1953.

Trimble, G. X. "Let not thy right hand." *New England J. Med.*, 1959, **260**, 46.

Trist, E. L., & Bamforth, V. Some social and psychological consequences of the Congwall method of coal-getting. *Hum. Relat.*, 1951, **4**, 3–38.

Tuckman, J., & Lorge, I. The best years in life: A study in ranking. *J. Psychol.*, 1952, **34**, 137–149.

Tuddenham, R. D. The constancy of personality ratings over two decades. *Genet. Psychol. Monogr.*, 1959, **60**, 3–29.

Tyler, D. B. Psychological changes during experimental sleep deprivation. *Dis. nerv. Syst.*, 1955, **16**, 293–299. (See also Vernon et al., 1956.)

Ullman, L. P., Krasner, L., & Collins, B. J. Modification of behavior through verbal conditioning: effects in group therapy. *J. abnorm. soc. Psychol.*, 1961, **62**, 128–132.

Underwood, H. W. The validity of hypnotically induced visual hallucinations. *J. abnorm. soc. Psychol.*, 1960, **61**, 39–46.

van Ree, F. Prediction of syndromes under LSD-25. *Adv. Psychosom. Med.*, 1960, **1**, 209–212.

von Felsinger, J. M., Lasagna, L., & Beecher, H. K. Drug induced mood changes in man. 2. Personality and reactions to drugs. *J. Amer. Med. Ass.*, 1955, **157**, 1113–1119.

von Felsinger, J. M., Lasagna, L., & Beecher, H. K. The response of normal men to lysergic acid derivatives. (Di- and Mono-Ethyl Amides.) *J. clin. exp. Psychopath.*, 1956, **17**, 414–428.

von Senden, M. *Space and sight: The perception of space and shape in congenitally blind patients, before and after operation.* Leipzig: Barth, 1932; Eng. transl., London: Methuen, 1960.

Vernon, J., & Hoffman, J. Effects of sensory deprivation on learning rate in human beings. *Science*, 1956, **123**, 1074–1075.

Vernon, J. A., & McGill, T. E. The effect of sensory deprivation on rote learning. *Amer. J. Psychol.*, 1957, **70**, 637–639.

Vernon, J., Meltzer, M., Tyler, D., Weinstein, E. A., Brozek, J., & Wolff, H. *Factors used to increase the susceptibility of individuals to forceful indoctrination: observation and experiments. Symposium No. 3.* New York: Group for the Advancement of Psychiatry, 1956.

Veroff, J., Atkinson, J. W., Feld, S. C., & Gurin, G. The use of thematic apperception to assess motivation in a nationwide interview study. *Psychol. Monogr.*, 1960, **74** (Whole No. 499).

Veroff, J., Feld, Sheila, & Gurin, G. Dimensions of subjective adjustments. *J. abnorm. soc. Psychol.*, 1962, **64**, 192–205.

Verplanck, W. S. The control of the content of conversation: Reinforcement of statements of opinion. *J. abnorm. soc. Psychol.*, 1952, **51**, 668–676.

Volkart, E. H., & Michael, S. T. Bereavement and mental health. In Leighton et al. (Eds.), *Explorations in social psychiatry.* New York: Basic Books, 1957. Pp. 281–307.

Voth, A. C. An experimental study of mental patients through the autokinetic phenomenon. *Amer. J. Psychiat.*, 1947, **103**, 793–805.

Voth, H. M., Modlin, H. C., & Orth, M. H. Situational variables in the assessment of psychotherapeutic results. *Bull. Menn. Clin.*, 1962, **26**, 73–81.

Walker, A. M., Rablen, R. A., & Rogers, C. R. Development of a scale to measure process changes in psychotherapy. *J. clin. Psychol.*, 1960, **16**, 79–85.

Wallach, M. A., & Kogan, N. Aspects of judgment and decision making: interrelationships and changes with age. *Behav. Sci.*, 1961, 23–36.

Waller, W. W. *The sociology of teaching.* New York: Wiley, 1932.

Wallerstein, R., Robbins, L. L., Sargent, H. D., & Luborsky, L. The psychotherapy research project of the Menninger Foundation: Rationale, method and sample use. *Bull. Menn. Clin.,* 1956, **20,** 221–280.

Waltz, K. N. *Man, the state, and war.* New York: Columbia University Press, 1959.

Wapner, S., & Krus, D. M. Behavioral effects of lysergic acid diethylamide (LSD-25). Space localization in normal adults as measured by the apparent horizon. *Amer. Med. Ass. Arch. Gen. Psychiat.,* 1959, **1,** 417–419.

Washburn, W. C. Patterns of self-conceptualization in high school and college students. *J. educ. Psychol.,* 1961, **52,** 123–131.

Watson, J. B. *Psychology from the standpoint of a behaviorist.* Philadelphia: Lippincott, 1919.

Weisman, A. D., & Hackett, T. P. Psychoses after eye surgery. *New Engl. J. Med.,* 1958, **258,** 1284–1287.

Weitzenhoffer, A., & Hilgard, E. R. *Stanford hypnotic susceptibility scale.* Palo Alto, Calif.: Consulting Psychologists Press, 1959.

Welford, A. T. *Skill and age.* London: Oxford University Press, 1951.

Werner, H., & Wapner, S. Toward a general theory of perception. *Psychol. Rev.,* 1952, **43,** 351–357.

Werner, H., & Wapner, S. Sensory-tonic field theory of perception: Basic concepts and experiments. *Revista di psicologia,* 1956, **4,** 315–337.

West, L. J. (Ed.) *Hallucinations.* New York: Grune & Stratton, 1962.

Wexler, D., Mendelson, J., Leiderman, P. H., & Solomon, P. Sensory deprivation: A technique for studying psychiatric aspects of stress. *Arch. neurol. Psychiat.,* 1958, **79,** 225–233.

Wheaton, J. L. *Fact and fancy in sensory deprivation studies.* Aero-medical Reviews, Review 5-59, Air University School of Aviation Medicine, Brooks AFB, Texas, 1959.

White, R. W. An analysis of motivation in hypnosis. *J. gen. Psychol.,* 1941, **24,** 145–162.

White, R. W. *Lives in progress.* New York: Dryden, 1952.

Whitehorn, J. C. Studies of the doctor as a crucial factor for the prognosis of schizophrenic patients. Paper from the Henry Phipps Psychiatric Clinic of the Johns Hopkins Hospital, 1959.

Whiting, J. W. M., & Child, I. *Child training and personality.* New Haven: Yale University Press, 1953.

Whyte, W. H., Jr. *The organization man.* New York: Simon & Schuster, 1956.

Wiener, N. *Cybernetics.* New York: Wiley, 1948.

Williams, R. J. The biological approach to the study of personality. Presented to the Berkeley Conference on Personality Development in Childhood. University of California, May 6, 1960.

Winder, C. L. Some psychological studies of schizophrenics. In D. D. Jackson (Ed.), *The etiology of schizophrenia.* New York: Basic Books, 1960. Pp. 191–247.

Windle, C. The relationships among five MMPI "anxiety" indices. *J. consult. Psychol.,* 1955, **9,** 61–63.

Wolf, S., & Wolff, H. G. Evidence on the genesis of peptic ulcer in man. *J. Amer. Med. Ass.,* 1942, **12,** 670–675.

Wolpe, J. *Psychotherapy by reciprocal inhibition.* Stanford, Calif.: Stanford University Press, 1958.

Wooley, D. W. The revolution in pharmacology. *Perspectives in biology and medicine,* 1958, **1**, 174–197.

Yarrow, L. J. Maternal deprivation: Toward an empirical and conceptual re-evaluation. *Psychol. Bull.,* 1961, **58**, 459–490.

Yarrow, L. J. The effects of a change in mother-figures during infancy on personality development. *Annual Report,* Infant Research Project. Washington, D.C., 1962.

Yarrow, L. J. Research in dimensions of early maternal care. *Merrill Palmer Quart.,* 1963, **9**, 101–114.

Yarrow, L. J. Separation from parents during early childhood: Implications for personality development. In M. Hoffman and Lois Hoffman (Eds.), *Review of child development research.* Troy, N.Y.: Russell Sage College Press, 1964.

Yarrow, Marian R., Schwartz, Carlotte G., Murphy, Harriet S., & Deasy, Leila C. The psychological meaning of mental illness in the family. *J. soc. Issues,* 1955, **11**, 12–24.

Yarrow, Marian R., Campbell, J. D., & Yarrow, L. J. Interpersonal change: Process and theory. *J. soc. Issues,* 1958, **14**, 60–63.

Yarrow, Marian R., Scott, Phillis, deLeeuw, Louise, & Heinig, Christine. Child-rearing in families of working and non-working mothers. *Sociometry,* 1962, **25**, 122–140.

Yarrow, Marian R., Blank, P., Quinn, Olive, Youmans, G., & Stein, Johanna. Social psychological characteristics of old age. In J. Birren et al. (Eds.), *Human aging: A biological and behavioral study.* Public Health Service publication #986. Washington, D.C.: U.S. Government Printing Office, 1963.

Zajonc, R. B. Concepts of balance, congruity, and dissonance. *Publ. Opin. Quart.,* 1960, **24**, 280–296.

Zbrowski, M. Cultural components in response to pain. *J. soc. Issues,* 1952, **8**, 16–30.

Zimmerman, C., & Bauer, R. A. The effect of an audience upon what is remembered. *Publ. Opin. Quart.,* 1956, **20**, 238–248.

Zimring, F. M. The experiencing process. *Counseling Center Discussion Papers, IV,* No. 22. Chicago: University of Chicago Library, 1958.

Ziskind, E., Jones, H., Filante, W., & Goldberg, J. Observations on mental symptoms in eye patched patients: Hypnagogic symptoms in sensory deprivation. *Amer. J. Psychiat.,* 1960, **116**, 893–900.

Zubin, J. The measurement of personality. *J. counsel. Psychol.,* 1954, **1**, 159–164.

Zubin, J. A biometric model for psychopathology. In *Current trends in the description and analysis of behavior.* Pittsburgh: University of Pittsburgh Press, 1958.

Zubin, J. Psychopathology and the social sciences. In *Symposium on social psychology: Past, present, and future.* New York: Holt, Rinehart, & Winston, in press.

Zubin, J. Discussion of introduction to facet design and analysis by Louis Guttman. *Proc. of the Internat. Congr. of Psychol.,* Brussels, 1957, 135–138.

Zubin, J., Burdock, E. I., et al. *Experimental abnormal psychology.* New York: Columbia University Press, 1957.

Zubin, J., Fleiss, J., & Burdock, E. I. Methods for fractionating a population into homogeneous subgroups. Read before the seminar of Mathematical Methods in the Social Sciences, Columbia University, New York, March, 1962.

Zuckerman, M., Albright, R. J., Marks, C. S., and Miller, G. L. Stress and hallucinatory effects of perpetual isolation and confinement. *Psychol. Monogr.,* 1962, **76**, No. 549, 1–15.

Zuckerman, M., & Cohen, N. Sources of reports of visual and auditory sensations in perceptual isolation experiments. *Psychol. Bull.,* 1964, in press.

Name Index

Subject Index